LIFE OF ROSSINI

SOCRATES:

But let your thoughts range freely through the air,
*Like chafers with a thread about their feet.**

Aristophanes, Clouds

Vie De Rossini,

PAR

M. De Stendhal;

Ornée des Portraits de Rossini et de Mozart.

Laissez aller votre pensée comme cet insecte
qu'on lâche en l'air avec un fil à la patte.
SOCRATE. *Nuées d'Aristophane.*

PREMIÈRE PARTIE.

Paris,

CHEZ AUGUSTE BOULLAND ET Cᵗᵉ, LIBRAIRE,
RUE DU BATTOIR, N° 12.

1824.

LIFE
OF
ROSSINI

by

STENDHAL *, pseud.*

Marie Henri Beyle

New and revised edition

Translated and annotated by

RICHARD N. COE

THE ORION PRESS

NEW YORK, 1970

Frontispiece: The title-page of an early edition of 'Vie de Rossini', signed by Stendhal. Reproduced by courtesy of the Trustees of the British Museum.

TABLE OF CONTENTS*

* Indicates *Notes* at end.

CHAPTER VII

Of the Wars between Harmony and Melody

The sweet succulence of a peach is finally *not* preferred to the harshness of more adult tastes—chronological list of the major representatives of the Italian school.

CHAPTER VIII

Of the Invasion by the Blunt-Minded, and of the Ideology of Music

Careless scoring by Rossini indicated by a + — the composer who complicates his accompaniments restricts the freedom of the singer—Rossini's accompaniments are dangerous, not so much for their *quality* as for their quantity—the orchestra of the *Théâtre Louvois*—the indication *piano* considered as a sign of weakness.

CHAPTER IX

AURELIANO IN PALMIRA

A superb duet: *se tu m'ami, o mia regina*—DEMETRIO E POLIBIO, Rossini's first opera (spring, 1809)—opening of the new theatre at Como.

CHAPTER X

IL TURCO IN ITALIA

CHAPTER XI

Rossini in Naples

Rossini signs a *scrittura* with Signor Barbaja—concerning a certain Neapolitan *prima donna* and the influence of her voice upon Rossini's subsequent work.

CHAPTER XII

ELISABETTA, REGINA D'INGHILTERRA

CHAPTER XIII

ELISABETTA, REGINA D'INGHILTERRA (*continued*)

An Italian *Ode on the Death of Napoleon*, to be compared with

TRANSLATOR'S FOREWORD

HENRI BEYLE, whom the public was already coming to know as Stendhal, was about thirty-one years old, and had already experienced much of the world—including the retreat from Moscow—when he chanced to hear a German military band in Milan playing a curiously lilting melody in an unfamiliar idiom. He enquired after the composer, more from idle curiosity, perhaps, than from any other motive, and learnt that the *maestro* was "a young man named Rossini", and that the tune which had so intrigued him was the duet: *Mi rivedrai, ti rivedrò* . . . from an opera called *Tancredi*.

The year was 1814, and Rossini was enjoying the first upsurge of his amazing popularity; but Henry Beyle was a most obstinate individualist, and by no means inclined to echo the hysterical and unreasoning applause of the crowd. Rossini, admittedly, was a glorious sun compared with the dim candle-light of a Portogallo, a Zingarelli or a Simon Mayr; but what was Rossini beside a Mozart, a Cimarosa, or even a Paisiello? Rossini's brittle and superficial tunefulness was to be *enjoyed* rather than revered; and for some years, Beyle continued to be cool in his appraisal, and moderate in his judgment.

But if Rossini was all the rage in Italy, in France he was treated as an ill-bred *parvenu*, whose cheap popularity was an insult to a great musical tradition. So, if Beyle's refusal to move with the crowd had, while he remained in Milan, tended to make him cool in his attitude towards Rossini, this same contrariness, once he had travelled northwards over the Alps towards Paris, served to imbue him with the purest fire of Rossinian ardour. And, from 1821 onwards, he was in fact obliged to live in Paris, since the Milanese authorities, suspecting him of being a French secret agent, had requested him to leave the country. Thus it comes about that, in 1822, we find Beyle constituting himself the most fervent advocate of Rossinian opera in a society which is still puzzled by this new genius from Pesaro.

The first contribution which he was to make to the furthering of his newly-adopted cause was an article on Rossini written for an English journal published in France, the *Paris Monthly Review* (January 1822).

Proof that the subject was of interest to the general reader was not long in forthcoming, for the article was promptly pirated by two major English reviews of the period, *Blackwood's Edinburgh Magazine* (October 1822) and *Galignani's Monthly Review* (November 1822); while in Italy, not only did the substance of Beyle's study reappear in translation in a Milanese periodical, but this same version was subsequently re-printed in book form.[1]

If the French and English readers received their first survey of Rossini and his music, all in all, with favourable interest, the Italians were profoundly shocked; for Beyle, whose musical insight is both sensitive and profound, still obstinately maintained at least a part of his original critical position, and insisted that the music of the *Barber*, for all its piquant and delicious gaiety, was still less powerful, less evocative, and perhaps even less *permanent*, than the music of *Don Giovanni*. Such contempt for the national hero on the lips of an impu-dent foreign calumniator was hardly to be borne, least of all while the original *Rosina*, Signora Geltrude Giorgi-Righetti, was there to defend her adored *maestro*. The defence was published in Bologna in 1823, under the title of *Reminiscences of a sometime prima-donna, concerning the composer Rossini . . .*;[2] and this curious document constitutes one of the earliest authentic studies of Rossini by a person who had a compara-tively intimate personal knowledge of him.

Meanwhile, Beyle, encouraged by the unexpected success of his first venture, had decided to follow up this initial victory with a *History of Music in Italy, 1800–1823*, which he intended to have translated and published in England. For various reasons, however, the MS. was withdrawn at the last minute; reluctant to waste good work done, the author began to cast about for some means of using at least part of what he had already written in a new shape; and so the months from January to September 1823 were spent converting much of the material accumulated into a *Life of Rossini*.

Warned by his experience with Signora Giorgi-Righetti, who had not failed to point out the wretched "English journalist's" criminal ignorance in matters of detail, Beyle this time was at some pains to

---

[1] *Rossini e la sua Musica.* Milano, dalla tipografia di Felice Rusconi, contrada di S. Paolo, No. 1177 (1824).

[2] See *Bibliography*. The work (which is very rare in the original) has been reproduced in full in Henry Prunières' edition of the *Vie de Rossini*, vol. 2, pp. 433–474.

make certain of his facts; and a first draft of the book—based almost entirely upon this laboriously accumulated factual evidence—was ready in the spring of 1823. At about the same time, it began to be rumoured that Rossini was to visit England; and the English publishers, anxious to meet this sudden market with a "best-seller", hurriedly had the MS. translated, and published it as rapidly as possible (January 1824). Meanwhile, however, Beyle had taken up his original draft, which was neat, balanced, factual and dull, and was rapidly destroying every claim to neatness, factuality and balance which it had ever possessed, in the joyous process of turning it into one of the great masterpieces of musical criticism. In April 1824, when the first *French* edition appeared, the simple narrative of Rossini's career had almost disappeared beneath a most wondrous mass of anecdotes and descriptions, tables and footnotes, theatrical admonitions and philosophical speculations; and the volume which finally took its place on the bookshelves of enthusiasts in every country was well over twice the length of the little opportunist pamphlet which had been released on the occasion of Rossini's visit to London.

In 1824, when the *Life* was published, Rossini himself was thirty-two; and he had another forty-four years to live. Yet in spite of this, Beyle's analysis covers almost everything which is of lasting musical value in Rossini's work, with the exception of *Le Comte Ory*, *Guillaume Tell*, and the collection of miscellaneous musical satires and cameos entitled *Péchés de Vieillesse*, which Respighi, many years later, was to weave into the ballet-suite *La Boutique Fantasque*. As a pure biographer, obviously Beyle is at a greater disadvantage; nevertheless, the fact remains that the majority of those who have written subsequent *Lives* of Rossini have been quite content to dismiss the last forty years of the composer's existence in a final, abrupt chapter or so at the end of the book; with the result that this "amateur" biography, with all its inaccuracies and its fatal weakness for anecdote, has formed the basis for every serious study which appeared in print between the day of its original publication, and the day, over a century later, when Professor Radiciotti's authoritative three-volume *Vita* came at last to replace the delicious inaccuracies of the dilettante with the matter-of-fact realities of the scholar. But if Beyle is no longer satisfying as a factual biographer, he remains unrivalled in penetration and interest as a critic; for his criticism is not so much *analysis* as *interpretation*—the very personal interpretation of a man of genius, who was a rebel against the taste of his own century, and deeply sympathetic in his appeal to the imagination of our own.

Our last glimpse of Rossini in the *Life* is of his marriage to Isabella Colbran and his final farewell to Naples; the last opera which Beyle describes is *Semiramide* (Feb. 1823). In March 1822, the Rossinis had included in their honeymoon a four-months' stay in Vienna, where *Zelmira* had been produced on 13th April; this visit was the occasion of the famous meeting with Beethoven, and of a notorious outburst of jealousy and ill-temper from Weber, already broken by ill-health and overwork. The winter of 1822–3 was spent largely in Venice working on *Semiramide*; and in the autumn, after a quiet summer, Rossini and Isabella set out for London to fulfil a contract at the King's Theatre. En route, they had their first glimpse of Paris (where the *fêtes* and banqueting reached such proportions that they inspired a mordant little satirical vaudeville from Scribe: *Rossini à Paris, ou Le Grand Dîner*); and on the 7th of December, in a violent storm, they crossed the Channel.

Rossini's visit to England (then at one of its periodical musical low ebbs) was extremely profitable financially, and is rich in anecdote for the historian; but musically it produced nothing more valuable than an insignificant octet for voices: *Il Pianto delle Muse in Morte di Lord Byron* (9th June 1824)). Six months after his arrival, Rossini left these philistine shores with 175,000 francs already in his pocket, and the promise of a contract with the Italian Opera in Paris to convince him that his hand-to-mouth existence as a wandering musician was really ended. In the autumn of 1824, the contract was confirmed; he was to receive 20,000 francs a year to direct the Théâtre Italien in the place of his old rival Paër; yet, with unwonted tact or generosity, he insisted that Paër should remain his associate. Nevertheless, partly because of the re-organization required, and partly because of his own laziness, nearly a year passed before his first new opera was produced.

And even then, it turned out to be scarcely more than a *morceau de circonstance*: *Il Viaggio a Reims, ossia l'Albergo del Giglio d'Oro*, written for the coronation of Charles X (19th June 1825); such success as it had was short-lived, and Rossini soon discarded it, reserving its better numbers for incorporation elsewhere when the time came. The remainder of the year was taken up, ostensibly, with the first production of Meyerbeer's *Il Crociato* (September 1825), but in fact with a slow and important inner revolution: the assimilation of the French operatic tradition. Two milestones reveal the progress made by Rossini in this conscious process of de-italicization: *Le Siège de Corinthe* (9th October 1826), which is a French re-writing of the Italian *Maometto II*; and *Moïse* (26th March 1827), in which a similar process of transformation is applied to the older Italian *Mosè in Egitto*. Although both these operas were highly successful, and had something positive to contribute to the musical climate of the time (*Le Siège* has been called "the first Grand Opera"), neither is strictly speaking a new or original work. In fact, over five years separate *Semiramide* from Rossini's next major opera, *Le Comte Ory*, which was produced on 20th August 1828.

Le Comte Ory reveals the extent of the transformation which had taken place in Rossini's musical technique; for not merely was it designed specifically to please a French audience, but in fact it succeeded to such a degree that it may be considered as the source of a new genre altogether—the French *operetta* of the XIXth century tradition; and if, on the one hand, Rossini's influence may be traced in composers such as Donizetti, Bellini, Mercadante and even the young Verdi, on the other, his musical disciples must certainly be held to include Auber, Messager and Offenbach.

A year after *Le Comte Ory* came the second, and final, major opera of the Parisian period: *Guillaume Tell* (3rd August 1829). In *Le Comte Ory*, Rossini, for the first time since the *Barber*, had been blessed with a supremely competent libretto;[1] it is the tragedy of *Guillaume Tell* that Jouy's bathetic text based on Schiller's drama is almost beyond redemption. *Guillaume Tell* is a "musician's opera"; no student of Rossini can deny the power and originality of its score; and yet, somehow, like Victor Hugo's *Burgraves*, it seems to belong to that strange class of indigestible masterpieces whose greatness is so much beyond dispute that we would rather listen to something else. Yet it marks the climax of an epoch in more ways than one, for, on 13th August 1829, Rossini left Paris en route for Milan and Bologna. He was now thirty-seven, he had composed some thirty-nine operas in nineteen years, and he felt that he had earned a rest. The "rest" was to last until 13th November 1868—the day of his death.

[1] By Scribe.

Many reasons have been advanced to explain Rossini's "great renunciation". He himself insisted above all that he felt his music to be
dangerously out of harmony with the political drift of the eighteen-
thirties and eighteen-forties. Other biographers have maintained that
he had simply written himself out; that he was ill, disastrously ill, and
in fact had already been having serious neurasthenic attacks as early as
August 1825; that he was jealous of "the Jews" (Halévy and Meyerbeer); that the type of singer for whom he was accustomed to score his
works was to grow increasingly rare after 1830, and that this fact
upset the whole delicate balance of his musical sensitivity; that he was
violently offended by the cancellation of his Paris contract after the
revolution of 1830; or finally, that he was simply idle by nature, and
that, if poverty had forced him to work for a living in his youth,
success had taken from him the last obligation to exert himself at the
irksome and uncongenial labour of composition. The probable truth is
that all these were in some degree contributory causes to his ultimate
decision. However, the fact remains that, apart from one or two works
of a very different character (notably the *Stabat Mater* (1842), the
Petite Messe Solennelle (1864), and the delightfully miscellaneous *Péchés
de Vieillesse* (1857–68), to which reference has already been made),
Rossini's musical biography ends with *Guillaume Tell*.

The remainder of his life is strangely uneventful. His adored mother
had died in 1827; his father, to whom in the end he became scarcely
less devoted, followed her in 1839. The marriage with Isabella Colbran
was a disastrous failure, and was ended by an official separation (1836–7);
but already in 1832 Rossini had made the acquaintance of Olympe
Pélissier, a retired *demi-mondaine* with strong maternal instincts, who
was to become his most faithful mistress, companion and watch-dog,
and eventually (August 1846), after the death of Isabella, his second
wife. It was Olympe who nursed him through his terrible nervous
illnesses of 1852–5, and who, in the last calm period in Paris, organized
his household, "rationed" his constant flow of visitors, and presided
over the famous "Saturday evenings", whose informal music-making
was to be the envy of Europe. It was she who watched over her husband's table; for Rossini's final reputation as a *gourmet* was almost as
notable as his earlier fame as a composer; and *tournedos Rossini* still
frequently figures on the menu in those great houses where dining is
considered an art rather than a process. His intimate friends were the

composer Carafa, and (until his death in 1842) the banker Aguado; to the caricaturists of his day, he was an avaricious cynic with a biting, satirical wit; but to his closer acquaintances he was the patient and conscientious reformer of the *Liceo Musicale* at Bologna, and the generous patron and protector of Bellini, of the tenor Ivanoff, of Bizet, Gabrieli, and of that pious-minded and desperately serious young man from London—Arthur Sullivan. In 1836, he was so upset by a jaunt in a railway-train in Antwerp that he vowed never to travel again by this devilish means of locomotion; in 1848, a few insults hurled against his idle political indifference by a rioting mob in Bologna, soured for ever his delight in that great city; and henceforward he was to live in Florence and Paris until the end of his days. In 1860, he received a memorable visit from Wagner; and in 1868, he was serenaded by the soloists and orchestra of the Paris opera in the middle of the Chaussée d'Antin—for *Guillaume Tell* had just received its 500th performance. But on the whole few subjects interested him less than his own music; his modesty increased as his achievements receded; the more he heard of Wagner, the more he revered Bach; and in the end, when a visitor had the impertinence to ask him which he thought the greatest of his operas, he snapped back: *Don Giovanni!*

Such are the latter days of the boisterous, irrepressible practical joker, from whom, in Beyle's company, we take leave in 1823.

In this year 1968—the centenary of Rossini's death—many half-forgotten Rossinian operas have been performed, and many new facts have come to light about the great composer. Among the most important events of this notable year has been the publication of Herbert Weinstock's monumental *Rossini*: a study which makes all previous biographies, including even Radiciotti's, look out-of-date and amateurish.

Dr Weinstock does not approve of Stendhal very much. "In English as in French," he writes, "it is more interesting now as a psychological self-portrait of its author, a parade of enthusiasms and detestations, than as biography of the young Rossini. At least once in each three pages, it is magnificently, romantically—in a sense creatively—wrong." Since Dr Weinstock has levelled the accusation, I have ruthlessly exploited Dr Weinstock's own *Rossini* in order to establish the prosaic truth that lies hidden away behind Stendhal's romantic fictions. I hereby acknowledge my immense debt to this illustrious musicologist ... while still keeping to myself the obstinate reflection that, however often Stendhal may have been wrong, it is still remarkable all the same how often he was right.

In carrying out the American edition, I have altered the spelling of some of the proper names, in order to bring them into line with modern practice. The *Index* has been checked in the light of new information; and the *Bibliography* has been brought up to date. The *Notes* have been extensively brought up to date, so as to correct Stendhal's guesses, myths or mis-statements in the light of the most recent scholarship; and finally, instead of giving straight (and all too frequently meaningless) translations of the scraps and fragments of Italian libretti quoted by Stendhal in the original, I have tried in each case to trace the dramatic context in which the quotation is situated.

Stendhal is rightly contemptuous of the literary quality of the average libretto that Rossini, by contract, was required to set to music; on the other hand, writing in 1823, he could assume that Rossini's music would be sufficiently familiar for a mere half-line of abominable Italian to bring back a whole scene—aria, duet or finale—into his reader's mind. Today, unfortunately, this is no longer the case, except perhaps with the *Barber of Seville*. In an ideal world. I should have quoted the entire passage as given in the full vocal and orchestral score; failing this utopian possibility, I have appended extracts from the dialogue sufficient to give the reader at least a notion of the dramatic situation that Stendhal is discussing, even if the music is not there to give it life and meaning and beauty.

Yet there is hope, all the same. Rossini's music is certainly more familiar now than it was even ten years ago. When the English edition of this translation was published in 1956, few among us had ever heard any Rossinian opera at all except for the *Barber*, the *Italian Girl in Algiers*, the *Turk in Italy* and perhaps *Le Comte Ory*. Since that date, the musical climate has changed radically. Rossinian opera—*Il Signor Bruschino, L'Inganno Felice, La Pietra del Paragone, Otello*, even *Adina*—has proved to be the very stuff of which Festivals are made. And so, a hundred years after Rossini's death, Stendhal's "enthusiasms and detestations" are perhaps more relevant than they have been at any time since the great Romantic epoch, when Byron and Musset and Pushkin were one and all incurable Rossinomaniacs.

This translation of the *Vie de Rossini* is based on the critical edition by Henry Prunières (2 vols., Champion 1922), which is included in the *Œuves Complètes de Stendhal* under the general editorship of Paul Arbelet and Edouard Champion. Occasional corrections have been introduced from the edition by Henri Martineau (*Le Divan*, 2 vols., 1929). The text is given "complete and unabridged", with all its footnotes, digressions and irrelevancies; for only by such a translation can the true flavour of Stendhal's masterpiece be preserved. The only serious liberty which has been taken with the original occurs in the section devoted to *Otello*, where the final paragraphs of Chapter XVIII have been transferred to the beginning of Chapter XIX, in order that the reader who uses the book chiefly as a series of opera-analyses may find all the revelavant comments about *Otello* under one heading.

All Stendhal's critical writings are rich in references to contemporary personalities—so rich that, in order to avoid losing the original text altogether in a grotesque labyrinth of footnotes (Stendhal's *and* my own), I have preferred to compile an *Index* at the end which gives a certain minimum of necessary information. Such few footnotes of my own as have seemed indispensable are signed (*Trans.*); all others are Stendhal's own additions in the original French. For the section at the end headed *Notes* (to which references are indicated by an asterisk * in the text), I am heavily indebted to Henry Prunières, particularly in the matter of correcting Stendhal's many minor errors of fact.

RICHARD N. COE

LIFE OF ROSSINI

PREFACE

N<small>APOLEON</small> is dead; but a new conqueror has already shown himself to the world; and from Moscow to Naples, from London to Vienna, from Paris to Calcutta, his name is constantly on every tongue.

The fame of this hero knows no bounds save those of civilization itself; and he is not yet thirty-two! The task which I have set myself is to trace the paths and circumstances which have carried him at so early an age to such a throne of glory.

If the narrator of this epic may claim to deserve his reader's confidence, it is because he has lived for eight or ten years in those same towns and cities which Rossini was electrifying with his masterpieces; many a time the Author has journeyed a hundred miles and upwards to witness a first performance; and in those days it was rare indeed for him to miss even one of the countless anecdotes which ran like fire from mouth to mouth in Naples, Venice, Rome, or wherever you might find an opera by Rossini.*

The Author of this present Work has already composed two or three others*, and all upon no less frivolous topics. The critics have warned him that when a man takes to the business of writing, there are certain Precautions to be Observed, certain Rules of Style to be Obeyed, certain Academic Disciplines . . . *etc.*; that he will never learn to write a book unless . . . *etc. etc.*; nor ever achieve the most coveted distinction of being a *Man of Letters*. Excellent! Certain persons (whom the reader shall name, not I!) have committed such curious sins beneath the cover of this honoured title, that I can think of at least one honest gentleman who could imagine no greater good fortune than to avoid it altogether.

This work, then, is not a *Book*. After the fall of Napoleon, the Author of the following pages, finding it both stupid and unprofitable to fritter away his youth in political squabbles, left home, and set out to see the world; and, chancing to be in Italy during the epoch of Rossini's extraordinary triumphs, he had occasion to describe them in letters to certain Polish and English acquaintances.

Scraps and extracts of this correspondence, later copied out and patched together into a book—this is all that the reader will find before him in these pages; and if he reads them, it must be because he enjoys Rossini, not for any merit in the writing. History, it is said, constitutes an agreeable exercise, no matter what circumstances may have determined the writing of it; and *this* history was composed in the very presence of the manifold and trifling events which it records.

I should not be in the least surprised to discover some thirty or forty inaccuracies* among the countless masses of minute detail which go to make up this biography.

There is nothing so difficult as to write the story of a man still living —particularly when that man is like Rossini, whose career leaves neither trace nor monument, but only an ephemeral memory of passing pleasure in every heart. I could sincerely wish that this great artist, who is also a most charming man, would follow the example of Goldoni and write his own *Memoirs*; which, I suspect, would be decidedly more entertaining than those of Goldoni, since Rossini is at least a hundred times wittier, besides being quite preposterously irreverent. I hope that there may perhaps be just enough inaccuracies in this *Life of Rossini* to cause him a passing spasm of annoyance, and so goad him into writing the book himself. But before the storm of his annoyance breaks upon my head (if it does), I feel that I must assure him of my very real respect, which is deep and infinitely sincere, and is of a quality very different from that, say, of the respect I bear to some fine Lord whose greatness is the envy of all eyes. In the lottery of Nature, the noble Lord has drawn *his* prize in cash; but Rossini has won a name which cannot die, and genius with it, and, best of all, a splendid share of human happiness.

The present treatise was originally destined to appear in English*; and only the sight of a music-school just off the Place Beauvau* has inspired the author with the courage to publish it in France.

*Montmorency, 30th September 1823**

INTRODUCTION

I

Cimarosa

On the 11th of January, 1801, Cimarosa died in Venice, in consequence of the barbarous treatment* he had suffered shortly before in the dungeons of Naples, where he had been imprisoned at the instigation of Queen Caroline.

Paisiello, the charming and graceful, rather than forceful and dynamic composer of *il Re Teodoro* and *la Scuffiara*[1], lived on until 1816; but it is not unfair to maintain that, ever since the closing years of the previous century, the bright blaze of musical inspiration, which so often kindles young and burns out early, had died and turned to cold ashes within his heart.

The secret of Cimarosa's power to compel the imagination lies in his use of long musical phrases, which are at once fantastically rich and extraordinarily regular. There is an excellent illustration of this manner to be seen in the first two duets of *il Matrimonio segreto*, and more especially in the second:

Io ti lascio perchè uniti . . .[2]

The human soul can know no beauty more exquisite than these two melodies; yet observe their characteristic *regularity*, their symmetry so marked that the mind cannot fail to perceive it; this is a serious fault in Cimarosa, for as soon as the listener is sufficiently familiar with three or four such songs, he can, as it were, *predict* the pattern and develop-

---

[1] The reader is referred to the *Index* for information concerning the various personalities and works mentioned in the *Life of Rossini*. (*Translator's note.*)

    [2] *Carolina:*
        Io ti lascio, perchè uniti
        Ch'ei ci trovi non sta bene . . .
        Ah! tu sai ch'io vivo in pene
        Se non son vicina a te!
               (Act I, sc. i)

ment of all the rest from hearing the first few bars. All Cimarosa's weakness lies hidden in that single word *predict*; and, as we shall shortly see, Rossini's style and all his glory spring from his power to wrestle with this very problem.

Paisiello never disturbs such deep currents of feeling as Cimarosa; his music has no power to fill the soul with that mystic imagery whose joyous radiance can touch the innermost springs of passion; the spiritual resources at his command never rise above a certain quality of gracefulness. Yet, in the field which he has chosen, he excels; his gracefulness is the gracefulness of Correggio, gentle, rarely provocative, but with its own peculiar, irresistible attraction. Among examples of Paisiello's music which are familiar in Paris, perhaps the most typical is the famous quartet from *la Molinara*:

Quelli là . . .,[1]

from the scene where Pistofolo, the notary, in a most delightful sequence, undertakes to intercede with the Miller's wife on behalf of his two hated rivals, the Governor and his own Liege Lord, conveying their respective and impassioned declarations.

The most remarkable characteristic of Paisiello's style is his trick of repeating the same phrase or passage over and over again, yet adorned at each return with new and added graces which engrave it ever more deeply on the listener's imagination.

No musical style in the world bears less resemblance to that of Cimarosa, with its glittering array of comic verve, of passion, strength and gaiety. Rossini likewise tends towards repetition, but not with purposeful intent; and a mannerism which, in Paisiello, is a careful climax of exquisite writing, is, in Rossini, incarnate idleness in all its glory! Let me hasten to add, lest I be straightway counted among his detractors and critics, that Rossini alone among all modern composers

---

[1] *Rachellina (la Molinara):*
　　Dite in grazia! Quei signori
　　Che vi dissero di me?
Pistofolo:
　　Quelli là stanno in errore,
　　Lascia fare, io penso a te!
Don Caloandro:
　　Favellasti alla mia bella,
　　Averan di me pietà? . . .
　　　　(*La Molinara*, quartet from Act I, sc. ix)

has earned the right to be compared with these great masters, whose stars faded from the heavens in the early years of the XIXth century. If only we took the trouble to study their scores with the care and attention that they deserve, we should suddenly be startled one fine day to find ourselves perceiving and feeling qualities in their music, whose existence we had never even suspected! In all art, the road to appreciation lies through reflection.

II

Of Certain Differences between German and Italian Music

No music will remain deeply imprinted in the memory unless it is of the kind that lends itself to private rehearsal; and no man, alone in his chamber late at night and equipped with nothing but his own voice, can rehearse orchestral harmony.

Fundamentally, this is the real difference between German and Italian music. Take any young Italian, whose whole being is pre-occupied with some imperious passion: he may, while it is still at fever-heat, reflect upon it for a time in silence; but sooner or later he will start to sing, softly, perhaps some tune by Rossini; and quite unconsciously he will have selected, among all the tunes he knows, the one which seems most aptly to echo his own mood. Then, a little later, instead of singing softly to himself, he will begin to sing out loud; and, still all unsuspecting, his singing will begin to answer, in subtle shapes and shadings, the peculiar quality of the passion which is raging in his heart. His soul, as it were, has found an echo, and the echo is itself a consolation; his singing is like a mirror in which he can observe his own reflection; previously, he had been exasperated by the unkindness of fate, and his spirit was filled with anger; but now he can see himself, and his final mood will be one of pity for his own misfortune.

Our young Italian, then, sings to escape from his own obsessing thoughts; but after a while, he may suddenly grow aware of the strange, new individuality with which the song of his choosing has been coloured by the quality of his singing; it may fascinate him, enchanting his soul; then, once this odd, ecstatic mood has been created, it is only a step to the making of a *new* song altogether; and since the climate and the way of life of southern Italy have endowed the inhabitants with excellent voices, as often as not he will find himself well able to compose without a piano.[1] I have met with a score of young Neapolitans

[1] This is the origin of those wonderful, but generally plaintive, folk-songs which, for countless generations have been handed down from singer to singer

who could compose a song as unconcernedly as young men in London write letters, or young men in Paris pen sets of verses. There is nothing unusual, under the soft, delicious night-sky of Naples, in their going home after the day's work, sitting down at the piano, and whiling away half the hours of darkness with songs and improvizations. No thought is further from their minds than that of "writing music" or of "becoming a famous composer"; the only motive of their art, the only secret of their happiness, is to have discovered a way of expressing the living emotions within them. In England, a young man in similar circumstances would probably have stretched his hand towards the bookshelf, taken down a volume of some favourite author, and read until one or two o'clock in the morning; but his enjoyment would have been less *creative* than that of the Italian, his imagination would have been less actively engaged, and consequently his pleasure less real. Improvization at the piano is an exclusive occupation; the single problem of expression leaves no room for any other anxieties, and mere technical accuracy perforce goes by the board.

To become a competent violinist, a man must practise scales three hours a day for eight years; at the end of which time, callosities as tough as leather will have spread across the fingertips of his left hand, leaving it grotesquely deformed; but the notes extracted from the instrument will be perfect. Even the most skilled of violinists still requires his two-hours' daily practice; and if he should chance to miss it for three or four days, he will find that the purity of his tone is already degenerating, and that his touch is losing its sureness in the more brilliant passages. The degree of patience and perseverance required to perfect this kind of skill is very unusual in the southern part of Europe, and is rarely found in conjunction with an impetuous temperament*. The violinist or the flautist is perpetually conscious of the beauty or the accuracy of his *tone*, and scarcely ever of the emotional *expressiveness* of his music. Observe this distinction, for it provides a further key to the riddle, and explains some of the subtle differences between the two schools of music.

within the Kingdom of Naples. Those who know this lovely country will recognize, for example, the national anthem, *la Cavajola*; or *il Pestagallo*, which is peculiar to the Abruzzi. A folk-singer from Aquila, who was teaching me some of these songs, once remarked: *La musica è il lamento dell' amore, o la preghiera a gli Dei* (Music is the lamentation of Love, or a prayer to the gods). *Diary*, 12th May, 1819.

B

During the last century, there were harsh Italian fathers who would condemn an ill-fated son to make himself proficient on the violin or oboe, just as others used to sentence their children to become *castrati*; but in our own time, the art of instrumental music has wholly taken refuge among the peaceful, patient folk beyond the Rhine. Amid the sighing forests of Germany, this people, its spirit ever filled with dreams, needs no more than the beauty of pure sound, *even without melody*, to urge it on to ever greater feats of perseverance, and to populate its vagabond imagination with rich and wondrous visions.

There was an occasion, twenty years ago, when *Don Giovanni* was to be produced in Rome; and for a solid fortnight, the instrumentalists struggled like demons to master the complexities of the passage where three orchestras have to play simultaneously during Don Giovanni's supper-scene in the last act. But in vain; to the very end, the best musicians in Rome found such a score beyond the range of their technique*. Their very *soul* was in their playing, but *patience* was not their brightest virtue. But in contrast, less than two weeks ago, I went to the *rue Lepeletier*, and watched the orchestra of the *Opéra* give a superb performance of a positively diabolic symphony by Cherubini *at sight*; and then fail miserably in trying to accompany the duet from *Armida*, sung by Bordogni and Madame Pasta. The *Opéra* is populated with superlative talent, trained and cherished with boundless patience—and without an iota of genuine musicality.

In Rome, twenty years ago, it grew to be a unanimous opinion that foreigners thought far too highly of Mozart's works, and that the passage for three orchestras, in particular, was a piece of rank absurdity only worthy of the barbarous Teuton.

The probing and meticulous despotism[1] which, for two centuries

---

[1] In 1795, an intelligent and at that time very young man, Signor Toni, who has since become extremely well known as a printer and publisher, held a post under the Venetian government at Verona; it was a modest employment, carrying a salary of 1,800 francs, and he was happy and contented, spending his leisure courting the favours of Princess P***. Suddenly he found himself dismissed from his office and threatened with imprisonment. Hastily he set off for Venice, where, after three months of manoeuvring and intrigue, he eventually managed to slip a passing word to a member of the *Council of Ten*, who replied: "Why the devil did you have to tell your tailor to make you a *blue* suit? We took you for a Jacobin!" Incidents of a similar character are not unknown in Milan in 1822; in Lombardy, a fondness for Dante (who was writing in the year 1300!) is accounted good evidence of *carbonarism*; and any man who evinces too inordinate a delight

now, has wrapped its strangling tentacles about the genius of Italy, has forced the only criticism which the censorship will permit to take refuge in low-grade journalism of the most unspeakable scurrility and baseness*; it is quite normal to find a man referred to as a *scoundrel*, and *ass*, a *thief, etc.*, almost as one has grown used to it in London,[1] and soon will do in Paris, for all the good we are likely to derive from our own "freedom of the press" and other injunctions to despise coarseness and vulgarity, even in print. In Italy, the journalist himself is, by tradition, one of the leading agents in the service of the Police, who use him to hurl dirt at anyone who achieves distinction in any walk of life whatsoever, and hence to spread terror and subservience. But it is as true of Italy as it is of France, or of any other country for that matter, that public opinion in the field of drama requires the guidance of criticism in the press; the reaction of an audience is as evanescent as a thought unless there is someone on the spot to record it; and, if the first link in the chain of argument is missed, no one will ever manage to deduce the second.

I must beg the reader's pardon for having introduced so odious a topic; but I should be immeasurably distressed if this fair realm of Italy, this wondrous land whose earth has scarcely settled over the ashes of men as great as Canova and Viganò, should be judged by the raffish vituperations of its periodical press, or on the evidence of such barren and empty-headed balderdash as may be found in the few books which a fear-haunted populace still finds the courage to print. Until the day comes when the whole of Italy enjoys the blessings of a moderate government, such as that which has flourished in Tuscany for the last eighteen months, I would implore, desperately, but, I think, only in fairness, that the spirit of Italy should be judged only insofar as that spirit transpires through the medium of art. Nowadays, no one but a fool or an accredited informer may have a book published.

A few years ago, in 1816, I chanced to be staying in one of the greatest cities in Lombardy. A group of local music-lovers—men of means and substance—had founded a private theatre in the town, equipped and decorated with every imaginable luxury; and they

in this writer will find that, gradually, his *liberal* friends will seem less inclined to seek his company.

[1] See, for instance, the foul-mouthed insults recently hurled by one Philpott against the celebrated Mr Jeffrey, the editor of the *Edinburgh Review*, which is the finest periodical in existence.

thought that it would be fitting to organize a festival to celebrate the advent among them of Princess Beatrice d'Este*, the mother-in-law of the Emperor Francis. In her honour, therefore, they commissioned an entirely new opera, with original music and a specially-written *libretto* —a compliment which, in Italy, represents the highest honour which can be paid to anyone. The librettist had the notion of arranging one of Goldoni's plays, *Torquato Tasso*, in operatic form. The music was ready within a week, rehearsals were under way, and everything was going with a swing, when, on the very eve of the great occasion, the Princess' chamberlain appeared, and intimated firmly to the distinguished citizens who were desirous of the honour of performing in her presence, that to recall before a scion of the house of Este the abhorred name of *Tasso*, a man who had once upon a time actually insulted this illustrious race, would be a most criminal discourtesy.

But no one seemed in the least surprised at this arbitrary intervention, and the title was simply changed to *Lope de Vega*.

It is my considered opinion that music can only appeal to the spirit of man by conjuring up a pattern of imaginative imagery, which in some way corresponds to the passions by which the listener is already swayed. It will therefore be evident that music, indirectly perhaps, but none the less inevitably, will reflect the political structure of its country of origin, since the individual listener is himself determined by the political atmosphere in which he exists. In Italy, the tradition of tyranny which reigns supreme in the body politic has effectively annihilated every generous impulse in the human breast save one: love. Consequently, we find no sign of martial vigour in Italian music until the appearance of *Tancredi*, whose first performance did not take place until a good ten years had elapsed since the miraculous feats at Rivoli and at the bridge of Arcola*. Before the echo of those tremendous days came to shatter the age-old sleep of Italy,[1] war and feats of arms had no part to play in music, save as a conventional background to give still greater value to the sacrifices made to love; for indeed, how should a people, to whom all dreams of glory were forbidden, and whose only experience of arms was as an instrument of violence and oppression,

---

[1] *Cf.* Napoleon, *Correspondence* for the year 1796, description of the general state of morale in Milan and Brescia. The Milanese "army" consisted solely of some eighty villainous scallywags dressed up in scarlet and entrusted with the policing of the town. *Cf.* also, in the *Bulletins de l'Armée d'Espagne*, what Napoleon achieved with such a people!

have found any sense of pleasure in letting their imagination dwell on martial images?

In contrast, think of the tunes *Allons, Enfants de la Patrie* or *le Chant du Départ*, and observe the arduous heights scaled by French music, almost, as it were, from the first moment of its inception; yet during the last thirty years (or, in fact, ever since our composers started copying the Italians) nothing half so fine has been produced. The reason is plain; for, during all this time, composers have chosen blindly to imitate the Italian conception of *love*, whereas love, in France, is nothing but a feeble and second-rate emotion, entirely overwhelmed by *vanity* and stifled by the witty subtleties of *intellect*.

Now, whether or not there be any truth in this impertinent generalization, I think it will be universally acknowledged that music can achieve no effect at all save by appealing to the imagination. But if there is one faculty which can be guaranteed to reduce the imagination to a state of impotent paralysis, it is *memory**. If, upon hearing some tantalizing melody, my first reaction is to *recall* the tracery of images and all the little dream-adventures which I had woven about it on the last occasion when it had caught my fancy, then everything is lost, a black and deathly frost grips my imagination, and the all-powerful enchantment of the music is banished from my heart; or at best, allowing that I may be able to recapture some half-hesitating glimpse of the old magic, it can carry me no further than to some secondary consideration, perhaps inspiring a fleeting admiration for the technical virtuosity of the performer in the execution of some difficult passage, or distracting my attention with similar triviliaties of subordinate importance.

A friend of mine once wrote*, about a year ago, in a letter addressed to a lady who was then living in the country: *Soon we shall be able to see* Tancred *at the* Théâtre Louvois, *but I doubt whether we shall really be able to appreciate all the subtle enchantment of this fresh and extraordinarily martial music until we have heard it performed three or four times. However, once we have fully grasped all its beauty and meaning, the power of its fascination will grow steadily, reaching a climax of intensity over a period of some twenty to thirty performances, after which our capacity for enjoyment will rapidly become exhausted. The more violent our initial infatuation, the more frequently we shall have heard these wonderful melodies surging round and round inside our head long after the performance is over and the theatre shut and empty, then the more complete, ultimately, will be our saturation, if I may use the phrase.*

Musically speaking, no one can remain for ever faithful to his old loves. If *Tancredi* is still received with rapturous applause after fifty performances, it can only be because the audience has been completely renewed; because a new class of society, attracted by the press, will have found its way through the doors of the *Louvois*; or (more prosaic reason) because this particular theatre is so abominably uncomfortable that the delights of listening are only purchased at an exorbitant price of physical suffering in every other part of the listener's anatomy, this same bodily suffering causing a state of nervous exhaustion, induced so rapidly that the maximum quantity of opera which anyone is capable of assimilating on any one evening is reduced to *one* act; in which case, the "saturation-point" for *Tancredi* will be reached only after eighty performances, instead of the customary forty!

It is a sad, but probably true, reflection, that, in music at least, the *ideal* conception of beauty changes every thirty years*. Consequently, anyone who would attempt to describe the revolution in musical taste brought about by Rossini has no need to explore the past much beyond the epoch of Cimarosa and Paisiello.[1]

Towards the year 1800, when these great men retired from their labours, they had been feeding the *repertoire* of every theatre in Italy, and indeed throughout the world for over twenty years. Consequently, their style, their whole technique and vision, had lost its most precious quality: the quality of *unexpectedness*. When I was in Padua, Pacchiarotti*, then a wonderfully genial old man, used to take me round his fashionable *jardin anglais*, and show me the tower of cardinal Bembo with its magnificent furnishings all brought from London in so curious a manner; and, during the course of these visits, he used to tell me how, in Milan in the old days, his rendering of a certain aria by Cimarosa would receive as many as four consecutive *encores*, night after night; I freely confess that, before I could credit a whole people with such an infatuated degree of intoxicated extravagance, I needed further

---

[1] There is no need to remind the reader that Dr Burney has published a most excellent *General History of Music*. Personally, however, I regret to confess that the perfection of this magnificent work is marred by occasional traces of obscurity. It may be that the origin of this veil of opaqueness, which sometimes falls between the eye of the reader and the conceptions of the author, lies in the latter's failure to make any clear statement about his own musical *credo*. I rather think that he might have done better to give us *examples* of what he understood by the terms *beautiful, sublime, mediocre, etc.*

confirmation; but the evidence was there, from a crowd of people who had witnessed the phenomenon with their own eyes. When the human heart adores with such intensity, how should its adoration last for ever?

If we should happen to find ourselves still taking pleasure in a song which we first heard years ago, it can only be because the *quality* of that pleasure has been completely transformed; our present delight lies in reminiscence, in recalling the charming fancies which had enraptured our imagination of old; but the original intoxication itself has vanished for ever, and cannot be recaptured. Thus a single spray of periwinkle-flowers could remind Jean-Jacques Rousseau of all the glories of his younger days.

The quality in music, which makes of it the most enthralling pleasure that the soul can know, and which gives it so marked an advantage over even the finest poetry, over *Jerusalem*, for instance, or over *Lalla-Rookh*, lies in the powerful element of *physical* intoxication which it contains. The pleasure of pure mathematics is of an even quality, neither increasing nor decreasing violently with time or mood; but the pleasure of music is as opposite to this as anything within the range and compass of our appreciation. The joy which music affords is violent and intense, but curiously unstable and quickly evanescent. Ethics, history, novels, poetry—arts which, within the scale of our different pleasures, are set at varied intervals between the two extremes of pure mathematics and *opera buffa*—all furnish a degree of satisfaction whose durability is in exact inverse proportion to its intensity; and only delights which, in intensity, are comparatively weak, can offer us positive assurance that they will always remain undiminished no matter how often we return to them.

In music, by contrast, every element partakes of the frenzied uncertainty of an unbridled imagination; an opera may inspire the most disproportionate havoc of enjoyment one night, and three nights later, occasion nothing more than an infinite weariness of boredom or an infuriating irritation of the nerves. The causes of this revolution may be insignificant—a shrill-toned, yapping female voice in a near-by box; or over-heating in the auditorium; or a neighbour leaning back luxuriously in his own seat and communicating a series of steady, maddeningly regular jerks to your own; indeed, the enjoyment of music is in so large a measure purely physical, that, as the reader will have observed, it may depend upon the presence or absence of phenomena which, in description, seem unbelievably trivial.

As often as not, an evening which promises the exquisite delights of Madame Pasta, and the added luxury of a comfortable box, may be completely *ruined* by the hateful intrusion of just some such ignoble triviality. One might ransack one's brain for hours on end, exploring the most delicate intricacies of metaphysics, or the subtlest niceties of literary criticism, to explain why *Elisabetta* seemed suddenly so unpalatable, whereas the real reason is simply that the auditorium was too hot and that, as a result, one was feeling thoroughly uncomfortable. Incidentally, the *Théâtre Louvois* is unrivalled in providing draw-backs[1] of this character, and generally in obstructing the enjoyment of music; and whenever such an obstruction arises, one stops listening *naturally* and starts listening *academically*; one *feels it one's duty* not to miss a single note. O, what a phrase: to *feel it one's duty*! How unspeakably *English*! How anti-musical! It is as though one were to *feel it one's duty* to be thirsty!

Music exerts a certain pressure upon the nervous system of the ear, creating a given degree of tension, and thus producing a physical, purely *mechanical* type of sensory pleasure (as, for example, during the first-act *finale* of Mozart's *Così fan tutte*); and apparently this physical pleasure communicates a certain degree of tension or irritation to the brain, forcing it to produce a series of pleasurable mental images, or else to react, with drunken intensity twenty times more violent than usual, to mental images which, in normal circumstances, would have inspired nothing deeper than the most vulgar sensual satisfaction—just as a handful of nightshade berries, picked accidentally in the garden, can turn the brain to madness.

Cotugno, the most celebrated doctor in Naples, once remarked to me during the *furore* which first greeted *Mosè in Egitto*: *Among the many and glorious titles which may be showered upon your hero, you should include that of* murderer. *I could quote you more than forty cases of brain-fever or of violent nervous convulsions among young ladies with an over-ardent passion for music, brought on exclusively by the* Jews' Prayer *in the third act, with its extraordinary change of key!*

It was this same philosopher (for assuredly so great a physician as Cotugno deserves such a title) who observed that semi-darkness was an

---

[1] In English in the original. (*Trans.*)

essential condition of true musical appreciation. A too-bright light, he maintained, irritated the optic nerve; and it was impossible that conscious awareness should be fully present in the optic and auditory nerves *at the same time. You may choose one pleasure, or the other; but the human brain is not sufficiently powerful to cope with both. I might suggest another curious phenomenon,* added Cotugno, who was probably influenced by the theory of galvanism*: *to achieve the completest sensory satisfaction from music, it is essential to be isolated from the proximity of any other human body. It may be surmised that the human ear is surrounded by a kind of musical ether, of which I can offer no description, beyond suggesting that it may exist. Thus, to obtain perfect pleasure, it is essential to be situated in a kind of* isolated field, *as we observe in certain experiments involving electrical magnetism, which in practice means that it is necessary that the space of at least one foot should intervene between oneself and the nearest adjacent human body. The animal heat which emanates from a foreign body appears to me to have a most pernicious effect upon the enjoyment of music.*

Far be it from me to insist upon the scientific validity of this theory tentatively put forward by the Neapolitan philosopher; I suspect that I may not be sufficiently competent a scientist even to have stated it correctly!

The most that I can assert with confidence is that I know, from the experience of a number of intimate friends, that a series of fine Neapolitan melodies, for instance, will oblige the listener's imagination to furnish a series of specific mental pictures; and at the same time will make him abnormally sensitive in appreciating the peculiar beauty of these same images.

In early days, when the pleasures of music are a new discovery, the listener's most immediate reaction will be one of astonishment at the curious things which seem to be taking place within him; and he will be entirely preoccupied with savouring the unsuspected sources of delight which he has just stumbled upon for the first time; but later, when he has had many years' experience in the service of this enchanting art, he will find that music which is perfect will provide the mind with a series of mental pictures *wholly related to the particular emotions with which he happens to be already preoccupied*. It will now have been made abundantly plain that the entire pleasure of music consists in *creating illusions*; and that common-sense rationality is the greatest enemy of musical appreciation.

The only reality in music is the state of mind which it induces in the listener*; and I will not quarrel with the moralists, when they claim that this state offers a powerful inducement to day-dreaming and sentimental effusions.

III

History of the Interregnum between the Departure of Cimarosa and the Coming of Rossini (1800–1812)

AFTER the departure of Cimarosa, and during the period when Paisiello had retired from active composition, music in Italy lay dormant, waiting for the appearance of an original genius. Perhaps I should rather have said, that the *pleasure of music* lay dormant, for the theatres could always show their tally of enthusiastic applause and extravagant admiration; but, after all, a pretty young miss of eighteen will weep tears of emotion, even over the novels of M. Ducray-Duminil; and you may usually observe a few crowds cheering, a few handkerchiefs waving, at the entry of the very puniest of princes.

Certain of Rossini's compositions date from before 1812; but this was the year in which he first received the signal honour of composing for *la Scala*, the great theatre of Milan.

In order to appreciate the full extent of Rossini's glittering genius, it is absolutely essential to have some idea of the state of music as it was when he found it, and to cast a glance at some of the composers who enjoyed a certain range of popularity between 1800 and 1812.

Let me observe in passing, that if music is a living art in Italy, this is only because every one of the larger theatres is constitutionally obliged to put on a *new* opera at certain fixed dates in every year; without this legal clause, the local brand of pedant, under the pretext of *cultivating appreciation of the classics*, would without doubt or question have strangled or outlawed every up-and-coming genius at birth; and none but the dullest of plagiarists would have received his honorable permission to survive.

If Italy is the *Land of the Beautiful* in every branch of art, this is only because the public steadily refuses to be satisfied unless the *ideal of beauty* is constantly renewed; and further because, in a country where everyone relies on his own sensibility and judgment, the pedants are treated with every atom of the scorn that they deserve!

Between Cimarosa and Rossini, there are two names which claim some attention: Mayr and Paër.

Mayr, a German who came to Italy to complete his musical education, and who settled in Bergamo some forty years ago, produced about half a hundred operas between 1795 and 1820. He owed his popularity to one tiny streak of originality which fascinated the ear with its unexpected novelty. His peculiar gift lay in scoring his orchestral passages, together with the *ritornelli* and accompaniments of his arias, with all the new richness of harmonic effect which his contemporaries Haydn and Mozart were perfecting in Germany at that very time. He had scarcely a notion how to extract melody from the human voice, but he was very skilled in extracting music from his *instruments*.

His *Lodoïska*, which was first performed in the year 1800, was wildly acclaimed on every side. I saw it myself at Schönbrunn in 1809, admirably sung by the charming Signora Balzamini, who died very shortly afterwards, when she stood already poised on the threshold of a career which promised to make her one of the most distinguished singers in all Italy. Signora Balzamini owed her talent to her ugliness.

Mayr's opera *le Due Giornate* dates from the year 1801; in 1802 he wrote *i Misteri eleusini*, which acquired a reputation no less than that which is to-day enjoyed by *Don Giovanni*. At that time, Italy refused to countenance *Don Giovanni*, finding that the score was too difficult to read. *I Misteri eleusini* soon earned a reputation as the most powerful, the most dynamic work of the age—a reputation which is most strikingly indicative of the direction in which music was moving: the star of *melody* was paling, while that of harmony* was in the ascendant.

Italian composers as a whole were abandoning *simple, unsophisticated* music in favour of *complex* and *erudite** music. Mayr and Paër found the courage to execute boldly, and with real erudition, precisely what every other *maestro* in the country was attempting timidly, hesitantly, and with so little learning that every bar in the score creaked with the faults of its musical syntax; and thus these gentlemen acquired an illusory aura of genius. Moreover, to make the illusion complete, both possessed a very real and genuine musical talent.

Their greatest misfortune was that Rossini appeared upon the scene some ten years too early. Operatic music, to judge by past experience, may hope to enjoy a life of about thirty years; and so these composers may with some justice bear a grudge against fate for refusing to allow them to live out their days in peace. If Rossini had waited until 1820 before beginning his career, poor Mayr and Paër would probably have held a place in the history of music beside that of Leo, Durante, Scarlatti and the rest, as major composers of the first order, whose popularity survived until well after their death. The opera *Ginevra di Scozia* belongs to the year 1803; it is a version of the *Ariodante* episode, which forms one of the most delightful passages from Ariosto's wonderful *Orlando Furioso*. In fact, the very reason for Ariosto's phenomenal popularity in Italy is that his style contains precisely those qualities which must unfailingly seem satisfying to a musical race; whereas, far away at the opposite end of the poetic scale, I dimly perceive the dwarfish figure of the abbé Delille!

As we might have expected from a German, all the impassioned arias of love and jealousy sung by Ariodante and his beautiful Scottish maiden, whom he believes to have betrayed him, owe almost every vestige of their power to *orchestral* effects in the accompaniment. Not that the Germans are an unemotional race—God forbid that I should perpetrate so gross an injustice towards the country which has given the world a Mozart!—but none the less, their emotionalism (to take an instance from this year 1823) is of that most curious variety which joyously leads them to believe that the French Revolution, together with all its consequences, is to be found complete to the last detail in the *Book of the Apocalypse*![1]

German emotionalism, too airy, too free of earthly trammels, too lightly fed on dreams, may only too easily degenerate into what we in France would call sentimental silliness.[2] Impassioned hearts, in Germany, seem strangely divorced from logical heads, and so the honest Teuton is never too slow to assume the existence of anything whose existence seems desirable.

The theme of *Ariodante* is so magnificently suited to opera, that even Mayr found himself inspired on three or four occasions; as, for instance, in the chorus sung by the group of pious hermits in whose midst Ariodante, in his despair, has come to seek asylum. This chorus, which depends for its effect upon harmonic contrasts, upon groups of voices

[1] An historical fact. Basle, 1823.
[2] *Vide* the famous German tragedy *Schuld*, by Müllner. I should feel extremely loath to recruit the hero, one Hugo, Graf von Oerindur, as a corporal in any regiment of mine!

set one against the other, rather than on soaring melody, is magnificent. Or again, Naples to this very day has not forgotten the duet between Ariodante, his face concealed by the lowering of his vizor, and his mistress, who fails to recognize him. In this scene, Ariodante is due to engage his own brother in single combat in an attempt to save his mistress; and he is just on the point of making a full confession to her of all his suspicions, and of revealing his identity, when the sounding of trumpets summon him to the battle. This situation, as moving, perhaps, as any that the most stirring of all the passions in the human breast could have furnished, is so superb that it is hard to imagine music so harsh, so grating, so grotesquely unmusical, that, in such a context, it could fail to bring tears to the eyes. In point of fact, the music which Mayr *does* give us is masterly.

In Italy, so many tender hearts have taken this duet under their protection, that the least hint of criticism breathed against it is received as irrefutable proof of odious bad taste. Therefore I will offer only one reflection: what *might* it have been, fired by the dynamic inspiration of a Cimarosa or suffused with the ineffable sadness of a Mozart? We might have had a second version of the *Sarah* scene from the oratorio *Abraham*. This scene between Sarah and the shepherds, to whom she has turned in her search for tidings of her son Isaac, who is already on his way to the Mountain of Sacrifice, is Cimarosa's masterpiece in the pathetic manner, and infinitely superior to the finest arias of Grétry or Dalayrac.

Year after year, Mayr would turn out two or three new operas, and was met with rapturous applause in the most famous theatres in the land. How could he fail to believe himself the equal of the great masters? In 1807, an opera entitled *Adelasia ed Aleramo* promised to be superior to anything which the worthy Bavarian had previously achieved. *La Rosa bianca e la Rosa rossa*, an opera based on a magnificent theme borrowed from English history (the Wars of the Roses), enjoyed immense popularity in 1812. Walter Scott had still to reveal the inexhaustible sources of superb drama which a people may discover by digging into the forgotten history of its own civil wars in the late mediaeval period; moreover, *la Rosa bianca* provided the tenor Bonoldi with a sublime opportunity to display the full potentialities of his remarkable voice.

But the opening *allegro* passage from the overture is only too typical of the abysmal depths of triviality which yawn with horrid persistence beneath the feet of any German composer who dare go in search of *gaiety*!

The recognition-scene between Enrico and his friend Vanoldo is filled with a pure and naïve grace, of a character which Rossini never quite achieved, because its very perfection depends upon the absence of even rarer qualities. This particular duet, incidentally, is by Paër.

A perfection of the same order is to be observed in the celebrated duet,

È deserto il bosco intorno . . .[1]

This is Mayr's finest achievement, and would indeed stand among the musical masterpieces of all ages were it not for a certain lack of expressive power in the concluding passages. In the scene of Vanoldo's treachery towards his friend Enrico, the librettist has furnished his composer with a device so deliciously ingenious as to be truly worthy of Metastasio. Enrico, learning that his friend has been attempting to win the favours of the lady with whom he (Enrico) is in love, cries out

Ah, chi può mirarla in volto
E non ardere d'amor![2]

Mayr was fortunate enough to light upon an Italian folk-tune to express this delightful inspiration; and so this duet, far sweeter than the more dynamic music of Cimarosa or Rossini, must surely be the fondest heart's-delight of every gentle, sentimental nature.

In *opera buffa*, on the other hand, Mayr reveals all the clumsy, elephantine gaiety of a good, dull-witted burgher.

Gli Originali is an opera which can be quite amusing if one has almost forgotten the sound of real Italian music. The theme is that of

[1] *Vanoldo:*
　　　È deserto il bosco intorno,
　　　Spunta appena incerta luna;
　　　Tutto tace, l'aria è bruna,
　　　Densa notte più si fa . . .
　　　　　　　　　(Act II, sc. xi)

[2] *Enrico:*
　　　Tu, Vanoldo! . . . E m'eri amico!
　　　Tu, Clotilde? . . . Ohimè! che ascolto!
　　　(Ah! chi può mirarla in volto,
　　　E non ardere d'amor?)
　　　　　　　　　(Act II, sc. xi)

melomania. When this opera first appeared, in 1799, it merely served to stress the bitter absence of Cimarosa, who was at that time already lying in prison in Naples, and, according to popular rumour, already hanged. If Cimarosa had had the setting of such a theme, people asked, what delightful arias in the style of

Sei morelli e quattro baj . . .,[1]

or of

Io quand'ero un fraschettone . . .[2]

or of

Amicone del mio core . . .,

might there not have come of it?

The genuine *melomaniac*, a farcical character who is rarely to be met with in France, where his obsession is usually no more than a snobbish affectation, is to be encountered at every step in Italy.

When I was garrisoned in Brescia*, I was introduced to a certain gentleman of the neighbourhood, who was a really extreme case of excessive musical sensibility. He was exceedingly well-educated, and by nature very gentle; but whenever he sat at a concert, there would come a point when, in sheer delight at the music, he would proceed quite unconsciously to remove his shoes. Then he would sit quietly, shoe-less, until the coming of some really *superb* passage, at which, unfailingly, he would fling both shoes over his shoulders into the crowd of spectators grouped behind him.

At Bologna, I have watched the most notorious miser in the city

[1] An aria inserted by Cimarosa into Paisiello's *Zingari in Fiera*. An old man tells a young girl what advantages she may expect from pleasing him:

Sei morelli e quattro baj,
Due carozze ricche assai—
                    Che carozze!—
Per adesso son ducati
Quattro mila cento e tre [. . .]
Tutto questo, gioia mia,
Tutto è fatto sì per te!

[2] An aria by Cimarosa inserted into Anfossi's *Gli Artigiani*.

Bernardo:
Io quand' ero un fraschettone,
Sono stato il più felice;
Ogni ninfa in sul balcone
Era l'idol del mio cor.
Più di cento trenta cinque
Sono state le mie belle . . .

fling his gold about the floor and gesticulate like a dervish when the music happened to touch some supreme fibre in his being.

Mayr's "melomaniac" merely reproduces on the stage forms of behaviour which can be observed any day in the auditorium. But in any case, the very tone of the lamentations which arose on all sides over the absence of Cimarosa betrayed the fact that this fine man and great artist was soon to pass from fashion. Even if he were to have continued composing, the majority of the *dilettanti*, instead of yielding with unconscious simplicity to the naïve charm of his songs, would soon have allowed *memory* to usurp the throne of *imagination*, and the magic of surrender would have been violated by intrusive reminiscences of a twenty-years' series of enchanting masterpieces.

Mayr, besides being the most prolific composer of the interregnum, is also the most erudite; every bar he ever wrote is of impeccable correctness. The curious reader might take up the scores of *Medea*, *Cora*, *Adelasia*, *Elisa*, etc., and search them microscopically from end to end without detecting a single slip in the process; Mayr's perfection has the exasperating faultlessness of a Boileau, and the only puzzle is to discover why one is not more deeply moved. Yet you have only to pick up any opera by Rossini to find yourself in a new and undiscovered country; the clear, refreshing winds of the high mountains are stirring about you; the air is purer to breathe; you seem to be born again in a new world, and the thirst for genius is upon you. Rossini flings down whole handfuls of new ideas with careless condescension, sometimes hitting his mark, sometimes missing altogether; his music is a jumble, a conglomeration, an indescribable profusion of negligent luxury, all thrown together pell-mell with the incautious profligacy of inexhaustible wealth. I repeat: Mayr is the very genius of correctness; but Rossini is the very spirit of genius.

I shall not dispute the fact that Mayr has incontestably written some eight or ten numbers which have a deceptive glitter of genius about them, at least during the first three or four performances; as, for instance, the sextet from *Elena**. There was a time once, I remember, when I used to credit even Dalayrac with an occasional stroke of inspiration, in spite of the chronic disorganization which always marred his ideas; but, since then, I have taken the trouble to study Cimarosa rather more seriously, and have discovered the source of the majority of Dalayrac's more striking "inventions"; one may suspect, therefore, that a careful study of Sacchini, Piccinni, or Buranello might likewise suggest an origin and sufficient explanation for the occasional flashes of genius which light up the scores of our worthy friend Mayr. But with one important difference: for the German is undoubtedly a man of very considerable talent, while his erudition is as genuine and as solid as Dalayrac's is superficial and elementary; and consequently one may assume that Mayr, if he *did* borrow, will have disguised the fact most admirably.

However, there was certainly one occasion, in Venice, when Mayr did *not* bother to disguise his borrowings. The victim, in this particular instance, was Cherubini, and our worthy composer simply turned to the music-copyist attached to the theatre for which he was working, and told him blatantly: *Here is Cherubini's* Faniska; *please copy out the score from page* ... *to page* ...! The "loan" ran to some twenty-seven pages, and was reproduced note for note down to the last ♭

Mayr was to music what Dr Johnson was to English prose; he created a style which was heavy, turgid and a thousand removes from the natural beauty of simple speech, but which, nevertheless, had a certain quality of its own, particularly when one had struggled and struggled and eventually got used to it. But it was above all the *turgidity* of Mayr's style which enabled Rossini to obliterate his reputation in the twinkling of an eye; and indeed, some such sudden annihilation is the ultimate fate of all aesthetic artificiality, for, one fine day, the eye will light upon *natural* beauty, and be astonished that the opposite has managed to deceive it for so long. It is not hard to understand why our own *classicists* are so determined that Shakespeare shall never be performed, and so eager to set the whole pack of "young liberals" at his heels. What awful fate awaits our modern tragedies the day that Paris is allowed to see *Macbeth**?

After Mayr, I suppose that no composer of the interregnum enjoyed so wide a European reputation as *Paër*, a musician who, in spite of his German-sounding name, was in fact born in Parma. The reason for this success may perhaps be due to the fact that Paër, besides possessing an undeniable, and indeed quite remarkable, flair for composition, is an extremely shrewd individual, of great intelligence, and fully cognizant of all the secret arts which make a man respected in society. It has been said that one of the most striking proofs of Paër's shrewdness is the way in which, for eight whole years, he successfully concealed all knowledge of Rossini's existence from the people of Paris. Incidentally, if ever there was a man born who seemed predestined to delight the average Frenchman, that man is Rossini—Rossini, the *Voltaire* of music!

Every one of Rossini's works which has so far been performed in Paris has been completely ruined by the absurdity of the production*. I still shudder with horror whenever I think of the first performance of *l'Italiana in Algeri**; and shortly afterwards, when it came to giving *la Pietra del Paragone*, the most scrupulous care was observed to cut out specifically those two numbers, the aria

Eco pietosa . . .,

and the *finale*

Sigillara . . .,

which, in Italy, had earned this masterly opera its most thunderous applause*. Even the delightful chorus from the second act of *Tancredi*, in the scene where the Knights of Syracuse stand and sing on the bridge in the forest, was reduced to a bare half of its proper length, apparently from motives of "prudence".[1]

One of Paër's earliest works was *l'Oro fa tutto* (1793), but his first major success came with *Griselda* (1797). What is there to be said about this famous opera, which has been played on every stage in Europe? Everybody knows by heart the wonderful tenor aria, just as everybody admires *Sargino* (1803). I have no hesitation in placing these two operas in a category of their own, far above the remainder of Paër's work. *Agnese*, for instance, seems to me to belong to an altogether inferior order, and only owes its European reputation to the facile and ghastly trick of copying the actions, words and gestures of madmen—unfortunate wretches, whom nobody is going to submit to the troublesome test of a realistic study when such a study would involve setting foot in the grisly asylums to which they are confined by public charity. The listener's mind, horror-stricken by the gruesome sight of a father driven mad by his daugher's desertion, is an easy prey to the blandishments of musical suggestion. Many fine singers, including Galli, Pellegrini, Ambrogetti, and Zucchelli, have excelled in the rôle of this madman; but even the remarkable popularity of the opera cannot shake my con-

[1] As this page is being copied ready for the press, I notice that the great comic part of Isabella in *l'Italiana in Algeri* is to be sung by Signorina Naldi.

viction that it is profoundly wrong for art to deal with purely *horrifying* subjects. The madness of Shakespeare's *Lear* is made tolerable by the most touching devotion of his daughter Cordelia; but I personally feel that there is *nothing* to redeem the ghastly and pitiable condition of the heroine's father in *Agnese*. The immediate effect of music being to plunge the mind into a state where impressions are felt with an intensity which is multiplied a hundred-fold, I find this scene horrifying beyond endurance; and *Agnese* always remains with me as a thoroughly disagreeable memory, which is only the more unpalatable for having a theme which is based on reality. It is like the subject of *death*; it will always be easy enough to frighten men with the idea of death; but, for all that, to use the subject of death as a weapon in an argument is, and will always remain, a fool's trick, or a piece of selfish, priestly calculation. Since death is inevitable, let us rather forget it!

Camilla (1798), although similarly owing part of its popularity to the fashion for spine-chilling tales which, at that time, had spread far and wide under the influence of the "gothic novels" of Mrs Radcliffe, is nevertheless a better opera than *Agnese*; the theme is less gruesome, and more genuinely tragic. Bassi, one of the finest *buffi* in all Italy, achieved a masterly performance as the servant in the scene where he lies flat between his master's legs, and sings at the top of his voice to awaken him, crying:

> *Signor, la vita è corta,*
> *Partiam per carità . . .*[1]

This entire opera is filled with interminable passages of *recitativo secco*, which is harsh, and the dreariest thing in the world, as it might be an opera by Gluck. Where there is nothing to *soothe the ear*, there is no music.

---

[1] [Loredano, accompanied by his servant Cola and others, encamps before the gates of a solitary and grim-looking castle.]

> *Cienza:*
> Doman se non s'arrende,
> L'assalto si darà [. . .]
> *Loredano:*
> Ebben, cosa m'importa?
> Doman si partirà.
> *Cola:*
> Signor, la vita è corta:
> Partiam per carità!
>   (Act I, sc. x)

The part of Camilla herself used always to be played in Italy by Signora Paër, the composer's wife, who was a highly-accomplished singer. She enjoyed an extraordinary run of success in the rôle, which lasted for ten years; but to-day I can see no one who could play Camilla with any real distinction, unless it be Madame Pasta. I wonder whether the genius of this great artist could give the opera a new lease of life and popularity? Now that Rossini has taught us to expect such an amazing wealth of musical ideas, and Mozart has taught us to look for profundity, I am afraid that it may be rather late in the day to start listening to music in the manner of Gluck.

Mayr and Paër are the two outstanding figures who dominate the interregnum which stretches between Cimarosa and Rossini; having discussed them, my only remaining task is to name a few of the lesser composers of the period. I prefer simply to relegate them to a footnote.[1]

[1] Anfossi, Coccia, Farinelli, Federici, Fioravanti, Generali, Guglielmi (*father and son*), Manfrocci, Martini, Mosca, Nazolini, Nicolini, Orgitano, Orlandi, Pavesi, Portogallo, Salieri, Sarti, Tarchi, Trento, Weigl, Winter, Zingarelli, *etc.*

IV

Mozart in Italy

I WAS forgetting that it is essential to add a word or two about Mozart,[1] before we turn our attention permanently and exclusively to Rossini.

For ten years, the musical scene in Italy had been dominated by Messrs Mayr, Paër, Pavesi, Zingarelli, Generali, Fioravanti, Weigl, and by thirty or more others whose names are now more or less forgotten, but whose reign was then placid and untroubled. These gentlemen believed in their hearts that they were the true heirs and successors of Cimarosa, Pergolesi, *etc.*, and the audiences shared their belief, and continued to do so until, suddenly, Mozart came striding like a colossus amid this lilliputian swarm of Italian composers, whose stature had only seemed formidable in the absence of true greatness.

Mayr, Paër and their imitators had for many years been seeking to adapt the style of German music to the taste of Italian audiences and, like all compromisers and advocates of the *mezzo-termine* who manage to satisfy the most tepid elements of either party, they achieved a flattering measure of success—flattering, that is to say, to anyone who is not finicking about the *quality* of the applause which he receives. In contrast to this, Mozart, who, like all great artists, had never sought to please anyone but himself and a few kindred spirits; Mozart, who like some Spanish conspirator, could boast of having set his aim at none but the highest aristocracy of the society in which he lived—Mozart had followed an extremely perilous course.

Moreover, he enjoyed none of the advantages of a dominating personality; he was not prepared to spend his life flattering the mighty in their high places, bribing the press, and puffing his own name on to the lips of the multitude; consequently, he remained almost unknown in Europe as a whole until after his death. Furthermore, in Italy, his rivals were in possession of the field, writing their music specifically to match the voices of their best singers, composing pretty little duets for the

[1] See also *Appendix I.* (*Trans.*)

current mistress of the local Princeling and manoeuvring for patronage in the most advantageous quarters . . . and yet, to-day, what is the standing of a work by Mayr or *** beside an opera by Mozart? None the less, in Italy in the year 1800, the position was precisely the reverse. Mozart was thought of as a *romantic*, as a crude barbarian, a vandal poised for invasion across the sacred frontiers of classical art. It is not to be imagined that the ensuing revolution in taste, which to us seems so natural and so inevitable, was to take place in a single day.

Mozart was still a boy when he composed two operas for la Scala in Milan: *Mitridate* (1770) and *Lucio Silla* (1773).[1] These two operas were not by any means unsuccessful, but it was scarcely likely that a mere boy should dare strike out on his own against the current fashion. Whatever the inherent qualities of these two works, they were soon swallowed up in the great popular torrent of music whose course was being determined by Sacchini, Piccinni, and Paisiello, and the two tiny successes left no trace in the minds of men.

But, in the year 1803, or thereabouts, rumours of Mozart's triumphs in Munich and Vienna began to trickle across the Alps and disturb the profound complacency of the Italian *dilettanti*, who at first refused to believe their ears. Who was this *barbarian*, that he should reap so goodly a harvest in the field of Art? His symphonies and quartets, of course, had been known for some time; but who was Mozart to meddle with the esoteric mysteries of *vocal music*? He was spoken of much as the more ferocious partisans of French classicism still speak of Shakespeare: *The fellow is a savage, of course, but, like most savages, physically powerful; even the muck-heaps of Ennius may hold a grain or two of gold; if only he had had the chance to take lessons from Zingarelli or from Paisiello, we suppose he might have done something.* And so Mozart was set aside and thankfully forgotten.

In 1807, a small *élite* of Italian intellectuals, who had been invited to form part of Napoleon's suite during his campaigns of 1805 and 1806, and who had spent a while in Munich, began once again to broach the subject of Mozart; and it was decided, as an experiment, to try out one of his operas—*die Entführung aus dem Serail*, if I remember rightly. But any performance of this opera demands a high degree of competence from the orchestra; above all, it requires instrumentalists with a strict

---

[1] Mozart, who was born in Salzburg in 1756, and died in Vienna in 1796*, was therefore fourteen when he wrote *Mitridate*.

sense of *rhythm*, who can be thoroughly trusted not to falsify the *tempo* of the music; for this music is very different from the kind whose tunes can be got by heart after a couple of hearings, like the little romance, *C'est l'amour*,[1] which is so popular in Paris at the moment, or like the aria

Di tanti palpiti . . .

from *Tancredi*.

The Italian orchestra, therefore, settled down to work; but, faced with the ocean of notes which lay blackly across the pages of this wild, foreign score, the poor players could make nothing of it. You see, it meant that each one of them had to play strictly *in time*, and, above all, that each instrument had to *enter* and *finish* exactly where Mozart had said that it should. The lazier players, in disgust, referred to this unfamiliar principle as *barbaric*; the epithet was beginning to gain ground, and the whole project was on the point of being abandoned, when one or two of the wealthier *dilettanti* of the town, whom I might name if I thought it worth while, and who were inspired by a spirit of proper pride rather than by the superficial pin-pricks of vanity, loudly asserted that it was absurd that Italians should let themselves be defeated by the mere difficulty of any music; and so, by threatening to withdraw their support from the theatre where rehearsals were in progress, they eventually secured a first performance of Mozart's opera. Poor Mozart! Certain persons who chanced to be at that famous *première*, and who, later, have learned to love this great composer, have assured me on their honour that never in their lives did they hear such an unimaginable witches-sabbath! The choruses, the *ensembles*, and above all the *finales*, were transformed into a cacophony of positively appalling dimensions; while the over-all effect was of some howling carnival of raging demons! In all, perhaps two or three arias and one duet managed to swim on the surface of this boiling sea of discords, and achieved a reasonably adequate performance.

By the very same evening, the town had split into two warring factions. *Backstairs patriotism** (to use a phrase coined by Turgot in 1763, on the occasion of the performance of a certain nationalistic tragedy

---

[1] This vulgar little tune (I confess it with a due sense of shame) seems to me to be considerably *less* horrid than the celebrated romances of Monsieur [Romagnesi] and so many others. At least it can boast a rhythm which corresponds in some degree to our national temperament.

entitled *le Siège de Calais*) is the most devastating moral malady of Italy; and now the raging mania of *backstairs patriotism* awoke in all its blind fury, and proclaimed in every coffee-house in the town that no man born beyond the borders of Italy would ever write a decent tune! Upon which a certain nobleman, M***, with that spirit of moderation which is so characteristic of him, remarked: *Gli accompagnamenti tedeschi non sono guardie d'onore pel canto, ma gendarmi.*[1]

The opposite faction, under the leadership of two or three young officers who had stayed in Munich, insisted that, although Mozart could offer nothing in the way of *ensembles*, one might discover in his works two or three little arias, or even duets, which carried the true stamp of genius, and, more important still, of genuine originality. Whereupon the good folk whose only creed was *My country, right or wrong!* proceeded to fall back upon their favourite argument, and to assert that anyone who could admire music written by a *foreigner* was a *suspect Italian*. In the midst of these alarums and excursions, the run of performances arranged for the Mozart opera reached its due conclusion, the orchestra having played progressively worse and worse as night succeeded night. But at this point, certain superior folk (and nearly every Italian town holds two or three such; profound, far-sighted men, but of a brooding Machiavellian disposition, sombre, suspicious and persecuted, who keep close watch upon their tongues in front of strangers, and a still closer watch upon anything they publish)—these superior beings, then, began to murmur among themselves: *Since we observe that the name of Mozart excites such tempestuous loathing; since a whole country-side is in a fever to prove that he cannot write a note of music; and since we observe that the insults addressed to him are more burning and bitter by far than ever those which were hurled at Nicolini or Puccita* (these being the deadliest and dreariest composers of the age); *we therefore may conclude that this poor foreigner is likely to harbour a spark of genius.*

This, at any rate, was the type of argument current among those who frequented the Princess Bianca, and hinted at in other groups which met at the theatre, in the box of this or that distinguished local notability, whose names I may not mention for fear of damaging their reputations. On the other hand, I had rather draw a veil of silence over the coarse and brutal insults which were published in the press, and penned by the

---

[1] Teutonic accompaniments do not constitute a guard of honour for the melody, but rather a police escort!

official agents of the police. The cause of Mozart's music seemed to be lost; and scandalously, irretrievably lost at that.

At this point, however, there entered upon the scene a certain *dilettante*, exceedingly noble by birth and furthermore exceedingly wealthy, who, none the less, was not blessed by nature with overmuch common sense, and in fact belonged to that class of persons who carve themselves out a little niche within the framework of society by standing forth regularly every six months and declaring themselves the apostles of some new paradox, which they then proceed to preach here, there and everywhere at the top of their voices. This gentleman, having learned from a letter which one of his mistresses had sent him from Vienna, that Mozart was the greatest musician in all the world, began to talk of him in a most mysterious manner. He gathered together the six most competent instrumentalists in the town, dazzled them with the luxury of his establishment, deafened them with the clatter of his English horses and the rattle of his barouches, which he liked to have specially constructed in London to his own specifications; and finally, in the utmost secrecy, ordered them to practise the first-act *finale* of *Don Giovanni*. His palace was immense; and he placed at their disposal an entire wing which looked out over his private gardens. If any of these poor musicians was to break the oath of secrecy, he was threatened with the most dire consequences; and in Italy, when a wealthy man utters such objurgations, he is pretty certain to be obeyed. Incidentally, the hero of my story happened to have in his service five or six Brescia *bullies*, to whom no deed of violence came amiss.

It took not less than six whole months for the Prince's unfortunate musicians to master the first-act *finale* of *Don Giovanni*; but at last they managed it strictly *in tempo*. Whereupon, for the first time ever, they actually discovered *Mozart*! The Prince then engaged half a dozen singers, upon whom, likewise, he laid a strict injunction to secrecy. After two months of unremitting labour, the singers also managed to learn their parts. Still in the deepest and blackest secrecy, as though engaged upon some political conspiracy, the Prince ordered a performance of the *finales* and of all the principal numbers of *Don Giovanni* to be given at his country residence. Like everyone else's in Italy, his ear for music was good; he listened, and approved of what he heard. Now confident of the outcome, he began to grow slightly less mysterious whenever the conversation turned to Mozart; he provoked his antagonists, and finally came to the point of engaging in a wager, sufficiently heavy to interest both his and his opponent's vanity, and sufficiently exciting amid the silent stillness of an Italian town, to become the nine-days' wonder of all this part of Lombardy. The bet was, that he would organize a performance of certain numbers selected from *Don Giovanni*, and that a panel of judges, whose names were agreed upon on the spot, and who were known to be impartial critics, would pronounce as their considered verdict that Mozart was a composer of more or less the same quality as Mayr or Paër, and that although, like them, he had a weakness for too much noise and general Teutonic brassiness, he was all in all not far beneath the composers of *Sargino* and *Cora*. Such brazen assertions, I am told, provoked ungovernable fits of laughter simply in the making. Upon divers pretexts, the Prince, who was by now thoroughly enjoying the anticipated triumphs of which his vanity was assured, repeatedly postponed the great day; but at last the memorable incident took place. The test was held at his country residence, and he won the bet upon a unanimous verdict; and for the whole of the two years that followed, he was more conceited by half than he had ever been before.

This incident caused a great deal of excitement, and Mozart began to be played in Italy. In Rome, in 1811 or thereabouts, *Don Giovanni* endured a noble mutilation. Fraülein Häser (later to play a very special part of her own at the Congress of Vienna, and who momentarily caused certain Great Personages to forget all about the *Apocalypse*) was among those who sang in this production, and she sang extremely well. Her voice was most accomplished; but unfortunately the orchestra never kept time except by luck or accident, and the instruments were perpetually chasing each others' tails across the score; the result, therefore, was not unlike a Haydn symphony played by amateurs (and Heaven preserve us from *that*!). Finally, in 1814, *Don Giovanni* was given at *la Scala*, and stunned the audience into applauding. In 1815, *le Nozze di Figaro* was presented, and on the whole better understood. In 1816, *die Zauberflöte* was an appalling flop*, and ruined Petracchi, the lessee of the theatre; but finally the revival of *Don Giovanni* created a *furore*, if one may dare to use the word *furore* of anything connected with Mozart.

To-day, Mozart is more or less understood in Italy; but his music is still very far from being *felt*. In the general opinion of the public, the principal result of his impact on music has been to throw into the shade Messrs Mayr, Weigl, Winter and company, together with all the rest of the "Teutonic faction".

In this respect, Mozart smoothed the way for Rossini; for Rossini's wider reputation only begins to emerge in 1815, and this meant that, when he finally did appear fully on the horizon, he found no rivals in possession of the field worthier than Messrs Pavesi, Mosca, Guglielmi, Generali, Portogallo, Nicolini and one or two other last despairing imitators of Cimarosa and Paisiello. These gentlemen had something in common with those last-ditch defenders of the 'magnificent' epic style and of the classically 'noble' scenes of Racinian tragedy who may yet be found in France today, still clinging desperately to their decayed traditions. They could invariably count on a good measure of applause, and be certain of receiving the warmest praise couched in the purest language; but their admirers were somehow always half-aware of a tiny grain of *boredom* germinating in the bottom of their souls, and this tended to make them extremely crotchety. Their triumphs in the field of opera resembled certain others in the field of drama—let us say, those of *Saül*, of *le Maire du Palais*, of *Clytemnestre* or of *Louis IX*—in that, no one in the theatre *daring* to admit that he was frankly bored, each man turned purposefully to his neighbour, and, stifling a yawn as he proceeded, set out to demonstrate that what he had just watched was truly beautiful.

V

Mozart's Style

To-day, in the year 1823, after putting up a courageous resistance which lasted for ten years, Italy has at length ceased to be hypocritical in talking about Mozart, and therefore her opinion deserves to be taken into account and her judgment treated with serious consideration.

Mozart in Italy will never enjoy the success which he has known in Germany or in England; the reason, which is simplicity itself, is that his music does not *reflect the temperamental characteristics induced by the Italian climate*; it is emotive music, destined above all to evoke images in a vein of tender melancholy, which fill the soul with memories of sadness and echo the dying languor of the sweetest of passions. But love is not the same in Bologna as it is in Königsberg; love in Italy is far more dynamic, more impatient, more violent, less dependent upon dreams and imagination. It is not a gentle and gradual tide which sweeps slowly, but for all eternity, into the farthest recesses of the soul; it takes the whole being by storm, and its invasion is the work of an instant; it is a frenzy*—but frenzy knows nothing of melancholy; it is a wild explosion of massed energies—but melancholy springs from a *dearth*, a *failing* of energy. No novel, as far as I know, has ever described love in the Italian manner; and Italy, as a natural consequence, is a land where the novel is unknown. Instead, Italy has her Cimarosa, who has used the true language of his own land to describe its loves, in every shade and variation, from the dreaming girl,

Ha! tu sai ch' io vivo in pene ...[1]

sung by Carolina in *il Matrimonio segreto*, to the old man whom love has driven half out of his wits:

Io venia per sposarti ...

But I must call a halt to these philosophical speculations upon the variations to which the phenomenon of love is subjected under the

[1] See above, p. 5.

influence of different climatic conditions, for they might tempt us into infinite regions of metaphysical abstruseness. Any mind which was destined by nature to understand notions of this character, which are scarcely *thoughts* at all, but rather an obscure awareness of the senses, will have understood me already from the few half-defined hints that I have given; for the rest, the infinite majority, they will never perceive anything in such speculations save an infinite weariness of metaphysics; or at best, if the notion should chance to fall in with the fashion, they might condescend to get by heart a score or so of sonorous quotations on the subject; but then *I* am in no mood to sit here polishing up quotations for the benefit of persons of *that* stamp.

So let us return to Mozart, and to the *violence* of his music, which is a phrase that all Italians tend to use. Mozart appeared upon the musical horizon of Italy almost at the same moment as Rossini, in 1812; but I am strangely afraid that *he* will still be known and loved when Rossini's star has faded into dust. For Mozart was an originator in every field, in everything he touched; he is like nobody, and nobody is like him; whereas Rossini yet bears faint resemblances to Cimarosa, to Guglielmi and to Haydn.

The science of harmony may eventually explore the obscurest and remotest frontiers of music; yet, at the end of each road which leads to new knowledge, the explorers will be amazed to discover that Mozart has been there before them. Thus, in the technical, purely mechanical aspect of his art, Mozart can never be surpassed; and any composer who attempted to out-do him on this count would be like a painter who tried to out-do Titian in the effectiveness and realism of his colouring, or like a dramatist who tried to better Racine in the purity of his verse or in the delicacy and restraint of his expression.

As to the spiritual qualities of Mozart's music, the tempest-wind of his impetuous genius will never lack the power to sweep away the dreaming, contemplative spirits of this world, nor to fill their souls with sad and haunting visions. Sometimes the impact of his music is so immediate, that the vision in the *mind* remains blurred and incomplete, while the *soul* seems to be directly invaded, *drenched*, as it were, in wave upon wave of melancholy. Rossini is always amusing; Mozart never; Mozart is like a mistress who is always serious and often sad, but whose very sadness is a fascination, discovering ever deeper springs of love; such women either create no impression at all, in which case they are

called prudes; or else, if they leave their mark but once only, the scar
bites deep, and heart and soul are lost to them completely and for ever.

Just at the moment, however, Mozart is a fashionable craze in high
society, which, although it is by definition passionless, is always
happiest in making a pretence of passion, in persuading itself that it is
passionately in love with the most passionate of passions; and so long
as this fashionable passion persists, we shall have no sure means of
judging the ultimate and lasting effect of Mozart's music upon the
human heart.

In Italy, there are certain distinguished *diuettanti*, who, although few
in number, will always manage in the end to determine public opinion
in the arts. Their success is due, *firstly*, to their sincerity; *secondly*, to
the fact that, very gradually, their voice finds an echo in all those minds
which, while being sufficiently well-equipped to hold a clear opinion,
need first to hear it formulated by someone else; and *thirdly*, to the fact
that, while everything else about them revolves in a constant state of
chaos and turmoil, following the multifarious whims of fashion, they
alone remain stable, never shouting to make themselves heard above the
din, but waiting until their opinion is invited, and then repeating,
modestly but inexorably, the same considered verdict.

Such people* found Rossini *amusing*, and hence they greeted *la Pietra
del Paragone* and *l'Italiana in Algeri* with enthusiastic applause; furthermore, they were deeply moved, for instance, by the famous quartet
from *Bianca e Faliero*, and maintained that Rossini had brought new
life into the *opera seria*; but in the bottom of their hearts they think of
him as a brilliant *arch-heretic*; he seems to them, perhaps, like some new
Pietro da Cortona, that most impressive of painters, who, for a while,
dazzled all Italy, and all but eclipsed Raphael, for Raphael seemed cold
and almost uninspired by comparison. Raphael, incidentally, had
much of the unostentatious perfection and many of the profound
spiritual qualities which characterize Mozart. Nothing is less *showy* in
the whole world of painting than the modest appearance and the
celestial purity of a *Virgin* painted by the great master of Urbino; her
divine gaze is cast downward upon her son; and if the canvas were not
signed *Raphael*, the mass of humanity would pass it by in scorn,
scarcely condescending to pause a single instant before a thing so *simple*,
before a thing so *commonplace*—or seeming so, at least to him, who
glances at it with a commonplace soul.

The same thing is true of the duet from *Don Giovanni*,

> *Là ci darem la mano*
> *Là mi dirai di sì . . .*[1]

If this were not signed *Mozart*, how many of our smart young dandies would find its slow *tempo* anything but unspeakably boring?

By contrast, these same young bucks are startled, almost *electrified* into awareness by Rossini's aria

> *Sono docile . . .*

from the *Barber of Seville*. What do they care if this aria implies a radical misinterpretation of Rosina's character and situation? Would they even *notice* it?

But if Mozart's reputation should prove to be enduring, there is one consolation for Rossini; namely, that Rossini's music and Mozart's music scarcely ever appeal to the same audience. Mozart might almost say to his brilliant rival what the aunt said to her niece in Dumoustier's comedy, *les Femmes*:

> *Va,*
> *Tu ne plairas jamais à qui j'aurai su plaire.*

These same distinguished arbiters of taste in Italy, to whom I was referring a few minutes ago, maintain further, that if Rossini is inferior to Cimarosa in the richness and fertility of his comic inspiration, he is vastly superior to the Neapolitan in the speed, viracity and *verve* of his style. Rossini's scores constantly show him telescoping* phrases which Cimarosa would unfailingly have developed to their remotest implications. If it is true that Rossini has never written an aria as profoundly comic as

> *Amicone del mio core . . .*

it is equally true that Cimarosa never conceived a duet as sparkling and as *rapid* as the song which Almaviva sings with Figaro:

> *Oggi arriva un reggimento,*
> *È mio amico il colonello . . .*
> (Barber, Act I).

or a duet as feather-light as that between Rosina and Figaro (*Act I*).

[1] Act I, sc. ix.

Such qualities are entirely foreign to Mozart; he has neither comic verve nor lightness; he stands almost as diametrically in contrast to Cimarosa as he does to Rossini. It would have been inconceivable for him to write the aria

Quelle pupille tenere . . .[1]

in *gli Orazi e Curiazi* without an all-pervading strain of melancholy. He never suspected that love could even exist without a hint of sadness or fear.

The more completely one surrenders to the music of Rossini and Cimarosa, the more one *gorges* on its richness, the more austere the discipline needed to appreciate Mozart; on the other hand, the more thoroughly one is *saturated* with Rossini's tinkling dance-tunes and cascades of grace-notes, the deeper the satisfaction to be experienced in returning to the momentous harmonies and the stately rhythms of the author of *Così fan tutte*.

Mozart, as far as I am aware, only allowed himself two instants of gaiety in the whole of his life; the first, in *Don Giovanni*, when Leporello invites the Statue of the Commander to supper; the second, in *Così fan tutte*. This exactly corresponds to the number of occasions on which Rossini let himself go so far as to be melancholy. *La Gazza ladra* tells how a young soldier is forced to stand by and watch, while his adored mistress is condemned to death before his very eyes and borne off to execution; but there is nothing *sad* in it. In the whole of *Otello* there is not a hint of melancholy, save in the duet between Emilia and Desdemona, in the *Prayer-scene* and in the *Willow-song*. I shall have occasion later on to mention the quartet from *Bianca e Faliero*, the duet from *Armida*, and even the superb orchestral passage from the same work which occurs when Rinaldo, prey to a thousand conflicting passions, leaves the stage only to return an instant later;

[1] *Curiace:*
> Quelle pupille tenere
> Che brillano d'amore
> Vedran di questo core
> Candida ognor la fe';
> Ma se il dover mi chiama,
> Ma se l'onor m' invita,,
> Non palpitar, mia vita,
> Non dubitar di me . . .
>   (Act I, sc v)

C

but here is the point: this duet, with all its magnificence, is not a musical portrait of *melancholy*, but a superb illustration of *love in the Italian manner*. It is a description of *passion*, sombre, forbidding, frenzied even—but still passion.

Between Rossini's real masterpieces, *la Pietra del Paragone*, *l'Italiana in Algeri*, *Tancredi* or *Otello*, and Mozart's operas, there is not one single characteristic idea in common. The resemblance, which at best is superficial, and goes no deeper than a few technical coincidences of style—this resemblance, if in fact it exists at all, came much later, when, in *la Gazza ladra*, for instance, or in the introduction to *Mosè in Egitto*, Rossini was making a conscious effort to imitate the *compelling* qualities of German music.

Rossini never achieved anything so deeply moving as the duet

Crudel, perchè finora farmi languir così?[1]

nor did he ever achieve anything so profoundly comic as

Io quand' ero un fraschettone . . .[2];

nor even anything quite like the duel-scene from Cimarosa's *i Nemici generosi*, which was so exquisitely performed in Paris, fifteen years or so ago, by the inimitable Barilli*.

But on the other hand, neither Mozart nor Cimarosa ever wrote anything quite so fantastically gay and light-hearted as the duet

D'un bell' uso di Turchia . . .,[3]

from *il Turco in Italia*. Nothing could be more sparklingly *Gallic*, in every glorious sense of the word!

These ideas, I feel, give some indication of the lines of thought which must be pursued if one is to acquire a true, exact and deep understanding of the distinctive styles of each of the three great masters, who, comet-like and trailing their respective tails of imitators, have come in our own day to share the dominion of musical Europe. He who hears can imitate; and so imitators abound. There are imitations even among the tinny little dance-tunes of the *Théâtre Feydeau*. But let us make an end of it at last, and turn to ROSSINI.

[1] *Don Giovanni*, Act III, sc. ii.   [2] See above, p. 24.   [3] See below, p. 150.

CHAPTER I

Early Years

GIOACCHINO ROSSINI was born on the 29th of February, 1792, in Pesaro,[1] a delectable little township in the Papal State, on the shores of the Gulf of Venice. Pesaro is a port, with a busy life of its own. It rises among wooded hills, and the woods stretch down to the very brink of the sea. The countryside shows no trace of that barrenness and sterility which so often betrays the scorching breath of the sea-wind. On the coasts of the great oceans, where towering waves and tremendous storms scar the land with the indelible marks of their dark and inhuman violence, every object seems to speak of desolation and calls to mind, as on the frontiers of some immense and despotic empire, the hand of the tyrant and of his fierce, inflexible authority; but the Mediterranean, this gentle inland sea with its sheltered, shaded banks, knows nothing of all that wild, unfettered energy; every vista is a paradise of sweet and sensual beauty—and nowhere is the landscape sweeter or more sensual than within the dreaming confines of the Gulf of Venice. There is evidence enough to remind the beholder that this was the cradle of civilization in our world. Under these skies, forty centuries ago, men discovered the earliest delights of ceasing to be savage; they were lulled into civilization by the sweetness and the sensual loveliness that they saw on every hand, and suddenly they came to recognize that there was more wisdom in loving than in killing ... an *error* from which poor Italy is not recovered yet, and which has caused her countless times to be invaded and humiliated. How much happier her destiny, if God had seen fit to make her an island!

The political state of Italy is not to be envied; nevertheless, for some centuries now, out of the many-sided *completeness* of her civilization have arisen all those great men who have brought delight into the world. From Raphael to Canova, from Pergolesi to Rossini and Viganò, every genius who, it was ordained, should

[1] His father was Giuseppe Rossini; his mother, Anna Guidarini, one of the loveliest women in all the Romagna.

hold the Universe spell-bound through Art, was born in this land of lovers.

The very defects of those curious forms of government, which are the bane and blight of Italy, favour the art of love, and so further the cause of art.

The Papal government, which exacts no obedience from its subjects beyond the payment of taxes and a strict attendance at Mass, makes no effort to introduce any element of *security* into the society for which it is responsible. Every citizen is his own master, to do and speak the first thing that comes into his head, and to satisfy his own peculiar interests in whatever way he thinks best; and whether the means he chooses to satisfy his desires should lead him to poison a rival or merely to parade a mistress, is a matter of supreme indifference to the authorities which preside over his destiny. The government, from time immemorial abhorred and despised, sways no opinion and wields no influence whatsoever; it straddles the society beneath it; but it is not *of* that society.[1]

In my own mind, I like to picture it as a kind of Leviathan, a fabulous dragon, puffed and venomous, crawling out of the ooze of some boundless swamp and looming up without warning over the smiling and flowered countryside; it is a noisome, brutal creature, appalling in its irresistible ferocity, and universally malevolent; at all costs, it must not be encountered; every decent man and woman should run from it, avoid it, take shelter and hide from it as soon as it appears. And yet, when all is said and done, it is fundamentally *futile*; it belongs to that category of senseless, inescapable, but basically insignificant evils, like hailstorms and earthquakes, against which no one but a fool would dream of protesting.

But I suppose, in the end, someone *will* take it into his head to protest; and that day will mark the end and death of art in Italy*. Instead, we shall be greeted by the cold blast of earnest political discussion, as though Venice were no longer Venice, but rather London, or Washington!

This unexacting little government, of which I have just sketched so libellous a portrait,[2] is infinitely more propitious towards the passions

---

[1] All this was twenty years ago now; many things may have changed since then.

[2] Sources: de Potter, *De l'Esprit de l'Eglise* (description of the state of the Church in 1781); Giannone, *History of Naples*. An exception must be made in

and their untrammelled development than are the more sober govern-
ments of France or England, with their wary vigilance, their eye on
public opinion, and their tame journalists to prove that whatever they
do is right!

And the passions are the very stuff of art; that, of course, is one of the
main reasons why art cannot flourish in the sad, cold climate of the
North, where *Society* is the universal judge and arbiter of everything;
for *Society* is above all things *dispassionate*, ironical, and vain; while its
heart is so shrivelled and withered with the terror of ridicule that in the
end it is capable of nothing but cowardice in the most absurd degree.

To excell in art, the first essential is to have experienced the consuming fires of passion. A man may be gifted with the most brilliant intelligence, the sharpest wit, the keenest critical faculties, and yet it will avail
him nothing; for, unless he has first fulfilled the one essential condition,
which is at some time or other to have made himself unspeakably
ridiculous, he will never behold art otherwise than through the dim
folds of a veil. He may be filled with analytical penetration; he may,
respecting all other studies worthy of human attention, be a positive
mine of wisdom, sagacity, profundity, etc.—yet no sooner is he placed
before a work of *art* than he becomes blind to everything save to the
one part which is totally insignificant: the *material*. To him, a painting
is the canvas on which it was painted; while music, as he understands it,
is nothing but an offshoot of mechanical physics, a science of sounds
varied in combination. Such is *Voltaire*, when he writes of music or
pictures. These hard, insensitive northerners, faced with a Raphael, can
find nothing better to do than to *analyse* it, dissolving its sublimity into
a smart, practical talent for spreading colour on canvas. And as for
music . . . ! (Just glance at some of the articles which used to be perpetrated, day after day, in *le Miroir*!)

Obviously I am being uncharitable; yet the reason why I have
allowed my satirical instincts to run riot in this unkind manner is because these very same *intelligent* people, who have just been so harshly
victimized, are precisely the sort of critics by whom I hope that this
book of mine will be judged. Intellectually, that is to say, they are so

favour of the excellent *régime* which is at present (1823) furthering the happiness
and prosperity of Florence. But how long may we hope that such a government
will survive? In any case, it can render no services to art; *enthusiasm*, in Tuscany,
perished many years ago!

infinitely superior to everyone else in the world, that, as *judges of art described*, they have no conceivable rivals—even when the description may happen to deal with a work which, in the original, they can neither understand nor appreciate. If I were writing a history of music or painting, I should go to Italy to collect my material; but I should publish the finished work in Paris.

For whenever it is a question of the accuracy of some abstract conception, or the aptness of a descriptive epithet, then the men of the North, moulded by some two centuries of more or less untrammelled discussion, recover that undisputed superiority which had slipped from their grasp at the sight of a piece of sculpture, or in the presence of the *ritornello* of some great theme, *agitato*.

In France, the painter or the musician finds the throne of the passions usurped by unlawful rulers: either by the terror of offending against the established conventions, against a thousand-and-one artificial susceptibilities; or else by the obsessive cogitation which of necessity precedes the venturing upon a nicely-contrived pun.

In England, art has two dire and implacable enemies: Religion (of the Old Testament variety); and Pride. In the higher ranks of society, the passions, without exception, are constricted by an ailing timidity, which is but pride under another disguise; and elsewhere, among the majority of young men, all true emotion is overwhelmed by the appalling necessity of devoting an average of fifteen hours out of every twenty-four to some ungrateful labour, failing which the victims are condemned to starve for want of bread, and die in the streets.

It is easy to see why Italy, the land of love and of *dolce far niente*, should be at the same time the homeland of art; and why, on the other hand, thanks to the petty and suspicious tyrants who batten on that unhappy country, it is only in the North that men are sufficiently enlightened to be able to discuss and *judge*, when art is dissected into words.

The Romagna, where Rossini was born, is to be numbered among the wildest and least idyllic of all the lands in the peninsula. For many years, the sly government of the priesthood has borne upon it; and for a corresponding number of years, *generosity* has been stigmatized as the absurdest of suspect or vicious eccentricities.

Rossini's father was an impoverished and third-rate horn-player*, a member of that fraternity of nomadic musicians who, to earn a scanty living, wander from fairground to fairground, journeying from Sinigaglia to Fermo, from Fermo to Forlì, and from Forlì to all the other little towns in the Romagna or in the surrounding regions. It is their trade to band together into small, impromptu orchestras, which are then hired to play for the fairground operas. His mother, who was a beauty in her day, had been a competent *seconda donna**. The couple wandered from town to town, he playing in the orchestra, she singing on the stage, and there is nothing surprising in their inveterate poverty; but poverty seems to have become a family tradition, to which their son Gioacchino Rossini has remained quixotically faithful; for when, two years ago, he journeyed to Vienna, heralded by a name which went sounding like a bell throughout the length and breadth of Europe, he had not yet set aside a sum of money equal to the annual salary of any one of the popular actresses who sing in the opera-houses of Paris or Lisbon.

But life costs nothing in Pesaro, and so this family, for all its dependence upon so uncertain a trade, knew no sadness, still less worried about the future.

In 1799, Rossini's parents took him with them from Pesaro to Bologna*; but he did not actually begin to study music until the year 1804, when he was twelve years old. His teacher then was Dom Angelo Tesei. After a few months, the young Gioacchino was already earning a few *paoli* by singing here and there in churches. His fine treble voice, coupled with the childish liveliness of his manner, made him more than welcome among priests who had *funzioni* to organize. Under the direction of his teacher Angelo Tesei, Gioacchino became most proficient in singing, in the art of accompaniment, and in the theory of counterpoint. By 1806, he was perfectly well able to sing at sight any piece of music which might be placed before him, and his friends began to have high hopes of him; he was handsome, and it was thought he might make a tenor.

On 27th of August 1806, he left Bologna and set forth on a musical tour of the Romagna. At Lugo, at Ferrara, at Forlì, at Sinigaglia and in various other towns, he conducted a number of orchestras, while himself playing the piano parts. He continued meanwhile with his singing in church until 1807*; but in that year, on the 20th of March, he entered the *liceo musicale* at Bologna, and began to study music under the direction of padre Stanislao Mattei.

A year later (11th of August 1808) Rossini was sufficiently advanced to be able to compose a symphony and a cantata entitled *Il Pianto d'Armonia**. This was his first original composition for voices. Immediately afterwards, he was elected to the office of "director" of the *Accademia dei Concordi**, a musical society which then existed within the walls of the *Liceo Musicale* at Bologna.

By the age of nineteen, Rossini had grown so knowledgeable that he was chosen to present and conduct Haydn's *The Seasons*, which was being performed at Bologna; *The Creation*, which was being given at the same time (May 1811), was performed under the direction of the celebrated male soprano Marchesi*. Rossini's parents, whenever they had no engagement, used to come home to the poverty of their little house in Pesaro. In this town, certain wealthy music-lovers, members, I believe, of the Perticari* family, took a benevolent interest in the young Rossini. One charming lady, who, when I knew her, still possessed great beauty, had the happy idea of sending him to Venice; and while he was there, he composed a little opera in one act for the *teatro San-Mosè*, which he entitled *la Cambiale di Matrimonio* (1810). After a flattering taste of success, he returned to Bologna, where, in the autumn of the following year (1811), his next opera, *l'Equivoco stravagante**, was performed. Then he went again to Venice, and composed *l'Inganno felice** for the Carnival season of 1812.

In this last-named work, genius breaks through with unmistakable brilliance. The experienced critic can detect most plainly, in this little one-act opera, the germs of ideas which later, in a dozen or a score of major passages, were to send the fame of Rossini's masterpieces ringing through the world—among them, a fine *terzetto* sung by the peasant Tarabotto, the Lord of the Manor, and the heroine—a virtuous maiden with whom Tarabotto's master has fallen in love, and would have married, had he not previously had her driven into exile through failing to recognize her at the critical moment.

L'Inganno felice calls to mind those early works of Raphael, painted when he was still fresh from the school of Perugino; both betray all the defects and all the hesitancies of extreme youth. Rossini, twenty years old and still timid in the consciousness of the fact, dare not yet seek to please himself alone. Two elements go to the making of a great artist: a spirit which is at once exacting and sensitive, passionate and scornful; and a talent whose sole preoccupation is to satisfy that spirit, and to cater for its delight by the creation of original beauty. Meanwhile, however, Rossini's protectresses had secured him an engagement at Ferrara where, during the sacred season of Lent, in the year 1812, he composed an "oratorio", entitled *Ciro in Babilonia*—a work which contains many magnificent passages*; but which still somehow seems to lack the fire of the earlier achievement, *l'Inganno felice*. Once more, Rossini was invited to Venice; but on this occasion, the *impresario* of the *teatro San-Mosè*, not satisfied with having obtained, for the fee of a few paltry sequins, the services of a delightful composer, the idol of the fair sex, whose dawning genius was on the point of setting his theatre high in the blaze of fashion . . . this *impresario*, observing that he was poor, thought that he could afford to treat him slightingly. Without more ado, Rossini proceeded to give an exhibition of that eccentric side of his character, which has always earned him a certain notoriety, but with which, indeed, he need never have been saddled at all had he been born in a more sophisticated country.

It was Rossini's undisputed right, as a composer under contract, to have the members of his orchestra perform whatever he fancied to set down in his scores. He therefore gathered together into the newest of his operas, *la Scala di Seta*, which he had composed for this same insolent *impresario*, every freak, extravagance and musical oddity which he could manage to hatch out of his fertile and unquestionably eccentric imagination! In the *allegro* of the overture, for instance, the violins were required to pause at each bar, and to deliver a gentle tap with the bow against the tin reflectors of the stands holding the candles which lit the orchestra-pit. The surprise and exasperation of the huge audience, which had collected from every quarter of Venice, and even from the neighbouring mainland of Italy, to hear the young *maestro*'s new opera, may well be imagined! These spectators, who had been besieging the doors of the theatre two hours before they were opened, and had then had to sit patiently in anticipation for a further two hours inside the building, took the proceedings as a personal affront, and whistled with all that derisive vehemence of which an Italian audience in a fury alone is capable. Rossini, far from being upset, simply laughed outright, and enquired of the *impresario* what he thought to have gained by treating him in so cavalier a fashion; and then promptly set out for Milan*, where his friends had secured him an engagement. But a month later, Rossini was back again in Venice, where he composed two *farse* (one-act operas) in succession for the *San-Mosè*: *l'Occasione fa il ladro** (1812) and *il Figlio per azzardo* (Carnival season, 1813). It was during this same Carnival, in the year 1813, that Rossini composed *Tancredi*.

Of all the lands of Italy, Venetia stands supreme in the sureness of its taste and the keenness of its appreciation of music written for the human voice; the reader, then, can imagine for himself the success of this superb opera. Had the King-Emperor Napoleon himself thought to honour Venice with his presence, the excitement of his arrival could have done nothing to tear the people away from Rossini. *Tancredi* enjoyed a popularity verging on the delirious; it was a true *furore*, as the expression runs in Italian (that loveliest of languages created especially for the arts!). Everyone, from the humblest gondolier to the proudest lord in the land, was singing, singing ...

Ti rivedrò, mi rivedrai ...;*

and in the very courts of law, the judges were forced to call for order among the spectators, who were disturbing the proceedings by singing

Ti rivedrò ...

—in the *salon* of Signora Benzoni I have met hundreds of person who will bear out the truth of this fact!

There was a phrase current then, which the *dilettanti* used to use as a kind of greeting or password: *Cimarosa has come back among us!*[1] But the truth was better than the legend, for the music was *original* and the delights were *new*. Before Rossini, the *opera seria* had too often enclosed arid deserts of dreariness and monotony; admirable passages there were, but they were sparse and scattered, separated too often from the other by fifteen or twenty minutes of recitative and boredom. But here was Rossini, infusing into this type of composition all the fire and the vivacity and the perfection of the *opera buffa*.

The true *opera buffa*, with *libretti* in Neapolitan dialect by Tito di Lorenzi, grew to perfection through the works of Paisiello, Cimarosa and Fioravanti. In all the world there is no form of art more instinct with fire, life and genius; it is so *alive* that the temptation is well-nigh irresistible to join in the dialogue oneself. Man has, as yet, come nowhere nearer to perfection in art, than here. The spectator who

---

[1] Cimarosa, who was adored in Venice, and who had been a personal friend of many of the music-lovers in that city, had died there a few years earlier, in 1801.

beholds a good *opera buffa*, unless he have the misfortune to be born *phlegmatic*,[1] has no choice but to die, either of laughter, or else of sheer delight. Rossini's triumph was to have dislodged some portion of this divine fire from the *opera buffa*, where it had become affixed, and to have transposed it, not only into the *opera di mezzo carattere*, as in the *Barber of Seville*, but likewise into the *opera seria*, as in *Tancredi*; for it is not to be claimed that the *Barber of Seville*, for all its unmistakable hilarity, is a real *opera buffa*; it is still one degree removed from the ultimate regions of gaiety.

Outside Naples, the *opera buffa* is a style almost unknown; moreover, it would be difficult, for all the recent progress made in instrumental music, to add so much as a few touches of scoring for oboe or bassoon to the masterpieces of Fioravanti, Paisiello, and their fellow-composers. With such a *genre*, Rossini took the greatest care not to meddle, any more than a playwright would care to attempt a tragedy of murder after *Macbeth*. He attempted the *possible*, which was to instil new life into the *opera seria*.

[1] *Vide*, concerning the "six temperaments of man", the immortal treatise of Cabanis: *Des Rapports du Physique et du Moral de l'Homme*.

CHAPTER II

Tancredi

Since this delightful opera has already been completely round Europe within the space of four years, what is there to be gained by submitting it to a process of analysis and criticism? Every reader of this book, I fancy, is, and has long been, perfectly well acquainted with everything that he is supposed to think about *Tancredi*; the probability is, therefore, that he will flatly refuse to accept criticism of *Tancredi* in any terms which I might propose, preferring rather to criticize *me* in terms of *Tancredi*. Furthermore, thanks to the art of Madame Pasta, *Tancredi* is now to be seen in Paris in a performance which no other capital in the world can equal.

Indeed, it seems scarcely credible that a young woman, herself scarcely of the age when the passions are beginning to stir, should readily possess, not only the sweetest of voices, but in addition, talents as a tragic actress almost as outstanding as those of Talma—and yet, how *different*, how much simpler!

Nevertheless, to be faithful to my obligations as an historian, and to escape any accusation of incompleteness, I must attempt a sketch of *Tancredi*.

The opening bars of the overture are both charming and dignified; but I hold that the first real breath of genius is felt in the *allegro*. It is fashioned with an originality and a boldness, which, at the *première* in Venice, captured every heart in the audience. Rossini had not dared to take his seat at the piano, as it was customary, and as indeed his contract obliged him to do. He was scared of being greeted with an outburst of derisive whistling, for the national honour of the Venetian audience was still tingling with the reverberations of that *obbligato* accompaniment upon the tin reflectors which had graced his previous opera. In childish apprehension, the composer had hidden away beneath the theatre in the passage leading to the orchestra-pit. The leader of the violins searched high and low for him; but at last, seeing that it was already late, and that the audience was beginning to show those signs of impatience, which, except at *premières*, always seem so absurd to the actors themselves, resolved to begin the performance. The first *allegro* of the overture, however, was so well received that, while every corner of the house echoed with clapping and cheering, Rossini crept out from his hiding-place, and screwed up sufficient courage to edge into his seat at the piano*.

Two elements contribute to the brilliance of this *allegro*: the massive grandeur of *pride* chiselled down into the fine contours of *elegance*. Here, assuredly, is music fitting for the chivalrous hero whose name is Tancred; music worthy of the Knight whose lover was a lady of high renown and higher integrity; music, finally, which embodies the genius of Rossini in all its purity. Let him be but himself; then there is no mistaking the qualities which lie in him—all the elegance of some young French hero, some new Gaston de Foix; not strength or forcefulness, as you would find it in Haydn. To realize the "high ideal" of antiquity, strength is imperative; and Cimarosa had discovered the secret of it in the themes of his opera *gli Orazi e Curiazi*. But Rossini, unconsciously following in the footsteps of Canova, ceded the place of this *strength*, which was so indispensable and so admired in the art of Ancient Greece, to *elegance*; he was instinctively aware of the trend of his own century, and he abandoned the "high ideal" of Cimarosa, just as Canova found the courage to abandon the "high ideal" of antique sculpture.[1]

In a later period, when Rossini has tried to imitate Cimarosa in his search for *strength*, the result has at times been merely *heaviness*; the reason being that, having failed in his attempts to achieve forcefulness through his melodic line alone, he has been obliged to turn for help to those *harmonic platitudes* so dearly beloved of Mayr, Winter, Weigl, and kindred composers of the Teutonic faction.

Perhaps my explanation is somewhat too metaphysical; true or not, however, the *fact* remains: when Rossini is being himself, his music combines elegance and wit; but it possesses neither the strength which is so characteristic of Haydn, nor any of that wild impulsiveness in the manner of Michelangelo, which is a feature of the music of Beethoven.

These considerations have been suggested to me primarily by the *allegro* from the overture to *Tancredi*. The main theme reveals various

[1] This provides a notable instance of a point of contact between sculpture and music. For the development of this somewhat abstruse notion, *cf. l'Histoire de la Peinture en Italie*, vol. II, p. 133.

original devices, all alive with a grace and a subtlety which are peculiarly French; but the pathetic element is wholly missing.

As the overture comes to an end, the curtain rises, and we witness the entry of the Knights of Syracuse, who sing in chorus:

Pace, onore . . . fede, amore . . .[1]

As a chorus, it is charming; but is that really the epithet which it should have inspired? Is it not precisely that *strength*, with which I have just been concerned, that is lacking—that same *strength* which is sensed at every turn in Haydn's music? This particular chorus has a sweetish, insipid flavour about it, which is scarcely in its place in any context, but least of all amid a company of Knights from the Middle Ages!

Cinq chevaliers français conquirent la Sicile,

sings the poet; yet it is these wild-willed Knights (I had almost written *wild beasts*), of whom Walter Scott has recently given us so life-like a portrait in the character of the Knight-Templar Boisguilbert in *Ivanhoe*, and who are shortly to take the daughter of one of their own order and send her to a cruel death . . . these same "parfit gentle" Knights, who have proceeded to coo to us, in dove-like tones, a little lullaby of

Pace, onore . . .!

Had it been a scene set among the poetic shepherds of *l'Astrée*,

Où, jusqu'à je vous hais, tout se dit tendrement,

a scene depicting the hand-clasp which pledges eternal peace, the event might most fittingly have been celebrated by just such a chorus; but is music of this character really appropriate to the uncontrollable energy of the Middle Ages? The steel-armoured Knights of those barbaric days, even in the act of sealing a peace, would probably have suggested nothing less rugged than the grimness of a lion resting, or the stony severity of the Old Guard marching back into Paris after the battle of Austerlitz.

[1] *Coro:*
>Pace, onore . . . fede, amore,
>Regni, splenda, ogn'alma accenda;
>Spento il rio civil furore,
>Siracusa esulterà!
>
>(Act I, sc. i)

Rossini's exculpation must be, that in Raphael's early paintings one likewise seeks a sign of strength, and seeks it in vain, even when the design cries out for it most urgently.

This *introduction*[1] to *Tancredi* invariably fails to produce any marked impression, in spite of its lilting melody. Were it not that the very notion of correcting *any* work, let alone one which has achieved success, is a thousand miles removed from Rossini's temperament, he could profitably spend a few minutes' labour over this chorus of the Knights of Syracuse.

By contrast, Rossini takes a most splendid and overwhelming revenge in the *ritornello* and the passage of vocal music which heralds the entry of Amenaide:

Più dolci e placide . . .[2]

Hitherto, no music had ever expressed so perfectly that simple and noble elegance which befits a young princess born into the Age of Chivalry.

Amenaide's *cavatina*,

Come dolce all' alma mia . . .[3]

lacks that strain of melancholy which Mozart would have infused into it, and the embellishments are garnished with too much prettiness for the music to be truly in character. A maiden whose soul has some strain of nobility, dreaming of her lover who is outlawed and banished, should be portrayed in a vein of sadness; Voltaire appreciated the nuance, and strove after it. But Rossini was still too young to feel the

---

[1] The term *introduction* covers everything that is sung between the end of the overture and the first recitative.

[2] *Coro:*
>   Più dolci e placide spirano l'aure
>   In sì bel giorno;
>   Fra tanta gioja, sembra, che s'animi
>   Tutto d'intorno,
>   Or che trionfono concordia e amor.
>   (Act I, sc. iii)

[3] *Amenaide:*
>   Come dolce all'alma mia
>   Scende il suon de' vostri accenti!
>   Come a'vostri, a'suoi contenti
>   Va esultando questo cor!
>   (Act I, sc. iii)

lack of it; or rather (not to launch out too early into the language of panegyric), an emotion was involved which perhaps never, to the very end, penetrated into his soul. Later on in life he might, for instance, have imitated Mozart; but at eighteen, he was writing in a style whose simplicity was dictated by his genius alone; and that genius, while it surely understands tenderness, has, I feel convinced, no inkling of the kind of tenderness which is inseparable from melancholy.

And so, at last, we come to the celebrated entry of Tancred himself. This landing of Tancred and his followers upon a deserted, lonely beach requires all the technique of Italian stage-craft if it is to retain any shadow of dignity. The scene, as it was performed at the *Théâtre Louvois*, with the characters scrambling out of a sort of skiff, whose agitated convulsions (it being but forty paces away from the audience) were clearly visible in every detail, needed every iota of the magnificent *portamento* of Madame Pasta to redeem it from utter absurdity; the more so, as the "shore" was constructed out of ridiculous little bits of painted cardboard, in such a way that the "trees" threw shadows *against the sky*! In the same scene, in the version which is given in Milan, the landing of Tancred and his Knights is half-glimpsed in the dim distance, which is indeed the way in which such scenes *should* be presented to the imagination. The *décor*, too, is a masterpiece in the Milanese production; it is by Sanquirico or Perego, and the very wonder of it compels the eye to forget to enquire too critically into the physical details of the action. Fortunately, however, Parisian audiences are not finicking about the settings of the plays which are served up to them, and absurdity, unnoticed, ceases to be absurd.

For the performance in Venice, Rossini had composed a magnificent aria to be sung at the entry of Tancred. Signora Malanotte, however, took a dislike to it;[1] moreover, being then in the flower of her beauty, and at the height of her powers and eccentricities, this admirable *prima-donna* chose to communicate her distaste for the aria to the composer only upon the very eve of the *première*.

The *maestro's* despair may be imagined! The calamity belonged to that order of disasters which drive young men of that age and in that position to very madness. (Happy age, at which one *can* be driven to madness!) *If, after the pantomime of my last opera*, muttered Rossini,

---

[1] Madame Pasta recently inserted this aria into the first act of *la Rosa bianca e la Rosa rossa*, where there is a similar situation.

they now whistle at the entry of Tancred, the whole of this opera va a terra (*will be a flop*)!

The wretched young man walked back to his cheap lodgings, sunk in thought. Then an idea struck him, and he scribbled a few lines of music; and these few, hurried jottings heralded the birth of the famous aria:

Tu che accendi . . . ,[1]

which has enjoyed a wider and more universal popularity than perhaps any other aria in the world. There is a legend current in Venice, which relates that the first seed of this delightful *cantilena*, which so admirably conveys the happiness of lovers meeting after long separation, sprang from a Greek Litany, and that Rossini had heard it chanted a few days earlier at Vespers in a church on one of the little islands in the Lagoon. The Greeks have managed to preserve the old *happiness* of their great Mythology despite all the menace and the gloomy terrors of the Christian religion!

In Venice, this aria is known as the *aria dei risi*. The title, I admit, is somewhat undignified, and I confess to a certain feeling of embarass-ment in recording the (gastronomic rather than poetic) little anecdote to which it owes its origin. The name *aria dei risi*, since it must be revealed, means *rice-aria*. In Lombardy, every dinner, from that of the highest in the land down to that of the obscurest little *maestro*, begins invariably with a dish of rice; and since rice is eaten for preference very much under-cooked, four minutes precisely before the course is due, the chef invariably sends a minion with this momentous query: *bisogna*

---

[1] *Tancredi:*

Tu che accendi questo core,
Tu che desti il valor mio,
Alma, gloria, dolce amore,
Secondate il bel desio.
Cada un empio traditore;
Coronate la mia fe'.
Di tanti palpiti,
Di tante pene,
Da te, mio bene,
Spero mercè!
Mi rivedrai . . .
Ti rivedrò . . .
Nè tuoi bei rai
Mi pascerò . . .

Act I, sc. iv)

mettere i risi? On that famous evening when Rossini, plunged into despair, walked slowly back to his lodgings, the *cameriere* asked the usual question; the rice was set to cook; and before it was ready, Rossini had completed his aria:

Di tanti palpiti . . .

Thus the title *aria dei risi* commemorates the speed with which it was composed*.

What is there to be said about this superb *cantilena*? Talking about it to those who already know it would seem to me to be as absurd as talking about it to those who have never heard it—if indeed, in the whole of Europe, there may still *be* people who have never heard it!

But only those who have seen Madame Pasta in the rôle of Tancred may realize that the *recitative*:

O patria, ingrata patria!¹

can be yet more sublime and more moving than the aria itself. Madame Fodor once took the aria, dressed it up in quadrille-rhythm, and used it for the singing-lesson scene in the *Barber of Seville*. A good voice can render the most dismally mediocre of arias in fine style, the singer being nothing more than a sublime barrel-organ; but a recitative taxes the resources of the human soul. And even in the aria, the passage setting the words *alma, gloria* will never really be sung properly by anyone born north of the Alps!

Without the experience, or the memory of the experience, of the madness of love, as love is known in the happy countries of the South, it is quite impossible to interpret the phrase *mi rivedrai, ti rivedrò**. The nations of the North might devour twenty *Treatises on the Art of Poetry* as learned as that of La Harpe, and still have no understanding why the words *mi rivedrai* precede the words *ti rivedrò*. If any of our fashionable critics could understand Italian, they would surely detect a *lack of breeding*, if not indeed a *total contempt for the delicacies of social intercourse*, in Tancred's behaviour towards Amenaide!

    ¹ Tancredi:

Oh patria! o dolce ingrata patria!
Alfine a te ritorno! . . . Io ti saluto,
O cara terra degli avi miei, ti bacio!
(Act I, sc. iv)

Upon Tancred's entry, the orchestration reaches a superb climax of *dramatic harmonization*. This is not (as it is foolishly believed in Germany) the art of employing clarinets, 'cellos and oboes to re-echo the emotions of the characters on the stage; it is the much rarer art of using the instruments to voice nuances and overtones of emotion which the characters themselves would never dare put into words. When Tancred lands on his deserted beach, he needs no more than a phrase or two of speech to portray his emotions; voice and gestures express something; but completeness requires an instant or two of silence, while he contemplates, with mingled sensations of pleasure and sadness, the ungrateful country to which he has returned. If he should speak in this instant, Tancred would dissipate our interest in him, and shatter, in our entranced imagination, the perception which we have of the thoughts deeply stirring in him, as he looks again upon the land which is the home of Amenaide. Tancred *must* not speak; but while he is contained in a silence so perfectly expressive of the feelings raging within him, the sighing horns of the orchestra conjure up a new portrait of his spirit, and echo emotions which, perhaps, he hardly dare acknowledge to himself, and which certainly will never find form in words.

An achievement of this character is something new in music; it was unknown in the times of Pergolesi and Sacchini, and it is still unknown to our worthy Teutonic friends. They use *their* instruments to furnish us, as crudely as possible, with certain necessary information which the singer on the stage should, properly speaking, convey to us in words. Their vocal passages, on the other hand, being either wholly expressionless, or else hopelessly overburdened with expression, just as reproductions of paintings by Raphael are normally overburdened with exaggerated colour, serve largely to give the imagination a rest from the ideas suggested by the orchestra. Thus their operatic heroes act very much like those Sovereigns who, filled brim-full with the finest intentions in the world, yet find themselves unable, with their own tongue, to utter anything but commonplaces of the worst order, and so are constantly referring the petitioner to their Ministers-of-State whenever some question arises which requires an important answer.

Every instrument in the orchestra, like every individual human voice, has its own distinctive characteristics; for example, in Tancred's aria and recitative, Rossini scores for the flute*; the particular virtue of the flute lies in its ability to portray joy mingled with sadness;[1] and this complex mixture of emotions is precisely that which Tancred experiences when his eye lights once more on that ungrateful land to which he can no longer return save in disguise.

If this conception of the relationship between orchestral and vocal music can be made any clearer by an analogy, I would suggest that Rossini successfully employs a device invented by Walter Scott—that same technical device which, perhaps, was responsible for all the most astounding triumphs of the immortal author of *Old Mortality*. Just as Rossini uses his *orchestral harmony* to prepare the way for, and to reinforce, his passages of vocal music, so Walter Scott prepares the way for, and reinforces, his passages of dialogue and narrative by means of *description*. Consider, for instance, the very first page of *Ivanhoe*, with its magnificent description of the setting sun; how its rays, already losing strength and falling almost horizontal, struggle through the lowest and thickest branches of the trees which conceal the dwelling of Cedric the Saxon. And then how, in the centre of a wood-land glade, this dying-diminishing light picks out the curious garments worn by Wamba the Jester and Gurth the Swineherd. Before the great Scottish writer has even completed his description of this forest lit with the departing beams of a sun already lying on the tree-tops, and of the curious garments worn by these two characters—characters surely lacking in "nobility", and whose appearance in the story at all is a violent offence against all the rules of "Classical Dignity"—already we find ourselves disposed, prophetically as it were, to be affected by the words which they have yet to utter. And when at last they do speak, their least syllables are rich with infinite significance. Imagine the opening of this chapter, which itself opens the novel, rewritten, with the dialogue *un*prepared by the description: the whole effect would be ruined.

Composers of genius, then, relate orchestral harmony to vocal

[1] It might be suggested that there is a certain analogy to be drawn between the *flute* on the one hand, and on the other, those great *ultramarine-coloured* draperies which a number of famous painters (amongst others, Carlo Dolci) have tended to employ so lavishly in paintings of scenes where tenderness mingles with gravity; however, a suggestion of this nature, which might well pass for an illuminating flash of genius in Bayreuth or in Königsberg, would certainly be treated in Paris as mere rubbish! O happy nations, within whose boundaries there is known no stronger guarantee of a reputation for sublime profundity, than a talent for being obscure and incomprehensible!

melody in precisely the same manner as Walter Scott relates description
to dialogue in *Ivanhoe*; the rest (for example, the learned M. Cherubini)
tumble their harmony in pell-mell, just as M. l'abbé Delille, in his
poem *de la Pitié*, piles up description upon description. Cast your mind
back for an instant, and remember his episodic characters—how pale
and colourless they seem; and yet how brilliant Paris found it all, in the
year 1804. Since then, our sense of critical appreciation has advanced by
leaps and bounds; so let us hope that soon we may make similar progress in musical appreciation, and that "harmony" in the German sense
will go the same way as verses in the *style Louis XV*. Our authors in
bygone ages, La Bruyère, Pascal, Duclos, Voltaire, never dreamed of
describing nature, any more than it occurred to Pergolesi or Buranello
to use orchestral harmony. The poets of our own generation have
recovered from this particular blindness, only to fall into an excess of the
opposite character; and in the same way, music is all set to drown itself
in harmony. Let us hope that we shall grow out of the sentimental
prose of Madame de Staël, just as we have grown out of the passion for
unbridled description so dear to the bard of *les Jardins*, and that we shall
reach a stage when we shall be able to refrain from effusion over the
touching beauties of nature, save when our hearts are themselves sufficiently cool and objective to observe them properly and to appreciate
them.

Walter Scott is for ever interrupting and reinforcing his dialogue
with description, at times even in a manner which is decidedly irritat-
ing, as, for instance, when the entrancing little dumb girl, Fenella, in
Peveril of the Peak, is trying to stop Julian leaving the castle of Holm-
Peel in the Isle of Man. Here we have a clear case where the mind of the
reader is exasperated by the descriptions, just as the ear of the average
Italian listener is exhausted and irritated by German-style orchestration;
nevertheless, when description is properly employed, it works on the
mind, creating an emotional state in which it is admirably susceptible to
the impact of the simplest dialogue; and it is indeed thanks to the art of
such wonderful descriptive passages that Walter Scott found the courage
to be *simple*, to abandon the rhetoric which Jean-Jacques and so many
others had made fashionable in the novel, and, finally, to risk a kind of
dialogue which was in very truth *borrowed from nature*.

Perhaps, as a result of this long digression, I may have succeeded in
giving some notions of the respective positions which Pergolesi, Mayr,

Mozart and Rossini occupy upon the Mount Parnassus of music. In Pergolesi's day, description of nature, whether grave or gay, was un-dreamed-of in any novel; Mozart was the Walter Scott of music, bringing to the use of description an exquisite sense of artistry, but occasionally—albeit very rarely indeed—laying slightly too much emphasis upon it. Mayr, Winter, Weigl, the musical counterparts of M. l'abbé Delille, fling in description by the cartload, compensating for its intrinsic lack of interest by its *academic correctness* (it being grammati-cally unimpeachable, and most subtle in its linguistic mechanics!). Rossini, finally uses description in the manner which has the greatest popular appeal, with brilliant colouring and a peculiar quality of picturesqueness in his lighting; unfailingly he arrests the eye, but some-times he tires it.

In *la Gazza ladra*, for instance, one is for ever longing to silence the orchestra, the better to appreciate the singing. The effect is powerful and harsh, appealing only to the sensibility of the trained ear; whereas the *dilettanti* would prefer more charm, more sweetness, more simple and lilting melody entrusted to the human voice.

Rossini was very far from this failing when he composed the wonder-ful score of *Tancredi*; he seized unerringly upon that exact balance between richness and luxuriance, by which beauty is made more beautiful still, and yet not concealed, not damaged, not overlaid with useless ornament. Whenever the mind is over-dinned with noise or else bored with an excess of simplicity, it should return to the entrancing music of *Tancredi*, and be refreshed.

The feature of this opera which sent Venice into such transports of delight was the *originality of its style*, and the entrancing quality of the songs, which were, if I may so express myself, "decked out" with the oddest, newest, most unexpected accompaniments, which perpetually stung the ear into wakefulness, and added spice even to the most ordinary-looking of daily dishes; and yet, with all this, these accom-paniments achieved their fascinating effect without ever threatening to encroach upon the voice. *Fanno col canto conversazione rispettosa,*[1] remarked one of the wittiest music-lovers in Venice, the celebra-

---

[1] *They make respectful conversation with the melody . . . i.e.,* the accompaniment never trespasses beyond the bounds of respect in relation to the voice, and always sinks into a polite hush whenever the singer appears to have something important to say; in German music, by contrast, the accompaniments are grossly insolent.

ted Buratti (author of those most delicious satires, *l'Uomo* and *l'Elefanteide*).

"The first-act *finale* of *Tancredi* has its defects," I was told one evening in Brescia by Signor Pellico (a charming man, and the finest tragic poet in Italy, but now sentenced to fifteen years imprisonment in the fortress of Spielberg): "In particular, those uncouth and startling *leaps*, when the melody lurches from one note to the next!" "But," I replied, "are we *never* to be allowed to hear anything startling? If you want to make discoveries, you must occasionally allow your ships to venture into uncharted waters. If the 'uncouth' had been forbidden by law, how could Beethoven, with his wild impetuosity and his outlandish music, have been there to catch up the torch as it fell from the hands of the measured and noble Haydn?"

If, in Act I of *Tancredi*, Rossini still fails to draw fully upon all the resources of orchestral harmony in the luxuriant German style, he is completely the master of those charming phrases of shapely and entrancing melody in the style of Cimarosa, which, later, will be encountered ever less frequently in each successive work. Mark especially, in the superb quintet from Act I, the phrase:

Deh! tu almen . . . ,[1]

which Amenaide addresses in succession to her father, to Tancred and to Orbassano. In the same act, a respite from the strain of listening to orchestral harmony is provided by the unaccompanied quartet; both these numbers are masterly in their effect. In the quartet, the part sung *sotto voce* by Orbassano is delicious; this fine melody in the bass seems to lead one ever onward towards unknown emotional adventures, so

[1] *Amenaide:*
    Padre amato! . . .
Argirio:
              Ed osi ancora
    Di fissar sù me le ciglia!
    Una rea non è mia figlia:
    Non ti son più genitor.
Amenaide:
    Deh! tu almen . . . (*a Tancredi*)
Tancredi:
    La fe', l'onore
    Tu così tradir potesti!
    Va! . . .

                    (Act I, sc. x)

that, without ever understanding whither one is being guided, the
journey itself becomes a pleasurable experience.

At the very outset of the second act, there is a delightful phrase:

Nò; che il morir non è ...;[1]

but this is soon forgotten, swept away by the entrancing duet:

Ah! se de' mali miei ...,[2]

whose proud and chivalrous inspiration contrasts so magnificently with
the music which has gone before.

In this fine section of the score, the predominant characteristic is the
fiery spirit of war-like knight-errantry, shot through with the stirring,
irresistible frenzy of the Middle Ages, which, in nobler minds at least,
transformed the brutal fact of war and its accompanying dangers, which
we have degraded to a *methodical and mathematical nastiness,*[3] into a thing
of the *spirit*. This triumph of Rossini's art is not to be analysed in terms
of any mere physical or technical devices which he selects and uses,
successfully or otherwise; such secondary considerations scarcely concern us here. Mark rather the *originality* of what he chooses to depict.
Tancred's part in the duet

[1] *Amenaide:*
> No, che il morir non è
> Sì barbaro per me,
> Se moro per amor,
> Se moro pel mio ben!
>
> (Act II, sc. i)

[2] *Argirio:*
> Ah! se de' mali miei
> Tanta hai pietà nel cor,
> Palesa almen chi sei,
> Conforta il mio dolor.
>
> *Tancredi:*
> Nemico il ciel provai
> Fin da primi anni ognor;
> Chi sono un dì saprai;
> Ma non odiarmi allor
>
> *Argirio:*
> Odiarti ... ?
> *Tancredi:*
> Oh! son sì misero ...
>
> (Act II, sc. iii)

[3] *Vide: la Tactique*, by M. de Guibert. Bayard invariably refused the supreme
command.

Ah! se de' mali miei . . .,

which begins in a strain of profound, heroic melancholy:

Nemico il ciel provai,
Fin da primi anni ognor.
....
Oh! son sì misero . . .,

ends upon a brilliant note of triumph, of courage which has learned to face a sea of troubles with stoical determination. Thus, after a brief moment of despondency, a hesitation due to human weakness and to human love, which is both natural and moving, Rossini bursts forth into a heroic vision of *modern national idealism*, in the best sense of the term—a conception which no Italian composer could have so much as dreamed of before the events of the Bridge of Arcola and the March to Lodi. These immortal names must have been among the earliest that Rossini heard in childhood; they date from 1796, when Rossini was five; and in that year, in Pesaro, he could have watched the immortal battalions marching through, fired with the quintessence of military ardour, sinewy, stripped bare of silks and silver, medals, orders and crosses, striding onward to Tolentino, to the conquest of that wealth of paintings, statues, and still greater works of art which, in later days, when our strength had been sapped by the lapping luxury of royalty, were wrested back from us at the stirring of a finger*! Fired by that same lofty inspiration which Tancred experiences at the touch of the spur of *national honour*, should we not swear that one day we shall have vengeance, and seize our trophies again into our own hands?

In the course of this war-like duet, Rossini uses his trumpets with infinite skill, worthy of the most consummate master; he, by instinct and at the age of seventeen, had discovered secrets which others may scarcely learn, by theory or by practice, even after years of painstaking study.

The melodic period:

Il vivo lampo . . .[1]

[1] *Argirio, Tancredi:*
    Ecco le trombe!
    Al campo, al campo!
    Di gloria avvampo
    E di furor!

which accompanies the instant when Tancred draws his sword, is, I believe, the finest thing that Rossini has ever written. It possesses every quality: nobility, truth and originality.

I should like to advise all singers, even Madame Pasta, to be sparing in the use of roulades in these immeasurably brief instants of extreme passion, as, for instance, when Tancred exclaims:

Odiarla! o Ciel, non so . . .[1]

Any character who, in such moments of passionate intoxication, still finds time to be elegant—that is to say, still finds time to remember that other people exist, to calculate how he may stand in their opinion, and to court their approval—in my belief can boast of nothing but a most insensitive disposition. The truly passionate character, on such occasions, forgets all elegance save that which has become second nature to him. By contrast, when roulades are used to accompany the words:

Di questa spada . . .,

the effect is incomparable.

Allow me, by the way, to remark that our learned literary friends, who so fondly imagine that by studying Boileau they can grow into connoisseurs of Italian opera, have sworn an oath of undying hatred towards *all* roulades, flourishes and ornaments in music. *Their* ideal is above all severity—stylistic *asceticism . . .*

Non raggioniam di loro, ma guarda e passa*.[2]

The first dozen bars which Tancred sings when he is brought back in his triumphal chariot are delightful; they bring both freshness and

> Il vivo lampo
> Di questa spada
> Splenda terribile
> Sul traditor!
> (Act II, sc. iii)

[1] *Argirio:*
    Ma pugnerai per lei?
Tancredi:
    Sì! morte affronterò!
    (L'ingrata odiar dovrei . . .
    Odiarla? o Ciel, non so!)
                (Act II, sc. iii)

[2] Do not let us talk about them; cast a glance and pass on. (The line is spoken by Virgil to Dante, as they journey through the Inferno of the *half-hearted*.)

respite. The chorus of the Knights who have gone to seek Tancred in the forest,

Regna il terror ...,[1]

is, in a different vein, almost as fine as the aria: *il vivo lampo* ... Here in my opinion, the combination of Italian melody with German-style orchestration touches perfection; it marks the point at which our present revolution, which is hurtling us headlong towards harmonic *complexity*, should be arrested.

The dynamic force which is urging this revolution forward lies in one very simple phenomenon, which is this: among the nations of the North, out of every score of charming young ladies who indulge in the luxury of music-lessons, nineteen learn to play the piano; one alone learns to sing, and consequently the nineteen others come in the end to believe that nothing can be beautiful unless it is *difficult.* In Italy, the *Ideal of Beauty* (in so far as music is concerned) is universally sought by way of the human voice.

I should grow infinitely tedious if I yielded to the temptation of setting down my impressions concerning every separate passage in *Tancredi*; or rather, not *my* impressions, but the impressions which were abroad in Naples, or in Florence, or in Brescia, or wherever I happened to see this particular opera; for no one has a deeper mistrust than I of *personal* impressions, which, even when they are sincere, are all the world to him who holds them, and supremely indifferent, if not downright absurd, to the next man, who happens not to share them. I implore the reader to believe me, when I state that throughout this book the personal pronoun *I* is simply a conventional device, which might at any time be replaced by a different phrase, such as: *It used to be said in Naples, among those who frequented the Marchese Berio* ...; or else, *One day, in the company of Signora Benzoni, Signor Peruchini, that most cultivated of Venetian music-lovers, whose very opinions are law, remarked that* ...; or else, *This evening, amid the group which gathers in the theatre around Signor Antonini, the lawyer, I heard Signor Agguchi maintain*

[1] *Coro:*

> Regna il terror
> Nella città   !
> Tancredi di dolor
> Dunque morrà !
> Ove sarà ?

(Act II, sc. ix)

that harmony in the German style . . .; and Count Giraùd agreed with him; which opinion, however, Signor Gherardi, who is a personal friend of Rossini, proceeded to refute point by point. . . . The rare impressions scattered throughout this work which are wholly of a personal nature, are hemmed in with all manner of doubts and qualifications, which indeed reflect the attitude of the Author himself; and besides, the Author here confesses that, in composing this *Life of Rossini*, he has unashamedly borrowed his judgments concerning this great man and his works from all manner of sources, and amongst others, from countless German and Italian periodicals*.

In this way, at Bologna, in the box of Signora Z***, I recorded the following opinion from my friend Gherardi: *In* Tancredi, *the most striking feature is the youthfulness of the music. Elsewhere, audacity is one of the most remarkable characteristics of Rossini's compositions, as indeed it is of his personal character. But in* Tancredi, *this audacity, which thrills and astounds me in* la Gazza ladra, *or in* il Barbiere, *is missing. There is nothing but purity and simplicity in every note; not an atom of embellishment, just genius in all its primitive innocence; genius which, if I may be permitted the expression, is still virginal. I adore everything in* Tancredi, *even a curiously archaic suggestion which I detect here and there in the melodic line of some of the songs; they seem to retain something of the form which was familiar to Paisiello and Cimarosa—those long, shapely phrases which somehow manage to elude us only too easily, enchanting the imagination . . . and escaping, ensnaring the soul . . . and vanishing! In short, I love* Tancredi *as I love Tasso's Rinaldo, for both betray the still-virginal sensibility of a man of genius.*

Rossini, whose audacious insult to the Venetian public with that famous *obbligato* upon the tin reflectors was still very recent, was obviously in no mood now to retreat timidly among the melodic and harmonic platitudes which disfigured the scores of the majority of his rivals. I cannot detect in *Tancredi*, at least in performance, one single specimen of those harmonic *clichés* which form, as it were, the stock-in-trade of the average composer of the German school, and which, in later years, Rossini employed only too frequently in his German-style operas, *Mosè*, *Otello*, *la Gazza ladra*, *Ermione*, etc. For in Naples, when such men as Zingarelli and Paisiello (great men once, but now in their dotage, and a prey to pedantry and jealousy) accused him of ignorance, Rossini reacted by seeking the approval of the protagonists of the *ascetic style*. Now, the phrase *ascetic style*, when it is employed by artistic charlatans, and echoed and repeated parrot-fashion, mechanically, by woolly-minded enthusiasts, turns out almost invariably to mean a style stuffed with harmonic platitudes; which style only too often deceives the uninitiated, amongst whom, in Milan in 1817, I must count myself, having been utterly hoodwinked and taken in by Soliva's opera *la Testa di Bronzo**.

I could easily compose twenty lines of commentary upon every one of the arias or *ensembles* of *Tancredi*. Reflections of this nature, when they are delivered seated at the piano, have their value; for, by analysing impressions while they are still fresh in the mind, the analysis may serve to intensify the sensation experienced, and, more especially, may help to give it some permanence, and to establish it more definitely in the world of memory. But these same reflections, transplanted into a book and delivered far away from any piano, can soon grow intolerably boring. And yet I need to be threatened with that terrible word *boredom*, with all its tragic implications, before I can constrain myself to curtail my enthusiasm for *Tancredi*.

It may well be imagined that, in a land such as Venice, Rossini's glory as a composer was easily equalled by his triumphs as a man. It was not long before la Marcolini, a delightful *cantatrice buffa*, and, at the same time, a woman in the fullest flower of her youth and talent, swept him away from the great ladies who had been his first protectresses. The gossips whispered of base ingratitude; and there were many tears shed. Moreover, there is an anecdote—somewhat intricate, but exceedingly amusing—relating to this adventure, which provides a beautiful illustration of Rossini's character, his audacity, his gaiety, and above all his ability to make quick decisions; but, to tell the truth, it is an anecdote which I dare not set down in print. To baffle the curious, I might change names until they were utterly unrecognizable; yet the circumstances of the tale are so extraordinary that there is not a man or woman in all Italy who could fail to pick out the real actors; so we must wait a year or two. Incidentally, it is said that la Marcolini, not to be outdone by Rossini, made him the sacrifice of prince Lucien Bonaparte.

And indeed, it was for la Marcolini, for her ravishing contralto voice and for her magnificent gifts as a comic actress, that Rossini composed the superb comic rôle of the *Italian Girl in Algiers*, which we poor

northerners have beheld so nobly distorted. There is a certain actress*
(yet, in deference to her beauty, she shall be nameless) who transforms
this young creature with her southern temperament, this joyous,
irresponsible, gay, passionate young woman, who, let it be admitted,
has but the most fleeting regard for her reputation, into a stolid York-
shire miss, whose most deep-seated care, in every situation, is to merit
the approbation of all the old wives in the parish, failing whose good
opinion, she must be for ever left high and dry without a husband. Is
there *no* refuge, where a man may seek asylum from the furious pursuit
of virtue? Do I patronize the *opera buffa* in order to enjoy the *noble
prospect*,[1] the monumental delineation of female perfection? I suppose
I should be held guilty of "shocking the tone of our serious-minded
generation", or of "offering flagrant insults to the laws of decency" *etc.*,
etc., if I dared suggest that, the more our manners and morals grow
dingy, strait-laced and hypocritical, the better claim we have to some
compensating debauch of *frivolity* in our entertainments!

[1] In English in the original. (*Trans.*)

CHAPTER III

L'Italiana in Algeri

However, let us rather consider *l'Italiana*, not as it was seen in Paris (thanks to the machinations of certain very clever persons*, who were stubbornly set on poisoning whatever delight we might have been prepared to take in Rossini), but as it was given in Italy, where its appearance immediately lifted its young composer straight into the front rank among *maestri*.

There is more permanence, more persistence and solidity in the sheen of the rainbow than in the emotions which music is able to awaken in the human soul; music itself has no stable element of reality; and since its enchantment stems wholly from the imagination, it needs no more than some slight, even involuntary, association of contaminating ideas to stifle the success of a masterpiece. This was the fate of *l'Italiana* in Paris; and it has been spoiled to such an extent, that it can never hope now to inspire unreserved delight in that city. Before the audience so much as sets foot in the theatre, it is intolerably prejudiced, unshakably persuaded beforehand that it is doomed to endure an evening of grim mediocrity. A prejudice of this nature would necessarily be fatal to the finest of music in any country in the world; judge then of its effect in the heart of a nation where a man thinks it neither odd nor ignorant to enquire of his neighbour: *Pray, Sir . . . am I amused?*

The overture of *l'Italiana* is charming, but it is too frivolous; and that, indeed, is a *great* fault!

The *introduction* is admirable; it is a true and profound portrait of the sorrows of a woman abandoned. The aria which underlines this mood,

Il mio sposo or più non m'ama . . .,[1]

[1] *Elvira:*
   Ah, comprendo, me infelice!
   Che il mio sposo or più non m'ama.
Zulma:
   Ci vuol flemma: a ciò ch'ei brama
   Ora è vano il contraddir.

(Act I, sc. i)

is delightful, and the sorrow is sorrow without a hint of tragedy.

However, before we go any further, let us stop an instant and consider; for these few words imply, without any qualification, *perfection* in the style of the *opera buffa*. No other living composer has earned this praise; and even Rossini was soon to cease to covet it. When he composed *l'Italiana in Algeri*, he was in the full flower of his youth and genius; he was not afraid to repeat himself; he felt no urge to create *powerful* music; his home was the delightful province of Venetia, the gayest land in all Italy, if not in all the world, and assuredly the least tainted with pedantry. The glittering reflection of the Venetian character falls across the texture of Venetian music;[1] and musical Venice, rating lightness of heart above depth of passion, looks first and foremost for songs which entrance the ear. In *l'Italiana*, the prayers of the people of Venice were abundantly granted; no race did ever witness an entertainment better suited to its own character; and, of all the operas which were ever composed, none was more truly destined to be the joy and delight of *Venice*.

Thus it came about that, travelling through the province of Venetia in the year 1817, I found *l'Italiana* being performed simultaneously in Brescia, in Verona, in Venice itself, in Vicenza and in Treviso.

It must be confessed that, in not a few of these towns, (in Vicenza, for example), the music was performed by singers who would have been honourably flattered by comparison with the least distinguished among our own; but for all that, there was a thrill, a *verve*, a *brio* in their performance, a sweeping excitement over all, the like of which is not encountered in any opera-house beneath our cold and reasonable skies. I used to observe how, from the very opening of the first act, at the earliest, slightest burst of applause, a kind of musical frenzy would take hold of orchestra and audience alike, sweeping one and all away in waves of uncontrollable delight. I too participated in this strange delirium, which could fire a blaze of joy in a third-rate theatre where

---

[1] Schiller, in a novel entitled *der Geisterseher: aus den Papieren des Grafen von O . . .*, gives us a sketch of the Venetian character of unrivalled charm and brilliance. Here is a problem worthy of the most serious philosophic enquiry: the gayest nation in Europe, the happiest, the least constrained, is that whose written constitution is the most abominable! (*Vide l'Histoire de Venise*, by M. Daru: Constitutions of the State Inquisition.) The gloomiest city in the world is undoubtedly Boston—precisely that where the political state is all but perfect. Could it be that *Religion* is the key to the enigma?

the highest attainment was unqualified mediocrity. How it came about, I cannot explain. Yet this enchanting opera held no hint to evoke the *reality* or the *sadness* of life; and most assuredly there was not in all the audience a single head which held a notion of submitting sensual delight to the test of *critical judgment*. The singing, the *décor*, the liveliness of the orchestra, the perpetual improvising of the actors—there was nothing in all this to chain or fetter the spectator's imagination, which, at the slightest touch of encouragement from within, could start away into a world far removed from our own, and gay as our world is not. But all this has to be witnessed in the flesh, and acquires nothing in the telling save an ill-seeming flatness.

On these occasions, the music would seem to transport us bodily into its most frenzied realms of fantasy. The performers, encouraged and inspired by the uncontrolled outbursts of applause and by the cheering of the audience, would dare feats of virtuosity which, I am certain, they would never have dreamed of attempting at the next performance. I have heard that exquisite *buffo*, Paccini, who used to play messer Taddeo at the teatro San-Benedetto in Venice, confess privately at the end of an evening of wild success and wilder frenzy, that, compared with such a performance, the most exquisite banquet, the sweetest delights of an excursion by gondola, all the most brilliant, the gayest experiences in the world, were as nothing, as dust in the mouth!

Following the plaintive song of poor Elvira, abandoned by the Bey, I know nothing compounded of more brilliance and less cruelty, nothing more expressive and (in Italy) more natural than Mustafà's song:

> *Cara, m'hai rotto il timpano . . .*[1]

To the life, this is a portrait of a lover tired of his mistress; and yet it is all without malice, and self-respect is spared the indignity of humiliation.

Observe that here, as indeed everywhere, I am concerned with the music, never with the words, which, to tell the truth, I do not know.

[1] *Elvira:*
>> Signor per quelle smanie
>> Che a voi più non ascondo . . .
> *Mustafà:*
>> Cara, m'hai rotto il timpano,
>> Ti parlo schietto e tondo.
>>> (Act I, sc. i)

D

It is my invariable habit to rewrite the words of any opera for my own satisfaction. I take the plot which the librettist has invented, and I require further from him one word, and *one only*, to give me the key to the mood of the scene. For example, I take Mustafà to be a man who is bored with his mistress and his own greatness, and yet, being a sovereign, not devoid of vanity. Now, it is not improbable that, if I were to follow the dialogue as a whole, this general impression would be ruined. So what is the remedy? Ideally, of course, the answer would be to have had Voltaire or Beaumarchais compose the *libretto*; in which case it would be as delightful as the music, and never a breath of disenchantment in the reading of it! But happily (since Voltaires are rare in our imperfect world), the delightful art which is our present study can well continue without the services of a great poet ... provided always that one avoids the sinful indiscretion of reading the *libretto**. At Vicenza, I observed that, on the first night, it was customary to skim through it just sufficiently to gain some notion of the plot, glancing, as each new episode opened, at the first line, just so as to appreciate the emotion, or the shade of emotion, which the music was supposed to suggest. But not once, during all the forty performances which came after, did it occur to one single member of the audience to open that slim little volume with its gilt-paper binding.

Still more apprehensive of the disagreeable impression which might be gleaned from the *libretto*, Signora B***, in Venice, used to refuse to allow anybody at all to bring it into her box, even at the *première*. She used to get someone to prepare her a summary of the plot, some forty lines in all; and then, during the performance, she would be informed, in four or five words, of the theme of each aria, duet or ensemble, which had previously been numbered 1, 2, 3, 4 ... *etc.*, as each item was introduced in the performance; for instance, simply: *Ser Taddeo is jealous; Lindoro is passionately in love; Isabella is flirting with the Bey, etc.*— this condensed summary being followed by the first line of the aria or duet which happened to be in question. I observed that everyone approved of this procedure, and thought it most suitable. In such a fashion should all *libretti* be printed for those—to tell the truth, I hardly know how to find an epithet which does not merely appear conceited! —for those who appreciate music as music is appreciated in Venice.

The *cavatina* sung by Lindoro, the favoured lover in *l'Italiana in Algeri*,

Languir per una bella . . .,[1]

is perfect in its simple originality; the effect is powerful while the music remains uncomplicated. This *cavatina* is one of the finest things that Rossini has ever composed for a pure tenor voice. I shall never forget the impression which Davide, the greatest, or rather the *only* true tenor of our generation, produced in his rendering of the part. It was one of the noblest triumphs of the art of music. The audience, carried away by the provocative gracefulness of this elegant, pure and full-toned voice, grew mindless of all else in the world. The great advantage of this *cavatina* is that it is not too richly imbued with passion; it is not over-dramatic. We are still in the opening scenes; undistracted by the more or less intricate complexities of the plot, we can surrender whole-heartedly to the tide of delight which sweeps over us. It is the most *physical* music that I know.

This delicious instant is renewed a moment later; but, of necessity, even though the pleasure set before us for our delectation be not a whit inferior in quality, its effect will be less intense. The duet between Lindoro and Mustafà,

Se inclinassi a prender moglie . . .,[2]

[1] *Lindoro:*

Languir per una bella
E star lontan da quella
È il più crudel tormento
Che provar possa un cor.
(Act I, sc. iii)

[2] *Lindoro:*

Se inclinassi a prender moglie
Ci vorrebber tante cose;
Una appena in cento spose
Si potrebbe combinar [. . .]
Per esempio la vorrei
Schietta . . . buona . . .

Mustafà:

È tutta lei.

Lindoro:

Due begli occhi.

Mustafà:

Son due stelle.

Lindoro:

Chiome . . .

Mustafà:

Nere.

is as charming as the *cavatina*, but already there is a hint of something new, a suggestion of something more serious, more dramatic. Lindoro protests against having to accept the wife whom the Bey is attempting to thrust upon him. Our grave and weighty critics in the *Journal des Débats* have given it as their considered opinion that the whole plot from beginning to end is an insult to the rational faculties of man—not realizing, poor fools that they are, that if it were otherwise, it would be totally unsuited to this type of music, which is indeed but un-reason organized and perfected.[1] If these, our worthy men of letters, insist upon right reason and deep passion, let them turn to Mozart. In genuine *opera buffa*, passion is permitted to intrude only now and again; its function, as it were, is to give us respite from too much hilarity; and at such moments, let me add in passing, a skilful portrait of one of the tenderer emotions becomes well-nigh irresistible, combining as it must the charm of the unexpected and the fascination of contrast. For it is a characteristic of *good* opera, that no passion can leave us with a mere half-impression; and so, if the outpouring of emotion were uninterrupted, it would preoccupy us to the point of exhaustion—and then, farewell for ever to the extravagant delights of the *opera buffa*.

Mustafà's reply to Lindoro,

Son due stelle . . .,

in which he insists that the woman he is to love should have exquisite eyes, is a riot of laughter. Lindoro's reflection:

D'ogni parte io qui m'inciampo . . .,

is the finest music ever written; no other composer could have breathed such *freshness* into his melody. However, Mustafà's rejoinder,

Lindoro:
> Guance . . .

Mustafà:
> Belle.

Lindoro:
> (D'ogni parte io qui m'inciampo.
> Che ho da dire? che ho da far?)

Mustafà:
> Caro amico, non c'è scampo;
> Se la vedi, hai da cascar.
>   (Act I, sc. iii)

[1] *Cf.* Metastasio, who aims to create a similar impression in the serious drama. *Vide: Vies de Haydn, de Mozart et de Métastase*, p. 374.

Caro amico, non c'è scampo . . .,

shews the first, faintest trace of Rossini's most serious musical defect. The part which Mustafà has to sing is scored for *clarinet*; it achieves nothing more than a broken succession of chords, contrived solely to bring out the glittering splendour of the wonderful *cantilena* held by the tenor. Cimarosa understood the art of making this type of second-voice delightful to listen to, if by any remote chance the listener's attention should so far wander as to give a moment's thought to it. But in this instance, when at last, after the fourth or fifth performance, the poor listener remembers to be curious about the second-voice (Mustafà), he is confronted by the most banal scoring imaginable—*orchestral* scoring—and his delight, in consequence, withers. As I record this defect in Rossini's music, my regret is as poignant as that which I might feel if I were to observe, upon the fair features of a girl of eighteen, that tiniest fold in the skin beside the eye, which, ten years from now, will grow into an anxious furrow.

In this duet, Rossini betrays the first symptoms of that fatal complaint (whether of idleness or self-mistrust) which eventually was to drive him to write music for the concert-platform instead of music for the *drama*.

Isabella's aria

Cruda sorte! amor tiranno . . .,[1]

is flat and uninspired; by contrast, however, no praise is too superlative for the famous duet

Ai capricci della sorte . . .[2]

The music of this passage seems to be framed in a pattern of grace and elegance which is without parallel in Cimarosa; and it is this simple, noble gracefulness which makes Rossini the composer *par excellence* for

[1] *Isabella:*
    Cruda sorte! amor tiranno!
    Questo è il premio di mia fe' . . .
                  (Act I, sc. iv)

[2] *Isabella:*
    Ai capricci della sorte
    Io so far l'indifferente,
    Ma un geloso impertinente
    Io son stanca di soffrir.
                  (Act I, sc. v)

a French audience. This particular and original quality, which is something quite new in the history of music, springs perhaps from the fact that there is less *passion* in this duet than there would have been if Cimarosa had been the composer. The transition passage

> Messer Taddeo . . .
> Ride il babbeo . . .,[1]

is a thing of unqualified delight!

Following hard upon such a storm of extravagance and absurdity, it was essential to allow the audience some respite; and in this, the *libretto* is well-advised, affording as it does two whole scenes of recitative for us to wipe away the tears which wild tempests of laughter had brought to our eyes.

There is likewise a wonderful moment of *respite* in the great scene where the Bey Mustafà welcomes Isabella; it is provided by the chorus singing

> Oh! che rara beltà![2]

It was a stroke of genius to include a fleeting instant of church-music in an *opera buffa*; but Rossini, terrified of boring his audience, made it exceedingly short.

The *cantilena*

> Maltrattata dalla sorte . . .,[3]

is a masterpiece of coquetry; to the best of my belief, this was the first time that coquetry had ever been depicted on the Italian stage in its true colours. Cimarosa has a tendency to make his coquettes speak with

---

[1] *Taddeo:*
　　Donna Isabella?
　Isabella:
　　　　　　Messer Taddeo . . .

　Taddeo:
　　(La furia or plàcasi.)
　Isabella:
　　　　　(Ride il babbeo.)
　　　　　　(Act I, sc. v)

[2] Act I, sc. x.
[3] *Isabella:*
　　Maltrattata dalla sorte,
　　Condannata alle ritorte . . .
　　Ah! voi solo, o mio diletto,
　　Mi potete consolar.
　　　　　　(Act I, sc. xi)

a trace of the accent of true love, and that, perhaps, is the only weakness of which that great composer may be held guilty in all his skilled portrait of the feminine heart. Isabella's aria had to contain, at one and the same time, enough of love to deceive her unhappy victim, and enough of mockery to amuse the audience.

The quartet with Taddeo, in the *finale* of the first act, is excellent. Mark particularly the comic thrust:

> *Ah! chi sa mai, Taddeo?*[1]

Here we have indeed an exquisite demonstration of the achievement of the *opera buffa*, the perfection of comedy realized through the medium of music—and Rossini sweeps his paint on to his canvas with strokes as broad as can be imagined!

And when, at that very instant, Lindoro appears, together with the poor, deserted woman and her companion, never was there a song of greater delicacy and contrasting freshness than:

> *Pria di dividerci da voi, signore . . .!*[2]

The contrast is admirable, and the total effect, with its movement and its sweeping enchantment, one which Mozart and Cimarosa might well have envied!

It is my belief that the greatest fools in Christendom may legitimately grudge our worthy literary critics the crass ineptitudes which they have perpetrated with regard to the latter part of this *finale*! Admittedly (and why deny it?) the Bey *does* say:

> *Come scoppio di cannone*
> *La mia testa fa bumbù . . .;*[3]

[1] *Taddeo:*
  (Ohimè! . . . qual confidenza! . . .
  Il turco un cicisbeo
  Comincia a diventar.
  Ah, chi sa mai, Taddeo,
  Quel che or ti tocca a far?)
                                (Act I, sc. xii)

[2] *Lindoro, Elvira, Zulma* (together):
  Pria di dividerci da voi, signore,
  Veniamo a esprimervi il nostro core,
  Che sempre memore di voi sarà.
                                (Act I, sc. xiii)

[3] Act I, sc. xiii.

and, further, Taddeo *does* express himself in the words:

> *Sono come una cornacchia*
> *Che spennata fa cra, cra . . .*[1]

But did these miserable, benighted creatures never consider that, even if Marmontel or M. Etienne had written, expressly for this *finale*, ten or a dozen lines each, of unsurpassed exquisiteness, delicacy and charm, this contribution in itself would have done nothing to help the *music*, which, in all probability, would have been no worthier than some tinny tune by Dalayrac or Mondonville? It is as though a critic of Raphael's *Transfiguration* were to be at pains to applaud, above all else, the care which the artist took to paint his pictures on the very finest, first-quality Dutch canvas!

In Venice, where this *finale* was sung by Paccini, Galli and Madame Marcolini, the audience, by the end, were struggling and gasping for breath, and wiping the tears from their eyes.

And the impression created, moreover, is precisely that which persons of discerning taste *expect* from an *opera buffa*; the whole effect is extremely powerful; *therefore* the work is a masterpiece. This is a plain, straightforward argument, and neither in Venice nor in Vicenza was one obliged to stoop to hair-splitting quibbles over its details; through the gales of laughter, the audience rose unanimously to its feet and cheered: *Sublime! Divine!*

The outstanding characteristic of this wonderful work is its speed, its extreme economy and its lack of turgidity. It is just not possible to say more with such limited vocabulary—but how on earth are you to start explaining *this* to fools who understand nothing but the *libretto*? Rousseau undertook to supply the answer. At one point in his works, we find the following phrase, written in Italian: *Zanetto, lascia le donne, e studia la matematica!*[2]

ACT TWO

I know nothing more exciting than the entry of Taddeo in the second act:

[1] *Ibid.* To have criticized the opera on the evidence of these lines reveals a level of intelligence in the critic equal to that betrayed by the librettist!

[2] *Les Confessions.*

Ah! signor Mustafà![1]

The librettist shows some skill at this point; a powerful situation is created, sketched in a few words, and set out with great clarity and superb comic effect. It would be hard to discover a scene of greater liveliness and gaiety than the aria and pantomime of

Viva il grande Kaimakan![2]

However, if this effect is to succeed, it requires the essential courage to exploit the *pantomime*—and this is precisely what was *not* done in Paris! The scene could hardly be less offensive, but ... dignity, dignity at all costs!

The end of the aria

Qua bisogna far un conto ...[3]

is worthy of Cimarosa in his most perfect mood of farcical inventiveness, and yet the style is utterly different—more wit and less passion.

I enjoin upon you a most careful study, both of the *cantilena* itself, and of the accompaniment, in the passage where the wretched Taddeo, reduced to the dire extremity of making a choice between impalement and the sacrifice of his love for Isabella, proceeds to reason out the pros and cons. The setting of the words

Se ricuso ... il palo è pronto,
E se accetto ... è mio dovere
Di portargli il candeliere;
Kaimakan, signore, io resto!

[1] *Taddeo:*
　　Ah! signor Mustafà!
　Mustafà:
　　　　　　　　　　Che cosa è stato?
　Taddeo:
　　Abbiate compassion d'un innocente.
　　Io non v'ho fatto niente ...
　　　　　　　　　　(Act II, sc. iv)

[2] *Chorus:*
　　Viva il grande Kaimakan,
　　Protettor dei Mussulman.
　　Colla forza dei leoni,
　　Coll'astuzia dei serpenti ...
　　　　　　　　　　(Act II, sc. iv)

[3] *Taddeo:*
　　Qua bisogna far un conto:

is admirable. An achievement of this character is the prerogative of *genius* alone; study, labour and conscientious application to duty, far from providing inspiration, merely stunt and baulk the composer's imagination; this is one of those triumphs undreamed-of in the German school!

There was only one method by which an aria of such stupendous gaiety could fittingly be brought to a close; the rule, in fact, could have been found in any *ars poetica*, for the dullest and most banal of composers to read and obey: what is required is *a sudden lapse into a vein of sadness*. But here is the problem: how is the composer to create an atmosphere of profound sadness, and at the same time maintain his tone of complete simplicity, and all this—prime necessity of all—*without losing speed*? Rossini found the answer with the sublime (and *apparently* elementary) phrase:

> *Ah Taddeo! quant' era meglio*
> *Che tu andassi in fondo al mar!*[1]

No one who has ever been at Court can miss the point of these artificial congratulations showered with studied politeness upon one to whom official advancement has brought nothing but despair; the situation is a most eloquent portrait of the absurdest dilemmas which arise in that strange society. The impression which the scene creates is so moving that there are days when one pities Taddeo, for all the absurdity of his rôle as the rejected lover.

Following upon an aria and a chorus so rich in pure comedy, a longish period of respite was essential, and this is provided with great ingenuity by the librettist.

Isabella's aria:

> *Per lui che adoro . . .,*[2]

> Se ricuso . . . il palo è pronto.
> E se accetto? è mio dovere
> Di portagli il candeliere.
> Ah! . . . Taddeo, che bivio è questo!
> Ma quel palo? . . . che ho da far?
> Kaimakan, signore, io resto,
> Non vi voglio disgustar.
>
> (Act II, sc. iv)

[1] *Ibid.*
[2] *Isabella:*
> Per lui che adoro,

was intended once again to depict a nuance of coquetry; but on this occasion, Rossini was less successful than in the duet from Act I. Isabella's roulades, elegant and repetitive, produce no response in the listener's imagination save one of stony indifference. The primary musical material is so poor that no one can fail to be aware that all this embroidery is strewn upon it merely in order to disguise its inherent worthlessness, rather than to enrich its splendour and enhance the magnificence of its effect.

However, Rossini fully recaptures his inspiration in the quintet

> Ti presento di mia man'
> Ser Taddeo Kaimakan . . .[1]

This passage is perhaps the crowning achievement of the whole opera. Every note of the music is pre-eminently dramatic. Nothing could be more provocatively gay nor, at the same time, truer to nature, than Isabella's thrust:

> Il tuo muso è fatto apposta . . .,

nothing could be more coquettish, more deceitful, than the line:

> Aggradisco, o mio signore . . .

Poor Mustafà with his importunate sneezing succeeded in moving even the Parisian audiences to laughter. The stubborn obstinacy of a fool set on his high horse is admirably characterized in the lines:

> Ch'ei starnuti finchè scoppia,
> Non mi muovo via di qua!

>> Ch'è il mio tesoro,
>> Più bella rendimi,
>> Madre d'amor . . .
>> (Act II, sc. v)

[1] Mustafà:
> Ti presento di mia man'
> Ser Taddeo Kaimakan.
> Da ciò apprendi quanta stima
> Di te faccia Mustafà.

sabella:
> Kaimakan? a me t'accosta,
> Il tuo muso è fatto a posta.
> Aggradisco, o mio signore,
> Questo tratto di bontà.
>> (Act II, sc. vi)

and then, just as one is about to feel the first warnings that too much laughter and unmitigated farce might in the end become boring, Rossini gives us the delightful phrase:

Di due sciocchi uniti insieme . . .,[1]

to bring rest and refreshment to the listener's exhausted mind. But, at the very end, poor Mustafà's song,

Tu pur mi prendi a gioco . . .,[2]

is weak and platitudinous, the music consisting of nothing but dull, broken sequences scored for clarinet; this is school-boy stuff, and written by an idle pupil at that!

However, to restore the balance, the trio round the mysterious word *pappataci* is both brilliant and powerful; the contrast between the tenor part of Lindoro and the *basso-profondo* of Mustafà:

Che vuol poi significar?
. . . A color che mai non sanno . . .,[3]

is a pure delight to listen to—and moreover, provides a perfect instance of a fine operatic effect which is completely independent of the *libretto*,

---

[1] *Taddeo:*
　　　(Ch'ei starnuti finchè scoppia.
　　　Non mi muovo via di qua.)
　　Isabella, Lindoro:
　　　(L'uno spera e l'altro freme.
　　　Di due sciocchi uniti insieme
　　　Oh! che rider si farà!)
　　　　　　　　　　　(Act II, sc. vi)

[2] *Mustafà:*
　　　Tu pur mi, prendi a gioco;
　　　Me la farò pagar.
　　　Ho nelle vene un foco,
　　　Più non mi so frenar.
　　　　　　　　　　　(Act II, sc. vi)

[3] *Mustafà:*
　　　Ma di grazia, Pappataci
　　　Che vuol poi significar?
　　Lindoro:
　　　A color che mai non sanno
　　　Disgustarsi col bel sesso,
　　　In Italia vien concesso
　　　Questo titol singolar.
　　　　　　　　　　　(Act II, sc. ix)

and which, in consequence, must be completely invisible to those who insist upon approaching vocal music exclusively through the medium of the words.

The end of the trio:

Fra gli amori e le bellezze . . .,[1]

is a triumph of merriment and *verve*; yet, in the middle of this unparalleled deluge of farce and comedy, there intrudes one instant of nobility, of delicacy, almost of tenderness, which affords the most brilliant of contrasts:

Se mai torno ai miei paesi . . .[2]

The scene of the oath-taking is, if anything, finer still; in the Parisian production, it was cut out altogether, and one would really like to know *why**? Was it envy? Or is the reason to be sought in a principle enunciated on one occasion by one of the directors of the *Théâtre Louvois*, in the course of a conversation with certain *dilettanti*:

I would have it clearly understood, gentlemen, that our theatre is not a fair-ground show-booth, to be used for the antics of clowns and jugglers!

I decline to proceed with the discussion of this insignificant mystery; if there exist people who cannot understand how to get their true money's-worth of entertainment, so much the worse for them. All the same, these identical people are never short of a fine phrase to eulogize the superior excellence of the theatre which, every evening, enjoys the privilege of opening its doors to them. *In the whole of Italy*, they assure each other fervently, *you would never find anything comparable to this!* Who am *I*, to spoil their beatitude? It is so naïve, so innocent! It

---

[1] *Mustafà:*
     Mia spiegatemi, vi prego:
     Pappataci che ha da far?
  Lindoro, Taddeo:
     Fra gli amori e le bellezze,
     Fra gli scherzi e le carezze,
     Dee dormir, mangiar e bere,
     Ber, dormir, e poi mangiar.
                    (Act II, sc. ix)

[2] *Taddeo, Lindoro:*
     Se mai torno ai miei paesi
     Anche questa è da contar.
                    (Act II, sc. ix)

happened on one occasion that I found myself at table, confronted by a straggly bunch or two of mean, green and sourish grapes, served up ceremoniously at dessert in the dining-hall of a noble castle near Edinburgh. What was the point in seeming ungrateful? It would surely have betrayed nothing but the grossest ill-breeding on my part, to have disillusioned the wealthy epicure who was my host, and who, at huge expense, had introduced these grapes into his enormous hot-houses. The worthy individual had never known the great grapes of Fontainebleau, the famous *chasselas*; and his powers of intellect had needed to be far more developed than is usually befitting to millionaire hot-house-owners before he could have grasped the purely abstract notion that, in lands where the vine grows freely in the open air, there *may* be grapes which are better and tastier than those which are cultivated with such trouble and expense in artificial forcing-houses. Had I spoken my mind, I should have seemed just as absurd as some eccentric gardener returned from a far country with his head all stuffed with new methods of gardening; *he* propounds the schemes—but there is no one but himself to answer for their excellence!

The extreme docility of the audiences who patronize the *Théâtre Louvois*, and who have not the necessary minimum of moral courage to demand their Rossini *un*-mutilated, is the more exemplary, in that there exists surely somewhere an official statute expressly forbidding all cuts in any work performed in the Royal Theatres*. And in any case, statutes or no statutes, it is to be conceived that an artist of the stature and reputation of Rossini, who, by general admission, is a man of some considerable talent, may claim the right to see his works performed at least once *as they were written*, instead of chopped up into unrecognizable little bits and pieces! But in that case, what would happen to our worthy friend the "arranger", his office and his valuable privileges? Let us leave this amenable public to its self-congratulatory smirks and its good manners, still preening itself over its much-vaunted right (which, imperceptibly, has been taken away from it) to whistle long and loud whenever it disapproves, for in all conscience, it shows little enough discretion in the exercise of its right to *applaud*! Yesterday (June 1823), I watched four French actresses* performing together in an *Italian* opera, *le Nozze di Figaro*. What a triumph, what a flattering instant of glory of our *National Honour*! National Honour did indeed applaud wildly, voicing the enthusiasm of its manifold delights—

amongst which, surely, the pleasure of *variety* must rank extremely high, since every one of the four good ladies had sung sharp, each in her own style and individual manner! But these are mere peccadilloes, of which our *liberal press* dare not take cognizance, for fear of jeopardizing its popularity!

Genius, in the *Italiana in Algeri*, has its final fling with a magnificent trio—which was deemed to be "too frivolous" for the taste of the Parisian audiences. The final aria is two things at once; firstly, it is a *tour de force*, to the eternal glory of Signora Marcolini—where else would you hope to find a *prima-donna* with enough strength in her lungs to master so mighty an aria, with all its fantastic wealth of decoration, at the very end of so exhausting an opera? This in fact is one of the problems which causes a certain amount of anxiety in Italy, and sometimes mitigates against the *Italiana* in performance; no such anxieties, however, ruffle the smooth, untroubled brow of the management of the *Théâtre Louvois*, and Signorina Naldi dealt with this aria precisely as she had dealt with all the rest!

Secondly, this aria is remarkable for its historical content and implications. You may rightly wonder exactly what "historical implications" are liable to be encountered in the *finale* of an *opera buffa*; but alas! gentlemen, it is true! It may be against the rules, but none the less this outrage, this audacity *exists*!

> *Pensa alla patria, e intrepido*
> *Il tuo dovere adempi;*
> *Vedi per tutta Italia*
> *Rinascere gli esempi*
> *D' ardir e di valor.*[1]

The ardour of patriotism, banished from the soil of Italy ever since the capture of Florence by the Medici in 1530, under pain of twenty years' imprisonment, had only recently been revived by Napoleon. Rossini knew his audience, read into its secret heart, and feasted its imagination on the delights which it craved. None the less, here as elsewhere, Rossini is extremely careful not to make too prolonged a demand on the response of any one emotion or enthusiasm; with the result that the noble melody

[1] Act I, sc. xi. The three quotations on this page form one continuous passage in the libretto. (*Trans.*)

Intrepido
Il tuo dovere adempi . . .

—a melody calculated to fetch forth everything which is most noble in the human heart—has scarcely been heard once, when he immediately feels the need to allow his audience to relax, and so transforms his patriotic mood into

Sciocco! tu ridi ancora?

Then comes a passage in which the base ignominy of a certain political party, which had denounced the rebirth of generosity in the hidden heart of Italy, is castigated in the words:

Vanne, mi fai dispetto . . .

—words which, when the opera was first produced, were invariably drowned in a roar of applause. As against this, however, the passage

Rivedrem le patrie arene . . .[1]

is gentle and musing; the language of patriotism is at length overlaid with the accents of a different, more intimate love.

And these are the last dying echoes of this most delightful opera. It is a masterpiece which never fails to give pleasure, and it has been acclaimed in every city in Europe save in Paris (where, I am most firmly convinced, there was *high treason* abroad!) But just try to imagine *Andromaque* performed at the *Théâtre Français* with the great clown Montrose in the rôle of Oreste . . . yet the disparity is no greater than that between Signorina Naldi and the part of the merry-mad Isabella. So charming a creature should confine her talents to the rôles of Amenaide or Juliet, where she may be certain of pleasing our ears as well as our eyes.

But all this, you will accuse me, *is much ado—worse, much* serious *ado —about nothing, about a mere game, a pastime, an* opera buffa! . . . I plead guilty. The subject-matter is futile, and the dissertation has been lengthy. If a child were to offer an analysis of the art of building card-

---

[1] *Isabella:*
     Qual piacer! Tra pochi istanti
     Rivedrem le patrie arene.
     (Nel periglio del mio bene
     Coraggiosa amor mi fa.)
               (Act II, sc. xi)

castles, collapsing at a breath and yet towering two storeys high, do you not suppose that the learned exposition of such a difficult matter would take a little while to complete? And furthermore, would you really be so surprised to find that a subject which, for the child concerned, was so fascinating, so utterly absorbing, should be treated with a good deal of seriousness? Well then, I am just such a child. Admittedly, no discussion on the art of music will furnish clear and rational principles of impeccable logic, or even of proven practical utility; but for all that, if Heaven has granted you a heart to feel beauty, you may nevertheless derive some pleasure from it*.

CHAPTER IV

*La Pietra del Paragone**

I BELIEVE that it was Signora Marcolini* who caused Rossini to be "offered a contract" (*scritturare*)¹ at Milan for the autumn season of

¹ The *scrittura* is a little two-page agreement, normally printed, which sets out the reciprocal obligations of the composer or the singer on the one hand, and of the *impresario* who engages them on the other. Where first-rate artists are concerned, innumerable petty intrigues are liable to develop around the *scritture*, which afford a great deal of general amusement; I strongly advise the traveller in Italy to look closely into this special branch of diplomacy; it frequently calls for considerably more wit and ingenuity than the *other* sort! As regards the *technique* of this diplomacy, we may observe something in common with the technique of art; that is to say, the customs and traditions of the country where art was born have freely intermingled with the pure, abstract theory, and often help to explain many of its peculiarities. At any given period of his career, Rossini's genius has almost always betrayed traces of the influence of the particular *scrittura* which he happened to have signed. If only there had been some Maecenas, some Prince to guarantee him a steady income of 3,000 francs a year, Rossini would have then been able to sit and wait for the breath of inspiration before taking up his pen and sitting down to compose; and this simple revolution would have given a totally different character to every single composition which his genius was to produce. Our French composers, MM. Auber, Boïeldieu, Berton, *etc.*, have this advantage, and compose at their leisure, producing about one opera a year; whereas Rossini, in a manner reminiscent of the Golden Age of painting, wrote four or five operas a year throughout his youth, turning them out (as Guido Reni used to turn out pictures) to pay the inn-keeper and the washerwoman. I blush at the necessity which forces me to ferret about among such vulgar details, and I entreat the reader's pardon; but I would remind him that I *am* writing a biography . . . and such is the truth. Every art is faced with the same problem; the artist is confronted with gross material indissolubly rooted in vulgarity, and it is his task to surmount it, even though the coarseness of the details makes it impossible for the powers of imagination to come to the rescue. But it is precisely amid such circumstances that Rossini maintained his genius in all its freshness and vigour; although it is also true that, since the manners of modern Italy are a product and direct consequence of those which were in vogue in the mediaeval republics, poverty carries no stigma, and certainly not the stigma which it carries in *monarchic* France, where right-seeming (*parestre*) is everything, as the Baron de Fœneste so accurately maintains.†

If there is one thing in Italy which passes for a miracle, it is an *impresario* who fails to go bankrupt, and who observes some regularity in the payment of salaries to his singers and his composer-conductor. When one observes closely what poor devils these *impresari* in fact are, one is truly moved to pity on behalf of the

the year 1812. In any case, it was there that he composed *la Pietra del Paragone* for the opera-house of *la Scala*. He was twenty-one; and he was lucky enough to hear his music sung by la Marcolini and by Galli, Bonoldi and Parlamagni, all at the height of their powers; and each one of these artists was immensely successful in his or her respective part. The generosity of the audience even embraced poor old Vasoli, an ex-grenadier from Napoleon's Army of Egypt, but now almost blind and, as a singer, hardly even third-rate, who made his undying reputation in the aria: *Ombretta sdegnosa del Missipipì** . . .

La Pietra del Paragone is, to my mind, Rossini's masterpiece of unadulterated *opera buffa*. I implore the reader, however, not to take fright at such extravagant expressions of adulation; I have no intention whatsoever of risking another analysis such as that which I have just given of *l'Italiana in Algeri*. *La Pietra del Paragone* is unknown in Paris; certain Very Clever Persons had the best reasons in the world for making sure that, if it had to appear there at all, it should be given only in a severely mutilated version; consequently it fell flat, once and for ever*.

The *libretto* is excellent; once again the situations are powerfully conceived, one following upon the heels of the other with breath-taking speed; they are worked out clearly and with a minimum of dialogue; and such dialogue as there is, is usually highly amusing. These various situations, however lively, however direct and forceful their appeal to the passions, habits and mannerisms of the crowd of characters involved, none the less maintain contact all the time with the realities of life, and reflect the social patterns and manners of Italy—

wretched *maestro*, who, to live at all, must wait upon the salary which these ill-dressed persons are supposed to pay him! The first idea which springs to mind on meeting the average Italian *impresario* is that, if ever he should chance to set eyes on a round sum of twenty sequins, he would rush off to buy a new set of clothes, and disappear for good with the change!

† *Le Baron de Fœneste*: a most curious novel by Agrippa d'Aubigné, almost as fascinating as the *History of his Life*, written by himself. This *History* paints the portrait of Henri IV almost as faithfully as *Quentin Durward* depicts that of Louis XI. I discovered there a whole store of anecdotes concerning Henri IV, none of which I dare quote. There is no question but that this monarch was a great man; but he was most certainly *not* a milk-and-water saint. There are some most striking resemblances between Henri IV and Napoleon; and also between the *Life* of d'Aubigné and the *Mémoires* of Las Cases. Even the motives are identical in the two cases—except one: Henri IV adored women as Napoleon adored battles!

of this happy land of Italy, which is so fortunate in its inner, intimate life of the heart, and so desperately unfortunate in the petty tyrants who rule over it. In such a land, there is no fairer test of skill than to create situations like these, which, for all their realism and forcefulness, never for a moment depict life as a thing of gloom and despondency tricked out with the thinnest, the most superficial *veneer* of gaiety,[1] but rather manage to interest the mind without giving rise to a single depressing reflection. On the other hand, however, it would be futile to expect from an Italian *libretto* any trace of the flashing wit which sparkles and glitters in the type of play which is put on at the *Théâtre du Gymnase*, and which is so brilliantly amusing the first time you go to see it (and occasionally the second time too!).

This opera is entitled *the Touchstone*, because it is the tale of a young man, Count Asdrubale, recently heir to a considerable fortune, who invents a test to "prove as with a touchstone" the hearts of those friends, and even mistresses, who had descended upon him at the same time as his new wealth. A man of commoner clay would have been well satisfied with the concert of flattery and attention which played about Count Asdrubale; all the world smiled upon him; yet he could not be happy in his own heart, for that was set upon the Marchesa Clarice, a young widow, who, together with a train of thirty-odd companions and friends, had come to spend the season of the *villeggiatura*[2] at his country-house, situated near Rome, in the centre of the Forest of Viterbo; and yet—who could tell?—it was quite possible that Clarice herself loved nothing in him so much as his glittering wealth and his great estate.

Every traveller will recall the Forest of Viterbo and its magnificent scenery. This was the country whence Claude Lorrain and Guaspre Poussin drew such a wealth of wonderful material for their landscapes. The charm of the *décor* makes a perfect background for the pattern of stirring emotions which is to be woven among the various characters staying in the great mansion. Count Asdrubale has an intimate friend,

---

[1] *Cf. Le Solliciteur*, or *l'Intérieur d'un Bureau*, which, by the time one has seen them twice, leave one with a sense of overwhelming pity for the "heroes". Yet the plays named represent the only *real* comedies of our generation. "Comedy", as it is played at the *Théâtre Français*, is nothing better than a *Serious Epistle*, chopped up into dialogue and stuffed with moral maxims. *Cf. la Fille d'honneur, les Deux Cousines, les Comédiens*, etc.

[2] The country-holiday season.

a young poet touchingly free of academic vanity, unversed in insincerity and affectation, but not unversed in the art of love. Giocondo—for such is the name of this wild young dreamer—is also in love with Clarice. He suspects that Asdrubale is a favoured rival; whereas Clarice for her part conjectures that, if she allows her love for Asdrubale to be seen, he may believe—even while he accepts her hand in marriage—that she is not wholly averse to claiming a share in a noble fortune, nor to cutting a fine figure in society.

Among the swarm of parasites and flatterers of all sorts and species who swarm and buzz about in the count's domain, the librettist has given place of honour to one don Marforio, the local journalist. In France, there are no finer intellects in all the land than those upon whom devolves the daily responsibility of addressing us through the newspapers;[1] but in Italy, the case is very different*. Don Marforio, an intriguer, a coward, and above all a *braggart*, spiteful but by no means foolish, is responsible for the comic element of the plot, in conjunction with one don Pacuvio, an implacable gossip-writer, perpetually burdened with secrets of unspeakable importance, which he insists on confiding to every one in turn. The absurdity of such characters, whose existence would be almost inconceivable in France, thanks to the comparative (if limited) freedom of the press which we enjoy, is common enough to meet with in Italy, where newspapers are subjected to a censorship of intolerable severity, and where governments think nothing of flinging into gaol a dozen or more poor gossips, whose only crime was to have sat in a coffee-house bandying about some insignificant snippet of local news—nor of keeping them there indefinitely, until one by one they choose to confess the source of their criminal information, which, more often than not, is nothing but the dullest item of libellous invention.

Don Pacuvio, then, the gossip-writer, and don Marforio, the journalist, both citizens of Rome, come to Asdrubale's residence in quest of conversation, and discover two young ladies, relatives of the count, neither of whom would be averse to catching him as a husband. To this end, they employ every petty ruse which current practice permits in such circumstances, and don Marforio becomes their intimate adviser.

[1] MM. Jouy, de Lamennais, Etienne, Chateaubriand, Benjamin Constant, de Bonald, de Pradt, de Marcellus, Mignet, Buchon, Fiévée, *etc.*, *etc.*

As the curtain rises, a superb chorus touches off the action among this vast crown of characters in a manner as lively as it is picturesque. Don Pacuvio, that intolerable gossip, has some private information of unparalleled importance, which he absolutely insists upon sharing with the whole host of friends and acquaintances who have gathered about the count, and even upon imparting to the determined pair of young ladies who are after his hand. But the poor pamphleteer meets with a cool reception, and ends up by making himself such a nuisance that he sends everyone scurrying for safety to avoid him—whither, however, quite unperturbed, he continues his relentless pursuit.

Giocondo, the passionate young poet, and don Marforio, the journalist, now step on to the stage, and sing a "literary duet", which, as may well be imagined, is of a most lively, satirical character. *At a single stroke of my critical pen*, claims the scribbler, *a thousand poor poets fall flat in the dust!*

> *Mille vati al suolo io stendo*
> *Con un colpo di giornale!*

Treat me properly, on the other hand, and I shall reward you with glory! But the young poet is not to be tempted: *At such a price*, he exclaims, *glory would be utterly despicable! What have I in common with a newspaper?*

This duet is delightfully pointed and satirical, and only Rossini could have managed it. Its most admirable qualities are its fire, its wit, its lightness of touch, and its completely dispassionate, almost indifferent emotional attitude. The sly journalist, realizing that Giocondo is immune to temptations which aim to flatter his literary vanity, abandons him with a Parthian shot directed against his disappointed love for Clarice. *Tilting against millionaires*, he remarks, *with no better weapon than a heart enslaved, is a sport which often betrays a noble character, but which rarely leads to success!* This depressing truth decidedly upsets the young poet; both characters leave the stage, only to make way at last (after so much chatter *about* her) for the adorable Clarice, who sings the *cavatina*:

> *Eco pietosa tu sei la sola . . .*

In Italy, this aria is as well-known as the famous song from *Tancredi*; nevertheless, the most prudent management of the *Opéra-Bouffe* in Paris had the wondrous common sense to suppress it altogether! If there is one field in which music excels, it is in the portrayal of a *hopeless passion*; and in this case, especially, since the preceding scenes have already given us an intimate glimpse of the passion in question, the portrayal is unusually perfect. We are not concerned here with the old, platitudinous story of a love thwarted by some prosaic, external obstacle—a father, or a guardian, as the case may be—but with the analysis of a love thrown into despair by the anguished torments of *fear*. Clarice's fear is that, in the eyes of her lover, she shall appear to possess nothing but a base and mercenary soul. To a person of discriminating taste, the difference between these two dramatic motives is incalculable:

> *Eco pietosa* (exclaims Clarice) *tu sei la sola*
> *Che mi consola nel mio dolor* . . .

Indeed, who else is there for poor Clarice to confide in? In circumstances like these, could any truly noble lover bear the vulgar consolations of "talking it over" with a friend? If she had turned to her companions, one and all would certainly have urged her: *Marry, marry quick, no matter how, and let love come later, if God will it so!*

While Clarice is still singing, the count, who happens to be close at hand, concealed in a neighbouring glade, has a fancy to play the echo*; the plan is crazy, and quite at variance with all his previous careful scheming; but in the end, the temptation is too strong. So, when Clarice sings:

> *Quel dirmi, o dio, non t'amo* . . .

the count provides the echo: *amo*. This is a dramatic variation which it had not occurred to Rossini to exploit in the aria from *Tancredi*; and it is not hard to imagine the impact which a device of this character, so admirably suited to the characteristic requirements of opera, and enhanced with all the dreamy gentleness of Rossini's music, might have created in Paris. But no; our prudent *directors* naturally appreciated the danger at once!

Clarice enjoys one fleeting moment of happiness; but the count's tender avowal was only an ephemeral weakness; when she meets him again an instant later, he as agreeable, as light-hearted, but as distant and reserved as ever. He is in fact meditating his great "test", and we are allowed to behold him issuing final instructions to his steward, who is to aid and abet him. Having observed Giocondo's unrequited love for Clarice, he is delighted to have the chance of discovering precisely how long it is likely to remain unrequited in his absence. At last, the count vanishes out of sight, only to reappear a moment later disguised as a Turk. This "Turk" now proceeds to confront the steward with a bill of exchange, duly and correctly signed by Asdrubale's father, for the round sum of *two millions*—a debt which, when paid off, will swallow up the greater part of the count's estate. The steward in due course formally recognizes and acknowledges the signature of his employer's father, verifies that it is genuine and valid; and the general belief grows rapidly that the count is completely ruined. The stage is now set for this gentleman himself to make his entry, still heavily disguised as a Turk; and at this point Rossini launches out into the most perfect *buffo finale* that he ever composed.

The "Turk" (played by Galli) has a vocabulary which is restricted to one solitary word, which he employs with indiscriminate persistance to confound every objection which is raised up against him—a barbaric, semi-Italianized word: *sigillara! Let the seals be affixed!* This baroque expression, which the "Turk" has ever on his lips, repeating it willynilly in every context and with every manner of inflexion (since it is the only reply he seems to know to every question or demand which is addressed to him), created such a *furore* among the Milanese, among this nation of *born connoisseurs*, that the opera was accredited with a new title in consequence. In Lombardy to-day, if you happen to mention *la Pietra del Paragone*, no one will understand what on earth you are talking about; you must always refer to *il Sigillara*.

This is the *finale* which was cut in the Paris production*!

The "Turk's" retort to the journalist, who attempts to protest when the bailiffs want to affix the seals to *his* room, is famous throughout all Italy, echoing the unquenchable outburst of laughter which it provoked at the time:

> *Don Marforio:* *Mi far critica giornale*
> *Che aver fama in ogni loco.*
> *Il Turco:* *Ti lasciar almen per poco*
> *Il bon senso a respirar!*

The audience was hugely delighted with this *finale* and its *Sigillara!* and the opera inaugurated a whole epoch of enthusiastic and ecstatic performances at *la Scala*; Milan was invaded by hordes of opera-goers

from Parma, from Piacenza, from Bergamo, from Brescia, and from
every city within a distance of twenty leagues. Rossini became the
greatest figure in all the land; he was overwhelmed with visits from
admirers; and love could not long deny him his just reward. Dazzled
by so much glory and fame, the loveliest of lovely women in all
Lombardy, hitherto a model of conjugal fidelity, and a high and
honourable example to every young married woman, forgot every
scrap of duty she owed to her house, her husband and her reputation,
and publicly carried Rossini off in her arms under the very nose of la
Marcolini. Rossini, for his part, transformed his young mistress into
the finest musician you might hope to find in all Italy; and it was at
her side, upon *her* piano, and within the walls of *her* country-house* at
B[ologna], that he composed by far the larger part of the arias and
cantilenas, which, in time, were to form the crowning glory and
triumph of his thirty operatic masterpieces.

At that date, the province of Lombardy was enjoying a period of
unparalleled prosperity. Milan, the brilliant capital of a new-founded
kingdom, whose liberal king exacted from his subjects a lighter *tribute*
of *stupidity* than any of his royal neighbours, was simultaneously alive
with every imaginable variety of activity, with every opportunity for
making money or for procuring pleasure. And, for a State just as much
as for an individual, happiness consists not so much in possessing money,
as in making it! Milan had adopted a new code of manners, bearing
such a stamp of vigour as had not been seen since the Middle Ages;[1]
yet there was no affectation, no prudishness, not yet any mere blind
adulation of Napoleon; for if Napoleon ever wanted servile flattery,
he was certainly made to pay for it in good, ringing money.

But this wonderful period of prosperity, which reigned in Lombardy
in 1813, was all the more pathetic and moving, in that it was on the
point of being obliterated. It was as though some vague prophetic
instinct was already whispering to an apprehensive people to listen for
the thunder of cannon away in the far North. Even before the last
echoes of the wild triumph of *la Pietra del Paragone* had died away, our
armies were in full retreat along the Dnieper, and Black Reaction* was
bearing down upon us.

[1] *Cf.* the *Bulletins de l'Armée d'Espagne*; the generals Bertoletti, Zucchi,
Schiassetti, *etc.*; Count Prina, Minister of State; the painter Appiani; the poet
Monti, *etc., etc.*

For all Rossini's habitual and perhaps studied indifference, there come times when even he can barely keep out of his voice an occasional trace of deep excitement; and so indeed it happens whenever he is brought to talk about the great happiness he experienced during this long, fair summer of his youth, when he, in the company of a whole nation which, after three hundred years of black oppression, was slowly coming out of darkness into the light of a new dawn, discovered the thrill of being alive.

ACT TWO

The second act of *la Pietra del Paragone* opens with a quartet which is without parallel in all the rest of Rossini's works; it catches to perfection the accents and the indefiniable charm of a conversation among a group of people, each one of whom is in the grip of some intense and vital emotion, and yet all of them strenuously deny themselves the actual pleasure of talking about their secret feelings.

There then follows a comic duel between don Marforio, the journalist, who has had the temerity to make amorous suggestions to Clarice, and Giocondo, the young poet, who still worships her unavailingly, and who now claims the right to act as her champion and avenge her.

The journalist, with all the desperation of cowardice, pleads with his opponent:

> *Dirò ben di voi nel mio giornale!*

to which the latter replies:

> *Potentissimi dei! sarebbe questa*
> *Una ragion più forte*
> *Per ammazzarti subito!*

Further complications weave a new web of entanglement about this duel, beginning with the intervention of the Count, who likewise insists upon obtaining satisfaction in respect of an insolent article which the journalist had published concerning his mysterious adventures. The great trio which eventually emerges from this imbroglio may well bear comparison with the famous duel-scene from Cimarosa's *i Nemici generosi*; the difference between the two composers being, as always, that the one is impassioned where the other is witty.

The somewhat wry facetiousness of the cowardly journalist, who would give a great deal to wind up the business in a spirit of universal friendship and good-will,

> Con quel che resta ucciso
> Io poi mi batterò . . ,

is musically delightful; and the song:

> Ecco i soliti saluti . . .,[1]

which is sung by the two friends while they accept swords offered to them upon silver platters by a pair of footmen in full livery, and then proceed to the formal salutes of the fencing-schools, is utterly delicious! The language of the dialogue is just sufficiently serious to deceive an otherwise intelligent man who is momentarily stupefied with terror.

This trio, which is delightful on any stage and in any country, was greeted in Italy with the wildest enthusiasm: for, in every petty little provincial town, the satire found its mark ad hominem, in the person of some wretched, miserable, official journalist who, despite the best efforts of his highly-placed "protectors", periodically lands himself in the middle of some scrape or other, or gets caught up in some undignified riot, where (as Scapino satirically remarks) "blows fall thick as hail-stones". In Milan, where everyone knows everyone else, the enthusiasm was wilder than anywhere, for the actor who played don

---

[1] Count Asdrubale and Cavaliere Giocondo decide to fight with swords to decide who is to have the honour of first fighting Don Marforio with pistols:

Marforio:
Prima fra voi, coll' armi,
Il punto sia deciso:
Con quel che resta ucciso
Io poi mi batterò.
Asdrubale, Giocondo:
Ebben, l'acciar decida,
Chi primo ha da pugnar.
Marforio:
(Comincio a respirar.)
Asdrubale, Giocondo:
Ecco i soliti saluti!
(Del duello inaspettato
Si consola il maledetto,
E non sa che per diletto
Lo faremo ancor tremar!)
In the Paris version, this duel was transferred to the end of Act II. (Trans.)

Marforio had somehow or other procured a full suit of clothes, which, as all the town knew only too well, had been worn on a certain occasion by the "official journalist" employed by the Police!

La Pietra del Paragone, like *l'Italiana in Algeri*, finishes with a mighty aria. La Marcolini had at some time expressed a wish to appear on the stage in male attire; and so Rossini had persuaded his librettist to contrive the plot so that Clarice, still pursuing her schemes to wrest a confession of love from the Count, should disguise herself as a Captain of Hussars.

Not a single voice in all Milan—not even that of the pilloried "official journalist"—was raised in protest against the palpable absurdity of such a plot, where a young lady of noblest Roman birth and of the highest social pretensions, chooses to amuse herself by dressing up as a Captain of Hussars, and indulges a whim to salute the audience, sabre in hand, at the head of her entire squadron. No doubt, if la Marcolini had insisted, Rossini would cheerfully have had her singing away on horseback! The aria itself is fine enough; but, when all is said and done, it is really all *bravura*; and just at the point where the dramatic interest should rise to a climax, Rossini clumsily allows the tension to relax completely, with the result that the listener's imagination, which had been screwed up to a pitch of electrified intensity in anticipation of the great moment, is just left dangling limply; and, in the end, the audience is reduced to applauding a series of virtuoso roulades, just as though it were listening to a concert, for want of anything better to applaud.

It was while Rossini was in Milan that he "borrowed" the device known as the *crescendo* (later to become so notorious) from a composer by the name of Giuseppe Mosca*—to the latter's unspeakable disgust.

CHAPTER V

Conscription and Envy

AFTER such a remarkable run of successes, Rossini returned to Pesaro to visit his family, to whom, incidentally, he is still passionately attached. In all his life, he has written but to *one* person: his mother—and the letters which he writes to her bear the following superbly uninhibited superscription*:

*All'onoratissima signora Rossini, madre del celebre maestro,
in Bologna.*

Thus the man, thus his character; half-seriously, half jestingly, he acknowledges his own halo of glory, and scarcely deigns to cloak himself in the petty robes of academic modesty—a phenomenon which convinces me that, in Paris, he could never hope to enjoy any real personal popularity. Blessed with genius in the midst of the most impressionable people in the whole universe, intoxicated with adulation ever since his earliest adolescence, he abides firmly by his faith in his own ability and fame, and sees no valid reason why an individual of the stature of a *Rossini* should fail to rank, not by special concession and privilege, but simply by a dictate of natural law, with a Lieutenant-General or a Minister-of-State. They, apparently, have picked a winning number in the lottery of ambition; he, in the lottery of native genius. The aphorism is of Rossini's own invention; I heard him formulate it one evening in Rome, in 1819, while the whole company which had assembled at the house of Prince Chigi was deliberately being kept waiting for him.

At about the same time as his journey to Pesaro, he achieved another success, which was very rare indeed at the time: the terrible conscription-laws were relaxed for him, as a special concession to his dawning genius. The Minister of the Interior for the Kingdom of Italy proposed to Prince Eugène* that an exception be made in his favour; and the Prince, notwithstanding the abysmal terror with which he contemplated any directives sent from Paris, yielded to public opinion. Redeemed from military service*, Rossini went on to Bologna, where there awaited him further adventures in the same vein as those which he had recently encountered in Milan—audiences to deafen him with their acclamations, and the fairest of fair women to crown him with their love!

The musical purists of Bologna, however, who are notorious throughout the length and breadth of Italy, and who stand in much the same relation to music as the members of the *Académie Française* stand in relation to the "three unities" of classical tragedy, accused him (and rightly so) of occasional infringements against the laws of composition*. Rossini acknowledged that indictment: *I should be guilty of fewer faults,* he replied to this wretched swarm of pedants, *if ever I re-read my own manuscripts; but you must realize that I am lucky if I have six weeks in which to write a whole opera ... and even so, I usually spend the first month simply enjoying myself! But then, when else do you* expect *me to enjoy myself, if not now, while I am both young and successful? Am I supposed to wait until I grow old and jealous? And so the time passes, until we get to the last fortnight, during which, every morning, I sit down and compose a new aria or a duet, which we then put into rehearsal the same evening. How do you expect me to be able to spot every little syntactical slip in the accompaniment* (l'istrumentazione)?

These so-called "grammatical slips" stirred up a great fuss in certain quarters of Bologna. A generation or two ago, similar pedants had got into the habit of proclaiming that Voltaire did not know how to spell. *So much the worse for spelling!* retorted Rivarol.

In Bologna, where the pedants were railing and fulminating so bitterly against Rossini, on account of his repeated "violation of the rules of musical composition", Signor Gherardi supplied the retort: *Tell me, please, who invented these famous "rules"? And, supposing these "inventors" to be men of genius, is their genius more resplendent that that of the composer who created* Tancredi? *A load of stupid nonsense doesn't cease to be a load of stupid nonsense, just because it is grown ancient and taught in the schools!*

Here we have a set of notions, which they have chosen to call "rules"; let us examine them closely. However, before we go any further, tell me this: what sort of "rules" are these, which may be violated or discarded at will, without the listener growing one whit the wiser, nor his pleasure one iota the less?

In Paris I believe it was M. Berton (*de l'Institut*) who revived this old quarrel.[1] Yet the fact is that these "faults" pass totally unperceived

[1] I am most profoundly worried, lest certain spiteful persons should feel the urge to cast doubt upon the deep and sincere respect which I feel towards *all* French composers in general (ancient as well as modern), and towards M. Berton in particular. In due fairness, both to M. Berton, and to myself, I could not do better than to reproduce here the most singular correspondence to which I have just referred in the text. My most tormenting anxiety is lest I be accused of being a *bad Frenchman*; and you will agree that it would be a terrible fate, if something so frivolous as a book on music should blast and obliterate for ever my reputation as a *sound patriot*.

LETTER FROM M. BERTON

L'Abeille, 4th August, 1821.

Mr. Rossini possesses a brilliant imagination, tremendous vivacity, much originality, and a plentiful fertility of invention; nevertheless, he himself is as well aware as anyone, that his style is occasionally faulty and incorrect; moreover, for all the protests of certain persons in this matter, purity of style is not a quality to be lightly dismissed, and faults of syntax, whatever language one happens to be using, are never excusable. This, of course, is nothing new to M. Rossini, which is the reason why I have taken the liberty to discuss the problem in these pages. Moreover, since it has grown customary for writers in the daily press to constitute themselves music-critics, I, who have graduated through the schools of Montano, of le Délire, of Aline, etc., may safely claim, I feel, the right to pronounce my own opinion ex professo. Furthermore, I state my ideas frankly and openly, above my own signature, which is more than can be said for certain persons whose furious pastime of making and un-making reputations is pursued strictly incognito. My only motives in writing as I have done are, firstly, an unsullied love of art for its own sake, and, secondly, a sincere consideration of M. Rossini's own interests. No one would question the fact that this composer is the most outstanding genius who has appeared in Italy since Cimarosa; but a man may be widely, and indeed justly renowned, without necessarily achieving the distinction of a Mozart.

I must renounce the satisfaction of transcribing at length passages from a treatise by M. Berton, entitled *De la musique mécanique et de la musique philosophique, par M. Berton, membre de l'Institut royal de France* (1821, p. 24), which clearly puts Rossini in his proper place. "This Italian", apparently, never rises above "mechanical music". In another little essay, of a mere seven pages this time, which appears as an article in *l'Abeille* (vol. IV, p. 267), M. Berton proceeds to prove that the composer of *Otello* has achieved nothing more profound in music than a number of *arabesques*. Similarly, in Italy, a certain Signor Majer, of Venice, has recently established the same remarkable truth.

REPLY TO M. BERTON

Le Miroir, 11th August, 1821.

Evidently my opponent is no longer the inexperienced editor of some obscure periodical: nor am I called upon to defend my opinions against the pricks and prods of some unknown drawing-room amateur. An athlete, well-trained and crowned with the laurels of more than one recent victory, has now stepped into the arena, and flung down the glove in formal challenge. The composer of Montano, Aline and le Délire challenges in me the admirer of Tancredi, Otello and the Barber. The serried ranks of the anti-Rossinian host have at last brought forward a champion upon whose strength they may place firm reliance. Here is one of the leading figures of the living theatre ready to expound the learned cause and yet more learned prejudices of the Academy itself: the protagonist of the musical counter-revolution has proved to be a member of the Institut de France.

M. Berton *precludes his initial skirmish with a volley of words whose ring of lofty disdain, unfamiliar in the field of literary polemic, betrays a deep and intimate conviction of his own incontestable superiority. I observe this phenomenon; but far be it from me to see in it a matter of reproach. On the contrary, I have the most profound admiration for such plain and frank assertions of god-like self-confidence; an antique hero is entitled to an attitude of proud bravado, and a touch of swagger in the vocabulary is not misplaced as a prelude to a duel. Moreover, M. Berton is not content merely to admire the ancients; he is set upon imitating their noble deeds; he knows that, in those heroic combats, of which Homer and Virgil have left us such brilliant descriptions, no protagonist did ever come to grips with his opponent, unless the pair had first exchanged a broadside or two of threatening and disdainful epithets. It is true, of course, that the most presumptuous was not always the most valiant; witness Paris, who day by day provoked the most illustrious warriors of the Grecian camp, only to flee like a startled fawn at the critical instant of combat; but clearly such cautious reservations can in no way detract from the time-honoured respectability of the tradition, nor diminish the value of an antique example in the eyes of so convinced an adulator of antiquity. As for myself, who, unlike M. Berton, profess no such relentless and exclusive cult of the manners, men and arts of ancient times, it is understandable that I should not, in my defence, borrow the same tone which he has seen fit to use in his attack. His weapon is a boastful vainglory refurbished from the Greeks; mine, the modest politeness of a later age. He will find that I can easily manage without his armoury of withering sarcasms and imperious sneers, no matter whether I am stating my opinion concerning the score of* Otello, *or whether I am expressing my considered verdict upon Racine, whose glorious sun (in the opinion of this learned musician) plunges the pale star of the author of* Brutus *and* Mahomet *into inglorious eclipse.*

M. Berton *accuses me of failing to sign my articles; but surely the illustrious professor has exaggerated the significance of our little contest. He seems to have forgotten his own epoch, imagining himself carried back in time among the heroic disputes between Gluck and Piccinni; a musical argument, to him, is nothing less than an affair of honour; moreover, he is forgetting that I have never once mentioned him by name in any of my articles, and that he, and he alone, is the aggressor. If it were a question of anything but a literary duel, I should be only too pleased to make myself known at the earliest possible opportunity: but while the subject of our quarrel turns upon the respective merits of Racine and Voltaire, the respective superiorities of Mozart and Rossini, I shall continue to take every precaution which may serve to conceal my identity. M. Berton's signature is well-known and highly-respected; and an article from his pen, even if its intrinsic value is approximately nil, might still find readers, thanks to the name which commends it to the public; whereas my own name is so obscure, that its publication would probably serve only to weaken the good opinion which my articles, by their own unaided merits, have already widely earned. I conclude, therefore, that my honorable adversary is not wrong to publish his signature: and that I am equally justified in refusing to publish mine.*

In the opinion of M. Berton, it is an unspeakable blasphemy to have asserted that Rossini is more dramatic than Mozart; and to the uttering of this blasphemy (if blasphemy is should indeed prove to be!) I plead completely guilty. Very well, then: the nature of the crime having been established, it remains to be seen whether the accusation can be substantiated, and whether the public, who constitute the only jury whose powers I recognize as valid, will decide that I have truly merited reproof by uttering the words for which I have been denounced. If I were to stand upon my rights, I might well refuse to analyse the various characteristics of Otello *which make it* more *dramatic, since M. Berton has carefully refrained from pointing out any which make it* less; *but the learned academician to whom this answer is dedicated, having once asserted that he had "graduated through the schools of* Montano, le Délire*", and even (one might add) of* les Rigueurs du Cloître*, seemed to think that he had established the privilege of being believed upon his own unsubstantiated word whenever he saw fit to assign rank and status to any given composer.* Voltaire, *writing his commentary upon* Corneille, *or even* La Harpe *and* Lemercier *in the pulpit of the* Athenæum, *analysing the works of our greatest writers, usually condescended to furnish us with* some *proofs of their assertions: and yet they too might be said to have "graduated", the first with a good score of undisputed masterpieces, the second with* Warwick *and* Philoctète, *the third with* Pinto, Plaute *and* Agamemnon. *But it seems that learned professors of the* Conservatoire *acquire through their "graduation", titles and privileges which are peculiar unto themselves, and in which mere ordinary men of letters have no share. Yet I have always believed, at least until now, that when they claimed the most important privilege of all, which is to say everything and prove nothing, this privilege extended no further than to their own erudite scores.*

Rossini *is not content simply to make assertions: he proves what he is asserting; and in this short sentence lies the highest praise that his genius can merit. This is both why and how he is dramatic: he creates his characters, he follows the development of his plot, as though he had completely forgotten the helping presence of the librettist at his side. The restlessness, the sparkling wit of* Figaro, *the surly and suspicious cunning of* Rosina's *tutor, the strange mixture of fury and tenderness which characterizes the love of* Othello— *these are examples of true dramatic beauty, these characters who, even if the support of the libretto were to be suddenly withdrawn from them, would still retain the greater part of their charm or grandeur. That there may exist elsewhere such qualities as richer harmony, greater stylistic severity, correctness or restraint, finer shades of obedience to the* Rules of Composition, *etc., I will not deny; but, from the point of view of the dramatic impression, all these very real qualities are no more than handy auxiliaries: they can never furnish the fundamental, constituent features of a great dramatic imagination. Be sincere and honest: silence your school-bred prejudices, and forget for once the despotic authority of a great name; listen to* Mozart *with your mind as well as your ear; and then tell me truly, whether, in your heart of hearts, you find the* Figaro *of* le Nozze *as original, as amusing, as "good theatre" as the* Figaro *of* il Barbiere. Opera *is drama; when I go to the theatre, I go to witness a* dramatic *performance; and what intimation of the dramatic do I receive from hearing Count* Almaviva's *steward sing a series of wonderful arias, none of which has anything but the sketchiest, the most tenuous connection, either with his character or with the development of the plot? If I want to hear beautiful music as such, I can go to a concert; when I go to the opera, it is because I want emotional stimulus, because I want to be moved to laughter or to tears. Whether the author of the drama which is being performed before me call himself* dramatist, composer *or* choreographer, *whether the medium he employs consist of words, notes or steps, it makes no significant difference; in every case, he will have achieved the first objective of his art, he will have fulfilled his promise and satisfied my expectancies, if, by a faithful portrayal of life and manners, by the construction of a coherent plot, by the dramatic truth of his situations and the psychological truth of his characterization, he so handles the "Art which imitates Nature", that I am persuaded to forget, once and for all, that the performance which I am watching is nothing more than an ingenious pastime, and induced to accept as true that which I know to be a lie told within certain accepted conventions. It is this illusion which* Rossini *has created more often than any other composer, and which he has brought to a pitch unsurpassable within the narrow limits of the art*

E

which he has chosen as his medium; which, finally, has procured him such numerous and resounding triumphs. In Mozart's operas, the libretto *is essential, providing the spectator with an indispensable translation; in those of Rossini, it is nothing more than a subsidiary accompaniment: the Figaro of* The Barber *is a great and profoundly comic figure; the Figaro of* le Nozze *is only a brilliant musician.*

In spite of the opinion of my illustrious antagonist in this matter, I do not believe that Rossini (whom he is pleased to call Mr Rossini) will repudiate the praise which I have bestowed upon his admirable compositions. If he were to do so, the author of Otello *would prove himself scarcely a man at all, but a very prodigy; for he would combine a will-power of stoical severity with a genius for tropical luxuriance. This double miracle is scarcely possible. A fundamentally modest composer is almost as rare as a fundamentally dramatic one.*

SECOND REPLY (No. 173)
on the occasion
of
OTELLO

Otello *continues to draw the multitudes; the brilliance of this opera is by now a matter of common consent, except among a few academic piano-teachers, musical anatomists, in whose opinion the qualities of wit, originality and true dramatic* verve *all pale into insignificance beside the monstrous fault of some technical irregularity in a finale, or some syntactic weakness in a quintet. The general public, which is far too reasonable to look for any virtue in the theatre other than its own pleasure and satisfaction, will be the very last body to criticize a favourite composer for his so-called infringement of laws laid down by the Conservatoire, or of theories studiously invented by erudite professors. It declines to sit and wait for permission from the purists of the* rue Bergère *before it decides to enjoy itself; and its applause bears little relationship to the sufficiency of the composer's exercises in academic counterpoint.*

The quarrel which has arisen between those who admire Rossini's genius, and those who stand by the tradition and authorities of the old régime in music, may be due, perhaps entirely, to the fact that both sides have used terms without bothering to define them. It has been asserted that the author of Otello *and* The Barber *possessed in his music a greater instinctive sense of what was essentially* dramatic *than the majority of his rivals or predecessors. This assertion, wrongly understood, has set the professorial party by the ears. Yet a single glance at the* Dictionnaire de l'Académie *would have sufficed to smooth over all the differences. It would there have been made quite plain, that dramatic qualities, as such, have nothing to do with stylistic perfection or its opposite, still less with servile obedience to the rules of composition. Not that Rossini, even on this double count, is in any way as criminal or as incompetent as his detractors have insisted— far from it; but even if it were to be conceded that in this respect he had fully deserved every reproach which had been hurled at him, it nevertheless remains quite clearly demonstrated, in practice if not in theory, that the music of this renowned composer is more eloquent, more expressive and more* popular *than that of the most famous masters who have ever lived. When I use the word* dramatic, *then, this is what I mean (and it is impossible to discover any other interpretation):* Music is an art whose technical resources are narrow and limited; music is used to interpret words, but words also help to interpret music; and if you rob music of the assistance of words, you will transform it into a sort of hieroglyphic idiom, decipherable by a small circle of initiated adepts, but totally unintelligible to the vast majority of the audience. *Now, he who succeeds, by the use of particular combinations of those sound-symbols which are the alphabet of music, in achieving a degree of expressiveness which, more closely than any other, corresponds to that of the* normal spoken language, will have achieved, as a composer, not merely the highest dramatic quality, but the nearest approach to truth. And this achievement is precisely that which Rossini has accomplished. Among all known composers, he is the one who is least dependent upon his librettist; he has, as far as it lies within the nature of his medium to do so, liberated his art from the inglorious fetters of a necessity which left it shorn of half its glory. He is like some delightful foreigner who is intelligent enough to make himself understood without the need of an interpreter; he is like an instinctive writer of genius, who has learned to triumph over the obscurities of the language in which he is writing, and who can be read and understood by normally educated people without invariably requiring the notes and glosses of a commentator.

Mozart may be richer, more harmonious; Pergolesi may be more correct, more polished; Sacchini may have greater gravity, his style may be more chaste—all this may be true; and yet neither I nor the general public is therefore necessarily wrong to conclude that Rossini speaks more clearly to out understanding, that he holds the key to the innermost secrets of our delight and sensibility. Rossini's music is fired with an indescribable, intangible element of reality and living emotion, which is somehow lacking in all the grandeur of Mozart; his colours, perhaps, are less brilliant, but the pattern he paints is more faithful to the original, and, in the theatre, a faithful resemblance is the first, the most essential requirement. The operatic composer is nothing but a portrait-painter who paints in music.

If there should appear to be any truth in these reflections, they may well serve as the preface to a peace-treaty which I am only too willing to conclude with my learned antagonists. Let them continue to think of Mozart as the greatest of musicians who ever wrote music, while we continue to put our faith in Rossini as the greatest of musicians who ever wrote opera. I am sure that this ingenious distinction will make us all friends again.

This settled, my final task must be to drum some semblance of reason into the thick skulls of those who decry Italian music as such—that is, of those who suffer from this new and curious brand of insanity and chauvinism, which includes the nationality of the composer among the vital elements which go to determine the aesthetic quality of a romance or a quartet. These worthy patriots would flatly prohibit cosmopolitanism in entertainment: but they seem to forget that there is no such thing as French music, or Italian music, or Spanish music, or German music, but only good music and bad music—and nothing else. Its passport can add not one jot of merit to its qualities, nor subtract one iota of badness from its defects. When all is said and done, there are only two kinds of music: music which pleases, and music which does not.

Let it be said at once, that Rossini's compositions would unfailingly have been placed in the former of these two categories even without the added attraction of talented singers to which the management of the Théâtre Louvois has seen fit to entrust their execution; nevertheless, these artists well deserve to be applauded in their own right, and it is perhaps fair to say that never before has Italian opera in France been seen at such clear advantage, nor has it been performed by so unexceptionable a company. Madame Pasta has made very real progress since her début, while Garcia, as Otello, shows unusual powers, not only as a remarkable singer, but as a considerable tragic actor; no one could show a finer grasp of every thread in that infinitely subtle web of thought and feeling which goes to make up the violent and impassioned character of Desdemona's lover.

Anyone who is sufficiently intelligent to appreciate a good sound argument buttressed by a solid structure of irrefutable logic will be grateful to me for having reproduced this interesting letter by M. Berton (de l'Institut), and in particular for having introduced them to l'Abeille, the periodical in which this great composer has, on various occasions, inserted his judgments concerning Rossini, and

when Rossini's operas are heard in performance. It is as though one were to denounce Voltaire for failing to employ the same turns of phrase, the same stylistic *idiosyncrasies* as La Bruyère or Montesquieu. In point of fact, it was the second of these two writers who used to say that *a Member of the Academy writes as one should write whereas a man of true discernment writes as he should write.*

The fact is that something like half a hundred *accredited* composers, finding themselves relegated into the utmost regions of outer darkness in the course of a few months by the masterpieces of a twenty-year-old, irresponsible hot-head, urgently needed a pretext to give some rational justification to their instinctive reaction of jealousy. This kind of accusation, maintained by a whole *class* of critics, never fails to have a certain effect, and we shall find it occurring over and over again—in fact, just as long as there are still audiences to applaud Rossini. Any detailed discussion of Rossini's "syntactical howlers" would be bound to run on for forty pages or more, and in the end grow desperately boring; so I omit it. A mere technical exposition of the point to which the purists have seen fit to object would fill a good ten sheets of manuscript; so it would be a great deal better if the reader would make an expedition himself to the *Théâtre Feydeau* any evening when M. Berton's opera *Montano et Stéphanie* is on the bill; and then, the day following, go and see *Tancredi*. I am convinced that M. Berton has conscientiously eschewed every one of those dreadful "syntactical howlers" of which he so loftily accuses Rossini; so I may quite confidently request every reader to place his hand upon his heart, and to tell me honestly: what is the *real* difference between the two works?

In every town in Italy you could unearth a score or so of wretched keyboard-hacks, who, for some very small consideration, would be only too delighted to correct every one of these dreadful "syntactical howlers" in whichever of Rossini's scores you cared to propose to them.

recorded the advice which, out of his great goodness of heart, he is prepared to offer "this Italian".

Yet, however forceful his dialectic, M. Berton keeps still another weapon up his sleeve; and recently he has made public a new and even better reply to the author of *Otello* and the *Barber*—this time still more crushing, annihilating and irrefutable. This thunderbolt is the score of *Virginie*, a Grand Opera of *impeccable* academic rectitude, which, at this very instant (July, 1823), is playing to thunderous applause at the Royal Academy of Music, and is destined to sweep the capitals of Europe. But where, oh where, in all Italy, is there to be found an actor to sing the part of Appius *quite* in the style of M. Dérivis? *That* indeed is a problem!

Yet this is not all, for there is still another objection which I have heard voiced against Rossini. Certain critics (blessed are the poor in spirit!), having read his scores, stand aghast with horror at the thought that he should not have *developed his ideas to greater advantage.* Here is a man who is rich and happy; and so he flings a whole golden *louis* to a little farm-girl in exchange for a bunch of roses—but the *misers* call this *madness*! Not everyone is blessed enough to appreciate the joys of pure irresponsibility.

While in Bologna, however, poor Rossini found himself entangled in a worse web than any that the purists had woven for him; for his Milanese mistress, abandoning in one blind moment of frenzy her household, her husband, her children and her reputation, turned up one fine morning at his lodgings, which were, to say the least of it, modest. The first instant of reunion was most tender and touching; but hard upon the heels of the first lady came a second, the fairest, the most renowned in all Bologna (Princess C . . .). Rossini, after an instant of hesitation and perplexity, solved the dilemma by bursting with laughter, and singing a comic aria—after which, he promptly vanished, leaving both good ladies high and dry! Passionate love is *not* his strong point.

CHAPTER VI

The Impresario and his Theatre

WHILE he was staying in Bologna, which is the headquarters of musical life in Italy, Rossini was offered commissions from every single town in Italy which is proud enough to boast a theatre. *Impresari* were everywhere granted their contracts on the express condition that they should succeed in commissioning an opera from Rossini. He was paid on an average about a thousand francs for each work,* and he composed about four or five operas a year.

Let me explain the inner workings of the theatrical system in Italy. A *contractor*—usually the wealthiest burgher of some petty township, for this particular office carries with it considerable social prestige and not a few other advantages, although it frequently turns out to be financially ruinous!—undertakes to run the theatre in the town whose leading citizen he has the honour to be; so to start with, he forms a company, which consists invariably of: a *prima-donna*, a *tenore*,[1] a *basso cantante*, a *basso buffo*, a second (female) and a third (male) *buffo* singer. Next, the *impresario* engages a *maestro* (composer) to write an original opera for him, having always due regard, in the setting of his arias, to the particular characteristics of the voices of the singers who are to perform them. The *impresario* then purchases a text (the *libretto*: always in verse), which may cost him anything from sixty to eighty francs, the author being usually some wretched *abbé* parasitically attached to one of the wealthier households in the neighbourhood; for in Lombardy, where the meanest of petty provincial towns invariably counts some half dozen landed estates bringing in a hundred thousand *livres* a year and upwards, the undignified profession of *parasite*, so brilliantly satirized by Terence, still flourishes in all its glory. Next, the *impresario*,

---

[1] The term *tenore* signifies a voice with strong *chest*-notes in the upper register. Davide is famous for his *falsetto*, that is to say, for his powerful *head*-notes. Generally speaking, *opera buffa* and *opera di mezzo carattere* are written for tenors with a normal voice-range, and such singers, taking their title from the works in which they most frequently perform, are known as *tenori di mezzo carattere*. The true tenor generally appeared to best advantage in *opera seria*.

himself the owner of one of these estates, proceeds to hand over all the business management of the theatre to his agent, who is usually a lawyer, and in fact the same arch-scoundrel who manages his personal business in private life; while *he* (the impresario) is more properly occupied in falling in love with the *prima donna*; at which point, the great question which arises to tickle the curiosity of the entire neighbourhood, is whether or not he will offer her his arm in public.

Thus "organized", the company eventually gives its first performance, but not without previously having survived a whole month of utterly burlesque intrigues, thus furnishing an inexhaustible supply of gossip to entertain the entire countryside. This *prima recita* is the greatest public happening in all the long, dull existence of the town concerned —so momentous indeed, that I can think of nothing in Paris which could offer anything like an adequate comparison. For three weeks on end, eight or ten thousand persons will argue the merits and defects of the opera with all the powers of sustained concentration with which heaven has seen fit to endow them, and above all, with the maximum force of which their lungs are capable. This *première*, unless blasted at the very outset by some scandal of positively catastrophic dimensions, would normally be followed by some thirty or forty others, at the conclusion of which the company disbands. A run of this type is usually called a "season" (*una stagione*); and the best season is that which coincides with the Carnival. Any singers who have not been engaged (*scritturati*), usually hang about in Bologna or in Milan, where they have theatrical agents who make it their business to secure them contracts, and to rob them unashamedly in the process.

Furnished with this little sketch of the life and manners prevailing in the Italian theatre, the reader will now have no difficulty in picturing the singular existence which Rossini led between the years 1810 and 1816, and which has no equivalent in France. One after the other, he visited every town in Italy, spending some two or three months in each. As soon as he set foot in the place, he would be welcomed, banqueted and generally adulated by every *dilettante* in the neighbourhood, so that the first two or three weeks would be gaily frittered away in the consumption of gala dinners, spiced with sighs and shrugs over the unspeakable imbecility of the librettist. Rossini, over and above the extraordinary and penetrating intelligence with which he was gifted by nature, was indebted to his earliest mistress (the countess

P***, in Pesaro) for a thorough training in literary appreciation, which he had perfected through reading the works of Ariosto, the comedies of Machiavelli, the *Fiabe* of Gozzi, and the satires of Buratti; and in consequence, he was exquisitely sensitive to the nicer absurdities of the average *libretto*. *Tu mi hai dato versi, ma non situazioni*,[1] is a complaint which, more than once, I have heard him thunder at some wretched literary hack, who is thereupon reduced to utter apologetic dissolution, and returns a couple of hours later with a penitent sonnet, *umiliato alla gloria del più gran maestro d'Italia e del mondo*.

After two or three weeks spent in these and similar dissipations, Rossini begins to refuse invitations to banquets and *soirées musicales*, under the pretext that he must seriously give his attention to studying the vocal potentialities of his company. With this end in view, he commandeers a piano, and makes them sing; and on such occasions the observer may witness the depressing spectacle of a great composer compelled to distort and mutilate the finest flights of musical inspiration which have ever been known, for the simple reason that the *tenore* cannot reach the note which some noble vista of creative imagination has suggested, or else because the *prima donna* invariably sings off pitch in the course of transition from one key to the next! Frequently the only competent singer in the whole company turns out to be the *basso*.

Finally, three weeks before the *première* is billed, Rossini, who is by now quite sufficiently familiar with the voices of his company, starts to compose in earnest. He rises late, and settles down to work through a perpetual barrage of conversation maintained by his new-found acquaintances, who, despite every protest he can venture to make, obstinately refuse to leave him in peace for a single instant during the whole of the live-long day. He dines with them at the local *osteria*, and as often as not, sups with them as well; he returns home late at night, his friends convoying him back to the very door of his lodgings, all singing at the tops of their voices some song which he has improvised during the course of the evening; on occasions, they have even been known to indulge in an impromptu *miserere*, to the inexpressible scandal of all pure and pious church-goers in the neighbourhood. But eventually he does manage to retreat to the peace of his own room, and this is the hour—often towards three in the morning—when his most brilliant musical inspirations tend to come upon him. He scribbles them

---

[1] You have provided me with verses, but not with *situations*!

down, hastily and without a piano, on any odd scraps of paper which may chance to be handy, and tosses them aside until the morning, when, amid the roar and hubbub of convivial conversation, he may find time to "instrument" them (to use his own favourite expression). He must be pictured as a spirit of quicksilver agility, as a character of the most fiery temperament, perpetually subject to new impressions, perpetually on the alert for new ideas; the sort of man for whom nothing ever seems too difficult. Thus, latterly, while he was working on his *Mosè in Egitto*, an acquaintance chanced to remark: *Since you intend to have a Chorus of Jews, why not give them a nasal intonation, the sort of thing you hear in a synagogue?* Struck by the notion, Rossini promptly sat down and composed a magnificent chorus, which in fact does open with a most curious harmonic combination strongly reminiscent of the Jewish synagogue. To the best of my knowledge, there is only one thing which reduces this ever-brilliant, ever-fertile, ever-active genius to a state of utter paralysis, and that is the importunate presence of some pedantic *purist*, in whose conversation flattery alternates with an airing of theories, and who is only happy if he can overwhelm his victim with compliments decked out in academic verbiage. On such occasions, Rossini's temper tends to get the better of him, and he launches out promptly into a string of sarcasms which, generally speaking, are likely to be more remarkable for their grotesque imagery and energetic phraseology, than for their stylistic perfection and classical purity of diction. In Italy, where there are no idle and disdainful courtiers to while away their time by "purifying the language", and where no one would dream of considering his dignity and position rather than simply enjoying himself, the number of things which are accounted "coarse" or "in bad taste" is infinitely small; and so it comes about that we have the peculiar colourfulness of a poet like Monti—poetry which is certainly noble, and which can even be sublime, but which is yet a thousand leagues removed from the silly scruples and timid pruderies of the *Hôtel de Rambouillet* or its modern equivalents. If you desire to bring out the contrast, compare the works of M. l'abbé Delille; the very meaning of the word *noble* is different in France and in Italy.

One such pedant, a full-blown *monsignore* by trade, who, in order to badger him with civilities, had tracked him down right into the very bedchamber of the inn where he was staying, and had effectively prevented him from getting out of bed, received the following admonition:

"*Ella mi vanta per mia gloria* . . . you are pleased to mention my celebrity; yet do you know, Monsignor, wherein lies my *fundamental* claim to immortality? I will tell you: it is because I am the handsomest man alive! Canova has promised me that, one day, he will use me as a model for a statue of Achilles!"—saying which, Rossini leapt eagerly out of bed, and stood before the dazed stare of that noble prelate in the very costume in which Achilles is usually depicted, and whose public exhibition, in Italy, is considered monumentally disrespectful. "Observe, my Lord, this *leg*," he went on. "When a man possesses a limb so exquisitely turned, is he not *certain* of immortality? . . ." The remainder of the harangue, I omit; for once launched on a thoroughly bad joke, Rossini gets drunk with the sound of his own voice, intoxicated with the wild gusts of laughter which are inspired by his own grotesque fancies; he seems to be inexhaustibly fertile in the invention of nonsensical inanities, which usually veer rapidly towards the obscene; and once he is set on *that* course, nothing in the world can stop him. The pedantic prelate soon discovered that there was no alternative but to retreat.

Composing, according to Rossini, is mere child's-play; the real drudgery of the job comes with *rehearsal*. Then begins the agony, for on such distressing occasions the poor *maestro* has to endure the torments of the damned, as, one by one, he hears his most inspired ideas, his most brilliant, his suavest *cantilenas*, distorted and disfigured in every key the human voice can embrace. "It is quite enough," Rossini maintains, "to make one want to boo oneself out of the profession for good and all." Invariably, after each rehearsal, he falls into a fit of black depression, utterly disgusted with music which, only the previous day, had seemed delightful.

Nevertheless, these rehearsal-sessions, painful as they must be for any sensitive young composer, are to my mind symbolic, for they reflect the triumph of Italian musical sensibility. On such occasions, gathered together around some evil, broken-backed piano in a decrepit shanty, known as the *ridotto*, belonging to the local theatre of some unspeakable little provincial town—say Reggio or Velletri—I have watched eight or ten fourth-rate, down-at-heel opera-singers proceeding to rehearsal, invariably to the accompaniment of a full concerto for saucepans and roasting-jack from some neighbouring kitchen and, under such appalling circumstances, both *experience* and *express* the subtlest and the most intimately moving emotional nuances of which the art of music is capable; and it is precisely on occasions such as these that we cold Northerners must stand amazed to see a plain set of ignorant dolts, all totally incapable of picking out a simple waltz on the piano, or of telling the difference between one key and the next, singing and accompanying *by instinct alone*, and with such magnificent *brio*, music which is new, original and completely unfamiliar to them, and which, in fact, the *maestro* himself composes, alters and re-arranges before their very eyes while they are actually in course of rehearsal. They make countless mistakes, of course; but in music, mistakes which are due to over-enthusiasm are soon forgotten and forgiven—as quickly as the lover forgives his mistress faults which arise from loving too well. I, personally, was completely fascinated by these sessions; however, I have no doubt that M. Berton (*de l'Institut*) would have found them *scandalous*!

No truly honest observer, venturing into Italy from abroad, could dare for one instant to deny the hopeless absurdity of presuming to train singers or composers elsewhere than under the shadow of Vesuvius.[1] In this land, which is the very homeland of beauty, the child at the breast is lulled to sleep with singing; nor are the songs it hears mere nursery-rhymes like *Malbrouck s'en va-t-en guerre* or *C'est l'amour, l'amour*. Beneath a burning sky, oppressed by an inexorable tyranny under whose dark shadow all speech is perilous, joy and despair alike find expression far more naturally through the complaint and burden of a song than through the writing of a letter. The only subject of conversation is music; the only opinions one dare hold, or express with the least semblance of fire and frankness, are opinions which concern music. Everybody without exception, however, does read and write *one* thing, namely, satirical sonnets composed in the local dialect,[2] and directed against the Governor of the city; whereupon the Governor, given the first opportunity, retaliates by locking up every poet in the neighbourhood, on a charge of *carbonarism*. This is literal fact, completely devoid of exaggeration; I could quote a score of names and cases, if it were prudent to do so. All the same, reciting satirical sonnets aimed at the Governor or the King is *far* less dangerous than discussing

---

[1] *Tu regere imperio populos, Romane, memento.* Virgil.

[2] *Eg. Sonnet,* by . . . (Reggio); *Count Prina's Vision* (Milan, 1816); *Satirical Poems,* by Buratti (Venice), *etc.*

political theory or arguing about historical problems. For should the abbé ***, or the *Cav. di M****, or whomsoever the police may happen to be employing as their local informer at any given moment, return to the Chief of Police (who, in most instances, is an intelligent man, usually a renegade liberal), and report to him the bare bones of some argument which he claims to have overheard, and which seems to hang together more or less adequately, and to offer some semblance of rational logic, this very fact furnishes all the evidence that is required, and the case against the victims is complete; for the informers, the *abbé* ***, the *Cav. di M****, etc., are so fantastically and inconceivably uneducated, that it is manifestly impossible that they should have *invented* any such argument out of their own heads! The sequel is inevitable: the Prefect of Police summons you into his presence, and gravely accuses you "of having conspired against my master the Governor *by having presumed to talk!*"[1]

On the other hand, since the sin of dabbling in satirical sonnets of a topical character is practically universal; and since the subject-matter in general does not usually transcend the known (limited) intellectual ability of the informer to grasp its rudimentary outlines; it follows that anybody may reasonably plead *calumny* in his defence.

When we last saw Rossini, he was busy directing rehearsals of his latest opera to the accompaniment of an abominable piano in the *ridotto* of some wretched theatre in some third-rate town such as Pavia or Imola. If it is true that this dismal little penthouse is the revered sanctuary of unadulterated musical genius, the very holy-of-holies of pure aesthetic enthusiasm, devoid alike of bombastic pretensions and of any sense of the absurd, it is likewise true that this same unmentionable piano is the focal point about which the most fantastical ambitions and the most inglorious squabbles, fired by the most naive and the most utterly outrageous vanity, are shamelessly unleashed. In the midst of all which, of course, it is not unknown for the piano itself to disintegrate, having been physically battered to smithereens, each separate smithereen then becoming a missile for hurling at the head of some detested rival! I strongly advise any traveller in Italy who has any claim to be considered a genuine lover of art to witness this noble spectacle.

---

[1] *Peccano in quel che dite.* "The citizens under my jurisdiction are guilty of potentially seditious activities; the fact that *you* have been talking proves it!"— this accusation is historically true, and dates from 1819.

The private lives of the company (it goes without saying) furnish an inexhaustible supply of gossip for the entire community, whose eventual pleasure, or the contrary, during the most exciting month out of all the months in the year, must depend wholly upon the success or failure of the new opera. When a town falls under the spell of this intoxication, the rest of the world may roll by unnoticed; moreover, during these anxious crises of uncertainty, the rôle of the *impresario* is most exquisitely gratifying to his vanity, for he is, literally, the Most Important Personage in all the land. I have known skinflint bankers happily fling away a round sum of fifteen hundred golden *louis*, and write off the deficit as money well lost in the purchase of so flattering an eminence. The poet Sografi has written a charming little play in one act, based on the adventures and the vanities of an operatic company of this type; among the characters involved, I remember especially a German tenor without a word of Italian, who provides the most uproarious comedy, and the whole thing is worthy of Regnard, or even of Shakespeare. The entire set-up, in the life and the flesh, is so utterly *outrageous*, so fantastic the sight of these Italian opera-singers, all drunk with the divine fire and the passion of music, squabbling like children over the prerogatives of their immortal vanity, that the dramatist's main concern must have been to *dilute* the extravagance of his raw material, to water it down by three parts at least, and somehow to constrict it within the narrow limits of truth, probability and nature, rather than to add touches of artificial dramatization. The most faithful of portraits, sketched with the severest eye to realism, must necessarily have appeared nothing but a caricature of the most fantastic improbability.

Marchesi (the famous Milanese male-soprano), during the latter part of his stage career, refused point-blank to sing at all unless his first entry in the opening scene of the opera were made either on horseback, or else on the top of a hill. Furthermore, whichever alternative was eventually agreed upon, the cascade of plumes which surmounted his helmet was required to be at least six feet high. In our own time, Crivelli still refuses to sing his opening aria, unless the librettist agrees to provide him with the words *felice ognora*, which are particularly convenient for the execution of certain series of roulades.

But we are in danger of forgetting all about our little Italian township, which we last beheld tense with anxiety, one might almost say possessed with *frenzy*—the frenzy which heralds the great day of the *première* of its own specially-composed opera.

The critical evening arrives at last. The *maestro* takes his seat at the piano; the auditorium is stuffed to bursting-point. The crowds have come pouring in from every town and village within twenty miles' radius; enthusiasts bivouac in their open carriages in the middle of the streets; the inns have been overflowing ever since the previous day, and the customary Italian courtesy of these establishments is showing a tendency to wear a bit thin. Everyone has downed tools long ago. As the hour of the performance draws near, the town seems like a deserted, hollow shell; the passions, the wavering hopes and fears, the entire life of a whole thriving population is focused upon the *theatre*.

As the overture begins, you could hear a pin drop; as it bangs its way triumphantly to an end, the din bursts with unbelievable violence. It is extolled to high heaven; or alternately, it is whistled, nay rather *howled* into eternity with merciless shrieks and ululations. There is no parallel in Paris, where cautious vanity anxiously eyes a neighbouring vanity beside it;[1] these are men possessed of seven devils, determined at all costs, by dint of shrieking, stamping and battering with their canes against the backs of the seats in front, to enforce the triumph of *their* opinion, and above all, to prove that, come what may, *none but their opinion is correct*; for, in all the world, there is no intolerance like that of a man of artistic sensibility. If ever you chance to meet, in artistic company, an individual who seems fair-minded and reasonable, change the subject quickly; talk to him about history, or about political economy, or about some related topic; for whereas there is every possibility that he may one day turn out to be a distinguished magistrate, a fine doctor, a good husband, an excellent academician, or indeed whatever you will, he can *never* become a true connoisseur of music or painting. Never.

Each aria of the new opera, in its turn, is listened to in perfect silence; after which, the cataclysm is let loose once more; and the bellowing of a storm-tormented sea is nothing but the feeblest comparison. The audience makes its opinion of the singers on the one hand, and of the composer on the other, distinctly audible. There are cries of *Bravo Davide! Bravo Pisaroni!*, or on other occasions, the whole theatre will echo with daemonic shrieks of *Bravo maestro!* Rossini rises from his

[1] All first-nights are grim and chilly at the *Théâtre Louvois*.

seat at the piano, his handsome face assuming an unwonted expression of gravity. He bows thrice, submitting to storms of applause, and deafened by a most unlikely variety of acclamations, for whole sentences of adulation may be flung at his unresisting head; after which, the company proceeds to the next item.

Rossini always appears in person at the piano for the first three nights of each new opera; but, at the conclusion of this statutory period, having received his salary of seventy *sequins* (about eight hundred francs) and attended a grand farewell dinner given in his honour by all his new friends (that is to say, by the entire population of the town) he at length drives away in a *vettura*, his bags up beside him stuffed more tightly with music than with personal belongings, only to begin the same procedure all over again at the next port of call, perhaps forty miles distant. Normally, on the evening of the *première*, he writes a letter to his mother, sending her, for her own use and for that of his old father, two-thirds of the meagre salary which he has been paid. When all is said and done, he is lucky to have as much as eight or ten *sequins* in his pocket; yet it needs no more to make him the happiest of mortals, and if heaven but grant him on the road to fall in with a *fool*, the urge to play practical jokes grows supremely irresistible. On one occasion, when he was driving in a *vettura* from Ancona to Reggio, he pretended to be a music-master possessed of the bitterest undying hatred towards *Rossini*, and spent the whole journey singing the most execrable tunes (which he invented on the spur of the moment) to the words of his own most famous arias—tunes which he then proceeded to hold up to general scorn and ridicule as examples of the "so-called masterpieces" of that "unmentionable toad Rossini", whom certain tasteless individuals were imbecile enough to call a genius!* Incidentally, nothing was further removed from mere vanity on Rossini's part than his thus turning the conversation into musical channels; in Italy, there is no subject with greater popular appeal, and conversation, after a brief reference to Napoleon, reverts inevitably to this one obsessing topic.

CHAPTER VII

Of the Wars between Harmony and Melody

At this point, I must beg the reader's permission to intrude with a digression, which may help considerably to abridge the discussions to which we shall shortly be introduced as we follow Rossini in his stormy career, and as we recall the quarrels which gathered about him as soon as the pedants found him sufficiently successful to honour with their vituperation—whereupon all other composers, great and small alike, banded together against him.

It was in Bologna that the storms of jealousy first began to gather about Rossini's head; and, once aroused, made it impossible for him to repeat the easy successes of earlier days.

Rossini has always flouted the pedants; none the less, despite his sneers at individuals, the tribe as a whole has managed to exert no inconsiderable influence upon his work; and that influence has proved fatal.

In order to analyse the somewhat vague connotation which critics of all nations have attributed to the word *taste*, it is a fairly common trick to go back to the most elementary meaning of the term. Properly speaking, the "pleasures of taste" are the sensations experienced by a child which has been given a ripe peach by its mother.

I intend, in order to further the art of musical appreciation, to follow up the phenomenon of the child's delight in its ripe peach; for soon enough it will begin to lose this primitive taste for sweet and sickly delicacies; I can visualize this same child, now grown up into a strapping lad of sixteen, gulping down beer with the greatest of relish, notwithstanding the taste of the brew, which is bitterish, and at first fairly revolting, but in the end stimulating. The student, eagerly clamouring for beer after violent exercise, would simply be nauseated by the sickliness of anything sweet and sugary.

A few years later still, this acquired taste for astringents will no longer stop short at beer; the distaste our young man feels for what he would now call *insipidity* drives him to indulge in a German speciality called *sauerkraut*, which outlandish word merely signifies *sour cabbage*. The distance between this, and the peach, whose tempting smell made his mouth water at the age of three, is incalculable. To round off my analogy with a few nobler instances, I would remind the reader that Voltaire's friend Frederick the Great, in his old age, developed so passionate a liking for spiced and highly-seasoned dishes, that the honour of dining at the King's table grew to be something of a torture for those young French officers, whom fashion had brought to the elegant reviews at Potsdam.

As a man ever grows older, so, gradually, he loses the taste for fruit and other sweet things, which had been his delight in childhood, developing instead a craving for tastes with *bite* and *strength* in them. Brandy would be torture for a six-year-old, were it not counter-balanced by the joy and pride at being allowed to drink out of Daddy's glass!

This ever-growing passion for all that is sharp and stimulating, this increasing distaste for all that is sugary and insipid, offers an exact, if somewhat vulgar, analogy with the revolution in musical taste which took place between 1730 and 1823. The charm of simple *melody* may be compared with the sweetness of some luscious fruit, which all children adore. Harmony, on the other hand, is the musical equivalent of those sharp, stimulating, highly-seasoned dishes which the jaded palate of middle-age craves to satisfy its blasé sensibility. It was in Naples, in the neighbourhood of the year 1730, that composers such as Leo,[1] Vinci,[2] and Pergolesi[3] devised the suavest arias, the most lilting melodies, the most luscious *cantilenas* which have ever bewitched the human ear.

---

[1] Composer of that sublime aria which stands alone among all the music of this earlier period, *Misero pargoletto* (from the opera *Demofoonte**).

[2] *Vide: Artaserse* (based on Metastasio), which is Vinci's masterpiece.

[3] The aria: *Se cerca, se dice** remains even to-day unsurpassed as an example of music in the pathetic style. It belongs to the opera *l'Olimpiade*. *La Serva Padrona* is an admirable *opera buffa*: if you added a new set of accompaniments and took out some of the recitatives, all Paris would flock to see it to-morrow. Foreigners have a great advantage over ourselves: Pergolesi's music escapes from the absurd category of the out-moded. Our grandfathers, as they appear in their portraits, with their coats all embroidered in the fashion of Louis XV's time, seem plainly ridiculous; but our remoter ancestors, with their doublet-and-hose and the armour which it was customary to wear in the days of François I, are invested with a splendid aura of romantic mystery, as they gaze severely down upon us from their vast portraits.

But between 1730 and 1823,[1] the musical public, following a line of development parallel to that of a child which grows first into a brilliant young man, and later into a blasé old dotard, has grown to be nauseated by things which are smooth and sweet, instead craving ever more urgently for things which are rasping and harsh. Setting aside its ripe and luscious peaches, it has, so to speak, besieged the great composers who supply it with sustenance, clamouring for *sauerkraut*, curry and *kirschwasser*, and offering them fame and glory in payment for goods received. I am only too well aware that these analogies are not exactly *noble*; but at least they seem *clear*.

This revolution, which occupies a period of some ninety years in the annals of the spirit of man, has passed through a whole series of quite distinct *phases*. Where will it stop? I cannot tell; I only know this much, that each phase (and each one has lasted some twelve or fifteen years, corresponding more or less with the vogue of some popular composer) has witnessed the belief that the end of the revolution was at hand.

I too, therefore, am probably just as much the dupe of my own immediate senses as any of my predecessors, when I maintain that the *perfect equilibrium* between the ancient craft of melody and the modern craft of harmony was achieved by Rossini and exemplified in the style of *Tancredi*. The magician who bewitched me as a young man with the most entrancing delights I ever knew, has cast a spell upon me, making me, by reaction, unjust towards *la Gazza ladra* and *Otello*, which are less caressing, less enchanting to the senses, but more stimulating, and (perhaps) more dynamic.

Henceforward, whenever I use the words *delightful, sublime, perfect,* etc., I beg the reader to bear in mind this "profession of faith". In my cooler moments of philosophical reflection and respect for the dry judiciousness of others, I fully realize the absurdity which may attach to such words; nevertheless, I employ them for the sake of convenience.

It is customary in France to distinguish a certain shade of political opinion by calling a man *un patriote de 1789*;[2] in the same style I denounce myself as a *Rossiniste de 1815*! This was the year in which

[1] I omit minor historical details which, by distracting the reader's attention from what is essential, would blur the clear general outline which I am trying to indicate.

[2] Literally, *a patriot in the style of 1789, i.e.* a man of unadulterated revolutionary fervour, uncontaminated by the influence of later and more sordid events. (*Trans.*)

Italy granted its most fervent admiration to the *style* and the music of *Tancredi*.[1]

However, I suspect that a music-lover of the vintage, say, of 1780, who had quite rightly learned to appreciate the style of Paisiello and Cimarosa above all others, would find *Tancredi* just as *noisy* and as *over-orchestrated* as I find *Otello* and *la Gazza ladra*.

Far from laying claim to any absurd and impracticable ideal of impartiality in art, I boldly proclaim a principle which, incidentally, appears to be highly fashionable at the moment: I declare that I am thoroughly biased. Impartiality in art, like reasonableness in love, is the prerogative of a frigid disposition and a luke-warm temperament. In consequence, I insist on being *partial*, as far as is consonant with the duties of a comparatively *good-natured* critic. The distinction is, that I have no craving actually to hang anyone, not even Herr Maria Weber, the author of *der Freischütz*, that Teutonic opera which is at the present moment evoking such unbridled and hysterical enthusiasm on the banks of the rivers Spree and Oder.

In the eyes of any ardent partisan of *der Freischütz*, I must seem a typical ancient phogey with an infinite capacity for declining to be bored, who probably nurtures some secret, esoteric reason of his own to explain his cult of the primitive and the barbaric. Such a person would probably describe *me* in the sort of terms—embellished to a greater or lesser degree with euphemisms, depending on the class of the critic—which I am in the habit of employing to state my own opinion concerning the kind of people who, around 1750, could manage to find fascination in the interminable recitatives of some "comic" opera by Galuppi.

To make myself quite plain, I suppose that the best thing that I could do would be to set out, here and now, a list of all those "miraculous geniuses" successively acclaimed in Italy as revolutionaries who have pushed their art to the farthest frontiers which it is capable of attaining, and who have achieved *unsurpassable perfection in the realm of the Beautiful*.

On the appearance of each new genius, violent—and of course in-

---

[1] In music, just as in literature, a work may be excellent in *style* and platitudinous in *content*—or *vice versa*. I prefer Rossini as a *stylist*, although I find more *genius* in Cimarosa. The first-act finale of Cimarosa's *il Matrimonio segreto* is an example of perfection in both form and content.

soluble—quarrels break out between the middle-aged in their forties, who *remember better days*, and the younger generation in their twenties; for any composer of talent always writes in the *style* (*i.e.*, with a given proportion of melody to harmony) which he happens to find in vogue at the moment of his entry upon the theatre of the world.[1]

Here, then, is the list* of those fashionable composers, whose names have all, in due course, been pounced upon by their immediate successors and stigmatized in terms of the vilest abuse:

Porpora was in vogue in	1710[2]
Durante	1718
Leo	1725
Galuppi, nicknamed *il Buranello*, because he was born on the little island of Burano, a cannon's-shot from Venice	1728
Pergolesi	1730
Vinci	1730
Hasse	1730
Jommelli	1739
Logroscino, who invented the *finale*	1739
Guglielmi, who created the *opera buffa*	1752
Piccinni	1753
Sacchini	1760
Sarti	1755
Paisiello	1766
Anfossi	1761
Traetta	1763
Zingarelli	1778
Mayr	1800

[1] *To have good taste*, even in literature, invariably means that one has mastered the secret of dressing up the intellectual content of one's work in whatever disguise may chance to be the latest fashion—or rather, in whatever happens to be the latest fashion *in fashionable society*. In 1786, M. l'abbé Delille represented the very acme of good taste!

[2] Very often a composer's earliest works remain his most satisfactory achievements. Musical genius tends to develop extremely young; but public taste needs a good four or five years' careful training before a new composer can effectively cause the talents of his immediate predecessors to be relegated to complete oblivion. I reckon that most of the celebrated composers included in the list here set out, were first launched upon the *fashionable* period of their career at an average age of five-and-twenty.

Cimarosa	1790
Mosca	1800
Paër	1802
Pavesi	1802
Generali	1800
Rossini⎫ Mozart⎭	1812

I have bracketed the last two names together for, under the combined influence of distance, of the difficulty experienced in reading Mozart's scores, and of the average Italian's utter scorn for any artist of foreign origin, it may legitimately be claimed that Mozart and Rossini made their *début* simultaneously in the year 1812.

To-day, there is a new *maestro* who has captured the whim of fashion and who has outrivalled the creator of *Tancredi*; this new star in the firmament is the author of *la Gazza ladra*, of *Zelmira*, of *Semiramide*, of *Mosè in Egitto*, of *Otello* . . . the Rossini of 1820.[1]

I beg that I may be allowed to draw a further analogy.

Two majestic rivers may have their sources in lands widely separated; each may flow through regions of completely varying character; and yet, in the end, the waters of both may come to mingle in the same stream. If you wish for a specific example, take the Rhône and the Saône. The Rhône comes pouring down off the glaciers of the Saint-Gothard range, on the borders of Switzerland and Italy, whereas the Saône draws its first waters from the north of France; the Rhône falls in a series of cascades and rapids down the narrow, picturesque gorges of the Valais, whereas the Saône waters the fertile plains of Burgundy. Yet, beneath the walls of Lyon, these two great streams eventually meet and mingle, to form that swift and majestic river, the finest in all

---

[1] Here are the exact dates of some of the major composers of recent times: Alessandro Scarlatti, born at Messina in 1650, died in 1730 (the founder of modern music); Bach, 1685–1750; Porpora, 1685–1767; Durante, 1663–1755; Leo, 1694–1745; Galuppi, 1703–1785; Pergolesi, 1704–1737; Handel, 1684–1759; Vinci, 1705–1732; Hasse, 1705–1783; Jommelli, 1714–1774; Benda, d. 1714†; Guglielmi, 1727–1804; Piccinni, 1728–1800; Sacchini, 1735–1786; Sarti, 1730–1802; Paisiello, 1741–1815; Anfossi, 1736–1775; Traetta, 1738–1779; Zingarelli, b. 1752; Mayr, b. 1760; Cimarosa, 1754–1801; Mozart, 1756–1792; Rossini, b. 1791; Beethoven, b. 1772; Paër, b. 1774; Pavesi, b. 1785; Mosca, b. 1778; Generali, b. 1786; Morlacchi, b. 1788; Paccini, b. 1800; Caraffa, b. 1793; Mercadante, b. 1800; Kreutzer (of Vienna), b. 1800 (the hope and promise of the German school).

†These dates are not all accurate. *Cf. Index. (Trans.)*

France, which rushes swirling beneath the arches of the Pont-Saint-Esprit, and can awaken terror in the breasts of the very boldest of pilots.

This description exactly befits the history of the two greatest schools of music, the German and the Italian; they originate in towns separated from each other by an immense distance, Dresden and Naples. Alessandro Scarlatti founded the Italian school; the German school was created by Bach.[1]

These two great streams of divergent opinions and distinctive pleasures, which in our own time are represented by Rossini and Weber respectively, seem now to be on the point of mingling, to form eventually one single school; and in all probability, this ever-memorable coalition is about to take place under our very eyes, in this notable city of Paris, which despite every threat from the censorship on the one hand, and from austerity (political and economic) on the other, is now more than ever before the *Capital of Europe*.[2]

Since fate has chosen to place us on the very brink of this great meeting-place, planting us high upon the promontory which still separates the two majestic torrents, let us observe these water-masses in their last heaving floods, in their last swirling torrents, before they are lost in each other for ever.

On the one hand, we see Rossini producing *Zelmira* in Vienna in 1823; on the other, Herr Maria Weber triumphantly acclaimed in Berlin on the same day* with his production of *der Freischütz*.

In the Italian tradition as it was in 1815, and more specifically, in the opera *Tancredi* (which I have chosen as a typical product to illustrate the characteristics of this school, so as to avoid any vague or obscure conception), the melodic line suffers no injury from its harmonic accompaniment.

Rossini discovered the secret of selecting, with unerring judgment, that precise degree of *harmonic chiaroscuro** which is required to provoke

[1] I have no intention of defending every single detail of my analogy against potential critics.

[2] If this prophecy is to be realized, it depends admittedly upon the fulfilment of one essential condition: the reorganization, on more or less rational lines, of the *Théâtre Louvois*. As things stand, in this year of grace 1823, it would appear that the secret of secrets is to let the place disintegrate altogether. Every attempt is being made to fill us with undying nausea for *Otello, Romeo, Tancredi, etc.*; what is needed is Madame Fodor, and a new tenor.

a gentle, but not aggravating, irritation of the aural nerves. This word *irritation*, which I have just employed, is borrowed from the vocabulary of the physiologists. Experiments have shown that (in Europe at least) the aural nerves always feel the need to come to rest upon a *common chord*; on the other hand, the whole aural system is *irritated* by dissonance (carry out the experiment yourself upon the nearest piano, if you doubt my word), and in such cases, a return to the common chord grows rapidly into an overmastering desire.

CHAPTER VIII

Of the Invasion by the Blunt-Minded[1]
and
Of the Ideology of Music

SHOULD harmony attract notice on its own account, *distracting* our attention from the melody; or should it merely increase the effect of the melody?

Personally, I confess, I favour the last solution. I have observed that, in the domain of art generally, all the really superb effects are produced through one medium of extreme beauty, and not by a whole series of manifestations in separate media, each one in itself of mediocre beauty. Human emotions tend to remain obstinately tepid when their reactions are interrupted by the necessity of choosing between two different categories of pleasure, each of a different quality. If I were to feel the urge to listen to a resplendent display of pure harmony, I should go and hear a symphony by Haydn, Mozart or Beethoven; but if I were to desire *melody*, I should turn to *il Matrimonio segreto* or to *il re Teodoro*. If I wanted to enjoy both these pleasures simultaneously (insofar as it is physically possible to do so) I should pay a visit to *la Scala* for a performance of *Don Giovanni* or *Tancredi*. But I confess that, if I were to plunge any deeper than this into the black night of harmony, music would soon lose the overwhelming charm which it holds for me.

It requires something like positive genius to fail to write a melodic phrase correctly; but there is nothing easier than to fall down irredeemably over the scoring of a mere ten bars of harmony!

Harmony requires *scientific knowledge*. This requirement in itself has proved fatal, for it has provided a heaven-sent excuse for all manner of fools and pedants to meddle in the art of music.

While I have no particular wish to launch a spiteful epigram against the learned professions, anyone with the slightest knowledge of the world will agree with me, that if Voltaire's masterly *Histoire de Charles*

---

[1] A phrase which Stendhal frequently uses in English. (*Trans.*)

XII were to be submitted to-day, anonymously, for the annual prize offered by the *Académie des Inscriptions*, the members of that learned body would find nothing worthier of comment than one or two inaccuracies of detail and, for all its most delightful quality, it would most certainly *not* win the competition. It is in precisely this same spirit that our musical scholars tend to analyse the works of Rossini. Yet permit me to do them justice; their insults are at least offered in good faith![1]

The science of singing, as it is envisaged to-day at the *Conservatoire de Paris*, teaches how to produce a series of words correctly linked according to the purest rules of syntactical grammar; but as to putting any *meaning* into those words . . . !

Rossini on the other hand, overwhelmed by the multiplicity and the vividness of all those infinitely varied shades and nuances of emotion which come crowding all at once into his mind, has been necessarily guilty of a certain number of minor grammatical errors. In the original scores, he has nearly always noted them with a cross +, adding in the margin the comment: *per soddisfazione de' pedanti*.[2] Any competent student, after six months' training at the *Conservatoire*, could have spotted these examples of sheer carelessness, which in any case, are in certain instances deliberately experimental.

So what remains is to take a look at the science of musical grammar as it is understood to-day. Are Rossini's errors in fact *real* errors? And who formulated the grammatical rules in the first place? Musicians whose genius was unquestionably superior to that of Rossini? This is not a case, as it is for instance in linguistic grammar, for a careful study of colloquial usage; those who have written in the language of music are far too few in number for there to exist, properly speaking, anything in the nature of an *accepted practice*. Music is still awaiting the coming of its Lavoisier, the genius who will eventually submit the whole system of the aural nerves, and indeed the human heart itself, to a series of accurate scientific tests and experiments. Everyone is aware that the sound of a saw being sharpened, or of a piece of cork being cut, or even of a sheet of paper crumpled in the hand, is quite enough for certain people, and can easily set a peculiarly delicate nervous system completely on edge.

[1] *Cf. L'Abeille* (1821); *la Pandore* (23 July and 12 August 1823).
[2] For the satisfaction of the pedants.

However, there do exist certain *contrasts*, or harmonies, of sound, which, as distinct from the unpleasant reaction produced by the squeal of cut cork or the squeak of crumpled paper, inspire sensations which are categorically *agreeable*.

This *musical physicist** to whom I have just referred, this new Lavoisier, whom I have potentially endowed with a remarkably sensitive nervous system in respect of such phenomena, will need to devote himself to a series of experiments protracted over many years, from which, in the end, he will be enabled to work out the laws of music by a process of pure *logical deduction*.

In this noble treatise, under the heading *Anger*, for instance, we should find a table setting out those twenty *cantilenas* which, in his opinion, most satisfactorily express this particular emotion; similarly under the headings *Jealousy*, *Requited Love*, *Torments of Separation*, etc., etc.

It frequently happens that an accompaniment will manage to evoke in our imagination some finer shade of emotion which the voice unaided is not able to express.

The superior being whose existence we are postulating would therefore be obliged to tabulate the series of arias, previously selected as illustrative of the most adequate expression of the emotion of Anger, *in the context of their accompaniments*. Under such conditions, it should be possible to determine, for instance, whether the emotional reaction produced is more violent *with* or *without* accompaniment; or further, to what precise degree it is permissible to complicate the accompaniment without proportionately diminishing the intensity of the emotional reaction.

All these major problems, once resolved *by the methods of experimental science*, will eventually lead to the establishment of a *scientific theory of music* based upon the *observed data of emotional psychology* (European sub-species) and upon an analysis of the *habitual reactions of the aural nerves*.

At the moment, however, the majority of the laws (so-called) which bear down so tyrannically upon the native genius of the composer, belong to the same category of groundless fantasmagoria as the philosophies of Plato and Kant; they are just so much mathematical nonsense, concocted with a greater or lesser degree of inventiveness and imaginative ability, but one and all requiring urgently to be tested in the crucible of experiment.[1] They are arbitrary decrees, based upon vacuity and hot air;[2] they are consequences deduced from first principles which cannot be ascertained; but unfortunately, the authority of these "laws" derives from the same source as the authority of the average King—that is to say, both are hedged about by a multitude of powerful officers, who have the strongest personal motives in the world for insisting upon the infallibility of the government! If ever this "respect for the laws" should chance to be disturbed; if ever anyone were to assume the scandalous temerity to enquire scientifically into their fundamental *right* to be laws, then good-bye to the pompous vanity and the inflated self-satisfaction of all our Professors at the *Conservatoire*!

Some of these gentlemen, however, are reasonably intelligent. How do they fare under the present régime?

At a certain stage of their career, those exceptional specimens who manage to retain some semblance of reasonableness—I might instance M. Cherubini—realizing suddenly that the whole logical structure which they are in process of erecting with such sweat and effort has no foundations whatsoever, are seized with panic; hurriedly, therefore, they abandon all attempt to study emotional reactions, and bury themselves instead in philosophical analysis. Instead of building fine columns and elegant porticos, they wear out the best years of their lives digging deep down in the cellars and excavating the foundations. And when at length they emerge, all smeared with grime, from their subterranean passages, they have at least the satisfaction of having acquired a head stuffed to bursting-point with demonstrable mathematical certainties about music; but the fine flower of youth has withered away in the process, and their hearts are drained dry of the last trace of emotion; yet emotion alone was in the end all that mattered, for nothing but emotion could inspire music like the duet from *Armida*:

Amor possente nome . . .[3]

Some harmonies possess a meaning which is unmistakable; which is, so to speak, as expressive as the spoken word; in such cases, a single

[1] Bacon would certainly have included *music* under the authority of his dictum: *Humano ingenio non plumae addendae, sed potius plumbum et pondera.*

[2] *Cf.* Socrates' arguments in favour of ascetism, in M. Cousin's *Platon*, vol. I, p. 200.

[3] See below, p. 392.

hearing is enough to convince the listener of their peculiar quality. Any music-lover of genuine and profound sensibility should make the experiment of analysing his own reactions to chords of this character. Nevertheless, I must add a warning; there is a precipice to be avoided, towards which we are liable to be tempted by that natural element of human impatience which we all share: one delightful experiment does *not* constitute a science; and there is always the danger that we may be led to mistake a charming romance for a factual history.

Nothing is more heartbreaking than a scientific discipline of doubt and analysis applied to something one loves. The more enthralling, the more voluptuous the pleasures of music may be, the more odious and painful the processes of objective criticism are likely to prove. And when the critic has been reduced to this state of enervated exasperation, the least flicker of a *theory* seems irresistibly seductive.[1] Just as, in the sciences of rational speculation, it is essential to retain sufficient control of one's mental faculties to be perpetually on the alert for the first symptom of that besetting sin of the intellect, which is the urge to leap blindly to conclusions; likewise, in the theory of aesthetics, the soul, which is always apt to sacrifice objective analysis to personal pleasure, must be continually disciplined.[2]

But there is a further danger to be avoided, this time of a very different order, and promising certain shipwreck for the unwary vessels of the *blunt-minded*.[3] Such rash mariners, setting out into these uncharted waters in quest of *eternal truths*, are liable to go blind halfway towards their goal, and in the majority of instances, end up by mistaking the *difficult* for the *beautiful*.[4]

The reader will appreciate that I cannot do more than brush the fringes of these vast problems. At best, I may be able to touch lightly upon the *moral* aspect of the question; that is to say, upon the aspect which deals with the relationship between certain specific musical

[1] This is the whole story of the young German Romantics; their soul caught fire with the love of virtue; but other, less scrupulous, persons took advantage of this instant of spell-bound enthusiasm to pump their heads full of undemonstrated—and therefore absurd—logic.

[2] Well and good! Tread the primrose path of dalliance, if you simply want to enjoy yourself; but in *that* case, stop laying down the law!

[3] In English in the original. (*Trans.*)

[4] This lamentable fate, I suspect, was that which overtook one of the most learned musical geniuses of our time.

phenomena and the emotive psychology of the human race, or the tendencies of our particular European imagination.

As somebody must make a beginning some day, I suppose that in the end I may pluck up the courage to give the public a *scientific* treatise upon these vital questions. But, over and above the fact that any such treatise would necessarily be exceedingly abstruse, I am afraid that it might also prove to be exceedingly ridiculous. I could heartily wish that the only persons permitted to read it should be those who can prove that they have wept at a performance of *Otello*.

Meanwhile, I shall have pleasure in offering the patient reader a specimen or two of the more intelligible conclusions of that "science" as it is *now* practised, in whose argument the most clearly-demonstrated truths are still inextricably bound up with the wildest and most baseless assertions. The *logical deductions* which follow from such a science lead one incessantly to the most preposterous conclusions, which can be disproved with five fingers on the tiniest spinet.

But if *you* had spent four whole years digging for diamonds in the darkness of a mine, and if you then discovered, in the depths of the blackest shaft, some little nest of bits of coloured glass with which an ingenious confidence-trickster had salted the holding, would not *you* be tempted to take them for diamonds of the finest water, as fine as the Koh-i-Noor? Under such circumstances, visual evidence goes by the board, corrupted and destroyed by the natural vanity of man. For it would require a rare greatness of soul to admit that four whole years had been thrown fruitlessly away and that, in all this time, you had never once had a clear sight of those fantastical treasures which the confidence-tricksters (*i.e.* the Professors of the *Conservatoire*) had been dangling before your expectations, day in and day out, with a *Can't you see perfectly plainly that such a chord will* not *harmonize with such another?* —and you committing yourself ever deeper and deeper, every time you agreed!

Proportionately as the accompaniment grows more complex, the liberty of the singer is restricted; it ceases to be possible for him to give free rein to his personal genius for musical decoration, as he could have done if the accompaniment had been simpler. With accompaniments in the German style, any singer who risks a scrap of embellishment runs instantly into the grave danger of producing a discord.

Ever since *Tancredi*, Rossini has been moving steadily in the direction of complexity.

In this, he imitated Haydn and Mozart, just as Raphael, a few years after leaving the school of Perugino, sought to *strengthen* his painting by imitating the work of Michelangelo. Instead of delighting mankind with the charm of his natural gracefulness, he preferred to threaten it with terror and apprehension.

Rossini's orchestration has grown steadily more obtrusive, spoiling the melodic line of his voices. However, the real defect in his later accompaniments lies rather in their *quantity* and not, like those of the German school, in their *quality*. Let me make my meaning clearer: an accompaniment in the German style imposes a *total* restriction upon the liberty of the singer, making it impossible for him to decorate the melodic line in the natural way which his genius might have dictated. A singer of the character of Davide, for instance, is inconceivable in the context of German-style *istrumentazione*, which, as Grétry put it, is perpetually *prodding at* the melody, imperiously forbidding the singer to exploit the fullest powers of expression which his medium can afford. Davide's colourful palette owes its peculiar richness to the infinite variety of embellishments and *fioriture* which he normally employs.

This fundamental difference between accompaniments which, *superficially*, sound equally noisy, indicates yer another distinction between the German and the Italian musical traditions.[1]

Almost any composer to-day could demolish Rossini's reputation, and thrust that genius back into the obscurity whence he emerged, simply by composing an opera in the style of *Tancredi*—a style which is a thousand leagues removed from that of *Mosè in Egitto*, *Elisabetta*, *Maometto* or *la Gazza ladra*.

I shall have occasion in a subsequent chapter to relate a few of the innumerable anecdotes which were abroad concerning the Court of Naples, and which, directly or indirectly, induced Rossini to alter his style. Even if, by some unheard-of chance, Rossini could for once be

[1] Twenty years hence, when Parisian audiences will unquestionably have made enormous strides forward in the science of musical appreciation, and in the *destruction of fashionable prejudices*, everything that I have just written will necessarily appear antiquated, and men will have acquired the courage to delve deeper in search of truth. Undoubtedly, Signor Massimino will ultimately rank as one of the principal authors of this happy revolution. His method of teaching deserves the highest commendation. See the brochure by Signor Imbimbo.

persuaded to talk seriously about music, I doubt if he would offer any other explanation of this stylistic revolution. Nevertheless, there is one explanation which might be suggested, and that is, that several of his later operas were composed for vast and extremely noisy theatres. At the *San-Carlo* and at *la Scala*, there is ample room for three and a half thousand spectators. Even the pit is comfortably provided with broad, fully-backed benches, which are replaced every other year. Another point is, that Rossini was often obliged to write for singers whose voices were tired or strained. If he had allowed them to sing solo or thinly accompanied (*scoperte*),[1] or if he had provided them with broad, sustained melodies (*spianati e sostenuti*) to execute, he would have had to fear lest their technical weaknesses, falling too much in evidence, or being too distinctly audible, should prove fatal to singer and composer alike. On one occasion in Venice, when someone commented reproachfully on the lack of fine, well-developed melodies in slow tempo, Rossini retorted: *Dunque non sapete per che cani io scrivo?*[2] *Give me a Crivelli, and* then *see!* It is a fairly generally accepted principle that, for large theatres, it is essential to increase the proportion of *ensemble* numbers. *La Gazza ladra*, which was composed for the enormous auditorium of *la Scala*, seems much *heavier* than it really is, when it is performed in a tiny theatre like the *Louvois* and, incidentally, by an orchestra which seems to specialize in a mood of superb disdain towards all subtlety of shading, and which treats any passage marked *piano* with a sneer of inexpressible disgust![3]

[1] *Lit.*: revealed.

[2] Then you don't realize the sort of dogs I write for?

[3] I am well aware, of course, that any generalizations as sweeping as those which I have propounded in this chapter must necessarily leave me completely naked and defenceless against the artillery of *dishonest* criticism. To have spiked the guns of sarcasm, I should have had to increase the length of this chapter, which is in all probability *quite* dull enough already, by fifty pages of parenthetical and explanatory clauses; which I refuse to do. And so, with truly Roman stoicism, I sacrifice myself for the eventual salvation of my reader!

CHAPTER IX

Aureliano in Palmira

I SHALL say very little about *Aureliano in Palmira*, the main reason being, that I have never seen it performed. This opera was composed for Milan in 1814, where it had the good fortune to be sung by Velutti, the last of the great *castrati*, and by la Correa, who could claim one of the finest voices of any woman during the last forty years.

I believe that I am correct in stating that *Aureliano* has never been performed outside Milan. I can certainly vouch that it was never given in Naples in my time; moreover, during the vogue of Rossini's *Elisabetta*, hostile critics began to allege that the music of this latter opera was nothing other than the *Aureliano* music served up cold. The only truth in this assertion concerned the overture. Rossini, knowing perfectly well that the Neapolitans had never heard his *Aureliano*, borrowed it without further ado*.

I know only one duet from this opera:

Se tu m'ami, o mia regina . . .,[1]

scored for contralto and soprano. This winter, in Paris, I had the good fortune to hear it performed by two voices which are assuredly as fine, if not finer, than the most perfect, the most delicate that were ever formed in Italy. But I knew already, without this additional proof, that France could produce voices as exquisite as any in the world; the trouble is simply that our teachers of singing are no Crescentinis, and

[1] *Arsace:*
    Se tu m'ami, o mia Regina,
    Tornerò di te più degno,
    Sola in Asia avrai tu regno,
    Come regni sul mio cor.
  Zenobia:
    Ah! soltanto il Ciel che invoco
    Te conservi, o mio guerriero;
    Perderò corona e impero
    Pur che a me tu resti ognor.
                (Act I, opening duet)

that the average provincial town is firmly convinced (as indeed is the *Conservatoire* itself) that there is no singing quite as fine as really *loud* singing!

Entranced by the perfect harmony of these two delightful voices,

Se tu m'ami, o mia regina . . .,

I caught myself more than once meditating, whether this is not the finest duet that Rossini has ever written. Of one thing at least I am certain: that, by plunging the listener into the remotest, most mysterious depths of reverie, it performs the miracle which is the surest hall-mark of truly great music.

It happens sometimes that memories from the past come crowding in upon us, awakening in us, in some secret fashion, the echoes of dead and vanished emotions; and when, at such a time, we suddenly come to recognize, perhaps in some *cantilena*, a true portrait of the half-forgotten image which is stirring in our own hearts, then we *know* that the music has the quality of true beauty. This phenomenon, setting the mood of the song against personal experience, seems to offer a kind of *verification*, which results in a more detailed awareness of the subtlest shades of feeling within ourselves, or even in a completely *new* awareness of shades of feeling which hitherto we had not known to exist. Such, if I am not mistaken, are the "mechanics" of the process by which music feeds and flatters the pinings of unrequited love.

Another opera by Rossini, which I saw only once, was his *Demetrio e Polibio**, and that was in Brescia in 1814. One day in June, towards seven in the evening, we were all sitting in the garden of the contessina L***(*), beneath the great trees which make it a haven of delight in this burning climate, eating ices. This garden, rising slightly above the level of the huge plain of Lombardy, is so situated that it takes shade from the woods on the green hill-side which juts out over the town. One of the ladies of the company started singing to herself, and the tune must have struck the assembled guests, for everyone suddenly stopped talking. "What were you singing?" somebody enquired, as soon as she had finished. "One of the songs from *Demetrio e Polibio*," she replied; "To be precise, the famous duet:

Questo cor ti giura affetto . . ."

F

"Is that the same *Polibio* as the one which is being given in Como to-morrow, with the Mombelli daughters in the cast?"

"The very same; Rossini composed the opera especially for them, in 1812, while old Mombelli, their father, used to sit by and point out the passages which were particularly well suited to his daughters' voices."

"But," put in one of the ladies present, "is it certain that Rossini *did* in fact write the opera? There are rumours that all the music was arranged by old Mombelli."

"He may perhaps have furnished Rossini with a tune or two—old-fashioned things, which were popular when he, Mombelli, was at the height of his fame, round about 1780 or 1790. There is a rumour, too, that the Mombelli daughters are related to Rossini."

"Why shouldn't we all go over to Como for the opening of the new theatre?" suggested the mistress of the house.

"Let's go to Como! Let's go to Como!" came voices from all sides; and so, within half an hour, four carriages harnessed with galloping post-horses were away on the road to Como, by way of Bergamo. The highway runs through some of the finest upland scenery which you could hope to see anywhere in Europe. Haste was essential, if we were to reach Como before the heat of the sun grew intolerable on the morrow; and that was how it came about that we drove recklessly onwards, despite our misgivings on account of the highwaymen who always infest the neighbourhood of Brescia and Bergamo—they having, so the rumour goes, even established a permanent network of intelligence agents in the former of these two towns. The terror and apprehension which possessed the ladies of the party seemed only to add to the thrill of the journey; and, upon the pretext of "distracting their attention", we abandoned ourselves to the unbridled pleasures of extravagant and imaginative fantasy, to metaphysical arabesques and baroque speculations inconceivable beneath other skies, and tinged not a little with the madness which flies abroad through the darkness of a fine, starry night. In this wondrous climate, even the blue of the heavens is different from the blue that *we* know. The chains of lakes, the mountains mantled with great chestnut-woods, with orange-orchards and groves of olives, which stretch from Bergamo to Domo-dossola, form what is probably one of the finest landscapes in all the world. But since no traveller has yet sung its praises, it remains almost unexplored; nor will *I* describe it, lest I be accused of exaggeration. I am already more than a little apprehensive, lest I be accused of this weakness respecting the miracles which I tend to attribute to music.

We reached Como at nine in the morning. The sun was already scorching; but I happened to be a personal friend of the landlord of the *Angelo*, an inn overlooking the lake (in Italy, mark you, no friendship is too humble to neglect!); he gave us rooms which were pleasantly cool, and the waves of the lake came lapping at the walls beneath our windows, a few feet below the level of the balconies. Rowing-boats shaded with awnings appeared in an instant, for those of our company who wanted to bathe; and so, at length, towards eight in the evening, we found ourselves, refreshed and in the highest of spirits, seated in the new theatre of the town of Como, which that very night was opening its doors to the public for the first time. The crowd was indescribable! People had come flooding in from the *monti di Brianza*, from Varese, from Bellagio, from Lecco, from Chiavenna, from *la Tremezzina*, from every nook and corner perched on or about the shores of the lake, which is a good thirty miles long. Our three boxes cost us forty *sequins* (450 francs), and even then we only managed to secure them as a special favour, thanks to my invaluable friend the landlord of the *Angelo*.

Every person of reasonable means, both in Como itself and in all the surrounding country, had contributed to the fund which had been set up to build this new theatre, which, architecturally, has inherited the noblest and simplest traditions of Italy, and which to-night was holding its very first performance. A huge portico, supported by six great Corinthian columns surmounted by bronze capitals, forms a convenient shelter where the patrons of the theatre may dismount from their carriages, thus fulfilling the condition which decrees that, in architecture, *utility* is a necessary complement to *beauty*. This portico fronts on a charming little *piazza*, just behind the magnificent cathedral, which can best be described as "modified gothic". On the left of this *piazza* rises a tree-clad hill which bars the southern extremity of Lake Como. We discovered that the interior of the theatre, with its bold and simple lines, fully justified the forceful, male beauty of the façade. The whole edifice had been built in three years by individual initiative —and *that* in a town of some ten thousand inhabitants, where there is grass growing in most of the main streets! Involuntarily there sprang

to my mind a picture of Dijon and its new theatre, which I observe
every time I pass through the city, and have been observing for the
past twenty years; its walls have risen to a height of exactly ten feet
from the ground! Admittedly, the city of Dijon has given us a score of
first-rate intellects and fine writers: Buffon, de Brosses, Piron, Crébillon, *etc., etc.*; but, since *intellectual* superiority is our national *forte*, let
us be satisfied with our triumphs in literature, and allow the beautiful
land of Italy to rule like a queen in her own kingdom of art.

A pleasant-mannered and extremely handsome young officer, Signor
M*** (aide-de-camp to General L***), whom, by a most fortunate
chance, we came across in the *atrio* of the theatre, and who turned out
to be an acquaintance of the ladies in our company, readily vol-
unteered us information about all the innumerable little details which
invariably excite curiosity upon one's first visit to an unfamiliar
theatre.

"The company which you will be watching to-night," he informed
us, "are all members of one single family. There are two Mombelli
sisters; the one, Marianna, always takes male rôles and sings the *musico*
parts; the other, Ester, whose voice boasts a greater range, although
perhaps it is less perfect in tone than that of her sister, is the *prima donna*
of the troupe. In the opera *Demetrio e Polibio*, which the Committee of
the local Musical Society has chosen to mark the opening of its new
theatre, old Mombelli, who was in his day a noted tenor, plays the
King. The part of the Leader of the Conspirators will be played by
an old fellow called Olivieri, who has for years been attached to
Signora Mombelli, the mother of the two girls, and who, to make
himself useful to the family, is a kind of general *utility-man* on the
stage, as well as cook and *maestro di casa* off it. Without being exactly
pretty, the two Mombelli daughers are quite pleasant to look at; they
are, however, virtuous to the point of ferocity. It may be presumed
that their father, who has ambitions (*è un dirittone*), has plans for marry-
ing them off."

Thus acquainted with the petty gossip of the theatre, we at length
watched the curtain rise upon *Demetrio e Polibio*. I have, I believe, never
before experienced so vividly the quality of Rossini as a *great artist*.
We were *transported*—there is no other word for it. Each successive
item was a positive banquet, a miracle of singing at its purest, of melody
at its most enchanting. In a moment we seemed to be spirited away

among the shady walks of some enchanted park—it might have been Windsor—where each new vista seemed fairer than all that had gone before, until at last, reflecting upon one's own wondering astonishment, one realized with something of a shock that one had bestowed the supreme award for beauty upon twenty different objects.

Is there anything in all music more languorous and more touching—yet touching with that peculiar tenderness, innocent alike of melancholy and of premonition,[1] which is born only beneath the blue heaven of Italy, and which is nothing but the softer aspect of a noble and virile nature—is there anything more affecting than this *cavatina* sung by the *musico*:

> *Pien di contento in seno* . . .?

Moreover, the *style* in which it was sung by Marianna Mombelli (now Signora Lambertini), was a revelation to us; we had never before appreciated the full potentialities of the *canto liscio e spianato*.[2] At this distance in time, I cannot recall the plot of the *libretto*; but I remember as clearly as though it were yesterday, that when we reached the duet between the *soprano* and the *basso*:

> *Mio figlio non sei,*
> *Pur figlio ti chiamo* . . . .,[3]

we were so deeply plunged into reverie, reflecting that nothing on earth could better depict the deep-felt and moving love of a father for his son, that we completely forgot to applaud the music. In style,

---

[1] Compare the landscapes of Switzerland with those of the fair land of Italy. *Vide: le Journal des Débats** (29 July 1823), which contains a charming description of the town of Varese.

[2] Simple and pure, stripped of pretentious ornamentation; the style of Virgil, for instance, as compared with that of Madame de Staël, in whose art each sentence is loaded to the hilt with every arabesque and flourish known to philosophy or sensibility!

[3] *Polibio:*
> Mio figlio non sei,
> Pur figlio ti chiamo,
> Lo merti, lo bramo,
> Chiamarti così.

Siveno:
> Son grato al tuo dono,
> Rammento chi sono.
> Son figlio infelice
> Che vive per te.

Demetrio e Polibio ranks with *Tancredi*; but in content, it is something far finer. Such, at least, was our verdict.

When we reached the quartet

Donami omai, Siveno . . .,

our admiration, like that of the remainder of the audience, knew neither bounds nor language in which to find expression. To-day, nine years after this memorable evening, during which time I have listened to a great deal of music (usually for want of anything better to listen to!), I do not hesitate to assert that this quartet must number among Rossini's most masterly inventions. I know nothing anywhere which can surpass it. If Rossini had composed nothing, save this one quartet, Mozart and Cimarosa would still have recognized in him a man who was their equal as an artist. Incidentally, one of its most fascinating qualities is a curious lightness of touch (the sort of thing a painter would describe as 'created out of nothing") which I have never encountered in Mozart.

I remember that the effect upon the audience was so instantaneous that, not content with calling for one *encore*, they were on the point of reviving an ancient practice, and calling for a second, when a personal friend of the Mombelli family stepped down into the auditorium, and appealed to the enraptured *dilettanti*, explaining that neither of the Mombelli girls was particularly strong in health, and that if they insisted upon a second *encore* for the quartet, there was a very real danger that the singers might not be able to get through the remainder of the opera. "But," protested the *dilettanti*, "is there anything still to come which is worth hearing, compared with *this*?" "Most assuredly there is!" answered the family friend. "There is the duet* between the lover and his mistress,

Questo cor ti giura amore . . .,

and at least two or three others besides." This argument at last took effect upon the pit, and sheer curiosity conquered the wilder manifestations of enthusiasm. Moreover, the family friend was fully redeemed in the promises he had made on behalf of the duet

Questo cor ti giura amore . . .,

for it is impossible to portray the mystic sweetness of love with greater delicacy, or with less poignant sadness.

A factor which strongly contributed to the charm of these perfect *cantilenas* was the unobtrusiveness and, if I may use the term, the *modesty* of the accompaniments. These songs were the first fragile blossoms of Rossini's genius; the dawn of his life had left the dew still fresh upon them.

Later in his career, Rossini was to journey towards the cold and dismal lands of the North, where gaping chasms yawn blackly on the edge of every summer landscape, inspiring melancholy and *horror* in the beholder; and this *horror* was to become an integral part of his later conception of beauty.[1]

By resorting to crude contrasts for his effects, Rossini succeeded in winning the applause of the *blunt-minded*, and of all musicians who think of music as the Germans do, in terms of dust and learning. If all the composers (Mozart excepted) born outside Italy were brought together in one vast congress, and kept there until the end of time, their whole united effort could never produce one single quartet half as fine as

Donami omai, Siveno . . .!

[1] *Cf.* the accompaniment to the scene of the arrival of Moses, in the opera *Mosè in Egitto.*

CHAPTER X

Il Turco in Italia

IN the autumn of this same year, 1814, Rossini composed *il Turco in Italia* for *la Scala* in Milan, in response to a demand for a sequel to *l'Italiana in Algeri*. Galli, who for some years* had been giving admirable performances as the Bey in *l'Italiana*, was entrusted with the part of the young Turk, who, driven out of his course at sea by a great storm, struggles ashore in Italy, and falls in love with the first pretty girl whom chance sets in his path. Unfortunately, this particular pretty young thing already possesses, not only a husband (don Geronio), but a lover (don Narciso) into the bargain, who turns out to be in no mood to step down in favour of *any* Turk! However, the lady, who is named donna Fiorilla, being gay and flirtatious by nature, is delighted by the impression she has made on the handsome foreigner, and jumps at the double chance of tormenting her lover and of making a fool of her husband.

Don Geronio's *cavatina*

> *Vado in traccia d'una zingara*
> *Che mi sappia astrologar,*
> *Che mi dica, in confidenza,*
> *Se col tempo e la pazienza,*
> *Il cervello di mia moglie*
> *Potrò giungere a sanar,*

is in the purest comic vein. This delightful song is a perfect example of music in the tradition of Cimarosa, notably in the reply which poor old don Geronio returns to his own question:

> *Ma la zingara ch' io bramo*
> *È impossibile trovar!*[1]

Nevertheless, if the thematic structure of this *cavatina* reveals a direct

[1] Act I, sc. iii.

ancestry in the songs of Cimarosa, the stylistic treatment is entirely original. The part of don Geronio is one of those in which the famous *buffo* Paccini acquired his great reputation. Every evening, I remember, he used to think up some new and original interpretation for this passage; one night, he would give us a husband genuinely in love with his wife, and driven to distraction by her irresponsibility; the next, a cynical philosopher who would be the first to shrug his shoulders at the singular whims of the helpmeet which fate has foisted upon him. At one performance (I forget whether it was the fourth or the fifth), Paccini risked a piece of absurdity so foreign to our present code of manners that I hesitate even to describe it, for fear of shocking my readers' susceptibilities. You must know, then, that on that particular evening, society gossip was exclusively preoccupied with the fate of one particular husband, who was very far from accepting with philosophic fortitude the distressful accidents peculiar to his state. The boxes of *la Scala*, almost without exception, were buzzing with chatter over the circumstances of his misfortune, of which, indeed, he had become aware for the first time that very day. Paccini, irritated by the fact that no one seemed to be paying the slightest attention to the opera, suddenly began, right in the middle of his *cavatina*, to mimic the unmistakably individual gestures and the wild despair of the unlucky husband. This highly reprehensible piece of impertinence succeeded beyond all belief; the audience was seized by a spasm of merriment, which, starting *pianissimo*, grew rapidly into a reverberating *crescendo*. To begin with, only one or two persons seemed to realize that there was a remarkable similarity between Paccini's histrionic despair on the stage, and that of the Duke of *** in real life; but one by one, the entire audience came to identify the gestures of that poor cuckolded aristocrat, and in particular, his handkerchief, which he never failed to hold in his hand whenever he mentioned his wife, to wipe away the tears of distress which poured from his eyes. But how can I describe the outburst of universal hilarity which echoed through the huge building, when the luckless Duke himself entered the theatre and, in full view of the entire audience, found a seat in a friend's box scarcely above the level of the pit itself? The audience to a man screwed its neck round to the point of positive discomfort, in order to extract the last ounce of delight from his presence. However, the unhappy husband not only remained entirely oblivious to the sensation he was creating; but to crown it all, the audience was soon permitted to deduce from his gestures, and in particular from the pitiful fluttering of that abominable handkerchief, that he was indeed "telling the tale anew" to the occupants of the box which he was visiting, and that he was being careful to omit not one of the degrading circumstances of his previous night's discovery!

One needs to realize just *how* small, from the point of view of gossip, scandal and amorous intrigue, are Italy's greatest cities, in order to appreciate the hysterical convulsions of laugher which overwhelmed the audience, sharp-tongued and cynical as it was, at the spectacle of the ill-fated husband in his box, and of Paccini on the stage, gazing at him steadily while he sang his *cavatina*, and instantly mimicking his slightest gesture with a flourish of grotesque exaggeration. The orchestra forgot to accompany, even the police grew mindless of their "duty to quell a riot". Fortunately in the end, some spectator less giddy than the rest made his way to the box, and succeeded—though not without some pains—in extricating the still-tearful Duke.

Galli's magnificent voice found full scope for its powers in the paean of greeting which the Turk, scarcely come to land, addresses to the fair realm of Italy:

> *Cara Italia, alfin ti miro,*
> *Vi saluto, amiche sponde!*[1]

The librettist had built into his text a special virtuoso scene for Galli, who was worshipped in Milan, and who was now making his first reappearance on the stage of *la Scala* since his return, after a year's absence, from an engagement in Barcelona.

The reverberations of Galli's voice echoed like thunder in the huge auditorium of *la Scala*; but the audience felt that Rossini, who was at the piano, had for once not lived up to his reputation in this particular duet. This unfavourable verdict was made clear in the distribution of the applause, for, while the house shouted itself hoarse with *Bravo Galli!*, there was scarcely a single voice to ring the changes with a

---

[1] *Selim:*
> Cara Italia, alfin ti miro!
> Vi saluto, amiche sponde;
> L'aria, il suolo, i fiori e l'onde,
> Tutto ride e parla al cor.
>   (Act I, sc. vi)

Bravo maestro!—it is worth remarking that, at the *première* of any opera, the applause for the singers and the applause for the composer are always kept perfectly distinct. As you may well have guessed, nobody gives a damn for the librettist; for who indeed, unless it were a *French* critic, would dream of judging an opera by the *words*?

The enthusiasm which greeted the delightful duet:

> *Siete turchi, non vi credo;*
> *Cento donne intorno avete,*
> *Le comprate, le vendete*
> *Quando spento è in voi l'ardor ...,*[1]

was so boundless that it wholly transcends my powers to describe it with any semblance of accuracy. Incidentally, I have been unable to resist the temptation to set down the whole of this quatrain, because every phrase, every word even, catches such unexpected charm from Rossini's perfect setting. One hearing is enough; thereafter the tune sticks, and the words too, which sound so deliciously provocative on the lips of that particular young lady, who utters them as a pretext for rejecting advances and who, in reality, is desperate to see the pretext rejected instead.

The Turk's reply[2] is as charming as a madrigal by Voltaire.

No composer on earth save Rossini could have written such music, which reflects the last dying struggles of flirtatious provocation as, gradually, flirtation is transmuted into love. Fiorilla's words are still brilliant with the bantering laughter of a coquette, but the first tremors of *love* are already stirring in the accompaniment which chatters long beside them. Nothing can subdue the irrepressible lightheartedness of this wonderful *cantilena*, until we suddenly become aware of the first deep murmurs of dawning passion.

How can I describe the taunting subtlety of the reproach:

> *le comprate, le vendete ...,*

---

[1] Act I, sc. ix.
[2] *Selim:*
> Ah! mia cara, anche in Turchia
> Se un tesoro si possiede,
> Non si cambia, non si cede,
> Serba un Turco anch'egli amor.
>> (Act I, sc. ix)

as it is repeated again and again, and each time with a hint of variation in the underlying expression, by the exquisite voice of Luigina C***, with all its delicacy of tone and its pure precision? O fortunate land of Italy, where love is understood as in no other clime!

Don Geronio, who is only too well aware of Fiorilla's dawning passion, brings up the heavy artillery:

> *Se tu più mormori*
> *Solo una sillaba,*
> *Un cimitero*
> *Qui si farà!*[1]

If such notions seem ridiculous to us in Paris, it must be remembered all the same that in Italy they represent a model example of the librettist's art. The meaning is clear; the emotion is intense; there is comedy in the style of the expression; and, last but not least, there is no trace of that super-refined, elaborate preciosity which we associate with Marivaux. Every instant spent in appreciating such *finesse*, in admiring and applauding it, is just so much time lost for the appreciation of the *music* and, worse still, would continue to distract the attention for a long time to come. To enjoy the *finesse* of verbal wit requires *critical penetration* at an intellectual level; but critical penetration is the very faculty which must be jettisoned for good and all if we are to allow music to weave its elusive web of dreams about our soul; the two pleasures of sense and intellect are distinct, and the belief that both can be enjoyed at once, a dangerous hallucination. Nobody, save a *French literary critic*,[2] could stubbornly persist in this illusion, which can be dispelled by one single comment: *In music, the same word or phrase is subject to constant repetition, each successive re-statement infusing the spoken material with new meaning.* Yet somehow it still passes the

---

[1] Act I, sc. x. Subsequently, Rossini transferred the whole of this scene bodily to *la Cenerentola* (Act I, sc. vi); consequently, it is not found in modern texts of *il Turco in Italia*. (*Trans*.)

[2] *Eg*. MM. Geoffroy, Hoffman, the Editors of *la Pandore, etc., etc*. M. Geoffroy, the most enlightened of these miscellaneous gentlemen, used to refer to Mozart as *a tin-pot and pan-handle composer of more-or-less barbaric tunes*. His successors, however, have been much more severe in their attitude towards Mozart: they have *analysed* and *commended* him. *Cf. l'Abeille* (vol. II, p. 267); *la Renommée; Le Miroir, etc*.

understanding of our venerable literary gentlemen that, in poetry proper, a single repetition of this character can murder the verse, the rhythm and the rhyme, and that the most brilliant shaft of wit, repeated, or even *pronounced slowly*, would normally disintegrate into complete inanity.[1]

In opera, *verse* is confined to the published *libretto*, and exists only by the good graces of the type-setter, who disposes his words in an artificial order on the printed page; in the theatre, once the music escapes from the narrow bonds of recitative into the impassioned flights of song, the ear hears nothing but prose; a man who was blind would never for one single instant recognize the succession of sounds which came to his awareness as verse.

The quartet, from whose text I have just been quoting, may seem arid enough and completely barren of wit from a French point of view; but for all that, it is most admirably suited to music; and its concluding section leads straight into a *cantilena*:

> *Nel volto estatico*
> *Di questo e quello . . .*[*,2]

sung by the four main characters, donna Fiorilla, her lover, her husband and the Turk, which is a perfect example of the fusion of comedy with dramatic verisimilitude.

In the production at *la Scala*, Paccini played the husband and Galli, the Turk; the lover who is so determined to "stand upon his rights" in the face of the newcomer was played by Davide; while Signora Festa played Fiorilla. The *ensemble* was perfect.

In the second act, the pointed little duet:

---

[1] An inquisitive and tactless bore once buttonholed M. de T[alleyrand] in the heat of a political crisis: "Well now, Monseigneur, what has fortune brought you to-day?" "Ill luck, Sir . . . *you*, Sir!" came the retort. Set this rejoinder to music, and it becomes just about as witty and amusing as the nonsense which is printed in the musical articles of *la Pandore*.

[2] *Selim, Fiorilla, Don Narciso, Don Geronio:*
> Nel volto estatico
> Di questo e quello
> Si legge il vortice
> Del lor cervello
> Che ondeggia e dubita
> E incerto stà.
>
> (Act I, sc. x)

D'un bell' uso di Turchia
Forse avrai novella intesa . . .,[1]

in the course of which the young Turk quite bluntly puts it to the
husband that he should *sell* his wife, is just as delicious in every respect
as the earlier duet from Act I. The text provided such a perfect foil for
Rossini's own peculiar sense of humour, that he could not help but
give it a supremely perfect dramatic setting in music. It is impossible
to conceive a more effective combination of lightness, merriment, and
that unique and brilliant *gracefulness*, of which *il Pesarese* may claim to
be the undisputed master. This duet may boldly invite comparison
with any of the melodies invented by Cimarosa or Mozart; for these
two great composers may indeed have written music as fine, but certainly not *finer* than this. And for sheer lightness of touch, the *cantilena*
is, and will always remain, absolutely without parallel. It has something
of the delicacy of the arabesques which Raphael executed for the
loggias of the Vatican. Nowhere, perhaps, save in the scores of Paisiello,
might one hope to light upon a passage which could rival the perfection
of Rossini's music in this number.

I suspect, however, that any reader who chanced to hear this duet
when it was performed in Paris will promptly be tempted to accuse me
of the most unbridled exaggeration; but I would hasten to point out in
my defence, that it is imperative that the performance should be as
perfect as the material; a singer of the quality of Galli is absolutely
essential. If the singers should reveal the faintest hint of fumbling or
hesitation, the gracefulness is gone for ever.

The ball-room scene is another masterpiece. I have no information
whether the high-minded directors who preside over the destinies of
our own *Opera Buffa* dared to include it for the gratification of Parisian

---

[1] *Selim:*
      D'un bell' uso di Turchia
      Forse avrai novella intesa:
      Della moglie che gli pesa
      Il marito è venditor.

   Geronio:
      Sarà l'uso molto buono,
      Ma in Italia è più bell' uso:
      Il marito rompe il muso
      All'infame tentator.
                            (Act II, sc. ii)

audiences*, when they had the temerity to offer them an "amended version" of *il Turco in Italia*.

The quintet:

> *Oh! guardate che accidente;*
> *Non conosco più mia moglie . . .*[1]

is perhaps the finest thing I have ever heard in any *opera buffa* by Rossini; the secret lies in the exquisite balance maintained between *technical simplicity* on the one hand, and *expressive characterization* on the other. But if music of this quality is to be appreciated in all its perfection, a certain degree of spiritual intoxication is essential in the listener; and we all know that nothing can appear more obnoxious, or in worse taste, than the hilarity of others when we ourselves for one reason or another are in no mood to share it. In such circumstances, the obstinately unamused know full well how to get their revenge: *Idiotic buffoonery!* they grunt, *Music-hall nonsense!*

I have no need to explain that, if the Milanese received Rossini's latest masterpiece with a shade of coldness, the reason was *not* that they found it "too flippant". The trouble lay in what they felt to be an insult to their national pride. They maintained that Rossini had plagiarized his own earlier work, and served it up to them as something original. In some petty provincial theatre, the liberty might have been connived at; but at *la Scala*, the finest theatre in the world (so thundered the worthy citizens of Milan), the composer might at least have taken the trouble to write something which was not *stale*. Four years later*, *il Turco in Italia* was revived in Milan, and on this occasion was enormously successful.

> [1] *Geronio:*   Oh! guardate che accidente!
>   Non conosco più mia moglie!
>   Egual Turco, eguali spoglie.
>   Tutto eguale . . . che farò?
>
>   *Narciso:*   No, partir di qui non posso
>   Senza roi, Fiorilla mia.
>
>   *Zaida:*   Ma comprendere non posso
>   Qual sarà la sorte mia.
>
>   *Selim:*   Deh! seguitemi in Turchia.
>   Là, mia sposa vi farò.
>
>   *Fiorilla:*   Persuadermi il cor vorria,
>   Ma risolvermi non so.
>
>   (Act II, sc. xii)

CHAPTER XI

Rossini in Naples

B<small>Y</small> 1814 or thereabouts Rossini's fame had spread as far south as Naples, which displayed a great show of astonishment and disbelief that there could exist in all the world a major composer who had had the temerity not to be born a Neapolitan. The *impresario* in Naples was a certain gentleman by the name of Barbaja, by birth a Milanese, a sometime waiter in a coffee-house who, by gambling, and more especially by holding the bank at faro and by running a gaming-house, had amassed a fortune worth several millions. Signor Barbaja, who had received a thorough early grounding in business methods in Milanese commercial circles, among the host of French army-contractors who were making and losing fortunes every six months in the wake of the battalions, had, and still has, a good eye for the main chance. He realized at once, from the way in which Rossini's musical reputation was spreading abroad in society, that here was a young composer who might be good or bad, but who, rightly or wrongly, was going to be the coming figure in the world of music; so off he went post-haste to Bologna to fetch him. Rossini, who was used to dealing with the seediest of fourth-rate *impresari* in a perpetual state of flagrant bankruptcy, was astonished to find himself sought out by a millionaire who, in all probability, would count it beneath his dignity to embezzle the customary twenty *sequins* out of his salary. The millionaire offered him an engagement, which was accepted on the spot. Later on, in Naples, Rossini signed a *scrittura* for several years. He undertook to compose for Signor Barbaja two original operas *per annum*; and, in addition, to arrange the scores of all other operas that Signor Barbaja saw fit to put on, whether at the main theatre in Naples, the *San-Carlo*, or at the secondary theatre, known as the *teatro del Fondo*. For which services, Rossini was to receive an annual remuneration of 12,000 francs, and to hold shares in certain gaming-houses, of which Barbaja was the official lessee—shares which were to bring in a further 30–40 *louis* a year to the young composer.

The musical direction of the *San-Carlo* and *del Fondo* theatres, for which Rossini had so lightly assumed the responsibility, was an enormous undertaking, a positive drudgery of manual labour involving the transposition and "arrangement" of an unbelievable quantity of music, either to suit the voices of the singers, or else simply to gratify the whims of their "protectors". Such a task, by itself, would have been sufficient to blast any fragile and melancholy genius, any unhardened talent depending upon the delicate inspirations of a highly-strung nervous system; a Mozart would simply have been suffocated. But Rossini possesses a tough and congenitally cheerful temperament, which carries him as unconcernedly over importunate obstacles as it does over the barrages of hostile criticism. An "enemy", to him, promises nothing more formidable than a fresh chance to make a fool of someone, or simply to get up to a few more monkey-tricks and practical jokes, if I may be allowed to lapse temporarily into a style of speech as downright vulgar as the subject.

Rossini cheerfully shouldered the immense burden with which he now found himself saddled*, in much the same spirit as Figaro (in his own *Barber*) undertakes the commissions which rain upon him from all sides "as thick as hailstones". He did the job he was paid to do, and laughed, and in particular continued to exhibit the most pointed irreverence and disrespect towards everyone with whom he came in contact; an attitude which was to earn him a host of enemies, among whom, in this year of grace 1823, we may name Signor Barbaja himself, who was to become the victim of a practical joke in the worst *imaginable* taste when Rossini proceeded to marry his mistress*. In spite of this, however, Rossini's contract with Barbaja lasted until 1822, and exercised an inestimable influence upon his genius, his happiness and his whole career.

Fortunate as ever, Rossini made his *début* in Naples in the most brilliant manner imaginable with an *opera seria* entitled *Elisabetta regina d'Inghilterra* (October 1815).

However, to understand the reasons for this particular success, and more especially, to grasp the nature of the doubts and hesitations which had besieged him at the moment of his arrival in the lovely city which is the home of the Neapolitans, it is necessary to go back a few years into the past.

The Royal Personage* who rules over Naples is a great huntsman, a mighty football-player, a tireless horseman, an intrepid fisherman; the physical man is the whole man; he knows perhaps one emotion, and one only (and that is the direct outcome of his physical prowess)— a passion for enterprise and daring. For the rest, his total lack of positive enthusiasm for crime being equalled only by his similar lack of positive enthusiasm for virtue, he remains a being utterly devoid of the least semblance of moral consciousness, as indeed it becomes a true hunts-man to be. Rumour asserts that he is a miser, but this is an exaggeration; he detests having to pay out money in cash, but he will happily sign away anything one cares to ask for, provided that the money is in the form of bonds drawn on the treasury.

For nine long years this King Ferdinand had languished in the island of Sicily, a kind of prisoner in the hands of a people who could think of nothing better to do than to pester him with *parliamentary govern-ments, economic principles, balances of power*, and other such revolting and unintelligible nonsense. No sooner had he escaped from this chill exile and arrived in Naples, when one of the fairest jewels in all his Neapolitan kingdom, one of the flowers which, glimpsed from afar, had made him pine most desperately in his alien surroundings—the magnificent *San-Carlo* theatre—was destroyed utterly, and in a single night, by fire*. This blow, so they say, affected him more deeply than defeat in a dozen pitched battles or the loss of a whole realm.

And while he lay thus, and the sickness was upon him, there cometh a man unto him, saying "Lord, behold this great theatre, which the flame at this very hour devoureth; yet despair not, for in nine months I will build it for thee again, and it shall be more beautiful than it was, even in all its glory!"

And Signor Barbaja kept his word. On the 12th day of January 1817, when the King of Naples at length set foot in the new *San-Carlo* theatre, he was able to feel, for the first time in twelve years, that at last he was really a King. From that instant onwards, Signor Barbaja was the greatest man in the kingdom. Now it happened that this greatest-man-in-the-kingdom, theatrical-manager and gaming-house-keeper was also the "protector" of Signorina Colbran, his own *prima donna*, who amused herself by making a fool of him all day long, and conse-quently had him exactly where she wanted him. Signorina Colbran, who is to-day *Signora Rossini*,* was between 1806 and 1815 one of the most celebrated sopranos in all Europe. In 1815, however, she began to "suffer from a strained voice", an affliction which, in singers of lesser distinction, would have been vulgarly termed *singing off key**. From 1816 to 1822, Signorina Colbran revealed a marked tendency to sing either above or below the required pitch, and her singing became what (in inferior mortals) would certainly have been termed *execrable*; but God forbid that one should have suggested anything of the kind in Naples! In spite of this minor indisposition, however, Signorina Colbran retained her position as *prima donna* at the *San-Carlo* theatre, and was invariably applauded whenever she appeared on the stage. This, to my mind, represents one of the most flattering victories ever achieved by rank despotism; for, if there is one passion which outstrips all others in the breasts of the inhabitants of Naples—the most emotional, irrepressible people on earth!—it is incontrovertibly their passion for music. And yet, for five whole years, from 1816 to 1821, this un-quenchable race was obliged to endure the most excruciating and tyrannical oppression, directed specifically at those activities to which it was accustomed to look for its most fervent and coveted pleasures! But Barbaja was under the thumb of his mistress; and *she* was the pro-tectress of Rossini. Barbaja, sitting at the King's right hand, held the purse-strings; and if he paid anyone, it was only "them as had earned it" (as they used to say vulgarly in Naples at the time); he basked in his sovereign's favour, and he put up as best he could with his mistress.

If I have sat once in the *San-Carlo* theatre, I have sat a score of times, and listened to Signorina Colbran embark upon an aria, which after the first few bars, would tail off into the most excruciating, the most insupportable cacophony; and one by one I have watched my neigh-bours creep out of their seats, shaking, neurotic, their patience frayed and their endurance exhausted—yet all in dead silence, without a word! And after *that*, let anyone deny that terror be the principle of despotic government*—if anyone dare! Or deny that, as a principle of *any* government, it can work miracles! . . . when it can compel silence upon a crowd of furious Neapolitans! ! On those occasions, I used to accompany my neighbours outside the theatre, and together we would take a stroll around the *Largo di Castello*; and then, some twenty minutes or so later, we would return sheepishly to our seats, just in case we might happen to hit on some odd duet, some forgotten *ensemble*, which the fatal *protégée* of the King and of Signor Barbaja was not, for once, devastating and laying waste with the noble ruin of her voice. During the ephemeral rule of the constitutional government of 1821, Signorina Colbran never once dared show her face upon the stage without first sending on a prologue to grovel in abject apology; and the audience, to show their opinion of her, found especial amusement in building up a tremendous reputation for a certain Mademoiselle Chaumel (known in Naples as la Comelli), who was well known to be her detested rival in every respect.

CHAPTER XII

Elisabetta, regina d'Inghilterra

ACT ONE

B Y the autumn of 1815, however, when Rossini arrived in Naples and produced his *Elisabetta*, matters had not yet reached this completely scandalous pass; the public was very far from execrating Signorina Colbran, and never before or since did she possess greater beauty than at that time. It was a beauty in the most queenly tradition: noble features which, on the stage, radiated majesty; an eye like that of a Circassian maiden, darting fire; and to crown it all, a true and deep instinct for tragedy. Off-stage, she possessed about as much dignity as the average milliner's-assistant; but the moment she stepped on to the boards, her brow encircled with a royal diadem, she inspired involuntary respect, even among those who, a minute or two earlier, had been chatting intimately with her in the foyer of the theatre.

Walter Scott's novel *Kenilworth* was not published until 1820; nevertheless, its existence makes it superfluous for me to give a full analysis of the plot of Rossini's opera, although in fact *Elisabetta* was produced five years earlier. The very name *Elizabeth* conjures up so clear a picture of the character of this illustrious queen, that there is nothing I need add—a queen in whose nature the noblest virtues of a great sovereign are from time to time eclipsed by the human weakness of a beautiful woman gazing regretfully at the shadow of her departing youth. In the libretto, as in the novel. Leicester, Elizabeth's favourite, is on the point of mounting the steps to the throne, and of receiving the offer of the queen's hand; he however, being in love with a lady of sweeter disposition and less imperious demeanour, whom he has had the temerity to wed in secret, has only one hope, which is to deceive the sharp eyes of a love which is not only jealous, but which is moreover armed with the sovereign power and authority. In the opera, the secretly-wedded wife is not called Amy Robsart, but Matilde. The libretto is a translation from a French melodrama*, perpetrated by a

Tuscan-born gentleman by the name of Smith, whose home was in Naples.

The opening duet*, in the minor key, between Leicester and his young wife, is not only magnificent, but extremely original. *Elisabetta* was the first music written by Rossini which had been heard in Naples, and his great reputation, acquired exclusively in the northern provinces of Italy, had predisposed the Neapolitan audiences to be hypercritical in their standards of judgment; none the less, it may justly be claimed that this first duet,

Incauta! che festi?[1]

determined not only the success of this particular opera, but also the wider triumph of its composer.

A courtier by the name of Norfolk, jealous of the high favours which the Queen's love has heaped upon Leicester, betrays to Elizabeth that the unworthy man, whom her royal pride already rebukes her for loving, has audaciously entered upon a secret marriage. He reveals that her favourite, newly returned in triumph from the Scottish wars (and whose victorious arrival provides the setting for the opening scene of the first act), has brought back with him his newly-wedded wife, concealed among a party of youthful hostages whom the Scots have despatched to Elizabeth, and whom the Queen has recently admitted as pages into her own household. Thus, Norfolk continues, she has unwittingly made her young rival, who is disguised in man's costume, a guest at her own court. The instant of fury and profound deception which follows is musically superb. Pride and love, the Queen's two obsessing passions, struggle most cruelly for the possession of her soul. The duet between the Queen and Norfolk,

Con qual fulmine improvviso,
Mi percosse irato il cielo![2]

[1] *Leicester:*
　　Incauta! che festi?
　　Seguirmi perchè?
　　Gli effetti son questi
　　D'amore e di fe'?
　　　　　　　　(Act I, sc. iv)

[2] *Norfolk:*
　　Perché mai, destin crudele,
　　Costringesti il labbro mio?

was received just as enthusiastically in Paris as it had been earlier in Naples. Its temper is at once fiery and majestic—an excellent combination in any portrayal of pride; but the love-element is disappointing, appearing merely as so much ranting and raging.

The Queen, beside herself with fury, commands the Lord Marshal of the Court to draw up the guards, and to warn them to be ready to carry out her orders promptly and implicitly, whatever these may be. At the same time, she commands him to have brought into her presence all the Scottish hostages, and finally to summon Leicester, whom she desires to see instantly. Having issued this swift series of commands, in a breathless, *staccato* rush of words, Elizabeth remains alone. In this instant, it must be confessed, Signorina Colbran was magnificent; she allowed herself no gestures; she simply paced up and down, unable to control herself, to force herself into stillness while she awaited the setting of the stage and the arrival of her false lover; her eyes alone betrayed that her mind was burning with the single word which inexorably would send her lover to his death. This is precisely the sort of situation which operatic music requires and thrives on!

At length, Leicester appears; but at the very same instant, the Scottish hostages are introduced into the audience-chamber. Elizabeth, her eyes blazing with fury, scans the crowd of pages to pick out the object of her hatred; and Matilde's confusion soon betrays her. Broken, unfinished sentences and phrases hint at the violence of the passions which are at stake; but in the end, recitative gives place to singing, and the first-act *finale* beings. The Queen, understanding that she has been betrayed by everyone and everything around her, gives secret instructions to one of the guards, who shortly afterwards reappears carrying a cushion draped in a veil. Elizabeth, with a final glance at Matilde and Leicester, sweeps this veil angrily aside. There, on the cushion, lies revealed the crown of England; and Elizabeth offers it to Leicester, together with her own hand.

> Ma fedel a te son io,
> Mentre accuso un traditor.
> *Elisabetta:*
> Con qual fulmine improvviso
> Mi percosse irato il cielo?
> Qual s'addensa orrendo velo
> Che mi colma di terror?
>
> (Act I, sc. vii)

As a pure dramatic climax, this scene is magnificent. In straight tragedy, a technical piece of business of this character may be out of place; but in opera, which thrives on the melodramatic and the visual, it is superb and unbelievably effective on the stage.

Elizabeth, who extracts a kind of grim pleasure from her own fury, mutters to herself:

> *Qual colpo inaspettato*
> *Che lor serbava il fato,*
> *Il gelo della morte*
> *Impallidir li fè![1]*

But Leicester, in rash disobedience, rejects the Queen's offer; she, in ungoverned fury, snatches at the young "page", and drags him forward to the front of the stage, hoarsely shouting at her lover: "So *this* is the vile creature who has taught you to become a traitor!" Matilde and Leicester, realizing that they have been betrayed, are overwhelmed with confusion, replying in broken phrases to Elizabeth's accusations. Elizabeth summons her guards, in whose wake there enters the entire court, which therefore is able to witness every detail of the tragic crisis, including the resounding disgrace of Leicester, whom the Queen orders to surrender his sword.

No librettist could have imagined a more inspiring *finale*, at least from the composer's point of view; music, divine art as it is, cannot depict political upheavals; try as it may to illustrate dramas of this character, private crises invariably submerge public revolutions. But in this instance, all the emotions concerned—*jealousy*, which is tormenting Elizabeth to the very brink of madness; *despair*, growing ever blacker in Leicester; and *love*, unbelievably sad and touching in his young wife—are all intimate and personal, and therefore admirably suited to the purposes of music. None the less, it would be quite false to suggest that it was the *libretto* which was chiefly responsible for Rossini's triumph. At the *première*, the Neapolitans simply went mad with delight. I shall never forget that first evening. It was a gala-day at Court; but I remember observing that the party (which included myself) gathered in the box of the Princess Belmonte to witness the opening performance, was at first inclined to be decidedly severe in its

---

[1] Act I, sc. ix (quartet sung by Elizabeth, Leicester, Matilde and Matilde's brother Enrico).

welcome to this new *maestro*, who had been born far from the shores of Naples, and who had acquired his resounding reputation among "foreigners".

But, as I have already mentioned, the opening duet, in the minor key, between the ambitious Leicester (Nozzari) and his young wife (Signorina Dardanelli) disguised as a page, disarmed the severest critic, and Rossini's entrancing style had soon completely seduced the most stubborn resisters. *Elisabetta* offered all the great emotional tension and drama of the *opera seria*, without exacting the usual toll of dreariness and boredom.

The circumstance that it was a gala-day also prevailed in favour of the maestro. There is nothing like the brilliant ceremonial of a festival at Court to whet the appetite for flamboyant splendour, or to banish the preoccupations of solitary grief and unrequited love. And it must be admitted that, musically speaking, *Elisabetta* tends considerably more towards *magnificence* than towards pathos; not an episode but where the voices blare away like clarinets; and the most thrilling passages often turn out, on analysis, to be nothing but *music scored for the orchestra*.

But at the first performance, we were a thousand leagues removed from the cold rationality of such criticism. There is only one phrase to describe our reactions with any semblance of adequacy: we were literally swept off our feet!

Having discussed this superb first-act *finale* at some length, I have just realized that I forgot to mention the overture. Yet it was the overture which heralded the triumph of the whole opera. Nevertheless, I recall a certain Signor M***, a connoisseur of the highest order, coming round to Princess Belmonte's box and remarking: "You know, this is precisely the same overture as he used for *Aureliano in Palmira*, with just a few new touches in the orchestration!" It turned out later, of course, that nothing could have been more correct. A year later still, when Rossini went to Rome to write the *Barber of Seville*, his laziness tempted him to make use of this identical overture for yet a *third* time! Thus the same music is pressed into service to portray, in the one instance, the struggles between love and pride in one of the noblest minds of which history has ever left record; and in the other, the inanities of Figaro the Barber! Yet it is true that the slightest change of *tempo* will often suffice to transform the merriest jig into the saddest and most melancholy of pavanes. Try the experiment yourself, by singing Mozart's aria,

Non più andrai farfallone amoroso . . .[1]

in increasingly slow time.

In *Elisabetta*, the principal themes of this overture, which Rossini was to call so repeatedly into service, form the concluding statement of the first-act *finale*.

[1] *Nozze di Figaro,* Act I, sc. viii.

CHAPTER XIII

Elisabetta, regina d'Inghilterra

(continued)

ACT TWO

THE second act opens with a scene which is quite magnificent. Elizabeth, terrible in her fury, commands her guards to summon the trembling Matilde into her presence. Her purpose is revealed in the fateful words:

> *T' inoltra, in me tu vedi*
> *Il tuo giudice, o donna!*[1]

Reasons of State decree that death and ignominy shall be the lot of any woman who, being a known enemy of the realm, shall dare introduce herself into my court in the treachery of disguise. Yet a grain of mercy still lies concealed in my soul. Take up this pen, and renounce, once and for ever, any claims you may imagine you hold over the heart and fortunes of ambitious Leicester. Recant and save yourself!

This recitative, with its full orchestral accompaniment, is superb. On the first night it sent terror thrilling through every heart. It is impossible, without having watched Signorina Colbran in this scene, to understand the *furore* which she inspired in Naples, and the mad things which were done in her name at this time.

An Englishman, one of Barbaja's rivals, had had sent out from England a set of extremely accurate sketches, which made it possible to reproduce exactly, and in every detail, the costume of this severe-minded monarch. These XVIth century dresses turned out to be exquisitely becoming to the wondrous figure and classical features of Signorina Colbran. Everybody in the audience knew the story of the costumes, and of their historical accuracy; and so all the prestige of history lay like a sacred mantle over her majestic presence, adding still further to her astonishing beauty. *Kenilworth* itself, filling a romantic

[1] Act II, sc. iii.

imagination with exalted dreams, never conjured up a more splendid or a more queenly Elizabeth. In all the huge arena of the *San-Carlo*, there can scarcely have been a man who had not, at that moment, thought death an insignificant price to pay for a glance from so beautiful a Queen.

Signorina Colbran, as Elizabeth, used no gestures, did nothing melodramatic, never descended to what are vulgarly called *tragedy-queen poses*. The immensity of her royal authority, the vastness of events which a single word from her lips could call into being, all this lived in the Spanish beauty of her eyes, which at times could be so terrible. Her glance was that of a queen whose fury is restrained only by a last rag of pride; her whole presence was that of a woman who still has beauty, and who for years has grown accustomed to beholding her first hint of a whim followed by the swiftest obedience.[1] When Signorina Colbran

---

[1] *Il celere obbedir.*

The phrase comes from Manzoni's *il cinque Maggio*. I know no other poem which is worthy of its noble subject*:

> Ei fu. Siccome immobile,
>   Dato il mortal sospiro,
>   Stette la spoglia immemore
>   Orba di tanto spiro,
>   Così percossa e attonita
>   La Terra al nunzio sta,
>
> Muta, pensando all' ultima
>   Ora dell' uom fatale;
>   Nè sa quando una simile
>   Orma di piè mortale
>   La sua cruenta polvere
>   A calpestar verrà.
>   . . . .
>   . . . .
>
> Dall' Alpi alle Piramidi,
>   Dal Manzanarre al Reno,
>   Di quel securo il fulmine
>   Tenea dietro al baleno;
>   Scoppiò da Scilla al Tanai,
>   Dall' uno all' altro mar.
>
> Fu vera gloria? Ai posteri
>   L'ardua sentenza; nui
>   Chiniam la fronte al Massimo
>   Fattor, che volle in lui
>   Del creator suo spirito

talked with Matilde, it was impossible to escape the irrefutable conviction that this woman had reigned for twenty years as a queen whose
authority was absolute and supreme. It was the *ingrained* acceptance of
the manners and mannerisms bred by despotic power, it was the unmistakable absence of the least shadow of doubt concerning the devoted
obedience which would greet the most insignificant and capricious of
her commands, which characterized the acting of this great artist; all
this wealth of exquisitely-observed detail could be read into the
statuesque calm of her every gesture. And when, rarely, she did move,
it was as though the breaking of the stillness were forced upon her from
within, by the clash of turbulent passions in her soul; not once was it
merely to threaten, to impress, to constrain obedience to her will. The
very greatest of our tragic actors, even the great Talma himself, are not
exempt from the weakness of imperious and theatrical gestures when
they play the parts of tyrants and despots. It may be that this theatri-
cality, this characteristic *genus* of tragic swagger, is merely a sop flung

> Più vasta orma stampar.
> . . . .
> . . . .

> E sparve, e i dì nell' ozio
> Chiuse in sì breve sponda,
> Segno d'immensa invidia,
> E di pietà profonda,
> D'inestinguibil odio
> E d'indomato amor.
> . . . .
> . . . .

> Oh ! quante volte al tactio
> Morir di un giorno inerte,
> Chinati i rai fulminei,
> Le braccia al sen conserte,
> Stette, e dei dì che furono
> L'assalse il sovvenir !

> Ei ripensò le mobili
> Tende, i percossi valli,
> E il lampo dei manipoli,
> E l'onda dei cavalli,
> E il concitato imperio,
> E il celere obbedir.
> . . . .
> . . . .

to the exacting tastelessness and vulgarity of the pit which, in France and elsewhere, decides the fate of tragedies; but, for all the wild applause they may elicit, extravagant mannerisms and gestures in this tradition are none the less absurd. No man in the world uses *fewer* gestures than a despotic monarch;[1] why *should* he rant and gesticulate? He has for so long been accustomed to implicit obedience, that emphatic movement is merely superfluous; swift as lightning, an imperceptible nod brings fulfilment to his every wish.

The superb scene in which Signorina Colbran displayed such greatness as a tragic actress comes to an end with a duet between the Queen and Matilde:

> *Pensa che sol per poco*
> *Sospendo l' ira mia . . .,*[2]

which soon changes into a trio with the entry of Leicester.

The story runs that it was Rossini's own inspiration to have Leicester make his entry between the two women, the one scarcely holding back her seething outbursts of fury, the other exalted to a state of unnatural violence by the despair which true love has wrought in the heart of a girl of sixteen. Given the exigencies of the medium, the conception is indeed something near to pure genius.

Following this great trio come two arias, one by Norfolk (originally played by Garcia), the second by Leicester (Nozzari); both are reasonably well written. The quality of the singing needs no description; suffice it to say that two great tenors, ardent rivals in their art, were appearing together upon a great and solemn occasion before an audience comprising all the great personages in the land, and all the most sophisticated connoisseurs in Naples. On the other hand, considered purely as pieces of composition, both arias had a faint flavour of the commonplace, and seemed to fall rather below the high standard of the rest of the opera.

Leicester is imprisoned and condemned to death by the High Courts of the Realm. A few instants before his execution, Elizabeth is seized with intense horror at the prospect of losing for ever the one man who had succeeded in awakening softer feelings in a heart wholly devoted to ambition and to the sombre enjoyment of power. At the last minute

---

[1] Alfieri, *Vita:* portrait of Louis XV.
[2] Act II, sc. iii.

she decides to visit Leicester in prison, whither the traitor Norfolk had preceded her, only to hide behind one of the pillars of the dungeon upon her arrival. The two lovers talk; and gradually, as they come to understand that Norfolk was the villain who had attempted to destroy Leicester, are reconciled. Norfolk, realizing now that he has been unmasked, and that there is no hope of pardon, draws a dagger and rushes at Elizabeth. But Matilde, Leicester's young wife, who had come to bid him a final adieu, cries out a warning, and so succeeds in saving the Queen's life.

Elizabeth, already half-converted as a result of her conversation with Leicester, pardons the young lovers; and Rossini makes amends for the two rather unsatisfactory arias of the preceding scene with one of the most magnificent *finales* that he ever composed.

When the Queen cries out:

> *Bell' alme generose . . .,*

the enthusiasm of the audience knew no bounds. Fully fifteen performances had to be witnessed before we were finally restored to a state of sanity, and able to submit our delight in this superb passage to the tempering judgment of rational criticism*.

Elizabeth pardons Leicester and Matilde in the following phrases:

> *Bell' alme generose,*
> *A questo sen venite;*
> *Vivete, omai gioite,*
> *Siate felici ognor.*[1]

When, in the end, we *had* sufficiently recovered our senses, so as to be capable of criticizing and examining, we discovered that the music of this passage had all the still, sweet calm of the hush that follows the storm. On the other hand, I would like to suggest that, in the short space of these 20–30 bars, Rossini has included a specimen of every one of those aggravating defects which tend to mar his style. The principal melodic line is smothered beneath cascade upon cascade of ill-assorted ornamentation, beneath a rolling lava-stream of *roulades* which show every sign of having been designed for wind-instruments rather than for the human voice.

However, when all is said and done, we must give him his due as he

[1] Act II, sc. x.

deserves. Rossini had just arrived in Naples; and, being determined to succeed at any price, he had necessarily to cater for the tastes of his *prima donna*, since it was she who held Barbaja, the theatre-manager, in the hollow of her hand. Now Signorina Colbran's *repertoire* had never included any particular talent for pathos; her genius, like her person, was all magnificence and splendour; she was a queen, she *was* Elizabeth; but it was the Elizabeth who issued commands from the height of her throne, and not the Elizabeth who could pardon with a generous heart.

Even if the natural bent of Rossini's own inspiration had been towards the pathetic (which I am very far from admitting to be the case), he would have been obliged to curb and restrain this natural tendency because of the vocal limitations of the celebrated *prima donna* to whom the rôle of Elizabeth was to be entrusted.

In the passage:

> *Bell' alme generose . . .*

Rossini resorted to the somewhat naïve device of heaping together all the vocal ornaments which Signorina Colbran had a flair for executing effectively, into one huge, formless amalgamation, regardless of their character or origin. We were regaled with a sort of illustrated catalogue of all the technical accomplishments which that magnificent voice could master; and the result provided an unrivalled demonstration of the value of pure technical virtuosity in music; for this fantastic conglomeration of embellishments was handled with such superb skill that, in spite of the patent absurdity of the entire conception, it took fully fifteen to twenty performances before we were at last able to realize that the whole lot was entirely out of place.

Rossini, who is never at a loss for a retort, had an answer ready to meet our criticism. "Elizabeth," he maintained, "remains a queen, even in the act of granting a pardon. In so proud a heart, mercy is never a pure act of undiluted generosity; it is always, in part at least, a political gesture. Furthermore, can you tell me of *any* woman, let alone a queen, who can *genuinely* forgive the insult of seeing another woman preferred to herself?"

At this point in the argument, the *dilettanti* began to get angry. "Every note in the whole opera," they maintained, "is vitiated by this same lack of pathos; the music is magniloquent, but nothing more . . . just like the talent of your *prima donna*! The rôle of Matilde, for example, should be steeped in tenderness; yet—with the solitary exception of the opening bars of the trio,

Pensa che sol per poco . . .

—you have given us nothing in that vein at all; and even those few bars have the plain simplicity of a nocturne, rather than the tender warmth of a lover's aria. All the same, this isolated passage does give the listener an instant of respite amid all the surrounding splendour; and in fact, four-fifths of the pleasure which it inspires are due solely to the fact of this contrast. Now, why not admit frankly that, throughout the work, you have consistently sacrificed both dramatic emphasis and expression to la Colbran's passion for embroidery?"

"I have sacrificed to one idol, and to one *only*," retorted Rossini, with that streak of pride which becomes him so admirably. "I have sacrificed to *success*!"

At this point, the genial archbishop of T(rento) rallied to Rossini's defence.

"In Rome," he said, "when Scipio was accused before all the people, the only reply he would vouchsafe to his enemies was: *Romans! Ten years ago, on just such another day, I destroyed Carthage; therefore let us go now to the Capitol, and render thanks to the immortal gods!*"

One thing is certain: the impression created by *Elisabetta* was prodigious. And although it is greatly inferior to *Otello*, for example, yet it contains many passages which are bewitchingly fresh and original.

To-day, looking back upon the occasion with a cool and detached mind, I would say that it was a mistake to have written the parts of Norfolk and Leicester for *two tenors*. However, I can answer for Rossini's rejoinder to *that* criticism: "I happened to *have* two tenors at my disposal, whereas I had no *basso* to play Norfolk." But the truth is that, before Rossini's time, it was a tradition that major parts in *opera seria* should never be given to the bass. Rossini himself was the first composer ever to score difficult parts for this type of voice in *opera di mezzo carattere*, as, for instance, in *la Cenerentola, la Gazza ladra, Torvaldo e Dorliska, etc.*; and it may truly be claimed that it is to his music that singers such as Lablache, Zucchelli, Galli, Remorini and Ambrosi owe their real origin.

G

CHAPTER XIV

The ten Operas of Rossini's "Neapolitan" Period

I<small>N</small> the space of one year, Signorina Colbran sang in Rossini's *Elisabetta*, in Caraffa's *Gabriele di Vergy*, and in Mayr's *Cora* and *Medea*; in each part she was magnificent, performing miracles of pure virtuosity with her voice. At that period, the *San-Carlo* was the scene of a musical banquet rich and varied enough to satisfy the most ardent and the most hypercritical of music-lovers; for Signorina Colbran's supporting cast included the younger Davide, Nozzari, Garcia and Siboni. But alas! this season of glory was short-lived; in the following year, 1816, Signorina Colbran's voice began to show signs of wear, and soon it became an unparalleled piece of good luck to hear her get through an aria without disaster. Even when she did sing in tune, the lurking awareness that she might at any moment go wrong was enough to kill all the delight which one might otherwise have gathered from her singing—so true it is that, even in music, an instant of pleasure can only be truly consummated while the critical faculties are lulled into silence. In France, this major truth will never be understood; for the Frenchman will never forsake his belief that the spirit of criticism is the only fitting spirit in which to approach the Temple of the Arts.

We used to wait eagerly, until the critical moment arrived when Signorina Colbran was to embark upon her opening bars; then if we found that she was firmly resolved to sing out of key, we likewise took a firm resolve, and chatted away ostentatiously among ourselves until it was all over, or else escaped outside into a coffee-house and ate ices. After a few months of these and similar excursions, the audience began to grow bored with the whole thing, gave up the pretence of deluding itself that poor Signorina Colbran was all she had been in her younger days, and waited expectantly for the management to get rid of her. Nothing happened. Naturally, there was a little grumbling—and this was the point at which the fatal "protection", of which la Colbran enjoyed the privilege, began to show itself in its true colours: the harshest of tyrants robbing a whole nation, not only of its favourite delight, but also of the notable wonder which had been its traditional source of pride and self-esteem before all other peoples. The public found a thousand different outlets for the deep-felt protests of its exasperation; but notwithstanding, the unlimited powers of despotism proceeded with their dark machinations, and iron fingers throttled the indignation of the most clamorous people on earth into sudden silence. This one act of favouritism on the part of the King towards his beloved Barbaja earned him a greater measure of unpopularity than the accumulated insults and arbitrary injustices of an entire reign, heaped without restraint by the scornful hand of tyranny upon a race which will need to live and struggle for another century at least, before it grows fit to assume the vast responsibilities of freedom.

In the year 1820, one thing alone would have made the Neapolitans happy; not the gift of a Spanish constitution, but the elimination of Signorina Colbran!

Rossini himself took the greatest care not to meddle in Barbaja's intrigues; moreover, the Neapolitans very soon realized that no man in Italy could have been less tempted by his natural inclinations to involve himself in machinations of this character, nor more deficient in the powers of concentration and foresight which they require. Nevertheless, since Rossini had come to Naples under contract to Signor Barbaja, and since, on top of this, he was known to be in love with la Colbran, it was almost inevitable that the people of Naples should occasionally make him suffer in revenge for the humiliations heaped upon them. Thus it came about that his Neapolitan audiences, who were always the first to be swept off their feet by his genius, were at the same time always the first to insult him with their disapproval. He on the other hand, no longer able to rely upon la Colbran's voice, plunged deeper and deeper into German-style harmony, and, more especially, retreated ever further from the *true art of dramatic expression*. Moreover, Signorina Colbran used to plague him incessantly to decorate his arias with the type of embellishment to which her voice was accustomed.

One can now understand by what fatal chain of circumstances it came about, that poor Rossini sometimes seems to exude a faint aroma of *pedantry*. He is a great poet—a great *comic* poet—forced against his will and judgment into the paths of *erudition*, and obliged to display this erudition over sombre and serious matters. Imagine a Voltaire who, to earn a living, was compelled to write a *History of the Jews* in the style and manner of Bossuet!

Yet, even if Rossini has sometimes plunged into the depths of *Teutonism**, his Teutonism somehow contrives to remain genial and sparkling with life.[1]

After the production of *Elisabetta*, Rossini made a hasty journey to Rome, where, in the same Carnival season (1816), he composed *Torvaldo e Dorliska* and *il Barbiere*; after which, he came back to Naples, and produced *la Gazzetta*, an insignificant little *opera buffa*, which succeeded only moderately, and immediately afterwards, *Otello*, at the *teatro del Fondo*. After *Otello*, he returned to Rome for *la Cenerentola*, and squeezed in an extra journey to Milan for *la Gazza ladra*. Finally, he returned once more to Naples, and there, almost before he had had time to settle, produced *Armida*.

In spite of the superb duet which it contains, *Armida* was a comparative failure, since, at the *première*, the audience chose to take their revenge upon the composer for the vocal shortcomings of Signorina Colbran. Acutely disturbed by the coldness of his reception, Rossini determined to work out a formula for success which should leave him independent of the handicap of Signorina Colbran's voice; and so, following the example already set by the German school, he proceeded to exploit ever more fully the resources of his orchestra, gradually transforming accessory into principal. The failure of *Armida* was splendidly redeemed by the triumph of *Mosè in Egitto*, which enjoyed a prodigious success. But from this point onwards, Rossini's artistic vision tends to grow progressively more distorted. He had already written twenty operas, and it was no longer any too easy to invent a really original *cantilena*; but he could—and still can—produce light and witty harmonic patterns without so much as an instant's thought. And so laziness became the accessory of necessity; and between them, they conspired to drive him out into the harsh wilderness of Germanic music. *Mosè in Egitto* was followed immediately by *Ricciardo e Zoraide*, *Ermione*, *la Donna del Lago* and *Maometto II*. Every one of these operas

---

[1] I offer my apologies to the German people for having referred so disrespectfully to their opera; my only excuse is my *sincerity*. In all other respects, the esteem which I profess for the race which could produce a *Martin Luther* is beyond doubt or question. Moreover, Germans may take consolation from the fact that I am none too generous towards the music of my own country, even at the risk of appearing unpatriotic.

received a triumphant ovation, with the solitary exception of *Ermione*, which was an experiment, Rossini having decided to imitate the declamatory style* which Gluck had popularized in France. But music which has no immediate sensual appeal to the ear is doomed to half-hearted appreciation among the Neapolitans. Besides, in *Ermione*, the *dramatis personae* spent every instant they were given on the stage in losing their tempers with each other, with the result that the entire opera was fixed in one obstinate mood of anger, which in the end proved very monotonous. *Anger*, as thematic material for music, is valid only as a contrast to something else. There is an axiom current among the *dilettanti* of Naples, to the effect that, in opera, the raging outbursts of some bad-tempered Tutor should always be used to set off the tender aria of the pretty young ward!

In the last group of operas referred to above, Rossini had an additional resource to draw upon in the superb contralto of Signorina Pisaroni, who was incontestably a performer of the very highest quality.

The male voices which he had at his disposal during this period were those of Garcia, the younger Davide and Nozzari, all three being tenors. Davide is still the finest tenor of his whole generation; his technical ability is merely the foundation of something like true genius, which gives him a quite incredible fertility in the art of improvization, but which sometimes leads him badly astray. Garcia is remarkable for the astonishingly *assured* quality of his singing; Nozzari, finally, in spite of having been endowed by nature with the least perfect voice of the three, has nevertheless proved to be one of the finest singers in Europe.

CHAPTER XV

Torvaldo e Dorliska

Aꜰᴛᴇʀ the brilliant success of his *Elisabetta*, Rossini was invited to spend the Carnival season of the year 1816 in Rome, where he wrote two works: for the *teatro Valle*, a poorish *opera semi-seria* entitled *Torvaldo e Dorliska*; and for the *teatro Argentina*, his masterpiece, *il Barbiere di Siviglia*. The former of these two, *Torvaldo*, was composed expressly for Galli and Remorini, the two most renowned *bassi* in Italy at that time (1816), when Lablache and Zucchelli were still almost unknown. His tenor was Domenico Donzelli, then at the height of his powers, and especially remarkable for the *fire* which he could instil into his singing.

There is one passionate outburst in Dorliska's great aria

> *Ah! Torvaldo!*
> *Dove sei!*

which, if it is sung with a more than ordinary degree of zest and attack, invariably creates a very remarkable impression. But the remainder of this aria, together with a trio between the tyrant, the lover, and a farcical porter,

> *Ah! qual raggio di speranza!*

or, one might rather say, together with the opera as a whole, while it would make the reputation of any normal composer, adds nothing whatsoever to that of Rossini. One might perhaps compare it with some *bad* novel by Walter Scott, the only figure whose European reputation is as vast and as undisputed as that of *il Pesarese*. To be sure, if some unknown were to have written *the Pirate* or *the Abbot*, this feat alone would have set him high above the common level of ordinary scribblers. But the feature which distinguishes the *real* master is the sweeping audacity of his design, the brave impatience revealed in his contempt for niggling detail, the grandiose touches which characterize his creative vision; he knows how to husband his reader's attention, shielding it lovingly against the danger of vain distractions, only to hurl it with greater impetus upon the traces of what is really essential. Walter Scott will cheerfully use the same word three times running in a single sentence, just as unscrupulously as Rossini will give the same passage in three separate repeats, once on the clarinets, once on the violins and once on the oboes.

The merest sketch by Correggio, in my own personal opinion, is preferable to the most laborious, the most detailed painting by Charles Lebrun or by such another of our "grand-manner" painters!

Torvaldo e Dorliska, which, to judge by the unmitigated idiocy of the *libretto* (whose style, apparently, is intended to achieve *sublime eloquence*!) and by the total dearth of originality and individuality in the characterization, suggests a translation of some Boulevard melodrama, none the less contains one superb *agitato* passage, sung by the tyrant, and based on one of the finest melodies which a true *basso* could wish for; consequently Galli and Lablache rarely omit it from their respective concert *repertoires*. To console the reader who may never have heard it, I would add that this aria is nothing other than an earlier version of the famous *Letter-Duet* in the second act of *Otello*:

Non m'inganno, al mio rivale ...

CHAPTER XVI

Il Barbiere di Siviglia*

WHEN Rossini arrived in Rome, he found the *impresario* of the *teatro Argentina* desperately pestered by the police, who were relentlessly censuring every *libretto* which he thought of using on the grounds that it contained "allusions". Of course, if you are dealing with a race which is at once dissatisfied and witty, everything soon becomes an "allusion".[1] In a fit of exasperation, the *impresario* suggested to the Governor of Rome that he might be allowed to use the *Barber of Seville*, a pretty little *libretto* which, unfortunately, had already been used by Paisiello. The Governor, who happened on that particular day to be bored to tears with the very mention of *morals* and *decency*, agreed. His consent, however, plunged Rossini into the most disturbingly embarrassing position, for he was far too intelligent not to be genuinely modest when confronted by real merit. He wrote off hastily to Paisiello, who was then living in Naples; and the ageing *maestro*, who was not entirely devoid of a somewhat spiteful humour and who, besides, was mortally jealous of the success of *Elisabetta*, wrote him a most polite reply, expressing his sincere approval of the aesthetic taste exhibited by the Papal police. There can be no doubt that Paisiello was counting upon a resounding and catastrophic flop*!

Rossini wrote an extremely modest little note of explanation* to be prefaced to the *libretto*, exhibited Paisiello's letter to all the *dilettanti* in Rome, and settled down to work. In thirteen days*, the music of

---

[1] When the police declare war on ideologies, the inevitable outcome is a kind of burlesque melodrama. In this very year, 1823, Talma has been refused permission to perform *Tibère*, a tragedy by Chénier (who died ten years ago!), "for fear of allusions". Allusions *to whom*, may one enquire? (particularly on the part of a poet who died in 1812, and who abominated Napoleon!)

Just recently, in Vienna, Caraffa's charming opera *Abufar* was "suspended", for fear lest it "incite the population to illicit love". But, to begin with, there is no "illicit love" in the plot, since Farhan is not Salema's brother; and further, would to God that nothing worse than *emotion* could corrupt the light ladies of Vienna! I sadly fear, however, that it is not *love* which is such a menace to their virtue, but the temptation of *shawls** and such other tangible inducements!

the *Barber* was ready. Rossini had imagined himself to be writing for a *Roman* audience; but it turned out in the end that what he had created was to be the greatest masterpiece of *French* music*, if by this term one may understand music which reflects the character of the people of France as they are to-day, and which is so conceived as to afford them the greatest pleasure imaginable, in so far as the general characteristics of the race as a whole have not been altered out of all recognition by a generation of civil war.

The artists whom Rossini had at his disposal were Madame Giorgi* for the part of Rosina, and Garcia for that of Almaviva; while Zamboni was to play Figaro, and Botticelli was to be the first Dr Bartolo. The *première* took place at the *teatro Argentina* on the 26th of December 1816*, which is in fact the day when the *stagione* of the Carnival begins in Italy.

The Roman audience found the opening scenes of the opera boring, and greatly inferior to Paisiello's version. They were disappointed not to find the naïve and inimitable graces of that composer, nor his style, which is a miracle of simplicity. Rosina's aria:

Sono docile . . . [1]

struck the listeners at first as being out of character, and the young *maestro* was accused of having transformed an *ingénue* into a virago. The opera to some extent recovered from this disastrous beginning with the duet between Rosina and Figaro, which, with all its exquisite lightness of touch, is a triumphant display of Rossini's style at its best; and the aria of *la Calunnia* was averred to be both magnificent and original (in 1816, Rome had not yet learned to appreciate Mozart).

But after don Basilio's great aria, the absence of the naïve and somewhat excessive graces which had become associated with the opera through Paisiello bred a rapidly-mounting sense of disappointment, until, finally exasperated by the trivia at the beginning of Act II, and deeply offended by the lack of dramatic expression, the audience

[1] *Rosina:*
> Io sono docile—son rispettosa,
> Sono obbediente—dolce, amorosa;
> Mi lascio reggere—mi fo guidar.
> Ma se mi toccano—dov'è il mio debole,
> Sarò una vipera—e cento trappole
> Prima di cedere—farò giocar.
> (Act I, sc. ix)

forced the management to bring down the curtain. By this gesture, the Roman public, which is so inordinately proud of its musical connoisseurship, committed an act of intolerance which, as so often happens, turned out later to be (as well) an act of singular stupidity. For, on the following evening, at the very next performance, the *Barber* achieved a resounding triumph; the audience *this* time being pleased to observe that, if Rossini was deficient in some of the virtues of Paisiello, he was also completely deficient in the *dullness* which too often afflicts the latter's style—a perilous defect, which comes near to ruining many of the works, both of Paisiello and of Guido Reni, who, in their different media, share many characteristics in common. During the twenty or thirty years which had passed since the hey-day of the older *maestro*, Roman audiences had to some extent forsaken the habit of using the opera-house as a kind of club and general centre for conversation; consequently, it suddenly dawned upon them that the everlasting recitatives which, in the average opera composed around 1780, stand like barriers separating the purely musical passages from each other, were singularly *tedious*. It was as though our own race of playgoers, some thirty years hence, might suddenly find itself flatly unable to understand the purpose of those eternally-dragging intervals which customarily divide up the acts of a tragedy in any modern performance, for the simple reason that, in due course, somebody is bound to devise a means of keeping the audience *entertained* during these periods, whether it be with organ-music (on two or three different keyboards, either in concert, or in dialogue), or else with demonstrations and scientific experiments in physics, or else simply with a little mild gambling. To whatever degree of perfection *we* may have brought the arts in general, we must be resigned to the fact that our heirs and successors will certainly have the impertinence to invent something of their own!

The overture to the *Barber* caused great amusement in Rome; the audience heard—or rather, *imagined* that it heard—a musical dialogue compounded of all the threats and bluster of the elderly, jealous and enamoured guardian, and all the plaintive sighs of his pretty ward. The miniature trio:

Zitti, zitti, piano, piano[1]

[1] *Rosina, Almaviva, Figaro:*
Zitti, zitti, piano, piano,

of the second act became phenomenally popular. "But," remonstrated the party hostile to Rossini, "it is indeed *miniature* music; granted that it is pleasant and tinkling—but it doesn't *express* anything. Rosina discovers that her Almaviva is faithful and loving, instead of the scoundrel whom she had had portrayed to her, and what happens? She knows no better way of expressing her thrilled astonishment and delight than through a set of silly little roulades:

> *Di sorpresa e di contento*
> *Son vicina a delirar . . .*[1]

Yet the fact is, that these same roulades, which seem so curiously misplaced in such a context, and which all but killed the opera in Rome, even at the second performance, have become desperately popular in Paris; Paris, as usual, prefers pretty compliments to true love. Incidentally, the *Barber*, with its easy and attractive music, and in particular, with its plain, accessible *libretto*, marks the turning-point in the conversion of many people to Rossini's operatic style. It was first performed in Paris on the 23rd of September 1819*; but the routing of the pedants, who had rallied round Paisiello as round one who possessed the genuine authority of an *ancient*, dates only from January 1820.[2] I have no doubt that there will always be some sophisticated persons to reproach me with wasting time over the repetition of useless platitudes, but I must beg them to re-read some of the newspapers of that time (and even some of to-day's, for all that public taste and musical discernment have made tremendous advances during the last four years); I can promise that they will unearth more than one palpable absurdity!

The whole art of operatic music, in fact, has likewise made immense progress since Paisiello's day; it has rid the stage of the intolerable, interminable recitatives which burdened the style of the earlier epoch;

> Non facciamo confusione;
> Per la scala del balcone
> Presto andiamo via di qua.
> (Act II, sc. xi)

[1] *Rosina (stupefatta, con gioia):*
> Ah! qual colpo inaspettato!
> Egli stesso? o Ciel, che sento?
> Di sorpresa e di contento
> Son vicina a delirar.
> (Act II, sc. xi)

[2] *Vide: la Renommée*, a "liberal" journal of the period.

and it has learned the essential secret of mastering the *ensemble*. "It is absurd," maintain certain poor, passionless, *blunt-minded* creatures, "for five or six people to sing all at once". Agreed. It is supremely absurd for even *two* people to sing at once; for when does it ever occur that two people, even supposing them to be dominated by the most violent of passions, should go on speaking simultaneously for any length of time? Rather the opposite, if anything; the more extreme the passion, the greater the attention we should normally pay to the protests of that antagonist, whose conversion to our own point of view appears to be a matter of such dire consequence. This observation holds good, for instance, even of the poor Indian savages,[1] or of the heathen Turks; yet nothing is further from their minds than any longing to be thought intelligent or sophisticated. Is not this an admirably logical argument? Could anything be more reasonable? And yet experience proves it false from top to bottom. In practice, there is nothing more delightful than a duet. Therefore, O poor but well-meaning literary critics, you who are so busy applying your invincible critical dialectic to arts in respect of which you are all as blind as bats, run away and write us a thesis or two to prove that Cicero is a riot of innocent merriment, or else to demonstrate that M. Scoppa has eventually discovered the only true rhythm of the French language, and learned the ultimate secrets of the art of writing poetry!

It is precisely the mounting excitement, the *crescendo*, of these ensembles, which dissipates the boredom of those poor, unfortunate, *right-thinking* people, whom fashion, pitiless and implacable as ever, has hounded into the *Théâtre Louvois*,[2] and prods them into some semblance of wakefulness.

Rossini, who was full well aware that, in writing the *Barber*, he was deliberately challenging one of the most noble figures in the whole history of music, had the good sense (whether by luck or by sound reasoning) to be pre-eminently *himself*.

Should we ever feel ourselves beset by the urge—which might or

[1] *Vide: Mœurs et Coutumes des Nations Indiennes*, translated from the English original (by John Heckewelder) into French by M. du Poncet.

[2] *The German, who lives by theories, treats music as material for erudition; the sensual Italian turns to it in search of pleasure, violent but yet ephemeral; the Frenchman, ever vain rather than impressionable, may on occasions succeed in exploiting it as a subject of witty conversation; whereas the Englishman simply pays his money down, and takes good care to have nothing further to do with it!* (from *Raison, Folie*, vol. I, p. 230).

might not, ultimately, contribute to our deeper appreciation—to pry rather more curiously into the intimacies of Rossini's style, the *Barber* is the place where we should seek. In this opera, one of the most notable characteristics of his style stands revealed with merciless clarity; for Rossini, who is so completely the master of the finale, the ensemble and the duet, becomes merely insipid and pretty-pretty in those arias which seek to combine *passion* with *simplicity*. *Il canto spianato*—here we have the *real* stumbling-block!

The Roman audiences used to maintain that, if Cimarosa had composed the music of the *Barber*, it might have suffered slightly in brilliance and *verve*, but it would have stood to gain most decidedly in comic atmosphere, and even more markedly in dramatic expression. And yet . . . suppose you had enlisted with the colours, and trekked half-way about the world; and then, one strange and unexpected day, had come back at last to the little German spa of Baden. And there, as fate decrees, suppose that you were suddenly to rediscover a charming long-lost mistress whom, a year or two earlier, in Dresden perhaps, or maybe in Bayreuth, you had adored with undying passion. Imagine the first instant of that reunion—its tender joys, its inexpressible delight! But the days go by; and three days, four days later, there seems to steal upon you a *surfeit* of kisses and caresses, a strange satiety of bliss. The unbounded adoration and devotion, the very sweetness and charm of this delightful German lady seem to fill you with a vague and languorous regret, which you may hesitate to acknowledge even to yourself—regret for the excitement of a creature from the South, for the whims and caprices, the tempestuous disdains and unpredictable humours of a woman whose veins are burning with the sun of Italy. This, precisely, is the reaction which I myself have recently experienced, listening to the admirable music of *il Matrimonio segreto*, when it was revived the other day in Paris, for the benefit of Mademoiselle Démery. Rossini, as I left the theatre after the first night of the revival, had shrunk in my imagination to the dimensions of a pygmy. Yet I remember saying to myself at the time: I must not judge too hastily; I must not formulate any rash and sweeping verdicts, for I am still under the spell. Yesterday (19th August 1823), as I came away from the fourth performance of *il Matrimonio*, I found myself staring hard at the immense obelisk which stands outside the theatre—and that obelisk had grown into the symbol of Rossini's glory and musical stature. The

feature which makes the second act of Cimarosa's opera almost un-
bearably insipid to our ears is its lack of *dissonance*. There is despair,
there is tragedy—but they are vignettes, insipid as icing-sugar. We
have learned a great deal about tragedy since 1793.[1] The great quartet
from Act I, for instance,

Che tristo silenzio![2]

seems merely wearisome; in a word, Cimarosa is more prolific in
musical ideas than Rossini, and his ideas are better, more original and
imaginative; but Rossini is the greater *stylist*.

In the realm of love, it is the thrilling, unpredictable temperament
of Italy and the South whose absence dulls the delight of soft German
caresses; in the theatre of music, by some contrary freak of fortune, it is
the thrilling dissonance of German enharmonic modulation whose
absence dulls the sweet, caressing graces of Italian melody. Think for
an instant of the passage:

Ti maledico . . .[3]

from the first act of *Otello*; and then recall *il Matrimonio segreto*, and in
particular the scene where old Geronimo, the merchant, his head
stuffed with wild dreams of some aristocratic alliance, discovers that
his daughter Carolina has secretly married a clerk. The great defect of
Cimarosa's music in this passage, I feel, is the *lack* of some hint of
harshness, the absence of Rossini's stirring discords.

Like the Astrologer in La Fontaine's fable, who gazed so fixedly at
the stars that he fell down a well, I am constantly in danger of falling
into errors of fact; and knowing this, I submitted this chapter to a
certain knowledgeable *dilettante* of my acquaintance, so that he might
discover and correct any slips which might have crept into the text.
His chief comment, however, was simply: "Is *this* what you call giving

---

[1] *Il Matrimonio segreto* was first performed in Vienna in 1793. The Emperor
Joseph was so impressed that he commanded a second (private) performance the
very same evening.

[2] *Carolina, Fidalma, Elisetta, the Count:*
Che tristo silenzio!
Così non va bene,
Parlare conviene,
Parlare si de'!

(Act I, sc. xvi)

[3] *Otello*, Act I, sc. xi. See below, p. 227.

an analysis of the *Barber*? I can't find anything here but froth and padding, like whipped cream on the top of a trifle. What do you expect me to be able to get hold of, in all this maze of words? Come, settle down to work properly, open the score, and let me play the principal themes for you; while you, Sir, proceed with your promised analysis, step by step, in dense and closely-reasoned argument!"

ACT ONE

The chorus of serenaders, which forms the *introduction* to the opera, leaves one with the unmistakable impression that one is watching Rossini about to engage in single combat with Paisiello; there is grace, there is sweetness, but there is also a great lack of simplicity. Count Almaviva's aria is platitudinous and empty;* his love belongs to the seventeen-nineties, to the days of the powdered *galants* who bowed themselves in and out of the salons of Paris. By contrast, however, everything that is genuinely Rossinian bursts out in a glorious blaze in the chorus:

Mille grazie, mio signore![1]

and the opening liveliness quickly works up into a *crescendo* of real *verve* and *brio*—a transmutation which Rossini does not always succeed in bringing off. In this passage, his soul seems to have flared up into a kind of brilliant bonfire, touched off by the sparks of his own wit. At the sound of Figaro's approaching footsteps, the Count retreats into the distance, remarking as he goes off:

Già l'alba appare e amor non si vergogna

—a comment which is beautifully and typically Italian! All things, claims Almaviva, are permitted to the lover; even though we, the audience, know well enough that *love*, in the eyes of the impartial observer, may seem nothing so much as a convenient excuse to cover a multitude of sins. But in the cold North, love is timid and hesitant, to the victims and to the indifferent spectators alike.

Figaro's *cavatina*:

Largo al factotum . . .

[1] The text and story of the *Barber* are so well known, that it seems unnecessary to set Stendhal's quotations in their dramatic context. (*Trans.*)

(especially as it was sung by Pellegrini), is, and will remain for many a day, the perfect masterpiece of music for *French* ears. What a fortune of wit, fire and delicacy in the passage:

> *Per un barbiere di qualità . . .!*

what a wealth of expressiveness in the phrase:

> *Colla donnetta . . .*
> *Col cavaliere . . .!*

In Paris, this song was greeted with rapturous applause, when it might easily have met with vociferous disapproval, on account of the some-what spicy innuendoes in the *libretto*. I am not aware that Préville's interpretation of the part of Figaro differed essentially from that of Pellegrini. In the first act, this inimitable comedian managed to convey all the gracefulness, all the sleekness, all the cautious and mischievous agility of a kitten; and later, in the scene where Figaro tricks his way into Bartolo's house, his expression alone would have tempted a judge to hang him on the spot. I would dearly love to see the part performed on the straight stage of the *Théâtre Français* as well as it was played by Pellegrini. It is one of the pet maxims of our highly-respected literary critics, that the members of any *operatic* company performing at the *Louvois* should be written off as a set of provincial clowns, utterly incapable of the most elementary notions of dramatic verisimilitude or expression, and from whom, logically, it would be sheer impertinence to expect anything of interest or permanent value. Only yesterday, I heard someone expounding this theory. A supercilious gentleman with his hair trimmed *à l'ancienne*, was explaining it all most meticu-lously to a couple of wretched young ladies, who were all nods and dutiful agreement—and *that*, actually inside the theatre which had just witnessed Act II of *la Gazza ladra* acted by Galli, not to mention Madame Pasta as Romeo, Desdemona, Medea and in countless other parts.

Should we not ourselves begin to look as absurd as our own worthy pedants, if we undertook to argue with them? True pathos, it is asserted, dwells nowhere save on the boards of the *Théâtre Français*; therefore, I beg you, go there and watch a performance of *Iphigénie en Aulide*, from which, I suppose, you will learn to discover all the gems of that abominable ranting tradition, which in fact wants nothing but an *obbligato* on the double-bass to transmute it into a bit of fourth-rate Gluck!*

The plot of the balcony-scene in the *Barber* is ideal, as far as opera is concerned; and the dialogue is unrivalled in its graceful simplicity and tenderness. But Rossini hurries over it in his urgent haste to arrive at the magnificent *buffo* duet which follows:

> *All' idea di quel metallo* . . .

The opening bars give us an impeccable character-sketch of Figaro's belief in the irresistible powers of gold; on the other hand, the Count's exhortation,

> *Sù, vediam di quel metallo* . . .

is beautifully and realistically evocative of the young aristocrat who is not so preoccupied by love that he cannot derive some passing amusement from Figaro, and from the greed of the lower orders in general at the sight of gold.

I have commented elsewhere upon the admirable rapidity of the dialogue:

> *Oggi arriva un reggimento* . . .
> —*Sì, è mio amico il colonnello.*

This passage seems to me to be, of its kind, the best thing that Rossini has ever done, and consequently the best thing that has ever been done in the entire history of music. However, there is an unfortunate hint of vulgarity in

> *Che invenzione prelibata!*

but, by contrast, the following passage from the Count's drunken-scene is a model of true comic dialogue:

> *Perchè d'un ch'è poco in se,*
> *Che dal vino casca già,*
> *Il tutor, credete a me,*
> *Il tutor si fiderà*

I have always particularly admired the quality of assuredness in Garcia's singing when he reaches the passage:

> *Vado . . . oh, il meglio mi scordavo . . .,*

which necessitates a change of key executed far upstage, where the orchestra cannot be heard properly—a feat of the greatest technical difficulty.

To my mind, the latter part of this duet, from the words

La bottega? non si sbaglia . . .

to the end, is beyond all possible praise. This is the duet which is fated to sound the death-knell of French *grand opera*; and surely it must be agreed that never did a weightier antagonist fall prostrate before a lighter assailant! What did it avail that the great Paris *Opéra* should have been deafening persons of taste with intolerable nonsense for a solid hundred-and-fifty years—in fact ever since the days of La Bruyère? Yet it had held out valiantly against the reforming zeal of half a hundred different ministries! Only one conspirator was strong enough to deal it a final death-blow and that, when at last it did appear upon the scene, was a true school of music destined for the ears of the French nation. In this respect, the most notable "assassins", after Rossini himself, have been MM. Massimino, Choron and Castil-Blaze.

It would not surprise me in the least if, driven to desperation, the partisans of our *grand opera* should manage to have *opera buffa* shut down altogether; its cause is already partially betrayed—witness the scandalous manner in which Cimarosa's *gli Orazi e Curiazi* has recently been revived!

Rosina's *cavatina*:

Una voce poco fa . . .

is delicious; she herself is gay and lively, but rather too cock-sure. There is a good deal of unnecessary self-assertiveness in the song of this innocent young ward, and a good deal too little love. Possessed of so much intrepidity, how can she fail to outwit her wretched guardian?

The paean of victory to the words:

Lindoro mio sarà
. . . .
Una vipera sarò

is a potential triumph for a really fine voice. Madame Fodor sang it so exquisitely as to be, in my humble opinion, perfect. Her magnificent singing sometimes holds a note of harshness (French style!); but a little harshness is not wholly out of place in the utterances of so resolute a young lady. Although, personally, I feel that such a tone is a calumny against nature, nevertheless it furnishes yet another proof of the infinite distance which separates the yielding, soft and melancholy love of those Teutonic beauties whom one may meet walking in the ornamental parks beside the Elbe, from the temperamental and domineering passions which burn like fire in maiden breasts from the further south of Italy.[1]

The celebrated "calumny" aria,

La calunnia è un venticello . . .

inspires me with the same reflections as the famous duet from the second act of *la Cenerentola*,

Un segreto d'importanza . . .[2]

I have already made bold enough to suggest that, without Cimarosa and his duet for two bass voices in *il Matrimonio segreto*, we should never have had the *Cinderella* duet; I am now going to defy the imputation of paradox for the second time. The aria known as *la Calunnia* seems to me to be nothing less than a blatant borrowing from Mozart, made by a man of considerable intelligence who is himself a competent composer. The aria itself is too long within its particular dramatic context; on the other hand, it provides an admirable contrast to the frothiness of everything immediately preceding it—the sort of contrast which is missing, for instance, in *il Matrimonio segreto*. In Milan, at *la Scala*, this aria was beautifully performed by M. Levasseur, who achieved a great personal triumph through his interpretation of it. Unfortunately, this artist, although French by birth, and the star pupil of the *Conservatoire*, failed lamentably when he appeared at the *Théâtre Louvois*; he sings without assurance, and in consequence the only impression which he manages to convey across the footlights is a sense of acute anxiety lest he should hit the wrong note! It was Voltaire who remarked that success in any of the arts, but above all in the theatre, depends upon owning the temperament of a man possessed.

[1] *Cf.* the sketch of the various love-affairs of la Zitella Borghese, as presented by the Président de Brosses in his *Lettres sur l'Italie* (vol. II, p. 250):

Et sequitur leviter
Filia matris ier.

[2] See below, p. 258.

Messrs Meyerbeer, Morlacchi, Paccini, Mercadante, Mosca, Mayr, Spontini, and many others among Rossini's contemporaries, would doubtless ask nothing better than to be able to imitate Mozart; yet not one of them, in all the scores which Mozart ever left, has managed to discover an aria as fine as *la Calunnia*. Without necessarily claiming to set Rossini on the same scale of genius as Raphael, I might mention that it was in the same spirit that Raphael imitated Michelangelo in the magnificent "Prophet Isaiah" fresco which is to be seen in the church of Sant' Agostino, in the piazza Navone, in Rome.

There is nothing in the whole score of *il Matrimonio segreto* as powerful (in its own gloomy style) as

E il meschino calunniato . . .

In the duet:

Dunque io son . . . tu non m'inganni?

we are offered the portrait, *not* of a girl of eighteen, but rather of some good-looking woman, perhaps twenty-six years of age, ardent in temperament and more than a little inclined to flirtation, debating with a confidant upon the ways and means to grant an assignation to a man who has caught her fancy. I refuse to believe that, even in Rome, the love of such a creature as Rosina should be so utterly devoid of the slightest suggestion of melancholy, or even, I might dare to add, of certain finer shades of fastidiousness and hesitation.

The phrase:

Lo sapevo pria di te . . .

musically speaking embodies a conception which, north of the Alps, might seem out of character. In my own opinion, Rossini made a decided mistake in thus allowing a chance of graceful and charming invention to slip through his fingers; even the most passionate of loves cannot thrive without a touch of modesty, and to strip it of this essential element is to fall into the vulgar error, common to sensual and unrefined persons in every land, of thinking all women alike. I admit that, when one has already some sixteen operas upon one's conscience, the search for originality may tend to become an obsession: that fine old man, the great dramatist Corneille, confessed to a similar obsession in his *Examen de Nicomède*; but I do not believe that this is the true explanation of the curious *tastelessness* which Rossini seems to have exhibited in this aria. While he was in Rome, and more particularly, while he was actually in the throes of composition, working on the scores of *Torvaldo* and *il Barbiere*, he had some curious personal experiences, much more nearly in the style of *Faublas* than in that of Petrarch. Subconsciously, and in direct consequence of that abnormally developed impressionability which is characteristic of the true artist in any medium, the women he depicted were the women who happened to be attracted to him at the moment—women to whom, perhaps, he himself might not be wholly indifferent. Without realizing it in the least, the arias which he composed at three o'clock in the morning would tend, as it were, to be fashioned to the taste of the company he had kept during the rest of the evening, and to echo the brazen laughter of a kind of women in whose opinion, without question, modesty and fastidiousness would have appeared as ridiculous as the crude ignorance *di un collegiale*.

Some of Rossini's most incredible and flattering successes are directly attributable to his own abnormal coldness and indifference. The *Barber* itself, together with several of the operas written at a later date, arouses my suspicions by its very popularity; for (dare I suggest it?) Rossini seems to owe his unparalleled success largely to his fundamental inability to draw any fine distinction between one woman and another. I am half-afraid that his personal conquests among certain distinguished ladies of Rome may have stifled in his soul the last spark of genuine susceptibility, the ultimate awareness of true feminine grace. In the *Barber*, wherever the scene requires a note of natural and profound emotion, Rossini offers us instead *preciosity*, or *elegance*, with never a hint of weakening self-control; his lovers seem to speak the language of Fontenelle. Such mannerisms are doubtless invaluable in the practical context of real life; but they contribute nothing to the glory of genius. In my opinion, there is far more *verve* and passionate unconstraint in Rossini's earlier works: compare *la Pietra del Paragone*, *Demetrio e Polibio* or *Aureliano in Palmira* with the *Barber*. I diagnose a slight attack of *scepticism* in sentimental matters—which, for a young man of four-and-twenty, represents no small advance along the hard road to philosophy and worldly wisdom. Rossini's peace of mind will benefit, unquestionably, from this advance; but I suspect that his genius is liable to suffer proportionately. Neither Canova nor Viganò ever completely vanquished their absurd, their *ridiculous* tendency to fall in love.

Once we accept that the general tone and atmosphere of the *Barber* is to be that of a novel by Crébillon *fils*, it is impossible to imagine a more brilliant display of wit, nor of the peculiar and piquant originality which is the whole essential charm of gallantry, than that which is to be observed in

> *Sol due righe di biglietto*
>
> . . . .
>
> *Il maestro faccio a lei!*
> *Donne, donne, eterni Dei!*

This is another instance of music in the "French tradition", displayed in all its purity and with all its glittering brilliance. Two tyrannical forces, pox and party-politics, have done their worst to make us serious; yet many years have still to roll away before we shall find ourselves—in some respects at least—cleared of the old and well-established charge of *frivolity*. Our younger generation is still a hundred years behind the times, compared with Claverhouse, or Henry Morton, as they are described in Scott's *Old Mortality*. Praise heaven, France is still, and will remain for many years to come, the land where love is charming because it is empty-headed, and delicious because it is artificial. And so long as compliments and kisses continue to be symbolic of our social life and national character, the *Barber of Seville*, and in particular the duet:

> *Sol due righe di biglietto . . .*

will remain the unchanging models of French music. It is perhaps worth observing that, if we simply think of Rosina as being twenty-eight years old and a widow, like Céliante in *le Philosophe marié* or Julie in *le Dissipateur*, the tone of her love is quite above reproach. Observe further, however, that music can no more portray affectation than painting can paint masks. And observe finally, that Rossini is for ever obsessed with the fear that his musical ideas, however charming in themselves, are in the end liable to grow boring. If you compare this duet with the one which Farinelli composed* and inserted into Cimarosa's *il Matrimonio segreto*, between the Count and Elisetta (sung by Pellegrini and Signorina Cinti, the same two performers who sing the duet in the *Barber*), you cannot fail to be struck, time and again, by the number of phrases, particularly towards the end, which Rossini would have cut short, for fear lest the audience should grow bored.

In the passage:

Fortunati affetti miei!

there is a ring of genuine happiness, but it is still the happiness of a brisk young widow, and not that of a girl of eighteen. Considering this piece as a whole, we may conclude that there are very few duets indeed, even in Rossini's tragic operas, where he attained to such splendid heights of originality and dramatic expression. I should maintain on this evidence, that if Rossini had been born to an income of 50,000 *livres* a year, like his colleague, Herr Meyerbeer, he would have dedicated his genius entirely to *opera buffa*. But he had to live; further, he chanced to fall in with Signorina Colbran, who performed exclusively in *opera seria*, a *genre* which reigned unchallenged in Naples at that time; and further still, it is to be remembered that, throughout the remainder of Italy, the police administration, which is as absurd in its meticulous attention to detail as it is futile in its large-scale projects, had decreed that theatre-tickets should cost one-third *more* for *opera seria* (such as *Agnese*) than for *opera buffa* (such as the *Barber*); all of which goes to show that fools, of whatever nationality, and whether literary critics or policemen, imagine that it is easier to write comedy than to write tragedy! (Could it be that they have some dim, subconscious inkling of the rôle which they themselves play in the world, and of their own multitudinous ubiquity?) Incidentally, it was this same police-administration, established forty years ago now, by Leopold, Grand-Duke of Tuscany, which, at the very dawn of its career, and in a moment of unsurpassable inspiration, robbed Italy for ever of its magnificent indigenous theatrical tradition, the *Commedia dell' Arte*—the tradition of plays which used to be performed *impromptu*, and which Goldoni, with his bald and platitudinous dialogue, was firmly convinced that he was superseding. The last remnants of true comedy still left in Italy survive to-day in the marionette-theatres*, which, in Genoa, in Rome and in Milan, are truly excellent, and where the plays, having no written text, slip past the censor, and genuinely reflect the inspiration of the moment and the interests of the day. It seems scarcely credible that a statesman as intelligent as Cardinal Consalvi, a man blessed with talent enough to control his own sovereign to begin with, and to rule the State passably well on top of it, and who, moreover, had at one time sufficient ability to become an intimate friend of Cimarosa, could

personally devote three solid hours to censoring the *libretto* of some
wretched, third-rate *opera buffa* (historical fact, 1821)! Yet even now,
the reader can have no idea of the true and full extent of this absurdity;
for his Eminence saw fit to pick a quarrel with the word *cozzar* (to
struggle), which, he maintained, recurred too frequently within the
text! So much concern did this worthy prelate display, out of the pure
goodness of his Christian heart, for the moral welfare of the people of
Rome, and for their preservation in a state of Grace and unblemished
purity.

Further than this, I dare not set down my meaning in plain black and
white, nor even hint at it; but I appeal to all travellers who have
wintered in Rome, or who may chance to have heard, for instance,
one or two of the anecdotes which concern the advancement of Popes
Pius VI and Pius VII; *these* are fair samples of the people whose morals
are in danger of being "corrupted" by the *libretto* of an *opera buffa*! In
heaven's name! If you want to "raise the moral standard", then raise
four extra companies of *gendarmes*, pick out annually the twenty judges
who shall have proved the most corrupt, and hang them! ... *that*
would "raise the moral standard" indeed, and a thousand times more
effectively. Setting aside the whole question of robbery in broad daylight, venality in the courts, and other such rubbishy nonsense, just
consider what must happen to the morals of a state where the entire
Court and ever single civil servant is compelled by law to be, and to
remain, unmarried—in such a climate, and with such opportunities,
too! Since the shock of Voltaire's cynical onslaught, it is true, we no
longer behold any save prudent and discreet dotards raised to the office
of Cardinal; but these same venerable gentlemen have been in Holy
Orders ever since they reached the roaring age of twenty! ... not to
mention the example of the pleasures of libertinage which they most
certainly observed under their own father's roof! The wretched people
of Rome have been so firmly shaped and moulded by a few centuries
of this *régime* which I dare not describe,[1] that the very virtue of surprise
has gone from them, and they have no quality remaining to them save
their *ferocity*. Several of the bravest of Napoleon's officers came originally from Rome, and a new Julius II would still be able to recruit there
an excellent army; but two solid centuries of Napoleonic despotism

---

[1] *Vide*: Burckhardt, *Mémoires de la Cour du Pape* (in which he held the post of
major-domo); Potter, *History of the Church*; Gorani; *etc.*

would probably still be insufficient to establish in such a city a code of morals as pure as that which reigns in Nottingham, say, or Norwich, or any other little English town. But, to get back to the *Barber* … "Haven't we wandered rather a long way from it?" I can hear someone complaining. Not so far as you might think. Have you ever watched a trickle of spring-water, clearer than glass and full of curious medicinal properties, bubbling out of the ground at the foot of some tall range of mountains? Can you say by what processes, hidden deep in the heart of the mountain, it was formed? Some day, perhaps, a scientist will find the answer, and prove it by theory and experiment; but until then, I shall continue to maintain that every peculiarity of the whole range, the contours of the upper valleys, the lie of the forests, *etc.—everything*, every known material factor, may have some influence* upon the formation of that pure and refreshing spring of water, where the hunter comes to quench his thirst and finds, as by a miracle, a source of new and vigorous energy. Every government in Europe maintains its *Conservatoire*; many sovereigns are genuinely fond of music, and cheerfully fling their entire revenue upon its sacrificial altar; yet somehow, even *that* seems to be no certain guarantee that they can conjure up a singer like Davide or a composer like Rossini.

There must, therefore, exist some undetermined but essential element, deep-hidden at the very heart of life and society in the beautiful land of Italy, or among the German forests. It is considerably warmer in the *rue Lepeletier* than in Dresden or Darmstadt; why, therefore, are the inhabitants less civilized? How does it come about that any orchestra in Dresden or Reggio can execute a Rossini *crescendo* with divine perfection, whereas Paris finds it brutally impossible? And above all, how does it happen that these German and Italian orchestras understand the art of *accompanying*?[1]

Bartolo's aria:

A un dottor della mia sorte …

is finely done*. I should like to hear it sung by Zucchelli or Lablache. The only comment I have to make is one which I have probably made rather too often already concerning these arias in the style of Cimarosa;

[2] On the one hand, perhaps—love and sincerity; on the other—vanity, and unceasing attendion to others.

they have more wit, and their style is crisper; but they fall far behind their model in *verve*, passion and real comic inspiration. As I am writing this, my eye has chanced to fall on a passage in the *libretto*:

> *Ferma là, non mi toccate!*

To anyone who is familiar with Rome, its politics and way of life, this passage seems to stand out like a symbol, the very incarnation of that whole world of suspicion and mistrust, in which the Romagna, and all those other provinces which, for three centuries, have suffered under the temporal yoke of the "Church Militant",[1] exist and move and have their being; I would be ready to wager that the librettist had never lived in the gentle plains of Lombardy!

The entry of Count Almaviva disguised as a soldier, and the beginning of the first-act *finale*, are models of wit, brilliance and lightness of touch. There is a delicious contrast between the weighty self-complacency of Bartolo, with this three-fold, emphatic repetition:

> *Dottor Bartolo!*
> *Dottor Bartolo!*

and the Count's aside:

> *Ah! venisse il caro oggetto!*

This wish on the part of the young lover is charming in its sentimental artificiality. The *finale*, piquant and light as a feather, is unrivalled; this section of the score alone contains musical ideas in such profusion as to fill out a whole full-length opera of the variety which holds the stage at the *Théâtre Feydeau*. But gradually, as the action moves relentlessly onwards towards the catastrophe, the *finale* is transformed by an unmistakable undercurrent of seriousness—a mood which is already discernible in considerable measure in Figaro's warning to the Count:

> *Signor, giudizio, per carità!*

The chorus:

> *La forza,*
> *Aprite qua . . .*

is both picturesque and striking. At this point, Rossini gives us a

[1] In the Papal States, religion is the only living law. Compare Velletri or Rimini with the first Protestant state which you may happen to visit. The chill spirit of Protestantism is fatal to Art; *cf.* Geneva or Switzerland. But, after all, art is only a luxury in life; the essentials are honesty, reason and justice.

marked *pause*, an interval of silence and respite, of which the listener, after the deluge of pattering prettiness to which he has previously been subjected, stands desperately in need.

The passage for three, and subsequently for five voices, in which the characters explain to the Commandant of the Seville police what all the disturbance is about, was the only part of the whole opera which received an indisputably *bad* performance in Paris. The general musical shape of the scene is slightly reminiscent of that episode in *il Matrimonio segreto*, where everything is explained to Geronimo (end of Act I). This is the one serious criticism which may be levelled at the *Barber*; any spectator who is in the least knowledgeable about opera tends to be worried by a certain lack of originality; the impression one gathers is always that of listening to a new edition—corrected, perhaps, and stylistically more exciting, but still a *new edition*—of some score by Cimarosa which one has heard, and loved, long ago; and you know as well as I do, that nothing is so fatal, so crippling to the imagination as an appeal to memory.

The arrival of the Count, and his subsequent release, followed by the obsequious apologies on the part of the police, remind me irresistibly of the police methods which were current in Palermo a few years ago. A young Frenchman, handsome without being dandified, and at least as remarkable for his amiable disposition as for his undisputed courage, was grossly insulted in the public theatre by a man of considerable local prestige and influence—which insult he promptly avenged. The young man's friends, however, urgently warned him to be on his guard as he left the theatre; and in effect he was set upon by the Sicilian aristocrat. The Frenchman, who chanced to be an unusually skilful swordsman, managed to disarm his adversary without killing him; and, forgetting that he was not in Paris, summoned the watch. The watch had in fact witnessed the assault, and hastened to arrest the would-be assassin; but no sooner had the latter haughtily revealed his identity than the watch scattered with countless expressions of grovelling apology; another word from the assailant, and they would most obligingly have arrested the victim! This proves at least that there is nothing intrinsically improbable in this scene from the first-act *finale* of the *Barber*; but what *is* highly unlikely is the startled immobility to which Bartolo is reduced by the sight of the curious methods of justice in his own land. He should in any case have been quite accustomed to them by now; but further, it is a marked characteristic of dry and dishonest natures like his, far from letting themselves be terrorized by the arbitrary injustices of government, to exploit them deliberately in order to feather their own nests; such people are invariably born profiteers.

In my experience, Bartolo's petrified immobility, which he maintains while all the others gather about him, singing:

> *Freddo ed immobile*
> *Come una statua . . .*

unfailingly produces an unsatisfactory impression. Immediately the audience has an instant to realize that the absurdity is overdone, the laughter dries up; and this alone is sufficient to prove that the farce is badly written. The spectator must be stunned into uncritical acceptance, as he is by Molière or by Cimarosa; but this is one of the most difficult things to achieve in all the art of music. For music, by its very nature, *cannot hurry its own development*; whereas the development of the intrigues and machinations of farce, if they are to succeed at all, must move with the rapidity of lightning. Music must somehow manage to convey *directly* comic suggestions of the same order as those which, in the straight theatre, might be conveyed by the speed and sheer acting ability of a first-rate comedy.

ACT TWO

I feel that the duet between the Count (in clerical disguise) and Bartolo is slightly dragging; when a composer loses his susceptibility to passion, the danger is always the same: he may continue to be provocative and amusing, but as soon as the spark of hilarity dies down, he grows dull. There are too many repetitions of the Count's phrase:

> *Pace e gioja . . .,*

and in the end, the wretched Bartolo himself could scarcely be more exasperated than the audience. For Rosina's music-lesson, it is traditional in Italy to use the charming little aria:

> *La biondina in gondoletta . . .,*

which, unfortunately, has been sung so often by now that it has become rather hackneyed. Incidentally, while on the subject of traditional Venetian music, there are innumerable comments which I should like to make—enough to make a book within a book. Stylistically speaking, the music of the Venetians might be compared with the paintings of Parmigianino, as contrasted, for example, with the severity and restraint of a Poussin or a Domenichino; it is like a dying echo of the voluptuous paradise of sensuality which reigned in Venice around 1760. However, if I were to follow up the conclusions of this theory, checking my deductions against the evidence of examples, I should find myself committed to a major treatise on political theory.[1] Paris has had the opportunity for hearing Signora Nina Viganò*, who is the finest performer of songs in the Venetian tradition; her whole style of voice-production differs utterly from that which is normally practised in France. Yet if we were to make our music *natural*, this is the way in which we should sing, and most decidedly *not* in the style of Madame Branchu.

In a properly-organized production, Rosina would be given a different song for the music-lesson scene every two or three performances. In Paris, Madame Fodor, who, incidentally, sang the part to perfection, perhaps better than it has ever been sung before, invariably gave us the aria from *Tancredi*:

Di tanti palpiti . . .[2]

arranged as a *contre-danse*, which sent the more venerable members of the audience into positive ecstasies of delight; as soon as the tune started, you could watch every powdered wig in the whole theatre bobbing up and down in rhythm!

Rossini himself maintains that Bartolo's aria:

Quando mi sei vicina . . .

was intended to be a kind of pastiche of an older musical tradition; "and," he usually adds, "I have certainly done it justice, if not more than justice!" I would not doubt Rossini's sincerity for an instant; and indeed, it might easily pass for a quotation from Logroscino or Pergolesi —minus the passion and minus the genius. These great old masters

[1] *Vide:* Carlo Gozzi, *Mémoires*, in particular his unending controversy with Signor Cratarol; nothing could offer a more marked contrast with Giacopo Ortiz. *V.* Signora Albrizzi, *Opera*.
[2] See above, p. 57–8.

appear to Rossini rather as Dante used to appear to Metastasio and the generation of poets around 1760, when the relentless efforts of the Jesuits had half-succeeded in dimming the glory of the *Divine Comedy*.

The great quintet belonging to the scene of don Basilio's intrusion and dismissal is a considerable milestone in the whole art of musical composition. Paisiello's quintet in the same context is a masterpiece of grace and simplicity, and no one was more acutely aware than Rossini of the veneration in which it was held throughout the length and breadth of Italy. At the most recent revival of Paisiello's *Barber*, which had taken place at *la Scala* in 1814, this passage alone had been triumphantly applauded, while the remainder of the opera had been received with comparative indifference. I would strongly urge all genuine lovers of opera to arrange an actual performance of these two quintets, one after the other, within the space of a single evening; in this way, one may learn more intrinsic and fundamental truths about music in quarter of an hour than I could set out in twenty chapters. The older master's composition is designed to stress, with comic and original effect, the *unanimity* of the injunction *Go back to bed*, which is hurled at the wretched Basilio from every quarter; and it is this particular aspect of the music which provokes such a roar of laughter from the audience —a roar as rollicking and as irrepressible as the mirth of the Gods themselves. By contrast, Rossini's setting strikes a note of admirable dramatic truth, especially in the phrases:

Ehi, dottore, una parola . . .,

and in:

Siete giallo come un morto . . .,

and in:

Questa è febbre scarlatina . . . .

But observe that this note of dramatic truth is seldom—indeed scarcely ever—struck in scenes portraying deep emotion; perhaps this may even be one of the reasons for Rossini's incredible popularity. Walter Scott's novels are original and unexpected, precisely because they dispense completely with the traditional love scenes which had formed the basis of every other successful novel for two hundred years.

The conclusion of this scene, where Figaro wards off Bartolo's indignation by slashing at him with a towel, used to be played by Bassi, the renowned *buffo*, in so singular a manner that, in the end, the audience almost began to feel sorry for Rosina's ill-fated guardian, so cruelly deceived he was, and so utterly miserable.

The aria:

Il vecchiotto cerca moglie ...

which is sung by Berta, the elderly governess, is extremely witty. This is one of those arias which Rossini himself sings with extraordinary polish and comic effect. I even suspect a trace of coquettish vanity in such displays; Rossini seems to find particular pleasure in showing off a splendid aria which might otherwise have passed unnoticed, and whose worth alone would have brought fame and fortune to Morlacchi[1] or to many another among Rossin's rivals.

The storm scene towards the end of the second act of the *Barber is*, in my opinion, greatly inferior to the similar scene in *la Cenerentola*. During the storm, Count Almaviva makes his way secretly into Doctor Bartolo's house, and we see him clambering up on to the balcony. Rosina believes him to be a villain, and not without reason, since he did in fact hand her letter over to her guardian. Almaviva, falling at her feet, undeceives her; but this climax, with all that it implies in the way of emotional tension, inspires nothing more moving or profound in Rossini's imagination than another froth of roulades which, on the whole, are even more trifling than usual. On the other hand, I would stoutly maintain that the finest music in the whole opera occurs in the concluding section of this same trio, whose beginning is so tediously reminiscent of the love-scenes in *Quentin Durward*:

Zitti, zitti, piano, piano!

I naturally hesitated to make so extravagant a claim, until I learnt that, in Vienna, where the audience this season (1823) has had the rare good fortune to hear Madame Fodor, Davide and Lablache in the same cast, it has become almost traditional to insist upon an *encore* for this little number. I entertain the most lively respect for the musical taste of the

---

[1] I have before me a most curious treatise, by one Signor Majer*, of Venice, which informs us that Signor Morlacchi (di Perugia) is the greatest composer of our time. On the other hand, a certain Parisian gentleman, of some note in the world of letters, and an influential correspondent in the daily press, assures us (particularly since Rossini had the impudence to turn down his *libretto*, entitled *les Athéniennes*) that the greatest composer of our age is Signor Spontini. One eagerly awaits the oracular pronouncement of M. Berton (*de l'Institut*) on this thorny problem.

Viennese, for it is their unique triumph to have fashioned a Haydn and a Mozart. It was Metastasio, living among them for forty years, who fired the highest circles of Viennese society with so passionate a love of art; in Vienna, moreover, the nobility, which includes in its ranks some of the wealthiest and most truly "gentlemanly" aristocrats in Europe, does not disdain to furnish directors for the Opera House.*

The only fault which mars the undeniable perfection of this inspired little trio—and a trifling fault it is at that!—is that it holds up the action for an unconscionable time just at the point where the plot demands hurry and bustle. If one could only transplant it elsewhere, using it in a different setting, it would be irreproachable. It is the very incarnation of the happy ending, particularly of some charmingly stylized, artificial love-affair; it would be admirably suited to a *libretto* based on one of those infinitely fragile comedies by Lope de Vega.

If the present volume is still extant, say in 1840, I trust that the reader will hasten to throw it on the fire; remember, for instance the fate of all those political pamphlets published in 1789—how dull and flat they seem to us to-day! Yet in 1840, when the company is gathered together in the *salon* of Madame Mérilde (Mérilde is exactly ten years old now, and disarmingly pretty, and adores Rossini, but secretly likes Cimarosa better), all this stuff which I have just spent the last hour writing will seem certainly no less stale and unprofitable. The revolution in music, whose beginnings we are now witnessing, foretells the total extinction of all the good old ways and traditions which are the very essence of French taste. Shame indeed! The critical revolution which has transformed the average audience in the *Théâtre Louvois* during the course of the last four years is already positively alarming; my evidence, moreover (the sales of Messrs Paccini, Carli, *etc.*), is statistical, scientific, and therefore unimpeachable. Even by 1833, many of the ideas contained in this volume, which now seem obscure or decidedly *avant-garde*, are bound to appear platitudinous and common-place. The partisans of the old *régime* have but one last resource—to banish Italian opera from the soil of France, or else to supplant its native singers with a sprinkling of well-picked French *prime donne*. A few nice voices, whose owners have never been properly taught how to use them, would soon throttle the life out of any opera!

CHAPTER XVII

Of the Public in General, Considered in Relation to Art

In music, as in everything else, the population of France is divided into two classes, with the result that never before has there been so wide and universal a scope for the average Frenchman to exercise his natural bent for sarcasm. One class consists largely of persons over forty; and these people, who have all made fortunes in business, wear powdered wigs, admire Cicero and are regular readers of *la Quotidienne*, *etc.*, *etc.*, may talk and argue themselves hoarse before they will ever convince me that they *really* like any kind of music except music-hall ballads and ditties with a good tum-ti-tum rhythm. Such persons, whom I cherish most reverently as quaint and venerable relics of a generation which is vanishing and of a way of life which is dying out, will never in a thousand years be converted to Italian music. Before the Revolution, Paris (and by *Paris*, I mean the sovereign judge and arbiter of all art and music in France) was nothing but an immense meeting-place for the idle. I beg you, for one instant, to stop and consider the following isolated, but incalculably significant circumstance: prior to 1789, the King was *not responsible for one single appointment in all the realm.*

In the Army, posts were filled in accordance with a most strictly-observed order of seniority; and thirty years of peace had transformed every officer into a very model of idleness. In the Law, once the aspirant had bought himself his judgeship, or purchased his title of *conseiller au Parlement*, he was established, immutably, for the rest of his natural days. As soon as a young man had made his first entry into the world, or rather, as soon as he was comfortably installed in the post which his father had purchased for him, the further prospects of his profession held neither interest nor excitement, and there was nothing left for him to do in all the world but to amuse himself as best he might; his career was predestined, charted, ordained and predetermined by outside forces; the robes of the office usurped the place of the man, and decided his fate in spite of himself. The only influence which could

H

conceivably, in the rarest of instances, alter this arrangement, was the *personal favour* which a young man might conquer in high places; thus M. Caron, the watchmaker's son, become the celebrated M. de Beaumarchais; but his was a special case, for he had taught the guitar to *Mesdames de France*, the old King's daughers*.

Life in those days was spent wholly in public; in public one lived, and in public one died. But the same Frenchman who, in 1780, had forgotten how to exist outside the crowded gatherings of the *salons*,[1] now hides away in the secret depths of his own home. Yet, in a society which spent its whole waking day either talking or listening, a ready wit came naturally to rank as the foremost advantage; a young man, upon his first entry into the world, might well have no ambition to become a Marshal of France; but the temptation to become another d'Alembert was far less easily resisted.[2]

The government of that epoch was extremely tolerant, and would never have dreamed of sending journalists to prison chained in a gang of common malefactors*; such barbarous behaviour would have shaken society to its very foundations. The authority which controlled the destinies of men was an insane conglomeration of warring and incompatible elements, of scattered fragments of mediaeval customs, of feudal and military traditions in a better or worse state of preservation; and the result, in art, was the emergence of a whole series of false and thoroughly artificial standards of taste.[3] Since *enthusiasm* of any kind, that is to say, any genuine interest in anything, was growing daily rarer in occurrence, it soon ceased to be urged that a sentence should convey a *meaning* clearly or distinctly; instead, language was required to be attractive *in itself*, and every utterance had perforce to contain some quaint or original turn of phrase. Moreover, as France gradually became transformed into a nation of cynics, it was to be observed that the

[1] Nowadays, the average bachelor dines alone in a restaurant on at least three hundred evenings out of every year; whereas in 1780, he would scarcely have shown his face there twice a month. The younger generation, in those days, used to think it beneath their dignity to be seen in a *café*. Supper-parties used to take up a quarter of one's whole life; but supper-parties have now ceased to be.

[2] *Vide:* Marmontel, *Mémoires*; Morellet, *Mémoires*; Madame du Deffand, *Correspondance:* Mademoiselle de Lespinasse, *Lettres, etc.*

[3] We, in the year 1823, may call them *false* and *artificial:* but in 1780 they seemed very *real* and very *natural*. The fairest thing that one can say, is that the maximum quantity of *potential emotion* in any individual (which emotion represents the raw material of art) was extremely limited.

powers of concentration which come naturally to any man of reasonable intelligence seemed to evaporate. Battles or banquets were planned with a similar nonchalance.[1] As soon as any situation arose which required the slightest integration of rational effort, the result was catastrophic; the firework-display, for instance, which was arranged to celebrate the marriage of Louis XVI (1770), ended in murder and rioting in the Champs Élysées—yet the following evening, the *Prévôt des Marchands** who had been responsible for the "organization" was not ashamed to appear, in the full regalia of a Knight of the Order of the Holy Ghost, at the *Opéra*! And gossip made a comic catch-phrase out of the plight of the Maréchal de Richelieu, who, caught up in the riot where two thousand people were being crushed to death, could do nothing but cry out piteously: "Gentlemen! Gentlemen! Come to the rescue of a Marshal of France!"[2]

Or would you have a more recent example? Then study the security measures which were taken to safeguard the secret of Louis XVI's flight to Varennes, and the behaviour of the various people concerned. The zeal of those involved in this tragic farce is unquestioned; their incompetence, positively astounding—yet typical of a whole generation.

This same generation, though in itself elegant and frivolous, had no words of praise lyrical enough for the energetic literary manner of a Bossuet or a Montesquieu; yet the most self-opinionated admirers of these great writers would have recoiled in horror before the strong familiarity of their language, while the suggestion that they should use such a style themselves would have left them petrified with apprehension.[3] To judge by appearances, the literary world gave its preference to its Bossuets and its Montesquieus, rather than to its Delilles, its

---

[1] *Vide:* Besenval, *Mémoires* (description of the battle of Fillinghausen); also descriptions of the battles fought by the Prince de Clermont and the Prince de Soubise. *V.* also: Lauzun, *Mémoires*, with the detailed account of his American expedition.

[2] *Vide: Mémoires* of Madame du Hausset, lady-in-waiting to Madame de Pompadour; *Mémoires* of Madame Campan (particularly the section prudently suppressed by certain cautious editors).

[3] "Sulla", writes Montesquieu in his *de la Grandeur des Romains et de leur Décadence*, "knew properly what he was about when he took such a step". Yet Marmontel would never have *dared* use so plain an idiom; and even to-day our older generation of writers is no bolder. Think of the acid comments and criticisms which have been levelled at M. Courier on account of his admirable *Hérodote*— it is Herodotus, apparently, whom our learned academicians wish to save from danger!

La Harpes, its Thomas, its Dorats or its abbés Barthélemy; yet in the event it was the last-named who alone supplied it with fare dressed and spiced to its taste, and furnished it with the only pleasures which its blasé and jaded palate was still in any fit state to appreciate. In the midst of this brilliant and depraved society, of which we to-day can form no conception, nothing could have appeared more absurd, more monstrous nor more perverted than a man of simple affections, capable of sincere and genuine emotion. M. Turgot, whose devotion to the welfare of the realm was inspired by sincere and unfashionable motives precisely of this nature, needed all the protection and influence of one of the most intelligent and highly-placed women in France before he could escape blatant ridicule; and even so, in the Faubourg Saint-Germain, there is some doubt still whether he got away entirely unscathed.

In a society where any man of true feeling and emotional integrity was pursued from childhood by sarcasm and ironical taunts, I leave it to the reader's imagination to fathom what fate befell that faculty which is known as *creative imagination*.

At the first sign or stirring of originality, it was pelted with ridicule; and of necessity, therefore, it took refuge in prettiness and preciosity; yet there was worse to follow, for soon enough it found itself compelled, before venturing on the least ambitious flight of fancy, to take a surreptitious glance around the *salon*, lest its enthusiasm should present its neighbours with a heaven-sent pretext for malicious irony.

With *imagination* fallen into this state of paralysis, it needs no great powers of diagnosis to visualize what fate, in France and in the year 1770, must have overtaken the art of *music*. Its principal function was to provide a measure for dancing to at balls; its secondary rôle, to cause astonishment at the opera with its "mighty screeching", which effect was aided and abetted by the *plain, hygienic style* of French singing.[1] There was, however, one event which, insignificant as it was, yet had some indirect effect on music: namely, the arrival of a young and lovely Queen straight from Vienna. Now the Germans are a sincere people, and as such they have imagination and, consequently, music. It is to Marie-Antoinette that we owe Gluck and Piccinni, and the excellent, provocative controversies which raged between the

[1] *Vide:* Madame d'Epinay, *Mémoires* (details of the morning's occupation of M. d'Epinay).

"King's party" and the "Queen's party". These controversies* lent music weight and prominence, without, of course, making it any better understood; for, once again, to create understanding would have meant refashioning the sensibility of an entire race.

Let me now recapture the thread of my argument. In 1780, the public of Paris was a public of idlers; to-day, not only would it be extremely hard to find a score of genuine idlers in the whole hive of Parisian society, but furthermore, thanks to the spirit of partisanship which has sprung up over the past four years, we may actually be standing on the threshold of a new era of passionate enthusiasms. A change of so radical a character, obviously, would resolve the entire problem.

Out of this whole, immense maelstrom of events, whose general outline I have just been tracing, it is my intention to isolate one single, tiny current; I shall beg the reader to observe one thing only: namely, the revolution which all this prodigious upheaval in the lives and manners of the public may have produced in Art—and not even in *all* the arts, but in one alone, which is the art of Music.[1]

The revival of music in France will inexorably be brought about by the efforts of a number of young ladies who, at the age of twelve or so, are now the pupils of Mademoiselle Weltz and Monsieur Massimino, and who are moveover fated to spend some eight months out of every year in the dreary solitude of the country. Brothers and sisters rarely encourage one's vanity; they are already only too familiar, both with one's *best tartan dress* and with one's *grand fantasia* on the piano. In fact, all that is really needed is a good spell of civil war; for the enforced isolation which attends such calamities might at least restore to France something of the old energy her people once possessed in the days of Henri IV and of Agrippa d'Aubigné; and then (like characters out of Walter Scott) we should all grow earnest, impassioned and sincere. Under the scourge of war, the frivolousness of the French character would at last know some restraint, and *imagination* would flourish as of old; nor would music be far behind in this refashioned world. In any corner of the earth where *solitude* and *imagination* go hand in hand, men learn soon enough to love music;[2] for the law admits no excep-

---

[1] *Vide: Racine et Shakespeare* (1823).

[2] *Eg.* Zurich. *Solitude* and *singing in church*: such are, at bottom, the original sources of *opera buffa*.

tions, and it is this same law which decrees that it is logically impossible to expect any enthusiasm for music among a people who live perpetually in each other's society, and who feel bored, and indeed all but ridiculous, so soon as they are left alone for a single instant.[1] Let us therefore be tolerant towards the older generation, if, with all the noble passages of *Tancredi* or *Otello* to choose from, there is really nothing that they manage to enjoy save those empty, pretty little quadrilles which certain well-intentioned *arrangers* have managed to "adapt" for the light-orchestras of Beaujon or Tivoli. What should a man do to escape from the tyranny of his own generation? But the phenomenon which gives me faith in the inevitable, ultimate triumph of true music in France is that, in spite of all the machinations engineered by the *Théâtre Feydeau* and the *Opéra*, our present generation of young ladies has grown impertinent and now, at the age of twenty, having been brought up in the *new* society, is gaily snapping its fingers at the venerable admirers of Gluck and Grétry.[2] The *Barber*, for instance,

[1] *Vide:* Volney, *Tableau des Etats-Unis*, p. 490.

[2] The older generation, however, will not be baulked of its revenge: *v. les Annales littéraires*, which is the organ of all right-thinking intellectuals, who treat Rossini as they treat Voltaire! These genuine representatives of the good old French traditions have little or no real feeling for music; but since, on the other hand, they suffer from no lack of self-esteem, there is nothing so absurd that they cannot be induced to swallow it, if one takes the slightest trouble to push it down their throats. Thus it happened that the *Journal des Débats*, one of the most influential papers of this persuasion, referring to Monsigny, decorated the poor old boy with the title of the "Finest Composer in Europe", supporting its assertion to the length of four close columns of print. It is really most aggravating for Europe that, until this very hour, she had completely failed to guess the name of her Finest Composer! I beg my readers to believe me, when I protest that I am in no wise lacking in the proper respect which is due to our honorable press; newspapers are invaluable—but above all as *thermometers*, whereby one may gauge the present temperature of public opinion in Paris. Any public which can endure with patience, let alone with enthusiasm, three theatres such as the *Variétés*, the *Vaudeville* and the *Gymnase* (which not only keep going, but thrive and flourish and play to full houses night after night, on a diet which consists of four solid hours of unmitigated bad singing) must logically abandon all serious claim to soundness or subtlety in its musical taste.

(I would observe, however, that it is the *men* of the *older generation* who maintain the fortunes of the *Vaudeville*, and not the aristocratic young ladies of the newer.)

The city which could nurture a Voltaire and a Molière may rightly, in my opinion, claim to be entitled the wittiest in the world. Italy, England and Germany might all be flung pell-mell into a crucible, without the result of such a distillation ever producing one single novel of the quality of *Candide*, or even a handful of songs like those of Collé or Béranger; but it is precisely this very phenomenon

owes its unheard-of popularity, not so much to the charming and infinitely flexible voice of Madame Fodor, as to the abundance of waltz-tunes and quadrilles which it has supplied to our dance-orchestras! After the fifth or the sixth society-ball, the *Barber* suddenly begins to sound strangely familiar; and *then* a visit to the *Théâtre Louvois* becomes a real pleasure.[1]

I should really turn now to the situation as it is in the Provinces, but I feel qualms at the thought of tackling so solemn, so majestic a theme. In theory, the enforced solitude which results in such places from the terror of compromising one's reputation by being seen in a street or a *café* should foster vast sincerity and immense depth of feeling, and spur the imagination onwards to flights of unparalleled daring. But in practice this does not happen: for, even to-day, the poor provincial locked away in the solitude of his study is still terrified of one thing above all others, which is *ridicule*; and the object of his profoundest hatred, mistrust and jealousy, as well as of his unstinted, but uncritical admiration, is still, as it always was, *Paris*. The precious fancies which sprang from the perverted taste of the glittering *salons* of the capital in 1770 or thereabouts, still reign in undiminished splendour in the provinces. But the real sting of the joke is that these conceptions and ideals *never were* anything but artificial, even in 1770; they never once sprang naturally from the genuine feelings and aspirations of the inhabitants of Issoudun or of Montbrison.[2]

A musical scholar of great erudition and wide experience, M. Castil-Blaze, recently had the happy inspiration of providing new *libretti*, in *French*, for Rossini's operas. But this high-spirited, swift, airy, *brittle* music, with all its pre-eminently French qualities, might have been as dull as ditchwater instead of original and exciting, and *still* have been greeted in the provinces with the same enthusiastical applause; "for"

which explains France's unspeakable obtuseness in matters *musical*. Representatives of the old school give all their attention to the words of a song, and none of it to the *tune* to which those words are sung; the emotional content, for them, lies in the text, *and not in the music*.

[1] If only someone would have the notion of squeezing a *ballet* into the interval between the first and second acts of every Italian opera which is performed at the *Louvois*, thus warding off the headaches and the fainting-fits which tend to develop during Act II, the *Louvois* would prove as popular as it is interesting, and the *Théâtre Français* would be doomed. But oh! the *blow* to national pride!

[2] *Cf. le Spleen*, short-story by M. de Besenval, which gives a beautiful portrait of provincial life in Besançon.

(say the men-folk) "isn't this the same *Barber* which *Paris has gone mad about?*" Whereas the women (who alone in France have any real feeling for music) in any case have had Rossini's music lying about on the piano for the last five years! The provinces, I feel certain, are fated to acquire a whole, positive, flourishing *host* of civic virtues many years before they have the first inkling of genuine aesthetic taste, or show themselves capable of any real artistic appreciation, or learn to derive from art any genuine and lasting emotional satisfaction. Is it not strange to think, that people so full of their own importance, so little given (apparently) to bashful hesitations and uncertainties, should, in the event, prove to entertain the deepest mistrust of their own personal impressions and reactions, and to be the least prepared to enquire simply and naturally whether such and such an experience causes them delight or displeasure? The provincial, preoccupied, to the exclusion of all else, by the figure he may cut in some *salon*, fears nothing so much in all the world as to find himself isolated in his own opinion; and he will scarcely dare to assert that it is cold in mid-January, or that *le Renégat* bores him stiff, until he has seen the fact stated in black and white in the Parisian newspapers.[1]

The provinces, I suspect, are not likely to find any early cure for this plague of aesthetic cowardice. They will sooner breed more heroes like Desaix or Barnave, Drouot or Carnot, than father a race of men gifted with *simple* tastes based exclusively upon personal impressions and upon a sincere insight into their own favourable or unfavourable reactions.

The general attitude towards art and music thus being determined, M. Castil-Blaze's lucrative inspiration will assuredly bring about a revolution in musical taste in the provinces similar to that which the teaching of M. Massimino has already effected in Paris. The *Théâtre Feydeau* will be dead ten years from now, and the *Grand Opéra* itself twenty years later. The government will be forced to instal Italian opera in the rue Le Peletier; and there will be ballets* in the interval between the acts, to delight us with the artistry of the most consummate dancers in Europe. Then, at last, Grand Opera in Paris will be a sight without parallel in all the world. Imagine, if you can, *Otello* sung by Madame Pasta, Garcia and Davide; and between the acts, the ballet

---

[1] I understand that, rather disastrously, many smaller provincial towns have taken *literally* the ironical praise which the critics meted out to *la Caroléide* and *Ipsiboé*.

les Pages du Duc de Vendôme, danced by Mlle Bigottini, Mme Anatole, Mlles Noblet and Legallois and MM. Paul, Albert and Coulon.

This chapter, which you have just been reading, replaces another, in which I had originally attempted to write a detailed history of the struggle between the two *Barbers of Seville* on the Parisian stage, and of the eventual victory of Rossini's version, the whole narrative to have been based upon contemporary periodicals, and upon the accounts of persons who assiduously witnessed every performance—not only those in which the part of Rosina was played by the brilliant and attractive Signora de' Begnis*, but also those which followed later, when the character was taken over by Madame Fodor, who enjoyed such a magnificent and well-deserved success in the rôle.

But in the end, instead of bothering with all these details, which might have grown more than a little tedious before I had done with them, I have preferred to pursue some research into the origins of musical taste in France, and to trace the drift and direction of that revolution now in progress in the field of entertainment which is the subject of this study.[1]

[1] Were it not for the tyranny of certain professional *literary autocrats*, this aesthetic revolution would advance both faster and more effectively; but, since we are doomed to suffer the burden of an *Académie Française*, let our estimate of this institution be *neither higher nor lower* than it deserves. Let us try to control our natural exasperation at the pig-headed opposition of certain learned Doctors, who claim to speak *with superior authority*;† and if our opponents should chance to be a shade pedantic, let us look to it that we do not ourselves become *outré*!

† Quoted *verbatim* from the *Journal des Débats* in its account of the elegant insults levelled at the *Romantics* by the celebrated M. de Villemain, I forget whether at the beginning or at the end of his course of lectures.

CHAPTER XVIII

Otello*

THE theme of serious love is as foreign to Rossini as it is to Walter Scott; and indeed, when one knows nothing of love as a passion except through what one has read in books* (*Werther*, perhaps, or the *Nouvelle Héloïse*), it is no easy task to paint a successful portrait of jealousy. It is necessary to have loved as implacably as the Portuguese Nun, and with all the unquenchable ardour of which she has left us so vivid an echo in her immortal *Letters**, if one is to have any understanding of the kind of jealousy *which is powerful enough to move an audience in a theatre*. In Shakespeare's tragedy, we are made to feel that Othello *cannot* go on living when once he has killed Desdemona. Even if we imagine that the sombre Iago were to have perished in some hazard of war, at the very same moment as Desdemona herself, and that Othello were thus doomed for ever to believe in Desdemona's guilt—even so, life could have held no more savour in his eyes (if I may indulge a taste for mixed metaphor, *à l'Italienne*); Desdemona dead, why should Othello live?

I trust, dear Reader, that you will agree with me when I affirm that, if the passion of jealousy is to be effectively conveyed through the medium of art, it must first be rooted in a soul possessed of a love as desperate as that of *Werther* himself—of a love which may be *sanctified* by self-inflicted death. Any love which fails to rise to this degree of intensity has, in my opinion, no right to be jealous; where love is tepid, jealousy is a mere impertinence.

Love which is not passionate, but simply *fancy* or *infatuation*, can contribute nothing to art save an atmosphere of hilarity and general merriment. The kind of jealousy which often accompanies love of this "secondary" quality may indeed be just as violent as a jealousy with very different origins; yet it cannot touch the artistic sensibility. Its characteristic feature is *vanity*; and jealousy of this category is invariably farcial (like the infatuated dotards in the old comedies)—unless the sufferer happens to be a personage of autocratic rank and power, in which case wounded vanity must be appeased by blood, and usually receives its satisfaction soon enough. But in all the world, there is nothing more abominable, nor more revolting, than blood shed out of vanity; and our minds turn immediately to the calendar of crimes committed by Nero, by Philip II, and by all the other monsters who have worn crowns and sat on thrones.

Before we may be truly stirred by the tragedy of *Othello*, before we may judge him *worthy* to kill Desdemona, one thing is essential: not a shadow of doubt must remain in our mind (or in that of any other spectator who should chance to consider the question) that, should Othello remain alone in the world after the death of his lover, he must necessarily and immediately strike *himself* with the same dagger. Unless I find this conviction firmly rooted in the bottom of my heart, Othello becomes indistinguishable from somebody like King Henry VIII, who, having chopped off the head of one of his wives, in accordance with the most just and lawful sentence delivered by the Courts of the time, feels nothing but intense relief; he would be the moral equivalent of one of our modern "dandies", who think it the merriest sport to stand by and laugh while some woman who adores them dies of grief.

This *prophetic vision of Othello's death*, which is not only a moral necessity, but the absolute condition upon which our sympathy in the tragedy depends, is entirely absent in Rossini's *Otello*. This Othello is too patently shallow to convince me beyond reasonable doubt that it is not simply vanity which makes him seize the dagger. And once this uncertainty is allowed for an instant to take root, the whole theme, which is perhaps richer in emotional implications than any other conception springing from the fundamental phenomenon of love, is liable to degenerate with appalling rapidity into some insignificant and sordid little trifle borrowed from the *Tales of Bluebeard*.

However, I should imagine that any considerations such as those which I have just been analysing would have appeared supremely ridiculous to the unmentionable literary hack* who prepared the Italian *libretto* which Rossini was expected to use; *his* job was to turn out seven or eight neatly-contrived scenes, all vaguely related to Shakespeare's tragedy, and all competently equipped with sufficient plain narrative to make sure that the public understood what was meant to be happening on the stage. Moreover, out of the total of eight scenes, not more than two or three could safely have *rage* as the dominant *motif*, for music does not possess the power to express fury for any length of time without degenerating into unrelieved monotony.

In Shakespeare's version of *Othello*, the first scene shows us Iago, accompanied by Roderigo, the rejected suitor of Desdomena, on his way to rouse the Senator Barbarigo[1] and to warn him that Othello has abducted his daughter. This situation holds potential material for a chorus.

The second scene shows us Othello himself, who, in an attempt to justify his love in the eyes of his old comrade-in-arms, Iago, is unwise enough to betray the real extent of his passion. Here we have potential material for an aria by Othello.

The third scene shows us Othello telling the "plain, unvarnished tale" of his love before the assembled members of the Senate of Venice, before whom he is summoned to answer a charge of abduction. It was a stroke of genius on the part of the poet to have created a situation where a narrative episode of this character, which is always so delicate to handle and lends itself so easily to absurdity, becomes in point of fact a *dramatic necessity*. Othello is accused of witchcraft; his Moorish origin, the darkness of his skin, the superstitions of the XVIth century —everything conspires to lend an air of plausibility to the accusation which is brought against him by old Barbarigo the Senator, Desdemona's father. In his defence, Othello tells of the simple means which he used to win the heart of his young bride; how he ran through the story of his life from year to year, filled with "the most disastrous chances" and "moving accidents". At last, one of the Senators[2] exclaims: "I think this tale would win my daughter too." Desdemona then enters, summoned at her father's insistence; and there, before the whole Assembly, this timid maiden, no longer obedient to the voice of her own father, throws herself into Othello's arms; at which, the aged Senator, in a fit of passion, cries out:

> Look to her Moor, have a quick eye to see:
> She has deceived her father, may do thee.
>
> (I. iii. 293–4)

This, I feel, provides admirable material for a quintet; it is rich in varied emotional elements, including the passions of love, anger and

---

[1] *Brabantio* in Shakespeare's text. (*Trans.*)
[2] The *Duke of Venice* in Shakespeare's text (I. iii. 172). (*Trans.*)

revenge; it follows a marked line of dramatic development; it provides for a chorus of Senators desperately moved by this strange scene which has come to trouble their midnight deliberations—and nothing of all this which the spectator cannot grasp and appreciate *directly*.

Here, then, we have three consecutive scenes, all of which gradually build up a portrait of an Othello obsessed by love, while at the same time they capture our interest in the quality of this love, by telling us in detail how, despite the copper-colour of his skin, he was able to win the heart of Desdemona—information which is more than necessary, for, once we see him as a lover deliberately preferred above all other rivals, his physical disabilities cease to be of any importance. If *such* a man should murder his beloved, it is inconceivable that the cause should be mere vanity; and so this disastrous suspicion is for ever banished from the picture. And what, may we be so bold as to enquire, did our Italian librettist invent as a substitute for the perfection of this scene where Othello, in our very presence, recounts the history of his love? A "triumphant entry of a victorious general"!—an inspiration so new, so *original*, that, for a whole century and a half, it has furnished the gala-attraction of every single Grand Opera ever committed in France, and made dazzled provincials gape with astonishment and admiration!

This "triumphal entry" is followed by a recitative and a full-scale aria,

Ah! sì, per voi già sento . . .[1]

—a positively supreme blunder, whose immediate consequence is to give us, right from the very outset, a picture of an Othello filled with pride and superb disdain for the enemy whom he has vanquished. And let me repeat, that a *proud*-hearted Othello is the very last conception in all the world which should be foisted upon the audience at this particular moment!

Following upon an initial howler of such devastating magnitude, involving the meticulous selection of that particular platitude which is best calculated to make specific nonsense of the whole plot, the less

---

[1] *Otello:*

Ah! sì, per voi già sento
Nuovo valor nel petto;
Per voi d'un nuovo affetto
Sento infiammarsi il cor.
(Act I, sc. i: Otello addresses the
Doge and Senators of Venice)

said about the rest of the *libretto*, the better. It would have needed every scrap of genius which Rossini possessed to save the opera, not merely from the banality of the text (for nothing is more normal), but from the *illogicalities of the plot*, which set another, and far thornier problem.

To perform such a miracle, Rossini would have had to master certain specific qualities which, in all probability, he simply does not possess at all. I confess myself obsessed by the overwhelming suspicion that Rossini himself has never known what it means to love someone *to the pitch of absurdity*. Ever since it has become fashionable in High Society to have *Grand Passions*,[1] and owing to the corollary, that it is every man's ambition to behave "like High Society", I have been finding myself increasingly reluctant to believe in the genuineness of any *Grand Passion*, until it has given proofs of its sincerity and good faith by inducing the victim to make himself ridiculous.

Poor Mozart, for instance, spent the greater part of his life—a life, it is true, which ended before he was six-and-thirty—in perpetual and imminent danger of plunging into this abysmal heresy of ridicule. Even in the *Marriage of Figaro*, which is the most light-hearted of all his operas, he cannot so much as glance at the subject of jealousy without making it sombre and deeply-moving; think, for example, of the aria:

> *Vedrò, mentr' io sospiro,*
> *Felice un servo mio!*[2]

or of the duet:

> *Crudel! perchè finora . . . ?*[3]

In the presence of this kind of music, the audience is instantly and instinctively aware that, if such jealousy should lead to a crime, the fault must be attributed, not simply to *wounded vanity*, but to the delirium of a mind unbalanced, distraught by the most intolerable anguish which the human soul can experience. But Mozart's characters speak a language which is unknown to Rossini, and the whole of *Otello* is barren of the faintest trace of any such *obsession*; instead of deep grief, we are asked to accept mere *fury*—and to make the best of it we can;

---

[1] The abbé Girard, a most sharp-witted observer of his fellow-mortals, wrote in 1746: "Custom, which permits a married woman to indulge in open flirtation with her suitors, forbids her the least hint of *passion*; for, in such circumstances, passion would be merely ridiculous" (*Synonymes*, article entitled *Amour*).

[2] *Nozze di Figaro*, Act III, sc. iii.

[3] *Ibid.*, Act III, sc. ii.

again and again we are shown the *injured vanity* of a creature who sways the power of life and death over his victim; never once the anguished and piteous misery of a passion betrayed by the object it worships.

The librettist *should* have given Othello *two* duets with Iago. In the first of these, the "damn'd inhuman dog" would have sown the first seeds of suspicion in Othello's heart, while Othello would have replied to the perfidious insinuations of his persecutor by exalting Desdemona ever higher in the mystic enthusiasm of his love.

Thus all the "sound and fury" would have been reserved for the duet in the second act; and even at this point, we should have had two or three passages in which Othello would have reverted to his obsessing adoration. But the librettist was a man far too well-versed in his academic theories to deign to imitate the monstrous imaginings of a "barbarian"* like Shakespeare; instead, he daringly resorted to our dear, familiar friend, the "unaddressed letter", which provides the standard *dénouement* in Voltairian tragedy—a platitudinous piece of confidence-trickery, which in our own day would scarcely serve to swindle a stock-exchange speculator out of a paltry couple of hundred, but which, for all that, is assumed to be deep enough to deceive men of the calibre of Orosmane, Tancred and Othello! Moreover, some petty consideration of *backstairs patriotism* (which earned him great favour in Venice), induced our worthy poet to revert to the original Italian legend[1] which had provided Shakespeare with the basic plot of his tragedy. However, *all* the pillaged material, whatever its source, is handled with such unspeakable ineptitude, that he completely fails to suggest the faintest nuance of hesitation, or even to hint at the last glowing sparks of love in Othello's breast; and I fancy that, in all the orgy of blunders composing this so-called *libretto* which Rossini was supposed to manage, none is more fantastic than this. The feeblest of novelettes making the crudest of claims to psychological realism would have furnished our highly-respected scribbler (whom I have the unpardonable audacity to criticize!) with the information that the average human heart struggles more than once, experiences more than one fleeting instant of doubt and hesitation, before it agrees to an eternal renunciation of the greatest, the most god-like happiness which exists on earth—the belief in the untarnished perfection of the beloved object.

[1] G. B. Giraldi Cinthio, *Cento Novelle*, Part I, 3rd Decad, 7th tale (ed. Venice, 1608, pp. 313–321).

One factor alone contrives to redeem Rossini's *Otello*, and that is *our* reminiscences of Shakespeare's *Othello*! Shakespeare created, in the person of Othello, a character who is as true, as historically *real*, as Julius Caesar or Themistocles. The very name of Othello is as vivid a symbol of impassioned jealousy as the name of Alexander is symbolic of indomitable courage; so much so, indeed, that if some misguided writer were actually to *show* us Alexander fleeing in panic before the onslaught of his enemies, we should still refuse to think of him as a coward; we should merely conclude that the writer did not know his job. Since the music of *Otello* is admirable in every respect bar one (*dramatic expression*), we can easily allow our imagination to supply the one specific virtue which is missing; for this faculty is never so well-disposed to furnish non-existent qualities as when it is overwhelmed by sudden admiration for a set of qualities which *do* exist—a secret which is perfectly familiar to Italian actors, brought up in the tradition of *improvization*. We are so astounded to hear verse declaimed on the spur of the moment with the speed and facility of normal speech (a feat which, to us, appears quite incredibly difficult), that the resulting "poetry" unfailingly sounds most impressive while we are actually listening to it; which is not to say that we should not find it quite intolerably flat on the day following, if anyone should have the double impertinence, firstly to write it down at all, and secondly to show it to us!

In *Otello*, we are so electrified by the magnificent musical quality of the songs, so spellbound, so overwhelmed by the incomparable beauty of the theme, that we invent our own *libretto* to match.

In Italy, the performers themselves are usually so completely dominated by the magic which Shakespeare attached to the fatal name of Othello, that unconsciously as it were, traces of simple and spontaneous emotion—features which are only too often missing from Rossini's music—creep into the interpretation of their recitatives. In Paris, the various performers who have sung the part of Othello have all been actors of too much talent to quote as examples of this primarily *subconscious* phenomenon which results from contact with the great name of Othello; but I may state with conviction that I have never yet heard an insignificant performance of Desdemona's recitatives. There can scarcely be a single music-lover in the whole of Paris who could forget Madame Pasta's entry on the line

Mura infelici, ove ogni dì mi aggiro![1]

and the desperate simplicity in the inflection of her voice. Given actors of such outstanding ability, the illusion of beauty is not difficult to catch, nor is it long before we are sincerely convinced that this score, which is indeed almost overpowering in its torrential impetuosity and a masterpiece in the "grand manner",[2] is also deeply emotional, and carries with it that sense of fatality, that mark of impending disaster, which impelled Virgil to write of Dido, that she had *the pallor of death that was to be.*[3]

If we insist on looking for *love* in Rossini's works, we should be well-advised to turn to his earliest composition, *Demetrio e Polibio* (1809*); for by the time of *Otello* (1816), Rossini had forgotten the haunting echoes of *real* love, except, perhaps, in the scoring which surrounds the part of Desdemona, and in particular in the charming duet,

Vorrei, che il tuo pensiero . . .;[4]

for I must repeat (at the risk of sounding not merely boring, but utterly paradoxical) that, in general, the tone of Rossini's *Willow Song* is one of despair rather than of sincere and moving *tenderness*. Ask any lady with some experience in the gentle art of courtship which of the two moods is harder to portray!

Signor Caraffa, who, as a composer, is not in the same class as

[1] *Desdemona:*
> Mura infelici, ove ogni dì mi aggiro,
> Dopo più lune, incerta e oppressa, ah! voi
> Più al guardo mio non siete
> Come lo foste un dì, ridenti e liete . . .
> (Act I, sc. iv)

[2] The paintings of Paul Veronese (*e.g. Venice Triumphant*) are likewise masterpieces in the *grand manner*—a manner which certainly has a more immediate and popular appeal than the style of Raphael; yet, in the end, if we seek an artist who can give us a *natural portrait* of the passions, it is to the halls of the Vatican that we must ever return.

[3] Pallida morte futurâ [*Aeneid*, VI, line 643].

[4] *Desdemona:*
> Vorrei, che il tuo pensiero
> A me dicesse il ver.
Emilia:
> Sempre è con te sincero:
> No, che non dei temer . . .
> (Act I, sc. v)

Rossini, has nevertheless written a *farewell aria*,[1] which is used at the end of the first act of Viganò's ballet, *les Titans*, and which immediately creates an atmosphere of tender sympathy in the highest degree. If only Othello, bidding adieu to Desdemona after some secret meeting fraught with danger and difficulty, had a similar duet somewhere in the first act, the whole audience would be moved to tears; and this instant of tenderness and love would be all the more heart-breaking, since no one in the entire house could fail to be aware of the kind of death which is ultimately reserved for poor Desdemona. As it is, however, Othello's rages seem to betray nothing save congenital bad-temper—and, what is worse still, bad-temper springing from wounded vanity.

[1] This aria actually belongs to the opera *Gabriele di Vergy*, which is one of Caraffa's best works. It comes out of the duet:

O istante felice!

CHAPTER XIX

Otello (continued)

ACT ONE

THE main theme and the *crescendo* of the overture are brilliant rather than tragic; the *allegro* is extremely vivacious.

I approve most highly of this emotional device at the very opening of so tragic a tale; for what interests me is the *development* which takes place within the soul of Othello who, as we watch him escaping with his beloved at the beginning of the first act, stands upright on the highest peak of happiness, only to sink, in the last act, to the uttermost degradation of murder, and to become a symbol of the accumulated misery of the whole race of man. Such a contrast is sublime, because it is in the very nature of things, and because there is no truly passionate lover in all the earth whose soul is completely free of the fear of such a fate; but, I insist, to interpret this contrast in terms of opera, it was essential that the work should open on a note of joyous delight, portraying in the most vivid and striking fashion imaginable the supreme happiness of Othello, and the devotion and tenderness of his love. If we accept this pattern of emotional development, the raging would be confined to the end of Act II, while, in Act III, when the die is already cast, Othello should proceed grimly with his predestined sacrifice.[1]

The solo clarinet passage*, which occurs in the overture, suggests a mood of heart-rending pity, quite distinct from the kind of "pity" which is inspired by commonplace misadventures, and which is the normal reaction produced by the average contemporary sentimental

[1] *Cf.* the admirable manner in which the last act was played by Kean, and the unfathomable depths of love revealed in Othello's exclamation: *Amen! Amen! With all my soul,*† when he listens to Desdemona's prayer. The English, in my opinion, are unrivalled in two spheres of art: dramatic declamation and landscape gardening.

† Original text: *Amen, with all my heart!* (*Trans.*)

drama (assuming that it produces any reaction at all!). This passage is instinct with fine and delicate spirituality.

Again, it is delicacy and spiritual grace rather than majesty and grandeur which, to my mind, characterize the opening chorus:

Viva Otello, viva il prode![1]

the music of which is sparkling and infinitely ingenious.

When Othello steps forward, on the words

Vincemmo, o padri![2]

his recitative is half-shadowed with hints of sadness in the accompaniment. At the very instant when the melodic line of the song rises in triumph, the accompaniment is muttering: *You are to die!* For Rossini, having once resigned himself to the grim duty of following the non-sequiturs of the *libretto*, was obliged to abandon any ideas he may have had about depicting the initial state of *happiness* which surrounded Othello, and was required to suggest cadences of melancholy from the very moment of the first aria:

Ah! sì, per voi già sento . . .[3]

Nozzari, who sang the part of Othello, which Rossini had originally composed for Garcia, achieved a rare felicity of expression in suggesting the nuance of sadness which dwells in the lines:

Deh! amor dirada il nembo
Cagion di tanti affanni![4]

[1] *Chorus of Senators:*
Viva Otello, viva il prode,
Delle schiere invitto duce!
Or per lui di nuova luce
Torna l'Adria a sfolgorar!
(Act I, sc. i)

[2] *Otello:*
Vincemmo, o padri. I perfidi nemici
Caddero estinti . . .
(Act I, sc. i)

[3] See above, p. 213.

[4] *Otello:*
Deh! Amor dirada il nembo,
Cagion di tanti affanni,
Comincia co' tuoi vanni
La speme a ravvivar.
(Act I, sc. i)

His magnificent stature, which could convey so stirringly an impression of grandeur tinged with melancholy, was extremely valuable to him in expressing certain aspects of the part, and in interpreting conceptions of which the librettist had probably never dreamed. I well remember the astonishment with which the Neapolitan audiences reacted to the pure beauty of his gestures, and to the general impression of rare and graceful majesty which was characteristic of Nozzari in the part; incidentally, the style of his acting on this occasion was quite outside his usual repertoire. It may perhaps be claimed that *any* part which portrays *extremes* of emotion is relatively easy to act. The rôle of the Father, for instance, in Paër's opera *Agnese* is always excellently played; and at this very moment, in Paris, it is not difficult to enumerate at least seven or eight competent actors (I might name MM. Perlet, Lepeintre, Samson, Monrose, Bernard-Léon, *etc.*) who, let it be observed, are all magnificent in "heavy" parts; whereas I cannot recall ever having seen on any stage a competent straight *jeune premier* who can play the standard "young lover". Yet few of us have actual experience of extreme emotions, whether tragic or farcical; whereas we meet young lovers every day.

There is plenty of fire in the duet between the sombre Iago and the "young quat", Roderigo:

> *No, non temer: serena il mesto ciglio;*
> *Fidati all' amistà, scorda il periglio ....*[1]

Incidentally, however, there is one thing of which I am completely convinced; and that is, that whoever the young composer may be who is ultimately destined to eclipse Rossini, the great secret of his triumph will be found to lie in the *simplicity* of his style, and in the sincerity and completeness of his revolt against the complex*. If you are going to use your orchestra so violently and so rowdily in a simple duet between two minor characters who, to make matters worse, show not the slightest inclination to be quarrelsome, what can you hope to have left for Othello's raging and for the great dialogues with Iago?

The most outstanding quality of this score of Rossini's, which is unquestionably his finest achievement in the heavy Germanic style, is its fiery urgency: "volcanic" was the term which was popular at the *San-Carlo* theatre. But the disadvantage is that there is always a certain

---

[1] Act I, sc. iii.

sameness about the dynamic violence of this kind; shades and nuances of expression are swallowed up in the general welter of noise; we miss the middle road between grave and gay, the transitions from joyous daylight to severe darkness; the listener is condemned to live in constant intimacy with the trombones. And there is another factor which aggravates the monotony of this "violent" style, universally revered by our musical philistines as the very perfection of perfection: the absence of standard recitatives. In *Otello*, all recitatives, without exception, are reinforced with full orchestral accompaniments, as is the habit in French *grand opera*. But this device implies a waste of emotional reinforcements which should have been held in reserve until the final act. Viganò* displayed far truer inspiration in his ballet *Otello**, when he had the superb impertinence to use a simple *forlana*[1] in the opening scene. In the second act, moreover, Viganò had the intelligence to insert a major scene in a calm and dignified key, a scene where Othello holds a revel by night in his garden, in the course of which the first seeds of jealousy are implanted in his soul. In consequence, by the time we reached the concluding scenes of Viganò's ballet, we were not *surfeited* with ranting and terror; and soon the whole audience was moved to tears. But I have rarely seen anybody similarly moved at Rossini's *Otello*.

In the version of *Otello* which was specially arranged for the Paris production, Madame Pasta's* magnificent rendering of her recitative:

Mura infelici, ove ogni dì mi aggiro . . .[2]

to some extent redeemed the utter idiocy of the *libretto* at this point, and rescued Rossini from the pitfalls into which he had been lured by its ineptitudes. But the credit for this achievement rests exclusively with Madame Pasta herself; for the same recitative, declaimed by some northern singer, no matter how celebrated (*e.g.* Madame Mainvielle), might well pass completely unnoticed, and would no longer contribute that delicate suggestion of gentle, sighing melancholy, the absence of which, in my opinion, so cruelly weakens Rossini's score. Madame

[1] A kind of lively dance, traditional in the district of Friuli; the gaiety of the main section, however, is counterbalanced by the extreme melancholy of the subsidiary section. Viganò was a pure genius, in spite of the fact that his reputation never went beyond the borders of Lombardy, where he died in 1821, after having created the ballets *Otello*, *Myrrha*, *la Vestale*, *gli Uomini di Prometeo*, etc., etc.

[2] See above, p. 217.

Pasta contrives a subtlety of embellishment which is beyond praise;
with the result that the audience applauds her even more warmly in
the recitative than in its continuation, the aria

> O quante lagrime
> Finor versai . . .,[1]

which the arrangers have borrowed from *la Donna del Lago*, and which
was originally composed by Rossini for the superb contralto voice of
Signorina Pisaroni. I cannot find words eloquent enough to describe
the effectiveness of Madame Pasta's style, as she declaims the following
lines:

> Ogni altr' oggetto
> È a me funesto,
> Tutto è imperfetto,
> Tutto detesto.[2]

O happy, beautiful language of Italy, in which such words as these may
be spoken without fear of extravagance or risk of absurdity! And yet
these words *do* convey, without extravagance and with a maximum of
straightforward simplicity, a specific nuance of sensibility, an *epoch* of
feeling (if I may so express myself), which invariably accompanies the
deepest manifestations of love. In itself, the aria is magnificent; yet,
personally, I find it too *intense*, too severe in its melancholy. The opera
as a whole would have created a deeper impression if Madame Pasta
had selected, at this point, an aria whose dominant note was *tender*
love; something less harsh and perhaps more moving. It may be,
however, that the "arrangers" were more concerned to forestall the

---

[1] *Desdemona:*

> Palpita incerta l'alma,
> Dal cor svanì la calma [. . .]
> O! quante lagrime
> Finor versai,
> Lungi languendo
> Da tuoi bei rai!
> Ogni altr' oggetto
> È a me funesto,
> Tutto è imperfetto,
> Tutto detesto . . .
> (Act I, sc. iv)

[2] There is such *fire*, such a world of suppressed emotion in Madame Pasta's
utterance of the word *detesto*, which she gives on the lowest note of all her superb
range, that the echo of it reverberates in every heart.

accusation that the opera lacked *variety*; for the ideal characteristics which I have just enumerated are precisely those which Rossini was to give to the delightful duet:

> *Vorrei, che il tuo pensiero . . .*[1]

whose opening bars, unheralded by the usual *ritornello* introduction, are a stroke of genius. This duet, on the rare and fortunate occasions when it is properly performed, has always struck me as the finest thing in the whole opera. Stylistically, its purity and simplicity are reminiscent of the Rossini who was the composer of *Tancredi*; yet there is more fire, more boldness in the line of the *cantilena* than could have been expected in the earlier work. Unfortunately, I have never heard it performed to its best advantage on the actual stage. This very winter, however, by a fortunate accident, I was privileged to hear it sung *once* to absolute perfection, in the intimacy of a *salon* in Paris; the singers, let me hasten to add, were both French and their rendering had all the technical mastery of a Signora Barilli, with, perhaps, a certain additional warmth of feeling which this great artist sometimes failed to achieve.

There are further entrancing reminiscences of *Tancredi*, with all its ardent youth and brilliant stylistic freshness, in the chorus:

> *Santo Imen, te guidi Amore!*[2]

which seems to combine the gentle enchantment of dawning genius with a new and vigorous masculinity which the composer had not dared display in *Tancredi* or in *Demetrio e Polibio*. Given a good set of voices, this chorus is one of the finest of all works which can be selected for concert-performance; and incidentally, it is also an example of the perfection which may result from an exact balance exquisitely maintained between German-style orchestral harmony on the one hand, and the melodic genius of fair Parthenope[3]* on the other.

---

[1] See above, p. 217.

[2] *Wedding Chorus:*
> Santo Imen, te guidi Amore
> Due bell' alme ad annodar!
> > (Act I, sc. ix)

[3] . . . . tenet nunc
Parthenope.
> *Virgil.*

The *finale* which follows,

Nel cuor d'un padre amante . . .,

is usually acclaimed as one of Rossini's most masterly achievements;
and it may safely be asserted that there is not a single one among all
the great man's rivals who could have even approached such musical
eminence. In Paris, however, it has never been heard in any performance as accomplished as that which was given at the *San-Carlo* in
Naples, when Davide played Roderigo and Benedetti, who was a
magnificent *basso*, sang Desdemona's father. It is not that the voice of
M. Levasseur, which was heard in Paris, is basically unsound in any
way; but the actor himself is hesitant and uncertain.

Davide reached heights beyond praise in the passage:

Confusa è l'alma mia . . .,[1]

and in all the subsequent part of the *finale*.[2] Despite the sublime inanity
of the text, he was nothing less than divine in

Ti parli l'amore:
Non essermi infida!*[3]

[1] *Elmiro:*
   Nel cuor d'un padre amante
   Riposa, amata figlia;
   È l'amor, che mi consiglia
   La tua felicità.
Rodrigo:
   Confusa è l'alma mia
   Tra tanti dubbi e tanti,
   Solo in sì fieri istanti
   Reggermi Amor potrà.
                                        (Act I, sc. x)

[2] Unfortunately, a very slight deterioration in health, even in the case of so
eminent an artist, may easily render all these comments horribly inapt. I am referring to Davide *as he was in 1816 and 1817*, and I must beg the reader to apply a
similar qualification to all comments concerning the relative merits of this voice
or that which may be found throughout this biography.

[3] *Elmiro:*
   Se al padre non cedi,
   Punirti saprà.
Rodrigo:
   Ti parli l'amore:
   Non essermi infida.
   Quest'alma a te fida
   Più pace non ha . . .
                                        (Act I, sc. x)

This trio between Signorina Colbran, Davide and Benedetti has qualities enough to satisfy the most exacting of *dilettanti*. Whole years may pass by, even in the most eminent theatres, before one may hear a passage sung with such unparalleled beauty in effect. In Paris, for instance, where we have at different times heard both Galli and Madame Pasta, the only times these great artists have ever appeared together was in Paër's *Camilla*.

Othello's entry is superb. Here, at long last, the librettist has contrived a situation which has all the characteristics of good opera; and it must be generally agreed that Rossini could scarcely have treated it with a more effective display of pure fireworks. The situation is one to which all the colour and ostentation of stylistic and harmonic splendours *à la Mozart* are ideally suited; my only criticism, which springs from my own personal impression and preferences, is that such splendours should never have been allowed to intrude *earlier* into the dramatic pattern. In the Parisian version, Garcia manages the part of Othello extremely well; his acting is full of fire and fury; he is most truly the *Moor*.

The contest between the two tenors, Nozzari and Davide, was beyond praise, notably in the dialogue-passage

> RODRIGO: *E qual diritto mai,*
> *Perfido! su quel core*
> *Vantar con me potrai,*
> *Per renderlo infedel?*
> OTELLO: *Virtù, costanza, amore.*[1]

In the *cantilena* which forms the setting of the last three words, *Virtù, costanza, amore*, Rossini may be hailed as a serious rival of Mozart; that is to say, he managed to scale the same heights as the great German composer precisely in that field where Mozart himself came nearest to perfection. There can be nothing finer in all the art of music, nor truer, not more exact in reproducing the natural ring of passion, nor more dramatically effective, than this passage; but once again, to hear a performance barren of the glorious rivalry of some Nozzari and Davide striving to outdo each other in perfection, goaded higher and ever higher in achievement by the spurs of emulation, is to hear nothing. As far as Desdemona is concerned, Madame Pasta sings the

[1] Act I, sc. xi.

part, and above all *acts* it, twenty times better than Signorina Colbran. Her rendering of

È ver: giurai,

is quite supreme.

Everyone knows the famous

Empia, ti maledico!

—the very compass of the art of music has no means to produce a more powerful impression. Haydn himself wrote nothing more splendid.[1] The chorus which follows,

Ah! che giorno d'orror![2]

is most nobly conceived; incidentally, however, if the unspeakable incompetence of the librettist did not defy every attempt to find a category low enough to hold his so-called "poetry", the musical setting of the words:

Empia, ti maledico!

should logically have accompanied some phrase such as:

[1] Rossini stole the inspiration of this passage from Generali's opera *Adelina.*

[2] The quotations on this, the previous and the following page are all more or less continuous in the opera:

> Otello:
> Virtù, costanza, amore,
> Il dato giuramento.
> Elmiro:
> Misero me! che sento!
> Giurasti?
> Desdemona:
>   È ver: giurai [. . .].
> Elmiro:
> Empia! ti maledico!
> Tutti:
> Ah! che giorno d'orror!
> Incerta l'anima
> Vacilla e geme,
> La dolce speme
> Fuggì dal cor [. . .]
> Smanio, deliro e fremo . . .
> Desdemona:
> Smanio, deliro e tremo.
> No, non fu mai più fiero
> D'un rio destin severo
> Il barbaro timor.
>   (End of Act I)

Out of my sight! I do no longer love thee!

which Othello, blinded with rage, should have thundered at Desdemona as he confronts her with the fatal handkerchief which she has given to his rival Roderigo.[1]

Furthermore, what earthly right has the Senator Elmiro, Desdemona's father,[2] to intrude his vanity and bad-temper into the midst of such a theme? What have these petty exasperations got to do with the emotions and the heart-stirring conflicts of so terrible a situation, where an impassioned lover is driven to a frenzy of cursing in the face of the woman he worships, and to planning her eventual murder? There is no lover on earth, whatever his present happiness, who is entirely free from the fear of a similar catastrophe, or who, if his love is unadulterated and sincere, can truly say that he has never once glimpsed it in the distant dimness of the horizon; besides, all great passions are fearful and superstitious. This is the supreme manifestation of dramatic insight which the imbecile librettist has chosen to fling away in favour of the vanity and cantankerous ravings of an aged Senator filled with Cassandra-like prognostications, who is mainly worried lest his daughter should marry below her station. I feel so strongly about this disastrous incompetence that I sincerely hope that one day some charitable soul may devise a new set of words, which shall in the end make *some* sense out of Rossini's music.

The passage:

Incerta l'anima . . .

expresses with rare felicity the first moment of respite after the human soul has passed through an instant of indescribable horror—the respite which comes through sheer exhaustion, through the brutal impossibility of sustaining emotions a moment longer at such a pitch. In such passages, the dynamic qualities of Rossini's genius serve him admirably. Mozart, in similar scenes, tends now and then to miss a certain running undercurrent of vivacity and speed.

Desdemona's lines:

Smanio, deliro e tremo . . .

provide a fitting conclusion to this magnificent *finale*. I must stop

[1] It seems scarcely necessary to point out that the details of the Marchese Berio's *libretto* bear very little resemblance to those of Shakespeare's play. (*Trans.*)
[2] Shakespeare's *Brabantio* becomes *Elmiro Barbarigo* in the libretto. (*Trans.*)

writing, stop eulogizing, lest I be suspected of mere extravagance. The passage is so exquisite that it defies praise and description alike. Suffice it to mention, however, that despite the triumphant reception which greeted this *finale* at the *Théâtre Louvois*, we in Paris have seen nothing but a copy, and a pale, washed-out copy at that, of the original. Without a Davide in the part of Roderigo, or a Father who, in the scene where Othello is arraigned before the assembled Senators, can sing with all the unrestraint of a Galli in the second act of *la Gazza ladra*, nothing is quite the same.[1]

ACT TWO

The lack of a sufficiently competent artist to sing the part of Roderigo has led, in the Paris version, to the omission of the aria:

Che ascolto! Ahimè! che dici?[2]

This is a brilliant sketch in miniature of the dramatic situation which Corneille used and developed so powerfully in *Polyeucte*—the theme of the lover who, at the climax of his passion, learns that the woman he adores is already married. In this instance, Roderigo receives the fateful news from the lips of Desdemona herself.

In the great duet between Othello and Iago:

Non m'inganno; al mio rivale . . .,[3]

[1] Some scholars have maintained that the trio in the Act I *finale* of *Otello* is modelled on a similar trio in *Don Giovanni*, particularly with regard to the similarity of the clarinet-accompaniments. It is further asserted that the orchestral accompaniment, played while Othello reads the fatal letter which Iago has given him (duet, Act II) is extracted from a Haydn symphony in *E flat*.

[2] *Rodrigo:*
Che ascolto! Ahimè che dici?!
Ah! come mai non senti
Pietà de' miei tormenti,
Del mio tradito amor?
                                          (Act II, sc. i)

[3] *Otello:*
Non m'inganno; al mio rivale
L'infedel vergato ha il foglio;
Più non reggo al mio cordoglio,
Io mi sento lacerar!
Jago:
(Già la fiera gelosia

the tyrannical librettist at length relents sufficiently to allow us to enjoy
at least one of the great situations implicit in so magnificent a theme.
Here at long last we *do* see Iago tempting the wretched Othello towards
the abyss. The music is good. There is a great deal of dramatic expression, besides considerable dramatic truth, in the dialogue:

> JAGO: *Nel suo ciglio il cor gli veggo.*
> OTELLO: Ti son fida. . . . *Ahimè! che leggo?*
> JAGO: *Quanta gioja io sento al cor!*

At a performance which I saw yesterday (26th July, 1823), and which
was one of the most entrancing which Madame Pasta has ever given,
the part of Iago did at last receive a reasonably competent performance
in the hands of a newcomer to the stage, who thoroughly deserves to
be encouraged by the public;[1] he was particularly excellent in the
beautifully natural passages of the *cantilena*:

> *Già la fiera gelosia . . .*

On the other hand, there are no words harsh enough to describe the
catastrophic collapse of the trio:

> *Ah veni, nel tuo sangue . . .,*[2]
>
>> Versò tutto il suo veleno,
>> Tutta già gl'inonda il seno,
>> E mi guida a trionfar!)
>
> *Otello (legge):*
>> Caro bene . . . e ardisci ingrata?
>
> *Jago:*
>> (Nel suo ciglio il cor gli veggo!)
>
> *Otello:*
>> Ti son fida . . . Ahimè! che leggo!
>> (Quali smanie io sento al cor!)
>
> *Jago:*
>> (Quanta gioja io sento al cor!)
>>   (Act II, sc. iv)

[1] Signor Giovanola, from Lodi. He reminded me slightly of the incomparable
Bocci, who used to dance Iago in Viganò's ballet.

[2] *Rodrigo:*
> Ah! vieni, nel tuo sangue
> Vendicherò le offese:
> Se un vano amor ti accese,
> Distruggerlo saprò [. . .]

Desdemona, Rodrigo, Otello:
> Tra tante smanie, e tante
> Quest'alma mia delira;

which, in Naples, used to be so divinely sung by Davide and Nozzari. Madame Pasta alone has the talent to carry off the closing passages of this fine trio:

Tra tante smanie e tante . . .

Her acting in the fainting-scene is unrivalled in its natural simplicity, and she manages to bring real interest into what is fundamentally a dramatic platitude, a physical accident belonging probably to that category of phenomena which have been so degraded by our modern passion for cynicism, that the dramatist is forced to abandon any attempt to handle them on the stage, leaving them to the only domain in which they remain truly impressive—real life.

Desdemona's aria, at the instant when her waiting-women come in to her:

Qual nuova a me recate?[1]

contains a fine orchestral passage, *agitato*. This aria introduces a tantalizing instant of joyous happiness, impressive by very reason of its contrast with the oppressive and threatening atmosphere which dominates the remainder of the second act:

Salvo dal suo periglio?
Altro non chiede il cor . . .[2]

Rossini rises magnificently to the height of the occasion, particularly in the passage:

Vinto è l'amor dall'ira,
Spira vendetta il cor.

(Act II, sc. v)

[1] *Desdemona:*
Qual nuova a me recate!
Men fiero, se parlate,
Si rende il mio dolor.

(Act II, sc. viii)

[2] *Coro:*
Che mai saper tu vuoi?
Desdemona:
Se vive il mio tesor?
Coro:
Vive, serena il ciglio . . .
Desdemona:
Salvo dal suo periglio?
Altro non chiede il cor.

(Act II, sc. viii)

Se il padre m'abbandona . . .,[1]

which, thanks to the great artistry of Madame Pasta, has become famous throughout Paris. This was one of the scenes in which I became most acutely conscious of the superiority which this fine actress holds over her rival, Signorina Colbran.

Were we not already acquainted with the curious workings of our librettist's mind, we might at this point reiterate the complaint which we had recorded earlier: "What the devil, Sir, have we to do with the *Father's* worrying and grousing? You would oblige us by remembering that the human heart is not made to hold more than one all-absorbing passion at a time, and therefore that it is to her lover, half-mad as he is in his jealous obsession, and *not* to her father, that Desdemona, her family lost and her reputation gone, must address her complaint:

> *Se Otello m'abbandona,*
> *Da chi sperar pietà?*

ACT THREE

The plot of the third act is contrived with far greater skill than in either of the other two. The succession of griefs which overwhelm poor Desdemona is developed with a reasonable show of competence. In the still of the night, she appears in her chamber; she confesses to her companion the anxious thoughts which have possessed her ever since the news of her husband's banishment (for the Council of Ten has newly pronounced his exile from the State of Venice); a song drifts up from

[1] *Elmiro:*
> Qui . . . indegna!
Desdemona:
>   Il genitore!
Elmiro:
> Del mio tradito onore
> Come non hai rossor?
Coro:
>   O Ciel! Qual nuovo orror!
Desdemona:
> L'error d'un' infelice
> Pietoso in me perdona!
> Se il padre m'abbandona,
> Da chi sperar pietà?
>   (Act II, sc. viii)

the lagoon, where a passing gondolier sings these wonderful lines from
Dante:

> Nessun maggior dolore
> Che ricordarsi del tempo felice
> Nella miseria.[1]

Unhappy Desdemona, beside herself with strange fears, crosses to the
window, calling out: "Who art thou, who singest thus?" But it is her
companion who answers her with these moving words:

> È il gondoliere che cantando inganna
> Il cammin sulla placida laguna,
> Pensando ai figli, mentre il ciel s'imbruna.[2]

There is a touch of great charm in the conception of this little recitative
with its accompaniment on the orchestra. The gondolier and his singing
remind the ill-starred Venetian girl of the fate of her nurse, the faithful
slave who was purchased in Africa, and who died far from her own
land, after watching Desdemona's childhood. Desdemona, pacing un-
certainly about her room, comes by chance upon her harp which, on
the big stages of the Italian theatres, usually stands in a permanent
position on the left of the stage, while the fatal bed occupies the centre.
Seeing the harp, Desdemona is tempted to stop and play; she sings the
old song which her nurse, the African slave-girl, had sung in her
childhood:

> Assisa al pie' d'un salice . .[3]

The arrangement of the text of this song could hardly have been better
—let me say this at once to the honour of the librettist, the marchese
Berio, a man who is as charming a companion in society as he is unfortunate and abominable as a poet! But the music adds little to Rossini's
reputation. The song is well-written, correct, inoffensive ... and
nothing more. Any impression it creates in performance (and this is

[1] *Inferno* V. 121–123.
[2] Act III, sc. i.
[3] *Desdemona:*
> Assisa al pie' d'un salice,
> Immersa nel dolore,
> Gemea trafitta Isaura
> Dal più crudele amore ...
>> (Act III, sc. i. "Isaura" is Shakespeare's
>> "Barbara". *Trans.*)

I

considerable) is due entirely to its context and, in Paris at least, to the
magnificent interpretation of Madame Pasta.

Half-way through the song, the ill-fated Desdemona, distracted
with grief, forgets how the verse continues; and at the same instant, a
violent gust of wind shatters a pane of glass in the great Gothic window
of her chamber. This simple coincidence seems to her grief-stricken
mind an omen of dire and terrible significance.[1] She sings another
snatch of her song, but choking tears prevent her from singing more.
Hastily she abandons the harp, and dismisses her companion. Any
scene of this character inevitably puts the listener in mind of Mozart;[2]
but memory induces comparison, and comparison, in this case, profound regret.

Alone in her chamber in the depths of this terrible night, while the
palace which is her home is shaken from cellar to attic by the crashing
of thunder, Desdemona turns to heaven with a short prayer, which
again (musically speaking) is not all that it might be, but which nevertheless, in performance, seems greatly superior to the *Willow Song*.

And then she moves towards her bed; and the curtains, falling behind
her, hide her from the audience.

At this point, in the larger Italian theatres, the orchestra plays a
magnificent *ritornello*, which was of necessity omitted at the *Théâtre
Louvois* in Paris, thanks to the parsimony and shoddiness of the *décor*.
During this *ritornello*, far away in the uttermost depths of the stage, and
incredibly distant, we glimpse Othello, a lantern held high in his hand,
and his naked *cangiar* under his arm, tip-toeing towards his wife's
chamber, down the winding staircase of a tower. This stairway, which
winds downward in a spiral, gives us glimpses of the fearful visage of
Othello, a lonely point of light picked out by the lantern in the midst
of this infinite ocean of darkness, appearing, disappearing, and then
appearing again as he follows the twists of the little stairway which is
his only path; now and then, the light catches the blade of the un-
sheathed *cangiar*, and the gleam of steel flashes a chill warning of the
coming murder. After an infinite length of time, Othello reaches the
front of the stage, moves across to the bed, and parts the curtains. At

---

[1] As this scene was played in Naples, where the superstition of the *jettatura* [the
evil eye] still persists, the effect was electric.

[2] *Cf.* the song of the Statue of the Commander in *Don Giovanni*; or the despair
of Doña Anna when she comes upon the body of her father.

this climax, no description could be anything but a superfluous piece of impertinence; let it be enough simply to recall the magnificent stature of Nozzari, and his profoundly moving acting. Othello sets down his lantern; a gust of wind blows it out. He hears Desdemona cry out in her sleep: *Amato ben!* Flashes of lightning chase each other now across the sky in an ever-quickening succession, as in some southern storm; and their light flickers into the fateful chamber. With any luck, the audience will fail even to catch the fatuous imbecility of the librettist, who has chosen *this* moment of all moments to show off his pretty talents as a wit! Othello cries out:

> *Ah! che tra i lampi, il cielo*
> *A me più chiaro il suo delitto addita!*[1]

Desdemona wakes up; and there ensues a duet which is hardly worthy of the situation. Othello seizes his *cangiar*, while Desdemona flies for safety to the bed, and receives the fatal stroke just as she reaches it. The curtains fall together, and hide the rest of the terrible deed, which takes place in the darkest recesses of the stage. Simultaneously, the whole chamber is shaken with the noise of battering on the door, and the *Doge* appears . . . the rest of the story is common property.

It was in Venice, on the occasion of just such a performance of Othello, during one of those evenings stilled into sadness, or rather into a kind of pensive melancholy, which sometimes, in these strange lands of the South, steal like ghosts into the merriest feast of life, that we fell to talking about the tragedies which have overtaken *real* lovers; and Signora Gherardi, of Brescia, told us the tale of Hortensia and Stradella. At the time, it affected us with an impression which perhaps may not survive the re-telling now, and in any case, the story is well known; but in spite of all these disadvantages, here it is. It is indeed a "plain, unvarnished tale"; the facts are historically true, and not without significance for the student of the manners, and even of the political state of Venice at the time.

Alessandro Stradella*, in 1650, was the most celebrated singer in Venice, and indeed in all Italy. In those days, the art of musical com-

---

[1] This is supposed to mean that the lightning has shown Othello that Desdemona is asleep, and therefore that the words *caro ben* ("my well-beloved") are spoken in a dream to a man whom she loves, and not to him (Othello), who is there, but whom she cannot see coming, because she is asleep.

position was extremely primitive. The *maestro* created scarcely more than the sketch of an idea; the real burden of creation lay far more heavily upon the singer than it does to-day, and it was *his* genius which had to invent almost everything that was significant or characteristic in the music which he executed. It was actually Rossini who was the earliest composer to whom it occurred to write down, in precise detail, all the embellishments and all the *fioriture* which the singer was to perform. But in Italy, in the neighbourhood of the year 1650, the situation was very different. The natural consequence was that the attraction of music was far more closely bound up with the individual personality of the singer; and in the general opinion of the day, among all those who enjoyed a certain measure of popularity, there was none who could so much as rival Stradella; it became proverbial to say that "he could master the hearts of all who heard him". One day he came to bask in his own celebrity in Venice, which at that date was the most brilliant of all the capitals in Italy, and the city which was famed above all others for the pleasures which were to be had within its boundaries, and the fastidious freedom of its manners and morals. Stradella received an eager welcome in the most distinguished families, and the highest-born ladies in the city would quarrel over the privilege of taking lessons with him. It was in this society that he first met Hortensia, a lady of Roman birth and aristocratic breeding, who was at that time a widow, and publicly courted by a noble Venetian belonging to one of the most powerful families in the Republic. Stradella won her love. Signora Gherardi took us, on the day following the one on which she told us the story, to see his portrait which hung in the palace of one of her friends; and we beheld his proud features deeply imprinted with melancholy, and his black eyes burning with those *subterranean fires*, whose secret life is so disturbing. The art of the portrait-painter, brought to perfection in Venice through the school of Titian and Giorgione, permits us even to-day to study every detail of Stradella's face. It is not hard to believe that such a man, ennobled by the added distinction of a great talent, should have been loved with passionate sincerity and should, in spite of his own poverty, have seized his prize out of the very grasp of a great and powerful *Seigneur*; and in fact he did steal Hortensia away from the noble Venetian. There was only one course which the two lovers had open to them: to escape as quickly as possible from the territory of the Republic. They retreated to Rome, where they lived, giving themselves out to be a married couple. But, still fearing the vengeance of the frustrated Venetian lover, they were afraid to travel directly and openly to Hortensia's estates; instead, they journeyed by the most circuitous routes and, even when they arrived in Rome, they took lodgings in the most deserted quarter of the town, and studiously avoided showing themselves in public places. The hired assassins, whom the Venetian nobleman had set on their tracks, took many months to discover them. After having vainly scoured all the most important towns in Italy, they eventually arrived in Rome one evening when there happened to be in progress a great *funzione*, with music, in the church of San Giovanni Laterano; and there, entering with the rest of the congregation, they chanced to perceive Stradella. Overjoyed at the freakish coincidence which had found them their victim just when they were about to despair of ever encountering him, they resolved to waste no more time and to carry out the task for which they were hired; but first they began a thorough exploration of the church, seeking in every corner, in case Hortensia might chance to be among the assembled faithful. They were still busily employed in their search, when certain other musical items executed by artists of lesser repute came to an end and Stradella himself began to sing. In spite of themselves, they stopped dead; and some force seemed to compel them to listen to the divine voice. Hardly had they been listening for more than a few minutes, when they felt themselves profoundly moved; in all the world there was but one artist who could command such exquisite perfection, and they were to extinguish for ever a voice of such unparalleled beauty! Stricken with horror, they began to shed tears of remorse, and long before Stradella's singing had come to an end, they had no further thought but to rescue those very lovers whose death they had sworn upon the Holy Gospels at the instant when they received the salary for their hire. At the conclusion of the ceremony, they watched patiently for Stradella outside the church; and in the end their patience was rewarded by the sight of him leaving the building, with Hortensia, by an inconspicuous little doorway at the side. Going up to him, they thanked him for the pleasure he had just given them, and confessed that he literally owed his life to the impression which his voice had made upon them, and to the manner in which he had melted their hearts; further, they explained the dreadful mission of their journey, and advised him to escape from Rome without a moment's delay, so that they might convince the jealous Venetian lover that they had arrived too late.

Stradella and his mistress were not slow to grasp the significance of this advice; and so, that very same evening, they chartered a ship, set sail down the Tiber, journeyed by sea as far as La Spezia, and thence made their way to Turin by the most unlikely roads. The Venetian nobleman, for his part, having received the report submitted by his *buli*, was fired to a still higher pitch of fury and, there and then resolving to take the responsibility of vengeance upon his own shoulders, set off directly for Rome, to call upon Hortensia's father. Here he succeeded in convincing the old man that nothing could wash away the stains of his dishonour save the blood of his daughter and of her seducer. Italy at that time had inherited from the old mediaeval Republics that vengeful spirit of the *vendetta*, which to-day has lapsed so completely into oblivion; *revenge*, in those barbarous times, represented the only honour which was known, the only additional safeguard over and above the common laws, the only means to which an injured party might resort in a land where duelling would merely have seemed absurd.[1] Thus the Venetian and the aged father fell into complete agreement, and together instituted a search throughout every town and village in Italy, When, finally, they received news from Turin that Stradella had taken refuge there, the old Roman aristocrat who was Hortensia's father, accompanied by two hired assassins particularly renowned for the skill which they displayed in the exercise of their craft, set out for Piedmont, having first taken care to supply himself with several letters of introduction to the Marquis de Villars, who was at that time French Ambassador to the Court of Turin.

Stradella, for his part, was now forewarned by his adventure in Rome, and had taken steps since his arrival in Turin to acquire protection in high places. His talents had earned him the favour of the Duchess of Savoy, who at that period was Regent of the kingdom. This princess undertook to help the two lovers to escape from the fury of their enemies; Hortensia was allowed to retreat into a convent, while Stradella received the title of First Singer to the Royal Household,

---

[1] *Vide:* Benvenuto Cellini, *Memoirs*; also the excellent *History of Tuscany* (1814), by Pignotti. This last is a very sincerely-written book, and greatly superior to that by Signor Sismondi, who has no gift whatsoever for describing the social and moral background or the true *physiognomy* of an historical period.

and thus was permitted to live actually within the precincts of the royal palace. These precautions seemed adequate; and so for several months, the two lovers had basked in a warmth of tranquillity and perfect happiness; they were indeed almost tempted to believe that, after the fiasco in Rome, the Venetian had grown tired of the pursuit, when one evening, Stradella, who was taking the air upon the ramparts of Turin, was set upon by three men who left him for dead with a stab-wound in the chest. The assailants proved to have been Hortensia's father, that venerable Roman citizen, together with his two hired assassins, who all retreated immediately after the crime to seek asylum in the Residence of the French Ambassador. M. de Villars, who wished neither to protect them from the consequences of a murder which was a nine-days' wonder throughout all Turin, nor to hand them over to justice after his own Residence had been invoked as asylum, took the third course, which was to connive at their escape.[1]

Against all probability, however, Stradella recovered from his wound, albeit with the total loss of his exquisite voice; and thus for a second time, the Venetian saw all his plans frustrated. Nevertheless, he still continued to cherish his scheme for vengeance. Now, however, with a prudence learnt from failure, he took an obscure name, and settled down in Turin, satisfied for the moment to set a horde of spies to watch Hortensia and her lover.

Such insatiable and bloody perseverance may seem almost incredible; but such was the *code of honour* of the time; if the Venetian aristocrat had renounced his right to revenge, he would himself have been pilloried by public scorn.[2]

In this manner, a whole year went by; at the end of which the Duchess of Savoy, who had grown meanwhile ever more deeply interested in the fate of the two lovers, resolved to legitimize their union and to crown it with the consecration of marriage. After the ceremony was over, Hortensia, who was bored with convent-life, had a wish to see the Geneose riviera. Thither Stradella took her; they arrived in Genoa; and the following morning, both were found dead in bed—stabbed.

[1] An identical situation arose in Chambéry in July, 1823.
[2] A friend of mine in Bergamo* [Radichi] tells how he was *forced* by public opinion to shoot and kill, in the open street, a *sbirro* who had surveyed him with a look of undisguised suspicion. He escaped justice for the offence by means of a self-imposed exile to Swiss territory, which lasted six weeks.

CHAPTER XX

La Cenerentola

THE first time I ever heard *la Cenerentola* was in Trieste*, where it received a superb performance from Madame Pasta, who can be as tantalizing in the rôle of Cinderella as she is tragic in *Giulietta e Romeo*; from Zucchelli, whose voice with its magnificent tonal purity is sadly under-appreciated by our Parisian audiences; and finally from that unrivalled *buffo* singer, Paccini.

It would have been hard to remember a finer production of any opera —such, in any case, was the verdict given in Trieste, where the public kept *la Cenerentola* running for a hundred performances on end, instead of the thirty for which Madame Pasta had bargained.

Nevertheless, in spite of the talented acting and the enthusiasm of the audiences (which last is a necessary condition, essential to the true enjoyment of music), I was greatly disappointed with *la Cenerentola*. On the first occasion, I was convinced that I was unwell; subsequently, however, as performance after performance left me cold and unmoved, while the crowds around me cheered to the pitch of delirium, I was forced to admit that my dissatisfaction must have its roots in some permanent personal idiosyncrasy. The music of *la Cenerentola*, beautiful as it is, seems to me to be lacking in some essential quality of *idealism*.

Many opera-lovers—perhaps the majority—are little concerned with the technical difficulties of the score; their delight lies in allowing the music to flow gently and caressingly over their imagination, there to conjure up whole castles of glittering and romantic fantasies. If the music is simply bad, the imagination remains lifeless and immobile; but if it is barren of *idealism*, there will be no lack of fantasies in the imagination, but they will be harsh, prosaic and revolting and the soul, repelled by such intrinsic vulgarity, will eventually seek its satisfaction elsewhere. Whenever I see *la Cenerentola* announced on the theatre-bills, I feel impelled to say, in the words of the Marquis de Moncade: "To-night I shall rub shoulders with the *hoi polloi*!" The music clutches at my imagination and willy-nilly drags it down to its own level, among the petty hurts and pettier triumphs of *snobbishness*, among the titillating satisfactions of appearing at a ball in faultless evening dress, or of being nominated major-domo to some minor scion of royalty. Now, I, having been born and lived long in France, may freely confess that I am heartily sick of snobbishness and vanity, sick of its little victories and defeats, sick of *braggadocio* and *gasconades*, sick of every one of the five or six hundred musical comedies dealing with the foiled expectations of snobs and braggarts which I have had to sit through in my career. Since the death of our last great writers of genius, Fabre d'Eglantine and Beaumarchais, our entire dramatic tradition has come to rest upon one foundation, and one only: vanity. Society itself, or at least nineteen parts out of twenty of that society, including everything that is vulgar and bourgeois, turns and turns again about one axis: vanity. Without wishing to seem unpatriotic, I believe I may legitimately record that I am by now utterly nauseated by this passion, which, in France at least, seems to have usurped the prerogatives of all the rest put together.

I went to Trieste in the hope of discovering something new; but when I saw *la Cenerentola*, I felt that I was back in Paris, at the *Théâtre du Gymnase*.

Music is incapable of sustaining rapid dialogue; it can portray the subtlest shades of the most ephemeral emotions, shades so fine and delicate that they may elude even the greatest of writers; it might even be suggested that the real domain of music begins only where the domain of the spoken word finishes; but music has one vital limitation: it cannot *sketch* an idea. In this respect, music shares the disadvantages of sculpture, as compared with sculpture's rival among the visual arts, painting; the majority of objects which strike us as remarkable in real life are valueless as subjects for the sculptor, for the simple reason that the chisel cannot leave anything half-said. The brush of a Veronese or of a Rubens can create a magnificent portrait out of some famous warrior in full armour; but nothing is heavier, or more absurd, than the same subject under the sculptor's chisel. If you want an example, take the statue of Henri IV in the courtyard of the Louvre.[1]

---

[1] Sculpture is to painting, rather as a letter to an intelligent and not unattractive mistress is to an informal conversation; the sculptor and the letter-writer have the same problem, which is fundamentally, how to avoid spoiling a suggestion by over-emphasis.

Imagine some idiotic braggart retailing gaudy and totally unfounded anecdotes of battles, wherein he, the hero of heroes, has won immortal crowns of glory; in musical terms, the *melodic line* would give us, in all sincerity, his own estimate of himself; but the *accompaniment*, all the while, would be full of mockery and disbelief. Cimarosa has created a score of little masterpieces founded upon some principle of this sort.

Melody can do nothing with emotional half-tones and suggestions; these qualities are found only in the under-currents of orchestral harmony. Yet note that even *harmony* cannot convey any but the most fleeting, the most ephemeral of images, for, as soon as harmony starts to claim too much attention in its own right, it threatens to kill the melody, as indeed does happen in certain passages of Mozart; in which case harmony, having now usurped the dominating rôle in the partnership of composition, becomes itself incapable of suggesting the half-expressed and the half-perceived. I ask pardon for this brief excursion into metaphysics, which I could certainly contrive to make less obscure if only I could play a few illustrations on a piano.[1]

I was attempting to explain how it happens that music is so ill-equipped when it comes to depicting *vanity*, and the *superficial* triumphs which pertain to it, together with all the rest of the bag of pretty little tricks so popular in France—the material from which, over the last ten years, every theatre in Paris, has been churning out its nauseating harvest of *spicy entertainment*,[2] its glut of cheap plays and shoddy operas, any one of which grows worse than intolerable after the second hearing.

The triumphs of vanity are rooted in a process of contrast, in a series of comparisons, deft-fingered and drawn with lightning rapidity,

---

[1] A fine example of this relationship between melody and accompaniment is to be heard in the Moor's *cavatina* in *Otello*: the melody is triumphant; but the accompaniment whispers insistently, *Othello, thou shalt die.*

[2] *Eg., le Faux Pourceaugnac, le Comédien d'Etampes, les Mémoires d'un Colonel de Hussards, etc., etc.*; or at Drury Lane, *the Deceiver deceiv'd, etc.* The so-called high-life† of every society in Europe is compounded of nothing but vanity. This is probably the reason why this same *high society* which, outside Italy, is the only social class which cultivates music at all, is at bottom so utterly antimusical; and why, on the other hand, it is so passionately fond of French novels.

A Russian aristocract from Saint Petersburg knows nothing more perfect in wit, intelligence and delicacy of feeling than Marmontel's *Contes Moraux* (*v. De la Russie*, by Passavant and Clarke).

† In English in the original (*Trans.*).

between oneself and *other people*. Vanity is inconceivable without *other people*; and this factor alone is quite enough to paralyse the imaginative faculty, since true imagination cannot spread its mighty wings unless it be in solitude, and cut off from *other people* by a black barrier of oblivion. Therefore no art whose principal appeal is to the imagination should risk its chances by meddling with the portrait of vanity.

La Cenerentola dates from 1817; Rossini composed it for the *teatro Valle*, in Rome, for the Carnival season 1816–17 (26th December 1816, lasting approximately until the middle of February 1817). The singers at his disposal were more or less unknown: they included Signora Righetti*, Signora Rossi, Guglielmi (*tenor*) and De' Begnis (*buffo*).

The *introduction* to *la Cenerentola* consists of a passage for Cinderella and her two unkind sisters: the elder is seen practising dance-steps in front of her cheval-glass; the middle sister is adjusting a flower in her hair; while poor Cinderella, faithfully fulfilling the rôle which we have heard attributed to her ever since our earliest childhood, is busy heating up the fire with a pair of bellows to make coffee. The whole of this *introduction* is witty and amusing; the song of Cinderella herself contains a few "touching" passages, but they are to be classed with those similar "touching" scenes which form so indispensable a part of our good old middle-class melodrama, where the audience is driven to weep hot tears by the very commonplaceness of the misfortunes. From beginning to end, this whole section is emotionally superficial, as though written under the influence of the proverb: *Let sleeping dogs lie*. The music itself is pre-eminently Rossinian. Neither Paisiello nor Cimarosa nor Guglielmi ever touched so ethereal a degree of feather-lightness.

But at the words

Una volta, e due, e tre![1]

---

[1] La Cenerentola's little song:
  Una volta c'era un re,
  Che a star solo s'annoiò . . .
taken up mockingly by the Ugly Sisters:
  Cenerentola:
  Una volta . . .
  Clorinda:
          E due . . .
  Tisbe:
              E tre!
              (Act I, sc. i)

the melody seems to me to degenerate into utter triviality. From this point onwards, the music invariably afflicts me with a faint feeling of nausea; and this reaction, which is never entirely dissipated, recurs periodically throughout the opera, and with increasing violence. In Trieste, to console myself for feeling as splenetic as the proverbial Englishman, sitting in morose and solitary gloom amid an audience seething with excitement, I used to analyse my own reactions, and eventually reached the conclusion, that *idealism* is as essential to music as it is to other arts; and further, that the scenes which music conjures up in our minds, and the fancies which it kindles in our imaginations, should *always* eschew banality in any marked degree. I cannot take any pleasure, for instance, in the comedies of M. Picard; I despise his heroes too intensely. I am not denying, mark you, that there may be dozens of *Philiberts* and of *Jacques Fauvels* in this world of ours; I am merely saying that I should refuse positively ever to degrade myself sufficiently in my own estimation as to speak to them!

Whenever I hear the tune:

Una volta, e due, e tre!

I receive the impression of having wandered by accident into the back of some shop off the *rue Saint-Denis*. The Polish pedlar of a shop-keeper may not disapprove of what he hears spoken on his own premises; nor, apparently, is the average inhabitant of the city of Trieste liable to be disagreeably impressed; while even *I* am quite prepared to pray that happiness should descend, like manna in the wilderness, upon every dirty little back-shop in France ... *provided that* I am not required to associate with the inmates of such establishments who, assuredly, would think *me* even more repellent than I should think them.

Don Magnifico's *cavatina*:

Miei rampolli femminini ...[1]

when it is sung by Galli or by Zucchelli, is a positive orgy of vocal sensuality. Its enormous popularity has been largely due, however, to its admirable suitability as a vehicle for displaying the rich delights of

[1] *Magnifico:*
Miei rampolli femminini,
Vi ripudio! mi vergogno!
(Act I, sc. ii)

a full-toned and resonant bass voice; further than this, it is nothing but
a *pastiche* of Cimarosa, *minus* the genius!

Ramiro, the prince-in-disguise of *la Cenerentola*, has a duet which
I find a slight consolation for don Magnifico's *cavatina*: the pretty
impertinence of the music is still somewhat reminiscent of some win-
some little milliner from the *rue Vivienne*, but many sins are forgiven
to a pretty woman; and beauty soon obliterates vulgarity. The passage:

> *Una grazia, un certo incanto . . .*[1]

has a certain charm, and I find a pleasant suggestion of wit in

> *Quel ch' è padre, non è padre*
> . . . .
> *Sta a vedere che m'imbroglio!*[2]

[1] *Cenerentola, Ramiro:*
> Una grazia, un certo incanto,
> Par che brilli su quel viso.
> Quanto caro è quel sorriso!
> Scende all' alma, e fa sperar.
> > (Act I, sc. iv)

[2] *Ramiro:*
> Ma, di grazia, voi chi siete?
Cenerentola:
> Io chi sono? Eh, non lo so.
Ramiro:
> Nol sapete?
Cenerentola:
> > Quasi no.
> Quel ch'è padre, non è padre . . .
> Onde poi le due sorelle . . .
> Era vedova mia madre . . .
> Ma fu madre ancor di quelle . . .
> Questo padre pien d'orgoglio . . .
> Sta a vedere che m'imbroglio.
> > (Act I, sc. iv)

Whenever, with brazen shamelessness, I appear to be conscientiously offering
to the most critical literary public in Europe some poetic monstrosity of even
more preposterous ineptitude than usual, this said offering being extracted from
the Italian *libretto*, it is to be clearly understood that my only object in so doing is
to remind the ear of the melody and accompaniment which Rossini has composed
to a given text. In any case, how should I conceivably manage to do what I am
setting out to do, unless I can assume that the reader has been to the *opera buffa*
at least *once* within the last six months? Further, if any reader, during the last six
months prior to reading this note, shall prove to have a total of less than ten visits
to the *Théâtre Louvois* to his credit or shall be unable to furnish evidence that he
has read at least one book or serious treatise upon the principles of art at some

In this scene we meet Rossini in the fullest display of his powers and in the most triumphant field of his talent. Yet how sad it must seem, to those whose sensibility is of a rarer quality, that with all his resplendent wit, he could not manage to squeeze out a drop or two of *dignity*! It should be remembered, however, that this opera was written specifically for the citizens of Rome, from whose manners every trace of dignity and refinement has been banished[1] by three centuries of Papal government, and by the Machiavellian politics of a Pope Alexander VI and of a Ricci!'[2]

The *cavatina* sung by the lackey Dandini, who comes on disguised as the Prince:

Come un' ape ne' giorni d'aprile . . .[3]

is extremely amusing. In this instance, the servants'-hall vulgarity which

time within the last two years (*e.g.*, Dubos, *la Poésie et la Peinture*; Paine Knight, *the Principles of Taste*; Alison, *Essay on Beauty*; or some noble treatise in German upon the subject which our Teutonic neighbours love to call *die Ästhetik*)—*if* there be any such person among my readers, then I take the strongest objection to him!

[1] An admirable portrait of the manners of this period is afforded, in a most naïve and curious fashion, by the comedies of Gherardo de' Rossi. His description of the world he knew omits *nothing*, save one or two of the less acceptable social improprieties, such as revenge by arson, or murder by poison, or a few other misdemeanours of similar character which, considered purely as material for comedy, are perhaps a little awkward to manage, and which, if depicted as part of the normal routine of daily life on His Holiness' personal estates, might have compromised the further peaceful existence of Signor de' Rossi, who is a banker in Rome. These comedies, together with the *Confessions* of Carlo Gozzi, are the sources which I have consulted every time that I have come to set down in these pages some characteristic detail concerning this curious country, which, amid all the surrounding *aridity* of this modern age in which we live, still produces its Canovas, its Viganòs and its Rossinis, whereas we in France, with the rarest of exceptions, can turn out nothing but charlatans of greater or lesser agility in the wild scramble for an entry on the Pensions List and a contribution from the Privy Purse!

[2] *E.g.*, the poisoning of honest old Ganganelli who, seated in full sunlight in a window of his palace at Montecavallo, had been amusing himself by dazzling passers-by with points of light reflected in a mirror. Most singular consequence of Jesuitical poison!

[3] *Dandini*:

Come un' ape ne' giorni d'aprile
Va volando leggera e scherzosa;
Corre al giglio, poi salta alla rosa,
Dolce un fiore a cercare per sè,
Fra le belle m'aggiro . . .

(Act I, sc. vi)

pervades the whole style of the music is for once really in place; the score, like the *libretto*, contains just the thinnest veneer of guttersnipe-ish brassiness, exactly the right amount to remind us of Dandini's real status without shocking our sensibility by too extravagant a display of coarseness. Cimarosa would have preferred to show us the *passions* of his unsophisticated characters, rather than their social mannerisms, acquired as a direct result of contact with society at a particular level; but *then* he would have shown us how these passions were thwarted by the degrading circumstances of a humble social position.

In Paris, this *cavatina*, which is a sort of *concerto* for a good bass voice, is often performed—and most delightfully performed at that—by the excellent *basso* Pellegrini; and in particular the lines

> *Galoppando se 'n va la ragione*
> *E fra i colpi d'un doppio cannone*
> *Spalancato è il mio core di già,*
> *(Ma al finir della nostra commedia . . .)*[1]

are sung with infinite grace, and embellished with enchanting sprays of *fioriture*. The speed with which the music gallops away with the last line of this quatrain is genuinely thrilling. The Italian librettist, Signor Ferretti, of Rome, had the good sense to make no attempt to imitate the gallic wit of his original model—and this was a sacrifice which needed some courage, for it is common knowledge that *Cendrillon* is one of the most enchanting of all the delightful works which have come from the pen of M. Etienne.

So far, all that the opera has offered us is a broad display, if not of downright coarseness, at least of excessive vulgarity; and Rossini's music, far from striving to diminish the crude complexion of his material, has if anything served to intensify it. After such an orgy of emotional brashness, therefore, it is a most welcome refreshment to reach the scene where Cinderella runs after her father, catching him by the tails of his embroidered coat, and singing:

> *Signore, una parola!*[2]

[1] *Dandini:*
[. . .] (Ma al finir della nostra commedia,
Che tragedia—qui nascer dovrà !)
(Act I, sc. vi)

[2] *Cenerentola:*
Signore, una parola:

The acting of Madame Pasta, her uncontrolled, childish emotion in particular, is excellent. I confess that I find this quintet quite delightful; in music, as in painting, some hint of dignity seems to me to be an essential and constituent part of art; conversely, in respect of M. Teniers, *etc.*, I have the honour to acknowledge myself in complete agreement with the opinion expressed by Louis XIV.

In the song:

> *La bella Venere*
> *Vezzosa, pomposetta . . .*

it needed all the skill of Madame Pasta's stagecraft and acting to console me into forgiving the triviality of the music; but this slightly nauseating little tune vanished suddenly into

> (*Ma vattene!*) . . . *Altezzissima!*

As soon as don Magnifico begins to reveal the first undercurrents of *real* emotion, I suddenly lost my painful awareness of the trivial superficiality which characterizes all his behaviour. At this point, Galli's fine voice becomes really magnificent.

There is a pretty little tune to the words:

> *Nel volto estatico*
> *Di questo e quello . . .*[1]

although here again we come up against that intrusive note of *vulgarity.*

> In casa di quel Principe,
> Un' ora, un' ora sola
> Portatemi a ballar.
> *Magnifico:*
> Ih! ih! la bella Venere!
> Vezzosa, pomposetta!...
> Sguaiata, cova-cenere!
> Lasciami, deggio andar [. . .]
> [*He strikes at her with his stick*]
> *Ramiro, Dandini:*
> Fermate!
> *Magnifico:*
> Serenissima!
> (Ma vattene!) Altezzissima!
> Servaccia ignorantissima . . .
> (Act I, sc. vi)

[1] Act I, sc. vi. See above, p. 149.

In the following scene, don Magnifico's exit affords Galli a further opportunity to display the superb qualities of his voice on the line:

Tenete allegro il re: vado in cantina![1]

Stressing the literal meaning of the word *cantina*, he lets his voice, with all its rich and rolling reverberations, rumble slowly down to bottom A.[2]

The first-act *finale*, which opens with a chorus of courtiers attendant upon the Prince hauling a half-tipsy don Magnifico up from the depths of the cellar, and which proceeds with don Magnifico's aria, is a perfect *pastiche* of the older *buffo* style of Cimarosa—but without the essential undertones of deep emotion. I can only repeat what I have said before (perhaps far too often!), that when inferior characters are stripped of the dignity of true emotion, all the elements of unpleasantness pertaining to their humble social status break through; and I confess that, once I have seen Tiercelin in *le Coin de la Rue* or in *l'Enfant de Paris*, I find it unbearable to sit through the same experience a second time.

In don Magnifico's aria:

Noi don Magnifico . . .[3]

true passion is replaced, as usual, by the superficial brilliance of wit; and wit, in music, is never a sure guarantee against the creeping menace of the commonplace. The best that this aria can achieve is a sort of melodic prettiness; I find it sadly lacking both in *verve* and in inspiration; and, in my opinion, nothing is so catastrophic in farce as mediocrity of any sort. By contrast, the duet which succeeds it is bright and brisk, and in Trieste was acclaimed as the musical climax of the whole work. Ramiro asks his lackey Dandini, who is still disguised as the Prince, what impressions he has managed to gather concerning the character of the Baron's two elder daughters:

[1] Act I, sc. viii.
[2] There is an Italian idiom: *Canta in cantina*, which means *to sing inaudibly*.
[3] *Magnifico (osservando come scrivono)*:
    "Noi Don Magnifico . . ."
    Questo in maiuscole!
    Bestie! maiuscole!
    Bravi! così . . .
                                                        (Act I, sc. x)

Zitto, zitto; piano, piano . . .[1]

The part of the tenor (Ramiro) is delightful in its freshness and originality, and is deliciously expressive of the feelings of a young Prince, who has learnt from a friendly magician that *one* of the Baron's daughters is worthy of his heart and hand—the magician in question, of course, was referring to Cinderella. The pace and brilliance of this duet, which offers an unparalleled display of musical fireworks, are quite unique. Never before had music been known to bombard the listener with so rich, so glittering, so spontaneous, so *original* a succession of new and tantalizing sensations.

No one in a normal frame of mind who hears this duet can resist its impulsive urge to merriment; the soul is left defenceless before this boundless, flooding tide of fantasy—or rather, is wafted away into some seventh heaven of delight by the sheer enchantment which such fantasy brings with it in its wake. When Ramiro and Dandini are joined by the two elder sisters, the ensuing quartet:

> *Con un' anima plebea!*
> *Con un' aria dozzinale!*[2]

not only contains several passages of exceptional musical brilliance, but in addition represents a master-stroke of verisimilitude in the dramatic context of the scene.

[1] *Ramiro:*
> Zitto, zitto: piano, piano:
> Senza strepito e rumore.
> Delle due qual è l'umore?
> Esattezza e verità.
> (Act I, sc. xi)

[2] When Dandini (disguised as the Prince his master) suggests that, if *he* marries one of the Ugly Sisters, the other can marry his lackey (who is Prince Ramiro in disguise), the Sisters recoil in horror:
> *Clorinda, Tisbe:*
> Un scudiero! questo no!
> *Clorinda:*
> Con un' anima plebea!
> *Tisbe:*
> Con un' aria dozzinale!
> *Clorinda, Tisbe:*
> Mi fa male, mi fa male]
> Solamente a immaginar!
> (Act I, sc. xii)

The aria which accompanies Cinderella's entry into the assembly-room,

Sprezzo quei don che avversa . . .[1]

is not only graceful, but unusually witty into the bargain.

The second act opens with an aria, in which don Magnifico confides to us that, as soon as one of his daughters is safely married to the Prince, the profitable perquisites of office are bound to start rolling in to *him*:

> *Già mi par che questo e quello*
> *Conficcandomi a un cantone,*
> *E cavandosi il cappello,*
> *Incominci: Ser Barone*
> *Alla figlia sua reale*
> *Porterebbe un memoriale?*
> *Prenda: per la cioccolata,*
> *E una doppia ben coniata*
> *Faccia intanto scivolar.*
> *Io rispondo: Eh sì, vedremo;*
> *Già è di peso? Parleremo* . . .*[2]

[1] *Cenerentola:*
> Sprezzo quei don che avversa
> Fortuna capricciosa;
> M'offra, chi mi vuol sposa,
> Rispetto, amor, bontà
>   (Act I, sc. xiv)

[2] *I can already imagine someone or other taking me secretly aside into a corner, and taking off his hat, and beginning thus: "My Lord Baron, would you do me the favour of carrying a petition for me to your Royal daughter . . . and then, of course, you'll do me the honour of taking chocolate with me, won't you? . . ." And meanwhile, a well-minted doubloon slips unobtrusively into my hand. So I reply: "Ah yes . . . We'll see . . . is the coin full weight? Very well, then . . . let's discuss the matter".*

Such indeed is the accepted standard of behaviour in the wretched city of Rome, and such, in consequence, are the tasteless satires which may be perpetrated without risk of provoking an outcry; such, finally, *is* the normal way in which affairs are managed within the boundaries of the Papal State! In Paris, we draw a more becoming veil of discretion over such transactions. I recall two young gentlemen, who were already making handsome profits out of certain contracts with the Ministry of ***; but they had the notion that they might effectively double the number of fictitious accounts presented every month for signature if they could only succeed in inducing the *Citoyen Ministre* to agree to some acceptable gift. Accordingly, after a series of careful researches in the close neighbourhood of Paris, one of the two young gentlemen finally lighted upon a most

Ramiro's aria:

Se fosse in grembo a Giove . . .,[1]

which reveals the fact of his love, and his determination to discover the object of his admiration, is pleasant in an amusing sort of way; it is a brilliant show-piece for a competent tenor, and ideally suited to the concert-platform—a remark which reminds me that, while Rossini's imitators have often recaptured the *pace* of his work, which is easy enough to copy in music, no one has yet succeeded in reproducing his peculiar brand of wit.

The duet which follows:

Un segreto d'importanza . . .[2]

pleasant mansion surrounded by a fine park, not far from Mon. . . . Having purchased the property, they had the mansion furnished and decorated in the very latest fashion and with every refinement of elegance and taste. When all the alterations were complete, the parquet-flooring well polished, the clocks set and wound, one of the would-be profiteers said to his collaborator: "Why not enjoy ourselves for a week in our own Manor before handing it over to the Minister?" The outcome of this brilliant inspiration was the immediate installation of a score of beautiful women, complete with their *beaux*, and banquets every day, followed by balls every evening. But at length the fatal day dawned when this week of splendour had to end; one of the accomplices sadly locked up the mansion, carried away the keys, and laid them before the Minister. The latter accepted the "gift"; the only words of acknowledgement, however, that he deigned to utter were: "The place is bound to be damp, I warrant!" "Impossible, sir!" came the reply. "We have taken the precaution of living in it ourselves for a whole week before offering it to you." "And *who* were your companions during this time?" "'Fore God, sir, none but our usual friends, who proved most worthy guests." "By which," rejoined the Minister, "I understand that you have had the audacity to introduce women of doubtful reputation into *my* residence; I confess, sir, that I find you confoundedly impertinent! You may go free *this* time; but on another occasion you will be pleased to observe the proper respect which is due to a Minister of the Crown!" Having received this admonition, the honest contractor vanished; while the Minister ordered his horses, and set out to inspect his new property.

[1] *Ramiro:*
   Sì, ritrovarla io giuro.
   Amore, amor mi muove:
   Se fosse in grembo a Giove
   Io la ritroverò!
                    (Act II, sc. ii)
Mythology (as you may observe) falls like manna from heaven upon the bad poets of Italy (no less than in France!).
[2] *Dandini:*
   Un segreto d'importanza,
   Un arcano interessante

is a superb example of the art of *pastiche* or musical plagiarism. In all probability it could never have existed at all without a specific model, which is to be found in the second act of *il Matrimonio segreto*:

> *Se fiato in corpo avete ...*[1]

Yet, even if one is so familiar with Cimarosa's little masterpiece as to know it completely by heart, none the less there is still infinite delight to be had from listening to the imitation. If this claim seems extravagant, it can be verified any day in Paris, where Rossini's duet is excellently sung by Zucchelli and Pellegrini. The line:

> *Son Dandini, il cameriere!*

invariably gets a well-deserved laugh, partly because of the sudden impact of a return to realism, and partly as a result of the puncturing of the Baron's grossly-inflated sense of self-importance.

In Trieste, the part of Dandini was played by Paccini, that most exquisite of *buffo* actors; and it is one of my greatest regrets that I cannot convey even the sketchiest notion of the effects which he produced. But it is better to admit straight away that there is nothing to be gained by description, unless the reader should chance to have seen him with his own eyes—Paccini, laughing up his sleeve at the fatuousness of the Baron, as they enter together for their duet; Paccini watching him out of the corner of his eye, unostentatiously, yet with such concentration that he almost misses his own chair as he sits down, and comes within an inch of rolling ignominiously upon the floor; Paccini

> Io vi devo palesar:
> È una cosa stravagante,
> Vi farà trasecolar [. . .]
> Sono un uomo mascherato;
> Ma venuto è il vero principe,
> M'ha strappata alfin la maschera.
> Io ritorno al mio mestiere,
> Son Dandini il cameriere . . .
>
> (Act II, sc. iii)

[1] *Geronimo:*
> Se fiato in corpo avete,
> Sì, sì, la sposerete!
> Un bambolo non sono,
> Veder ve la farò.
>
> (*Matrimonio segreto*, Act II, sc. i)

striving with everything he knows—yet always in vain—to stifle his
laughter when he realizes just exactly how much significance the
Baron attaches to the secret which he is about to impart; Paccini concealing his irrepressible explosions of mirth by turning his head abruptly
to one side, which gesture plunges the Baron into nameless despair,
since he interprets it to mean that the "Prince" has withdrawn his
favour from him; Paccini, with some desperate and contorted effort,
pulling his face straight again . . . and then turning slowly back towards
the Baron with a countenance of indescribable gravity; Paccini, lacking
at last the iron will to sustain this mask of puritanical and reverend
gloom, raising his eyebrows to an unprecedented height upon his fore-
head, thus inspiring further torments of mortal anxiety in the bosom
of our poor provincial Baron, flabbergasted by the sudden appearance
of so profoundly horrifying an expression upon his Sovereign's august
features . . . The actor who played the Baron had no need to do anything, for the audience, choking with laughter and wiping the tears
from its eyes, had no attention to spare for *him*; the absurdity of *his*
character was ineradicably and for ever established by Paccini's
reactions to it; for indeed, Paccini's acting was so perfect and lifelike in
its characterization of a man who is getting a rise out of some oafish
imbecile, and extracting the very last ounce of enjoyment out of the
process, that even if the part of the Baron had been played by a Fleury
or a de' Marini or by any one of the masters of classical comedy, with
every shade and *nuance* of ingenuity, art and psychological profundity,
the audience would have found itself compelled, even in spite of itself,
to think of them as village idiots. Paccini's behaviour was so real and so
natural, that not for one instant could one conceive that any man,
whose face wore *such* an expression, could be in the presence of anybody save a genuine and authenticated *fool*!

Furthermore, this astonishing programme was varied at every
performance; what talent, what genius indeed, could ever give the
faintest impression of that endless, crowded sequence of doubtful and
malicious jibes, of gestures parodying the behaviour of his friends and
colleagues, of allusions to their private affairs, of references to the current
chronicle of gossip in Trieste, all of which, together, constituted
Paccini's "interpretation" of a part?

For instance, the inextinguishable burst of laughter, when, on one
occasion, after his line to the Baron:

Me ne vado sempre a pie' . . .[1]

Paccini suddenly took it into his head to add:

Per esempio verso la crociata!

But of course, *you cannot explain a joke*; and nobody knows that better than I do!—for, to explain it, you have to start telling it all over again, and the flimsiest of anecdotes which, in the telling, takes no more than half a minute (which is probably precisely what it is worth!), runs to three or four good pages of print in a book, the very sight of which fills me with so much shame and confusion, that I immediately tear it all up again!

Paccini, like Rabelais, is a volcanic eruption of broad and discreditable jokes; and whatever their effect upon the audience, there is no question but that he himself enjoys them more heartily than anyone; nor can the dullest of spectators have the slightest doubt of it, seeing how his delight stamps every move, gesture and inflexion with the very genius of *verve* and naturalness. To my mind, it is this unrivalled *natural* quality of his art, the undisguised ingenuousness of his perpetual buffoonery, which permits him to get away with the endless series of burlesque and satirical impertinences which he fearlessly flaunts upon the stage at every performance, and which, anywhere else, would land him in gaol. For instance, in Trieste, the twelfth of February is celebrated as the Royal Birthday; there is a sung Mass with full music in the Cathedral; and, as everybody knows, at such a festival, the climax is always a great *gloria in excelsis*. No member of the Faithful is excluded from participation in any of the offices of the Church—not even Paccini (and why should he be, since, in Italy at least, there is no sentence of excommunication pronounced against opera-singers?). So Paccini goes to church; and if, on his arrival, it is discreetly observed that his entire head from chin to crown is snowed white with rice-powder, is it to be assumed that this minor anomaly should prove any

---

[1] *Dandini:*
    Io non uso far de' pranzi,
    Mangio sempre degli avanzi,
    Non m'accosto a gran signori,
    Tratto sempre servitori,
    Me ne vado sempre a pie'.
               (Act II, sc. iii)

valid reason for his failing to join the rest of the congregation in singing the great *Gloria*, and in singing it well, moreover, and with irreproachable gravity?—yet the mere sight of Paccini, snow-capped, yet himself singing and serious, is at long last too much for this particular church-full of the Faithful, who disintegrate into one mighty cataclysm of laughter, ably led therein by the highest dignitaries in the land.

I have purposely chosen as an illustration one of Paccini's most discreditable performances. In Paris, it goes without saying, any such outrage would be treated as abominable and disgusting, inspiring nothing but undisguised indignation, instead of the almost universal laughter which we witnessed in Trieste. Yet this very *indignation* is significant in itself, and deserves some comment. If Paccini were to appear in France, he would assuredly provoke the most violent indignation, not only on account of the disreputable incident illustrated above, but, I boldly maintain, on account of numberless other jests which, in themselves, *are in no way reprehensible*.

I am profoundly convinced that, say Paccini were to appear as a member of the *Italian Opera Company* in London, his triumph would be as notable as his failure would be catastrophic in Paris, where, if he ever dared *be himself* on the stage of the *Théâtre Louvois*, he would certainly meet a chill and shocked silence, even if he were not frankly booed off the stage. The implication would seem to be that laughter has been banned for ever from the soil of France;[1] and this prompts me to make an enquiry: is this perhaps, not an *isolated* disaster, but a revolution which is inherent in any advanced state of civilization? Does this gross and inflated measure of self-importance represent an unavoidable stage through which every community must pass on its way to a more civilized condition? Or is it rather simply one more instance of the pernicious influence of the court of Louis XIV upon French taste and upon French aesthetic sensibility in general? Will the Federated Republics of America, when eventually they cast off the drabness of puritanism and the cruelty of their Old Testament heritage,

---

[1] We have already reduced our best comic actors, Samson and Monrose, to the ignominious position of having constantly to entertain us with jokes *which we know already*. Our supercilious prudishness refuses to countenance anything *new*. Potier is perhaps the only comedian left who enjoys the rare privilege of making us laugh *without reservation*; and this is simply because we make no attempt to conceal our contempt for his particular brand of humour!

come likewise, in about a hundred and fifty years' time, to this same stage of prohibited laughter*?[1]

Nevertheless, although we in Paris have never seen Paccini—although it is well-nigh *impossible* that we ever should see him—we have at least had a glimpse of Galli in the part of don Magnifico. But you should go to Milan, where he is the idol of his own laughter-loving audiences, if you want really to see the pontifical gravity of his expression as he sidles off into the *salon* to make sure that no one is eavesdropping; for this gravity alone is sufficient to stamp him indelibly as a complete fool about to hear a momentous secret. And the impetuosity, the admirable *impatience* in his characterization, as he scuttles back to his chair to hear what the Prince has to tell him—a man overwhelmed with obsequiousness, and yet so greedy of secrets that the conflict between respect and curiosity has left him exhausted, until in the end he stands swaying and weaving like a snake charmed by a pipe, and yet starting convulsively at every word the Prince utters; the portrait is perfect, for here, in front of us, lives and breathes a being eaten up, utterly gnawed away by passion—and yet this unquenchable passion is supremely *absurd*! But, before his audiences in Paris, whose solemn presence is a thing of terror to the poor Italian actors, Galli scarcely found the courage to display even half of his real dramatic abilities; for all Italians know that European reputations are won or lost in Paris. A musical article or review in *la Pandore*, which to *us* seems just so much nonsense tricked out in fine prose and which we therefore unashamedly skip in reading, is an oracle of terrifying authority to these miserable foreign actors. In the excess of their generosity, they are prepared to accept it as the true voice of the most highly-critical public in Europe. No Englishman, for example, is prepared to bow down before the throne of genius, and give his homage: *Wonderful! Quite amazing!*[2] until he has first read some *article* to guarantee the reputation. And the more frivolous, the more absurd even, the review in question, the more impressive it is bound to appear in the eyes of this or that insurgent against the tyranny of the serious.

[1] If any one of our worthy French *literary critics* ever reads this page, I shall expect an outburst of fury: *On the contrary, Sir, we have an unparalleled sense of humour; in point of fact, France is the only country in Europe which knows how to laugh at all!*

[2] In English (with mis-spellings) in the original. (*Trans.*)

The duet:

Un segreto d'importanza . . .

is rapidly followed by an orchestral interlude depicting a storm, in the course of which the Prince's coach is upset. As a storm, however, it is quite innocent of Teutonic implications, bearing not the slightest resemblance to Haydn's storm in the *Seasons*, or to the toil and trouble which accompanies the casting of the magic bullets in *der Freischütz*. Here we have no suggestion of tragedy; yet nature, for all that, is faithfully imitated, complete with miniature "horrific climax", exquisitely rendered. At all events, and even without making any great claims to tragedy, this unusual passage, right in the middle of an *opera buffa*, offers all the charms of contrast. I have never witnessed a single performance (except, of course, at the *Théâtre Louvois*; I am referring to orchestras which have at least *some* subtlety in interpretation, such as those of Dresden or Darmstadt) at which I did not feel spontaneously impelled to cry out: *Oh, the ingenuity of the thing!* Many a time I have become involved in arguments with German acquaintances about this passage, and I can readily understand that, in their eyes, this particular storm must seem nothing but a washed-out miniature; people who can be moved by nothing less impressive than the Michelangelo frescoes will obviously have little to say in favour of this kind of music; on the contrary, *their* ideal is bound to be something like the infernal din which emerges from the concluding passages of the scene in *der Freischütz*, referred to above, where the diabolical bullets are concocted in the furnace—all this affording yet another proof of the doctrine that, in music, the *ideal of beauty* varies with the climate. In Rome, whose unique and peculiar sensibility Rossini had in mind when he composed the storm for *la Cenerentola*, the human temperament is nervous and exceedingly sensitive, and men, who exist on their emotions, and detest most heartily all the serious business of living, nourish their systems on coffee and ices; whereas in Darmstadt, life is one long round of good-fellowship, fantasy and music,[1] in the midst

---

[1] The reigning Prince of Darmstadt calls to mind the good old days when the Emperor Charles VI was renowned as the finest contrapuntist in all his wide dominions. The sovereign ruler of Darmstadt, who is a great patron of the arts, has never been known to miss a rehearsal in his own opera-house, and beats time from the royal box; and all the players in his orchestra (which is excellent, incidentally) have received his personal decoration.

of which any man with a little business-sense and a due quota of scraping and bowing in the direction of the Sovereign, can make himself a pretty fortune; and in any case the staple diet is beer and *sauerkraut*, and the atmosphere is blurred with fog for six months out of every twelve. But in Rome, on Christmas Day, when I went to the Papal Mass at Saint Peter's, I found the heat most decidedly uncomfortable in the sun, and the twenty-fifth of December under Roman skies was like a warm mid-September day in Paris.

The storm is followed by a charming sextet:

Quest' è un nodo inviluppato . . .[1]

which is quite strikingly original. When I first heard it, I used to think even more highly of it than I do now, when long familiarity has made me conscious of a certain *drag* towards the conclusion of the *sotto-voce* section. Nevertheless, this sextet may well be justified in its claim to represent the musical climax of the whole opera, vying for preference with the charming duet from Act I between Ramiro and Dandini:

Zitto, zitto, piano, piano!

and if the duet finally wins the prize, it must ultimately be thanks to its sustained, magnificent *pace*, and because it is one of the liveliest things that Rossini has ever composed, at least in that brisk and impetuous style which is the most characteristic feature of his especial genius. This is the field which is peculiarly his own, and in which no other musician, not even the greatest, can claim to be his master.

The great aria from the *finale*, sung by Cinderella herself, is something more than the standard *bravura* exhibition; here and there one glimpses a flash of sincerity and real emotion:

Perchè tremar, perchè?

. . . .

[1] *Ramiro, Dandini, Magnifico, Cenerentola,*
  Tisbe, Clorinda:
      Quest' è un nodo inviluppato,
      Quest' è un gruppo rintrecciato,
      Chi sviluppa più inviluppa,
      Chi più sgruppa più raggruppa . . .
                          (Act II, sc. viii)

Figlia, sorella, amica,
Padre, sposo, amiche! o istante![1]

It must be admitted, however, that the principal melody which is woven about these flashes of intuitive feeling is remarkably commonplace. This is one of those arias which I have never heard so well sung by anybody as by Madame Pasta; her rendering held a note of pathos and true dignity which was admirably fitted to the situation (true virtue triumphant and forgiving after years of misery); and by this she dissipated the gnawing suspicions that the whole aria might, at bottom, be nothing more than a *bravura*-piece for the concert-platform. By comparison, when Ester Mombelli sang the same passage in Florence in 1818, it did indeed degenerate into the most shameless *bravura*, dignified only by the rare technical excellence of the performer. I have never heard anything clearer, more crystalline, than this exquisite voice of Signorina Mombelli, trained in all the ingenious graces of the old school; but it was like listening to a display of academic virtuosity; nor did it ever seem to occur to anyone to wonder about the motives which *might* have been stirring in Cinderella's breast, and which were most certainly *not* stirring in the music as rendered. By contrast, when Madame Pasta interprets Rossini, *she* brings to the music all those very qualities in which *he* is lacking.

It is worth noting, that Rossini has now given us three operas which conclude with a grand aria for the *prima donna*: namely, *Sigillara*,[2] *l'Italiana in Algeri* and *la Cenerentola*.

I must once more make it quite clear that I am utterly incompetent to set myself up as a critic of *la Cenerentola*. This disclaimer is made entirely in my own interest, lest the quality of my musical sensibility should lie open to question; and I am willing to be modest about anything save about my acute sensitivity to music. *La Cenerentola* has

---

[1] *Cenerentola (to Don Magnifico and the Ugly Sisters:)*
    No, no; tergete il ciglio,
    Perchè tremar, perchè?
    A questo sen volate,
    Figlia, sorella, amica,
    Tutto trovate in me [. . .]
    Padre . . . sposo . . . amico . . . oh, istante!
                       (Act II, sc. x)

[2] *La Pietra del Paragone. (Trans.)*

on the whole been more successful than the majority of Rossini's operas in France*, and I have no doubt that if, by some whim or other, our worthy directors had seen fit to engage Signorina Mombelli, Signorina Schiassetti or some other more or less competent *prima donna* for the title-rôle, it might even have rivalled the popularity of the *Barber*. In the whole score of *la Cenerentola*, I doubt whether there are ten bars which evoke the fantastic, extravagant and fascinating imagery which comes crowding in upon me from all sides whenever I have the good fortune to hear a performance of *Sigillara* or of *i Pretendenti delusi*.[1] In the whole score of *la Cenerentola*, I doubt whether there are really ten bars on end which wholly escape the taint of the sordid little shops in the *rue Saint Denis*, or are uncontaminated by the odour of those money-grubbing, gutter-minded business-men who, when I meet them in society, send me scuttling out of the back-door as soon as I see them coming in at the front. But these elements of vulgarity, which I find so inexpressibly distasteful, would, if only they had been reasonably well sung, have given Paris everything it ever asks for under the title of *comedy*. One must therefore assume that these recent Parisian audiences somehow failed to notice the very features which seemed so inescapable to me; otherwise I cannot see how a public, which regularly applauds and encourages such productions as *la Marchande de Goujons*, *l'Enfant de Paris* and *les Cuisinières*, can fail to have gone delirious with enthusiasm over *la Cenerentola*. In which case, the opera would have stood to benefit from a process of suffrage quite as complex as that of the double-vote system: it would have been borne in triumph upon two separate sets of shoulders, the ones belonging to those who adore Italian opera for its own sake, the others to those who habitually gorge themselves on the coarse vulgarity offered as a nightly attraction by the *Théâtre des Variétés*.

[1] One of Giuseppe Mosca's hundred operas.

CHAPTER XXI

Velluti

I REGRET that the announcement which I now have to make will be unpalatable even to the most favourably-disposed class of readers which this present biography may hope to secure. I am, moreover, deeply distressed by the duty incumbent upon me to make it, for I am well aware of the risk which I am taking; countless opinions, strange-seeming here in Paris, which I have expressed, but which so far will have been excused as the insignificant vagaries of an irresponsible mind, will suddenly be transmuted into indigestible paradoxes, into odious blasphemies whose last excuse, that of *relevance* to the matter on hand, will have been swept away from under them. Yet the Author, having sworn a most curious oath, which is to speak what he believes to be the truth on all matters whatsoever, even at the risk of offending simultaneously the only readers who are capable of appreciating his work, and the great artist himself whose life he is writing, is in a position of dire necessity to continue even as he has begun.

The sort of man who moves about in Society; who has visited the *opera buffa* some two hundred times in the course of his life so far; who is beginning to despise the *Académie Royale de Musique* except for its ballets; and who studiously neglects the *Théâtre Français*—such a man represents the most enlightened, the most well-disposed reader whose attention I am likely to secure. Now, a *dilettante* of this class may perchance recall, long ago, when the censorship was less tyrannical than it is in our own time, having seen a performance of Beaumarchais' glittering comedy, *le Mariage de Figaro*. Figaro, he will remember, is excessively vain of his exhaustive knowledge of the English language: which exhaustive knowledge consists of one word—*Goddam!* Well, to come to the point and risk everything in one throw, I maintain that the average *dilettante* in Paris has precisely the same kind of "exhaustive knowledge" of one of the most important aspects of singing, which is the art of embellishment or *fioriture*, as Figaro had of the tongue of Shakespeare. This whole realm of music, so utterly new and foreign to

Parisian ears, could only be explored, could only be made *familiar* through six good months spent in an intensive study of Davide or Velluti. Any explorer who arrives in a new country, after the first, and by no means disagreeable glance about him, is bound sooner or later to receive a violent shock, when he begins to notice the multitude of strange and unfamiliar objects which come crowding about him from every quarter. The best-tempered, the most genial of travellers is hard put to it to suppress some small manifestation of distaste. Such would undoubtedly be the reaction of any average Parisian *dilettante* face to face for the first time with the extraordinary technique of which Velluti is the master. I would suggest, therefore, to any such *dilettante*, that he should without further ado set out to make a study of the *Romance* from *Isolina*[1] in Velluti's interpretation.

Imagine a beautiful woman, whose supreme attribute is the perfection of her figure, sauntering along the *Terrasse des Feuillants* in bright December sunshine, wrapped in her finest mantle of furs; and now, an instant later, visualize this same graceful being setting foot in some fashionable drawing-room, which is handsomely furnished, filled with flowers, and warmed to a gentle, even temperature by some ingenious and artfully-concealed device; watch her, as she crosses the threshold, throwing off her furs, and standing forth in all the fresh and brilliant tracery of a spring-time *toilette*. The woman who walked on the *Terrasse des Feuillants* is the *Romance* from *Isolina* expatriated from Italy, exiled in the cold North, and there enunciated by some well-trained tenor; how, under such circumstances, such wrappings, are you to do more than guess at the secret and hidden graces, at the *true* elegance of form and movement beneath? Freshness of line, perfection of contour alike are invisible to him who sees but the envelope. But when, on the other hand, you hear the fluted voice of Velluti singing his own favourite *Romance*, it is as though your eyes were unsealed; and before your wondering gaze, divested at last of her heavy mantle, stands Beauty herself in all her delicate shapeliness and entrancing fascination.

The first three bars which Velluti sings are prayers addressed by a lover to his mistress in her displeasure; and the passage concludes with a sudden *fortissimo*, when the lover, tormented by the object of his love,

---

[1] Morlacchi's opera *Tebaldo e Isolina*, which contains the famous *Romance*, will be performed (with Velluti in the cast) in Leghorn in September, 1823.

implores her forgiveness in the name of memory—the memory of the first fair morning of their new-discovered joy. The two opening bars, in Velluti's interpretation, are filled to the brim with *fioriture*, expressing to begin with extreme timidity, and later profound despair; he strews every note with descending scales in semitones, with *scale trillate*; and then at the third bar, resolves them all into a clear, unembellished, strong and sustained *fortissimo* which, on the occasions when he is at the height of his powers, is a miracle of freedom and confidence. No woman who truly loved could resist such a *cri de cœur*.

Such a style may, at first, seem effeminate, if not actively disagreeable; but at least the average French opera-lover, if he is honest, must confess that this particular vocal technique is something which he does not understand, a *terra incognita* of whose existence he had received no inkling from the singers he had heard in Paris. I do not deny that here, in this country, we have vocalists who can execute *fioriture*, and execute them with precision; but I maintain, firstly, that the sounds produced by singing of this character are not usually pleasurable *in themselves*, *i.e.*, regardless of their context in the work as a whole; and secondly, that this type of singing, at least as we know it, is anti-musical, since it constantly associates effects which should not be heard in juxtaposition, and which injure each other by their close proximity. Even without exactly understanding the reason, any listener of true and natural artistic sensibility, whose ear has been trained through the medium of a couple of hundred performances at the *opera buffa*, is bound to feel vaguely dissatisfied with the impression created by the technique of ornamentation as it is normally interpreted in France; he may reluctantly accept it with his mind; but his heart obstinately remains unmoved. But if he were to hear Velluti, particularly on those occasions when this notable singer is at the height of his form, he would experience precisely the opposite impression, accompanied by a sensation of pleasure growing daily more exquisite. The celebrated Sassarini, a *castrato* attached to the Royal Chapel of His Majesty the King of Saxony, used to create the same sort of impression in his execution of church-music; and Davide comes near to achieving the same deliriously exciting result, or as near as is possible with the technique of a normal tenor. I will not confuse the reader by identifying a number of other fine singers who might have conjured up a distant echo of those angelic sensations which Velluti can inspire in our souls, had Nature but seen fit to accompany the gift of a flexible larynx with the second, but no less essential gift of a refined sensibility. It is by no means uncommon to hear singers of this latter category (who as usually greeted with wild applause by the vulgar run of humanity, which has no fault to find with them) reeling off whole strings of haphazard *fioriture*, sometimes of extreme technical virtuosity, but all radically incompatible with each other in meaning, in colour, and even in fundamental character. Imagine a Talma, complete with all his wonderful powers of dramatic characterization, in the grip of some horrible nightmare, and declaiming, in rapid and totally random succession, extracts from each of his most famous parts: first, four lines of frenzied passion, extracted from a speech by Orestes (*Andromaque*), followed by a couple of lines of sublime and dignified moral ratiocination, borrowed from Severus (*Polyeucte*), followed again, without a moment's pause, by a couple more lines of snarling tyranny scarcely repressing its lust for blood, and ultimately to be identified as Nero (*Britannicus*) . . . and all the while, the soulless masses, upon whom the significance of all this is utterly wasted, vowing that they have never seen more marvellous acting, and cheering themselves hoarse! Yet, without exaggeration, this sort of performance is precisely the kind to which we have been accustomed from our most celebrated singers—for instance, from M. Martin.

Whereas Velluti gives us a whole, coherent speech, every line of which is conceived *in the same character*.

K

CHAPTER XXII

La Gazza ladra

Tʜɪs black and platitudinous* melodrama was contrived for Rossini by Signor Gherardini, of Milan, who based his *libretto* upon a popular boulevard play of the same character by MM. Daubigny and Caigniez. To make matters still worse, it would seem that this disgusting little anecdote is based upon an actual happening: a poor servant-girl *was* in fact hanged on one occasion at Palaiseau, and in her memory a Mass, which came later to be known as the *Magpie Mass*, was instituted.

In Germany, where this world of ours is thought of as a perpetually unresolved enigma, and where the natives see fit to spend the thirty or forty years of their maturity counting the bars of the dismal cage in which Fate has chosen to place them; where the melodrama *Calas*, which likewise stems from our vulgar, popular boulevard theatre, is prized far above Schiller's great tragedies *Don Carlos* or *Wilhelm Tell* (the latter being deemed *too classical*!); where, in this year of grace 1823, there is still a widespread belief, not only in ghosts, but also in the "miracles" of the Prince of Hohenlohe—in Germany, audiences would relish nothing so much as the added little thrill of horror which this hint of *reality* brings to the depressing and melodramatic *fiction* of *la Gazza ladra*.

The Frenchman, on the other hand, being first and foremost concerned with the criteria of "good taste", argues as follows: This world of ours is so full of filth in any case, that further speculation upon the imbecility of Him who created it is nothing but one of the more sordid exhibitions of self-indulgence, a pastime which simply adds one more drop of nastiness to the whole raging ocean of metaphysical sewage; *reality* is a plague, to be avoided as one values one's sanity. Art, therefore, far from being concerned with *realism*, has as its main function to furnish sufficient *idealism* to purge the soul, as swiftly and as durably as possible, of every taint of this dung-heap world, where

Le grand Ajax est mort, et Thersite respire.
La Harpe.

But the Italian, as soon as he has shaken off his adolescence and the priests who conscientiously torment it, has little time or inclination for such intricacy of argument; he would soon lose himself in a web of subtlety and entanglement, and in any case, for centuries now, the police of his country have forbidden him the simplest elements of logic; but he has *passions*, and to these he blindly surrenders. Rossini has woven, for his especial delight, exquisite music about an abominable theme; he responds to this challenge by enjoying the music while he can, and by paying as little attention to the story as he can manage; and if some dismal critic were to come and point out the blemishes in the object of his pleasure, he would take to his heels and run, as though from a *seccatore*[1] of the most intolerable variety. If there *must* be discussion, the Italian will only have it of one kind: the kind which immediately and perceptibly increases his present delight.

La Gazza ladra is one of Rossini's most successful works. He wrote it in Milan, in 1817, for the spring season* (*la primavera*).[2]

Fourteen years under the rule of an inspired despot had made Milan, a city once renowned for nothing but over-eating, into the intellectual capital of Italy; and in 1817 it could still number among its citizens some four or five hundred individuals—the remnants of that army of administrators which Napoleon had recruited from every corner of Italy, from Bologna to Novara and from La Pontebba to Ancona, to hold high office in his Kingdom of Italy—who stood head and shoulders above the general run of their contemporaries. These sometime civil-servants, who remained in Milan, partly through fear of persecution elsewhere, but partly in answer to their own preference for the life of a capital city, were in no wise disposed to acknowledge the superior critical acumen of the Neapolitans in any field whatsoever. In consequence, the *la Scala* audience took its seats for the *première* of *la Gazza ladra* with the firmest intention of deafening the composer of the *Barber*, of *Elisabetta* and of *Otello* with a positive hurricane of displeasure at the very first hint of a lapse from grace. Rossini was not unaware of this prevailing mood of hostility, and was therefore extremely nervous.

But the triumph was so delirious, the opera created such a *furore* (I

[1] A bore.
[2] The opening dates of the various *stagioni* are as follows: *Spring*, on the 10th of April; *Carnival*, on the 26th of December, which is the second day of Christmas; *Autumn*, on the 15th of August.

find the dynamic quality of the Italian critical vocabulary quite indispensable!), that scarcely a moment passed without the entire audience rising to its feet as one man to shower Rossini with applause. That night, at the *Caffè dell' Accademia*, the composer declared that, notwithstanding his delight at the success of the work, he was utterly exhausted by the effort of bowing, literally hundreds of times, to an audience which, at every instant, had been interrupting the performance with its shouting and applause: *bravo maestro! evviva Rossini!*

The success, then, was unparalleled*; and it may fairly be claimed that no composer has ever better fulfilled his own specific intentions. Moreover, the applause was the more flattering in that, as I have said, the audience at this date (1817) still comprised the intellectual *élite* of the whole of Lombardy. Thus it was during this same Golden Age that the city of Milan was ennobled by the choreographic masterpieces of Viganò. Alas, this glorious epoch was soon to crumble into dust, to disintegrate, around 1820, in a welter of arrests and *carbonarism*.

I was myself in the audience for that first performance of *la Gazza ladra*; and it was one of the most glittering, the most single-minded triumphs I have ever witnessed. Furthermore, this same triumph, maintained at this same pitch of enthusiasm, continued for three months on end! Rossini was fortunate with his cast: there was Galli, who at that time possessed the finest, the strongest and the most expressive bass voice in all Italy, and who played the *Soldier* in a style worthy of Kean or of de' Marini; there was Madame Belloc, who sang the part of poor *Ninetta* with her pure and wonderful voice which seems to grow younger with the passing of every year (the rôle is not difficult, but she sang it with infinite grace and intelligence; and I remember that she seemed to add a touch of dignity here and there to the basic conception of the character, so that in the end we had, not so much a common serving-wench, but something much closer to the daughter of a gallant veteran, driven out into the world to seek employment on account of her father's misfortunes); there was Monelli, a pleasing tenor, who played the young conscript, *Giannetto*, who returns to his father's house; there was Botticelli, in the part of the old peasant *Fabrizio Vingradito* (the part which, in Paris, was so magnificently interpreted by Barilli); there was Ambrosi, with his glorious voice and his superbly-integrated acting, in the rôle of the villainous *Podestà*; and finally, there was the exquisite grace of Signorina Gallianis, which, in the part of *Pippo*, was quite inimitable, and lent a particular charm to the Act II duet between *Pippo* and *Ninetta*. As though by some common consent, all the actors did their best to bring some touch of true dignity to the story. By contrast, Madame Fodor's performance made the whole thing unspeakably vulgar.

ACT ONE

What is there to say about the overture to *la Gazza ladra*? In fact, I wonder whether there is anyone left who is not already completely familiar with this most picturesque little *sinfonia*.

Rossini's innovation of scoring for the *drums* as a major part of his instrumental pattern creates an atmosphere of *realism*, if I dare use the term, which I have never encountered elsewhere;[1] it is an experience which can scarcely fail to make a vivid impression. Again, it would be almost impossible to describe the enthusiasm and the delirium of the Milanese audiences on first hearing this masterpiece. The pit, having clapped and cheered to the echo, having shouted for five whole minutes on end, having in fact created such an uproar and pandemonium that no conceivable stretch of the imagination can visualize it, found itself in the end utterly exhausted, too physically weak to cheer a moment longer; and then it was that I observed each man turn to his neighbour and start talking—a phenomenon which is totally foreign to the suspicious temperament of the average Italian. Meanwhile, in the boxes, the crabbedest, the oldest, the most cantankerous of spectators were gasping and squeaking: *o bello! o bello!*—the same word over and over again, twenty times on end, and not addressed to anyone in particular (for, of course, to repeat the same word twenty times is rather odd as a normal conversational gambit), but rather, every man having by this time grown completely oblivious even of the fact that he *had* neighbours, expressing the thinker's own thought to himself. These cries of delight held all the vivacity and all the charm of a reconciliation; for the public, touchy in its vanity, still remembered *il Turco in Italia*; and I imagine that the reader will not have forgotten how this opera received an unfavourable welcome, on the grounds that it was "lacking in originality". Rossini was determined to over-

[1] *Cf.* the various treatises concerning this overture which were published in Berlin in 1819.

come this set-back; and his Milanese friends were in fact extremely flattered to find that he had created something so profoundly original for their especial pleasure. It is this underlying preoccupation at the back of the composer's mind which explains the drum-passages and the somewhat Teutonic rowdiness of the overture; it was absolutely essential for Rossini to create an overwhelming impression from the very first notes. But in the event, the first twenty bars of this fascinating *sinfonia* were quite sufficient to effect an unqualified reconciliation between composer and audience; before the end of the first *presto*, the theatre was a tempest of delight; and the public *en masse* was encouraging the orchestra with *extempore* accompaniments! From this point onwards, the opera went from triumph to triumph, and the performance was one long scene of delirium. At the end of each number, Rossini was forced to abandon his seat at the piano in order to acknowledge round upon round of applause; and in the end, it seemed that he would sooner grow tired of bowing than the audience would grow weary of manifesting its enthusiasm.

This overture, which begins with the young conscript, covered with medals and glory, returning to the bosom of his rustic family, soon takes on a note of sadness, suggesting the tragic events which are destined to follow; but even this sadness is shot through and through with fire and *vivacity*, for it is the melancholy of youth, not of age; and in fact, all the chief characters of the opera are young. The *introduzione* sparkles with life and movement, and with a peculiar brilliance which reminds me of Haydn's symphonies and of all the uninhibited *dynamism* which is so characteristic of this composer. Attention is drawn towards the Magpie with the utmost skill and ingenuity:

> *Brutta gazza maledetta,*
> *Che ti colga la saetta!*[1]

[1] *La Gazza:*
    Pippo! Pippo!
Pippo:
                Chi m'ha chiamato?
Coro:
    Non so niente.
La Gazza:
                Pippo!
Pippo:
                Ancora!

In this passage, from the very first bar, I am always struck by a note of rustic energy, by a strong flavour of the countryside, above all by a complete lack of urban sophistication—features which imbue this particular *introduzione* with a colouring, an atmosphere which is a world removed from that, say, of the *Barber*. I like to think that, if there were music in Washington or in Cincinnati—music which were genuinely national, and not merely imitative—it would betray the same characteristic absence of artificiality and sophistication.[1]

This suggestion of peasant energy pervades the whole of Act I. The sour temper of Lucia, the farmer's wife (or rather, the disastrous consequences which are to spring from this blemish which stains her character) is first hinted at in an extremely impressive passage:

Marmotte, che fate?[2]

A few touches such as these are quite sufficient to betray the hand of a great artist: the initial conception is broad and sweeping, perfectly developed, and unimpeded by a cluttering of irrelevant detail. The composer, clearly, has been bold enough for once to face up to the challenge of boring his audience, and to risk not pandering to the vulgar urge to be entertained with insignificant witticisms. The result is an effect which is truly grandiose.[3]

The reply which Lucia receives when she enquires for her husband:

> *Coro:*
>> Ve' chi è stato.
> *Pippo:*
>> Brutta gazza maledetta,
>> Che ti colga la saetta!
>> (Act I, *Introduzione*)

[1] This opening scene of Act I has the same characteristic flavour that one meets in the poetry of George Crabbe; and in certain passages, it has something of the energetic rhythms of Burns' *Ballads*.

[2] *Lucia:*
> Marmotte, che fate?
> Così m'obbedite?
> Movetevi, andate,
> La mensa allestite,
> Là, sotto alla pergola,
> Che invita a mangiar.

[3] The same principle applies to the paintings of Correggio, or to the majority of antique marbles. Some definitions of *the Beautiful* are equally valid for all the arts, from an *opera buffa* to the architecture of a dungeon. Grecian pilasters in a dungeon offer consolation . . . of a sort!

Tuo marito? . . .[1]

together with the little aria sung by Fabrizio, a cheery old gaffer, as he climbs out of the cellar waving a bottle—all this section is pre-eminently merry, rustic and thumping; and, stylistically, more and more reminiscent of Haydn. Once again, it is the *Magpie* who is made to reveal to the spectators the young conscript's love for the heroine; for when his mother declares:

Egli dee sposar . . .[2]

the Magpie burst in with a squawk:

Ninetta! Ninetta!

The verve and brilliance of the ensuing *tutti*:

Noi l'udremo narrar con diletto . . .

is quite astounding; I would remark, however, that the less a composer is concerned to sustain an atmosphere of dignity and distinction, the *easier* it is for him to keep up a pitch of merriment, vivacity and general

---

[1] *Lucia:*
     Ehi, Ninetta! quando io chiamo,
     Tutti perdono l'udito,
     E colui di mio marito,
     Dove adesso se ne sta!
   Coro:
     Tuo marito? Eccolo qua!

[2] *Fabrizio:*
     Certamente, ed ammogliato
     Lo vorrei, ben mio, veder.
   Lucia:
     A me tocca il dargli moglie,
     Questo affaire a me s'aspetta.
     Egli dee sposar . . .
   La Gazza:
               Ninetta! Ninetta!
   Fabrizio:
     Ah! la gazza ha indovinato! [. . .]
     L'ha seduto, l'amato Giannetto,
     A suo padre, alla sposa vicino,
     Or d'orgoglio brillar lo vedremo,
     Or di bella pietà sospirar [. . .]
     Noi l'udremo narrar con diletto
     Le battaglie, le stragi, il bottino
     E fra i brindisi, intanto faremo
     I bicchieri ricolmi sonar!

brio. Incidentally, there are two lines in this passage which have a fine martial ring about them:

> Or d'orgoglio brillar lo vedremo,
> Or di bella pietà sospirar ...

Ninetta's *cavatina*:

> Di piacer mi balza il cor ...[1]

resembles the overture in being one of Rossini's finest inspirations: is there indeed anyone who is *not* familiar with it? As a portrait in music of the boisterous and open-hearted merriment of a young country-wench, it is perfect. I doubt whether Rossini's genius has ever created anything more glittering, nor at the same time more *dramatic*, more true, or in closer harmony with the spirit of the *libretto*. This aria has all the forcefulness of Cimarosa, with something else that Cimarosa rarely achieves, namely, dynamic movement in the opening bars.

The only quarrel one might pick with this *cantilena* might be to criticize its slightly vulgar and bumptious rusticity. In this context, it is worth observing, that whenever Rossini aims at deep emotional sincerity, he is obliged to return to his older technique of *long phrases of lilting melody*. The phrase *di piacer* runs for eight whole bars; and such an extension is comparatively rare in Rossinian opera.[2]

There is, however, *one* suggestion of emotional sincerity, introduced with infinite finesse; this occurs in the line:

> Dio d'amor, confido in te ...

[1] *Ninetta:* Di piacer mi balza il cor;
               Ah! Bramar di più non so.
               E l'amante, il genitor,
               Finalmente rivedrò.
               L'un al sen mi stringerà:
               L'altro ... l'altro, ah! che farà?
               Dio d'amor, confido in te!
               Deh! tu premia la mia fe'!
               Tutto sorridere mi veggo in torno,
               Più lieto giorno brillar non può!
               Ah! già dimentico i miei tormenti,
               Quanti contenti alfin godrò!

[2] A single bar removed from Ninetta's first phrase immediately gives the listener the impression that something is missing; I can think of hardly anywhere else in Rossini's work (or at least in the operas belonging to his "second manner") where the same could be held to be true, except in certain passages in waltz-time.

just before the double-bar. With a generous effort, one can overlook the crass ineptitude of putting the words *God of Love* (*dio d'amor*) into the mouth of a farmer's daughter. The librettist, one supposes, was a *classicist*. When Madame Fodor sang this *cantilena* in the Paris production, the tone of her voice was unexceptionable; but unfortunately its pure beauty was not matched by any comparable sensitivity or subtlety in the expression. Like all artists of mediocre sensibility, whose "inward fire" (as the painters say) burns fitfully and low, Madame Fodor, in her interpretation of this *cavatina*, made up for a *beauty*, which she could not command, by a display of *opulence*, which she could. Armed with every virtuoso weapon from her technical armoury, she so peppered the composer's fundamental inspiration with roulades and ornaments, that in the end she managed to obliterate it completely. O notable triumph! If Rossini had been present to hear the performance, he would doubtless have told her what he had already told the celebrated Velluti on the occasion of the *première* of *Aureliano in Palmira* (Milan 1814): *Non conosco più le mie arie!* "I cannot even recognize my own music!"

A natural and lively feeling for dramatic expression, which yet never deviates from the line of pure beauty, is rare enough in Rossini to merit respect when it *does* occur. The opening phrase of the *cantilena*:

> *Di piacer mi balza il cor* . . .

should be sung in absolute simplicity, stripped of roulades, and in fact barren of every kind of ornament; all embellishments of this character should be saved up for the *end* of the aria, when Ninetta seems to be contemplating the excess of her own happiness. All manner of gay and glittering *fioriture* are in place when she comes to the phrase:

> *Ah! già dimentico*
> *I miei tormenti* . . .

—words which that charming little singer, la Cinti, pronounces with so tantalizing and so irresistibly provocative an accent!

In the Milan production, this and similar delicate points of interpretation were perfectly grasped by Madame Belloc. But I should merely risk boring my long-suffering readers if I were to describe the further tempests of enthusiasm which greeted this aria, which is so simple, so natural and so easy to understand. It marks the zenith of perfection in the rustic tradition. Indeed, I feel sorry that the scene is not set in Switzerland; no aria could fit better into the context of an opera like *Lisbeth*.[1] Spectators in the pit had clambered up on to their benches, and had called upon Madame Belloc to give them an *encore*; and they were already calling for yet another *encore* of this same *cavatina*, when Rossini intervened in person, addressing the front rows of the pit from his seat at the piano: "Gentlemen, the part of Ninetta is extremely heavy; and if you continue to treat Madame Belloc in this inconsiderate manner, she will be too exhausted to finish the opera". This argument, which was repeated from mouth to mouth, and argued from one end of the pit to the other, did at last, after an interruption lasting some fifteen minutes, produce an effect. My neighbours on either hand were arguing away among themselves with as much heat and sincerity as though they were old acquaintances; and in all Italy I have never since witnessed such fatal imprudence. Spontaneous discussion of this type gives the informer the very chance he is hoping for, to butt in, pick a side in the argument, and later denounce the contestants to the police—only too successfully!

Following this *cavatina*, which breathes all the joy and freshness of the forest, we tumble right back into the very meanest squalor of civilization, dragged thither by the song known as the *Jew's aria*, a piece of music which reeks of the most loathsome race on earth, the Polish Jews;[2] on the other hand, considered purely and simply *as an aria*,[3] it is excellent. All the sordid *realism* which it implies is re-

---

[1] *Lisbeth*: an opera which was immensely popular in France some twenty years ago, tastefully based on the theme of an unmarried mother deserted by her lover! Rossini's aria should be compared with Weigl's *die Schweizerfamilie*, a masterpiece of Teutonic "simplicity", which, however, appeared rather *too* naïve for the taste of the Milanese in 1819.

[2] To my mind, the Polish Jews are, in their own particular province of activity, not unlike the swindlers who plague the Kingdom of Naples; the blame, *the entire responsibility* for their nefarious activities, belongs to the respective governments of the two countries involved, whose short-sighted policies have *created* such individuals. In France, ever since the time of Napoleon, the Jews have come to be indistinguishable from all other members of the community, save in that they are slightly more miserly.

[3] *Isacco*:

> Stringhe, e ferri da calzette,
> Temperini e forbicette,
> Aghi pettini, coltelli,
> Esca pietre, e solfanelli ...
> Avanti, chi vuol comprar!

deemed and made palatable by the inspiration of Rossini's wit and ingenuity.

The chorus which heralds Giannetto's return:

Viva! Viva! ben tornato![1]

holds such a wealth of musical ideas, such an infinite, inexhaustible *luxuriancy*[2] (as they would say in England) of genius, that I find it almost impossible to conceive its existence. On the other hand, when the young conscript, arrayed in all his martial glory, returns at last to his native village, where the local papers have just published an article about him and his adventures, the aria which he sings is insipid and commonplace in the extreme, and in thoroughly bad taste into the bargain. In defiance of every dictate of common politeness, our young hero goes straight away to look for his mistress and then, leaving the entire village, including his own father and mother, standing rather uselessly in the background, he proceeds to make love to her under their very noses. Love, the most fascinating of passions, is utterly debased the moment it loses the virtue of modesty.

The aria:

Anche al nemico in faccia . . .[3]

is quite agreeable to listen to, despite its fundamental inanity and

---

[1] *Coro:*
  Viva! Viva! Ben tornato!
Pippo:
  È Giannetto!
Ninetta:
        Oggetto amato!
  Deh mi vieni a consolar!

[2] In English in the original. (*Trans.*)

[3] *Giannetto:*
  Vieni fra queste braccia,
  Mi balza il cor nel sen!
  D'un vero amor, mio ben,
  Quest'è il linguaggio!
  Anche al nemico in faccia,
  Mi ripresento ognor,
  Tu m'inspiravi allor
  Forza, e coraggio, e valor [. . .]
  Ma quel piacer che adesso,
  O mia Ninetta, provo,
  È così dolce, e nuovo,
  Che non si può spiegar.

pretentiousness. But what was really required at this point, both in the passage:

Ma quel piacer che adesso . . .

and even more urgently in the *ritornello*-section which introduces it, was some theme which was both joyous, gentle and deeply tender— the diametrical opposite of our French national brand of swaggering and volcanic passion. This is a case where it becomes absolutely imperative for Rossini to have at his disposal a Giannetto, whose voice can supply the feeling, the depth and the true sincerity which are so seriously lacking in the score. It would be best if Madame Pasta could take the part—and not only this one, but those of *all* the maestro's passionate lovers; her own personality has certainly no less a contribution to make towards the interpretation of these rôles than that which it has made already in the case of Tancred.

At the words:

No, non m'inganno . . . ,[1]

[1] The words: "No, non m'inganno" are omitted from the opening of Fernando's recitative in many versions.

Fernando:	Jeri, sul tramontar del sole,
	Giunse a Parigi la mia squadra.
	Io tosto del capitano imploro
	Di vederti il favor.
	Bieco e crudele, ei me lo niega!
	Con ardir, con fuoco, a detti suoi rispondo.
	Sciagurato! Ei grida;
	E colla spada già, già m'è sopra!
	Agli occhi mi fa un velo il furor;
	La sciabola impugno, m'avvento, e i nostri ferri
	Già suonano percossi, quand' ecco a noi sen' viene
	Pronto un soldato, e il braccio mio trattiene.
Ninetta:	E allora, padre mio?
Fernando:	Barbara sorte! Fui disarmato
	E condannato a morte.
Ninetta:	Misera me!
Fernando:	Gli amici, procurar la mia fuga.
	Il prode Ernesto
	Di questi cenci mi coperse,
	E scorta mi fù, sino al primo villaggio,
	Dove entrambi, piangendo, ci lasciammo.
	Amico mio, ei disse; e dir non più mi poteva: Addio.

(Act I, sc. vii)

which Galli sings to the accompaniment of a sweeping movement downstage, tragedy steps into the idyll, and joyousness has fled for ever.

When Rossini composed *la Gazza ladra*, he was in the thick of a violent quarrel with Galli*, who had successfully supplanted him in the favours of la M***. Now Galli, you must understand, has a magnificent voice; but in the whole of his range, there are just two or three notes which he can never strike perfectly, unless it is merely a question of sliding rapidly across them in some transition passage; if he is obliged to dwell upon them, he invariably strikes them out of pitch. Rossini was unable to resist the temptation to write him a recitative (the one in which he tells his daughter about the quarrel he had with the Captain of his regiment) specially contrived to compel Galli to spend most of his time lingering fondly over that particular selection of notes which he was completely unable to sing properly. In Paris, whenever he came to the passage:

Sciagurato!
Ei grida; e colla spada
Già, già, m' è sopra . . .,

this singular limitation became most clearly apparent, and Rossini's revenge was triumphantly successful! But Galli, who can sing with magnificent assurance throughout all the rest of the range of his tremendous voice, had a fit of pig-headedness, and positively refused to alter these unsingable notes in the performance, although nothing could have been easier than for him to do so. His querulous obstinacy caused him therefore to muff this particular entry in Rome and in Naples just as much as in Paris; and in the latter city, where musical taste is highly critical, and little given to rapturous surrender, preferring cold and faultless virtuosity[1] to the sublimest flights of beauty marred by a slight technical imperfection here and there in the execution, Galli

---

[1] *Magis sine vitiis quàm cum virtutibus.* A voice admirably qualified to meet with approval in Paris in the year 1810 was that of Signora Barilli. Since that date the critical faculties of the average *Louvois* audience have been immensely sharpened; but that is not to say that the worthy Signora Barilli would not still enjoy a very real popularity, even if she were to reappear to-day. The number of persons in Paris whose sense of musical appreciation has been genuinely *educated* may perhaps have risen to some four or five hundred; and these may now claim to be as expert in the science of musical appreciation as the *ten thousand* regular opera-goers of the *San-Carlo* and *la Scala* theatres.

never enjoyed the unqualified success which should have been his by right.

The derisive gasps from the audience only made Galli more determined than ever not to give in, and he refused point-blank to alter the ten fatal notes, with the result that the ensuing nervous apprehension affected the quality of his voice and so, in spite of every effort on his part, this entry, the opening sequence of so magnificent a rôle, was always ruined by the intrusion of three or four hesitant notes. On the other hand, in Naples, when Galli's part was taken by Nozzari, this particular recitative was the occasion of one of the latter's most notable triumphs, and each note was produced with impeccable purity and precision. However, as soon as Galli reached the *end* of this recalcitrant section:

> *Amico mio,*
> *Ei disse, e dir non più mi poteva: Addio!*

he used to recover his confidence, and would soon rise to the finest heights of tragic acting.

Incidentally, it is absurd that Galli, in the part of a soldier who has deserted from his regiment, where he has been condemned to death, should appear on the stage in full military uniform, scarcely bothering to attempt to conceal it beneath his greatcoat; such foolhardiness would unquestionably lead to his immediate arrest as a runaway by the mayor of the first village he happened to pass through! This is a typical problem of *staging*, an art which is closely allied to that of painting. If, however, as the *libretto* requires:

> *Il prode Ernesto*
> *Di questi cenci mi coperse . . .,*

Galli were to appear clad in beggar's-rags, the part might well *lose* in dignity and stature; for, in all opera, it is essential to appeal to the *eye*. In real life, if a condemned man were to chance upon an unhoped-for meeting with his daughter, he (*i.e.*, Galli) would certainly have not less than two or three thousand words to say to her; but in opera, selection is imperative; and it is the function of the music, having selected, out of all this mass of words, not more than a hundred or so, to make them convey all the wealth of emotion which would otherwise have been present in the full three thousand. It is obvious, therefore that, among the material which has to be discarded, the first to go will be the description of physical detail; and so, logically, the opera as a whole must supply this defect by speaking to the eye.

The duet which follows this recitative by Galli:

Come frenar il pianto . . .?[1]

offers a superb instance of stylistic *opulence*.[2] The short orchestral passage which follows the lines:

È certo il mio periglio;
Solo un eterno esiglio,
O Dio! mi può salvar . . .[3]

> [1] *Ninetta:*   Come frenar il pianto!
>   Io perdo il mio coraggio!
>   E pur di speme un raggio
>   Ancor vegg'io brillar!
>
>   *Fernando:* No, no, non v'è più speme;
>   È certo il mio periglio;
>   Solo un eterno esiglio,
>   O Dio, mi può salvar.
>
>   *Ninetta:*   Per questo amplesso, o padre,
>   Ah! regger non poss'io;
>   Chi vide mai del mio
>   Più barbaro dolor [. . .]
>
>   *Fernando:* Il nembo è vicino;
>   Tremendo destino,
>   Mi sento gelar
>
>   (Act I, sc. viii)

[2] *I.e.,* high-sounding rather than truly moving; the style of Paolo Veronese or of Buffon. It is a style whose *magnificence* represents unadulterated sublimity to the aesthetically insensitive, and which invariably creates a *furore* in the Provinces!

Some of the harmonies in the opening bars of this duet are reminiscent of the *introduzione* to the *Barber*. Certain sections of the *finale* of Act I have been criticized on the same grounds. There are further resemblances to be noted between the quartet from *Mosè in Egitto*:

Mi manca la voce . . .[*]

and the quintet:

Un padre, una figlia . . .

and it has also been asserted that the passage which follows the sentencing of Ninetta is similar to a chorus from *la Vestale*:

Détachez ces bandeaux . . .

[3] It is unthinkable that any *French* soldier should betray (in words, in any case) such an abysmal state of depressed morale. But the librettist was supremely indifferent to the petty nationalistic vanity of the land in which his scene was set, and in consequence there is an unfamiliar ring of *truth* about his portrait of human misery. It is precisely this type of "crudity" which our French connoisseurs have seen fit to complain of in the paintings of Guercino.

produces a truly *physical* sensation of terror. But after the phrase:

Più barbaro dolor . . .

there comes a brief instant of genuine tenderness.

The passage:

Tremendo destino . . .,

which occurs in the duet, towards the end of the repeat, is overwhelming in its power and menace. By contrast, in the concluding *ritornello*, there is an ephemeral suggestion of *idealism* which, by distracting the listener's attention, if only for a moment, from the sordid brutality of the tragedy, brings a glimpse of respite.

The *cavatina*, sung by the *Podestà*:

Il mio piano è preparato . . .[1]

is a brilliant show-piece for a first-rate bass voice. When it was sung in Milan by Ambrosi, the very power, the dynamic violence of this remarkable artist had the positive disadvantage of concentrating the audience's attention with unpleasant singlemindedness upon the atrocious character of the *Podestà*. Pellegrini, who sings it in Paris, serves the requirements of the opera as a whole much better by exploiting every facet of the delicacy and miraculous gracefulness of which his delightful voice is capable. In any case, given its context, the whole *cavatina* is far too long.

The scene in which the *Podestà*, who has lost his glasses, hands Ninetta the official description of the deserter and makes her read it aloud, is rich with all the poignant, breath-taking suspense of melodrama: it is a scene of sordid nastiness, unrelieved by *idealism* of any description. This is the sort of thing that the average German simply adores. I would not deny its dramatic power; but as it proceeds, the last spark of comedy is extinguished for ever.

The trio which follows:

Respiro—partite . . .[2]

[1] *Podestà:* Il mio piano è preparato,
          E fallire non potrà;
          Pria di tutto con destrezza
          Le solletico l'orgoglio!

[2] *Ninetta:* Respiro.

is sublime; and it is the early section of this passage which contains the
masterly prayer:

Oh! nume benefico!

But the fact is that, shortly before, Winter had produced an operatic
version (based on Voltaire's tragedy) of the story of *Mahomet*,
which contained a fine prayer for the combined voices of Zopiro,
who is praying alone in the depths of the temple, and of his two
children, as they enter downstage with the mission of putting him
to death. In consequence, Rossini insisted that the librettist should
provide *him* with a prayer, which he then proceeded to set *con
pegno.*

The *Podestà*, having watched the soldier depart, and believing
himself to be unobserved, addresses Ninetta in the following
words:

Siamo soli. Amor seconda
La mia fiamma, i voti miei.
Ah! se barbara non sei,
Fammi a parte nel tuo cor!

This is superb tragedy (I refer, obviously, to the music, and *not* to the
words!); and the trio as a whole deserves every laudatory epithet that
has yet been invented; if Rossini had written this and nothing else, it
would alone have been quite sufficient to establish his reputation
indisputably and for ever above the whole host of his competitors in
the field of musical composition.

Fernando's re-entrance is as violent as could be imagined:

Podestà:
　　　　　Mia cara!
Fernando:
　　Signora!
Ninetta:
　　　　　Partite!
Podestà:
　　Udite?
Ninetta:
　　　　　Partite, uscite di qua!
Fernando:
　　O nume benefico
　　Che il giusto difendi:
　　Propizio ti rendi,
　　Soccorso, pietà. (*Exit.*)

> *Freme il nembo* . . .
> *Uom maturo e magistrato,*
> *Vi dovreste vergognar!*[1]

But here, as elsewhere, violence and frenzy are more to the forefront than dignity, sensibility or artistic refinement; while, in the orchestral score, the outstanding characteristic is *noise*; thus, for instance, the passage:

> *Non so quel che farei,*
> *Smanio, deliro e fremo* . . .

is positively volcanic. In this section, Rossini's naturally *rapid* style seems to bring added fire to the unbelievable frenzy of the orchestral score, and the trio as a whole may be summed up as one of the finest things that the composer has ever written in this, his second ("heavy") manner. The problem of voice-grouping is handled with infinite skill; and there is a further quality, which is rare enough even in the greatest music ever composed: namely, a kind of *progressive development*, managed with the most extraordinary subtlety. By the end of the trio, in some mysterious fashion, one has actually *moved forward* from the original starting-point.

In the scene immediately following comes the actual episode of the *Thieving Magpie*; and we see the bird flutter across the stage and fly off into the wings with the fateful spoon. The timing of this scene is excellent; the audience is too deeply moved by what has gone before to laugh at this theatrical trick; and, since the flight is completely unexpected, no one has time to wonder how it is worked. Following the

---

[1] *Fernando:*
> Ah! mi bolle nelle vene
> Il furor e la vendetta!
> Freme il nembo, e la saetta
> Già comincia a balenar! [. . .]
> Vituperio! Disonore!
> Abbastanza ho tollerato!
> Uom maturo, e magistrato,
> Vi dovreste vergognar!

Podestà:
> Non so quel che farei,
> Smanio, deliro e fremo;
> A questo passo estremo
> Mi sento il cor scoppiar!

                              (Act I, sc. ix)

great tragic sequence, which we have just been analysing so imperfectly, the music suddenly recaptures all its airy lightness, all its inimitable gaiety, with even a new touch of elegance hitherto unexploited—and all this dances accompaniment to the interrogation of poor Ninetta:

In casa di messere Fabrizio . . .[1]

This whole section is delicious, and I firmly refuse to believe that any other composer living could have so much as *attempted* anything like it. It is almost fantastic that one of the most charming *cantilenas* ever written, which, for sheer beauty, rivals the finest achievements of the whole art of music, should be used as a setting for what is precisely the most sordid and infamous rejoinder of the whole trial-scene. When the young conscript, quite correctly, calls attention to the fact that the missing object has been

Rapito! no, smarrito!

the *Podestà*, with peerless melodic suavity, replies:,

Vuol dir lo stesso!

In truth, this light-hearted *insouciance*, this delicious and positively *monarchic* skittishness, has been recorded more than once, in recent years, among *real* judges, members of the highest social circles, who have passed elegant death-sentences upon the King's enemies to the tune of some flippant little witticism—or, more exactly, without interrupting for one single instant the ceaseless, merry round of their perpetually epicurean and nonchalant existence. Rossini's music, I feel, would be admirably suited to a comedy entitled *Charles II*[2] or *Henri III*, where the dramatist, in order to depict some of the more prosperous

---

> [1] *Podestà:*   In casa di messere Fabrizio
> Vingradito è stato
> Oggi rapito . . .
> *Giannetto:* Rapito? No, smarrito!
> *Podestà:*   Zitto! vuol dir lo stesso!
> Rapito, avete messo,
> Un cucchiajo d'argento
> Per uso di mangiar.

[2] *Vide* the excellent *Memoirs* of Mistress Hutchinson; the reports of the trial of Sidney, and many other, similar cases. *Vide* the details of certain French trials, as recounted by Voltaire. *Vide* . . .

moments of the reigns of these two sovereigns, should have drunk at the same source of inspiration which fired Lemercier to write his tragedy entitled *Pinto*.

Some of my readers may chance to have been born in lands where justice is treated with universal respect, and where everyone acknowledges such a state of affairs as not only right, but *normal*; I must therefore digress for a few pages, in order to make it plain to such persons that Rossini was born in the Romagna, and accustomed to judges appointed directly by the Church; and therefore, that every scene and every line that he gives to the *Podestà* in *la Gazza ladra* is a faithful and realistic portrait, drawn after nature. The reason why he decorated Ninetta's interrogation with such a wealth of junketing, nonchalance and light-heartedness, is simply that he was making a faithful musical sketch of his chief protagonist, the Judge, who was elderly, bawdy, merry and a thorough-going scoundrel into the bargain—and further, that he could not lose sight of the eventual *dénouement* of his opera, which, in the tradition of Metastasio, was obliged to be *di lieto fine*. When I was in Milan, a city where (between 1797 and 1814) Napoleon had brought some semblance of decency into the administration of justice, I actually heard Rossini countering the criticisms which were being levelled against his *Podestà* with the greatest of good humour: "The young conscript," he used to maintain, "is a fool, even though he is a Frenchman. Now, *I* have never been campaigning and tearing standards out of the enemy's hands; but if *I* had been in his place, and if it had been *my* mistress who was accused of theft, I should have cried out: *I stole that wretched spoon!* But, you see, in the *libretto* which I had foisted upon me, Ninetta, overwhelmed by the circumstantial evidence marshalled against her, is too dismayed to answer anything, and Giannetto is just a plain fool; therefore the principal character in my *finale* is necessarily the Judge, who is a rogue, I grant you, but a merry one for all that, and who, moreover, has not the least *serious* intention of condemning Ninetta; all *he* is after, during the entire course of the interrogation, is to sell his verdict of 'not guilty' at a thoroughly handsome profit, and meanwhile to see what sort of price he can get."[1] What Rossini (being an extremely cautious man, and clearly mindful

---

[1] *Cf.* the *Podestà's* lines: Ora è mia, son contento.
                           Ah! sei giunto, felice momento;
                           Lo spavento piegar la farà!

of the fate of Cimarosa) did *not* add, was: "Go and stay a while in the region where I was born, and take note of the verdicts which are delivered there every day. Do you realize that you are quite liable to be arraigned before the authorities, and actually brought to trial, for the crime of having *once* (say, a year or two ago) *eaten chicken on a Friday?* Every Friday, in fact, the priests send out spies into the back-gardens of all the *palazzi* to hunt for chicken-bones on the rubbish-heaps; the chamber-maid cannot receive absolution at her Easter confession unless she denounces secret carcass-hoards of sacrilegiously-consumed fowls —and you know as well as I do, that a wretched chamber-maid in Imola or Pesaro who fails to make her Easter communion is a doomed woman! Imagine a town of twenty thousand inhabitants—take Ferrara, for example—with a Commissioner of Police, seven or eight Assistant Commissioners of Police, and a dozen or more District Superintendents of Police, all as busy as bees, and with nothing better to do in all the wide world than to find out whether Signor *** is guilty of eating chicken on Fridays. The Papal Legate, his Secretaries and his Secret Agents (whose titles, in the preceding sentence, I have translated into their better-known equivalents) are all priests, and the civil administration lies entirely in their hands; but they are obstructed at every step and hated like poison by the ecclesiastical authorities proper, the Archbishop and his Grand-Vicars, the Canons, *etc.*, *etc.*, who are all the sworn enemies of the civil administrative hierarchy, and who are perpetually denouncing its members to the Holy See, and charging them with laxity of discipline. One solitary denunciation of this character can hold up a Legate's promotion to Cardinal at the next vacancy. *But*: every one of these powerful and conflicting interests, every one of these bitter rivalries, every one of these counsels of prudence can be reconciled and satisfied by the simple measure of denouncing some poor devil of an inhabitant of Ferrara who has succumbed to the temptation of eating chicken of a Friday!" ... I could fill twenty pages with solid corroborative detail, and my only embarrassment would be to tone down the garishness of the colours and to understate the truth; but I should hate to stumble into such a sordid mire of filth, which would indeed be the most disastrous of calamities for a book whose object is entirely *frivolous*.[1] Nevertheless,

---

[1] If the foundations of my argument should be attacked, I may well resort to publication, and give the world a few details of one or two specific cases, from

the ultimate conclusion to be drawn from all the anecdotes which I *could* retail concerning the Romagna would always be the same: namely, that Rossini, by decking out his licentious *Podestà* in such an incredible garb of nonchalant urbanity, had absolutely no intention of concocting some atrocious epigram in the style of Juvenal. Generally speaking, it is very rare indeed in Italy for scoundrelism to be denounced in writing; the literary result would tend to be both depressing and in bad taste—and, worst of all, *platitudinous*!

The unresponsive character of Ninetta's despicable lover emerges very clearly in the song:

> *Tu dunque sei real*
> *(Ed io la credea*
> *L'istessa onestà)* . . .

All the nonsensical sickliness which the silly, sentimental soul of the average shopkeeper in the *rue Saint-Denis* finds so lavishly echoed in his beloved melodrama, gushed forth in a mighty, oozing stream when Ninetta allows herself to be stricken dumb—

> *Non v'è più speme* . . .[1]

—just because the Jew asserts that on a certain piece of silverwear which she had sold him, he had noticed some letters engraved: an *F* and a *V*. This happens, of course, just after she had chanced to remark that her father's name was Fernando Villabella, whence, logically, the *Podestà* has concluded that the man who was with her just now, and for whose sake she had read out a false description from the official form, was this same father in person. Heaven forbid that Ninetta should frustrate the poor dramatist by employing so unworthy a stratagem as simply to say in plain language: *This set of spoons and forks was given to me by my father, and the letters F V form his cypher!* The wretched maiden would rather die! The most disastrous feature of this which, at present, I am content to draw conclusions of a general nature. Incidentally, this sort of behaviour was the normal state of affairs under the "moderate" government of Cardinal Consalvi! *Vide*: Laorens, *Tableau de Rome*; Simond; Gorani, *etc.*

[1] *Ninetta:*
> Mi sento opprimere,
> Non v'è più speme,
> Sorte più barbara,
> O Dio! non v'è.

libretto is that every character, without exception, is fundamentally banal. It is to be observed that here at least we have one defect which is *never* to be met with in German opera, where there is always *something* to feed the imagination.

None the less, this first-act *finale* is full of movement, of entrances and exits which capture the audience's interest straight away. It contains plenty of solo passages, and a number of charming little *ensembles*; and the grouping is such that, given the size of the canvas, the arrangement of all the separate elements upon it could hardly be better. The dialogue itself is adequate; I could wish it the reverse, with a situation finely and naturally contrived, and the words as absurd as you could wish—for who ever pays the slightest attention to the *words* in an opera? In Naples, this *finale* came in for a certain amount of criticism on account of its length; but the Milanese, more patient by nature, seemed to enjoy it. Personally, I would tend to side with the good people of Milan. Stylistically, the music is energetic, powerful and natural; yet, remarkably enough, it never loses its rustic character, save during the course of a few delightful bars at the opening of the interrogation. As a whole, this Act I *finale* reminds me repeatedly of that highly individual note of gaiety which pervades the *Autumn* movement of Haydn's *The Seasons*, where he sets out to depict the rollicking merriment of the grape-harvest.

If Mozart had had the making of this *finale*, it would have been atrocious, intolerable; for he would unerringly have fastened on to the underlying tragic implications of the theme. His gentle nature, without fail, would have driven him to take the part of Ninetta, and through her, of all oppressed and downtrodden humanity, instead of concentrating upon the *Podestà* and his plots which, after all, are licentious rather than bloodthirsty, as is only too clearly indicated in the final lines which he utters before his exit:

> *Ah, la gioja mi brilla nel seno!*
> *Più non perdo sì dolce tesor!*[1]

[1] This character, the *Podestà*, has been wittily and powerfully drawn by Duclos in his novel, *la Baronne de Luz*. Duclos' licentious judge is named Thüring; the version of the same character whom we meet in *la Gazza ladra* should be played with a heavy admixture of farce, which, however, no Italian actor has the courage to attempt before the cold and disdainful audiences of Paris, to whom low comedy is simply inconprehensible. It is essential to bring out the bacchic side of his character.

CHAPTER XXIII

La Gazza ladra (continued)

ACT TWO

IN Paris, every face that you pass in the street is subtly and fascinatingly alive with some slight suggestion of passion; most usually, in the middle-aged male, it is *preoccupied egoism*; amongst the younger men, a carefully-cultivated hint of *military ardour*; among women, the desire to appear attractive, or at the very least to show plainly the class of society to which they belong. An expression which is very rarely encountered is one of *boredom*; for boredom, in Paris, would merely seem absurd, and is to be detected, alternating with an expression of downright bad temper, exclusively upon the countenances of foreigners, or of travellers newly-returned from abroad. Finally, there is one expression which is never, *never* betrayed; and that is one which reveals some deep and sombre emotional disturbance. In Italy, on the other hand, it is common enough—in fact, only too common—to observe a face seamed with the ravages of boredom; and boredom, in this context, means the simple *absence of any sensations whatsoever*. Likewise, one may occasionally remark the signs and symptoms of a joy bordering close upon madness; and, fairly frequently, the revealing scars of dark and deep-seated passions. In consequence, when the citizen of Paris takes his seat at the opera, he comes with a mind exhausted, worn out during the long day by a thousand shifting preoccupations; whereas the citizen of Parma or Ferrara brings to his pleasures a spirit which, having remained blank and unruffled since early dawn, is pure, fresh and virginal; and yet this same spirit, when roused, is capable of housing the most violent emotions of which the human soul can become conscious. Walking along the streets, the Italian treats his fellow-pedestrians with the profoundest disdain; or else he simply fails to notice them. But the Frenchman deliberately courts their good opinion.

You cannot have your cake and eat it. The Parisian, from the first instant when he steps abroad in the early morning, finds himself entangled in a hundred different webs and worries, and his soul obsessed by a hundred ephemeral passions. But in any typical little Italian provincial town, nothing (since the day of Napoleon's downfall) ever has nor ever will come to trouble the deathly stillness, unless it be, perhaps once in six months, the arrest of some unfortunate *carbonaro*. Herein, I believe, lies the philosophical explanation of the frenzied artistic *furores* which occur so often south of the Alps, and never at all in France. Not only are the souls of men in the South filled with a fiercer-burning fire; but this same fire is intensified by being rarely kindled. We in France have ten different species of amusement to while away our evenings; but the Italian has one only: music. On the Parisian stage, a play is deemed to have scored a "resounding triumph" the moment it inspires the *dilettanti* with sufficient curiosity to come and criticize it, thereby arming themselves with sufficient store of conversation to dine out on for a whole month; the main attraction is invariably this *delight in criticizing*—never the more primitive pleasure of surrender, whether to tears or ecstasy.[1]

By contrast, among the good townsfolk of Milan, tears and ecstasy were the all but universal reaction at the *première* of *la Gazza ladra*. The audience was almost wholly concerned with its own delight and its own reactions, and scarcely had a thought to spare for Rossini's reputation. But after the first-act *finale*, the opening scenes of Act II seemed rather insipid, in spite of the fact that the part of Pippo was played by Signorina Gallianis, a young actress possessed of a remarkably dignified presence and of a magnificent contralto voice, which was heard to best advantage in the duet:

> *Ebben, per mia memoria,*
> *Lo serberai tu stesso . . .*[2]

[1] The pure and primitive reaction to *drama as such* is unknown among the present generation, save in the popular theatres of the *Porte-Saint-Martin*, the *Gaieté*, etc.

[2] *Ninetta:*
> Deh pensa, che domani, oggi fors'anco,
> Non sarà più mio quest'ornamento!

Pippo:
> Ohibò! Non lo credete!
> Esser non può! Mel dice il cor, tenete.

Ninetta:
> Ebben, per mia memoria,

—a song which Pippo sings with Ninetta when he comes to see her in prison. There are moving passages here and there in the episodes

Fin chè mi batte il cor . . .

and

Vedo in quegli occhi il pianto . . .,

but, towards the end of the duet, the effect is unfortunately marred by some loud and intrusive orchestral *hammering*, which has the undesirable consequence of directing the listener's attention to the technical means by which the result is achieved, precisely at the moment when he feels the strongest urge to surrender blindly to his own melancholy sensations. This duet invariably conjures up in my mind a picture of a certain kind of emotionally unresponsive person, who conscientiously assumes a wan and tearful expression whenever the situation seems to require it; individuals of this character always react to tragic surroundings by taking a firm resolution to do the correct thing, and to look as miserable as possible.

After hearing Miss Stephens sing in London, it occurred to me that Rossini should have written this passage in the traditional style of English vocal music. English music escapes almost completely from the tyranny of the metrical bar-line; it reminds me of the sound of a horn far, far away in the depths of the night, where some of the intermediate notes are lost in the infinite distance; I have never heard anything more profoundly thrilling; and in particular, I know nothing more diametrically opposed to the rest of the music of *la Gazza ladra*.

The *Podestà's* aria, and more especially, the chorus into which it merges at the conclusion, might have made the reputation of any

> Lo serberai tu stesso;
> Non ha più senso adesso
> Di rifiutarlo ancor.
>
> *Pippo:*
> Pegno adorato, ah sempre
> Con Pippo resterai!
> Compagno mio sarai
> Finchè mi batte il cor.
> Addio! [. . .]
>
> *Ninetta, Pippo:*
> Vedo in quegli occhi il pianto . . .
> Dove si trova, o Dio!
> Un più sincero amore,
> Un più sincero amor!

composer less renowned already than Rossini; but unfortunately I cannot make the same claim for Giannetto's duet:

Forse un dì conoscerete . . .[1]

Judging by the overpowering stench of vulgarity which is apparent here and there in some of these *cantilenas*, one is strongly tempted to believe that Rossini's chief ambition had been to transform himself lock, stock and barrel into a Germanic composer, and to write music like Weigl or Winter. Consequently, *la Gazza* is nowhere as popular as in Germany; in Darmstadt, for instance, its defects pass unnoticed (and perhaps some of its qualities too); whereas *Tancredi* is looked down on as "miniature music". The worthy Teuton needs to be struck with a sledge-hammer before he shows any reaction!

The entry of the deserter brings back into the second act something of the dark and smouldering fires which had burned in the heart of the first. Galli's interpretation of the whole of the concluding part of the drama is a magnificent piece of tragic acting, as great as anything by de' Marini or Iffland. Here in France, we have no actor whose genius lies anywhere near this particular field; even the great Talma is conspicuously mediocre in a play like *Falkland*, or in a part like that of Meinau in *Misanthropie et Repentir*.

Galli's aria:

Oh colpo impensato![2]

[1] *Ninetta:*
> Forse un dì conoscerete
> La mia fede, il mio candore,
> Piangerete il vostro errore [. . .]

Giannetto:
> Taci, taci, tu mi fai
> L' alma in sen gelar d'orror . . .

[2] *Lucia:*
> Chi è? Fernando? O Dio!

Fernando:
> Mia cara amica, che nessuno ci ascolti!
> Ov'è Ninetta?

Lucia:
>   Ninetta? Deh fuggite!

Fernando:
> Ma che vuol dir quel pianto?

Lucia:
> Ah! Non m'interrogate! [. . .]

Fernando:
> Oh colpo impensato!

is distinctly commonplace. Rossini, realizing that Galli was having an unsuccessful season in Naples, promptly made up his quarrel with his ex-rival, and wrote him this aria, which is admirably suited to the peculiar range of his voice.

The opening section of the recitative:

Che vuol dire quel pianto?

is perfectly adequate, and the words:

M'investe, m'assale ...

are clothed in an atmosphere of genuine tragic despair. The line:

Per te, dolce figlia ...

is illuminated with a lustrous iridescence of pure and wondrous idealism; but in bitter contrast, the setting of

Perchè amica speme ...?

is abominable; it is downright bad Rossini, totally lacking in true pathos, but tricked out instead with a glitter of spurious embellishment fit only for the concert-platform; moreover, to add insult to injury, these tinselly decorations are simply borrowed wholesale from the tradition of the *opera buffa*.[1]

However, the aria concludes upon a fine tragic note with the words:

Oh annunzio ferale!
Ahi! Tutto del fato
M'investe, m'assale,
L'acerbo rigor!
Per te, dolce figlia,
L'irata mia sorte
Con anima forte
Soffersi finor.
Perchè amica speme
Nutriva il mio cor? [. . .]
Scoperto, avvilito,
Proscritto, inseguito ...
Ohimè! che risolvere
Quest' alma non sa!

[1] This passage provides a striking instance of the most serious defect which tends to mar Rossini's "second manner"; he writes his arias first, and then proceeds to sprinkle them with whatever series of embellishments may chance to fall best within the repertoire of his singer.

> *Scoperto, avvilito,*
> *Proscritto, inseguito . . .*

Zucchelli is magnificent in his rendering of this scene; we are made to feel, quite sincerely, that we are listening to the natural language of a tormented soul in despair. The public has still to realize the full extent of the greatness of this singer.

To judge by the style in which Rossini composed this "reconciliation aria" for Galli, I suspect that he may still have been secretly sulking a little. Musicologists hasten to point out (as though they had just spotted something really new and original) that, towards the concluding section of this number, the orchestral accompaniment rises considerably higher than the line of the vocal melody,[1] without, however, drowning the voice; when scholars take to applauding such nursery-tricks as proof of "inventive originality", the awareness grows upon one unmistakably that musicology, as an exact science, is still in its swaddling-clothes!

The Judges' chorus:

> *Tremate, o popoli . . .!*[2]

is superb; it achieves the supreme ambition of the "Grand Manner" in music: it inspires *Terror*.[3] In fact, the effect of this chorus is so overwhelming that, even in the *Théâtre Louvois*, I have never heard a single sacrilegious guffaw at the absurd sight of an Assize Court in full session, ceremonially arrayed in sweeping legal regalia, standing up and singing

---

[1] This trick of raising the accompaniment *above* the line of the vocal melody is a device which Rossini employs time and time again, and which ensures that the accompaniment, *however over-orchestrated*, will not drown the singer. By contrast, Mozart very frequently fails to avoid this danger, for instance in the aria:

> Batti, batti, o bel Masetto . . .†

from *Don Giovanni*.

† Act I, sc. xvi.

[2] *Coro:*
> Tremate, o popoli,
> A tal esempio!
> Questo è di Temide
> L'augusto tempio!

[3] Even the least sophisticated can feel the full force of this particular passion—witness Bossuet's *Sermons*! In 1520, for every person who had learnt to appreciate Raphael, there were a hundred who were instinctively *terrified* by Michelangelo. Canova would have made no impression whatsoever upon the average *dilettante* of the year 1520.

at the top of its voice! This passage has been criticized on the grounds of a certain resemblance with one of the choruses from Gluck's *Orfeo*; personally, however, I should prefer to believe that, if it is imitated from anywhere, it is modelled rather on Haydn.

The entry of Ninetta and the reading of the death-sentence are two terrible instants which I will gladly forbear to recall to the reader's imagination—indeed, I would be only too thankful if I could finish my analysis of *la Gazza ladra* altogether at this point; but that would mean doing less than justice to Rossini.

The phrase:

> Già d'intorno
> Sibillar *la morte ascolto* ...

is enough to freeze the blood in one's veins, especially the word *sibillar*; I can well believe that the more nervous members of the audience tend to feel faint. Galli's entrance accompanied by the chorus:

> O là! fermate ...[1]

[1] (*Enter Fernando*)

Tutti:
> Gran Dio!

Guardie:
> O là! Fermate!

Fernando:
> Son vostro prigionere;
> Il capo mio troncate;
> Ma il sangue risparmiate
> D'un' innocente vittima
> Che non si sa scolpar!

Coro:
> La sentenza è pronunziata,
> Più nessun la può cambiar.

Fernando:
> Ma dunque ... ?

Coro:
> L'uno in carcere, e l'altro sul patibolo;
> La legge è inalterabile,
> Nessun la può cambiar.

Fernando:
> Che abisso di pene ...
> Mi perdo, deliro;
> Più fiero martiro
> L'averno non ha!
> Un padre, una figlia
> Fra ceppi alla scure;
> A tante sciagure
> Chi mai reggerà?

is sublime. We in France have beheld nothing comparable in our own
theatre (with the solitary exception of Mademoiselle Mars) since the
days of Monvel. Yet in Italy, I have seen both de' Marini and especially
la Pallerini, work up just as much dramatic tension; and Iffland,
playing in Berlin in 1817, had certainly one or two climaxes which
would have borne comparison with this great entry of Galli's.

As a general rule, in moments of acute dramatic tension, recitative
alone is quite sufficient; whereas a *cantilena* would be seriously out of
place. The next words which Galli utters furnish a startling proof of
this paradoxical truth, which is so contrary to popular belief:

> *Son vostro prigionero,*
> *Il capo mio troncate.*[1]

Ninetta, Giannetto, Fabrizio, Fernando:
Ah! neppur l'estremo amplesso,
Questa è troppa crudeltà!

[1] *I am your prisoner; cut off my head (but do not shed the blood of a poor and innocent
girl who is incapable of defending herself).* Fine words, undoubtedly; but what
should have been said is simply: "I gave my daughter a set of silver spoons and
forks to sell; organize a search for these objects, *etc. . . .*" Of course, I shall now
be accused of behaving like a typical *French literary critic,* for having launched a
wild assault upon a wretched little Italian *libretto.* But there is a distinction; for
the main object of the philippics which these learned literary gentlemen hurl so
mercilessly at the target of their scorn and contempt, lies in the *words* (witness the
cruel thunderbolts of Jove-like anger hurled by *le Miroir* against poor Taddeo's
Cra, cra! in *l'Italiana in Algeri*); whereas *I,* on the other hand, object, not to
badly-written dialogue, but to badly-contrived *dramatic situations.* All the dialogue of every *libretto* invariably seems to me to be excellent, for the simple
reason that I never listen to it. I confess that I have read the text of *la Gazza ladra*
for the first time *now,* while actually engaged in writing this present analysis; for
here, unfortunately, I have no better means at my disposal for indicating specific
passages of Rossini's *music* than to refer to the words which happen to go with
them. It would have seemed oddly pretentious if, instead of simply quoting a line
of text, I had filled the footnotes at the bottom of each page with snatches of
melody set out in musical notation every time I wanted to identify a specific
aria.

Beginning with the middle of Act I, the whole of the latter part of *la Gazza* is
gloom and unbelievable despondency; and, for light relief, we are offered *horror*—
the *Podestà* in the prison-scene, for instance, making indecent proposals to
Ninetta. Sedaine once treated a similar subject in *le Déserteur:* but he escaped
this black and melodramatic pitfall by creating the character of Montauciel, who
represents one of the boldest and most difficult dramatic experiments ever
attempted in the French theatre. Rossini deserved to meet a Sedaine. Indeed, had
fate decreed that the inspired little stone-mason [Sedaine] should have been born
a gentleman of leisure with a private income of two hundred *louis* a year, French
literature would certainly have numbered one further genius in its ranks.

When an audience is really moved, I believe its faculties are so preter-naturally sharpened that it can detect with unerring accuracy the genu-ine echo of Nature. At this pitch of emotion, an audience may grow dangerous; for, if Art should seek to embellish Nature with any of its usual tricks and subterfuges, it is liable to vomit them back in disgust.[1]

In two terrible lines:

> L'uno in carcere,
> E l'altro sul patibolo!

sung by the Judges in chorus and by the Praetor, with all the impressive-ness of a vast concourse of bass voices, Rossini's music rises to the same heights of menacing solemnity as the words; and in the passage which follows:

> Un padre, una figlia
> ....
> A tante sciagure
> Chi mai reggerà!

Galli's performance, which never fails to leave a lasting impression, even in Paris, was magnificent beyond all description. This outstanding scene, the most powerful in the whole of modern Italian opera, and the most compelling thing by far that Rossini himself has ever created, finishes on a worthy note with the passage:

The wrongs inflicted by chance might, in this case, easily have been repaired by intelligent protection accorded by the Minister in power at the time; by rights, every one of Sedaine's *libretti* should have earned him at least 6,000 francs. As it was, he had the greatest difficulty even in getting himself elected to the *Académie Française*. In all the realm of art, I know nothing quite so futile as the kind of "protection" which is normally accorded by wealthy philistines ... unless it be the establishment of *Academies*! The *outstanding* members of our own particular *Académie*, which all but refused to admit Sedaine, were Marmontel and La Harpe; be judge yourselves, then, what the *rest* were like!

[1] This is the secret and fundamental explanation of the hostility shown by the Romantic dramatists towards the *alexandrine*, and of their refusal to accept it as the basic metrical form of tragedy. Racinian dramatic verse is perpetually intro-ducing minor distortions into the *simple* and *indivisible* truth of the utterances of human emotion. But a hundred and fifty years of philosophic enquiry have at last taught us the secret of these utterances. Racine's distortions are perpetrated in the name of "ornamentation"; but this particular evidence of genius, which was so rigorously exacted by the conventions of 1670, is repugnant to those of 1823. Our taste insists upon a far more *faithful* reproduction of nature; Schiller's *Wilhelm Tell*, in a prose translation, gives us much greater satisfaction than Racine's *Iphigénie en Aulide*.

L

Ah! neppur l'estremo amplesso,
Questa è troppa crudeltà.

At this point I feel that I must rally to the defence of Rossini with a general statement of principle, which is, that the speed of music in waltz-time is symbolically expressive of the overpowering and inevitable speed with which the hammer of destiny may fall and strike. Among all the immediate sensations of a wretch condemned to die within the hour, none is more terrifying and more intolerable than this obsessive experience of the phenomenon of *speed*.

And if the rhythm of the waltz has come, in our convention, to be used as a dance-measure, that is no fault of the music. In thirty years' time, this ephemeral fashion may have died away; but the symbolism of the hurrying passage of time is eternal.

This argument alone seems to me to afford sufficient justification for the various passages in waltz-rhythm which are freely—indeed, almost liberally—scattered throughout the second act of *la Gazza ladra*; on the other hand, however, no argument in all the world could serve to justify

Sino il pianto è negato al mio ciglio,
Entro il seno si arresta il sospir.
Dio possente, mercede, consiglio!
Tu m'aita il mio fato a soffrir!

—and this song, with its rollicking melody, is twice repeated at different intervals.

At the fourth or fifth performance of *la Gazza ladra*, a general outcry was raised against this outrageous piece of absurdity. Among Rossini's critics in the matter of this *allegro*, the wittiest by far was a certain young man, one of the most charming representatives of the *jeunesse dorée* of Milan, whose premature death is recognized to-day as a tragic loss to the world of art. Had he been still alive, I could have counted upon his devotion to furnish this little treatise with a page or two from his own pen; in which case, I could then have been certain that the work was not wholly unworthy of public notice.

Rossini's supporters (for there were two camps, sharply distinguished one from the other) maintained that we ought to be grateful to him for having meticulously disguised the atrocious brutality of the theme by enveloping it in the softening veils of melodic gaiety. If Mozart, they asserted, had composed the music to *la Gazza ladra* as it *ought to have been* written, that is to say, in the style of the serious episodes from *Don Giovanni*, the opera would have been gruesome to the point of nausea, and nobody could have managed to sit through a single performance.

But the fact remains that in no other opera has Rossini ever been guilty of so many *palpable misinterpretations* as in *la Gazza ladra*. He was nervously apprehensive of the Milanese audiences, who had borne him a grudge ever since *il Turco in Italia*; he was determined to dazzle them with a positive galaxy of passages glittering with "originality"; and he left himself even less time than usual for revision. I once heard Ricordi, the best-known music-publisher in Italy at the time, who had built a great fortune out of Rossini's popular successes, telling a gathering in Florence how Rossini had composed one of the most splendid duets in *la Gazza* sitting in the back room of his music-shop, amid a hurly-burly of shouting and all the satanic din of a dozen or more music-copyists dictating or checking scores aloud to each other—and finished it in less than an hour!

The great passage which opens with the chorus:

Tremate, o popoli ...

is, in my opinion, much too long.

The crowd-scene chorus, which is heard as Ninetta, escorted by guards, passes across the stage on her way to the place of execution, is essentially well-conceived. In Italy, where tyranny, being both suspicious and implacable[1] (and thus radically different from the despotism of Louis XV), has stifled at birth every delicacy of feeling, there is nothing unusual in the sight of the public executioner donning a gendarme's helmet and striding along beside Ninetta, dragging her ruthlessly to her feet after the wretched girl has fallen on her knees to pray as the procession passes the village church. In the production at *la Scala*, the *décor* for this scene, which was designed by Signor Perego*, was superb; the little church was dark and intimate; yet it was dignified with just that touch of grandeur which was required to dissipate (in part, at least) the gloomy horror which we must feel at witnessing so terrible a ceremony. At the *Théâtre Louvois*, on the other hand, the *décor* was all tinsel and prettiness, and worthily topped off with a tree

[1] *Cf.* the imprisonment of the historian Giannone.

or two slung up in the clouds, and completely devoid of support on the earth beneath. But the taste of the *Louvois* audience in matters visual is too grossly uneducated to worry about a little trifle like *that*![1]

There was never a light-comedy number better-placed than that which occurs in the *finale*:

> *Ecco cessato il vento,*
> *Placato il mare infido . . .*[2]

Galli used to sing it with magnificent *verve* and joyousness; by contrast, Zucchelli brings to his interpretation a unique perfection of grace; and when he sings it thus, this empty-headed little jig-tune becomes a thing of outstanding beauty. I should dearly like to see this great singer in a proper baritone part—for instance, as Don Giovanni.

After a performance of *la Gazza ladra* as it is given at the *Théâtre Louvois*, the poor spectator emerges deafened and exhausted. This excessive nervous strain could easily be avoided by the insertion of an hour's ballet between the two acts of the opera. In Milan, we would be given *Mirra**, *ossia la Vendetta di Venere*, one of Viganò's masterpieces. The dream-fantasies of mythology came as a delightful relief after the *only-too-realistic* horrors of that sordid little episode extracted from the parish annals of Palaiseau, with its Judge and its gendarmes. I suppose that there has never existed any orchestra inspired with a greater respect for academic accuracy, or with a nicer sense of mathematical values, or with a stricter sense of what it conceives to be its bounden duty, than that of the *Louvois*; certainly there has never been an orchestra so totally devoid of any feeling for music*. But since it seems impossible to hope for any *feeling*, let us pray that, given time, it may eventually be possible, by dint of *theory and instruction*, for the students at the *rue Bergère* to grasp that a *crescendo* is most effective if it is begun

---

[1] In thirty years' time, scene-painters will be firmly requested to delete all the pretty little patterns of scrolls and arabesques with which, at present, they feel obliged to disfigure their backcloths. When that day dawns at last, it may be that we shall have exchanged a load of petty vanity for a scrap of real pride. We are not too proud to drink *coffee*, although it refuses to grow patriotically on the soil of France; so why should we not turn our attention towards Milan, and invoke the aid of *i Signori* Sanquirico, Tranquillo and their heirs and successors?

[2] *Ninetta:* Ecco cessato il vento,
Placato il mare infido;
Salvi siam giunti al lido,
Alfin respira il cor . . .

softly; and that there do exist certain elusive and super-subtle shades of expression, normally known as *piano*. O, how one longs for one or two of those poor, unskilled instrumentalists from Capua or Foligno! They make mistakes; but when they do, the cause is invariably ignorance; there are certain notes which their fingers just do not possess the necessary dexterity to strike correctly. Yet what fire! What delicacy! What soul! What a *feeling* for music! By contrast, there exists a certain brand of note, rather too loud, rather too brassy, rather too *shameless*, whose perpetration proves this, and this only: that he who shall be proved guilty of having insulted the listener's ear by producing it, is eternally disqualified from the legitimate membership of any orchestra whatsoever (except that of the *Grand Opéra*).

Taken individually, each and every member of the *Louvois* orchestra (and particularly of the violin-section) is probably superior to any equivalent performer in the respective orchestras of Dresden, Munich or Darmstadt*. And yet, what an overwhelming difference in the general impression! The inherent technical superiority of our academic friends only becomes apparent in certain symphonies of Haydn, where everything is *harsh*; but as soon as they encounter a single bar which requires a little grace, a little tenderness *con espressione*, they are out of their depth. If you want evidence, just listen to their performance of the passages of this character which are to be found in the overture to *la Gazza ladra*; and, for further corroboration, consider the treatment which has recently been meted out to the overture of Cimarosa's *gli Orazi e Curiazi*.

The first time I heard *la Gazza ladra* performed at the *Louvois*, I was utterly scandalized. The conductor, who, incidentally, is a very gifted man indeed, a talented musician, a first-rate violinist, and an artist who handles his orchestra excellently within the limitations of the style of playing adopted in France, had completely altered the *tempo* of nearly every one of Rossini's numbers. If ever Rossini himself visits Paris, and if he can resist the temptation of issuing blandly misleading instructions concerning the performance of his own music (a form of practical joke which I have more than once known him to indulge in, and to carry though with poised equanimity and outrageous success, to the supreme discomfiture of the wretched singers whom he happened to have picked on!), he will be *forced* into some kind of expostulation with the worthy gentleman in charge of the *Louvois* orchestra. Poor

Rossini! If there is an argument, he is bound to be defeated, indeed utterly routed—for *he* is not a MUSICOLOGIST!

Tempo, in music, is the very essence of expression. Take that delightful aria,

Enfant chéri des dames ...

which Devìène once filched from Mozart, and play it *adagio*; it will move you to tears! Among the numbers thus "arranged" in so indefensible a manner by the conductor of the *Théâtre Louvois*, I recall in particular the prison-scene between Ninetta and Pippo:

Ebben per mia memoria ...

Anything marked *piano* was transmuted into *allegro*; but since man was born to be just, and compensation is one of the fundamental laws of nature, the next pretty little *allegro vivace* which turned up in the score was religiously converted into a sad and sighing *andante*, in blithe disregard of the dramatic situation, and (if I may so express myself) of the tortured squeal of protest from the *libretto*. Moreover, Pippo's cry:

Guarda, guarda! avvisa, avvisa!

at the instant when, perched high on the steeple of the church, he discovers the magpie's hoard and the silver spoons—an *allegro* passage if ever there was one, and played as such under the composer's own supervision in Milan—is transmogrified in the *Louvois* version into a kind of funeral dirge which, considered as a *parody*, is highly entertaining.[1]

In eight or ten years' time, when our present musical revolution is accomplished, and when all our pretty little twelve-year-old, music-learning school-girls are grown up, married and thoroughly independent, the new *Louvois* audiences will insist first and foremost upon *fine singing* from the actors instead of upon *clever playing* from the orchestra; and consequently, at least in respect of the *tempo* of this or that passage, they will degrade the conductor into the humble servant of the vocalists. Once the singer is on the stage, *even if he is incorrigibly mediocre*, everything else must obey and give way to him; not—Heaven forbid!—out of respect for him as a person, but from due deference to the ears of the listeners!

---

[1] It is asserted that the main subject of the steeple-aria is borrowed from *Otello*.

CHAPTER XXIV

Of the Quality of Admiration in France
or
An Essay concerning Grand Opera

THIS evening, the 5th March 1823, I went to hear *le Devin du Village*. Stylistically speaking, this opera is a somewhat clumsy imitation of the kind of music which was fashionable in Italy round about 1730. But this particular fashion long ago surrendered to the masterpieces of Pergolesi and Logroscino; and these in their turn were superseded by those of Sacchini, Piccinni, *etc.*, which were later outmoded by those of Guglielmi, Paisiello, *etc.* . . . composers who, in their turn again, were pushed into obscurity by Rossini and Mozart.

In France, however, we will have none of this unseemly haste; nothing which has once been generally approved may ever be allowed to fade *gradually* into the background. On every single count it is necessary to give *battle*. As a good Frenchman, I am resolved and adamant that what I admired yesterday, I shall continue to admire to-day; for if not, what should I find to talk about to-morrow? So-and-so's opera is a *recognized masterpiece*; it therefore *is*, and will remain, "exquisite"; and if (incidentally) it bores me to tears, the fault lies exclusively in *myself*. Even before we were ten years old, we had had to learn the hard lessons of life from the family retainer who used to put our hair in curlers: "There is no way of being beautiful, young Master, without *suffering* for it first!"

Europe is in a state of upheaval, and the staidest of institutions have been overthrown; alone amid the turmoil, the regular public of the *Grand Opéra* offers us a unique phenomenon: it stands exactly where it stood before. Seventy years ago, it held out with unrivalled gallantry against Rousseau: the first violins selflessly offered to assassinate him as the *Public Enemy of Patriotism*;[1] Paris to a man rose up in arms against

---

[1] *Patriotism!* . . . *le Miroir* uses the same old worn-out arguments to-day as Rousseau's detractors used to use in 1765; and anyway, what is *Patriotism*? An argument used to catch the votes of anybody who is *too busy to think*, by appealing to his emotions!

him; and there was talk of a *lettre de cachet*. A year back, the same scenes were re-enacted down to the last detail at the *Porte-Saint-Martin*; witness our entire "liberal press" persuading the motley assembly of drapers' assistants who constitute its "enlightened public" that *Shakespeare* should be hounded for ever off the French stage, on the grounds that he was one of Wellington's *aides-de-camp*!

Any native literary instinct which we may possess has remained rooted exactly where it was in 1765; and *Patriotism* is still the mainspring of our vanity. Indeed, as a race, we are so riddled with vanity, that sometimes we even manage to persuade ourselves that we are proud!

Consider the changes that have taken place in the *political* field since 1765: the scene opens with Louis XVI issuing an invitation to *Philosophy* to take a seat upon his Council of State; and the grave Goddess accepts, appearing in that august company beneath the immortal features of *Turgot*. But Turgot falls, and in his place sits Maurepas, that decrepit old buffoon with his store of puerile frivolity. Close on his heels comes a new reign—the dictatorship of high finance, and the rule of middle-class complacency; all beneath the symbol of honest Necker. But here comes Mirabeau, under whose guidance France sets out in search of a Constitutional Monarchy; and here, hard behind him, comes Danton, wielding a Reign of Terror and a firm sword to defy the foreign invader. Next we see a swarm of robbers, all fighting to dispossess the rightful rulers and seize the helm of state—but the dawn is nigh for all that, the brave dawn of Frascati! Meanwhile, our armies in the field are tasting the unsettling thrill of winning victories, and of routing the Austrians in battle.

And while we were sitting listening to music in the *rue de Cléry*, there came a young hero to take possession of his bride, the fair land of France, and for three whole years to be her happiness. But one day, along comes some obsequious individual who, faced with the simple duty of delivering a letter, whisks off his plumed hat with a flourish of sweet courtiership, reverses it, and uses it as a salver. Dazed by such glittering ceremonial, the hero is overcome: *No one else understands the secret of service!** This one letter delights him more than a dozen victories; and from that instant, the hunt is up, and France is a mad scramble of men grovelling and grubbing back into the days of Louis XIV, ferreting in the old monarchic rag-bag for precious scraps of finery. Baronies and courtly orders burn brightest in the heart's-desire of fair France ... until at last, wearied of the insolence of the new-fangled Counts of the Empire, she returns in rapture to her old love— Louis XVIII! What changes in the old order! Since 1765, public opinion has veered from left to right and back again at least a score of times. But, as though to console the wounded dignity of *Patriotism*, one class alone has remained faithful and uncorrupted: the *habitués* of the *Grand Opéra*. They alone may claim to have nobly resisted that fatal surge of weathercock-restlessness which has raged back and forth over so many heads. Indeed, this very evening, the singing was of a badness *identical note for note* with the badness which reigned sixty years ago!

And this evening, upon returning from *le Devin du Village*, I chanced quite unthinkingly to fetch down off the shelf a volume of Rousseau's flamboyant prose, and opened it at random. It happened to be the volume which contained his writings on music. I was literally thunder-struck: for every word which he had written in 1765 is as vital and as true to-day, in 1823, as it was then. French orchestras, while remaining obstinately convinced that they are the finest orchestras in the world, are no more capable to-day of performing one of Rossini's *crescendi* than they were in days gone by. Faithful to the traditional parchment-lined eardrums of our venerable ancestors, they grow sick with fright at the mere thought of starting *too softly*, and despise the elementary nuances of tonal values as symptoms of unmanly impotence. Tech-nique, in a purely *physical* sense, has improved, and no one would deny that the present generation of violinists, 'cellists and double-bass players can perform feats of virtuosity unthinkable in 1765; but the *spiritual climate*, if I may risk the phrase, in which the players live, move and have their being, is the same now as it ever was. Our musicians some-how remind me of a man who, after a life of cramping poverty, suddenly inherits a vast fortune from a distant and forgotten relative dying in the Indies; his scope of activity, his range of influence, is transformed out of all recognition; but his own character remains precisely as it was before ... or, if anything, grows worse, for this same character, made bold by the new flood of wealth, is now tempted to cast aside its old restraint and modesty, and to parade its crudity in shameless nakedness. Our instrumentalists have inherited an analogous fortune in manual dexterity. If Rossini, as he intends, stops a while in

Paris on his way to London, just wait and see how they will cavil and argue about the *tempo* of the music which *he* composed, and claim to understand the whole problem a hundred times better than he does! As separate individuals, every one of these instrumentalists is a first-class artist in his own line, and equipped with a greater store of technical virtuosity than any other player in Europe; but group them all together in a band, and the resulting "orchestra" remains something irremediably rooted in the year 1765. We are flooded from every quarter with scientific musicianship; nothing is left undeveloped, save a basic feeling for music. I am haunted by infant prodigies, who, at the age of ten-and-a-half, can, and *do*, astound us with full concertos on the violin; and yet a whole orchestra-full of mature and adult violinists is incapable of performing the accompaniment to the duet from *Armida*!

Music, considered as a mechanical technique,[1] is moving rapidly towards a state of perfection; music as an *art* is perishing by degrees. One is forced to conclude that, with people such as these, any increase in knowledge is accompanied by a proportionate decrease in sensibility. Rousseau's ideas on political theory and on social organization are a whole century out of date; but his ideas on music, an art which the French as a whole seem to find decidedly more recalcitrant, are still alive with truth and immediacy. A certain scribbler (still heart and soul in the *ancien régime*) has publicly asserted that *the two most typically French composers are Spontini and Nicolo*—apparently without even grasping the hint supplied by their *names*, that Spontini comes from Jesi while Nicolo was born in Malta, and that neither of them settled in France until a score of attempts to achieve popularity in Italy had proved unavailing! On every side, absurdity is matched by pretentiousness; but pretentiousness wins in the end!

Could it mean that, at bottom, the French nation is among the most conservative and the *least* inconstant of all the races in Europe? Philosophers have arraigned us often enough on the familiar charge of frivolity; but could one swear that the observations which motivate

---

[1] On one occasion recently, during a performance of *Tancredi*, the *Louvois* orchestra played the accompaniment to the whole of the duet: *Ah! se de' mali miei* . . . one semi-tone *higher* than was written in the score; that is to say that, without the slightest difficulty, and acting upon a simple hint from the conductor, *it transposed the whole number at sight from C major to D major*. Whereas, in 1765, the Master of the Musick had been obliged to call out: "Gentlemen! Pray observe the change of key!"

their verdict ever really penetrate beyond the superficial phenomena of the cut of a coat or the style of a wig?

We sneer at the Germans, and taunt them with their "stolidity"; yet during the last thirty years they have experienced at least three major revolutions in philosophy and in dramatic theory. We ourselves, on the contrary, still stand indomitably by *that great French composer Spontini*, and by our *Patriotism*; and we gallantly rally to defend our own Grétry (from Liége in Flanders) against that intruding alien Rossini (from Pesaro in Italy)!

In 1765, Louis XV, for all his intelligence, retorted to the Duc d'Ayen, who had been uncomplimentary about Du Belloy's patriotic tragedy *le Siège de Calais*: "Sir, I believed you to be a worthier son of France!" The Duke's reply is well known*. Even Napoleon, in his *Mémoires*, is carried away by the fine old tradition of patriotic untruth, and sees fit to condemn any historian who has the temerity to record events discreditable to France.[1] Had his reign not been cut short, he would, he says, "have *destroyed all the evidence* of the military history of his own epoch, so as to be the *sole and absolute master of Truth*". There is a curious anecdote concerning General Vallongue and the battle of Marengo; but the gallant officer who whispered it to me in confidence is too much of a gentleman to make it public. I personally worship Napoleon the hero; but I despise Napoleon the despot giving audience to the Chief of his Secret Police.

In all the political revolutions from which the state has emerged, France has shown no signs of "frivolity"; on the contrary, the average Frenchman has followed the prospect of his own individual economic advantage with the most relentless persistence;[2] and in literature, he has shown a similar tenacity in the pursuit of ideas which satisfy his *vanity*. The dramatist knows no more potent spell for conjuring the menace of a *fiasco* than to plagiarize a line or two from La Harpe; and even in the *Quartier du Marais*, there is no more certain way of earning a reputation for infinite intellectual finesse than to spice the same plagiarism with a super-subtle *nuance* or variation once in a dozen pages. That which we admired yesterday, we shall doggedly continue

[1] Notes on a work by General Rogniat.

[2] On the morrow of the *18 Brumaire*, two thousand citizens of wealth and substance suddenly *found it in their interests* to become zealous supporters of Napoleon.

to admire to-day; for admiration accumulates like money in the bank; if it were not so, we should be forced to fit ourselves out every day with a new fund of conversation; and then we might find ourselves faced with problems and objections which we had failed to foresee, and for which we had no answer ready . . . O, calamity!

In France, the humbler classes of society are frankly content to admire what "Paris" admires, just as, formerly, they would admire what was admired by the Court. Provincial society, all too painfully aware that it is not in the vanguard of fashion, is desperately afraid of allowing any really *serious discussion* on any of the topics which it has tacitly agreed to regard as being *in good taste*. It receives its opinions ready-made from Paris—from that scarlet city of Paris which the Provinces contemplate with secret and silent loathing leavened with abject humility. It is worth observing that the only persons left in Paris who still possess a trace of masculine and virile energy are invariably provincials who make their way to Paris at the age of seventeen, burdened with a whole noisome baggage of fashionable literary opinions dating from 1760!

It follows clearly, therefore, that in the field of art at least, *inconstancy* is precluded by the quivering susceptibilities of *vanity*: *he who desireth Beauty must pass through the Vale of Suffering*. No one dare risk a confident appeal to his own independent judgment—least of all in the Provinces, where independence is the one sin for which there is no forgiveness.

Such was the cacophony of lèse-majestical thoughts which dinned in my ears this evening at the *Opéra*, at the sight of that vast congregation of *persons of taste* all bored to extinction by *le Devin du Village*, and yet utterly devoid of the moral courage required to confess as much frankly, even to themselves;[1] so horrible indeed is the stigma which attaches, in France, to the man who dares stand alone in his opinion.

[1] Most of the seats at the *Grand Opéra* are taken, either by members of the lower orders, or else by gaping provincials freshly disembarked from the stage-coaches —the two classes of mortals who are *by instinct* admirers of anything *expensive*. Add a sprinkling of newly-arrived English landed gentry (in the boxes), and a score or so of licentious rakes who have paid to stare at the *corps de ballet* (in the balcony): this, together with the annual subsidy of 600,000 francs voted by the Government, represents the total sum of support which the *Grand Opéra* receives in Paris. The first Minister who happens to retain a farthing's-worth of common sense will install the *Italians* in the *rue Le Peletier*; but I can't see it happening before 1830!

One evening last summer, I strolled into Tortoni's *pâtisserie**, and there I found the connoisseurs of ice-cream all crushed one on top of the other in a space about two yards square. Somewhat annoyed at not finding one of the little tables free to sit at, I called to Tortoni, with whom I shared a friendship based on our common enthusiasm for Italy: "I don't understand the workings of your mind," I said. "Why don't you lease further premises adjoining your present establishment? Then at least one might find room to sit down!" *"Non son così matto!"* came the reply. "I know you French people—you're never happy unless you're being crushed to death! Just you walk over to the door, and take a look at the crowds on the *Boulevard de Gand*!"

Obviously I failed to digest my Italian friend's judicious reply, for recently I found myself saying to one of the managers of the *Opéra Bouffe*: "Your theatre, Sir, is dying of inanition; so why not spend a bit more, engage three additional singers at 30,000 francs each, and put on a performance once a week at the *Grand Opéra*?" "We shouldn't get a soul to come and sit through it," he answered. "The pit would be empty and the boxes deserted; if we did what you suggest, we should be killing the goose that lays the golden eggs; we should be stifling that most profitable fashion which alone persuades the average poor citizen of Paris to spend his small weekly savings, not on seats for the *Opéra Bouffe*, where he *wants* to go, but on our beloved *Grand Opéra*, whither the dictates of convention drive him!"[1]

I suppose that it would be very hard to record two manifestations of social conformism more utterly *futile* than those which I have just quoted. Fashionable Paris crowds into Tortoni's, there to be *crushed* to death, for precisely the same reason that it crowds into the *Théâtre Français*, there to be *bored* to death; the principle is the same in either case. It is the same man compelled by the same motive at two different hours of the day. At seven in the evening, strolling past the doors of the *Théâtre Français*, he thinks to himself: "Ah . . . *Iphigénie*! Wonderful play—why not drop in and see another performance?" So he takes his ticket, muttering under his breath as he does so:

[1] *If we increased the size of our theatre, no would would come and sit in the audience* —this is the inevitable retort which you get whenever you go and complain that the boxes are so cramped that it is nothing less than sheer torture to sit in them, or suggest that, since the two adjacent buildings belong to the Administrators of the theatre in any case, it would be a simple matter to transform the existing corridors into boxes *à l'italienne*, and to construct a new set of lateral corridors.

Jamais Iphigénie, en Aulide immolée
N'a coûté tant de pleurs à la Grèce assemblée,
Que dans l'heureux spectacle à nos yeux étalé,
En a fait, sous son nom, verser la Champmeslé.[1]
                    BOILEAU, *Epître à Racine.*

And when so noble and revered a critic as Boileau writes lines like these, where is he, poor man, to find the moral courage to convince himself that it is utterly absurd to talk about *une rame inutile* "vainly exhausting" *une mer immobile.*[2] In any case, our man has never so much as made a trip in a steam-packet!

A true die-hard Parisian never goes to Tortoni's to eat ices *because it is hot* (how unspeakably vulgar!), but simply because it is the "done thing", simply because he wants to "be seen" in an establishment frequented by high society, because he himself wishes to catch a glimpse of this same high society, and last—distinctly *last*—of all, because there may be a faint suggestion of pleasure in consuming ice-cream when the thermometer appears to be fixed permanently at 80 degrees in the shade.

By contrast, if, by eight o'clock in the evening, there are still a few seats empty at the *Théâtre Louvois*, there is only one conclusion to be drawn: the *Théâtre Louvois* is clearly *not* one of those establishments in which "high society" sees fit to crush itself to death . . . so *I* won't go either!

In Spain or in Italy, every man has the profoundest contempt for his neighbour, and savagely delights in the pride of his own opinions. This, of course, is the reason why no really "fashionable" person could ever endure to live in either country.

This, and all that has gone before, explains the history of Rossini's reception in France; from the day when some shrewd *Director* of the *Opéra Bouffe* chose to disfigure *l'Italiana in Algeri*, to the day when, during the run of *il Barbiere*, every ingenuity was displayed to suggest disadvantageous comparisons with Paisiello, the authorities have clung

---

[1] Never did Iphigenia cost so many tears to the assembled peoples of Greece by her sacrifice in Aulis, as Mademoiselle de Champmeslé caused to be shed in her name during the course of the wonderful tragedy which we have recently beheld.

[2] Il fallut s'arrêter, et la rame inutile
Fatigua vainement une mer immobile
        Iphigénie, lines 50-1.

desperately to the hope of setting the public against "that Italian". The manoeuvre was adroit, and shrewdly calculated to flatter the particular literary prejudices of the race to which it was addressed. Men of letters, always ready to consider the privilege of criticizing music and painting as a legitimate appendage to their professional titles*, stuck fast by the traditions of the guild, and poured forth rabid articles extolling composers who were thirty years out of date and denigrating the composers of to-day. It was still Racine and Boileau whom they were defending; still (in their own minds at least), Schiller and Byron who were to be cast forth into the nethermost pit. Their inkwells never seemed to hold sufficient vitriol to hurl at the "indescribable impertinence" of *any* young man who dared cast aspersions upon the renown of an *Ancient*![1] But luckily for Rossini, the heyday of Geoffroy was long past; none of the surviving newspapers really carried weight with any considerable section of the public; and so our poor, worthy literary critics, now no longer enjoying their traditional and privileged monopoly of the pulpit, were suddenly aghast to discover that no one was taking any serious notice of them at all!

Rossini's popularity in Paris dates from the production of *il Barbiere* —a mere *nine years** after he had become the idol of the public, not only in every corner of Italy, but throughout large areas of Germany as well. *Tancredi*, for instance, was produced in Vienna immediately after the Congress (1814–15); three years later, *la Gazza ladra* was given, amid scenes of wild enthusiasm, in Berlin; and ever since, the presses of that city have been pouring forth volume upon volume of praise or abuse concerning the overture.

Paris, on the other hand, was not allowed to appreciate even one *half* of Rossini's qualities until (to the unutterable despair of certain Patriotic Persons) Madame Fodor took over Signora de' Begnis' part in the *Barber*; and for the other half, it had to wait until Madame Pasta was heard in *Otello* and *Tancredi*.

[1] *Vide: la Renommée*, issues dating from the first part of September 1819 (as far as I remember); also various other journals.

CHAPTER XXV

Of the Two Enthusiasts

SOME time ago, I was introduced to an elderly clerk from the War-Office who possessed the gift of perfect pitch to such a degree that, if he chanced to be passing a stone-mason's yard set up in the neighbourhood of some site where a large building was in process of construction, and where a couple of workmen, standing side by side, happened to be chipping a block of stone with their hammers, he could tell instantly (if anyone chose to ask him) the exact notes which the two sets of hammer-blows were emitting—and *that*, with such perfect accuracy, that he was never known to make a mistake in his assessment of the sound-value, nor in the musical notation which he would correctly and unhesitatingly assign to it. If he happened to come across a barrel-organ playing (like all barrel-organs) out of tune, he would proclaim, even while the gruesome apparatus was still functioning, exactly *which* wrong notes it was churning out. No less apt was his felicity and accuracy in the analysis of the tortured screeching of a badly-rigged pulley fixed at the top of a crane-arm and struggling with some enormous weight; or of the anguished ululations proceeding from the unoiled wheels of a farm-cart. It is superfluous even to mention that my new friend could draw unerring attention to the tiniest slip in the largest orchestra; he could name the offending note and point out the guilty player. The individual who had originally introduced us later requested me to sing an aria, which (whether by chance or on purpose I will not reveal) presented a number of extremely doubtful notes; and, to the astonishment of a professional musician who happened to be present, these same doubtful notes were found to be exactly reproduced in the notational version which our friend the army-clerk produced a moment or two later, and presented to the discomfited singer! This curious person can copy down any tune which he hears, just as a child can be persuaded to write out one of La Fontaine's *Fables* when some family friend, to test his progress as a scholar, chooses to give him a dictation. If the tune is unusually long, the clerk, not trusting his memory, may ask you to stop at a given point, so as to give him time to get down on paper what he has heard so far. There are many other tests of a similar character from which this odd acquaintance of mine has been known to emerge equally triumphant, but it would be tedious to enumerate them. Every sound in nature speaks to him in a language which (technically speaking) is of pellucid clarity, and he can transfer it to paper; but he has not the faintest inkling of its *real* meaning. It would, I suppose, be hard to discover anyone whose ear was more sensitively attuned to the physical phenomena of sound; but it would certainly be equally hard to find anyone who was deafer to the broadest suggestion of pleasure which such phenomena normally convey.

This poor old clerk, whose countenance, like that of Monsieur Bellemain in *l'Intérieur d'un Bureau,* is placid, calm and contented, has behind him some forty years of impeccable and industrious service; and he is the *driest,* the most insensitive man alive. A *note,* for him, is a *noise*; music, a dead language which he hears perfectly and understands not at all. I do honestly believe that he *prefers* the sound of his masons' hammers chipping away at blocks of stone to all the symphonies that were ever written. As an experiment, we have tried sending him tickets for two concurrent performances, the one lot for comic opera at the *Théâtre Louvois,* the other for straight comedy at the *Théâtre de l'Odéon* (or alternatively, one set for some serious operatic performance at the *Grand Opéra* and the other for straight melodrama at the *Porte-Saint-Martin*); and invariably he has chosen the theatre where there was no singing. Music, apparently, gives him no pleasure whatsoever, except as a plain exercise for his freakish gift, as a test in the identification of sound; as an *art,* speaking to the soul, it is meaningless—and in any case, he does not possess a soul. At the first hint that any conversation is showing a tendency to drift off towards a higher level, at the first suggestion of any idea or event which threatens to rise above the very lowest abysses of triteness and banality, he simply proceeds to exclaim, naïvely and with monotonous repetition: "Fancy! Just fancy!" He is the living incarnation of the *prosaic.*

By contrast, no one who ever came into contact with the court of Prince Eugène, the Viceroy of Italy, can fail to recall Count C***, a young Venetian nobleman of the most heroic bravery, whose many instances of gallantry in action had rapidly earned him promotion to the rank of *aide-de-camp* to the Prince himself. Not only was this charming young man to all intents and purposes tone-deaf; but he was incapable of singing four notes on end without committing the most excruciating cacophony. But the astonishing fact was that, in spite of being constitutionally incapable of singing in tune, he adored music with a passionate intensity which is rare to find even in Italy. While triumph after triumph was being showered upon him in every field, it was quite obvious that a considerable and vital part of his happiness was incomplete unless he had music. A similar instance is that of Graf Wenzel von Gallenberg, who, during the period of Rossini's successes at the *teatro San-Carlo*, was responsible for the music of the ballets which were performed in the interval between the first and second acts, and which earned him a popularity almost as phenomenal as that of Rossini himself; yet I am assured that Gallenberg had the greatest difficulty in distinguishing between a correct note and an incorrect one.

These are extreme cases, and consequently rare; but taken together with all the intermediate degrees lying between them, they cover every type of musician and music-lover. On the one hand you have people—musical pedants, as rabid in their pedantry as the old-school latinisers with their souls steeped in vanity, avarice and book-learning—whose perceptions of notes, modes and keys are sharpened to an incredible degree of accuracy, but whose souls, indifferent to suggestion or passion or hint of passion, remain for ever unmoved by sounds of any description. These creatures, in the field of music, are invariably the most learned and the most imperturbable of critics; never caught off their balance by the rushing winds of enthusiasm, they keep doggedly to the narrow paths laid down straitly and for ever among the comfortable landmarks of things once learnt; and above all, they are never reduced to blushing over the kind of exaggerations which, uttered in unguarded moments before a company ill-equipped to sympathize with them, become such a source of recurring shame to the genuine lover of music.

Compared with the pedant, your true music-lover strikes one as singularly ignorant, and may occasionally stumble into the rashest absurdities—particularly when he tortures himself into astonishing postures of pedantry and falsehood in order to give the impression that he really *is* an expert in the "theory of sound-classification" and such other monstrous musical technicalities. In France, no *amateur* of this type can so much as open his mouth to speak of the divine art to which he owes the most inspiring of all delights, without charging headlong into some learned pitfall or other, thereby making himself the butt and laughing-stock of all the "professionals"; if he has theories, they are usually picked up wholesale out of Reicha, and no more than half-digested at that. Any evening at the *Théâtre Louvois*, I can glance across the auditorium, and pick out specimens of either category: the genuine *dilettante*, for instance, is always slightly untidy in appearance, whereas the pedant is invariably dressed up to the nines, a veritable masterpiece of painstaking sartorial discipline, even at *premières*, when decent seats are only to be had at the price of a real tussle. The poor, misguided fellow who really *enjoys* music tends, unwisely, to start *talking* in moments of supreme emotion; and this, of course, is when he is most liable to lay himself open to the jeers and irony of his less sensitive neighbours; he grows angry, while they sneer with ever-increasing complacency as his abysmal ignorance of names and dates and places grows glaringly more obvious; whereas the withered pedant in the next seat acquires a brittle halo of glory at his expense by reeling off, in a slightly less nauseating form than usual, the entire history of musico-logy, interwoven with a vast rigmarole containing every detail of the vocal characteristics of every *prima donna* who has appeared on the Italian stage for the last twenty years, every date of every first appear-ance, of every *première* ... etc., etc. And yet, *why* does our poor *dilettante* have to expose himself to ridicule in this foolhardy manner? It can only be because there is still a trace of the old French attitude left in his character. Why *do* we start talking? Why do we feel impelled to appeal for sympathy to this vast *extinguisher** of enthusiasm and sensi-bility? *Because of our obsession with other people!* Compare the typical music-lover who frequents the *San-Carlo* or *la Scala*: preoccupied to the exclusion of all else by the intensity of his own emotional ex-perience, devoid of any urge to criticize, still less to translate his sensa-tions into well-turned sentences, he is completely indifferent to his neighbour's opinion, unsolicitous of his approbation, and as likely as not unaware of his existence. Lost in his private and ecstatic universe of contemplation, anger and impatience are the only reactions that he is likely to manifest towards the importunate intrusiveness of *other people* —towards anyone who is rash enough to come between him and the rapture of his own soul. From time to time an exclamation may spring to his lips, to be followed by a relapse into profound and sullen silence.

If he beats time to the music, if he so much as stirs a finger, it can only be because there are certain passages where the final consummation of pleasure demands movement. His mouth will gape half-open, and every feature bear traces of intolerable exhaustion—or rather, will seem utterly drained of the last thin drop of vitality; his eyes alone may give some insight into the fiery recesses of his soul, and even then, should anybody chance to advise him of the fact, he will bury his head in his hands, so desperate is his contempt for *other people*.

Many renowned singers belong to that category of musicians whose prototype I have sketched beneath the symbolic figure of my little army-clerk, with his analytical mania and his passion for the music of stone-dressers' hammers. But in the last resort, they are nothing but banal and prosaic lumps of humanity, endowed by sheer chance with an accurate ear, a flexible larynx and powerful lungs.

And if, in time, they end up by acquiring a veneer of intellectual polish, their immediate reaction is to cultivate an artificial crop of "fine feelings" and "enthusiasm"; the word "genius" will tend to occur rather too frequently in their conversation, and busts of Mozart may suddenly appear upon their desks. If they live in Paris, however, the intellectual veneer is not essential to the erection of this façade; the phrases which furnish their conversation are supplied ready-made by the daily press, and there are always furniture-dealers handy with a good selection of busts of Mozart.

Many an instinctive music-lover, on the other hand, may wallow in the blackest ignorance of music as a science; and yet the majority of musical combinations, from the simplest to the most complex, will have a *clear and forceful significance* to him, each representing some subtle but unmistakable *nuance* of emotion. No language, to him, can speak with greater clarity than the language of music; and, since his mind has not been equipped (and warped) with any rational system of control, this poor *dilettante* has no power within him to resist the fatal seduction. Mozart is the sovereign and master of his soul and, in the space of twenty bars, can plunge him into a reverie, or else transport him into a realm where the most prosaic happenings in all the world— say, a dog run over by a cab in the *rue de Richelieu*—are transmuted into great tragedies of Destiny and mysteries of the heart.

CHAPTER XXVI

Mosè in Egitto

Occasionally, when I was in Naples, I would stroll round after a performance, towards midnight or one o'clock in the morning, and join a gathering of old music-lovers, who used to meet on a terrace above the *riviera di Chiaja*, on the roof-garden of one of the *palazzi*. A number of fair-sized orange-trees had somehow been transplanted up there, on to this miniature esplanade, and we could look down upon the sea and upon every other roof-top in Naples; while, facing us, rose Mount Vesuvius, which, each evening, would produce some new and curious phenomenon to fascinate our gaze. Seated up there, high up on this mountain-top of a terrace, we used to await the first cool and balmy breaths of the night-wind, which rarely fails to awaken soon after midnight. The splashing of the sea, whose waves came and broke upon the shore scarcely twenty paces away from the foot of the *palazzo*, added a further suggestion of coolness, which, beneath this scorching climate, contributed greatly to our feeling of well-being. In these conditions, the delicious urge to "talk music" was well-nigh irresistible; and we felt endlessly tempted to re-enact its subtle miracles, either through discussion, which, when it takes the form of torrents of living language poured forth from the heart, can breathe new life, as it were, into old and dead sensation; or else, more directly, by means of a piano which stood hidden away behind three orange-tubs in a corner of the terrace. The majority of these elderly *dilettanti* had known Cimarosa as a personal friend; and they often used to reminisce about the spiteful tricks which Paisiello had played upon him in the days when these two great composers shared between them the homage of Naples and of all Italy; for Paisiello, with the genius of an angel, had the morals of an ape, and consequently Cimarosa never knew the pure and unsmirched triumphs of his successor, Rossini, who reigns like the God-one-and-indivisible over Italy and the whole universe of music. This astounding popularity, incidentally, was a constant source of wonder to my friends, who used to like to try and explain it. Many a time I have heard Rossini compared unfavourably with the great masters of the end of the last century—with Anfossi, Piccinni, Galuppi, Guglielmi, Portogallo, Zingarelli, Sacchini, *etc., etc.* The only quality for which Rossini received full credit was his *style*, that is to say, the art of writing in a manner which is *characteristically entertaining to the present generation*; but as to ideas, as to anything really fundamental, there was no comparison—so they used to say—between this modern upstart and those fine old composers of days gone by. Unfortunately, I do not *know* the operas which those fine old composers composed; and in any case, where should I look to-day to find any voices technically capable of performing them?[1] I have heard nothing except one or two of their most celebrated arias; and I confess that my attitude towards the majority of these great figures closely resembles my attitude towards Garrick and Le Kain; for almost every day I hear these actors extolled to the skies by men for whose judgment and intelligence I have the greatest respect; and yet, in the domain of art, I am tyrannized by a bad intellectual habit which I have imported from the field of politics—namely, I am prepared to talk without let or hindrance about any subject under the sun, but I will believe nothing except that which I have seen with my own eyes. For instance, before my visit to England, I used to *believe* that Talma was the greatest tragic actor of the century; but since then I have actually *beheld* Kean!

We were in Naples, then, and at the height of our arguments concerning the relative merits of Rossini and of his precursors (whose superior deserts, strangely, were not rewarded by a correspondingly greater success), when the play-bills heralded a new opera with a Biblical theme, to be given at the *San-Carlo: Mosè in Egitto* (1818). I must confess that I set out for the theatre on this occasion with a marked lack of enthusiasm for the Plagues of Egypt. *Libretti* based upon the Holy Scriptures may have their attraction for a Bible-reading nation such as the English,[2] or even in Italy, where they are sanctified

---

[1] See below, chapters xxvii–xxxiv, which deal with the art of singing as it was in 1770 and as it is to-day. The main ideas embodied in these chapters, incidentally, were gathered during the course of conversations with the group which I have just described.

[2] Out of respect for the Sacred Text of the Bible, it proved too risky to include *Mosè* in the season of Italian opera at the *King's Theatre*, London; but in 1823, the music was adapted to make a new opera, entitled *Peter the Hermit*. This is an experiment which interests me considerably, for there are four or five of Rossini's

by a tradition of miraculous aesthetic beauty, and by the memories of Raphael, Michelangelo and Correggio. Speaking purely as a man of letters and as a student of humanity, I entertain the greatest respect for the Holy Scriptures, which I revere as a work of art in the same category as the *Arabian Nights**; their comparative antiquity, the primitive levels of behaviour which they depict, above all the stylistic *grandeur* of the writing—all these I find fascinating. As a politician, I admit their considerable value as the prop, pillar and corner-stone of any aristocratic society, and as the ultimate justification of those gorgeous liveries flaunted by so many English Peers; yet this is still a somewhat *intellectual* appreciation. As a *moralist*, whenever I think of the Plagues of Egypt, and of Pharoah, and of the way in which *it came to pass, that at* midnight, *the Lord smote all the first-born in the Land of Egypt* (*Exodus xii, v. 29*), my memories race back relentlessly to those twelve or fifteen *priests* amongst whom I spent my childhood in the time of the Terror.

Thus it came about that I found myself at the *San-Carlo* in no very propitious frame of mind, feeling rather like a man who has been offered a front seat at an *auto-da-fé*, where the victims have been furnished by some low piece of political knavery manoeuvred by M. Comte.

The opera opens with the so-called *Plague of Darkness*, a plague which offers any number of facile pitfalls to the unwary dramatic producer, and consequently lends itself to absurdity—all you have to do is to dim the footlights and the overhead battens! When the curtain went up, I am afraid that I simply burst out laughing at the sight of all those wretched little groups of Egyptians, plunged into Stygian darkness by the *Plague of Dimmers*, lost in the wilderness of an apparently boundless stage, and praying like fury. Yet . . . before I had heard twenty bars of this superb *introduzione*, I could see nothing less profoundly moving than a whole population plunged into deep misery; it might have been the people of Marseilles in prayer at the outbreak of plague in 1720. Pharaoh, his obstinacy vanquished by the lamentations of his people, cries out:

operas whose plots, as they stand, are so absurd that the imagination staggers and recoils; but I have hope now that new and adequate *libretti* may be written for them. There are some thirty literary periodicals in England, and it would be difficult to pick out a single page among the whole collection which is unsanctified by some Biblical allusion; not to mention Mr Irving—a figure who is inconceivable in France, even in Toulouse!

Venga Mosè![1]

Benedetti, who was playing the part of Moses, entered, wearing a costume which was sublime in its very simplicity, and had been copied from Michelangelo's statue in the church of *San Pietro in Vincoli*, in Rome; and before his supplication to the Almighty had completed its first sentence, every shred of critical scepticism had departed from my soul; Moses was no longer a shoddy conjuror turning his rod into a serpent and playing cheap tricks on a primitive simpleton, but a great Minister of the All-Powerful, who could cause a vile tyrant to shake upon his throne. I can still recall the overwhelming impression produced by the first hearing of the words:

Eterno, immenso, incomprensibil Dio![2]

The score, in this scene of Moses' first entrance, is reminiscent of Haydn at his most sublime—perhaps too directly reminiscent. The *introduzione*, which extends over a good half of Act I, and which has the audacity to risk twenty-six consecutive repetitions of the same vocal formula, represented Rossini's most serious excursion into academic music up to that date. Such temerity, combined with such monumental patience, must have cost infinite pains to any genius so volatile as that of Rossini. The musical erudition displayed in this passage is as profound as anything in Winter or Weigl; but at the same time, the fertility of his invention[3] would have scared the wits out of either of these worthy Teutons, who would have thought themselves stark, staring mad! Rossini's grasp of his medium is so perfect, that one might suspect him of having *invented* the science of music, rather than of having learnt it. *Mosè* enjoyed an instantaneous triumph in

---

[1] *Faraone:*
> Rimprovero tremendo
> Non lacerarmi il petto!
> Oh, troppo il mio comprendo
> Reo, pertinace error!
> Venga Mosè!

[2] *Mosè:*
> Eterno, immenso, incomprensibil Dio!
> Ah! Tu che regni ognora, de' tuoi servi
> Allo scampo, e il popol' tuo
> Colmi di benefizi . . .

[3] "Fertility of invention" in a passage containing twenty-six repeats of the same musical idea? This sounds like really first rate academic nonsense!

Naples—a triumph, moreover, which was pre-eminently *French* in character. The overwhelming applause which greets a scene from Racine or Voltaire inspires, in the breast of any typical Parisian play-goer, a secret spasm of delight and self-congratulation over the extent of his acquaintance with Literature and the unequalled perfection of his own good taste; and, as each rolling Racinian period reverberates through the theatre, he calls over in rapid review all the excellent reasons with which the thundering demi-gods of the *Académie*, La Harpe, Geoffroy, Dussault, *etc.*, *etc.*, have furnished him to demonstrate with infallible logic *why* he should admire it. In Naples, no one cares a fig for academic learning, save only in music; and that is why, that evening, at the prospect of a markedly "academic" opera, Neapolitan vanity was rapturously flattered to have the opportunity of applauding something really *abstruse*. Among my neighbours, the one emotion which I could clearly observe peeping through a score of different disguises, was that of *vanity*, gratified beyond expression at being able to display its own erudition. Some would effuse over *this* chord on the 'cellos, others at *that* note on the horn, and its peculiar appositeness; while others again (for already there was some jealousy of Rossini abroad in the land) would temper their enthusiasm with secret spite, and hint that this "unspeakably beautiful *introduzione*" might have been borrowed from an (unspecified) German composer. The second half of the first act went off without a hitch; it deals with the *Plague of Fire*, represented on the stage by a somewhat damp-looking display of fireworks. The second act, which deals with the Plague of Heaven-knows-what-else, was received with enthusiasm, particular praise being reserved for a magnificent duet, at which cries of *bravo maestro! evviva Rossini!* echoed through the theatre from all sides. The Crown Prince, son of the Pharaoh of Egypt, is secretly in love with a young Jewish maiden; and when Moses leads his people out of the land, she comes alone to bid her lover an everlasting farewell. Nature has furnished music with no finer theme for a duet. If Rossini has failed to realize all the possibilities of the situation in his

Principessa avventurata . . .[1]

[1] *Elcia:* Quale ascolto, qual cimento!
Chi dà lena all' alma oppressa?
Osiride: Deh resolvi, a che perplesso
Fausto amor ci assisterà?

his attempt at least leaves the listener vividly aware of all its implications. It was performed with great skill and ability by Signorina Colbran and Nozzari; their only defect, which they shared with the composer, was a slight lack of genuine sincerity and pathos.

In the third act, I have forgotten exactly what sequence led Totola, the librettist, to introduce the *Crossing of the Red Sea*—completely oblivious of the fact that this "crossing" was not precisely as simple a problem for the stage-manager as the *Plague of Darkness*. Owing to the relative positions of the stage and the auditorium, no theatre is equipped to show the sea except on a back-cloth; but in this instance, it was absolutely essential to produce a sea, by hook or by crook, on the actual front-stage, since the narrative demanded that it should be *crossed*! The stage-technician of the *San-Carlo*, desperately intent upon finding a solution to an insoluble problem, had finished up by producing a real masterpiece of absurdity. Seen from the pit, the "sea" rose up into the air some five or six feet above its retaining "shores"; whereas the occupants of the boxes, who were favoured with a bird's-eye view of the "raging billows", also had a bird's-eye view of the little *lazzaroni* whose job it was to "divide the waters" at the sound of Moses' voice! In Paris, no one would have cared a jot;[1] but in Naples, where the *décor* is as often as not a masterpiece of art and skill, there is a certain sensitiveness towards the achievements or failures of this particular aspect of the production; and audiences refuse to acquiesce in any contraption which seems to them more than usually absurd or outrageous. Their perception of the ridiculous is exceedingly acute; consequently, the scene was greeted with a gale of laughter, and the general merriment was so frank and so open, that no one really had the heart to turn surly and whistle. In point of fact, however, scarcely a soul in the whole audience listened to the last part of the opera at all; everybody was far too busy discussing the astounding *introduzione*.

The next day, everybody was whispering that the real composer* was not Rossini at all, but some German or other, whose name I forget.

> *Elcia:*   Principessa avventurata,
>   Tu godrai sì caro oggetto;
>   E di Elcia la sventurata,
>   Giusto ciel, che mai savio
>   Destin ci opprimerà . . .

[1] We in Paris are quite accustomed to the sight of mountains which *throw shadows on the sky*; cf. *Don Giovanni*, scene i, as revived in 1823.

My own impression, I recall very clearly, was that the passage contained too many felicitious ingenuities, the orchestral scoring too much *nonchalant sleight-of-hand* (if I may be pardoned the expression, which seems curiously apt when applied to Rossini), for me ever to be convinced of its Teutonic origin. Nevertheless, since Rossini's laziness on the eve of a *première* is so proverbial that no plagiarism is too monstrous to be attributed to him, I followed the general trend of opinion, and suspended judgment until the moment, some six weeks later, when a reply was received from that poor devil of a German composer (whose name I still forget), protesting, upon the last shreds of his national honour, that never in his life had he had the miraculous good fortune to compose the fabulous *introduzione* which had been sent to him for inspection. This was the signal for *Mosè* to embark upon an unheard-of run of success, and the Neapolitans grew daily more rapturous at this rare chance which had been vouchsafed them to applaud *harmony* and *erudition* in the same opera!

The following season (so I am informed) *Mosè* was revived, to the same thunderous applause for Act I, and to the same ungovernable fits of laughter for the *Passage of the Red Sea*. I was not in Naples at the time; but I was there when a third revival was announced*. On the eve of the first performance, Rossini, who was as usual lounging in bed and holding court to a score or so of acquaintances, was interrupted (to the immense delight of everyone present) by the appearance of the librettist Totola, who came rushing into the room, utterly unmindful of the assembled company, and shrieked at the top of his voice: *Maestro! maestro! ho salvato l'atto terzo!—E che hai fatto . . .?* demanded Rossini, mimicking the curious mixture of burlesque and pedantry which made up the wretched poet's manner: "My poor friend, what on earth *could* you do? They'll laugh this time, just as they always do!" "*Maestro*, I've written a prayer for the Jews just before the passage of the Red Sea," cried the wretched, snivelling hack, hauling from his pocket an immense wad of papers, all docketed like a lawyer's brief, and handing them to Rossini, who promptly lay down again in bed to decipher the tangle of hieroglyphic jottings scribbled in the margin of the principal document. While he was reading, the silly little poetaster was circling the room with a nervous smile, shaking hands and whispering over and over again: *Maestro, è lavoro d'un' ora.*[1]

---

[1] Maestro, it only took an hour's work.

Rossini glared at him: *E lavoro d'un' ora, he!* The scribbler, half terrified out of his wits, and more than ever apprehensive of some catastrophic practical joke, tried to make himself inconspicuous, tittered awkwardly, and glanced at Rossini: *Sì, signor, sì, signor maestro!* "Very well, then," exclaimed the composer, "If it only took *you* an hour to write the words, *I* shall manage to write the music in fifteen minutes!" Whereupon he leapt out of bed and, sitting down to a table (still in his nightshirt), dashed off the music for the *Prayer* in eight or ten minutes at the most, without a piano, and undeterred by the conversation of his friends, which continued as loud as ever regardless of his preoccupations, everyone talking away at the top of his voice, as is normal in Italy. "Here's your music—take it!" he barked finally at the librettist, who promptly vanished, leaving Rossini to jump back into bed, convulsed with laughter at Totola's fright. On the following evening, I made a special point of going to the *San-Carlo*. The first act met with its customary enthusiastic reception; and when the curtain went up on the third—on the notorious *Passage of the Red Sea*—there were the usual witticisms, and the same irrepressible urge to laugh. In fact, the laughter was already bursting forth audibly from the pit, when the audience suddenly became aware that Moses was starting on an unfamiliar aria:

Dal tuo stellato soglio . . .[1]

—a prayer which all the people echo in chorus after Moses. Caught unawares by this innovation, the pit found itself listening, and the incipient laughter died away. This first chorus, which is a fine composition, is in the minor key; but then Aaron takes up the prayer, and his words in turn are repeated by the people. Finally Elcia, the Jewish girl, implores heaven with the same supplications, and the people reply again; upon which, all kneel, and with mounting fervour repeat the same prayer; the miracle is accorded, and the waters divide to make a passage for the people protected of the Lord. This final section is in the major*.[2] It is impossible to imagine the thunder-clap

[1] *Mosè:*
      Dal tuo stellato soglio,
      Signor, ti volgi a noi
      Pietà de' figli tuoi,
      Del popol tuo pietà
[2] Here we have the key to any successful production of this opera: the miracle must occur *during the Prayer*, upon a sign from Moses as he turns to face the sea.

which burst upon the theatre, echoing and re-echoing until it seemed that the very walls must give way. People stood up in their boxes and leaned out over the balconies, shouting to crack the vault of heaven: *bello! bello! o che bello!* I have never known such a triumph, such a *furore*—which was all the more tremendous since everyone had come expecting to laugh or jeer. The success of *la Gazza ladra* in Milan was striking enough; but, because of the national temperament in that cooler climate, was considerably more restrained. O happy land of Naples! This was no longer the applause of *satisfied vanity*, the self-congratulatory raptures of a *French audience*, as it had been in the first act; this was the pure and overflowing gratitude of hearts whose joy was perfect, towards the god who had poured out before them such abundance from his cornucopia of pleasure. Who will deny, in the light of such an experience, that music can provoke an immediate and physical nervous reaction? This *Prayer* all but brings tears to my eyes whenever I think of it.

In Germany, *Mosè* is considered to be Rossini's masterpiece—a verdict which, if flattering, is obviously sincere, for in this opera, Rossini has condescended to speak in the native language of Germany itself: *erudition*, combined with complete self-abasement before the sacrificial altar of *orchestral harmony*.

Personally, however, I confess that I find *Mosè* in many respects boring. I cannot deny that I received a great deal of pleasure from it during the course of the first ten performances which I saw, nor that I could pleasurably devote an evening to it, say, once a month, provided that I felt in the right mood, and provided above all *that the standard of performance were well above average*; nevertheless, I feel that it is basically *poor theatre*. There is a lack of coherence and continuity in the emotional characterization, and I lose the thread of sympathy.[1] Rossini's real masterpieces bear watching thirty times on

---

[1] The platitudinous loves and the all-too-ordinary emotions of commonplace mortals, which fill literally hundreds of new novels published every year, are the very stuff of which music is made; the miracle of music is that, proportionately to the genius of the individual composer, it can strip them of their crust of vulgarity, and whisk them off into new regions of sublimity. The superb epics of *Job* and of the *Levite of Ephraim*, or the episode of *Ruth*, lend themselves supremely well as material for the *opera seria*. From motives of respect, I forbear to include the Passion of Christ, which is one of the finest subjects which could be offered to any modern audience. The Author of this work has himself attempted a tragedy entitled *the Passion of Jesus*.

end, and still fill me with exquisite delight, even when they are poorly sung.

In spite of the German school (which has a branch-office in the *Conservatoire de Paris*), and in spite of all the fine Teutonic names which swarm in our orchestras and *salons*, I am convinced that such qualified success as this opera *did* achieve in France was due exclusively to the performance of Madame Pasta, who to some extent redeemed the part of the Jewish maiden Elcia. In particular, the turban she wore with her costume was hugely appreciated, and she was outstanding in her rendering of the duet:

Ah! se puoi così lasciarmi . . .[1]

The *introduzione* was applauded, thanks to some first-rate singing by Zucchelli, supported by the fine voice of Levasseur in the part of Moses; and the *Prayer* proved irresistible. Indeed, on days when one is in the right mood, this *Prayer* sticks in one's head, and sets one humming the whole evening.

Mosè was the first of Rossini's operas for which he received adequate payment; he sold it in fact for 4,200 francs. By comparison, *Tancredi* had brought in no more than 600 francs, and *Otello*, 100 *louis*. The convention which is observed in Italy is that a score remains for two years the property of the *impresario* who employed the composer in the first instance, after which it becomes public property. It was as a direct result of this ridiculous piece of legislation that the music-publisher Ricordi, of Milan, was able to make a fortune out of Rossini's operas, while the composer himself languished in comparative poverty. Far from drawing any fixed annual royalties from his operas, as would be the case in France, Rossini is forced to appeal to the obliging dis-

---

[1] *Osiride:*
  Ah! se puoi così lasciarmi,
  Se già tace in te l'affetto,
  Di tua man' pria m'apri il petto
  E ne squarcia a brani il cor.
 Elcia:
  Ma perchè così straziarmi?
  Perchè farmi più infelice?
  Questo pianto, o Dio! non dice
  Quanto è fiero il mio dolor!
Rossini has transformed the noble and moving passage for solo clarinet from the overture to *Otello*, into an aria for Pharaoh's son Osiris.

position of his various *impresari*[1], if at any time, during the first two years, he wishes his works to be performed at any theatre other than that for which they were originally written; and moreover, no production of this kind can ever bring him in a penny.

Rossini could certainly compose an opera of the type which is popular at the *Théâtre Feydeau* within three days; and at that, more heavily loaded with musical numbers (8 or 9 items) than usual. He has often been advised to come to France, and to compose new music for all the old light-opera *libretti* written by Sedaine, Hèle, Marmontel and other competent playwrights who knew how to handle a dramatic situation properly. In less than six months, Rossini could have accumulated a capital which would give him a regular income of 200 *louis* per annum—a sum which, before his marriage with Signorina Colbran, would have represented undreamed-of wealth. But leaving aside this aspect of the matter, no advice could have been more hopelessly wrong than that which urged him to come to Paris. Half a dozen years among us would have been quite enough to turn Rossini into the most commonplace of mortals; he would have been thrice decorated, and he would have forfeited half his gaiety and all his genius; his soul would have lost its resilience for ever. Compare, not our own great artists (for I have no malicious ambitions as a satirist), but, for instance, Goethe in his *Aus meinem Leben,** and in particular in his *Kampagne in Frankreich 1792*; here is glaring evidence of what happens to men of genius when they set foot in the Courts of Kings! Canova refused to live at the court of Napoleon; but Rossini, in Paris, would never be free of the importunity of courtiers. So far, he has known no one but singers and *impresari*; with the result that he, Rossini, a penniless Italian musician, betrays in his thought a consciousness of dignity and a sense of legitimate pride a hundred times more remarkable than anything which is to be seen in Goethe, who is a far-famed philosopher. For Rossini, a Prince of the Blood is nothing more than an ordinary man invested in the robes of some office or other, of greater or lesser importance as the case may be, whose functions he exercises with greater or lesser success.

If Rossini were to live in France, he would have to develop into an agile-tongued sophist, a manipulator of feminine intrigues and the

---

[1] I must beg the reader's pardon for keeping a number of words in the original Italian; they reflect aspects of life which have no equivalent in France, and any translation would necessarily be misleading.

Lord knows what else besides—even a *politician*! In Italy, the society in which he lives has allowed him to concentrate on being the only thing that mattered—a musician. A blue suit with a black waistcoat and a cravat—this is his unchanging morning attire, and you could present him to the most high-born princess in all the world without inducing him to alter it. Yet this barbarous unconventionality has never prevented women from finding him agreeable; whereas in France, one and all would have concluded: *He's just a boor!* And thus it comes to pass, that France is simply teeming with delightful little artists who can gaily turn their hand to anything . . . except to the job of creating masterpieces!

CHAPTER XXVII

Concerning the Revolution
which Rossini has brought about in the Art
of Singing

THE great singers of the past, la Gabrielli, la Todi, la de' Amicis, la Banti and their like, have disappeared for ever,[1] and nothing remains of the spell of their voices save an echo, fading every day a little towards silence, of the impassioned enthusiasm of their contemporaries; these great names, all household words, and yet from day to day awakening sparser and vaguer memories, are fated eventually to yield pride of place to other celebrities nearer our own time. The same fate awaits us one and all*: Le Kain and Garrick; Viganò, Babbini, Giani, Sestini and Pacchiarotti. Even the great Conquerors are not exempt: what remains of them? A name, a legend perhaps, perhaps the ashes of some burnt-out city . . . little more, in fact, than there remains of a once-famous actor. As you see, I take little stock of that popular veneration which haunts the souls of the unenlightened—souls which were born to revere *Authority* in an embroidered coat,[2] and who still

[1] I cannot resist the temptation, at this point, of setting down one or two of the ideas which were discussed in those Neapolitan conversations in which I occasionally participated, and which I found so enthralling. If, in this and the following chapters, the reader should find any notions which may be either agreeable or useful, their true originator, to whom all credit is due, is M. le Chevalier de Micheroux,* sometime Minister in Dresden. Moreover, I am deeply indebted to this enlightened music-lover for a number of corrections which he has been kind enough to make respecting certain errors of fact of which I had otherwise been guilty elsewhere in this biography. Music flourishes in Italy without leaving a trace; even articles which appear in the periodical press are invariably either paeans of praise or tirades of abuse, and furthermore, rarely commit themselves to any positive statement of any kind. Since this book is simply a monstrous conglomeration of minute particulars, it will inevitably contain many errors. To establish the exact date of the first performance of this opera or that may well cost me more hard labour than the writing of a score of letters; and in the end, I am probably none too confident of the date which I finally decide to adopt.

[2] People, for instance, like those who have recently been coming and cheering, during eighty consecutive performances, at the sight of Sulla insolently lording it over the populace of Rome . . . *i.e.* Napoleon scornfully riding roughshod over the people of France.

M

adore a King three thousand years after he is dead and buried, for no better reason than that *he was a King*; folk, I mean, who reverently raise their hats as they cross the threshold of the Tomb of Psammis the Pharaoh, Ruler in the Land of Egypt. But to return to heroes who truly deserve fame, how much more do we know about Marcellus, the *Sword of Rome*, than about Roscius the actor? And, fifty years from now, who will be the more famous, le maréchal Lovendhal or Le Kain? Furthermore, in estimating the renown of famous captains, allowance must be made for the contribution of luck and opportunity. If Desaix had been elected First Magistrate of France, is it not probable that he would have been simpler, nobler and better than Napoleon? And is it not fair to suggest that a good half of Napoleon's glorious soldiership, the devotion of his Guards, for instance, or the phenomenal marches which he forced upon his troops in 1809, may be due to the authority of the Sovereign Power which he held between his hands, and which enabled him to promote any plain colonel who happened to catch his fancy to the rank of Lieutenant-General within three months?

Having fired off this petard at those honest worthies who, as they sit complacently stroking their *Orders of Merit*, think that it well becomes their position to sneer at artists, let us come back again to those truly exalted beings who had the courage to turn their back on the ante-chambers of kings, who felt and knew the most ennobling passions which the human heart can contain, and who, through the magic of these very passions, delighted and charmed their contemporaries.

We in our generation have watched the birth of many new sciences and of a number of hitherto undiscovered arts; for example, the taste for the *picturesque* in landscape-painting, as in landscape-gardening, was still undreamed-of in the days of Voltaire—a fact to which our dreary *châteaux* built under Louis XV, with their paved courtyards and their mathematical avenues of denuded trees, bear eloquent witness. It is natural enough that the subtlest of the arts, those in fact which seek to delight the most highly-cultivated minds, should be the last to develop.

Who knows, therefore? Perhaps in our own day some genius will master the secret art of describing with sublime accuracy the rare and individual gifts of Mademoiselle Mars or of Madame Pasta; and so, a hundred years hence, these miraculous virtues will continue to live on in the memory of man, as intact and as sharply personal as ever.

An exact and individual record of the voices of our great *prime donne* (should such a thing become possible) would not only profit their own celebrity, but would open the road directly to vast and unlooked-for progress in the art of singing as a whole. Great philosophers have maintained that the characteristic which distinguishes the rational spirit of man from the marvellous instinct of certain animals, is precisely that faculty, shared alike by all members of the human race, of transmitting to succeeding generations whatever progress, however inconsiderable, may have been made in the arts, trades or industries to which the earlier lives have been devoted. This process of transmission is already fully-developed in respect of a Euclid or a Lagrange; for a Raphael, a Canova, a Morghen, it is no more than partially available; yet may we hope, one day, to see it fully established even for the art of a Davide,[1] a Velluti or a Madame Fodor? Perhaps the first step in the right direction may lie in the development of a new style of writing *about* singing—a style which is *simple* and free of turgid rhetoric. This is what I shall attempt to achieve in the course of the following pages.

If art is to be a source of genuine pleasure, the first and essential condition is for it to produce a powerful emotional reaction in the observer. Let me digress once more to remark that, generally speaking, the scholar, the *savant* who is distinguished, either on a national level or else within the narrower limits of a particular group or class, for his erudition, is never a member of that exalted band of mortals endowed by heaven with the rarer gifts of sensibility. A minute proportion of these favoured beings—for instance, among the Ancients, one might name Aristotle—may chance to possess the ability for working out an amazingly precise and detailed analysis of a series of aesthetic and emotional experiences from which, *in the past*, they have received indescribable pleasure. But the ordinary run of philosophers, whose mental equipment consists exclusively of a highly-polished technique of logical deduction—a technique which, in all other fields of learning, reason and human endeavour, is warranted to preserve them faithfully

---

[1] The elder Davide, father of the present artist, whose voice once enjoyed a reputation equal to that of his son, is constantly reproaching the latter for not singing with sufficient *sweetness*, and for sacrificing too much vocal quality in the cause of mere technical acrobatics. I heard the elder Davide sing in the opera-house at Lodi in 1820; he was said to be then seventy years old. He now lives in Bergamo, as does also our worthy friend Mayr, the composer of *Ginevra di Scozia*.

from the pitfalls of error—unfailingly find themselves overwhelmed as soon as they venture into the field of art (where the only necessary mental equipment consists of the accumulated experience of violent emotional reactions), and dragged, as it were by some irresistible force, into the blackest morasses of absurdity. Such, among our own scholars, was the fate of d'Alembert, not to mention the countless others whose worth was inferior to his.

In respect of painting, music, architecture, *etc.*, the distinction between one nation and another rests upon the intensity of pure and spontaneous *sensation* which the average representative of the race—even among its uneducated classes—derives from these arts.[1] For instance, a race which is dominated by an overmastering passion for bad music would be closer to the reality of good taste than a race of scholars who, by dint of mental application, had learned to appreciate sensibly, rationally and *moderately* the most exquisite music which was ever conceived. Thus a priest will feel greater sympathy towards a fanatical, superstitious and orgiastic devotee of the gods *Fo, Apis,* or other similar absurdities, than for a balanced and rational philosopher, whose over-riding concern is the well-being of the human race combined with an attitude of total indifference towards the means employed in securing it, and who, by the light of unaided reason, shall have postulated the existence of *One God*, the Avenger of the Just and the Destroyer of the Unjust upon this earth.

Canova used to tell a neat little anecdote, which he first heard from one of his American admirers. Some years ago a primitive savage had wandered into the town of Cincinnati, and found himself face to face with a wig-maker's dummy; and Canova used to be able to produce a document, some eight or ten lines long, which, he said, represented a literal translation of the exclamations of astonishment and enthralled wonder which had escaped from the savage's lips at this first glimpse of the artificial wooden head—the first representation of the human form which he had ever encountered. Canova was the mildest and simplest of men; and therefore what he, in his modesty, did not dare to add, we must add for him. Any man of taste, upon first beholding

---

[1] The peoples that live in the region situated between the Meuse and the Loire are disproportionately *insensitive* to music; musical perceptiveness is reborn, southwards, in the neighbourhood of Toulouse; northwards, in the area around Köln.

Canova's superb figure-group, *Venus and Adonis*,[1] in which the great sculptor has portrayed the goddess overwhelmed by dark forebodings of tragedy as she bids farewell for the last time to her lover, who is already poised for the fatal hunting expedition from which he is doomed never to return—any man, I say, be his taste never so refined, upon first beholding this wondrous masterpiece of ineffable grace and most exquisite feeling,[2] will of necessity express his wonder and astonishment in precisely the same terms as those which sprang to the lips of the savage confronted with the wooden head of his wig-maker's dummy. The explanation is simple; for in actual fact the sensation of extreme wonderment, the *physical* impact produced upon the soul, is identical in the two cases; the one real exception would arise in the (all too common) situation where the man who admires Canova turns out to be a *pedant*, whose only intrinsic concern is to be admired *himself* for the quality of his own admiration. All the *difference* lies in the *external phenomenon*, that is to say, in the object which excites identical degrees of admiration and rapture in the two observers, who, in all other respects, are so utterly dissimilar. From the foregoing passages, it will be only too evident that, in all aesthetic matters, an expression of admiration can never prove anything save the degree of emotional excitement present in the admirer*, and can have no possible bearing upon the degree of merit implicit in the object admired.

When somebody informs you that he "admires" a great *prima donna*, Madame Belloc, for instance, or Signorina Mariani (who in my humble opinion, is the finest contralto now living), the first point to be

[1] Owned by the Marchese Berio, in Naples.

[2] In music, it is the quality of *motion* which exalts the soul and floods the mind with visions of inexpressible delicacy, conveying such impressions even to minds which may be markedly coarse in texture. A rough-and-ready millionaire, once truly stirred by music, lives for a fleeting instant upon the same emotional plane as a man of genuine intelligence and refinement.

Sculpture, on the other hand, inspires the same infinitely subtle and intangible reactions through its essential quality of *immobility*. One evening when his perceptions were unusually sharpened, Rossini promised to try and interpret the sublime *Venus and Adonis* group, which we were all admiring by torchlight, through the medium of a duet. I recall clearly that the Marchese Berio made him swear to it, by the shades of Pergolesi.

One of these days, I hope I may find the courage to hand my printer a treatise upon the *Ideal of Beauty* as it is interpreted in each of the various arts. It is two hundred pages long, of doubtful intelligibility, and (most serious defect of all) desperately lacking in transition-passages, like the present chapter!

elucidated is whether the person concerned was brought up in a religion which has a fine tradition of singing in church. A man may be gifted with the most phenomenal musical sensitivity, as far as pure *sound* is concerned; yet, if he chanced to be born, say, in Nevers, how do you expect him to be able to admire Davide? He is inexorably *bound* to prefer Dérivis or Nourrit. Moreover, it is not hard to understand why: simply, because three-fourths of the *fioriture* which Davide normally executes are so subtle as to be completely outside the physical range of his perception. The good citizens of Nevers (who are excellent people, I assure you, in all other respects, but who may count themselves exceedingly lucky if they manage to hear decent singing once in three months) are as necessarily baffled by Davide as we ourselves once were, in Berlin, by a painter who had chosen to depict the whole battle of Torgau, one of the victories of Frederick the Great, upon a disc of ivory no bigger than a penny-piece. With the naked eye, and without the help of a magnifying-glass, nothing was visible at all. The "magni-fying-glass", for want of which the poor citizens of Nevers are in such bad case, is simply the pleasure of having stood and applauded some fifty performances of the *Barber of Seville*, each consecrated by the magnificent singing of Madame Fodor. By contrast, the average young German who has chanced to be born in the inconspicuous little town of Sagan, in Silesia, hears twice a week in church, and daily in the streets around his home, enough music, primitive if you like, but still performed with clarity and precision, to give his ear a most thorough education. And this, precisely, is what is missing in the lives of the good people of Nevers—which, incidentally, is a town of far greater size and consequence than Sagan.

CHAPTER XXVIII

Some General Considerations: the History of Rossini's Development, examined in relation to Developments in the Art of Singing

WHEN, on one glorious day, the larger part of the audience at any given opera comes to the conclusion that it need say no more to justify its applause than simply: *We enjoyed ourselves*, then music in France may boast of having taken an immeasurable step forward.[1] Some such answer the Athenians would have given, if a stranger among them had insisted upon some explanation of the enthusiasm with which they greeted the tragedies of Aeschylus; for the mouths of those with nothing to say were still sealed, and Aristotle had not yet appeared to unseal them. In our modern world, on the other hand, everybody is gnawed with the tormenting ambition to *analyse* his reactions, and the fine folk in the boxes at the *Théâtre Louvois* would wrinkle up their noses in merciless disdain at the wretched spectator who had not better sense than to reply simply: *I feel it that way*. But this is not the worst, alas; the roots of our tragedy run deeper still; for these same spectators, who feel nothing and criticize everything, have conjured up in their wake a whole crowd of artists—poets who blossom where La Harpe has trod, musicians springing fully-armed from seeds sown by the *Conservatoire*. The *salons* of Paris are swarming with such poor fools, whose only contribution to Art has been, in their youth, the barren inspirations of an arid soul, and in their maturity, the exhalations of a heart scorched into spite and irritability by the searing winds of frustrated vanity, and soured by the shame of five or six catastrophic literary flops. Occasionally one or two of these wretched brutes, desperately discouraged by the constant pandemonium of derisive

---

[1] *Cf.* the most curious arguments set out in to-day's *Journal des Débats* (18th Sept. 1823)*. No one for whom art is not an *experience* can ever arrive, by a process of pure ratiocination, at anything more mystical than the *theory of recitative*; the *art of singing* is forever beyond his ken; the way of feeling is closed to him, and the way of reason leads elsewhere.

whistling which greets them wherever they venture, and reduced, in my opinion, to the level of the unhappiest of mortals, turn *critic*; further, they appear in print; and thus, at the end of this long chain of circumstances, we may open *le Miroir* and stumble across *this* entertaining reflection: *The sepulchral voice of Madame Pasta . . .!* In musical language, this is just another way of denying the existence of light.

Nothing is better calculated to destroy a nation's art, or to strangle it at birth, than the existence of such a rabble of "critics", whose souls are stripped stark-naked of every thread of sensibility and *romantic extravagance*, but who, to make up for this strange deficiency, have pursued, with mathematical exactitude and with all the dogged perseverance of blind aesthetic numbness, every scrap of erudition which has been uttered by mouth or written in books concerning the unhappy art upon which they have chosen to inflict their ardour. In such instances, we may observe a literary platitude realized in the flesh: the blossoming of art is blighted by the frost of over-civilization.[1]

However, I refuse to be drawn into the odious particular consequences of these general considerations; instead, I shall plunge without further ado into the history of Rossini's development. In 1810, when this great composer first embarked upon his career, there was perhaps no art which had suffered so terribly from the calamitous effects of a whole decade of sublime wars and sordid reactions as the art of singing. Ever since 1797,[2] in Milan, in Brescia, in Bergamo, in Venice, and indeed throughout the whole of upper Italy, people had had plenty to worry about besides music and singing. In 1810, the Milan *Conservatoire* had failed to produce a single distinguished pupil.

Naples had once been renowned for its famous *Conservatoires*, to which all nations had learnt to turn for composers and artists trained to minister to their various pleasures, and to reveal to their eyes the secret powers of music; but of all these notable institutions, not a single one remained. Singing was taught nowhere, save in a few obscure churches;

---

[1] Unsuccessful composers are the most dangerous enemies of music. In France, by far the most penetrating and *genuine* critics are young ladies of five-and-twenty.

[2] *Vide:* Comte de Las-Cases, *Mémorial de Sainte-Hélène* (vol. IV): revolt and revolutionary fervour in Bergamo, Brescia, Verona, *etc.*; followed, in 1799, by thirteen months of murderous reaction, *Vide* also: *Lettere Sirmiensi* (1809), by Signor Apostoli, of Padua, where he describes the curious adventures of certain patriots deported to the *Bocche del Cattaro.*

and the two last representatives of that long line of geniuses which Naples had produced, Orgitano and Manfrocci, had been carried off by death at the very outset of their careers. Their succession was left vacant and nothing remained upon the banks of the river Sebete save the chill silence of nonentity, or the colourless futilities of utterly incurable mediocrity.

Babbini, that great singer, who still awaits a rival in the peculiar field which he had made his own, had lived long enough to see Rossini; but his voice, weakened by age, had been unable to recall the old miracles of the past. Crescentini was still at the height of his powers, but he was away at Saint-Cloud, where he was soon to provoke Napoleon into committing the only major blunder of which that great man was ever guilty in respect of his civil administration;[1] and thus, for all his high-sounding title of *Knight of the Iron Crown*, he was lost to Italy.

Marchesi had retired from the theatre.

Pacchiarotti, he of the sublime voice, was lost in bitter contemplation of the decadence of an art which had been the enchantment and glory of his life. Pacchiarotti was a true artist; imagine, then, the scorn and disgust which must have raged in his soul—he who had never been guilty of a single sound or of a single movement, unless it was carefully calculated to appeal to the *immediate needs* of the mind and heart of his audience, whose satisfaction was the only reward his conscience would allow—at the sight of a *cantatrice* who knew no worthier ambition than to mimic and outrival the mechanical dexterity of a violin[2] in a variation with thirty-two double-crochets to the bar! That which, in days of old, had been the most profoundly moving of all the arts, was being quietly transformed before our very eyes into a trade for rude mechanicals. After the epoch of Babbini, Pacchiarotti, Marchesi, Crescentini and their contemporaries, the art of singing degenerated to such a degree of impoverishment that to-day nothing is left of all its former glory save the cold and literal technique of rendering an exact and inanimate note. Such, in the year of grace 1823, is the highest accomplishment to which a singer's ambition may pretend. But the *ottavino**, the big drum, or even the *serpent* which is used in church-music, all have a

---

[1] *Natum pati et agere fortia*, a maxim specially designed for Saint Ignatius Loyola.

[2] Later on, Signora Catalani included in her repertoire a vocal arrangement of Rode's *Variations*; it is true, however, that God somehow forgot to place a heart within reasonable proximity of this divine larynx.

similar ambition, and may achieve a similar degree of success in realizing it. The glories of *spontaneous inspiration* have been banished for ever from an art whose loveliest achievements have so often depended upon the individual interpreter and his genius for improvization; and the man whom I accuse of perpetrating this terrible revolution is *Rossini*.

CHAPTER XXIX

Révolution

THIS and the following chapters offer every prospect of being the most boring in the whole book; I offer no guarantee to the contrary. In fact, I have purposely gathered together in one section everything that I felt I had to say about the art of singing, precisely in order that the reader might have less difficulty in skipping the whole lot, if he felt so inclined. It must be clearly understood that the following discussions are destined to prove an unmitigated and wearisome nuisance to anyone who is not a confirmed *habitué* of the *Théâtre Louvois*.

As we have seen, at the moment when Rossini stood poised on the brink of his career, political events in Italy during the previous decade had resulted in a catastrophic dearth of competent singers, and even the few who remained were on the verge of retirement from the theatre. However, in spite of this circumstance of impoverishment and decadence, which offered so marked a contrast to the prolific and luxurious abundance of talent which had attended earlier generations of composers, Rossini's earliest works are still written faithfully in the *style* of his predecessors; at this period, he fully respected the rights of the singers, and was satisfied provided only that he could secure predominance for the voice. This is the musical conception which underlies such compositions as *Demetrio e Polibio*, *l'Inganno felice*, *la Pietra del Paragone*, *Tancredi*,[1] etc. Moreover, since Rossini had chanced to fall in with *prime donne* of the quality of la Marcolini, la Malanotte, la Manfredini, and the two Mombelli sisters, he had indeed every encouragement to compose music in which everything was subservient to the exigencies of the vocal interpretation; the more so, since he himself is a first-class singer, and has only to sit down to the piano, and run through one of his own arias, to transmute all the glory of his known genius for melodic invention into a new, if less familiar, genius for practical interpretation. But at this point there occurred one of those apparently

[1] Also Rossini's *juvenilia*: *la Cambiale di Matrimonio*, *l'Equivoco stravagante*, *Ciro in Babilonia*, *la Scala di Seta*, *l'Occasione fa il Ladro* and *il Figlio per azzardo*.

insignificant little happenings, which transformed the young composer's entire outlook and turned his whole genius in a new direction, endowing it with strange and unfamiliar qualities, which later were doomed to become exaggerated out of all proportion to their original intent, until in the end they have become a source of desperate anxiety even to the sincerest of his admirers.

It was in the year 1814[1] that Rossini journeyed to Milan to work on his opera *Aureliano in Palmira*; and there he met Velluti, who was to have a part in the coming production. Velluti was then in the full bloom of his youth and vigour, at the very height of his genius, and, incidentally, one of the handsomest men of his century; and he made shameless abuse of his prodigious gifts. Rossini had never actually heard this outstanding singer on the stage; none the less, he sat down straight away and composed the main *cavatina* which was to belong to the rôle.

At the first rehearsal with the orchestra, Velluti* sang the aria straight through, and Rossini was dazzled with admiration; at the second rehearsal, Velluti began to embroider (*fiorire*) the melody, and Rossini, finding the result both exquisite in performance and well in keeping with his own intentions as composer, approved; but at the third rehearsal, the original pattern of the melody had almost entirely *disappeared* beneath the marvellous filigree-work of embroidery and arabesque. At last there dawned the great day of the *première*: the *cavatina* itself, and in fact Velluti's whole performance, created a *furore*; but Rossini found himself confronted with insuperable difficulties in trying to identify what Velluti was supposed to be singing; his own music, in fact, had grown completely unrecognizable. For all that, however, Velluti's performance was a thing of unparalleled beauty, and enjoyed untold popularity with the audience, which, after all, can never be blamed for applauding something which it so wholeheartedly enjoys.[2]

The young composer's vanity was deeply wounded; *his* opera was a flop, and all the applause had gone to Velluti, his soprano. Rossini was always quick to size up a situation, and instantly drew the inevitable

---

[1] He was then twenty-two years old.

[2] Nevertheless, the opera as a whole was a flop. Velluti had quarrelled with the famous conductor of *la Scala*, Alessandro Rolla, and sulked like a child during the entire run of *Aureliano*; childishness, in fact, is the predominant facet of his character, and a footman can lead him around like a bear on a string.

conclusions from an experience which had proved so unspeakably humiliating.

In this instance, he argued with himself, *I have been lucky in that Velluti possesses both intelligence and good taste; but what guarantee have I that next time I accept a contract, I shall not be confronted with another singer of this type, equally fortunate in the flexibility of his larynx, similarly obsessed with this mania for embroidery, but in all other respects mediocre, who will promptly ruin my music for good and all, not only by making it unrecognizable to me, but—infinitely worse—by sending the audience to sleep with his twiddles and roulades, or, at best, by merely tickling their curiosity with a handful of meretricious conjuring-tricks? Moreover, the danger which threatens my poor, ill-treated music is the more imminent, in that there are no longer any competent and recognized schools of singing in Italy. Nowadays, the average theatre is coming more and more to be filled with people whose entire acquaintance with music derives from some ignorant village band-master. It follows that this repulsive tradition of singing a melody as though it were a violin-concerto, of decking it out with an infinite series of variations, is bound eventually, not only to undermine the gifts of the singer, but also to corrupt the taste of the public. Before long, every singer in Italy will be doing his best to imitate Velluti, each in his own peculiar range and style. A normal, straight cantilena will soon become a thing of the past; the public will grow to think it dull and uninspired. The result will be a wholesale overthrow of musical traditions, affecting even the fundamental characteristics of the human voice; for once the habit of perpetual embroidery grows firmly established in the singer's repertoire, and once people get into the habit of sneering coldly at any cantilena, unless it lie crushed and back-broken beneath its load of unmanageable and elaborate ornamentation, the whole technique of voice-control, the whole art of producing long, sustained notes, will be irretrievably lost, and consequently the voice will no longer be able to master anything which is genuinely spianato e sostenuto. Obviously, there is not a moment to be lost, and I must fundamentally reconsider the whole conception of music which I have held up to this point.*

Now I know how to sing; everyone is agreed that I possess some talent in this direction; therefore any fioritura which I devise will be in good taste; furthermore, I, as the composer, am in a good position to spot straight away both the strong and the weak points of any of my singers, and so I shall never write anything for them which lies outside the range of their normal abilities. Very well, then: in future, no singer of mine shall ever have the slightest pretext for improvizing a single appoggiatura.[1] *Every scrap of ornamentation, every vestige of a* fioritura, *will constitute an integral part of the song itself, and the whole lot,* without exception, *will be noted down in the score.*

And another thing: since our honest impresari *seem to imagine that I am richly paid for the contribution of some sixteen to eighteen musical numbers, all destined for the leading* rôles, *when I am offered exactly the same sort of sum that my predecessors used to earn from no more than five or six similar items, I think I have devised the perfect and foolproof scheme of retaliation against this distasteful, if amusing, misconception; for, in every opera which I shall write from now on, I intend to include at least three or four major items whose sole originality will consist in the* variazioni, *which I shall compose myself, instead of leaving them to be invented on the spur of the moment by some third-rate performer; in consequence, they will be devised methodically and in perfect taste; and thus, once again, our scoundrelly* impresari *will in the end pocket all the profits which will come pouring in from the application of my new system.*

The reader will have surmised that, as an historian, I have been emulating Livy. I have credited my hero with a fine-sounding speech which he certainly never uttered in *my* hearing; nevertheless, at some stage or other during the opening years of his career, it is inconceivable that Rossini should *not* have conducted this argument-in-monologue with himself; his scores are there to prove it.

Later on, in Naples, when he was confronted with the exhausted voice of Signorina Colbran (the only remaining contribution which she had to make to his series of masterpieces),[2] Rossini found himself compelled to turn his back even more completely upon the traditional *spianato* style of singing, and to plunge ever more desperately into a welter of *gorgheggi*, the only aspect of the whole craft of singing from whose mysteries Signorina Colbran could still emerge with her honour more or less intact. A careful study of the scores belonging to Rossini's

[1] I know no language more admirable than French for pursuing experiments in the analysis of emotional nuances and of intellectual subtleties; but, by virtue of its very *qualities* in this field, it is unsuited to musical description. Since I have failed to discover any terms in French which can be used to translate *with precision and clarity* the names given to all the various kinds of roulades and embellishments, I beg the reader's permission to keep occasionally to the original Italian. The claims of *precision and clarity* make such a sacrifice truly essential.

[2] The works which Rossini composed while he was in Naples include nine of his major operas: *Elisabetta, Otello, Armida, Mosè, Ricciardo e Zoraide, Ermione, la Donna del Lago, Maometto secondo* and *Zelmira* (1815–1822).

Neapolitan period demonstrates conclusively the lengths to which he was prepared to go to indulge his passion for his intransigent *prima donna*; in all these operas, there is not one single passage *cantabile spianato*, neither for her, nor, *a fortiori*, for any of the other characters, who were subject to the most stringent injunctions never to eclipse *her*. Rossini seems to have been completely indifferent to his own reputation; no other composer can ever have been less concerned with such preoccupations. But one of the fatal consequences of his obsequious deference towards Signorina Colbran has been that every one of his nine Neapolitan operas suffers horribly as soon as it is put on at any other theatre.

If Signorina Colbran had had no idiosyncrasy peculiar to herself other than the abnormal range of her voice, other operatic companies with differently-constituted *prime donne* could have resorted to the simple expedient of transposing (*puntare*) the parts into a new key—an elementary procedure which would have been quite sufficient to eliminate the small number of extreme notes belonging to the odd and uncommon compass for which the *maestro* had deliberately composed his music. It is quite normal to find that a simple transposition will enable two singers, both equally good, but with completely dissimilar voices, to appear in the same part with equal success.[1]

But unfortunately, this is not the case with Rossini's Neapolitan compositions. The problem is not confined to the *range* of the voice, but extends to the *quality and character of the ornamentation*; and this represents a formidable, and in nearly every case insurmountable, obstacle. I appeal to any *amateur* who may have tried to sing from a score specially written for Davide or for Signorina Colbran.

We may sum up, therefore, by saying that it was Velluti, in the Milanese production of *Aureliano in Palmira*, who first sowed in Rossini's mind the seeds of that revolution which, some years later, was to transform his whole style of writing; and that it was Signorina Colbran, in Naples, who forced him to carry this same revolution to such lengths that, in my own conviction, the ensuing exaggerations will ultimately prove fatal to his reputation. The whole series of operas written in Naples for Signorina Collran belong to this characteristic "second manner".

[1] The aria: *Di tanti palpiti* . . . has recently been performed, here in Paris, in three different keys.

CHAPTER XXX

Of a certain Talent which will be out of date by 1840

THIS present chapter is inspired wholly by a feeling of deep-seated compassion towards a certain number of young ladies, now aged somewhere between twelve and fifteen, whose development I have been observing with the gravest concern, and for whom that ungrateful taskmaster, the *pianoforte*, seems to hold out the solace of ideal beauty and to promise eventual admission into the sweet paradise of music. Here and there you may meet one or two of these gentle creatures whom nature has blessed with the possession of a reasonable voice, and who, in consequence, have been advised to learn singing instead— but in vain! The advice was scorned. The result is, that in twelve or fifteen years' time, a whole generation is doomed to discover that it has spent the best years of its life painfully acquiring a talent which will prove in the end both useless and antiquated; much as their grand- mothers, who twenty years ago had learned very properly to play pretty little tunes on the spinet, would find this same aptitude quite valueless in our own time. Wrapt in beatific contemplation of their own virtuoso prowess at the keyboard *now*, the engaging young ladies to whom I have referred may undoubtedly feel happily flattered and self-complacent; but, if this emotion constitutes a certain kind of pleasure, it is none the less a pleasure which is half a world removed from the *true* delights and the sweet reveries which music *should* inspire in the human breast. A child may learn to play exquisitely upon the piano; it may be able to read music as fluently as it can read a nor- mal page of prose; yet if, in the end, it has learnt nothing else, its mind will be for ever closed to the shades and *nuances* of the human voice, and so the only truly *moving* part of music is fated to remain shrouded in eternal mystery. And to judge by the speed with which the revolu- tion, in the midst of which we are living, is accomplishing its destiny, in fifteen years' time this "eternal mystery", this land which, in our generation, is a *terra incognita*, will be the only one which it is fashionable to know. There are already serious protests against the wearisome prolixity of adequate pianists.

The young ladies in question, who have already ventured a little way into the mysteries of music, will readily understand that the subtler *nuances* of emotion, to which I have just referred, can be expressed by the *human voice alone*, which treats them (in part at least) as a matter of spontaneous improvization in immediate response to a *direct relationship with the audience*;[1] and further, that it is these same *nuances*, these delicately-shaded variations of the spirit, and nothing else, which constitute the essential miracle of music—a miracle which, in the inaccurate haste of everyday conversation, may afterwards be attributed to certain instruments, but which, in actual fact, these instruments are incapable of producing. Have you ever heard an audience shout for an *encore* of a piano sonata? Instrumental music rarely stirs so much as a tremor in the deeper recesses of the human soul, and seldom moves to tears; the pleasure which it gives belongs rather to that category of cold and unexhilarating abashment at the sight of the triumph of virtuosity over the recalcitrance of technique; consequently, no man born is too insensitive to appreciate a concerto. An ice-cold heart, backed by a neat, methodical brain, and reinforced by an overdose of solid Teutonic perseverance, can master the piano a hundred times more successfully than could a mere *dilettante* like Pergolesi, for all his divine inspiration. I am not ashamed to propound a paradox: the man who can give an adequate performance of Blondel's *Romance* from *Richard Cœur-de-Lion*, is a finer musician, in the true sense of the word, than the man who can sight-read a *Grand Fantasia* by Herz or Moscheles. Anyone who is able to achieve a perfect rendering of this simple little *Romance* is musically equipped to understand Rossini's entire operatic output, and to appreciate the subtlest vocal innuendoes of a Madame Fodor or a Madame Pasta. Whereas a pianist, even one who has mastered his technique to the highest degree imaginable, will have learned to appreciate *nothing* except Rossini's *orchestration*, and perhaps an odd violin-concerto.

[1] Marchesi used to change the whole pattern of *fioriture* in any given part at every single performance.

CHAPTER XXXI

Is Rossini more inclined to repeat himself than other Composers?

Rossini's "variation-technique" (*variazioni*) has often tempted him to plagiarize his own compositions; and, like all robbers, he has always hoped that no one would notice his stolen booty.

After all, why should a poor *maestro*, who is under contract to dash off an opera in six weeks regardless of his health or state of mind, be blamed for falling back upon an expedient of this nature in those inevitable moments when his inspiration runs dry? Mayr, for instance, or many another composer whom I will refrain from mentioning by name, escapes the dilemma of self-plagiarism—but at what a cost! Mayr, instead of repeating himself, engulfs us in a blanketing fog of *apathy*, close upon the heels of which comes sleep, bringing grateful forgetfulness of all our woes. Rossini, on the other hand, allows us neither truce nor respite; his operas may provoke indignation, irritation, what you will . . . but never somnolence. The effect produced may be one of startling originality, or it may simply conjure up charming memories; but in every instance there is always a new delight ready to follow hot-foot upon the traces of the last; never that barren desert of burning emptiness which one finds, for example, in the first act of *la Rosa bianca*.

No one will dispute the fact of Rossini's extraordinary fertility of creative imagination; and yet there are four or five obscure newspapers* which emerge anew every morning to reiterate (the half-baked speaking to the half-educated) that Rossini is "repeating himself", "plagiarizing himself", "lacking in inventiveness", *etc., etc.*; in respect of which assertions, I beg the liberty of requesting an answer to the following questions:

1. When the great masters of the past composed operas, how many *major musical items* did they include in each?

2. What proportion of the major musical numbers which they did include managed to catch the ear of the public?

3. What proportion of *these* numbers deserved ultimate popularity? Paisiello wrote something like a hundred-and-fifty operas, out of which, in all, about eighty full-scale musical numbers achieved fame. Rossini has written thirty-four operas, and can easily claim a hundred popular successes, each one of which is fundamentally original. A fool, catching his first glimpse of a crowd of negro slaves, may be silly enough to believe that they all look exactly alike; Rossini's arias are similar negroes in the eyes of similar fools.

The greatest error of the *Louvois* public, the last bandage which needs to be torn away from in front of its eyes before it can aspire to a taste in music as sure and as infallible as that of the *habitués* of *la Scala* or the *San-Carlo*, is the fundamental illusion that *every note is meant to be listened to*; as an audience, it insists, as it were, upon having its money's-worth; not a crumb is destined to escape its insatiable voracity; if it reacted to tragedy in the same way as it reacts to opera, every line and every word would need to be as dynamic and as forceful as the famous *qu'il mourût!* in *Horace*, or as the dramatic *Moi!* from *Médée*.

But such an attitude is frankly incompatible with the natural laws which determine the mechanism of the human emotions. No man of genuine aesthetic sensibility could take pleasure in a succession of three major dramatic climaxes in the space of a few lines.

Nevertheless, as critics, we owe our readers a fair assessment of the situation; and in the case of the *Louvois* audiences, the most serious hindrances which impede the growth of a competent standard of taste spring:

   i   from the cramped insufficiency of the auditorium;
  ii   from the imperfect screening-off of daylight in the hall*; and
 iii   from the failure to provide *any* private boxes.

In any *small* theatre, mass-enthusiasm soon degenerates into mass-hysteria and nervous exhaustion.[1]

I regret to have to insist upon this, because it is something which shocks our notion of public behaviour: but the fact remains that the human soul *requires* four or five minutes of whispered conversation to release itself from the tension which may be built up by some sublime duet; only then will it be in any fit state to appreciate the aria which follows next on the programme.

[1] *Why?* I submit the problem to the learned Dr Edwards.

In art, as in politics, no natural law suffers itself to be broken with impunity. I would give vanity another ten years, and no more, to hold out in support of the absurd conventions which I have just been attacking, and to continue to make people believe that to whisper during the performance of an opera is automatically to brand oneself a philistine. What is the outcome of all this well-bred silence and *uninterrupted* attentiveness? Simply, that fewer people enjoy the performance than would otherwise be the case. It is precisely those spectators who are deterred from coming by their fear of this kind of *physical* discomfort who are at bottom the ones whose nervous systems are sufficiently delicate in their adjustment to enable them to appreciate the voluptuous appeal of a fine aria and all the lingering fragrance of music. As things are, any opera given at the *Louvois* which consists exclusively of six major musical items, each exquisite in its own separate fashion, is certain of success; whereas if these same six brilliant passages were to be *embedded*, as it were, in a setting consisting of seven or eight *less intensely moving* passages, the opera would be doomed to failure—and yet, were it not for the pedants, we should realize quite clearly that the inferior music has its own task to perform (the indispensable task of allowing us respite between climaxes), thus, ultimately, *increasing our pleasure* in the opera as a whole.

The first time one looks at Rossini's scores, one's immediate impression is that the technical difficulties confronting the singer are so immense that none of these operas is ever likely to find more than a lonely handful of artists capable of interpreting it; but further study soon convinces one that this music combines so many *different* features, all calculated to answer the divers needs and requirements of an audience,[1] that even if a good half of Rossini's *fioriture* were to be omitted in performance (or alternatively, even if all the *fioriture* are used, but in a different order of distribution throughout the score), the opera will still manage to be successful. Rossini's operas, in fact, do not require great interpreters. The only indispensable virtue needed in the artist is *technical agility*; and provided a singer, no matter how mediocre he may be in all other respects, possesses this one quality, he can always be certain of enjoying a reasonable amount of success—at least in so far as Rossini is concerned! Rossini's melodies, whose fascination is never

[1] All calculated to satisfy the demands of *our* generation; no music is more eminently *Romantic**.

broken by any of those touches of violence or harshness which spring
from the common obsession with *powerful effects*; his accompaniments,
with their vivacity and their seductive rhythms—these things alone are
sufficient to conjure up vistas of pleasure so enthralling that, whatever
modifications and excisions the singer, circumscribed by the limitations
of his own vocal technique, be obliged to make among the *ornamental
superstructure* of Rossini's music, the result, in spite of these forced
mutilations, is invariably both tantalizing and a delight to listen to.
Things were very different in the golden age of improvization, in the
days of Aprile, la Gabrielli,[1] etc., when the composer used deliberately
to permit his interpreter as much freedom as he could possibly manage
in his arias, thus allowing the singer innumerable opportunities to
display his or her individual talents. In such circumstances, if the performer was merely mediocre, or if his or her only talent was limited
to the mastery of a certain petty, mechanical vocal agility (a quality
which, alone, is very far from guaranteeing ultimate perfection in the
art of singing), song and singer alike were doomed to experience the
most resounding *fiasco*.

If, in 1814, Rossini had found himself in a position to pick and choose
from among a wide selection of competent singers, one may well
wonder whether he would ever have dreamed of touching off the spark
of that revolution which, in the event, he *did* kindle; whether he would
ever have contemplated introducing a system which implied that every
note of every aria should be written out *in full*.

Certainly *his* vanity might well have wished it; but then the vanity
of the singers would have roused up the most lively opposition, just
as, in our own time, we find Velluti persistently refusing to sing
Rossini's music.

One might well enquire further, and ask, which of the two systems
is in fact preferable? My own reply would be: the old system, with
some concessions to the new. It seems to me quite wrong for the
composer to write in *all* the ornaments; but at the same time it seems
right that the total liberty of the singer to mutilate his text should
suffer some restraint. There is no justification for Velluti's having sung

---

[1] Caterina Gabrielli, a noted *prima donna*, was said to sing well only when her
current lover was present in the theatre. There are a hundred different legends
abroad in Italy concerning her fantastic whims and caprices. She was of Roman
origin.

the *cavatina* from *Aureliano in Palmira* in such a fashion as to render it all but unrecognizable to the composer, because, in that case, Velluti himself becomes the author of the works which he is supposed to be interpreting; and there is every advantage to be gained from maintaining a strict barrier of separation between two arts which are so completely different in character.

CHAPTER XXXII

Some Details concerning the Revolution inaugurated by Rossini

THE art of *bel canto* was created in the year 1680 by Pistocchi; and its progress was hastened immeasurably by Pistocchi's pupil, Bernacchi (*c.* 1720). The peak of perfection was attained in 1778, under the aegis of Pacchiarotti; but since that date, the race of male sopranos has died out, and the art has degenerated.

Millico, Aprile, Farinelli, Pacchiarotti, Ansani, Babbini and Marchesi all owed their reputation to this style favoured by the older composers, who, in certain passages of their operas, provided the interpreter with scarcely more than a framework or *canvas*,[1] upon which to work out his own conceptions; and there is scarcely a single one of these great singers who did not, in addition, enrich the lives of his contemporaries by fostering the talents of two or three first-class *prime donne*. The biographies of such fine *cantatrici* as la Gabrielli, la de 'Amicis, la Banti, la Todi and others, all reveal the names of the famous *soprani* from whom they had learnt the supreme art of managing a voice.

More than one of the leading *prime donne* of our own generation owes her talents to Velluti—Signorina Colbran, for instance.

The supreme qualities of the *soprani* and of their pupils were seen at their most resplendent in the execution of *largo* and *cantabile spianato* passages; and we have a beautiful example of this style of writing in the prayer-scene from *Giulietta e Romeo*. Yet this precisely was the type of aria which Rossini, ever since the moment when he arrived in Naples and adopted what is now known in Italy as his "second manner", has been at greatest pains to eliminate from his operas. In

---

[1] The great singers of this school never actually altered the *theme* of an aria; they gave it first in a comparatively simple rendering, and then proceeded to embroidery. At the end of each aria, they were normally given some twenty bars to be filled in *ad lib.* with *gorgheggi* and other light embellishments of this nature; and finally, the song concluded with a *bravura* passage; *v.* for instance, *pria che spunti . . .*, from *il Matrimonio segreto*. This particular aria belongs to a category known in Naples as *arie di narrazione*.

former days, a singer might train for six or eight years before being
able to achieve a true *largo*, and the patient perseverance of Bernacchi,
for instance, is proverbial in the history of the art. But once this degree
of perfection, purity and sweetness, which the generation of 1750 considered to be the *sine qua non* of good singing, had finally been attained,
the singer had nothing further to do but to reap his reward; his reputation and his fortune lay ready to hand. However, since Rossini has
appeared on the scene, success or failure in the execution of a *largo*
passage has become a matter of sublime indifference, and if ever such
a passage were to be offered to any of our own audiences to-day, I can
hear, even from where I now sit, the echoes of that little proverb about
the devil and his own funeral. .... That poor audience would be bored
to death; and the reason is simple—because it would find itself being
addressed in a foreign language which it *thinks* it knows, but which in
fact it needs to sit down and re-learn from the beginning.

The older style of singing could stir a man to the innermost recesses
of his soul; but it could also prove rather boring; Rossini's style titillates
the *mind*, and is never boring. It is a hundred times easier to acquire a
fair enough proficiency to give a competent rendering of one of
Rossini's great *rondo* movements (the *rondo* from *la Donna del Lago*, for
instance), than it is to achieve a similar standard in some great aria by
Sacchini.

The subtleties involved in sustaining a long holding-note; the art of
portamento; the technique of modulating the voice so as to make it fall
with equal stress upon every note in a *legato* passage; the skilled control
which enabled a singer to draw breath quite imperceptibly, without
interrupting the long-drawn phrases of vocal melody so typical of the
arias of the old school[1]—these and similar qualities represented formerly the most difficult and the most essential attainments of a good
performer. The mere agility, remarkable or otherwise, of the voice,
served only one purpose: it was employed in the execution of *gorgheggi*,
i.e., it represented a luxury, it was used for display or, in a word, for
supplying an element of superficial glitter, and *never* for providing

---

[1] I find it to all intents and purposes quite *impossible* to write adequately of the
art of singing in any language other than Italian: here is the passage which I have
just written as it would have appeared in the original: *Le ombreggiature per le messe
di voce, il cantar di portamento, l'arte di fermare la voce per farla fluire eguale nel canto
legato, l'arte di prender fiato in modo insensibile e senza troncare il lungo periodo vocale
delle arie antiche.*

those essential qualities which were to shake and stir the soul. Every aria was provided, towards the conclusion, with a *cadenza*, usually of some twenty bars, whose whole *raison d'être* was to allow the singer to perform tricks with the muscles of his throat,[1] and to indulge in *gorgheggi*.

Rossini has been responsible for a musical revolution; but even his sincerest friends blame that revolution for having restricted the boundaries of the art of singing, for having limited the qualities of emotional *pathos* inherent in that art, and for having rendered useless, and therefore obsolete, certain technical exercises, valueless in themselves, but which could ultimately lead to those *transports of delirium and rapture* which occur so frequently in the history of Pacchiarotti and other great artists of an earlier generation, and so very rarely to-day. The source of these miracles lay in the *mystic powers of the human voice*.

The revolution inaugurated by Rossini has killed the gift of *originality* in the singer. What incentive can any singer have nowadays for taking infinite pains to convey to his audience, firstly, the native and individual quality of his voice, and secondly, the precise shade of expression by which it may be endowed through his peculiar and original sensibility? In Rossini's operas he is doomed to wait for ever in vain for one single opportunity to display these rare qualities, whose acquisition may have cost him literally years of unrelenting labour. But in any case, the mere habit of expecting to find everything already worked out, already noted down in black and white in the music from which he has to sing, is enough to kill his own inventiveness, to quench the last spark of initiative within him, and to induce a fundamental attitude of laziness. The average modern composer makes no greater demands in his score than can be fulfilled by the exercise of a moderate degree of technical competence in a specifically *material* field: the field, in fact, of the *instrumentalist*. Rossini's attitude of *lasciatemi fare* (leave everything to me), which is typical of his relations with his interpreters, has now reached such a pitch, that the latter may not even dispose of the right to improvise on the last note of all; in almost every instance, Rossini will be found to have supplied his own embroidery.

In days gone by, the great singers, Babbini, Marchesi, Pacchiarotti,

[1] The word *gorgheggi* is associated with the verb *gorgheggiare*, to make warbling noises in the throat. *Cf.* French: *gorge* = throat; English: *gargle*. (*Trans.*)

etc., used to *compose* their own ornamentation whenever the musical context required an exceptionally high level of complexity; but in normal circumstances, they were concerned with *extempore invention.* All the various categories of simpler embellishments (*appoggiature, gruppetti, mordenti,* and so on) were theirs to dispose and arrange as they thought best, spontaneously, and following the dictates of their art and their inner genius; the whole art of adorning the melody (*i vezzi melodici del canto,* as Pacchiarotti used to call it, when I met him in Padua in 1816) belonged by right to the performer. For instance, in the aria:

Ombra adorata, aspetta . . .[1]

Crescentini would suffuse his whole voice and inflexion with a broad and indefinable colouring of *satisfaction**, because it would strike him, *while he was actually standing up and singing,* that an impassioned lover about to be reunited with his mistress probably *would* feel something of the sort. But Velluti, who perceives the situation rather differently, interprets the same passage in a vein of melancholy, interspersed with brooding reflections upon the common fate of the two lovers. There is no composer on earth, suppose him to be as ingenious as you will, whose score can convey with precision, these and similar *infinitely minute* nuances of emotional suggestion: yet it is precisely these and similar *infinitely minute* nuances which form the secret of Crescentini's unique perfection in his interpretation of the aria; furthermore, all this *infinitely minute* material is itself in a perpetual state of transformation, constantly responding to variations in the physical condition of the singer's voice, or to changes in the intensity of the exaltation and ecstasy by which he may happen to be inspired. At one performance, he may tend towards ornaments redolent of indolence and *morbidezza*; on a different occasion, from the very moment when he sets foot on the stage, he may find himself in a mood for *gorgheggi* instinct with energy and life. Unless he yield to the inspiration of the moment, he can never attain to perfection in his singing. A great singer is essentially

---

[1] *Romeo:*

Ombra adorata, aspetta;
Teco sarò indiviso.
Nel fortunato Eliso
Avrò contento il cuor . . .

(*Giulietta e Romeo,* Act III, sc. i; sung by Romeo when he discovers the seemingly dead body of Juliet in the Tomb.)

a creature of *nerves*; a great violinist, on the other hand, needs a temperament of a radically different quality.[1]

But in any case, it is fundamentally wrong for the composer to elaborate *all* the ornamentation, for the simple reason that he would have to possess a perfect and intimate knowledge of the voice for which his music is destined, whereas this knowledge is something which can be known only to the singer who possesses it, and who has spent perhaps twenty years studying it and training it to the required flexibility.[2] A single ornament, I will not say *badly*, but even *unenthusiastically* performed, rendered dutifully but without *brio*, can destroy in an instant every shred of enchantment which had ever existed. You had been in heaven; but now you come tumbling down into the prosaic world of a box-at-the-opera; and you can count yourself lucky if you have not landed bang in the middle of a singing-lesson!

[1] The greatest violinist in Italy, and perhaps in all the world, is *Paganini*, who is still a youngish man, thirty-five years old, with black, piercing eyes and dishevelled hair. This ardent creature did not stumble upon the secrets of his divine art by dint of eight years' dogged perseverance through the *Conservatoire*; a hasty impulse inspired by loving *too well* (so the legend goes*) resulted in long years of imprisonment; and there, solitary and abandoned in a dungeon which might well have had no issue save to the scaffold, he discovered that the only companion who could console him in his fetters was his violin. Gradually he acquired the art of expressing the very whispers of his soul in sound; and the endless, dragging evenings of captivity gave him ample time to perfect this new language. Paganini should not be heard when he is striving to emulate the violinists of the North in some mighty concerto; but rather on some informal evening when he is in the mood and playing *capriccios*. Let me hasten to add that these *capriccios* present just as many *difficulties* in execution as any concerto!

[2] Velluti always prepares *three different sets* of ornamentation for any given passage; so that, when the instant of performance arrives, he can choose the one which best suits his mood. This precaution ensures that his embellishments never sound forced (*stentati*).

CHAPTER XXXIII

Excuses

NOTHING is quite so futile as music; and so I can well understand that the reader may be scandalized at the ponderous gravity of the tone which I have adopted to scatter a few handfuls of inconsequential observations through these pages, or to retail a couple of singularly pointless anecdotes, grossly overweighted, moreover, with the monumental grandiloquence of terms such as *ideal Beauty, felicity, sublime, sensibility* and so on, to the use of which I am only too prone.

And yet, all in all, this refusal to take music seriously is a phenomenon of which I entirely approve; I am sick to death of *things which must be taken seriously**, and I regret the good old days when full colonels on the active list used to spend their time embroidering tapestries, and when fine literary *salons* used to break up into games of cup-and-ball. I know my own century only too well: it is a century of lies and liars.[1] And so, as a result of this conviction, if there has been one principle to which I have constantly adhered, it has been never to exaggerate what I have to say by *beautiful writing*, never (above all) to chase after some particular effect with the help of a series of arguments and metaphors whose "glowing sincerity" is nothing but artifice, and whose ultimate achievement is to stun the reader into a kind of ecstatic wonderment, so that, at the end of each rolling period, he puts the book down and exclaims: *Now, that's what I call literature!* To begin with, I entered late in life into the arena of *belles-lettres*, and heaven has studiously denied me any talent for veiling the nakedness of ideas beneath the graceful draperies of exaggeration; secondly, it is my personal opinion that there is no sin so unforgivable as exaggeration in matters affecting the deeper emotions of mankind. To-day's short-

---

[1] I met recently with a young man of two-and-twenty, the author of a tragedy which had just been accepted by the *Théâtre Français*; and yet, while he talked to me, his greatest concern was to poke fun at the whole conception of tragedy within whose framework he had been working.

lived advantage of an instant's amazement is soon to be annihilated by an over-mastering sense of repugnance; and to-morrow brings a strange and inexplicable reluctance to pick up the book which had been set down the night before; it is almost as though one were to reflect: *I don't think I feel in sufficiently* high spirits[1] *this morning to appreciate the humour of having my leg ingeniously pulled.* Art, I would most firmly contend, was not invented to give pleasure at moments when the soul is already on fire with excitement and happiness; on such occasions, art is entirely superfluous, and no one but a fool opens a book when he is feeling cheerful. The purposes of art are higher, less ephemeral, and far better adapted to meet the more commonplace hazards and happenings of life. Art was created for a *consolation* to man. When the soul is filled with regret, when life is moving relentlessly towards the first still, sad days of autumn, when mistrust stalks shrouded like a ghost behind every dripping hedgerow—these are the days when it is good indeed to be able to turn to music.

And, when the soul of man is in such a mood, nothing is more repellent than exaggeration. In every instance when I have chanced upon some brilliant notion, which seems to lend itself to a whole sequence of flowing and well-rounded phrases, I have deliberately *understated* what I felt to be the truth, in order that the temptation of some fleeting, glittering little epigram should not pave the way to suspicion and disgust a page or two later. A lady of taste and delicate understanding, who had recently lost a close friend, once found the courage to declare, with that spirit of unconventionality which is the charm of intimate social intercourse: *When I used to feel dispirited, the conversation of M. *** would give me the same sense of comfort as one finds sometimes in a good, soft, well-sprung divan, when one is utterly exhausted and desperate to lie down and rest.* This expresses something of the pleasure and consolation which it has been my lot to discover in music. Music, as an art, suffuses the soul of man with sweet regret, by giving it a *glimpse of happiness*; and a glimpse of happiness, even if it is no more than a *dream* of happiness, is almost the dawning of hope. Books, on the other hand—the quintessence of the rarest flowers of the genius of France—I have set down in disgust a score of times. Rhetoric! All *rhetoric*! I have not the faintest spark of Rousseau's illuminating eloquence; and so I have struggled constantly to set aside this tempta-

---

[1] In English in the original. (*Trans.*)

tion, this *defect* which turns my stomach whenever I read his works.[1] Yet . . . Rousseau wrote many burning pages on the sweet art of music; and so let us return to our own delightful subject.

I am sure that our modern *dilettanti*, born in Rossini's own generation and, so to speak, sons of the revolution for which he alone is ultimately responsible, will allow me to remind them of some of the advantages which the old traditions of respect for the personal rights of any singer worthy of the name used to procure for the art of expression, or, in other words, for the pleasure of the audience.

There is no less diversity among human voices than among human faces. This diversity, which is already remarkable in the *speaking* voice, is a hundred times more noticeable in singing.

I wonder if the reader has ever observed the *timbre* of Mademoiselle Mars' voice? Where might one hope to find a singer whose voice could realize one hundredth part of the miracles which Mademoiselle Mars seems to promise in some exquisite flash of delicate *marivaudage*?

Pity, fear, astonishment, etc., can produce radical and diverse transformations in the human voice—in the voices, say, of those three charming ladies who were of our company last time we were discussing music; the effect of *pity*, for instance, upon one of those voices, which, in simple speech, is nothing remarkable, may produce an intonation of heart-rending loveliness, a thrilling overtone of emotion, which, by some instantaneous, *electrical* galvanization of the nervous system, can plunge every listener into a boundless ocean of melancholy. Yet, under Rossini's influence, this individual diversity, this unique shading of the voice, is doomed to extinction. In *his* system, every voice is required to render, more or less competently, an identical series of notes, *and nothing else*: it follows logically, therefore, that the net result of Rossini's revolution is the *impoverishment* of art itself.[2]

The particular natural resonance (*metallo*) inherent in every voice leads to a more or less obvious tonal identification with this or that expressed emotion. By the term *metallo*, I mean the *timbre* of the voice,

[1] In Geneva, I understand, Rousseau has no great reputation; but by contrast, Voltaire, so frivolous, so cynical, so anti-religious, so anti-Genevan, seems to be growing daily more popular. The reason?—well, after all, Voltaire was enjoying an income of 60,000 *livres* a year by the time he died!

[2] Except, of course, in the case of the one particular voice for which Rossini happens to have specially devised his ornamentation. Signorina Colbran owes a considerable part of her reputation directly to Rossini.

its fundamental, native quality, which is in no way dependent upon any talent or training which the singer who *uses* the voice may have inherited or acquired.

A voice may be clear or opaque, strong or weak, full or *sottile*, strident or muted;[1] but in each case it embodies, deep down in its own nature, the raw materials of various expressive intonations which, in themselves, may or may not be immediately pleasurable to listen to.

It may be confidently asserted that any voice, provided only that it has a certain degree of *precision*, thus enabling it to sustain a note with reasonable firmness, may sooner or later find music sufficiently well-suited to it for us to be able to listen to it with relative pleasure, at least for a few moments. The composer has only to take the trouble to devise a melody which falls well within the expressive compass of the particular voice which he has in mind. To begin with, it is essential that the *situation*, initially sketched out by the dramatist, should not contradict the native emotional *timbre* of the voice concerned. For instance, the natural quality of the voice may be one of sweetness, softness and stirring warmth; but in that case, if the character and circumstances which it is required to portray are imperious and violent (as, for example, in the rôle of *Elisabetta*, in Rossini's opera of that title), it stands to reason that nothing on earth will ever enable it to display its finest qualities, or to give complete satisfaction to those who listen to it. Technically speaking, a singer may possess every gift under the sun, and a soul alive to the subtlest hint of a *nuance*; yet none of this can avail him a jot against the obdurate *metallo* of his voice. The purest miracles known to the art are only achieved when a voice, which long training has transformed into an instrument of infinite flexibility, is offered the rare gift of a *situation* which demands precisely the *metallo* (*timbre*, natural shade of expression) which happens to be native to it. The occasions when all these conditions are fulfilled simultaneously are so rare, that it is, practically speaking, impossible to foresee when the miracle will occur; and it is precisely because the occasion *was* in fact so miraculous that an audience at *la Scala* once made Pacchiarotti sing the same aria five times in succession.[2]

[1] The same sentence in Italian would run as follows: *Una voce pura o velata, debole o forte, piena o sottile, stridula o smorzata.*

[2] I owe these ideas to Pacchiarotti himself, who granted me the privilege of his conversation one day in 1817, on an occasion when he was showing me round his *iardin anglais*, and the tower, originally belonging to Cardinal Bembo, which he

Once the fact of distinct vocal individuality is recognized and admitted, it follows logically that the composer now has a duty to take advantage of the native qualities of each particular voice, and to avoid harping upon its weaknesses. Can one imagine, for example, any composer so obtuse as to saddle Madame Fodor with an impassioned recitative, or Madame Pasta with an aria overlaid with a tracery of elaborate and glittering decoration? One of the results of all this is the practice, commonly met with in Italy, for a second-rate singer[1] to travel about the countryside completely equipped with a special set of arias, usually referred to as *arie di baule** or *baggage-arias*, which are carried around permanently, as it were, like a change of underwear. In dealing with a singer of this category, a composer may write any music he cares, and insist with legitimate authority upon his performing it; but you may be certain that, by hook or by crook, the singer will find some way of dragging in his *baggage-arias*, and, if he cannot introduce them *in toto*, he will get them in in fragments—the whole procedure being regarded as one of the huge standing jokes of the Italian stage!

Reprehensible as such practices may appear, it must still be allowed that these mediocre hacks achieve what is after all the sacred objective of all art: *they delight the public*. How infinitely far removed from all this are the precepts and practice of our own *Louvois* orchestra, and indeed the whole conception of music as it is understood in that venerable institution!

Unfortunately, the slightest alteration in the *tempo* of the main theme of a *baggage-aria* is quite sufficient to revolutionize the entire emotional pattern of the music. A phrase which, in its original *tempo*, had depicted wild anger, may now express nothing more urgent than gentle scorn; and yet, in spite of this radical change in the quality of expression, dictated by the need for inserting the passage into a thoroughly incompatible musical context, our wretched repertory-singer, whose one and only advantage is a voice thoroughly acquainted with the passage or phrase in question, will still somehow manage to give an excellent performance, and even to hold his audience enthralled. The reason for this phenomenon is that the particular theme of his

owns near the *Prato della Valle*, in Padua. *Cf.* the Author's account of a journey entitled *Rome, Naples et Florence en 1817.*

[1] Even, on occasions, for a first-rate singer too; Crivelli and Velluti never stir abroad nowadays without packing a score of *Isolina* (an opera which they give everywhere) in their baggage.

choice is probably better suited than any other, (*a*) to the native *timbre* of the performer's voice; (*b*) to the peculiar natural shading of his own individual sensibility; and (*c*) to the exact degree of technical proficiency with which his academic training may have endowed him. Thus the *baggage-aria* tradition completely obviates the worst faults of strained (*stentato*) singing; and it is precisely such *strained* singing which represents the most serious weakness in the tradition of the *Théâtre Feydeau*—a tradition which, for all that, is a good forty years further removed from the dark ages of barbarism than that of the *Grand Opéra*.

The reader will not have failed to observe, that even a first-rate singer does not necessarily have to know how to read music. The art of reading, in fact, is completely divorced from the art of singing,[1] and demands nothing more profound or subtle than patience and a certain capacity for severe and methodical perseverance.

One successful *rôle*—or in some cases, one successful aria—can make the reputation of a competent singer in Italy; and before Rossini's time, even that of a supreme artist often hung upon no more than ten or a dozen arias. The art of singing is so delicate, the delight which it inspires is of so thistledown a quality, that no singer can hope to enjoy an absolute success unless he chance upon an aria which fulfils, in one sublime instant of perfection, all the essential conditions which we have already had several occasions to mention. It follows, then, that there is nothing better calculated to satisfy an audience than an *aria di baule*. The truth of the proposition can be demonstrated even in the rather different conditions of the spoken theatre: how many different parts combine to furnish the reputation of a Talma or a Mademoiselle Mars? The *baggage-aria* tradition is admirably devised, not only with regard to the undeniable mediocrity of the average performer—a mediocrity which is scarcely to be wondered at in an art so supremely difficult—but also with respect to the extreme poverty which haunts the resources of so many of the smaller Italian towns; for such places, despite the grotesque insufficiency of the municipal purse, still manage to achieve two or three extremely adequate productions every year, a miracle which is only made possible by the exploitation of the *baggage-*

---

[1] In Italy, singers who have difficulty in reading music are known as *orecchianti*; their opposites, by the term *professore*. Thus you may often hear it asserted in Florence, that *Zucchelli è un professore*—which is very far from meaning that Zucchelli gives music-lessons, but simply denotes that he has no difficulty in reading music.

N

aria, and by the engagement of two or three exceedingly mediocre artists, each one of whom is nevertheless capable of giving a really brilliant performance of *not more than two or three arias*.[1]

As soon as a composer forgets to take into account the *metallo* (inherent tonal quality) of his singers' voices, the type of emotional portrayal which comes most naturally to them on the stage, and the degree of technique (*bravura*) which they may have acquired in the pure mechanics of singing, he runs the almost certain risk of obtaining no more for the price of all his pains than a careful, correctly-sung opera which no one enjoys the least little bit.

There are plenty of singers who are constitutionally incapable of dealing with certain categories of ornamentation (*volate, arpeggi, salti* on a descending scale, *etc.*), save in the most stilted and unnatural (*stentata*) manner. With a singer of this type at his disposal, any composer who fails to make the necessary allowances in his score, making a clean sweep of every musical device belonging to the categories described, is courting disaster; for he is liable to find himself in the absurd situation, where his arias, in performance, will convey a series of impressions which are the diametrical opposite of what he had originally intended. If I may be excused for putting forward an example which is perhaps rather over-simplified, both in idea and in illustration, I will try to explain exactly what I mean. Imagine a composer who wishes to convey the idea of a sudden and uninterrupted downpour of rain, or rather, say, of some oriental despot commanding a slave to vanish instantly from his presence, and who therefore proceeds to decorate his fundamental musical theme with a *volata discendente*; nothing could look prettier *in the score*. But on the glorious day of the first performance, the audience, faced with a thoroughly incompetent singer, will miss all these carefully-prepared suggestions of an inexorable monarch issuing an order where disobedience means death, and instead, as with one mind, will behold a vision of a decrepit and ill-tempered attorney stammering with impotent and choleric rage in the dusty depths of his chambers. Even if the absurdity escapes this furthest limit of bathos, the slightest touch of incompetence in the

---

[1] In October of the year 1822*, I came upon a quite delightful production of an opera in Varese, an insignificant little township in Lombardy no bigger than Saint-Cloud, whose inhabitants, incidentally, are remarkable for their tradition of most perfect courtesy towards foreigners.

rendering of the *volata* will necessarily kill the impression of *rapidity*, which the composer was striving above all to convey to the audience; and in consequence, the poor despot, with his terrible command to vanish *upon the very instant*, will find himself translated into a constitutional monarch politely inviting some harmless exile to leave his court as and when it suits his convenience. I would observe that there is not one single embellishment of the type executed by Velluti, which might not lead to some similar, fantastic interpretation. Every time I am away from Italy, I am constantly hearing Rossini's music tortured into making the strangest confessions, almost always in flat contradiction to the truth which it is struggling so valiantly to express; and the only reason for this breakdown of musical logic lies in the fact that his score has coerced the singer into performing some ornament or other which is totally incompatible with the natural qualities of his or her voice. Whenever this happens, I, who know how Rossini's music *should* sound, find myself listening to no more than half, or at very best, three-quarters, of the melody as it was originally written. Now, it will be obvious that so monstrous and so absurd a situation could never have arisen for a moment under the older system, when the greater liberty of the singer was a major consideration. In pre-Rossinian music, the only obstacle liable to be met with might lie in the presence of one or two abnormally high-pitched notes—an obstacle which would only arise when the passage under discussion had originally been specifically destined by the composer for some singer with an extremely unusual range of voice; once free of this particular obstruction, however (and its removal would involve remarkably little really serious difficulty), the singer was then unreservedly free to select his own style of embellishment, and to use no ornament of which he was not reasonably sure; and so there would be nothing to prevent him from dazzling his assembled admirers with all the individuality and beauty of his own unique voice and technical virtuosity.

I imagine that some well-informed critic, who has indulged his love of music to the extent of making a careful study of the individual voices of all the singers who took part in the original productions of Rossini's nine Neapolitan operas, may well object that the composer frequently appears to have failed to take proper advantage of all the characteristics of each particular voice, even when he was able to study it specifically with a view to composing for it. I can only answer that, apparently, Rossini was so deeply enamoured of his *prima donna* that he was prepared to go to any lengths to ensure that she was never overshadowd by any other singer.

But with this one solitary exception, the scores of Rossini's Neapolitan operas are a biography of voices—not only giving us the vocal history of Signorina Colbran herself, but also that of Nozzari, Davide, Signorina Pisaroni and others. These scores make it quite clear that all the embellishments, which singers had hitherto claimed the right to distribute *ad libitum*, had now been transformed into an integral, necessary, *indispensable* constituent part of Rossini's music; but that does not solve the problem, how any singer is to perform this music when his voice does not happen to possess exactly the same characteristics as that of Nozzari or Davide.

The operas which belong to Rossini's "second manner" are never *boring*; they have none of the infinite and barren tedium of an opera by Mayr, for example; but they can never recapture the same extraordinary spell which they managed to cast in Naples, except when, by sheer chance and on the rarest of occasions, they may happen to be graced by a singer whose voice is a natural medium for exactly the same type of embellishments as were best suited to the specific artist for whom the *rôle* was originally composed, and whose *style* corresponds exactly to his.

All this should suffice to explain how it is, that certain operas which created an absolute *furore* in Naples, have been known to provide nothing but yawns at the *Théâtre Louvois*. Both audiences are right in their judgment; and there is no need to go off exploring the boundless infinite of metaphysics in order to find an explanation for so uncomplicated a phenomenon. The fault lies entirely with the management of the *Louvois*. Have you ever witnessed anything more *impertinent*, for example, than its latest production of *gli Orazi e Curiazi*? If it had happened in Italy, the audience would have refused to leave the theatre until the "management" had obeyed its imperious summons and appeared on the stage *in person* to be hooted at![1]

Rossini's genius, imagination and *verve* are such that he has never learnt how to be boring, whatever the convention he may choose to

---

[1] No *commercial* manager would ever have dared to put on *gli Orazi* with the kind of cast which *we* were offered! The *Louvois* ought to be run on a commercial basis, and put out to contract, like *la Scala*.

adopt; but I shudder to think at some of the curious results which may be obtained when his *imitators* start producing music, and when *this* music is performed in theatres other than those for which it was originally composed. Such music of this category as has already been written closely resembles Rossini's, in that it is almost wholly woven out of ornamental material which happens to suit the singers for which it is destined in the first instance; and this ornamentation is in fact an integral part of the thematic substance of the music. But it is precisely when thematic material of this type is badly performed by singers whose voices are incompetent to deal with it, that we dig right down to that very rock-bottom of mediocrity which is intolerable in any art, and doubly or trebly intolerable in music.

It goes without saying that none of this criticism of Rossini's music applies in any degree to the happy days when he was composing arias such as:

> *Eco pietosa . . .*

or:

> *Di tanti palpiti . . .*

or:

> *Pien di contento il seno . . .*

or:

> *Non è ver mio ben, ch' io mora . . .*

or:

> *Se tu m' ami, o mia regina . . ., etc.*

But the terrible thing is, that if only he had gone on making progress in the same direction, he would probably have written music besides which these sublime arias would have seemed pale and insignificant. There are, admittedly, one or two arias in *la Donna del Lago*, a work truly *Ossianic* in character, which suggest a return to the days of his youth; but at bottom, this opera is *epic* rather than *dramatic*.

Do I need to repeat that, while Velluti, the Prince of Singers of our own generation, is capable of performing the most astonishing feats of virtuosity, he is all too frequently guilty of *abusing* his natural gifts, sometimes devastating and distorting the music of some wretched composer until it becomes practically impossible to recognize? Velluti never affords us the supreme pleasure of listening to a *simple* melody; and he hardly ever performs Rossini's music. Velluti's main concern is to play to the boundless admiration of a worshipping audience; flattery has grown to be an indispensable part of his very existence. Now, it happens that one of the rare ornaments which Velluti has never quite mastered is the *scale in giù* (descending scales), a form of embellishment which Signorina Colbran could execute with consummate ease, and therefore one which Rossini has been accustomed to scatter lavishly throughout his work. Logically, therefore, none of the music which Rossini wrote for Signorina Colbran can ever be performed by Velluti, or at least, it could only be performed in a highly unsatisfactory manner, and could achieve nothing but a *succès d'estime*.

CHAPTER XXXIV

Concerning the various Qualities of the Human Voice

A HUNTING-HORN, echoing over the hills of the Scottish highlands, can be heard at a considerably greater distance than the human voice. In this respect, *but in this respect only*, art has outdistanced nature: art has succeeded in increasing the *volume* of sound produced. But in respect of something infinitely more important, namely inflexion and ornamentation, the human voice still maintains its superiority over any instrument yet invented, and it might even be claimed that no instrument is satisfactory except in so far as it approximates to the sound of the human voice.

I would suggest that if, in some moment of pensive stillness and brooding melancholy, we were to peer into the very depths of our soul, we would discover that the fascination of the human voice springs from two distinct causes:

(1) The suggestion of passion, which, to a greater or lesser degree, inevitably colours anything which is sung by living man or woman. Even the least impassioned of *prime donne*, le Signore Camporesi, Fodor, Festa, *etc.*, whose voices express no positive emotion, still radiate a kind of indeterminate *joy*. I make a half-exception only in favour of Signora Catalani, whose prodigiously beautiful voice fills the soul with a kind of astonished wonder, as though it beheld a miracle; and the very confusion of our hearts blinds us at first to the noble and goddess-like impassivity of this unique artist. Sometimes, in an idle moment, I like to imagine a creature who combined the voice of Signora Catalani with the impassioned soul and dramatic instinct of la Pasta—a fond, sweet chimaera, whose dream-quality leads only to sadness and regret for a thing which *is not*; and yet, whose very possibility leaves one convinced that music sways a greater power over the soul than any other art.[1]

[1] Imagine the rapture which might be derived from Romberg's genius on the 'cello, if only the player had the impassioned soul of a *Werther*, instead of the flat,

(2) The second advantage which the human voice possesses by comparison with the instrument lies in its command of *language*, which can, as it were, storm the imagination, and fill it directly with the kind of imagery which the music is to embroider and develop.

If the human voice is weak in tone, compared with certain instruments, it can claim the power of *graduating* sounds to a degree of perfection inconceivable in any mechanical device.

The human voice commands an infinite variety of inflexions (which is the same thing as saying that a *totally passionless* voice is a practical impossibility); and, to my mind, this particular quality is of far greater significance than its other distinguishing characteristic, the power to express itself in language.

To start with, the excruciating doggerel which forms the verbal skeleton of the average Italian aria is hardly ever recognizable as verse of any description, owing to the multiplicity of repeats; the language which greets the listener's patient ear is pure prose.[1] Furthermore, the beauty of poetry does not lie in its bold and melodramatic exclamations, such as *I hate you like poison!* or *I love you to distraction! etc.*, but in its shades and subtleties, in the skilled ordering or selection of words; and it is these *nuances* which convince the reader of the poet's sincerity, and which ultimately awaken his sympathy and understanding. But there is no room for *nuances* among the haphazard jumble of 50–60 words which go to form the text of the average Italian aria; and so language, *as such*, can never be anything more than a *bare canvas*; the task of decorating this canvas with all the glint and glitter of a thousand tints and colours lies with the *music*.

Would you like a further proof that words are fundamentally unimportant in relation to music, and that, in practice, they are nothing but *labels to stick on emotions*? Consider any aria you like, sung with all the deep and impassioned sincerity of a Madame Belloc or of a Signorina Pisaroni; and then consider the same aria sung an instant later by one or other of our book-learned, half-frozen tailor's-dummies from the North. The latter worthy, if frigid, songstress will undoubtedly utter the very same words:

prosaic spirit of a worthy Teutonic burgher! Fräulein von Schauroth is only nine years old at present, but her fame has already gone abroad, and her temperament promises all the tempestuous wildness of true genius.

[1] As an exercise, transcribe the words of the famous aria: *Quelle   pupille tenere* . . . as they are actually *sung* in the score of *gli Orazi*.

Io fremo, mio ben, morir mi sento . . .

as the great artist who has just preceded her; but what can *words* do to shatter the creeping rim of ice which has fastened on to our hearts?

Two words, three words . . . just enough to tell us that the hero is sunk into depths of despair, or else that he is winging across the infinite spaces of happiness—this is all we need to grasp; if we then catch, or fail to catch completely, the words of the rest of the aria, either way is utterly indifferent; all that really matters is that they should be *sung* with passionate sincerity. This is what makes it possible to listen with appreciable delight to a good performance of an opera in a foreign language, even though, in this case, the words may be entirely incomprehensible; so long as some kind neighbour gives one the key to the more important arias, nothing else is needed. The same principle holds good in the spoken theatre: it is quite conceivable to derive considerable pleasure from watching a great tragic actor playing in a language with which one has but the sketchiest acquaintance. The conclusion to be drawn from all these observation would seem to be, that the *inflexion* of the words is of far greater importance in opera than the words themselves.

No quality is more essential in a singer than his power of *dramatic expression*.

So long as this power remains totally, or even partially, undeveloped and inadequate, there is no victory to be won in the art of singing which can be more than ephemeral, no triumph which cannot be attributed to some accidental favour or partiality on the side of the audience—a partiality which, ultimately, will be found to derive from sources completely foreign to art as such: physical attractiveness in the performer, a coincidence of political sentiments, or similar extraneous considerations.

Italy is full of legendary prophecies, punctual to the day in the manner of their fulfilment. The tale is told of a Neapolitan *dilettante* who, referring to two fair singers, one of whom was idolized like the morning star by her audiences, while the other was scarcely tolerated on the stage, stood up in the middle of the *San-Carlo*, seized by one of those mighty paroxysms of indignation and passionate anger which are not infrequently met with in that city, and cried aloud: "In three years' time, you will be trampling your idol underfoot; in three year's

time, you will be worshipping the goddess whom you now reject!"
Scarcely eighteen months had rolled by before the prophecy was
accomplished, for the *cantatrice* who had sung *with expression* had
utterly supplanted the sometime *prima donna* whom nature had gifted
with an infinitely finer voice. One might draw a parallel between the
company of an extremely *handsome* man and that of an extremely
intelligent man. But even if the defeated *prima donna* had sung, not with
a superb *natural* voice (which is a free gift of chance), but with *bravura*
(which is largely acquired), the same revolution in the taste of those
Neapolitan audiences, the same revolt against the *absence of dramatic
expression*, would inevitably have occurred in the end, although perhaps a little more slowly.

CHAPTER XXXV

*Madame Pasta**

THE temptation to sketch a musical portrait of Madame Pasta is too strong to be resisted. It may be averred that there was never a more difficult undertaking; the language of musical description is ungrateful and outlandish; I shall find myself constantly baulked by inadequacies of vocabulary; and even on those occasions when I *am* lucky enough to light upon the exact word required to convey my thought, the chances are that it will awaken none but the vaguest associations in the reader's mind. Furthermore, there can scarcely be one single music-lover in all Paris who has not already invented his own epithets in praise of Madame Pasta; none, therefore, will escape the disappointment of failing to find his own thought reflected here; and even the most favourably-disposed of readers, in the heat of devotion which this great singer so deservedly inspires among her admirers, is bound to find any portrait of her from another hand flat, insipid and a thousand times less wondrous than he had a right to expect.

When chance ordained that Rossini should meet the charming and gracious Signora Marcolini, the outcome was *la Pietra del Paragone*; when it was decreed that he should fall in with the majestic Signorina Colbran, the result was *Elisabetta*; and when fate led him to the impassioned and melodramatic Galli, we were gratified with *rôles* such as Fernando in *la Gazza ladra* and Mahomet in *Maometto secondo*; but he has never yet composed anything expressly for Madame Pasta.

If this same chance were to present Rossini with an actress who is young and beautiful; who is both intelligent and sensitive; whose gestures never deteriorate from the plainest and most natural modes of simplicity, and yet manage to keep faith with the purest ideals of formal beauty; if, allied to such an extraordinary wealth of dramatic talent, Rossini were to discover a voice which never fails to thrill our very souls with the passionate exaltation which we used, long ago, to capture from the great masters of the Golden Age; a voice which can weave a spell of magic about the plainest word in the plainest recitative;

a voice whose compelling inflexions can subdue the most recalcitrant and obdurate hearts, and oblige them to share in the emotions which radiate from some great aria ... *if* Rossini were to discover such a world of wonder, who doubts but that the miraculous would happen, that he would shed his laziness like a garment, settle down unreservedly to a study of Madame Pasta's voice, and soon start composing within the special range of her abilities? Inspired by the sublime gifts of such a *prima donna*, Rossini would recover the ardour which burned like a bright flame in his soul at the outset of his career, and win back the secret of those delicious and simple melodies which laid the first foundations of his reputation. Imagine *then* what masterpieces would come to crown the glory of the *Théâtre Louvois*, and how little time would pass before Paris should stand forth before the dazzled eyes of all Europe as the Capital of Music, usurping the majesty now reserved for the audiences of Naples and Milan!

If Rossini were to hear one performance of the *Prayer-scene* from *Giulietta e Romeo*, a sure test and touchstone for any *prima donna*; if he had once been forced to acknowledge the superb assurance of Madame Pasta's *portamento*, the infinite skill and subtlety of her glides, the unparalleled artistry with which she can inflect, sustain and smoothly control an extended vocal phrase, I have no doubt whatsoever but that he would willingly agree to sacrifice at least part of his "system" in her honour, and to thin out the tangled undergrowth of grace-notes which has come creeping like ivy about the pure lines of his melody.

If Rossini were once fully convinced of the perfect intelligence, moderation and good taste, of which Madame Pasta gives ample evidence in her own *fioriture*; if he could once grasp the principle that no ornamentation is so sure and so effective as that which springs from the spontaneous invention and emotional response of the singer, I cannot see how he could fail to be cured of his apprehension, and so once more entrust the delicate art of embellishment to the inspiration of this truly great singer.

The few genuine lovers of music who frequent the *Théâtre Louvois*, not because it is fashionable to do so, but because they are capable of being profoundly moved by the art which they find there, and whom I credit (with a trust which I believe to be not misplaced) with being as delicately sensitive to every distinct manifestation of beauty as they are to every prompting of noble ambition, might well, I would suggest, reflect upon what they would feel if, suddenly, after the long, barren years in the Assembly when nothing has echoed from the Speaker's Tribune save the dusty squeakings of written perorations, they were to find themselves confronted in that august gathering by some new Mirabeau, some second Général Foy, thundering through the halls with all the untrammelled genius of *improvisation* . . . What a difference! —and yet, between a singer struggling as best she can with a tangle of ornament composed for someone else, with a score which denies her every scrap of liberty and every fleeting opportunity to display the genius of her own inspiration; between a singer in this grotesque situation, and the same singer basking in the sweet freedom of a *cantilena* written expressly for her own voice, *i.e.*, not only within her particular compass, but also within the range of her own individual palette of colours and her own pattern of virtuosity, the difference is assuredly no less striking!

Out of all the operas in which Madame Pasta has sung a part since she came to Paris, I know only the second and third acts of *Giulietta e Romeo* which are in the slightest degree suited to the characteristics of her voice or to the peculiarities of her style. If I were to go through every other work which she has sung since she has been with us, I doubt if I should find as many as three solitary arias which exactly fulfilled all the conditions which are essential for perfection; and yet, in spite of this, Madame Pasta has cast a spell upon every heart, even through the medium of a style which persistently contradicts the *timbre* of her voice, and compels her into feats of unnatural acrobatics.[1] There has perhaps never been such another singer, who has both achieved, and deserved, celebrity under such impossible conditions. And now, all you who truly love music in all its purity and sweetness, imagine *what might be*, if a Rossini were to compose expressly for so rare a spirit!

Only if and when such a miracle were achieved, could Madame Pasta's fairest gifts receive their due reward. It is not difficult to guess what satisfaction her vanity might receive, now that Paris has spread her reputation abroad through Europe, if she were to tour the various stages of Italy. If, four or five times a year, she were to sing in original works *specifically composed to match the qualities of her voice*, I have not the

[1] One *tour de force* of this type, which makes music-lovers gasp with astonishment every time it is repeated, is her ability to play Tancred one night, and Desdemona three nights later.

slightest doubt that, in two or three years' time, her gifts would appear to be twice as splendid as they are now. Her reputation is already such, that it needs no stretch of imagination to visualize the alacrity with which every struggling composer in the land, eager that she should appear in *his* opera, and so lay the foundations of *his* renown, would lay himself out to please her, and devote his whole life, if need be, to studying the characteristics of her voice in order to match them in his own music.[1]

I must now beg my reader to show even greater patience than he has done already, while I, for my part, make even more strenuous efforts to be clear and lucid; in any case, I promise to be brief.

Madame Pasta's voice has a considerable range. She can achieve perfect resonance on a note as low as bottom *A*, and can rise as high as *C♯*, or even to a slightly sharpened *D*; and she possesses the rare ability to be able to sing contralto as easily as she can sing soprano.[2] I would suggest, in spite of my atrocious lack of technical knowledge, that the true designation of her voice is *mezzo-soprano*, and any composer who writes for her should use the *mezzo-soprano* range for the thematic material of his music, while still exploiting, as it were incidentally and from time to time, notes which lie within the more peripheral areas of this remarkably rich voice. Many notes of this last category are not only extremely fine in themselves, but have the ability to produce a kind of resonant and magnetic vibration, which, through some still unexplained combination of physical phenomena, exercises an instantaneous and hypnotic effect upon the soul of the spectator.

This leads me to the consideration of one of the most uncommon features of Madame Pasta's voice: it is *not all moulded from the same metallo*, as they would say in Italy (*i.e.*, it possesses more than one *timbre*); and this fundamental variety of tone produced by a single voice affords one of the richest veins of musical expression which the artistry of a great *cantatrice* is able to exploit.

---

[1] I would like to prophesy that Madame Pasta is destined to make the fortune of that composer, whose ascendant star is fated eventually to eclipse the glory of Rossini. She is nowhere to be seen at better advantage than in the *simple manner**; and *simplicity* offers the key to any rival who attempts to breach the stronghold of the glory of the man who composed *Zelmira*.

[2] An ability of which she gave ample proof by singing, not only the part of Tancred, but also those of Curazio (in Cimarosa's *gli Orazi e Curiazi*), Romeo and Medea.

The Italians are accustomed to describe this type of voice by saying that it has several different *registers*,[1] that is to say, several *clearly-distinguishable physical aspects*, varying in accordance with the region of the scale into which the singer chances to venture. In an untrained voice, which possesses neither the very considerable technique, nor (more important still) the exquisite sensibility required to ensure that a correct use is made of these various "registers", the result is simply one of roughness and inequality, and the total effect, a grating discordance whose harshness kills every atom of musical enjoyment. On the other hand, Pacchiarotti, la Todi, and a large number of other outstanding singers of the old school long ago demonstrated how easily an apparent defect might be transformed into a source of infinite beauty, and how it might be used to bring about a most fascinating touch of originality. In fact, the history of the art might tend to suggest that it is *not* the perfectly pure, silvery voice, impeccably accurate in tone throughout every note of its compass, which lends itself to the greatest achievements of impassioned singing. No voice whose *timbre* is completely incapable of variation can ever produce that kind of *opaque*, or as it were, *suffocated* tone, which is at once so moving and so natural in the portayal of certain instants of violent emotion or passionate anguish.

I have frequently heard it asserted, in the company of certain outstandingly well-informed and enlightened *dilettanti*, who, when I lived in Trieste, did me the signal honour of admitting me to their gatherings, that la Todi,[2] one of the last representatives of the Golden Age of

---

[1] A clarinet, for instance, possesses *two* registers; a low note played on this instrument seems to belong to a different tonal family, compared with a high note. For the sake of interest, let me record here a phenomenon which was first observed in London this year: a high note on a clarinet (or on a piano) leaves certain wild beasts, such as lions, tigers, *etc.*, completely unmoved, whereas a low note on the same instrument will instantly set them all roaring with fury. In the case of the human being, I suspect that precisely the opposite is more likely to be the case. Perhaps the explanation is that the low notes resemble animal-roarings, and hence suggest a challenge. Compare this with the experiments which were carried out in the year 1802 in the *Jardin des Plantes*, when a concert was given to a group of elephants. I do not know whether the scientific investigators concerned had enough intelligence to record the results of this experiment in language sufficiently simple for a layman to understand, nor whether they were able to resist so exquisite an opportunity for exhaling clouds of pseudo-scientific eloquence. Scientists are terrible people whenever they start showing symptoms of stylistic ambition, or when, at the end of infinite vistas of magniloquent prose, they behold the coveted image of an *Order of Merit*.

[2] Luiza Todi was singing in Venice in 1795 or 1796, and in Paris in 1799. Some

singing, possessed a voice and a style both extraordinarily similar to those of Madame Pasta.

La Todi's rival, la Mara, was a miracle of art and nature; Gertrude Mara was not only endowed with an unusually lovely and *molta bravura* (wonderfully agile) voice, but she possessed in addition an excellent training in a great tradition and a fine range of expression. Nevertheless, by the general acclamation of all true-born lovers of the arts, whose opinions, after a year or two, invariably become those of the broader public, Signora Todi snatched the victory when it lay almost within the grasp of her rival; for it was *her* singing which had the more often succeeded in recapturing the echo of their own emotions.

Madame Pasta's incredible mastery of technique is revealed in the amazing facility with which she alternates head-notes with chest-notes; she possesses to a superlative degree the art of producing an immense variety of charming and thrilling effects from the use of *both* voices. To heighten the tonal colouring of a melodic phrase, or to pass in a flash from one *ambiance* to another infinitely removed from it, she is accustomed to use a *falsetto* technique covering notes right down to the middle of her normal range; or else she may unconcernedly alternate *falsetto* notes with ordinary chest-notes. In all such displays of virtuosity, she apparently finds as little difficulty in securing a smooth transition between the two voices when she is employing notes in the *middle* of her normal chest-range, as she does when she is using the highest notes which she can produce.

The characteristics of Madame Pasta's head-notes are almost diametrically opposed to the characteristics of her chest-notes; her *falsetto* is brilliant, rapid, pure, fluent and enchantingly light. As she approaches the lower part of this *falsetto* register, she can *smorzare il canto*

people, as you must know only too well, are determined to insist that the most *modern* music is invariably the *best* music; and, as far as orchestral music is concerned, there is considerable diversity of opinion as to which of the various epochs of the last century produced the finest work. By contrast, in the domain of *vocal* music, there is general agreement that the period between 1730 and 1780 represented the *Golden Age*. By the end of the XVIIIth century, however, the few survivors who still treasured the secrets of this wonderful art were already very old. To-day, the world of singing knows a fair number of fine voices, and perhaps five or six artists who have a really profound mastery of technique: Velluti, la Pasta, Davide, la Pisaroni, Madame Belloc, and a few others. Their taste is probably purer and less extravagant than that of the great *soprani* who flourished *circa* 1770, but their technique is probably inferior.

(diminish her tone) to a point where the very fact of the existence of sound becomes uncertain.

Without such a palette of breath-taking colour deep within her own being, and without such an extraordinary and compelling natural gift, Madame Pasta could never have achieved the over-mastering force of natural expression which we have learnt to associate with her—a miracle of emotional revelation, which is always true to nature and, although tempered by the intrinsic laws of *ideal Beauty*,[1] always alive with that unmistakable, burning energy, that extraordinary dynamism which can electrify an entire theatre. But think how much pure artistry, and how much discipline and training has been necessary before this enthralling singer learned to harness the restive secrets of weaving such divine enchantments out of two different and utterly contrasting voices.

Her art appears to be infinitely perfectible; its miracles grow daily more astonishing, and nothing can henceforth stop its power over the audience from growing progressively more binding. Madame Pasta long ago overcame the last of the physical obstacles which stood in the way of the realization of pure musical enjoyment; and her voice to-day is as fascinating to the listener's ear as it is electrifying to his soul. Each new opera in which she appears fires her audience with feelings of ever-deepening intensity, or surprises them with new and strange aspects of a familiar delight. She possesses the great secret of imprinting a fresh pattern of colour upon old music, not through the medium of the words, or thanks to her genius as a great tragic actress, but purely and simply *as a singer*; and thus she is able to transmute a rôle (such as that of Elcia in *Mosè*), which might seem comparatively insignificant, into a thing of new and splendid beauty.[2]

However, Madame Pasta, like every other singer without exception, occasionally comes across certain technical *awkwardnesses*, certain peculiar contortions of the voice, which she is physically incapable of mastering, or at least, which can only be mastered with such difficulty that it is invariably at the expense of that miraculous faculty—normally such an integral part of her artistry—for entrancing the ear with the sheer delight of music, and for stirring and bewitching the soul through

[1] This unusual *pacatezza* [sedateness] of voice and gesture serves to distinguish Madame Pasta from every other great *prima donna* whom I have ever seen.

[2] Madame Pasta's singing-master, Signor Scappa, of Milan, is at present in London, where his method is achieving uncommon popularity.

the sensual pleasures of sound. These occasions, rare as they are, turn our impatient imagination with ever greater longing towards the day when we shall hear her, were it but once, in an opera composed expressly for her own voice.

I think that I should despair of ever succeeding, were I obliged to describe one single embellishment normally used by Madame Pasta which is not a monument of classical grace and style, or which is unfit to stand as a model of unrivalled perfection. Extremely restrained in her use of *fioriture*, she resorts to them *only* when they have a direct contribution to make to the dramatic expressiveness of the music; and it is worth noting that none of her *fioriture* are retained for a single instant after they have ceased to be useful. I have never known her guilty of those interminable frescoes of ornamentation which seem to remind one of some irrepressible talker in a fit of absent-mindedness, and during which one suspects that the singer's attention has wandered far out into vacancy, or else that he had started out with one intention, only to change his mind upon the subject half-way through. I leave my reader to supply the name of this or that popular singer, who is only too liable to fall headlong into traps of this kind (which, incidentally, can be more than a little amusing to the cynical observer); I should be rather sorry to spoil the enjoyment of certain half-baked enthusiasts, who, I notice, usually applaud this sort of nonsense to the very skies! Not infrequently, a *gorgheggio* will begin lightly, rapidly, and in a style reminiscent of the purest farce traditions, only to tail off on to a note of tragedy, or to immerse itself in a fog of impassioned and unmitigated gloom; or else, the singer, after having opened in a strain of severe and unimpeachable gravity, will proceed to discover half-way through that his inspiration has dried up, and so will make a wild and desperate plunge into the nonsensicalities of *opera buffa*. Clearly, only a singer whose soul is utterly insensitive to the art which he is supposed to practise could be guilty of such atrocities; but his insensibility is no worse than that of the spectator who cannot see their absurdity. I know of no better test than this for detecting the enthusiast whose taste has been learned by rote from the text-books of the *Académie*. Every time I hear *gorgheggi* of this type being applauded, say, in *la Gazza ladra*, I am reminded of the well-known anecdote concerning a certain popular Minister-of-State, who, being closeted with the King in his work-cabinet for a whole hour, spent the entire time reading him an interminable report on the prerogatives of his office; the King seemed unduly delighted with this report, which, in all conscience, could scarcely be called entertaining; but the fact was simply that the noble Lord in question was holding his document upside-down, and thus had proved conclusively that he did not know how to read. I feel that this little story is symbolic of the type of *dilettante* whose enthusiasm knows no bounds and whose praise is unsparing for an embellishment whose two halves are mutually contradictory, and which starts off by proclaiming *white*, only to finish up by shouting *black*! The dramatic situation may be *either* tragic or comic, but it cannot reasonably be both; and so, in either case, the applause is equally absurd.

Where should I find words adequate to describe the visions of celestial beauty which spread before us in dazzling glory when Madame Pasta sings, or the strange glimpses into the secrets of sublime and fantastic passions which her art affords us? Ineffable mysteries, dreams which lie beyond the powers of poetry, vistas unknown, unfathomable, deep-hidden in the recesses of the human heart, which no mere Canova with his sculptor's chisel, no mere Correggio with his painter's brush, could hope to reveal to our enquiring souls! Who could recall without a shudder that terrible instant when Medea draws her children towards her, while her hand feels for the dagger . . . and then pushes them away, as though shaken by some invisible tempest of remorse? The suggestion is so subtle, so delicate, that it would cause even the greatest of writers, I feel, to despair of the crudity of his own medium!

Or should I remind you of the great reconciliation-scene between Enrico and his friend Vanoldo, in the famous duet:

> *È deserto il bosco intorno . . .*[1]

and the superb artistry which introduces the theme and leads to the climax of Enrico's forgiveness:

> *Ah! chi può mirarla in volto*
> *E non ardere d'amor?*[2]

In every rôle which Madame Pasta has sung, there are at least ten

[1] See above, p. 23. From Mayr's *la Rosa bianca*, as performed during the evening of the 2nd of October, 1823. Never before, perhaps, has the singing of Madame Pasta seemed more divinely inspired. Incidentally, in this version of *la Rosa bianca*, I recognized several embellishments borrowed from Desdemona's *Prayer-scene*.
[2] See above, p. 23.

passages which I should like to analyse. For instance, the twelve bars in *Tancredi*, which she sings after the death of Orbassano, when she appears mounted in her chariot, are musically nondescript; and yet, what subtlety in the interpretation! What a miracle of art, that can make *this* music different from any other that has ever been! How clearly one feels the *melancholy stillness* in the aftermath of a victory which holds no pleasure for Tancred, since the innocence of Amenaide is still unvindicated! What a wealth of tragic lucidity in the perception of the sudden loss of that fierce, that unrelenting urge to live, which had sustained the young warrior before the battle, when the need to save Amenaide was a burning fire in his breast, and when the smallest uncertainty of victory was enough to blind him to the full horror of his fate!

Madame Pasta may indeed sing the same *note* in two different scenes; but, if the spiritual context is different, it will not be the same *sound*.

These are the sublimest heights to which the art of singing can attain. I have seen perhaps thirty performances of *Tancredi*; but Madame Pasta's musical intonation is always moulded so closely upon the *momentary inspirations* of her heart, that I may claim to have heard the phrase:

Tremar Tancredi?[1]

for instance, sung on some occasions with an inflexion of gentle irony; on others, with a manly intonation of courage, with the intrepid accents of a hero assuring his followers that there is nothing to fear, and strengthening the uncertain heart of timidity; on other occasions still,

[1] *Amenaide:*	Ah! che veggo? Tancredi! . . .
Tancredi:	Sì, il tuo Tancredi [. . .]
Amenaide:	Oh qual scegliesti Terribil' ora? Sventurato! e dove Fier destino ti guida?
Tancredi:	Qual terror!
Amenaide:	È troppo giusto. I vili tuoi nemici . . ..
Tancredi:	Li sfido . . .
Amenaide:	Fuggi! Salvati!
Tancredi:	Che dici?
Amenaide:	Trema . . .
Tancredi:	Tremar Tancredi . . .?

(Act I, sc. vii)

with an air of disagreeable surprise already tinged with resentment ... and then, suddenly, Tancred remembers that it is his beloved Amenaide who is speaking, and the first growlings of the storm of anger vanish into the smiling sunlight of reconciliation.

There is no language in the world which can render all the shades and subtleties of *music*; and so, as the reader will have observed, I am trying to prove their real existence by describing the *nuances* of the *acting*—a crudish process, but one which has the advantage of replacing the seven or eight pages of close writing, into which I had originally tried (unsuccessfully) to condense my remarks upon three particular *nuances* in the interpretation of the part of Tancred, as it was varied from performance to performance. Anybody who possessed the patience to read those eight pages would certainly be the kind of person who could appreciate the *nuances* for himself—and probably many others besides, which I have overlooked. So at least, as it now stands, this book will contain that many fewer *exaggerations* to provoke the ribaldry of the philistines.

A shade, a delicate suggestion of colour or feeling, belonging to the type which I have just been describing, and varying, as happens when the interpreter is Madame Pasta, from one performance of *Tancredi* to the next ... this is an exact instance of that kind of *microscopic detail* which no composer can ever fully transcribe into his score. And even if he should attempt to do so, as Rossini has been attempting ever since 1815, the year which marks the beginning of his "Neapolitan period", it will be glaringly obvious that no specific *mordent*, no particular embellishment, however excellent *per se*, can be guaranteed to match the voice and the mood of any given *cantatrice* on any given evening— the 30th of September, to take a date at random. This being so, it is flatly impossible for the singer in question to stir her audience to the most hidden recesses of their souls on the evening of the 30th of September *by means of this particular ornament*.[1]

[1] The genuinely impassioned lover may often speak a language which he scarcely understands himself; there is an intercourse of the spirit which transcends the narrow physical limitations of vocabulary. I might suggest that the art of singing shares this mysterious and inexplicable transcendentalism; but just as, in love, *artificiality is repulsive*, similarly in music, the voice must be allowed to be *natural*—that is to say, it should be allowed to sing melodies which have been especially written for it, in whose company it can feel at home, and of whose enchantment the singer herself, deep within her being, may be spontaneously aware at the very instant when she sings.

The *philistine* section of the audience, faced with any given passage, demands primarily the ornamentation which it has *grown to expect*; and provided that its taste is gratified in this direction, it will applaud the interpretation, no matter how appalling. But I am not concerned with such people, nor is this book addressed to them.[1] For I am persuaded that even outside Italy, yes, even in countries where it is normal to sing out of tune in church, there must exist small groups of genuine music-lovers, whose sensibility is sufficiently delicate (if I may risk the comparison) to act as a kind of microscope, through which they may detect and observe the most infinitesimal *nuances* in the art of singing. To persons such as these, I need make no apology for my own extravagant enthusiasms. And yet I should have to devote many pages to the subject, if I were to analyse every one of Madame Pasta's creations—and by *creations*, I mean certain individual means of expression, which are of her own invention and which, I would be prepared to swear, the composer who wrote the *notes* of her part never so much as contemplated.

A first example which I might quote is the evocative *stress* which she embodies in the line:

> Avrò contento il cuor . . .[2]

from Romeo's aria: *Ombra adorata, aspetta . . .*, and the slightly increased *tempo* of the *cantilena* which follows.[3] There is a similarly exquisite in-

---

[1] *Vide: le Corsaire*, 3rd October 1823.

[2] (Romeo discovers the dead Juliet in the tomb)

> *Romeo:*
> . . . Ma che vale il mio duol? Mia bella speme,
> Io ti sento, mi chiami
> A seguirti fra l'ombre: ebben m'aspetta,
> Ti seguirò [. . .]
> Ombra adorata, aspetta!
> Teco sarò indiviso;
> Nel fortunato Eliso
> Avrò contento il cuor.
>
> (Act III, sc. i)

[3] This is one of those typical and perfectly legitimate "stratagems" which the singer is quite entitled to employ, but which the insensitive and academic rigidity of the *Louvois* orchestra treats with such cruel and cynical indifference. The players in this orchestra all possess a degree of technical ability a hundred times greater than that of the average Italian musician in 1780; but the orchestra as a whole would have effectively stifled every spark of genius in a Marchesi or a Pacchiarotti, and it will continue to thwart and hinder every great singer whom Paris may produce. And if the singers should be rash enough to show themselves

vention in the way in which the preceding lines in the same scene are
inflected:

> *Io ti sento, mi chiami*
> *A seguirti fra l'ombre . . . etc.*

Any of the regular *habitués* of the *Théâtre Louvois* will recall the evening
when Madame Pasta first ventured to use these extraordinarily original
variants in her interpretation, and the kind of electric shock, infinitely
more flattering than any mere applause,[1] which ran instantaneously
round the auditorium; and yet, at any one of the twenty or thirty
performances of the same opera which had been given earlier, the
audience might have sworn that this admirable *prima donna* had already
carried her part to a height of unsurpassable perfection.

Later, during the course of the same evening, Madame Pasta enthralled us still further by displaying the prodigious contrast of her two
voices; and it was on this occasion that a friend of mine, a charming
young Neapolitan with a wide reputation as a connoisseur of music
and a wider one still as an enchanting lover, spoke to me in a tone of
such burning enthusiasm that I would give everything that I possess
in the world to be able to reproduce it here in cold print:

*This wondrous voice, with its swift succession of tones which shift like
shadow chasing sunlight, seems to distil a rare quintessence of delight and
memory, conjuring up the half-forgotten softness of the night in our unhappy
land—of those pure, crystalline nights, when the pattern of stars lay like a
silver web across the deepest blue of the sky, when the moonlight fell in shafts
of silence, haunting the quiet of that enchanted landscape which lay in stillness
spread across the banks of the Mergellina . . . the Mergellina, which I shall
never see again! Lost in the infinity of distance lies Capri, alone and islanded
in its silver sea, whose waves move softly at the cool beckoning of the night-
wind. And then, imperceptibly, gently, a diaphanous mist begins to steal across
the Huntress of the Night; an instant, and her light falls more tenderly, more
caressingly; nature, half-darkened, stirs the spirit more deeply, and wakes a
strange awareness in the souls of men. But wait . . . behold! Purer, brighter
than ever in her naked loneliness, Diana stands forth again in the Heavens,*

intimidated by the only too undeniable *erudition* of our instrumentalists, there is
the most pressing danger that we shall *never* witness true *bel canto*, with its
miraculous gift of *improvization*.

[1] Any fool can applaud with the rest; but to be *spell-bound*, one must possess a
soul. This is rare.

and the shores of Italy lie bathed once more in the living innocence of her silver-silent light. Thus with Madame Pasta: her voice, changing from register to register, inspires in me the same sensation as this memory of moonlight, veiled an instant, darker, softer, more entrancing ... then shining forth anew, a silver shower a thousand-fold increased.[1]

Or again, think how, at sunset, as the day-star sinks to rest behind Posilippo, our hearts seem to yield insensibly to sadness, and to be borne away upon a gentle tide of melancholy; a strange, inexpressible seriousness steals over our minds, and the harmony of our souls longs to be at peace with the still sadness of the evening. Likewise, just now, when Madame Pasta sang the phrase:

Ultimo pianto ...

I experienced the same emotion, with this difference only, that the transition was perhaps a little more rapid. It is the same feeling as that which clutches at my heart, but more persistently in the reality of life, when the first chill days of September steal across the traces of summer, and a light mist hovering about the tree-tops heralds the approach of winter and the death of nature's loveliness.

As we leave the theatre after a performance during which Madame Pasta has held us spell-bound ever since the first curtain, our whole being is filled, to the exclusion of all else, with the deep and boundless emotions which her voice has called up in the recesses of our soul. It would be useless to attempt a more specific analysis of a type of sensation which is at once so profound and so extraordinary. There seems to be nothing tangible to analyse, to pin one's admiration upon. The *timbre* of Madame Pasta's voice is not in itself superlatively brilliant; her technique and control hold nothing astonishing; the range which she commands is by no means abnormal; her secret lies wholly in her deep and passionate sincerity,

*Il canto che nell' anima si sente,**

which, in the short space of a couple of bars, can enthral and fascinate the wariest spectator—provided only (be it but once in all his life) he shall have wept for something other than money or *Orders of Merit.*

I could enumerate a longish catalogue of all the physical obstacles which nature had set in the path of Madame Pasta, and which she has

---

[1] There is only one *rational* standard by which *ideal beauty* may be assessed in any art: the *intensity of emotion* in the beholder.

had to overcome before she could learn the secret of communicating with that great collective spirit, the audience, and of electrifying it through the medium of her *voice*. Every day brings her some new triumph, and sees her a step further along the road to perfection; and every one of these steps is marked by one or another of those little, individual "creations", of which I spoke earlier. Incidentally, I did once ask a knowledgeable musician to dictate to me a list of her achievements; but I have decided finally to omit it, since the average reader, unless he chance to have had a *technical training* in the theory of music, would never understand a word of it. My subject is *beauty*; and it is as a painter, *not* as an anatomist, that I intend to discuss it, if I can; and in any case, I, who am ignorant, have no pretensions to indoctrinate the learned.

People have frequently sounded Madame Pasta's friends as to who taught her her craft as an *actress*. The answer is—*no one*! The only instruction which she has ever received has come straight from her own heart, from her own acutely sensitive reactions to the most delicate *nuances* of human passions, and from her admiration, so boundless as to verge upon the limits of absurdity, for *ideal beauty*. Once, in Trieste, while she was walking beside the harbour with a company of friends, a little three-year-old beggar-boy came up to her and asked for alms on behalf of his blind mother; she burst into tears and gave him all she had. Her friends, who had witnessed this incident, immediately began to speak of her virtue, her charitableness and the compassion of her heart. But she merely wiped away her tears and turned on them angrily: "I refuse to accept your commendation!" she exclaimed. "And I am *not* virtuous! But when that child came begging to me, he begged like a great artist. In a flash, I could see in his gesture all the despair of his mother, all the poverty of their home, the clothes which they need and the biting cold which is their relentless enemy. If, when the scene called for it, *I* could discover a gesture so faithfully portraying every suggestion of indescribable misery, I should be a very great actress indeed."

I suspect that Madame Pasta's genius as a tragic actress is made up of a thousand-and-one little casual *observations* of the kind which I have just recorded, modelled upon a series of tiny incidents which she has been gathering since the age of six, remembering them with vivid distinctness, and using them on the stage when the occasion demands.

But I have also heard Madame Pasta remark that she owes an incalculable debt to de' Marini, one of the greatest actors of the Italian school, and to the brilliant Signorina Pallerini, the actress who was specially trained by Viganò to play the parts of Myrrha, Desdemona and the Vestal Virgin in the ballets which he himself had created.

As a singer, Madame Pasta is too young to have heard Signora Todi on the stage; nor can she have heard Pacchiarotti, Marchesi or Crescentini; nor, as far as I can discover, did she ever have occasion to hear them later, after their retirement, in private performances or at concerts; yet every connoisseur who ever heard these great representatives of the Golden Age voices the general opinion that she appears to have inherited their style. The only teacher from whom she has received singing-lessons is Signora Grassini, with whom she once spent a season in Brescia.[1]

[1] There is an interesting passage concerning Signora Grassini to be found in Las Cases' *Mémorial de Sainte Hélène* (Vol. IV). Incidentally, no less recently than yesterday, I was privileged to look at a set of twelve incredibly passionate love-letters, in the handwriting of Napoleon himself, and addressed to Josephine; one at least dates from before their marriage. There is a passage, referring to the death of a certain Monsieur Chauvel, who appears to have been a close friend of Napoleon, which contains a most curious tirade upon the subject of death, immortality, *etc.*, quite worthy of Plato, or even of Werther! Several of these intimately passionate letters are written on vast sheets of official note-paper, headed with the device *Liberté, Egalité*, like a state document. Napoleon shows complete lack of interest in his own victories; but, in revenge, a passionate anxiety over the possibility of any serious rivals for Josephine's favours. "If you *must* love them, you must!" he writes on one occasion, "But you will never find one of them to love you as *I* have loved you!" After which, he adds: "We had a battle, both yesterday and to-day. I got better sport out of Beaulieu [the Austrian general] than out of the rest, but I intend to beat him hollow all the same!" I am very much afraid, however, that after the death of M. le Comte de B***, this precious set of twelve letters is liable to go to settle the grocer's bill.

CHAPTER XXXVI

La Donna del Lago

I⟨T⟩ may be asserted that, after *Elisabetta*, Rossini's work in Naples owed its success exclusively to his own individual genius. In the eyes of the general public, his principal claim to distinction lay in the fact that his style was a veritable revelation, at least compared with that of Mayr and of the various other academic and uninspired composers who had been his forerunners. Moreover, Rossini had introduced a hitherto unsuspected dynamic force into the supremely boring convention of the *opera seria*. It is quite possible, however, that his besetting laziness would have tempted him to sit back and rest on his laurels, had it not been for the implacable hostility shown by the public towards Barbaja and everything connected with his organization. But Rossini could not bear failure, and I have seen him physically ill when one of his works was whistled off the stage. (This is saying a great deal, in respect of a man whose outward bearing is one of supreme indifference, and who, furthermore, is unshakeably convinced of his own merit.) The actual occasion arose during the *première* of *la Donna del Lago*, an opera based on a bad poem by Walter Scott.

In this instance, the initial reaction to the performance was one of delight. The *décor* of the opening scene showed a wild and lonely loch in the Highlands of Scotland, upon whose waters the *Lady of the Lake*, faithful to her name, was seen gliding gracefully along, upright beside the helm of a small boat. This set was a masterpiece of the art of stage-design. The mind turned instantly towards Scotland, and waited expectantly for the magic of some Ossianic adventure. Signorina Colbran, who contrived to display considerable grace at the tiller of her skiff, managed to put up quite a creditable performance in her opening aria, and the audience, which was bursting for an opportunity to create an uproar, was grievously disappointed. The next number, a duet with Davide, was sung with some skill, and even beauty. But at last came the moment of Nozzari's entrance; he was required to come on at the very back of the stage; and the back-drop on that particular evening, was separated from the footlights by an absolutely *prodigious* distance. His part began with a *portamento*; and, as he opened his mouth to deliver a bellow of sustained sound, the effect was magnificent, and the echoes could have been heard right outside in the *via Toledo*. Unfortunately, however, since he was at the back of the stage, and the orchestra was in the front, he could not hear the instruments; and so his glorious *portamento* just fell about a quarter of a tone below the required pitch. At this unhoped-for chance to storm the stage with wild derision, the whole audience went mad as hatters, and the yell of malicious glee which ascended from the pit is still ringing in my ears!—a cage-full of roaring and ravenous lions, and the doors flung open!—Aeolus unleashing the fury of the winds! ... *nothing* can give the least, the sketchiest idea of the rage of a Neapolitan audience insulted by a wrong note, and so given the chance to work off a long-standing score of accumulated hatred!

Nozzari's aria was followed by the entry of a group of bards, who had come to infuse some military ardour into the Scottish army on its way to the battlefield. Rossini had had the idea of trying to rival the ball-scene from *Don Giovanni*, with its three orchestras, and so he had divided his orchestral resources into two sections, *viz.*, an accompanied chorus of bards on the one hand and, on the other, a military march with trumpets; and these two different musical effects, after each has been first heard separately, come together and are heard simultaneously.[1] Now it happened that this particular day (4th October 1819*) was a gala-day; the theatre was illuminated, but the Court was not present; and so there was nothing to restrain the exuberance of the young bloods and officers whose *privilege* it was to occupy the first five rows of the pit, and who had earlier been engaged in drinking the King's health with faithfulness, loyalty and ... persistence. At the first note which sounded on the trumpets, one of these gentlemen snatched up his cane, and started imitating the sound of a galloping horse. Soon this brilliant notion was taken up by the rest of the audience, and instantly, the whole *theatre-pit* became a *bear-pit*, the audience a screaming crowd composed of fifteen hundred schoolboys all busily imitating the noises of galloping horses, with a maximum energy and in strict

[1] Mozart, I feel, has shown greater ingenuity in solving a complex technical problem; but the final result is both clearer and more enjoyable in Rossini.

rhythm. The poor composer's ear-drums were not made to stand up to so infernal a din; he collapsed and retired.

But that very same night, he had to take the coach and set off post-haste for Milan, to fulfil an engagement contracted some time previously. We learned a fortnight later that, not only when he reached Milan itself, but at every post-station along the route, he had spread the news that *la Donna del Lago* had been a resounding success. In all good faith, he was lying, and we must therefore accord him the maximum of honour which is due to a valiant liar; but in actual fact, he was telling the truth. For, on the *5th* of October, the fair-minded and enlightened people of Naples, having slept on the matter and eventually come to realize the intolerable measure of their own injustice, had decided to make amends by applauding the new opera just as it deserved to be applauded; that is to say, with violent enthusiasm. Incidentally, the number of trumpets in the accompaniment to the bardic chorus had been reduced by half; and it must be admitted that, at the *première*, they had been deafening.

I recall that night of the 5th of October, when later in the evening, at a *soirée* held at the house of the Princess Belmonte, we poor fools were commiserating: "If only poor Rossini might hear of his success at some point on his journey, just think how it would console him! Isn't it a *shame* to think of him travelling all alone, and so *unhappy*!"—how little did we know of Rossini, and of his love of defiant bravado!

If I were not thoroughly ashamed of the disproportionate size which this book has already attained, I should risk a full and regular analysis of *la Donna del Lago*. Its essential construction is epic rather than dramatic, and the music most certainly retains a kind of *Ossianic* flavour, and a certain barbaric energy which is characteristically stimulating. Once the *fiasco* of the first-night was over and done with, the duet:

O matutini albori . . .[1]

sung by Davide and Signorina Colbran, was warmly and regularly applauded; its outstanding features are its freshness and a suggestion of *emotional sincerity* which is truly charming.

[1] *Elena:*
O matutini albori,
Vi ha preceduti amor;
Dai brevi miei sopori
A ridestarmi ognor . . .

The chorus of women's voices:

> D'Inabaca donzella . . .;[1]

the miniature duet:

> Le mie barbare vicende . . .[2]

sung by Davide and Signorina Colbran; and the aria:

> O quante lagrime[3]!*

sung by Signorina Pisaroni, are all masterpieces; the first-act *finale* is an extremely remarkable composition, and of the highest originality.

In the second act, the most outstanding numbers include the trio:

> Alla ragion deh ceda![4]

and the aria:

> Ah si pera . . .[5]

sung by Signorina Pisaroni, who rose to the front rank as a singer as a result of the reputation which she made by her performance in this opera.

The passions involved are less *dramatic* in this work than in *Otello*,

[1] *Coro:*
> D'Inabaca donzella,
> Che fe' d'immenso amore?
> Struggere un dì tremor . . .

[2] *Elena:*
> Le mie barbare vicende
> Che ti giova penetrar.

Uberto:
> Forse! Ah! Di! non è l'oggetto
> Che tu adori?
> Un altro amante sospirar,
> Languir ti fa?

[3] See above, p. 223

[4] *Elena:*
> Alla ragion deh ceda
> L'alma agitata, oppressa,
> Ed all' amor succeda
> La tenera amistà.

[5] *Malcolm:*
> Ah si pera! ormai la morte
> Fia sollievo ai mali miei,
> Se s'invola a me colei
> Che mi vesse in vita ognor.
> Ah! mio tesoro! Io ti perdei . . .

but the melodies are, I think, finer. On the whole, the music is *simpler*, more *spianato*; take, for instance, the delightful aria:

Ma dov' è colei che accende?[1]

It was generally agreed among the *dilettanti* of Naples that *la Donna del Lago* marked a first step upon the return road towards the style of the earlier part of Rossini's career, towards the musical atmosphere which is prevalent in *l'Inganno felice* and in *Demetrio e Polibio*; in connection with which I would like to add that not only *Demetrio*, but in particular *Tancredi*, is composed in a style which, *in my personal opinion*, is the finest thing that Rossini has achieved, and which, as a result of a more perfect balance maintained between melody and harmony, is the better calculated to produce a pleasing effect. By this statement, of course, I have no intention of implying that *Tancredi* comes nearest to perfection in its musical ideas, less still that it is Rossini's greatest opera. Since the period of *Tancredi* Rossini has acquired far greater depth, and his music has achieved a forcefulness far more dynamic in character; but his ideas are to some extent vitiated by the influence of a falsely-conceived *theory*.

[1] *Rodrigo di Rhu:*
Ma dov'è colei che accende
Dolce fiamma nel mio seno?
De' suoi lumi un sol baleno
Fa quest' anima bear . . .

CHAPTER XXXVII

Concerning eight minor Operas by Rossini

Here follow a number of operas, about which I intend to write no more than a few words, either because I myself have never seen them, or else because they are totally unknown in Paris. I might say, for instance, that the aria:

O crude stelle!

from the opera *Adelaide di Borgogna* (Rome, 1818*), is a remarkable composition, delightful to listen to, and furnishing an exquisite portrait of despair in a heart of sixteen summers (in this particular instance, the despair of Walter Scott's "Miss Ashton"); but what conceivable meaning could an *ex cathedra* statement of this character hold for a reader who is probably hearing the title *Adelaide di Borgogna* for the first time at this very moment?

During the autumn season of the year 1817, an opera called *Armida* was presented in Naples. Nozzari played the part of Rinaldo, and Signorina Colbran, that of Armida herself. It was brilliantly successful*, and contains what must be one of the finest of all Rossini's duets, and certainly the most celebrated:

*Amor, possente nome!**[1]

Not infrequently it appears that the fundamental quality of some of Rossini's finest compositions is not true *emotion*, but *physical excitement*, developed to the most extraordinary degree; and this is so striking in this particular duet from *Armida* that, one Sunday morning, after a

[1] *Rinaldo:*
　　　Amor! possente nome!
　　　Come risuoni!
　　　Come su quel soave labbro
　　　Nel mio dolente cor!
　Armida:
　　　Sì, amor! Se un' alma fiera
　　　Ti diè natura in sorte,
　　　Recami pur la morte
　　　E in me fia spento amor.

truly superlative performance at the *Casino di Bologna*, I observed that many of the ladies present were actually too embarrassed to praise it*. And yet, towards the end of the first section, there are distinct traces of a certain lack of precision in the scoring, which might almost lead one to suspect that this duet is the work of an apprentice at the craft. In spite of its great triumph in Naples, there is no evidence that this opera has ever been revived on other stages. The librettist is culpably responsible for a serious flagging of dramatic tension in parts, and he has made a pitiable hash of Rinaldo's wonderful narrative. Some of the choruses, however, are excellent.

Ricciardo e Zoraide (1818, autumn season): original cast including Davide, Nozzari and Signorina Colbran. The *libretto* is by the late Marchese Berio, one of the most charming men in Naples, and is based on an episode from Ricciardetto's epic, with no more fundamental alteration than a change of names for the characters. I have only seen this opera once or twice; my only clear recollection is that it was extremely well-received. In the first act, the greatest applause was reserved for a duet between le Signorine Colbran and Pisaroni:

In van tu fingi, ingrata![1]

for a trio between the same two singers, *plus* Nozzari:

Cruda sorte . . .,[2]

and for Davide's *cavatina**:

[1] *Zomira:*
  Invan tu fingi, ingrata!
  No, che l'interno ardore
  Un labbro mentitore,
  No, che celar non sà!
 Zoraide:
  Che dura prova è questa . . .
[2] *Zoraide:*
  Cruda sorte!
 Agorande:
      (Oh! amor tiranno!)
 Zomira:
  Io sprezzata!
 Zoraide:
     Più non reggo!
 A tre:
  L'alma mia fremendo stà!

O

Frena, o ciel![1]

while, in Act II, the most successful number was the duet:

Ricciardo, che veggo?[2]

The style of the opera as a whole is impassioned and full of oriental grandeur; one of its features is the absence of an overture*. Rossini shows a distinct tendency to grow bored with the drudgery of writing overtures, and therefore has proved, with a fine display of logic and reason, that they are unnecessary.

Ermione (1819) was no more than a qualified success, and only an odd item here and there received any noticeable applause. This opera was an experiment, Rossini having been tempted to try his hand at a work in the French tradition*.

Maometto secondo (1820)—a work which I have not seen. At the time, I learned from various correspondents that it became fairly popular. Certainly it contains a number of remarkable *ensembles*. The *libretto*, to the best of my belief, is by the Duke of Ventignano, who enjoys the reputation in Naples of being the finest living Italian tragic dramatist. Galli, I am told, was superb in the part of Mahomet.

Matilde Shabran (Rome, *Teatro Apollo*, 1821). In this production the cast was led by that attractive little *prima donna*, Signorina Liparini. Execrable *libretto*, but pretty music—such was the general verdict.

Zelmira, which was first performed in Naples in 1822, created a *furore* both there and in Vienna. Stylistically speaking, nothing could be further removed from the original conception of *Tancredi* and *Aureliano in Palmira* than this opera, which should be compared with Mozart's *la Clemenza di Tito*, similarly as far removed as possible from the style of *Don Giovanni*. But these two giants of music have proceeded in opposite directions, for while Mozart would probably, had he lived, have grown completely *Italian*, Rossini may well, by the end of his

---

[1] *Ernesto:*
   Frena, o Ciel, nel tuo dolore
   Or che siamo a lui d'innante
   Quell' ardire che nel sembiante
   Suole imprimere l'amore!

[2] *Zoraide:*
   Ricciardo? Che veggo!
   Mancare mi sento!
   In tanto contento
   Son fuori di me!

career, have become more *German* than Beethoven himself! I have heard a concert-recital of *Zelmira*, but I have never seen it on the stage, and so I dare not offer any criticism.

But the degree of Teutonism revealed in *Zelmira* is nothing compared with that which is displayed in *Semiramide*, which Rossini produced in Venice in 1823. Rossini, I fancy, must have been guilty of a slip in his geographical calculations, for this opera, which in Venice escaped ignominy only by grace of the composer's sacred and untouchable reputation, would probably have been hailed, in Königsberg or in Berlin, as a miracle straight from heaven. I have never seen it in performance, but I am not irretrievably broken-hearted over this loss, since the extracts which I have heard in concert-arrangement have left me singularly unenthusiastic.[1]

Several of Rossini's operas, including among others *la Donna del Lago*, *Ricciardo e Zoraide*, *Zelmira* and *Semiramide*, are not suited for production in Paris, on account of the lack of a contralto with sufficient technique to execute music written for Signorina Pisaroni.[2]

In any case, I should not advise anybody to experiment with these operas at the *Louvois*. The finest passages have already been removed from their context and inserted in other works—for example, the aria:

Oh! quante lagrime . . .

from *la Donna de Lago* has been transferred by Madame Pasta into *Otello*—and besides, musically speaking, it is quite likely that these operas would seem feeble compared with *Otello* or *Mosè*.

I should hasten to add that these remarks in no way apply to *la Donna del Lago* itself, in whose superb and markedly original score Rossini, probably for the first time in his life, received some positive help from his *libretto*. Given favourable circumstances, this opera could crush every disparagement; but it is absolutely essential that it should be given a set designed and painted by artists imported from Italy. The utterly *absurd* staging of *gli Orazi* in the latest revival which we saw here recently, would be the surest guarantee of turning *la Donna del*

---

[1] Anyone who prefers *Mosè* to *Tancredi* will have a higher opinion than I of *Semiramide* . . . *e sempre bene!* So long as he remain sincere, we shall *both* be right.

[2] Unquestionably, there must *exist* a certain number of contraltos in France; but as soon as a young lady evinces difficulty in reaching G or A, she is invariably told that "she has no voice". *Cf.* an excellent article on the subject by M***, in the *Journal des Débats*, July 1823.

Lago (which to some extent *requires* visual illusion) into a complete *fiasco*. Moreover, it needs an unusually large stage, to accommodate the marching and counter-marching of the Scottish army, together with the famous bardic chorus. Incidentally, there is some resemblance with Lesueur's opera *les Bardes*; or rather, there would be, if Lesueur's *genius* happened to match Rossini's.

In 1819 (to the best of my recollection), Rossini also produced a Mass* in Naples, spending a good three days trying to dress up some of his noblest themes in a semblance of ecclesiastical dignity. The experience was delightful, as one by one all the composer's finest melodies passed in solemn procession before our eyes, each *slightly altered in form*, so that it became a most interesting game to try and identify them*! A priest who happened to be present was heard to exclaim to Rossini, in deadly earnest: *Rossini, my son, if you took this Mass and went a-hammering with it at the very gates of Paradise, St Peter himself couldn't find it in his heart to close the door in your face, sinner that you are!*—a sentiment which sounds delicious in Neapolitan dialect, owing to the grotesque forcefulness of its idiom.

CHAPTER XXXVIII

Bianca e Faliero

W E last caught a glimpse of Rossini on the night of the 4th of
October 1819, riding post-haste out of Naples, to the accompaniment
of a hail of derisive abuse. In the same year, on the 26th of December,
he was in Milan, producing *Bianca e Faliero*. The theme is very closely
modelled on Manzoni's tragedy, *il Conte di Carmagnola*.[1] The scene is
set in Venice. The *Council of Ten* has just passed sentence of death upon
a young general, whose victories have aroused the jealous suspicions
of the oligarchs; but Faliero is loved by Bianca, the daughter of the
Doge himself. The part of Bianca was excellently sung by Signora
Camporesi; that of Faliero, by Signora Carolina Bassi, the only singer
whose style in any way rivals that of Madame Pasta. The *décor*, which
represented the Council-Chamber of the *Ten* was a masterpiece of
dramatic atmosphere. The very magnificence of this hall, its gloom and
hugeness, its panels hung with drapes of purple velvet, its scattering of
candles in golden sconces providing a dim and fitful illumination—all
this alone was enough to strike terror into the heart of the observer.
One felt already in the presence of *Despotism*, all-powerful and inexorable. Let the poverty of our resources or the insensibility of our
souls protest as they will, there is no more evocative commentary upon
fine dramatic music than that provided by a fine dramatic *décor*; nothing
is better calculated to tempt the mind out of itself and send it forth
upon the first stage of its journey into the world of illusion; no
medium on earth is better fitted to prime the soul into a state of musical
receptivity than the little thrill of pleasure which runs through the
audience as the curtain goes up at *la Scala*, and the magnificence of the
set is revealed for the first time.

[1] M. Fauriel, whose style as a writer is a model of purity, and who, into the
bargain, is a man of the most alert intelligence, has recently given us a French
translation of *il Conte di Carmagnola* (1823). I wonder if there is any price that
the true theatre-lover would think too high to see *Shakespeare* translated in so
delightful a style? Incidentally, *il Conte di Carmagnola* contains the finest ode,
I fratelli hanno ucciso i fratelli! which has yet been written in the XIXth century—
at least, that is my opinion.

The design for the Council-Chamber of the *Ten* in *Bianca e Faliero* was one of Sanquirico's supreme achievements; but as to Rossini's music, the whole score was a hotch-potch of reminiscences which earned scarcely the thinnest applause, and indeed came close to being whistled at. The audience proved to be in a highly critical frame of mind, and a technically intricate aria rendered with frigid virtuosity by Signora Camporesi did nothing to disarm the prevailing hostility. This aria came later to be known as the *garland aria*,[1] because Bianca is holding a garland in her hand as she sings it. In actual fact, there was only one original number in the whole of *Bianca e Faliero*: a quartet—but, as though in compensation for the rest, this quartet (and in particular, the clarinet-part in the accompaniment) must rank among the noblest conceptions with which any *maestro* in the world has ever been inspired. I would maintain boldly, and if not with truth, at least with the fullest conviction, that there is nothing in the whole of *Otello*, nothing in the whole of *la Gazza ladra*, to stand comparison with it for a single moment. The music has something of the tenderness of Mozart, but without his profound pathos. I am prepared to poise this quartet[2] unashamedly upon the pinnacle and summit of Rossini's achievement, declaring its brilliance to be not a jot less than the finest things in *Tancredi* or *la Sigillara*.

Almost immediately after the initial run of this opera, the number was transferred to a ballet which was to be given in the same theatre; and thus the same audiences heard the same music continuously for six months on end without ever growing tired of it—in fact, as soon as it was due to be played, the house fell into an awed and impressive silence.

Whenever my conscience begins to accuse me of having uttered too many exaggerations in this little book on music, I hum over to myself the theme of this quartet; and immediately my self-confidence returns. Somewhere deep within me, there is a secret voice which whispers: *If there are people who cannot feel it as I feel it, so much the worse for them! Why should they go buying books which were not intended for them in the first place?*

[1] *Bianca:*
　　　Della rosa il bel vermiglio
　　　L'amor mio gli pingerà ;
　　　Il candor di questo giglio
　　　La mia fè gli mostrerà
　　　　　　　(Act I, sc. v)

[2] *Bianca:*
　　　Cielo il mio labbro ispira . . .

CHAPTER XXXIX

Odoardo e Cristina

A YEAR before the production of *Bianca e Faliero*, Rossini had played a singularly unscrupulous trick upon a certain Venetian *impresario*; the incident had reached the ears of the public in Venice; and the failure of *Bianca* was in large measure due to a widespread suspicion among the audience that they might be tricked into applauding music served up cold from another opera. In the spring of 1819, Rossini had been engaged by the *impresario* of the *teatro San-Benedetto** in Venice for the sum of four or five hundred *sequins,* which represented an enormous sum in Italy at the time. The *libretto* which the *impresario* forwarded to Rossini in Naples was entitled *Odoardo e Christina.*

At that epoch, Rossini was head-over-heels in love with Mademoiselle Chaumel (la Comelli); and he had not the strength of mind to tear himself away from Naples until precisely a fortnight before the *première* at the *San-Benedetto* was due to be given. However, to calm the growing impatience of the *impresario*, he had at odd intervals sent off to him a fair selection of quite creditable musical numbers. Admittedly, the words of the original text seemed to bear little or no resemblance to those of the songs which kept turning up in Venice— but who ever worries about the *words* in an *opera seria?* They are always the same, the identical nonsense from one *libretto* to the next, *felicità, felice ognora, crude stelle, etc., etc.,* and I doubt if a single person in all Venice ever read the text of a *libretto serio*; not even the *impresario* himself who had commissioned and paid for it! In any case, when Rossini *did* finally condescend to put in an appearance, there were no more than nine days left before the opening night. The early scenes of the opera were greeted with frantic applause; but unfortunately there sat in the pit a solitary Neapolitan business-man, who proceeded to provoke a frantic state of consternation among his immediate neighbours by singing the theme of every number *before* the performers on the stage had reached it. Everybody was naturally intensely curious to discover where he had already managed to hear this supposedly original music. "Where have I heard it before?" he exclaimed. "Why, in Naples, of course, six months ago, in *Ermione* and *Ricciardo e Zoraide*. It was very popular, you know! But the only thing I can't understand is, why did you go and change the title? In any case, the *cavatina* of your nice new opera is patched together out of the best phrases from a duet in *Ricciardo*:

Ah! nati è ver noi siamo . . .[1]

and Rossini hasn't even bothered to change the words!"

During the long interval and the ballet which filled it, this fatal piece of information was passed with lightning speed from table to table round the coffee-houses, where the foremost *dilettanti* of the land were busy arguing out the rational bases of their spontaneous enthusiasm. In Milan, the incident would have provoked all the furies known to outraged patriotic vanity; but in Venice, everybody burst out laughing instead. Ancillo, a charming man and a renowned poet, produced an impromptu *sonetto* lamenting the ill-fortune of Venice, compared with the good fortune of Mademoiselle Chaumel. Meanwhile, however, the poor *impresario*, who was likely to be financially ruined by the scandal, rushed off in a fit of uncontrollable rage in search of Rossini. At length he discovered him; but Rossini, with unexpected coolness and impudence, simply retorted: "What did I contract to do? *Merely* to provide you with music which should be applauded. *This* music *has* been applauded, *e tanto basta*. Furthermore, if you had possessed an atom of commonsense, you could hardly have helped noticing that the edges of the manuscript I sent you were already turning yellow with age, and therefore you could hardly fail to realize that the music which I was forwarding from Naples was already old. Any *impresario* worth his salt, Sir, should be sharper than an old Jew; whereas you, Sir, show every symptom of being as innocent as a babe in arms!"

If anyone other than Rossini had been guilty of such an atrocious piece of impertinence, the insult could have been avenged only by the stiletto; but this *impresario* was a true devotee of music, and he was so enraptured by what he had already heard (it being, for him at least, a

[1] *Ricciardo:*
    Ah! nati è ver noi siamo
    Sol' per amarci ognor!
    Ciò, che tu brami, io bramo;
    Noi non abbiam che un cor.

genuine *première*), that he promptly forgave the sins and omissions inspired by love in a man of genius.[1]

This expedient, designed to meet a particular emergency in Venice, was only an *extreme instance* of what has unfortunately become Rossini's normal practice. For several years now it has been his main concern to secure contracts for his operas in *different* cities; he then proceeds to compose one or two genuinely original numbers; and all the rest is concocted out of old ideas refashioned to suit the context. This explains how it has happened that the key-note of *originality*, which forms such an essential constituent of *beauty in music*, is often absent (if the listener should happen to be a man of any considerable experience in the field) from compositions which, in all other respects, are so lively and so entertaining.

This peculiar Rossinian habit, moreover, makes it excessively difficult to reply to the question, *which is his finest opera?*

(I intend to leave out of account the wider question, whether it is legitimate to prefer the simplicity of *Tancredi* to the stylistic luxuriousness of *Ricciardo e Zoraide*, with its ornamentation transmuted into thematic material.)

In the overture to the *Barber* there is a passage of quite entrancing deliciousness: but here is the rub—the idea had already been used once before in *Tancredi*, and a second time, rather later, in *Elisabetta*. In the latter instance it appears as the theme of a duet, and this is probably the happiest of the three different versions. Ideally, then, one's first encounter with this delightful musical idea should be in the duet-version; but that depends vastly on luck. If one happens to have met with it earlier, whether in *Tancredi* or else in the *Barber*, the odds are that one will find the duet merely exasperating. Given the loan of a piano, and of a competent pianist to go with it, I could give *thirty* examples of such typically Rossinian transformations.

There is a curious thesis still to be written—an analytical survey of all the musical items in Rossini's operas which are *really distinct and independent*; this to be followed by a second survey of all the items *based upon similar musical ideas*, with footnotes indicating in each in-

---

[1] A correspondent in Turin informs me that Madame Pasta has recently (1822) appeared in *Odoardo e Cristina* with breath-taking success. This version of *Odoardo* was compiled from a selection of the more popular numbers out of previous operas by Rossini which had not yet been heard in Turin.

stance the particular aria or duet which embodies the most satisfactory version.

Among my many acquaintances in Naples, I have met a score of young fellows who would be perfectly competent to complete a study of this kind in a couple of days, and with as much off-handed nonchalance as a Londoner might show in dashing off a critical essay on the eleventh *canto* of *Don Juan*, or a Parisian in giving birth to a ponderous and learned article on the *Theory of Public Credit* or a pretty little satire concerning some adolescent piece of devilry perpetrated by an Honourable Minister in Council upon a Senior President of the Courts. Amid the gay round of Neapolitan social life, one might meet a hundred young men, any one of whom, if really put to it, could write a light-opera at least as good as *Ser Marc Antonio* or *il Barone di Dolsheim*—and take no more than six weeks about it. The difference is, course, that no professional *maestro* who has gone through the regular discipline of the *Conservatoire* would dream of spending so much as a fortnight on any opera in this style or category.

My Neapolitan friends used to claim that it was the easiest thing in all the world to *resurrect* fifty masterpieces by Paisiello or Cimarosa. One merely had to bide one's time until they were all completely forgotten (a state of things which will be fully realized in a year or two: as it is, only one of all Paisiello's operas, *la Scuffiara*, survives in the normal repertoire); and then, along comes some neat-fingered and intelligent musical carpenter, some composer, say, who is taking a rest-cure, and who is forbidden by doctor's orders to put his mind to anything serious (Signor Pavesi, for instance); *he* takes hold of Paisiello's *Pirro*, lops off the recitatives, re-scores and re-orchestrates the accompaniment, and adds a new set of *finales*. Obviously the hardest part of the job would be to convert the most original passage in each act into material for a *finale*. I wonder how often it would occur, in the course of this experiment in musical joinery, that one would stumble upon tunes which seem to reveal a striking resemblance to the more popular successes of our greater living composers ...? I confess that, if the lovely quartet from *Bianca e Faliero* were to be among the forgotten treasures thus unearthed, I should be genuinely disappointed!

In the present phase of his career, Rossini stands most urgently in need of a few resounding and humiliating *flops*. Unfortunately, however, I can think of nowhere, other than Naples and Milan, where there are audiences who are *worthy* to call down a similar *fiasco* upon his head; in any other town, an incident of this nature might arise through hatred, but it could never represent a conscious critical judgement. Rossini spent the year 1822 in Vienna; and in 1824, so the rumour goes, London will have the privilege of being his host. But in London, far from the accustomed theatre of his glory, Rossini will find only greater license and liberty to give out old music for new; thus his natural weakness will receive nothing but encouragement.

If we are to see him really on his mettle, let us hope that the London *impresario* will confront him with the *libretto* of *Don Giovanni* or of *il Matrimonio segreto*, and tell him to set *that* to music!

CHAPTER XL

Concerning Rossini's Style

Before concluding, I must say a word or two about the characteristic features of Rossini's style—a duty which follows inescapably from the theme of this book. To compose a treatise upon painting, and to write in praise of pictures presents difficulties which are already almost insuperable; but pictures at least leave a distinct and tangible impression on the mind, even when that mind belongs to a fool. Consider, then, the proportionate difficulty in talking about music under the same circumstances! Is there any phrase so outlandish or so absurd, that it may not offer some sort of temptation to the poor critic at his wits' end? The reader may well imagine that he will not be forced to dig very deep in order to unearth a few specimens!

Great music is nothing but *our emotion*. It would appear that music creates a sensation of pleasure by compelling the imagination to sustain itself temporarily upon a peculiar kind of fantasy. The fantasies of music are neither *calm* and *sublime* (as they are in sculpture), nor *sentimental* and *musing* (as they are in the paintings of Correggio).

The most striking quality in Rossini's music is a peculiar *verve*, a certain stirring rapidity which lightens the spirit, banishing all those grave, half-conscious musings conjured up from the very depths of being by the slow, sad strains of Mozart. And close on the heels of this first quality comes a second, a kind of *freshness*, which evokes a smile of pleasure at every bar. As a result, almost any score seems dull and heavy beside one of Rossini's. If Mozart were to dawn unheralded upon the world to-day, such is the severe verdict that would be passed upon his music. To learn to appreciate him, we should have to listen to him every day for a fortnight; but, at the *première*, he would be hissed off the stage. If Mozart still manages to survive beside Rossini, if sometimes one even *prefers* him, it is because he is rich with the accumulated treasures of all our past admiration, and beloved for the delight which he has given us over the years.

Generally speaking, it is only those whose courage lies beyond the fear of ridicule who dare openly prefer Mozart. To the common run of *dilettanti*, Mozart occupies a position similar to that of Fénelon in the eyes of the common run of writers: they praise him religiously, and would die rather than imitate his style!

On the other hand, if Rossini's music is never ponderous, it is desperately easy to hear too much of it*. The most distinguished representatives of the *dilettanti* of Italy, who have now been listening to it for twelve years, have been beginning, in these last times, to ask for something fresh. What will happen in twenty years' time, when the *Barber of Seville* will be as old-fashioned as *il Matrimonio segreto* or *Don Giovanni*?

Rossini is rarely sad—but what is music without at least a *hint* of pensive melancholy?

> *I am never merry when I hear sweet music*[1]

—so writes the author of *Cymbeline* and *Othello*, he who, best of all the poets of the modern age, had sounded the secrets of the human soul.

In this unquiet, unleisured century of ours, Rossini has one further advantage: *his music demands no concentration.*

In any drama where the music makes a serious attempt to interpret the precise *nuance* or measure of feeling which is embodied in the text, the listener is obliged to concentrate before he can be moved, or, in other words, before he can begin to derive enjoyment from what he hears. There is even, perhaps, a still more stringent condition attached to the appreciation of music: before he can *feel*, he must possess a *soul*. But in Rossini's music, the contrary is true; Rossinian scores, full of arias and duets which, all too often, are no more than brilliant firework-displays for the concert-platform,[2] demand no more than the slightest, the most *careless* effort of attention, for the listener to harvest all the pleasure which they may afford; nor is it necessary, on all save the rarest occasions, to own that thing which some romantic fools have called a soul—an incalculable advantage!

I am only too well aware how urgently so wild an assertion cries out for justification. Very well, then; open the piano, please, and

---

[1] *Merchant of Venice.*
[2] Particularly in the operas written for Signorina Colbran during Rossini's Neapolitan period.

recall how, in *il Matrimonio segreto*[1] (Act I, scene i), Carolina, rich in the happiness of being reunited with her lover, reflects tenderly upon the bliss which might be their lot:

Se amor si gode in pace . . .[2]

These words, with their utter simplicity, have conjured up one of the loveliest musical phrases in the world. But, in the *Barber of Seville*, when Rosina, who had come to think of her lover as a prodigy of ingratitude and a monster of depravity, and had even suspected him of trying to sell her to "Count Almaviva", discovers after all that he is true to her, and so encounters one of those supreme instants of rapture and content, the like of which it is rarely given to the human soul to experience—in these circumstances, Rosina, thankless little wretch that she is, can find nothing better to offer us than a tinselly garland of *fioriture*, which (one suspects) simply happened to be those which Signora Giorgi (the original Rosina) was able to master with the least show of awkwardness. No one could call these *fioriture* (which, admittedly, would sound very nice on the concert-platform) in any degree *sublime*; but Rossini was determined that everybody should find them *amusing*, and he has succeeded. This is not only a fault, but an inexcusable one; it is an aesthetic blunder of the first magnitude to portray the deep contentment which I have just described as mere superficial hilarity; and incongruities such as this are typical of the worst defect of his "second manner"—his tendency to score his music by the elementary process of piling in lock, stock and barrel all the embellishments which his artists have been in the habit of using *ad libitum* to ornament the works of *other* composers. Very often a piece of music which had originally been nothing but a more or less charming frill is transformed into a feature of major importance—for instance, the *tremolo* passages which appear so frequently in parts written for Galli (*l'Italiana in Algeri*,

---

[1] If I seem to be quoting the *Secret Marriage* rather too frequently, it is merely because it is one of the three or four operas which I can assume to be thoroughly familiar to the four or five hundred serious *dilettanti* to whom this book is addressed.

[2] *Carolina, Paolino:*
        Se amor si gode in pace,
        Non v'è maggior contento;
        Ma non v'è ugual tormento,
        Se ognor s'ha da tremar.
                (Act I, sc. i)

Sigillara, il Turco in Italia, la Gazza ladra, Maometto, etc.). It could scarcely be denied that ornamentation of this character is uncommonly elegant, nor that it lends an air of great vivacity, often of the most seductive freshness, to the music; but it is no less true that any trio or aria so decorated will most assuredly lose whatever finer shades of feeling it once possessed, and degenerate into a show-piece of gilt and glittering virtuosity.

Or would you prefer to arrive at the same conclusion by way of a different argument? Rossini, in obedience to a generally-accepted convention, composed all his operas upon the assumption that his two acts would be separated by an interval of at least an hour and a half, perhaps containing a ballet. But in France, where people in pursuit of pleasure would do anything rather than dream of being *natural*, one would be left feeling that one's Rossini-worship was spurious and superficial unless one were prepared to spend three hours on end, without an instant's relief or relaxation, listening to his music. This surfeit of music, imposed with such *intelligence* and *foresight* upon a race which possesses less patience and better ballet-dancers than any other in Europe, becomes utterly intolerable in the case of *Don Giovanni*, or any other similar, deeply-moving work. After four un-interrupted acts of *le Nozze di Figaro*, there is not a single member of the audience who is not sick with head-ache and sheer exhaustion, and an experience of this devastating character is sufficient to put one off music altogether for a whole week; but such cantankerous and un-kind thoughts never enter one's head for an instant after listening to the two uninterrupted acts of *Tancredi* or *Elisabetta*. Rossini's music, which is perpetually slithering over the brink into the echoing abyss of concert-platform virtuosity, is ideally suited to this brilliant arrange-ment devised by the Parisian theatre for its long-suffering public, and emerges triumphant from such a searching test. In every conceivable sense, Rossini's music is *French* music; but for all that, it is bringing us every day nearer to a state of mind in which, eventually, we may deserve to hear the accents of *genuine passion*.

CHAPTER XLI

Concerning Rossini's Attitude towards certain Composers
among his Contemporaries
and
Concerning his personal Character

Rossini adores Cimarosa, and his eyes fill with tears whenever he mentions his name.

Among academic composers, his greatest respect is reserved for Signor Cherubini, of the *Conservatoire de Paris*. Who can guess what this noble composer *might* have achieved, if the growing influence of German music had not quenched the last spark of love in his soul, or rather, if it had not banished the last shred of feeling which he still retained for the melody of his native land!

If Mayr were still actively composing, Rossini would be terrified of him; but Mayr himself, in return for this proof of respectful humility, is charmingly fond of his young rival, loving him with all the clumsy affection of his honest Bavarian heart.

Rossini has the highest opinion of Signor Pavesi, who has produced work of uncommon power and character, and he is sincerely anxious about this composer's failing health, which, young as he is, has already driven him into retirement. Incidentally, it is interesting to hear the man who composed the *Barber* maintain that, in the particular *buffo* style which is known as *nota e parola*, there is no further progress possible after Fioravanti. I have heard him add that he could imagine nothing more absurd in all the world than the fatuousness of presuming to meddle with *opera buffa*, after the unsurpassed state of perfection to which this form had already been raised by Paisiello, Cimarosa and Guglielmi.

One thing which stands out clearly from this confession is that Rossini has no conception whatsoever of the emergence of a *new ideal of beauty*. Pursuing his original idea, he insists that no one can hope to propose any *new* aesthetic ideals, since, in the short period which has

elapsed between Guglielmi's day and our own, the nature of man has
had too little time for development. We shall have to wait another
fifty years, he maintains, before a new public emerges to make new
demands upon its artists; but when that happens, each of us will seek
to serve it, following the promptings of his own particular genius. To
some extent, I have had to condense Rossini's reasoning, but without
distorting the general sense of his argument. I once heard him pro-
pounding this point of view in an onslaught of spluttering fury directed
against some poor pedant from Berlin, who had had the effrontery to
stand there, armed with a few thin quotations from Kant, and oppose
the *instinctive feelings* of a man of genius! Yet, in connection with
Rossini, I could sincerely wish that the cold North would undertake
some serious reflection, and acquire, perhaps, a deeper critical awareness of itself on the one hand, and of Rossini on the other, of his gaiety
and of his musical ability. Certain northern critics have seen fit to
accuse some of Rossini's numbers of being "too frivolous";[1] I
shudder to imagine the distress which might seize upon these poor
pompous men of letters, if ever they were to find themselves confronted with a real *opera buffa*—with the aria:

Signor, sì, il genio è bello![2]

for instance, which is sung by the Pedant in Paisiello's *la Scuffiara*; or
with Cimarosa's aria:

Amicone del mio core . . .

etc., etc. If a person is obviously about as sensitive as a rotten tree-stump,

[1] *Vide: le Miroir* (December 1821), referring to the *cra-cra!* passage in the *finale*
of *l'Italiana in Algeri*; the style of which passage, however, is no more than *di
mezzo carattere*.

[2] *Don Gavino:*
   Signor, sì: il genio è bello;
   Non si nega, io son con te.
   Ma se va col campanello,
   Ma se mandi la trombetta,
   Mara figlia benedetta,
   Non lo peschi, non lo trovi
   Un tel mostro come me . . .
In the original Neapolitan *libretto*, the pedant apostrophizes the little dress-
maker in words something like this: "You couldn't have chosen anyone better
in the world to fall in love with than *me*, now could you? You could hunt through
America, you could search all Asia, you could go half-way round the world and
back again, and never find anyone quite like *me* . . ."

even to the least esoteric *nuances* of an aria, had that person not do better to hold his tongue?

Let the North busy itself with its *Foreign Bible Societies*, with its *Utilitarianism* and its *Finance*; let Peers of the Realm in England, rolling in their millions, spend the day from dawn to dusk in grave discussion with their agents concerning the problem of a twenty-five per cent reduction in the rents of their innumerable tenants; meanwhile, the poor Italian, who only finds his fetters more securely fastened, and the hideous injustices which he endures more tyrannously prosecuted, by the efforts, direct and indirect, of such pious and humanitarian folk, knows only too well what *he* should think of so much virtue.[1] *His* enjoyment lies in art; he has learned to appreciate *beauty* in every shape and form which nature has been pleased to bestow upon his surroundings; there is pity rather than hatred in his look as he scrutinizes the dreary features of the northerner. *What do you expect?* I heard one day from one of the most charming of the poor citizens of Venice: *These pious, gloomy folk treat Venice like a colony; we are eight hundred thousand people, and they give us orders, and call us barbarians, because we are uncivilized enough to prefer our sunshine to their snows! But we watch them being* bored, *and that is our revenge!*

Let the great lords of the earth look down from the clouded summits of their aristocratic pride and from their haunts of luxury, and cast a glance of pity upon poor Rossini, who, in thirteen years of unrelenting labour and self-denial bordering upon parsimony, has still not managed to set aside a mere sixty or eighty thousand francs against his old age*. Yet I might add that poverty is no hardship to *him*; he needs no more exotic entertainment than a piano or a fool. In Italy, no matter where, in the humblest tavern as in the most brilliant *salon*, the name of Rossini has only to be spoken for every eye to turn and look at him; the seat of honour is his by right, and where he is becomes the seat of honour; adoration and sincere respect surround him, such as the noblest lord can nowhere find in Italy, unless he be prepared to fling away a hundred thousand francs a year, and smile at his own enforced *largesse*. Rossini's fame brings him every advantage which could

---

[1] I would refer the reader to the accounts of the journeys made by Sharp and Eustace; to those of Lord Bentinck's proclamation to the Genoese; of the Admirals Nelson and Caracciolo; also to the anecdote of the "corpse which stood upright on the sea"*.

accrue from great wealth, and so he only remembers his poverty when he happens to think specifically of the number of gold pieces which he possesses. The unique position which he occupies in Italy is the main reason why it was so absurd to propose that he should come and live in Paris, where, after a brief blaze of glory as a nine-days' wonder, he would swiftly have found himself relegated behind the rank and dignity of half a thousand Ministers, Ambassadors and Generals, every one of whom would be reckoned a more important personage than he. Whereas, in Italy, society looks on public offices as little better than a masquerade, and values nothing in the Minister more highly than the salary he receives.

Before the time of his marriage with Signorina Colbran (1821), who brought with her a dowry of some 20,000 *livres* per annum, Rossini had never bought more than two suits of clothes in a year; for the rest, he was lucky enough never to be inflicted with such dull virtues as *prudence*—and in any case, what is "prudence" in the souls of the poor, except the *fear of going short*? (Take note, all you *reasonable* and *prudent* people, that the sweetness of your wise self-righteousness rests at bottom upon this worthiest of inspirations: *fear*!) Rossini, confident in the power of his own genius, lived simply from hand to mouth, and never dreamed of the morrow. Yet, although he may come to be a passing fashion in the North, Rossini can never grow to be intimately accepted by races who are dissimilar to him in every particular. The best that may be hoped for is that there will come eventually a new generation, less poisoned by literary snobbery, less prone to grovel before the altars of the *style noble*, less susceptible to shocks of horror when confronted by the famous *cra-cra!* passage from *l'Italiana in Algeri*. When that happens, France will at last begin to understand (i) Italian *joyousness*; and (ii) Italian *genius*.

Rossini, and in fact all Italians, have a great regard for Mozart; yet they do not adore him as we do; for they admire his incomparable qualities as a writer of symphonic music rather than his gifts as a composer of opera. They never refer to him except as one of the greatest geniuses who ever lived; yet, even in *Don Giovanni*, they are liable to detect the typical weaknesses of the German school—that is to say, *not enough vocal melody*; plenty of melody for the clarinet and plenty for the bassoon, but nothing, or next to nothing, for that finest of all instruments (when it is not shouting its head off!), *the human voice*.

There was only one genius in all the world, according to Rossini, who could have challenged his reputation, and built himself one no less universal, and that was Orgitano; and I have heard Rossini speak of him with deep sincerity and seriousness—which is saying a great deal. Orgitano, a brilliant young man, was already promising the world a successor to Cimarosa, when he was carried off in the flower of his youth, in 1803—a new instance of the dangers which beset a genius. "Genius" depends upon a nervous system of a most uncommon pattern, susceptible of recording every tremor of passion, its violence, its fire, its unreason; but beware lest this same passion should consume the mind and body in which it dwells, destroying both upon the very threshold of life! I am heartily ashamed of this sentence, which would sound *much* simpler in Italian.

Paisiello, in Rossini's frequently-expressed opinion, was the most *inimitable* of all composers. He was the very incarnation of purity, simplicity and naïve grace, and his style has come to be so closely identified with his own personality that all imitations are henceforth doomed to failure. Paisiello was the master of unparalleled effects managed with unbelievable simplicity, alike in his melody, his harmony and his accompaniments; and in Rossini's view, his "simple melody" is now forbidden territory. "You have only to start work on it, and before you know where you are, you are back with Paisiello, imitating him without even being aware of it." Rossini can talk with intimate knowledge of all the greatest composers; he has only to play a score through once on the piano to know it by heart, and thereafter never to forget it. In this way, he has made himself familiar with everything produced by all the many generations before his own; and yet, if you go into his room, you will never see a scrap of music save blank manuscript paper.

Whatever may be the ultimate verdict of posterity concerning Rossini and his work, there is one characteristic which can never be denied: Rossini is as unique in his *creative facility* as Paisiello is unique in his *melodic simplicity*.

Anecdotes

I SHOULD prefer to be certain that my readers would bear in mind that this book is nothing but a straightforward biography, a form of literature which permits the inclusion of the most ignominious details, before I record the following typical instance of Rossini's laziness. On one extremely cold day, during the winter of 1813, Rossini had bivouacked in the bed-chamber of a very ill-favoured inn in Venice, and was composing in bed to avoid the expense of having a fire. As he finished the duet he was working on (he was actually engaged at the time in scoring *il Figlio per azzardo*), the sheet of paper slipped out of his fingers and fluttered away down to the floor. Rossini peered over the edge of the bed to try and locate it—but in vain, for it had slid right under the bed itself. He stretched out an arm, and leant half out over the side to feel for it; but eventually, becoming suddenly conscious of the cold, he withdrew hurriedly under the blankets, muttering to himself as he did so: "I'd rather sketch the whole thing out again; it won't take a minute—I can remember it easily!" Strangely enough, however, his mind promptly went a complete blank, and there he sat for a good quarter of an hour, fuming with impatience, but obdurately failing to recall a single note. Finally he burst out laughing: "I'm a fool," he said. "I'd do much better to write another duet. Wealthy composers can have fires in their rooms if they choose, but I have my own private form of self-indulgence: I flatly refuse to crawl out of bed to go groping after errant duets—and in any case, it would surely bring bad luck!"

Just as he was putting the finishing touches to the second duet, a visitor appeared. "Would you mind picking up a duet which has slipped under the bed?" asked Rossini. The visitor retrieved the wayward duet with his cane, and handed it to Rossini. "Now listen!" said Rossini. "I'm going to sing you *both* duets, so that you can tell me which one you like best." The young composer's friend opted for the original one; the second, it appeared, was rather too lively in *tempo* for the dramatic situation (incidentally, the person who told me the story assures me solemnly that there was not the slightest similarity between the two compositions); so on the instant Rossini wrote a trio for the same opera and, as soon as it was ready, struggled into his clothes, swearing all the while against the cold, and accompanied his visitor down to the Casino to get warm and drink a cup of coffee—meanwhile handing duet and trio together to the waiter, and telling him to take them round to the music-copyist of the *teatro San-Mosè*, for which he was working at the time.

If you like Italy and things Italian, nothing is so delightful as Rossini's conversation, which is inimitable. His mind is all fire and quicksilver, darting here, darting there, and falling upon any subject under the sun to cull from it a store of amusing, accurate and grotesque observations. There is scarcely time to catch the gist of one idea, before another comes to leap upon its traces. This astonishing mental agility might easily become an object of curiosity rather than of delight, were it not that this volcanic surge of startling ideas is subject to constant interruption in the shape of charming and comparatively restful anecdotes. Rossini's incessant travelling, "twelve years of comings and goings", as he calls it himself in referring to his own career; his constant intercourse with singers and actors, the maddest of all mankind, and with the pleasure-loving, merry-making sections of the aristocracy—all this has furnished him with an inexhaustible supply of the weirdest anecdotes ever collected concerning that poor species known as man. "I should be an uncommon fool to tell lies and invent a pack of nonsense," declares Rossini,[1] whenever some acrimonious or jealous bystander feels inclined to spoil the pleasure of the company by challenging the truth of one or other of his anecdotes; "My profession has always brought me into contact with every kind and type of singer, and no one will deny that singers are temperamental, the men as often as the women; and the more I grew famous, the more, and the odder, were the exhibitions of temperament to which I have been subjected. In Padua, I was treated to the indignity of being made to come and *caterwaul* in

---

[1] If ever it should please Signor Rossini to challenge the truth of any statement contained in these chapters, I retract it in advance; I should be grievously sorry to be thought lacking in tact or delicacy towards one for whom I feel the most sincere and profound respect. I recognize only one *aristocracy*, the aristocracy of genius; to whose ranks are also admitted those who practise the higher virtues. Occasionally those who have done great things, or who possess enormous wealth, may be admitted, as a sort of afterthought.

the street at three o'clock in the morning whenever I wanted to gain admission to a certain house which I had particular reasons for wishing to visit; and just because I was a *maestro* who was particularly vain of his own voice, the door would only open to me on condition that I should serenade the lady publicly, nocturnally and *out of tune*. At different times I have met in my room (and I could have met them waiting in my ante-room, if I had had one) almost all the wealthy *amateurs* in Italy, of the kind who nearly always give way in the end and turn *impresario* for the love of some good-looking *prima donna*. Finally, it has been alleged that I have not failed altogether to win the favours of the fair sex; and I can assure you that the ladies in question were not the stupidest of the species. I have had to encounter some strange rivalries; I have changed towns and changed friends three times a year without fail ever since I was born; and thanks to my name and reputation, I have met and grown to terms of familiarity with everything that was worth while meeting and knowing anywhere within forty-eight hours of my arrival . . . *etc., etc.*

It is Rossini's undying misfortune to be constitutionally disrespectful towards everything except genius; he is prepared to humour no one, and no practical joke is too outrageous to be brought home to him; if he should chance to fall in with a fool, so much the worse for the fool; but he is not spiteful, and if the success of some undignified stratagem will send him off into mad fits of laughter, he will promptly forget all about it an instant or two later. On one occasion, in Rome, he was invited to sing at the residence of some cardinal or other; but, just as he was preparing to begin, a train-bearer sidled up to him, and insinuated that it would be appreciated if he were to include as few love-songs as possible in his programme. Rossini's immediate reaction was to give an entire programme made up of lewd ditties in Bolognese dialect, which no one understood—and then, when he had laughed his fill, he went and thought of something else. Without this fertile and quick-witted inventiveness, he could never have found time or energy to produce the works which in fact he *has* produced; for remember that he has never considered it a waste of time to enjoy himself; that, being poor, he has never been able to afford the least help in the routine-work of scoring; and that, in spite of all this, he has composed forty-four operas and cantatas, and is still not thirty-two years old.

Rossini has an incredible talent for mimicry, and no one is safe from

him in this respect. He is able to send the company into fits of laughter
by picking out absurdities of gesture and appearance, even among
those of his acquaintance who would seem to be the least precious or
eccentric in their behaviour. Vestris, the greatest comic actor in Italy,
and perhaps in all the world,[1] used to tell him that he had all the
makings of a first-class actor. Rossini has a special genius for parodying
de' Marini, a ranting but at times magnificent actor, who enjoys the
foremost reputation in all Italy. Whenever Rossini sets out to "take
off" de' Marini, the onlookers are first reduced to helpless laughter by
the uncanny resemblance of the portrait, and finally deeply moved—
assuming, of course, that the onlookers are people who appreciate the
sing-song declamatory style of the French dramatic tradition. For, just
as Alfieri, for all the insults which he hurled against France, proceeded
in conscious imitation of Racine and Voltaire, so also do the Italian
actors "sing" their lines in imitation of the style widely popularized by
the French theatrical company which, under the leadership of Mademoiselle Raucourt and with full imperial patronage, toured Italy in or
about the year 1808. They have this much in common with French
actors, too: they excel only in comedy, where the worst excesses of
the declamatory style are restricted by the speed of delivery. Alone
among the Italians, Vestris escapes this universal plague of affectation,
and he fully deserves a wider European reputation than he has at
present. I have deliberately set down two or three of these scattered
ideas in this chapter, because they very frequently cropped up in
arguments between Rossini and one in particular of his admirers—
Rossini, as an *Italian patriot*, insisting that everything in Italy was
perfect (with the exception of one or two obnoxious and unmentionable
individuals), and that any foreigner who questioned this assertion did
so for motives of mean and dishonest jealousy. I detect in this attitude a
certain resemblance to the tone adopted by *le Constitutionnel* and *le
Miroir*, with their perpetual bleating about *Music and National Honour*.
In the year 1820, Rossini, stimulated by the violent arguments of the
Italian *romantics*, who are the most formidable opponents of the
declamatory traditions of the Italian theatre, was persuaded to take

[1] The Italian conception of *comedy* consists essentially in observing the delusions
of those who set out with burning ambitions, and get lost on the way to their
fulfilment; moreover, the goal of these ambitions does *not* consist, invariably and
exclusively, in aping the manners of the aristocracy.

part in a *comédie bourgeoise*[1] in Naples, where the cast included a
number of young people from the highest ranks of society. De' Marini
himself was among the audience, and agreed, as indeed we all did, that
Rossini's acting was extraordinary. "He still needs a little practical
experience," said de' Marini, "but apart from that, I have never seen
a more realistic performance. I doubt if there are two actors in the
whole of Italy who could eclipse him in any part he chose to play."

Rossini is a fair poet, and can turn out reams of doggerel for his own
operas if required; and many a time he has toned down the bombastic
grandiloquence of various *libretti seri* which have been foisted on him.
No one is more acutely aware of the ridiculous possibilities of the
typical *libretto*, and often, when he has finished an aria, he will turn to
his friends gathered round the piano and, taking care not to sacrifice a
single pearl of its grotesque absurdity, give a dramatic recital of the
fantastic jargon, whose fame and fortune he has just established for
ever through the medium of his music—*E però*, he once exclaimed,
when he had finished laughing, *in due anni questo si canterà da Barcelona
a Pietroburgo: gran trionfo della musica!*[2] By some untutored instinct,
rare enough in the land where he was born, Rossini is the natural
enemy of bombast. It should be observed that *bombast* stands in the
same relation to art in Italy as preciosity, affectation, wit and studied
mannerisms do to art in France. All evidence points to the fact that
Nature, in creating Rossini, had intended to enrich the world of music
with a perfect genius for *opera di mezzo carattere*. But an evil fortune
decreed that he should travel to Naples, and there discover that the
reigning queen of the theatre was Signorina Colbran; and a greater
misfortune still was to follow when he fell in love with her; for if only,
instead of this tragedy-heroine, he had met a *comic* actress, la Marcolini
for example, or la Gafforini in the flower of her youth and beauty, we
should certainly have had less of the Plagues of Egypt and infinitely
more in the style of *la Pietra del Paragone* and *l'Italiana in Algeri*. But

---

[1] A type of drama originally inspired by writers like Lillo and Nivelle de la
Chaussée (of the *comédie larmoyante*). It was popularized in France by Diderot
and Sedaine, in Germany by Lessing and his followers, and was strenuously
advocated by the *pre*-romantics as an antidote to the meaninglessness and bombast
of degenerate classical tragedy. It was melodramatic, middle-class, sentimental,
and—in a primitive way—realist. (*Trans.*)

[2] And yet, in two years' time, this stuff will be sung from Barcelona to St
Petersburg: what a triumph for the music!

it is *our* duty to make ourselves worthy of our great men, and so we should school ourselves to appreciate the true nobility of genius despite the inevitable blemishes which individual passions, social conventions and the distorted tastes of contemporary audiences have imposed upon Rossini's work. Are we to think less of Correggio, because the more or less baroque taste of the worthy ecclesiastics of his time compelled him to paint nothing but cupolas, and to present great portraits in an extraordinary foreshortening of perspective, *di sotto in sù*?

A FINAL WORD

Light, lively, amusing, never wearisome but seldom exalted—Rossini would appear to have been brought into this world for the express purpose of conjuring up visions of ecstatic delight in the commonplace soul of the Average Man. The sad, sighing beauty of Mozart has a quality which he could not dream of emulating and, in the field of comedy, he is easily outdistanced by Cimarosa; nevertheless, Rossini's music stands unchallenged for its speed, its vivacity and its excitement, and for all the particular effects which derive from these general characteristics. There is no *opera buffa* quite like *la Pietra del Paragone*; there is no *opera seria* quite like *Otello* or *la Donna del Lago*. *Otello* has no more in common with *gli Orazi e Curiazi* than it has with *Don Giovanni*; it is a work on its own. Rossini has given us a hundred different portraits of the joys of love, and one at least (the duet from *Armida*) which resembles nothing so much as dreamed of before; he has occasionally toyed with absurdity, but he has never been boorish or platitudinous—not even in the silly little dance-tune from the *finale* of *la Gazza ladra*. Finally, Rossini, who is incapable of writing twenty lines of prose without a glowing crop of howlers ... Rossini, who is incapable of writing twenty bars of music without betraying the overpowering presence of genius ... Rossini has become indisputably, since the death of Canova, the greatest living artist of our time. As to the verdict of posterity—how should *I* know?

If you promise to keep a secret, I might whisper in your ear that Rossini's style is the musical embodiment, not so much of France as of *Paris*: it is not really merry, but it is supremely vain and excitable; it is never passionate, but always witty; and if it is never boring, it is very, *very* rarely sublime.

CHRONOLOGICAL TABLE*

of

the Works of Gioacchino Rossini,
born in Pesaro on the 29th of February, 1792

I<small>N</small> August 1808,[1] Rossini, while still a pupil at the *Liceo Musicale* in Bologna, composed a *sinfonia* and a *cantata* entitled *IL PIANTO D'ARMONIA*.

   1. *DEMETRIO E POLIBIO*; Rossini's first opera, which, according to himself, he wrote in the spring of 1809, but which was not performed until [the 18th of May] 1812, at the *teatro Valle* in Rome, where it was sung by the tenor Mombelli, his two daughters Marianna and Ester, and by the bass Olivieri. There is no evidence, however, to prove that Rossini's vanity may not have led him, in 1812, to touch up the music here and there in the light of his greater experience. Signor Mombelli, incidentally, is a relation of Rossini. The *libretto* was written by Signora [Vincenza] Viganò Mombelli, the mother of Marianna Mombelli, who is to-day Signora Lambertini, and of Signorina Ester Mombelli, who still sings, and in fact possesses an excellent voice (1817).

   2. *LA CAMBIALE DI MATRIMONIO, farsa (i.e.* comic opera in

---

[1] Music in Italy is born and dies, and leaves no memorial of its passing; I have often been obliged to send off at least twenty different letters in an attempt to discover the exact date of composition of any given opera; and frequently the replies I have received have suggested three or four equally probable alternatives. I have with me letters from which I may deduce that Rossini's opera *Ciro in Babilonia*, for instance, received its first performance in two different towns and in three different years. In view of these difficulties, I must beg the reader to be lenient, and to forgive an error of detail here and there; for to have produced an accurate history of Rossini, fortified at every point against criticism, would have taken a great deal more time than I have had at my disposal. The best that I may hope is that the general conclusions which the Author has drawn from the facts known to him will show that, within the limitations of his own processes of thought and feeling, the interpretation which he has laid upon these facts is reasonably correct.

This table should be compared with the list of works given in Appendix II. (*Trans.*)

one act), Venice 1810, written for the *stagione dell' autunno*.[1] This opera was the first of Rossini's works to receive a stage performance: it was given at the *teatro San-Mosè* and sung by Rosa Morandi, Luigi Raffanelli, Nicola de' Grecis and Tommaso Ricci [Clementina Lanari, Domenico Remolini].

3. *L'EQUIVOCO STRAVAGANTE*, Bologna 1811, *autunno*. Written for the *teatro del Corso*. Singers: Marietta Marcolini, Domenico Vaccani, Paolo Rosich [Angiola Kies, T. Berti, G. Spirito].

4. *L'INGANNO FELICE*, Venice 1812, *carnovale*; *teatro San-Mosè*. Singers: Teresa Belloc, Rafaele Monelli, Luigi Raffanelli, Filippo Galli [? Dorinda Caranti, V. Venturi].

Galli enjoyed an immense success in the part of the peasant Tarabotto*, the leader of the miners. This is the earliest of Rossini's works to find a permanent place in the general repertoire. It contains a celebrated trio written for Madame Belloc,[2] Galli and the tenor Monelli.

5. *CIRO IN BABILONIA*, oratorio [*i.e.* opera with religious subject which can be performed in Lent], 1812. Written in Ferrara during Lent, and first performed at the *teatro Communale* by Marietta Marcolini, Elisabetta Manfredini, Eliodoro Bianchi [A. and F. Savinelli, G. Layner, G. Fraschi].

6. *LA SCALA DI SETA*, *farsa*, Venice 1812, *primavera* [in fact, *autunno*]. Performed at the *teatro San-Mosè* in Venice by Maria Cantarelli, Rafaele Monelli (tenor), Tacci and de' Grecis—the latter an excellent *buffo cantante*, who is still to be seen on the stage to-day (1823). [Also: Carolina Nagher and Gaetano Del Monte.]

7. *LA PIETRA DEL PARAGONE*, Milan 1812, *autunno*. Performed at *la Scala* by Marietta Marcolini (*prima donna*), Claudio

---

[1] I have decided to leave the designations of the Italian theatrical seasons in the original language; we have no corresponding convention, and therefore any translation would be necessarily misleading. As has already been mentioned, the operatic companies are disbanded after each season, and re-formed for the next. The *stagione del carnovale* opens on the 26th of December; the *primavera*, on the 10th of April; and the *autunno*, on the 15th of August. In certain cities, the dates of the *autunno* and *primavera* are subject to slight variations; while Milan sometimes has an additional season, the *autunnino*. But the *Carnival season* begins invariably on the second day of Christmas.

[2] Madame Belloc is still singing (1823) at *la Scala*, and with great success; her voice to-day is as fine as it was ten years ago. Madame Belloc, who is the daughter of a Cisalpine officer who had been banished from his own country, began her career at Bourg-en-Bresse in January 1800.

Bonoldi (tenor), Filippo Galli, [Carolina Zerbini, Orsola Fei, Antonio Parlamagni, P. Rossignoli and Pietro Vassoli].

8. *L'OCCASIONE FA IL LADRO* [or *il Cambio della Valigia*], *farsa*, Venice 1812, *autunno*. Sung at the *teatro San-Mosè* by the beautiful [Giacinta] Canonici (who has since become the mainstay of the *teatro dei Fiorentini* in Naples, where she received lessons from Pellegrini); by the excellent *buffo* Luigi Paccini; and by Tommaso Berti [Carolina Nagher, G. Del Monte, Luigi Spada].

9. *IL FIGLIO PER AZZARDO* [or *I due Bruschini*], *farsa*, Venice 1813, *carnovale*. Performed by Teodolinda Pontiggia, Tommaso Berti, Luigi Raffanelli and de' Grecis. Both the latter are first-class artists. [Also Carolina Nagher, G. Del Monte, N. Tacci.]

10. *TANCREDI*, Venice, 1813, *carnovale*; performed at the *teatro della Fenice*. *Opera seria*, the first of this type attempted by Rossini (except *Demetrio e Polibio*, which was not performed until 1812). Sung by Signora Malanotte, Elisabetta Manfredini and Pietro Todràn. [Also Teresa Marchesi, Carolina Sivelli and L. Bianchi.]

11. *L'ITALIANA IN ALGERI*, Venice 1813, *estate* (summer). Sung at the *teatro San-Benedetto* by Marietta Marcolini, Serafino Gentili (tenor), [P. Rosich, Luttgard Annibaldi, Annunziata Berni-Chelli] and by Filippo Galli, who was so magnificent in the famous "oath-scene" from Act II—the scene which was censored in the Paris production at the instigation of jealousy aided and abetted by prudishness.

12. *AURELIANO IN PALMIRA*, Milan 1813, *carnovale*. Performed at the *teatro alla Scala* by Velluti, Lorenza Correâ, Luigi Mari (tenor), Giuseppe Fabris, Eliodoro Bianchi and Filippo Galli*. Act I is scored at a much higher pitch than Act II, the reason being that the first was written for Davide, who then caught measles and was unable to sing; whereas the second was written for Luigi Mari, who took over the tenor part originally destined for Davide. This particular company is one of the most outstanding which has ever been gathered together over the last twenty years. Velluti was popular in his part, but the opera as a whole was a failure, and Rossini, his vanity stabbed to the heart, decided upon a change of *style*.

13. *IL TURCO IN ITALIA*, Milan 1814, *autunno*; *teatro alla Scala*; moderate success only. Singers: Signora Festa Maffei, Davide, Galli, L. Paccini [Vasoli, G. Pozzi, Adelaide Carpano].

14. *SIGISMONDO*, Venice 1814, *teatro della Fenice*. In spite of my most earnest endeavours, I have been unable to obtain any details about this *opera seria*. Incidentally, this list has cost me the dreary work of writing over a hundred letters for information; and I have been sent specimens of music purporting to belong to *Sigismondo* which are almost worthy of Signora Catalini's tame composer, Signor Puccita! [Singers: la Marcolini, la Manfredini, la Rossi, Bianchi, Bonoldi and D. Bartoli].

15. *ELISABETTA REGINA D'INGHILTERRA*, Naples 1815, *autunno* [4th October]. Sung at the *teatro San-Carlo* by Signorina Colbran, Signorina Dardanelli, Nozzari and Garcia. The first work of Rossini's *Neapolitan period*. [Also Maria Manza and G. Chizzola.]

16. *TORVALDO E DORLISKA*, Rome 1816, *carnovale*. Sung at the *teatro Valle* by Adelaide Sala, [Agnese Loyselet, C. Bastianelli], Donzelli (tenor), and the two excellent basses Galli and Rainiero Remorini. To-day (1823) Italy can claim four first-class basses: La Blache, Galli, Zucchelli and Remorini; and, running closely behind them, Ambrosi.

17. *IL BARBIERE DI SIVIGLIA* [or *Almaviva*; or *l'Inutile precauzione*], Rome 1816, *carnovale* [5th February]. Performed at the *teatro Argentina* by Signora Giorgi Righetti, and by Garcia, B. Botticelli, and by the brilliant *buffo* Luigi Zamboni, who first created the part of *Figaro*. [E. Loyselet, Z. Vitarelli, P. Biagelli].

18. *LA GAZZETTA*, Naples 1816, *estate*; demi-failure. Sung at the *teatro dei Fiorentini* by two *buffo* singers of the first water, Felice Pellegrini and Carlo Casaccia (the *Le Brunet* of Naples), and by Pellegrini's pupil, the attractive Margherita Chabran. [Also Francesca Cardini, Maria Manzi, A. Curioni, G. Pace and F. Sparano.]

19. *OTELLO* [or *il Moro di Venezia*], Naples 1816, *inverno* (winter) [4th December]. Performed at the *teatro del Fondo* (a charming circular theatre which serves as a relief-theatre to the *San-Carlo*) by Isabella Colbran, Nozzari, Davide, and the *basso* Benedetti. [Cicimarra and Maria Manzi.]

20. *LA CENERENTOLA* [or *la Bontà in trionfo*], Rome 1817, *carnovale* [25th January]. Given at the *teatro Valle* by Geltrude [Giorgi] Righetti, Catterina Rossi, [Verni], Giuseppe de' Begnis, [Vitarelli] and Giacomo Guglielmi. [Also Teresa Mariani.]

21. *LA GAZZA LADRA*, Milan 1817, *primavera* [30th May].

Sung at the *teatro alla Scala* by Teresa Belloc, Savino Monelli, V. Botticelli, Filippo Galli, Antonio Ambrosi and Signorina Gallianis. [Also M. Castiglioni, F. Biscottini, P. Rossignoli.]

22. *ARMIDA*, Naples 1817, *autunno*. Sung at the *teatro San-Carlo* by Isabella Colbran, Nozzari, [Cicimarra, Bonoldi] and Benedetti. Contains the famous duet. [Also G. Chizzola.]

23. *ADELAIDE DI BORGOGNA* [or *Ottone*], Rome 1818, *carnovale*. Sung at the *teatro Argentina* by Elisabetta Pinotti, Elisabetta Manfredini, Savino Monelli (tenor) and Gioacchino Sciarpelletti. [Also Anna Muratori, Luisa Bottesi, G. Puglieschi.]

24. *ADINA*, or *il Califfo di Bagdad*. Rossini sent the score of this opera to Lisbon, where it was performed in 1826 at the *Saõ Carlos* Theatre.

25. *MOSÈ IN EGITTO*, Naples 1818. Sung during Lent at the *teatro San-Carlo* by Isabella Colbran, Nozzari, [Benedetti, Friderike Funk, Maria Manzi, G. Chizzola, Cicimarra], and Matteo Porto*, whose fine bass voice registered a memorable triumph in the part of Pharaoh. It was a great mistake not to have offered Porto an engagement at the *Théâtre Louvois*.

26. *RICCIARDO E ZORAIDE*, Naples 1818, *autunno*. Given at the *teatro San-Carlo* by Isabella Colbran, [la Pisaroni, la Manzi], Nozzari, Davide, Benedetti [Cicimarra and Raffaela De' Bernardis].

27. *ERMIONE*, Naples 1819. Performed during Lent at the *teatro San-Carlo* by Isabella Colbran, Rosmunda Pisaroni, Nozzari and Davide. The *libretto* is based on Racine's *Andromaque*. Rossini has attempted to imitate the style of Gluck, and the characters are, to all intents and purposes, given nothing to portray except bad-temper. Demi-failure. [Also Maria Manzi, De' Bernardis the Younger, M. Benedetti, G. Cicimarra and G. Chizzola.]

28. *ODOARDO E CRISTINA*, Venice 1819, *primavera*. Performed at the *teatro San-Benedetto* by Rosa Morandi, Carolina Cortesi (one of the most beautiful singers who has appeared on any stage in recent years), Eliodoro Bianchi and Luciano Bianchi [and V. Fracalini].

29. *LA DONNA DEL LAGO*, Naples 1819 (4th October). Sung at the *teatro San-Carlo* by Rosmunda Pisaroni (who is one of the ugliest actresses imaginable), Isabella Colbran, [la Manzi], Nozzari, Davide, [Orlandini], Benedetti [and G. Chizzola].

30. *BIANCA E FALIERO* [or *il Consiglio dei tre*], Milan 1820,

carnovale. Sung at the *teatro alla Scala* by Carolina Bassi (the only singer whose genius approaches that of Madame Pasta), Violante Camporesi, Claudio Bonoldi and Alessandro de' Angeli.

31. *MAOMETTO SECONDO*, Naples 1820, *carnovale.* Performed at the *teatro San-Carlo.* I have been unable to procure the names of the cast [la Colbran, la Comelli (Chaumel), Nozzari, Galli, Cicimarra and Chizzola], but I have heard that Galli was as memorable in the part of Mahomet as he had been as Fernando in *la Gazza ladra.*

32. *MATILDE SHABRAN* [or *Bellezza e cuor di ferro*], Rome 1821, *carnovale.* Given at the *teatro Apollo,* which is the only adequate theatre in the whole of this great city. It was built during the French occupation. The opera was performed by the attractive Catterina Lipparini, by Anetta Parlamagni. Giuseppe Fusconi, Giuseppe Fioravanti, Carlo Moncada, Antonio Ambrosi and Antonio Parlamagni. [Also Luigia Cruciati and G. Rambaldi.]

33. *ZELMIRA*, Naples 1822, *inverno*; sung at the *teatro San-Carlo* by Isabella Colbran, Nozzari, Davide, Ambrosi, Benedetti and Signorina Cecconi. [Orlandini and Chizzola.]

34. *SEMIRAMIDE*, Venice 1823, *carnovale* [February]; given at the *teatro della Fenice.* An opera in the German style, sung by Signora Colbran-Rossini, Rosa Mariani (a remarkable contralto), Sinclair (the English tenor), Filippo Galli and Lucio Mariani [and Matilde Spagna].

Rossini has also composed a number of cantatas, of which I have been able to trace nine:

1. *IL PIANTO D'ARMONIA* [11th August] 1808, performed at the *Liceo Musicale di Bologna.* This is Rossini's earliest work; in style, it bears resemblance to the weaker passages of *l'Inganno felice.*

2. *DIDONE ABBANDONATA*, written in 1811 for Signorina Ester Mombelli.

3. *EGLE ED IRENE*, Milan 1814, written for the Principessa Belgiojoso, one of Rossini's most adorable protectresses.

4. *TETI E PELEO*, Naples 1816, written for the wedding of Her Royal Highness, Madame la Duchesse de Berri, and sung at the *teatro del Fondo* by Isabella Colbran, Girolama Dardanelli, Margherita Chabran, Nozzari and Davide.

5. [*IGEA*], Naples 1819. Cantata for [three] voices written in honour of His Majesty the King of Naples, and performed at the

teatro San-Carlo [on the 20th of February] by Isabella Colbran, [Davide and Gio.-Bta. Rubini].

6. [*PARTENOPE*], Naples 1819. Cantata performed in the presence of His Majesty Francis I of Austria on the 9th of May 1819, when this sovereign paid his first visit to the *San-Carlo*. The cast included Isabella Colbran, Davide and Gio.-Bta. Rubini.

7. *LA RICONOSCENZA*, Naples 1821; a *pastorale* for four voices, performed on the 17th of December 1821 at the *San-Carlo*, on the occasion of Rossini's benefit-night. Singers: la Dardanelli, la Comelli (Chaumel), Gio.-Bta. Rubini and Benedetti. On the following day, Rossini left Naples and set out for Bologna, where he married Isabella Colbran.

8. *IL VERO OMAGGIO*, Verona 1822 [*in fact*, 1823]; a cantata performed during the congress, in honour of His Majesty the Emperor of Austria. It was sung at the *teatro dei Filarmonici* by a young and very beautiful singer, Signorina Tosi, the daughter of a well-known Milanese lawyer, and by Velluti, Crivelli, Galli and Campitelli.

9. A *Patriotic Hymn*, Naples 1820.

There was also a second *Patriotic Hymn*, composed in Bologna in 1815*. It was a similar crime which caused Cimarosa to be thrown into prison.

If the present volume runs to a second edition, I intend to cut out the larger part of the analyses of *Otello, la Gazza ladra, Elisabetta, etc.*; and instead, I shall insert at this point a rapid sketch of the abilities and achievements of all living composers and singers of both sexes who have attained to any degree of popularity in Italy.

If this were to be done, the present volume would then offer a complete survey of the contemporary scene in the entire field of Italian music. I should probably include articles of some length upon Saverio Mercadante, the composer of *Elisa e Claudio* and of *l'Apoteosi d'Ercole*; upon Caraffa, the composer of *Gabriele di Vergy*; upon Paccini, who has written a superb duet for *il Barone di Dolsheim*; upon Meyerbeer, Pavesi, Morlacchi* (to whom we owe *Isolina, Corradino, etc.*) and others. Unfortunately, however, all these gentlemen have so far confined their talents to imitating Rossini.

CHAPTER XLIII

The Utopia of the Théâtre Italien*

I⸱T is quite conceivable that this or that young man of twenty-six or so, who is now reading this chapter, will, in fifteen years' time, have risen to be a Minister of State, or at least a Trustee of the Royal Opera House.

A Minister of State has no serious concerns outside the rise and fall of the stock-exchange and the permanency of his own office. It is therefore perfectly futile to address any relevant observations to *His Excellency*; but a *young* man, who has just spent the evening ponderously making the Grand Tour of half a dozen or more exclusive *salons*, where he has been engaged in surreptitiously smoothing the way for his own eventual rise to power, may, upon returning home, be prevailed upon, by the sheer boredom of having nothing better to do, to open a book; and ah! blessed among books is the book which is opened at such an instant, for it must needs be fatuous beyond believing if it can fail to gain by contrast!

Let us suppose, therefore, that a man of sense and ability should become, say, Steward of the Royal Household; here are some of the facts and arguments which I could wish such a man to have assimilated in his youth*.

The present Board of Trustees of the *Opéra-Bouffe* is as uncommunicative about the details of its budget as though this were a vital state secret. The only fact which is publicly available is that it is entitled to an annual subsidy of 120,000 francs, payable from the Civil List. But what *happens* to this subsidy? Into whose pockets is it ultimately absorbed? Indiscreet questions! I have no personal contact with the Management of the *Opéra-Bouffe*; consequently, the figures which I intend to quote carry no authority beyond that of common-sense and mathematical probability. If the Trustees see fit to deny the validity of my calculations, they will of course realize that the only incontestable way of refuting them would be to publish the *truth* in fact and figure.

The box-office receipts on an average day vary between 900 and 1,800 francs. We can assume, therefore, that the average takings at any one performance will be about 1,200 francs; there are three performances a week; therefore the total receipts for any given year will amount to .. .. 122,800 fr.

The charges for the hiring of private boxes (which, since the changes introduced two years ago, are now all let out on an annual subscription basis) bring in approximately 2,400 francs for each performance, *i.e.*, an annual income of .. .. 345,600 fr.

Probable total annual income .. .. 468,400 fr.

BALANCE SHEET

showing the approximate details of the expenditure of the Opéra-Bouffe[1]

Salaries

Mme	Pasta (with a bonus of 15,000 fr.) ..	35,000 fr.
Mlles	Buonsignori	20,000
	Cinti	15,000
	Mori	10,000
	Démeri	7,000
	Rossi	5,000
	Goria	4,000
MM.	Garcia	30,000
	Zucchelli	24,000
	Pellegrini	21,000
	Bordogni	20,000
	Bonoldi	18,000
	Levasseur	12,000
	Bonoldi, *Lodovico*	6,000
	Graziani	8,000
	Proffetti	6,000

[1] My calculations are based upon the budget of the *Theatre Royal* (Italian Opera), London. These figures are extremely revealing. The total expenditure of the London company amounts to 1,200,000 fr. I have also had access to the accounts of *la Scala*, Milan.

Auletta	..	..	..	4,000
Barilli (*producer*)	..	..		8,000

Total of salaries paid out to singers	253,000 fr.
Chorus and orchestra	80,000
Costumes, props and *décor*	55,000
	135,000 fr.
Administrative expenses, heating (a field for rampant swindle!), lighting, fire-service, watchmen, *etc.*	60,000
Approximate total expenditure ..	448,000 fr.
Approximate total income	468,000
Balance	20,000 fr.

Assuming that these figures are more or less correct (and they cannot be seriously inaccurate), there must exist a credit balance of something like 20,000 fr. *What happens to the profit?*[1] And what is happening to the annual subsidy of 120,000 fr., which His Majesty is pleased to grant to the *Théâtre Italien*, which, before the Revolution, used to be the *Théâtre de MONSIEUR*? I defy anyone to give a satisfactory answer to either of these questions!

The most urgent need is to rescue the Italian opera from the clutches of its most implacable enemies—a Board of Trustees composed wholly of *French* musicians. And the only way to achieve this is to run the opera upon a contract-basis, to put the whole organization upon a business footing by auctioning the contract to the highest bidder.

It is essential to draw up a document specifying the articles and conditions of the contract, based preferably upon the articles and conditions which are specified in all contracts entered into by the *teatro alla Scala* in Milan, and which, under Napoleon, between 1805 and 1814, proved perfectly adequate.

[1] If I insist upon this sum of 20,000 fr., it is because I have every reason to believe that the factor which is causing the *junior* administrators of the *Théâtre Louvois* to tear their hair in anguish is that, in actual fact, the organization *should* be showing a profit.

The lessee of the theatre would thus undertake to adhere to all the conditions laid down in his contract. Il Cavaliere Petracchi, sometime First Secretary to the Minister of Finance of the Kingdom of Italy, and in whose name the contract of *la Scala*, Milan, was held for many years, became, in 1822, one of the Senior Trustees of the Italian Opera House in London. He is an expert in this particular branch of financial administration, and might well be consulted in order to help put the new organization upon a firm footing. It is very probable that he would accept a post at the *Théâtre Louvois*. Signor Benelli might also prove distinctly useful.

The first condition to be laid down by the terms of the contract should be the obligation to provide Paris with ten new operas every year, eight of which should be by composers still living, and, among these eight, *two should be written expressly for the cast of this particular theatre.*

I would call your attention to the fact that we have not yet seen at the *Louvois* one single opera composed specifically for Madame Pasta.

The second condition should be, that the contractor is required to provide forty new *décors* every year, all to be painted by artists who have had an absolute minimum of two years' experience, either with *la Scala*, Milan, or else at *la Fenice*, Venice, or else in Turin. Within a *maximum* period of eighteen months after the first performance at which it is used, every set *must*, by the terms of the contract, be either sold or broken down. (At *la Scala*, a *décor* painted by Sanquirico or Tranquillo costs 400 fr.; the same thing in Paris costs 3,000 fr.) (*A*).[1]

The subsidy which His Majesty is pleased to grant for the pleasure of all music-lovers in his capital, and indeed throughout Europe,[2] would continue to be paid by *monthly instalments* to the lessee of the *Théâtre Italien*; but it would be paid only upon the recommendation of a Committee, consisting of nine outstanding *dilettanti* nominated by a Convocation composed of all the lessees of boxes in the theatre for the current year.[3]

---

[1] See *notes* at the end of this chapter. (*Trans.*)

[2] The burden of this subsidy should be borne by the *City of Paris*, whose inhabitants receive the benefit of the music, and which, as a city, profits by the attraction of some ten thousand wealthy foreigners brought annually into the country as the indirect result of this grant.

[3] The election of these representatives could be carried out in the simplest manner possible merely by placing a book for recording nominations and votes in the Manager's office.

The membership of this committee would then be brought up to twelve by the inclusion of two members of the *Institut de France*, and of one lawyer, all three nominated by the Minister. The entire committee would be renewed annually, the Minister retaining the option to re-appoint the same representatives as the previous year. The lessees of the boxes would also have the right to re-elect the same candidates (*B*).

There would be an Annual General Meeting on the 20th of December each year (*i.e.*, coinciding with the opening of the Season), at which the committee would be required to render a report to the convocation of lessees concerning the present state of the management.

The contractor would have the right to engage French singers if he wished; but he would not be allowed to use them for more than *one* part in each opera. We have a right to demand some protection against the horror of performances such as that of *le Nozze di Figaro*** (13th December, 1823), at which we underwent the indescribable experience of listening to *five* French voices in the course of one single evening—four ladies, Mesdemoiselles Déméri, Cinti, Buffardin and [Blangy], and one gentleman, Monsieur Levasseur, who is, fundamentally, quite a competent singer, but who suffers from chronic nervousness, a characteristic which is not a major recommendation in the part of Almaviva. A further clause relating to this condition: the lessee *may* engage French singers, but at an annual salary *not to exceed* 6,000 *fr.* (*C*).

The "watch-committee" would meet on the 24th of each month, and would then hand the lessee a voucher for the payment of the next instalment of the subsidy *only* on condition that he should be able to show that, during the previous month, he should faithfully and zealously have fulfilled the terms of his contract. A balance-sheet showing the box-office receipts for each separate performance should be submitted to the scrutiny of the committee, which should additionally have the right to demand an individual report upon the voice and zeal of each singer. The contractor would be under an obligation to furnish the committee with any information which it might require.

For this system to be perfect, the permanent company should be required to give two performances a month from their Italian repertoire at the *Grand Opéra*. All actors who took part in these performances should receive a special bonus or *fee* (*D*).

The great disadvantage of any plan such as that which I have here sketched merely in roughest outline is that, by the time it had been in operation for twenty years or so at the *Théâtre Italien*, the *Opéra-Français* would fall into disuse, and the stage at the *rue Le Peletier* would be handed over entirely to companies performing Italian operas in two acts, with a ballet in the interval—in fact, just as in Naples!

When a Minister personally takes it into his head to draw up a set of rules and regulations for something or other, his primary motive is usually a sudden fit of vanity; he is nearly always full of good intentions; and, were it not for his unrelieved ignorance of all questions remotely related to the main problem involved, he might almost succeed in making his rules both just and efficient. But the invariable weakness of all such high-handed administrators lies in their inability to cope with detail. In the case of the regulations governing the various opera-houses, the signatures required to implement any *particular* decision are, in normal practice, invariably either given or refused in circumstances amounting to total irresponsibility, and obtained exclusively through intrigue, persistence and back-stairs manoeuvring. Say that the mistress of some theatre-manager should be ill-fated enough to sing out of tune; or rather, suppose that an audience should from time to time dare to show its opinion of this same manager by whistling at his productions—what better reason could any "administrator" wish for as an excuse to do everything in his power to ruin some *rival* theatre where the standard of singing is higher than he would like to see?

But under the lessee-system, those who control the fortunes of the theatre, far from being concerned primarily to perpetuate abuses, would have a present and active interest in *reforming abuses*. The reason for this miraculous transformation is obvious; for, under the new plan, no one would feel the charming repercussions of such abuses more acutely than the lessee himself; in which case, the management could have no interest nearer its heart than the somewhat ascetic one of making things as awkward as possible for all exploiters of abuses. It is perfectly clear that the appointment of a "watch-committee" nominated from among the box-holders in any given season would expose the management of the *Opéra-Bouffe* to the powerful forces of public opinion. And of course, once a particular artist, or a particular *décor*, had been passed with the approval of the committee, the members of that committee would necessarily be transformed overnight into twelve fervid apostles all on fire with the urge to justify in the eyes of the wider public the decisions which they have taken. It will certainly be objected that my proposal is tainted with *republicanism*; I can only reply that a similar system has been in operation for many years in a country which is most incontrovertibly *despotic* in character, but whose inhabitants have a deep and passionate love of music—in the Austrian city of Vienna* (*E, F*).

NOTES

upon the preceding chapter
supplied by a sometime Theatrical Administrator.[1]

A. The simplest solution, which would be to offer a direct engagement to Sanquirico and one of his pupils, offering him so much, either per annum, or else for each separate décor, *would already effect a considerable saving. I think that, at this point, a word or two should be inserted, pointing out the immense superiority of the Italian theatrical sets compared with our own, and adding a few precise details about the difference in cost. For instance, if it could be established as a fact that the* décor *for* la Lampe merveilleuse *cost 100,000 fr., and that the same number of flats, or, generally speaking, the same set, would have cost no more than 12,000 fr. in Milan; and if it could be further established that, from an aesthetic point of view, the Italian* décor *would have been infinitely superior, I believe that nothing more would be required to convince any reader unless he had a personal axe to grind. But how many people seem to have an active interest in concealing the very abuses which I am trying to expose! I suggest that M. Aumer, the composer of the ballet* Alfred le Grand, *might be asked about the cost of* décor *in Milan.*

If patriotic considerations make the engagement of Sanquirico himself out of the question, why not engage Daguerre? He is sufficiently talented—and incidentally he should be instructed to use size-paint and not oil-paint; also that every décor *should be laid aside after it has served for a hundred performances. There is an unpleasant, cheeseparing flavour about the Parisian theatres in their attitude towards the public. In Italy, all scenery is touched up after forty performances at the very most, often after three days*.*

[1] These notes were added in pencil to the margin of my original MS., and I have decided to leave them exactly as they stood.

The new ventilator recently installed at the Louvois cost 38,000 fr., and one still gets a head-ache within an hour. I should be curious to see the detailed accounts of this expenditure of 38,000 fr. The swindling which goes on over the purchase of logs for the heating-system is perhaps still more fantastic. The best thing would be to install twenty thermometers, and to get the police to see that they were kept up to a given level, determined in relation to the temperature in the street outside. Why do they need to light the stoves, for instance, when the temperature outside is not lower than 50 degrees? Heating by gas is extremely efficient.

B. Since the French tend to behave rather like a flock of sheep in anything to do with the theatre, this plan for the organization of a "watch-committee" should be supported by a number of examples showing the system already in action, and the Author should point out that, from time immemorial, the Court Theatre of Turin, one of the most important in Italy, has been managed by a Commission of the Nobility (dei cavalieri), the members of which fulfil approximately the same functions as the Author has thought fit to attribute to the one-year's-lease box-holders at the Louvois. I believe that the same is true of the teatro Communale at Bologna, the most important theatre in the city. Similarly, the teatro della Pergola in Florence is subject to inspection by a Committee of Notables, and I have heard that the same practice prevails in several other Italian towns. The King's Theatre, London, is controlled by members of the Aristocracy, who let it out on contract. There is nothing in the Author's proposal which is not eminently reasonable, or which has not been tried out elsewhere over a number of years, with the most satisfactory results. Incidentally, the names of those responsible for the management of the Italian Opera House in London for the year 1824 are as follows:

> Lord Hertford,
> Lord Lowther,
> Lord Aylesford,
> Lord Mountedgecumbe,
> and a Sicilian gentleman, Count Santantonio.

Between 1778 and 1788, the contracting impresari of la Scala included the Count of Castelbarco, the Marquis Fagnani, the Marquis Calderara and Prince Rocca-Sinibalda. At present, however, it has become more usual to commission an agent and have the contract held in his name (testa di ferro).

*C. If it is thought desirable that the taste for Italian music should be per-
fected in France, the Conservatoire should create posts for two teachers of
Italian vocal music, and organize a course in this subject; it should also appoint
a teacher of Italian language and dramatic diction. Pellegrini or Zucchelli
would be invaluable as teachers of singing; but I have no doubt that we should
soon see some Frenchman appointed to teach Italian vocal music! I am fully
persuaded that if the Conservatoire de Paris were to appoint Italian teachers,
it would soon produce the most distinguished pupils, who could then be sent
abroad to spend two or three years on the Italian stage and to perfect their
technique, as happened in the case of our own Madame Mainvielle-Fodor. It
would be best to place three or four Peers of France, wealthy men distinguished for their love of music, in control of the Conservatoire.*

*Another idea would be to send out scouts into the southern provinces of
France, particularly into the region of the Pyrenees, to recruit any children
between the ages of twelve and fifteen who show evidence of being potential
singers. There is no reason on earth why nature should have bestowed finer
voices south of the Alps than in the southern territories of France.[1] The only
difference is, (i) that the average Italian twelve-year-old lives in a perpetual
atmosphere of good singing, whether in church or in the streets and (ii) that he
hears the gift of a good voice praised loudly above all other gifts.*

*D. Obviously it is desirable that the Grand Opéra should make way for
two performances a month of Italian operas but the senior Administrative
Board would never consent in a thousand years. Before a single year (and not
twenty!) had elapsed, the Opéra Français would have been ridiculed out of
existence and abandoned for ever.[2] Still, the project might be presented as a
means of increasing the receipts of the Grand Opéra; or alternatively, as a
means of covering unusually high costs at the Opéra Comique.*

*E. I think that the chapter should be concluded by suggesting a way of
saving the Théâtre Italien, which, in my own personal opinion, could not
fail; and that is, simply to offer Rossini a two-year engagement, on condition*

---

[1] All honour should be paid to Monsieur Choron, who has made immense
sacrifices for no other motives than a disinterested love of music. Any Minister of
the Interior who was in the least jealous of his good name and the reputation of
his office, should offer adequate protection to so genuinely patriotic a citizen.

[2] In 1823, the *Grand Opéra* company is technically incompetent to perform a
quartet from *la Gazza ladra* or *Camilla*; the consequence is simply that the takings
of the theatre do not amount to a *third* of its running-expenses.

that he should write three operas a year for that particular theatre. If the terms offered were at all reasonable, Rossini would unquestionably accept. He could also compose for the Grand Opéra *and for the* Théâtre Feydeau. *For the latter theatre, he could turn out a new opera every week, and make a fortune out of it. Everybody knows that even Nicolo was making 30,000 fr. a year this way, so you can imagine what it would be like with Rossini.*

If Rossini were to come and settle in Paris, it would add enormously to the prestige of the Théâtre Louvois *abroad; well-known singers would squabble* a pugni *for contracts, and the company would be adequately filled in no time at all. Signor Caraffa, who is living in Paris, and whose* Gabriele di Vergy *rivalled the popularity of Rossini's* Elisabetta *for two years on end, would then consent to work for the* Louvois; *and if at last Paris should begin to develop a taste for new and original music, the fortunes of the* Théâtre Italien *would then be established upon unshakeable foundations. Italian librettists would be granted royalties up to half of what is paid to the authors of the musical-comedies normally played at the* Théâtre Feydeau; *at which price you could command the most distinguished writers in all Italy.*[1]

Productions of Rossini's own works which are already on the repertoire would benefit enormously from the actual presence of the maestro, *whose eye would detect a vast number of blemishes in performance, such as unjustified distortions of* tempo *by the orchestra, unwarranted hullabaloo-ing by same orchestra, etc., etc. Our perennial floating population of idlers would grow prodigiously infatuated, with due and beneficial repercussions at the box-office. If economy dictates that Rossini should not only be paid, but paid generously, without costing the theatre a penny, let all* premières *of his operas be held as* author's-benefit *performances at the* rue Le Peletier. *At a rate of three operas a year, this would give an annual income of 45,000 fr. Add to this* concerts, *incidental music written for the* Théâtre Feydeau, *and profits from the sale of his music, which in Italy is sheer piracy, but which, here in France, is an extremely lucrative business—the total annual income from all this could scarcely drop below the figure of 60,000 fr.*

F. Singers who might with advantage be offered contracts.

First and foremost, of course, Madame Mainvielle [-Fodor]. She sings

---

[1] I am personally aware of the existence of four or five *libretti* (both *serie* and *buffe*) by Signor Pellico, the finest living Italian tragic dramatist, who is at present imprisoned in the fortress of Spielberg. To my mind, they are masterpieces, filled with magnificent dramatic situations drawn in bold and sweeping lines.

exceedingly well, and she has the additional qualification of being French. Many people disapprove of the Louvois from patriotic motives.

Messieurs
> Davide, tenore
> Donzelli, tenore
> Lablache, buffo cantante
> De' Begnis, buffo comico
> Ambrosi, basso
> Curioni, tenore (*an extremely handsome man, which is something that never comes amiss in a singer*).
> Luigi Mari, tenore (*who sang most excellently in* Aureliano in Palmira *in Milan in 1814*).

Mesdames
> Pisaroni, contralto
> Schiassetti*, prima donna (*at present in Munich*)
> Dardanelli, prima donna buffa
> Schiva
> Fabbrica
> Ronzi de' Begnis, prima donna buffa
> Mariani, contralto (*excellent*)
> Mombelli*, prima donna

There are a number of others as well, who have made their début within the last year or two, but whose reputation has not yet crossed the Alps. Signor Benelli, who is one of the lessees of the King's Theatre, London, is at present (October 1823) in Italy, recruiting new singers. We suffer considerably from the lack of so skilled an agent as Signor Benelli; likewise from that of a general manager of the character of Signor Petracchi. This Venetian nobleman, himself the owner of the* teatro San-Lucia, *might well give us profitable advice; London did not disdain to consult the Marchese di Santantonio*.*

CHAPTER XLIV

Of the material Circumstances
which affect the Life of the Theatre in Italy

THERE are in Italy two theatres of major importance: *la Scala* in Milan and the *San-Carlo* in Naples. Their dimensions are not dissimilar, *la Scala* being only a few feet narrower than the *San-Carlo*; and since, to derive enjoyment from listening to music, the first condition is to achieve a state of imperturbable indifference concerning the figure one cuts and the part one plays in the eyes of others, and since the second condition is to feel perfectly at ease, it was a stroke of genius to have divided up the bulk of the auditorium into a hive of private and completely independent *boxes*. Certain hypocritical travellers, such as Eustace and other of the same kidney, have not hesitated to imply that there were very imperious motives behind this general practice of wishing to be screened from public curiosity during a performance; but the fact is that these desiccated philistines were simply too insensitive to realize that a certain degree of private self-communion is essential to savour the sublimest charms of music. In any case, a woman in Italy is always accompanied into her box by five or six other persons; her box, in fact, is a *salon* where she receives her acquaintance, and where her friends may call to pay their compliments as soon as they see her arrive, escorted by her lover.

The *teatro alla Scala* can hold three thousand five hundred spectators with the greatest of ease and comfort; and there are, if I remember rightly, two hundred and twenty boxes*, each seating[1] three people in

[1] If anyone decides to build a proper theatre in Paris (and the problem will inevitably have to be faced within the next thirty years), precise details concerning the architecture and dimensions of *la Scala* can be found in a book by Signor Landriani, published in Milan in 1819. The *façade* is greatly inferior to that of the *San-Carlo* theatre; the corridors are narrow and ill-ventilated, and the inclination of the pit is insufficient; but with these few qualifications, *la Scala* is still the finest theatre in the world. The *ideal* theatre would stand in a block of its own, like the *Théâtre Favart*; and it would be surrounded on all four sides by arcades, similar to those in the *rue Castiglione*. Such, I believe, is the construction of the State Theatre in Moscow, which, however, the Author only visited for one day. This

front, in a position to watch the stage; but, except at *premières*, there are never more than two people occupying these seats, the escorted lady and her recognized gallant and servitor, while the remainder of the box, or rather *salon*, may contain anything up to nine or ten persons, who are perpetually coming and going all the evening. Silence is observed only at *premières*; or, during subsequent performances, only while one or other of the more memorable passages is being performed. Anyone who wishes to concentrate on watching the opera right through from beginning to end goes and sits in the pit, which is vast, and luxuriously equipped with benches furnished with back-rests, where the spectator can make himself exceedingly comfortable—so comfortable, indeed, that serious-minded English travellers have been known to count up to twenty or thirty persons sprawling across *two* benches each, and soundly asleep! The normal practice is to subscribe to a season-ticket. A seat in the pit costs approximately fifty *centimes* a performance. The boxes are not owned by the theatre, but are the private property of individuals, and are let out on independent leases. To-day, the lease of a reasonably comfortable box at *la Scala* may cost about 60 *louis* a year; in the golden age of prosperity which once

simple architectural device allows a hundred carriages to draw up simultaneously and without congestion.

I could show you a magnificent site, eminently suitable for a theatre which should be worthy of the Capital of Europe, and indeed of the entire world, facing the *Boulevard de la Madeleine*, between the *rue du Faubourg Saint-Honoré* and the *rue de Surène*.

If you desire to build a *smaller* theatre, ideally suited for music, I would suggest that the *teatro Carcano* in Milan might well serve as a model, but with the addition of the *façade* from the municipal theatre of Como.†

But if you want to construct a rather *bigger* theatre, then nothing could be prettier than the delightful example which is to be found in Brescia (*prettiness* in Italy becomes *magnificence* in France; whereas *beautiful* Italian architecture tends to strike the typical Frenchman as rather *depressing*). On the other hand, if you want a positively *tiny* theatre, I would suggest that the ideal is to be found, either in Volterra or else in Como. There is no law against plagiarism in architecture, unless, of course, our own architects should prohibit it from motives of *patriotic sentiment*. Signor Bianchi, an architect from Lugano, has created a series of superb designs for theatres; it was he who restored the *San-Carlo* in 1817.

† Signor Canonica, himself a celebrated architect who has designed several theatres in Lombardy, once maintained, in the course of a conversation at which I was present, that the laws of *acoustics* are still largely undiscovered. The *teatro Carcano* in Milan has proved to be ideal for music, and the acoustics are infinitely better than in the *teatro Rè*; yet both were built with the same skill and care by the same architect, Signor Canonica himself. The auditorium of the *rue Le Peletier*, which is built entirely of wood, is extraordinarily resonant.

reigned in the *Kingdom of Italy*, they used to cost up to 200 *louis*. The actual *purchase* price of a box ranges from 18,000 to 25,000 fr., depending upon the tier in which it is situated. Boxes in the second tier are, generally speaking, the most convenient, and therefore the most expensive.

The teatro San-Carlo* in Naples was restored with unparalleled magnificence in 1817 under the direction of Signor Barbaja. The boxes have *four* seats in the front row, and are not screened off by curtains; generally speaking, they are reputed to be less convenient and comfortable than those at *la Scala*, and the absence of curtains makes it necessary for the ladies always to appear in full evening dress. Considered as a social amenity, the *San-Carlo*, which gives performances only on three evenings a week, does not serve quite the same purpose as *la Scala*,[1] which is used as a general *rendez-vous* every evening of the week by all the big bankers and businessmen of the city; but, on the other hand, it is infinitely better suited for listening to music.

These two theatres are generally accepted as being the foremost "reputation-makers"[2] in all Italy; that is to say, that nothing gives a singer so much status as to have been engaged by one or the other of these two leading stages.

In Rome, on the other hand, the public is immensely vain about its own critical prestige, and unspeakably conceited—qualities which, however, have somehow done nothing to cure the ugliness, discomfort and cramped inadequacy of its theatres, which are mostly still built of wood. There is in fact only one which is even passable*, and *that*

---

[1] Among the advantages of civilization offered by the City of Paris, this is one of the more serious amenities which is lacking. The best thing to do would be to increase the size of the *foyer* of the theatre in the *rue Le Peletier* to at least three times its present dimensions, and to lease all the corresponding storey of the adjacent building, so as to convert it into a sort of literary club, with its own *café*, billiard-tables, *etc.* The essential condition is that membership should be by subscription. In the interests of intelligent society (and *not* in the interests of the privileged classes as such), I propose a new form of privilege. The subscription to this "theatre-club" would be exceedingly high, but allowing a 25% reduction for all persons paying 1,000 fr. or more in annual taxation, for all members of the *Institut de France*, for all lawyers with chambers in Paris, *etc., etc.*—in fact, for all members of society who rise out of the common rut. In any *club* of this type, whose membership is open to the public at large, the indispensable requirement is to keep out the penniless rabble of uneducated young bucks, who would finish up by bringing the whole enterprise down to their own level of vulgarity.

[2] *di cartello*, literally: *of advertisement*.

because it was built under the French occupation.[1] Ever since the restoration of the Pope, the standard of singing in Rome has been of dire and almost unrelieved poverty. Cardinal Consalvi, a highly enlightened man, and himself one of the foremost *dilettanti* of Italy,[2] had to employ a quite extraordinary amount of tact before he could persuade the late Pope to consent to the re-opening of the theatres. Pius VII used to say, with tears in his eyes, "The theatre is the Cardinal's *only* heresy!" The *Argentina*, *Alberti* and *Tordinono* theatres are nowadays no longer considered as being *di cartello*, except during the Carnival season; but the halo of fame which once shone so brilliantly about the names *Alberti* and *Argentina* still reflects a little glory through the years, almost undimmed, because, during the Golden Age of Pleasure (*c.* 1760), when Princes, as yet undisturbed by anxious thoughts that there might be danger to their crowns, had no preoccupation in the world save that of their own enjoyment, *these* were the theatres for which the glorious masters of the time, Pergolesi, Cimarosa,[3] Paisiello and the rest, composed their immortal triumphs.

Singers in search of prestige and reputation think less of Rome than of the *teatro della Fenice* (the Phoenix Theatre) in Venice. This theatre, whose dimensions are approximately those of the *Théâtre de l'Odéon* in Paris, boasts a *façade* of striking originality, fronting on one of the main canals; arrival and departure is by gondola; and since all gondolas are painted the same colour, the *teatro della Fenice* is no place for a

---

[1] Rome owes the greater part of its architectural improvements, which were carried out under Napoleon, to M. Martial Daru, the *Crown Intendant*, who was a man of great intelligence and artistic sensibility, and a close personal friend of Canova; among other projects carried out under his direction was the work on Trajan's column.

[2] In 1806 he was known to come down to the theatre in person to demonstrate to the singers the correct *tempo* for the performance of certain passages from Cimarosa. He was a man of formidable intellectual ability; but, between 1818 and 1823, he began to grow afraid of the *extremist* party, and all his acts thenceforward reveal his overwhelming determination to *stay in office*, cost what it might.

[3] Cardinal Consalvi commissioned Canova to make a portrait-bust of Cimarosa, and in 1816 this bust was placed in the Pantheon, beside the bust and tomb of Raphael. But the cardinal, yielding more and more beneath the pressure of the *extremists*, and, to the detriment of his reputation, yielding also on matters of considerably greater importance than this, was prevailed upon to allow his friend's bust to be exiled to the Capitol, where it became lost and insignificant among many hundreds of others, largely antique sculptures. At the Pantheon it was a symbol, reaching the hearts of all those who were born with a love of art; but at the Capitol, it is nothing more than a trifling curiosity.

jealous husband! In the past, in the days of the *Government of St Mark's*
(as the Venetians call it), this theatre knew an epoch of magnificence
and glory; Napoleon revived its grandeur for a while; but to-day it is
sinking slowly into degradation, together with the rest of Venice. In
thirty years from now, this fantastic city, gayer than the rest of Europe
put together, will have degenerated into a mean and insanitary village,
unless Italy should awaken her out of her dream, and give herself a
King—*one* King, not *many*; and should this happen, I should cast my
vote for the "impregnable city" of Venice as his capital.

The Venetians are the gayest, the most carefree, and, to my mind at
least, the most *philosophic* of men; and so they take vengeance upon
their oppressors, and find consolation for all the evils that beset them,
in the excellent perfection of the *epigram*. I have known certain severe
moralists to wax indignant over their frivolity; but I might answer
these glum and atrabiliar critics in the words of the comic servant
from *Camilla*:

Signor, la vita è corta![1]

Since the day when Italy saw all her hopes crushed at a single blow
by the fall of the one man who could have transformed her into *one
undivided, autocratic state*, the Venetians have somehow continued to
prop up the tottering glory of their theatre by sheer force of wit and
gaiety. To the best of my belief, it was here, in 1819, that Madame
Fodor laid the first foundations of her reputation, singing in Caraffa's
Elisabetta. The Venetians struck a medal in her honour. In 1821, they
resurrected the half-forgotten reputation of Crivelli, in Pavesi's
Arminio*.[2] And yet somehow, at the root of all these wild outbursts of
enthusiasm, lies a deep and passionate urge to prove that Venice is still
alive.

In Paris, there is always *politics* to provide the day's excitement; in
Venice, there is instead the latest satire by Buratti, the only major
satirical poet whom Italy has produced for many years. I would
strongly recommend the reader to study *l'Uomo, la Streffeide* or *l'Elefanteide*. Buratti is probably most strikingly successful in the grotesque
physical caricatures which he draws of his heroes; and, in a land where
newspapers are rare, bad and censored, where to read even *these* with

[1] See above, p. 28.
[2] A fine *libretto*, full of tense dramatic situations; music, too, which is far from
devoid of genius.

too much attention makes a man suspect of *carbonarism*,[1] and where, as a result, everyone is slowly dying of boredom, this technique has all the impact of startling originality. Imagine, then, the infinitely, greater excitement which is aroused by the arrival of the latest *prima donna* who is to appear *alla Fenice*, and of the latest composer who is coming to *write* her an opera. This is the reason why a reputation gained in Venice is at least as important, in music, as a reputation gained in Paris. In Paris we have at our disposal every conceivable form of pleasure; in Italy, there is but one—the pleasure of *love*, and of *art*, which is only love in another language.

Next in importance after *la Fenice* in Venice comes the *Court Theatre* in Turin. This building is actually a part of the royal palace, and fronts on to the noble vista of the *Piazza del Castello*. The entrance to the theatre runs through a series of arcades; but since it lies within the precincts of the King's palace, it counts as *lèse-majesté* to come wearing a coat, even in the middle of winter, it counts as *lèse-majesté* to laugh; it counts as *lèse-majesté* to clap, unless the Queen has clapped first . . . in 1821, when Madame Pasta appeared on the stage here, the latter article of this exquisite protocol had to be placarded three or four times in succession by the Chamberlain-in-Waiting! This theatre, which is of a fair size, but where the wretched spectator is being perpetually harried by soldiers growling about *lèse-majesté*, is reputed to stand fourth in importance in all Italy, and is always *di cartello*. Performances are given during the carnival season, and occasionally during Lent as well.[2]

Florence, Bologna, Genoa and Siena likewise possess theatres, cramped and somewhat tawdry, but which are all *di cartello* in certain seasons. In one town, the *carnovale* constitutes the "good" season; in another, the *autunno, etc.* Bergamo has a magnificent theatre, which is *di cartello* during the annual fair; similarly Reggio enjoys its "fashionable" season during the statutory weeks when the regional fairs and markets are in progress; and the same is true of the beautiful new theatre at Leghorn during the summer months. Or at least, all this was perfectly true ten years ago; but since then, the whole situation has been slowly but surely deteriorating. The majority of these theatres used to

[1] The fortress where the *carbonari* are imprisoned is actually just near by, on one of the little islands off the shores of Venetia.

[2] Piety permitting. Well-known retort of a certain great nobleman: *Non voglio abbrucciar le mie chiappe per voi!*

be subsidized and protected by the various local potentates in the states to which they belonged, at least when these rulers had enough leisure to enjoy themselves. But nowadays, when such doubtful monarchs are almost permanently occupied, along with an army of priests and a few remaining nobles, in herding the vast majority of their subjects in directions which seem curiously unfashionable, they live, not in the love of their peoples, but in abject fear of them;[1] and music is the last thing on which they are ready to spend money—rather a nice public hanging any day, than a new opera! Both in Milan and in Turin, large numbers of the nobility, with a weather eye upon storms to come, are saving money as hard as they can; whereas in 1796, in Cremona, a little town in Lombardy whose only claim to fame lies in being mentioned in a line by Regnard:

Savez-vous bien, monsieur, que j'étais dans Crémone . . .

the family with the greatest pretensions to nobility used regularly to send 200 *louis* to the reigning *prima donna* on her benefit-night.

Of course, most sovereigns still subsidize the theatre to some extent, because such subsidies are traditional, and because it is not politic to stop doing what used to be done before; but the money which they give is given with a wry smile and a bad grace. The Emperor of Austria allows 200,000 fr. to *la Scala*; the King of Naples, round about 350,000 fr. to the *San-Carlo*; while the King of Sardinia has economically trusted the running of his theatre to one of his own chamberlains. As far as I know, the only sovereign who positively enjoys spending money on his Italian opera is His Majesty the King of Bavaria; and, if the respect humbly due to such a sovereign might permit the expression, I should say that he is a merry and a happy man. Anyway, even though a depleted treasury grievously restricts his spending, he is always furnished with excellent singers, for he is invariably polite and genial towards them; thus, in Munich last year, you could have found a company which included the charming Signorina Schiassetti; Zucchelli, whose noble bass voice searches the very depths of the soul; and the enthralling Ronconi, last and most precious survivor of the Golden Age of singing, who, I declare it boldly, is a very genius among singers.

[1] Compare the state of Cassel (1823, last months) with that of Darmstadt, where the latest opera is the most vital topic of conversation*.

The splendour and glory of *la Scala* and the *San-Carlo* have, in the past, rested firmly upon the sound economic foundations of the *public gaming-rooms*. In vast halls adjoining the theatres stood faro-tables and *rouge-et-noir*, and, the average Italian being a born gambler, the bank would usually show a more than handsome profit and so turn over enormous sums to swell the funds of the theatre.[1] Gaming played a particularly vital rôle in the history of *la Scala*, which, situated as it is in a city with a damp winter climate, soon grew to be a general meeting-place for the whole town. A well-heated, well-lit establishment, where one may be quite certain of meeting people on almost any evening in the week, is a most invaluable institution for any city. But the Austrian authorities in Milan have prohibited gambling at *la Scala**, while the transitory revolution in Naples closed the tables there too, and King Ferdinand has not yet seen fit to open them again. In consequence, both these theatres are doomed, and their great musical tradition will die with them. It was the profits from the tables which enabled Viganò to produce his wonderful ballets (Milan, 1805–1821)— an art which he himself discovered, and whose secret died with him.[2]

Every theatre in Italy has its ceremonial opening date fixed each year on the 26th of December, which is the beginning of the *stagione* of the Carnival, normally the most brilliant of all. Since the day when *Religion* stalked back into the land to reclaim its birthright, there is no opera performed during Advent (the sacred season which precedes Christmas, beginning on or about the 1st of December), with the result that, now, the old, tense anticipation of novelty is increased a thousand-fold by deprivation of the foremost requirement of life; and when at last the 26th of December *does* arrive, I honestly do not believe that the news that Napoleon himself had risen from the dead would cause a

[1] As a disinterested observer, I note that in Paris the profits of the public gaming-rooms go, among other things, to provide pensions for pious moralists who denounce the abuses of this, our most curious century!

[2] The works of Viganò include: *Coriolano* (1804); *Tamari* (1805); *la Vanarella* (1805); *les Strelitz* (1812); *Richard Coeur-de-lion* (1812); *Clotilde* (1812); *il Noce di Benevento* (1812); *l'Alunno della Giumenta* (1812); *Prometeo* (1813); *Samandria liberata* (1813); *les Hussites* (1815); *Numa Pompilia* (1815); *Myrrha ou la Vengeance de Vénus* (1815); *Psammi roi d'Egypte* (1815); *les Trois Oranges* (1815); *Dédale* (1818); *Otello* (1818); *la Vestale* (1818). Yet, of all these masterpieces, not a trace remains save the music in arrangements made by Viganò himself. I can recommend the reader to look at the scores of *Otello*, *la Vestale* and *Myrrha*, which he can purchase from the music-publisher Ricordi in Milan.

single mind to abandon its passionate preoccupation with *music*. Not a woman in the whole theatre, on that evening, but is decked out in the gayest and most gorgeous of her gala-dresses; and, if the new opera is a success, any box which has not yet been leased for the year will have doubled in price by the following day. I should merely be wasting my time if I were to attempt a description of the wild extravagance of these carnival *premières*.

A successful opera, in Italy, will normally enjoy a run of some thirty successive performances, which is about the number of times that it is profitable to listen to an opera of average competence.[1] There is a performance on every day of the week with the exception of Friday, the day of our Saviour's death, and with the further exception, in lands under Austrian domination, of about seventeen miscellaneous birthdays, death-anniversaries, *etc.*, of the present living and last three dead Austrian Emperors or Empresses. Traditionally, the *maestro* who wrote the opera is required to conduct the performance of his own music from the piano during the first three performances; I leave you to imagine the ignominious horror of this obligation if the opera should turn out to be a flop! In practice, an opera has to be absolutely *detestable* to be taken off before the third performance; the composer, in fact, can claim three as a right. I should dearly like to see this tradition, which is extremely sensible, established in Paris. More than once I have seen an opera pick up at the third performance; and in any case, organized opposition, knowing that its efforts will be comparatively usless, will necessarily be much less active at the *première*.

Normally, during each season (which may include eighty to a hundred performances), the company will give three different operas, of which two will be original works composed *apposta* (expressly) for that particular theatre; also four ballets, consisting of two full-scale tragic ballets, and two comic ones.

Every town in Italy has its theatre; and most of the theatres in the bigger cities, Turin, Genoa, Venice, Bologna, Milan, Naples, Rome, Florence, Leghorn, *etc.*, are governed by a constitution which lays it down as an express condition that at certain stated intervals original operas composed specially for the theatre concerned *must* be produced.

[1] If an opera is well sung, it will be slightly different at every performance, owing to variations in the emotional mood of the singer, and consequently of the musical embellishments used.

This tradition is the one factor which has kept music alive in Italy as an active form of art; for assuredly, if chance had in fact *not* ordained it so, the pedants, by the very weight of their adulation heaped mountains-high upon the old, *dead* masters, would have crushed the new, *living* ones at birth! Without this established practice, music in Italy would be as dead as painting. Any painter, even the most gifted, is obliged to go down on his knees and *beg* for commissions; but for the musician, the boot is on the other foot—it is the capitalist with the money who is forced to go and *implore* the famous composer to work for the theatre of which he happens to be the lessee. To be able to put on a new opera is a vast triumph for municipal vanity in Italy, and towns no bigger or more important than Saint-Cloud quite ordinarily commission original music two or three times a year. If Colbert had suggested to Louis XIV a law, by whose enactment, every year, on the 26th of December, the 20th of February and the 25th of August, a new and original tragedy *had* to be produced at the *Théâtre Français*, the art of tragedy would not by now be as dead as a door-nail in the land of France. Dramatists, obliged by law to *exist*, would soon have been compelled to realize that they could not *exist successfully* except by following the development of progress and enlightenment within the community which they were required to serve.

If we in France wish, not to conjure up *composers* (which, as Diderot[1] said, would not be to begin at the beginning), but to start by *forming an audience*, the first, necessary step is to lay down *by law* that each year, and at *pre-determined, unalterable dates*, three new and original operas composed expressly for the theatre in question shall be given at the *Louvois*. The audience itself might then have the pleasure of being critic. Rossini, according to the latest rumours, is soon to be passing through Paris*, in December 1823, on his way to London, where he is to write a new opera. If only we could manage to *hold* him on the journey![2]

[1] I should dearly like to see the publication of eight good volumes *in-octavo*, containing the two-thousand-odd letters in which Diderot wrote to his mistress a detailed account of all that was going on in Paris in his day. They are the finest things he did*.

[2] With the exception of Signor Dragonetti and one or two other composers of *orchestral* music, the *Théâtre Louvois* cannot boast any considerable talent. No race in Europe is less sensitive to music than the English, and yet London organizes its music much better than Paris. The reason is obvious: London is inflicted, neither with "organized opposition", nor with the plague of *aesthetic patriotism*.

Let me give an example of a typical Italian opera-programme—an example borrowed from the account of a well-known traveller. On the 1st of February, 1818, the performance at *la Scala* began at 7 o'clock in the evening. (In the summer, it begins at a quarter to nine). On this particular date, the 1st of February 1818, the programme consisted of the first act of *la Gazza ladra*, which lasted from seven o'clock until a quarter past eight; of the ballet *la Vestale*, by Viganò, with a cast including Signorina Pallerini and Molinari, and lasting from half-past eight until ten o'clock; of the second act of *la Gazza ladra*, which ran from a quarter past ten until a quarter past eleven; and finally, of a tiny comic ballet by Viganò, entitled *la Calzolaja* (the Cobbler's wife), which the public had originally treated to an exhibition of derisive whistling out of a pure sense of its own self-importance, and yet greeted with delight every time it appeared upon the programme, because it was fresh and original. (In comedy, anything really fresh or original is always greeted with derisive whistling at the *première* by any truly *self-respecting* audience.) This ballet concluded the programme, which eventually finished between midnight and one o'clock in the morning. Every week, the miniature concluding ballet was varied by the incorporation of a new dance-sequence.

At *la Scala*, each scene of the opera, and each scene of the ballets is set in a fresh *décor*; and there are invariably a great many scenes, since the author relies to some extent upon the audience's appreciation of new and original sets to ensure the success of his work as a whole. No set (*scena*) is ever used for two distinct spectacles; if the opera or ballet should prove a failure, the set, which may have been magnificent, is nevertheless ruthlessly painted out on the following day, even if it has only been seen at one single performance; for the same flats are used over and over again for new scenes. All scenery is painted with size-paint, and the set as a whole is built up on principles which are utterly different from those which are in vogue in Paris to-day. In Paris, it is all tinselly glitter, everything is a filigree of pretty, witty little arabesques, each enamelled in immaculate detail. But in Milan, everything is sacrificed to mass effects of form and colour, and to the *general impression*. It is David's own special genius transposed into the medium of *décor*. The result is that, sometimes, even the most frivolous sets seem to wear a strange and imposing dignity, which strikes the beholder immediately, and produces a strong impression of beauty. The reader's imagination may perhaps be able to conjure up some idea of the grandeur of these palaces, cathedral naves, mountain landscapes, *etc.*; but, since nothing even remotely resembling them has been seen on the stage outside Italy, there are no words capable of *describing* these settings (*scene*). At the very best, I might claim that the views of Canterbury and Chartres cathedrals as shown on the *diorama*, or Mr Barker's sublime *panoramas* of Berne and Lausanne, have some power of suggesting the perfection of certain *décors* at *la Scala*, created by i Signori Perego, Sanquirico and Tranquillo—with this difference, however: that the *panoramas* and *dioramas* can lay no higher claim to consideration than as faithful *reproductions of nature*, whereas the stage-sets, which are likewise faithful portraits of famous places, have the added virtue of being ennobled by the boldest and rarest ideals of *absolute beauty*. Travellers in Italy who have admired these masterpieces of the scene-painter's art—I might almost say, who have *felt their power*, for indeed these *scene* literally double the dynamic impact of any opera or ballet—such travellers, I maintain, will find it quite incredible to learn that the great painters Perego, Sanquirico and Tranquillo receive no more than 400 fr. for any one set of this quality.[1] It is true, of course that *la Scala* commissions a hundred and twenty or a hundred and forty new *décors* every year. What is there left to say about these masterpieces to anyone who has once seen them? Or—a far thornier problem—what on earth is it *possible* to say about them to anyone who has *not* seen them, without laying oneself open to the most serious charges of over-statement?* Like Viganò's ballets, these *décors* are the eternal stumbling-block of every traveller who tries to give an account of his experiences in Italy—yet with this difference, that at *la Scala*, when Perego died, Sanquirick[2] was ready as a worthy successor, while Tranquillo, Sanquirick's pupil, is already as proficient as his master; but when Viganò died, he carried his secret for ever with him to the grave.

[1] The precious and stylized *miniatures*, devoid alike of impressiveness and grandeur, which are foisted upon the wretched audiences of the *Louvois* and the *Grand Opéra*, cost five or six times as much. Do you remember the *View of Rome* scene from the revived version of *gli Orazi* (14th August 1823)? It is not hard to perceive that Louis David has been exiled; painting is in full spate of degeneration and comes crashing back at a gallop towards the good old *patriotic* style of Boucher! *V.* the *Industrial Exhibition*, 1823.

[2] *Sanquirick* is the Milanese pronunciation of the Italian word *Sanquirico*.

CHAPTER XLV

Concerning the San-Carlo Theatre
and the present moral Climate of Naples,
the Home of Music

PERSONS who have travelled in Italy, and whose minds, transcending the merely *useful* or *convenient*, have acquired that true degree of culture which seeks out only the *beautiful*, will surely call upon me to account for my constantly-manifested prejudice in favour of *la Scala*, whose qualities I am for ever commending above those of the *teatro San-Carlo*. At first sight, nothing could be more unjust; for whereas Naples is the very fount and birthplace of fine singing, Milan is already tainted by the evil and infectious presence of so-called "rational" ideas from the North.[1] If you were to make a list of the finest composers in the world, you would find that the first thirty would be born, almost without exception, beneath the shadow of Vesuvius, whereas scarcely one first saw the light of day in Lombardy. The orchestra of the *San-Carlo* is infinitely superior to that of *la Scala*, for the latter observes the same

---

[1] There is no evil more insidious than the misapplication of scientific knowledge; for the false scientist stalks down the highways of error in so obstinate a conviction of his own rightness that it touches on the absurd. Remember the preposterous application of mathematics to the theory of probability; remember likewise the attempt, which has already been mentioned (p. 180), of a certain French *philosopher* to rationalize over the theory of the duet !

The weakness of such persons, who, in all other respects, may command an excellent dialectical method, is their passion for constructing coherent and rational philosophies based upon data which they are unable to perceive. Rationalism, in music, leads nowhere, save to the theory of the *recitative with instrumental accompaniment*; vocal music proper, the *aria*, consists at bottom simply of an *original melody*, which can be *experienced* but not *deduced*. And it just happens that this particular form of experience is extremely rare in France anywhere north of the Loire, whereas it is very common in Toulouse or in the Pyrenees. Do you remember those ragged little urchins who sang beneath our windows once in Pierrefitte, on the road to Cauterets, and whom you called up into our room*? Toulouse, incidentally, has something in its singing, some strange and sombre colouring in its atmosphere, particularly in its religious atmosphere, which reminds me of some typical city in the Papal States. Toulouse is still trying to justify the murder of Calas, even now, in the year 1823 !

principles in the field of music, as do our modern painters of the French school in the field of art, thus accounting for the *resplendent* and *glittering* diversity of their palettes—that is to say, that the orchestra is so obsessed by an absolute *terror of ridicule*, that it finishes up by achieving a perfectly uniform effect of unrelieved monotony, just like our own modern and fashionable doctors, who would rather let the patient die than risk an unorthodox remedy which might earn them the title of *Dr Sangrado**.

Constantly pursued by the fear of failing to paint in *soft and harmonious* colours—*i.e.*, fundamentally, by that fear of ridicule which, in ultra-civilized communities, attaches only too frequently to any manifestation of violent energy, and hence to all originality—our French artists have been reduced in the long run to depicting everything, even the greenest of green grass, in flat and uniform shades of grey. Similarly at *la Scala*, the orchestra would think itself in imminent danger of eternal perdition if it should once rise above the sweet inoffensiveness of its gentle *piano*—a defect which is diametrically opposed to that of the *Louvois* orchestra, whose pride and glory it is, never to fall short of a magnificent *fortissimo* . . . and let the singers go hang! The orchestra of *la Scala* cringes before the singers, and is their humble, obsequious and most obedient servant.

To this point, therefore, everything appears to favour Naples; but the House of Austria, which rules in Milan, although an absolute monarchy in theory, is an oligarchic monarchy in practice—that is to say, it is reasonable, economical and calculating. The Austrian aristocracy both loves and understands music; and the Princes of the House of Austria have inherited kindly dispositions and a certain instinct for statesmanship; at least, they are always most careful to take no important step without first thrashing the matter out in long consultation with a Senate of venerable Counsellors who, if they are singularly uninspired, are nevertheless exceedingly cautious. By contrast, in Naples, the rule is one of unmitigated despotism—a despotism based upon pure favouritism, which, in the matter of Signor Barbaja and the *teatro San-Carlo*, was to be seen in all the effulgent glory of its unredeemed absurdity. Under Signor Barbaja, it happened not infrequently that the *San-Carlo* would remain closed for a whole week on end. Under Signor Barbaja, who was anxious lest he should upset the somewhat chancy voice of Signorina Colbran, the programme, which should have consisted of a two-act opera and a full-length ballet, has been known to have dwindled to *one* act of an opera only, and one ordinary ballet. Foreigners who have come to Naples have been known to live there for three whole months without *ever* seeing the second act of *Medea* or *Cora*. (Personally, I could have felt quite happy without these particular second acts, but these foreigners happened to be Germans, and seemed to *want* Mayr's music! In any case, both *Medea* and *Cora* were fashionable at the time.) For two months on end, you could go and watch the *first* act of *Medea*; and then, for a further two months, the *second* act of *Medea* ... perhaps; it depended upon the current stage of disintegration in Signorina Colbran.

Naples has even reached a stage when (*horribile dictu!*) there are whole days without any musical performances *at all*. In 1785, in the days before the Third Estate declared war on the Aristocracy, this would not have mattered, for the conversation of fifty fascinating *salons* would have been open to the idler in search of amusement; but now a most curious revolution has occurred. Ever since the massacres organized by Queen Caroline and Admiral Nelson*, the venom of hatred has grown virulent to such a degree, that the first secret and delirious pact agreed upon by any happy pair of Neapolitan lovers is ... *never to talk politics!* Should one of the lovers see fit to broach a subject which, between man and man, and provided that no sinister smell of the *informer* lies heavy on the air, is the only *interesting* topic of conversation in all the world—this is a sure sign that the match is to be broken off! When I was in Russia, I met a young man named R......; and in consequence, when I came to Naples, I received a most cordial welcome from the delightful family of the Marchese N***, a family consisting of two sons and one daughter. The elder son is a revolutionary *carbonaro*, whereas the younger is an ardent supporter of the existing government; the father is one of the old-time partisans of Murat, the *King of Naples*, with a passionate fondness for all things French; the mother is all priests and piety; and the daughter is an impassioned adherent of *moderate carbonarism*, which wants a constitution on the French pattern, with two Chambers *à l'anglaise* (I should guess that she has a lover in exile, who is living in London!). The consequence is that this extremely *correct*, and at bottom extremely *united* family, sits down to table in a chill of deathly silence, which at last is broken by innocuous chatter about the weather, the latest eruption of Vesuvius or the *novena* of Saint Januarius. The theatre itself, and even Rossini, have become matters of party-politics, and a meticulous silence must be observed in that direction unless you wish to provoke storms of execration; the torture imposed by such unnatural and self-inflicted restraint is a thousand times more excruciating in Naples than in our own cool, distant and reasonable climates. "*Mosè* is a fine opera," said the royalist younger son. "Indeed," added the elder, "and so beautifully *sung*, too! Last night la Colbran scarcely went wrong (*non calava*) at all; she can't have been more than a semitone off key."—Dead silence! To utter rude thoughts about la Colbran is to speak sedition against the King, and the two brothers had sworn a truce. The elder son, the *carbonaro*, told me on another occasion: "The revolution has destroyed everything—even the fun of making love! Along comes a pack of damned Frenchmen, with their pretty vanities and their prim, bourgeois habits—and look at the result! Not *one* of our wenches but sits at home now, smugly dutiful and smiling at her own husband. Is it surprising, then, that the *men* get bored and miserable, and start wanting Houses of Commons and tempestuous parliamentary debates, and so on?—not forgetting that we are bred on eloquence in the tradition of Poerio and Dragonetti![1] Everything in Naples has been destroyed and broken—everything except our ballets, which are still the finest in the world, and the banks of the Mergellina!" These are the exact words which my Neapolitan friend spoke to me. Incidentally, the ballets which are performed in Naples (and are worthy of M. Gardel) have nothing in common with those of Viganò, which represent one of these "newfangled *romantic* inventions", and thus are received with sharp derision by the Neapolitans. The art of theatrical *décor*, and in fact all the visual aspect of the drama, is twenty times better in Naples than in Paris; but unfortunately, an immutable geographical decree has determined that no traveller shall reach Naples without having first passed through Milan, and in consequence, the sets at the *San-Carlo* usually seem cheap and often garish by contrast.

There may still be something to hope for music, however, from Calabria, the provinces of the East, Taranto, and in general from all the country which lies in the hinterland of Naples. The reasons I have

---

[1] Eloquent speakers, whose genius is at least the equal of anything which is to be seen in France, or even in England since the death of Sheridan and Grattan.

for holding to this belief are rather awkward to set down, for they
would seem to shock both decency and common-sense.[1] Nevertheless,
it shall be attempted. The art of any community has its roots in the
physical constitition and in the material and moral culture of that
people as a whole; that is to say, art is composed of countless hundreds
of *habits*. Now, for more than a century, music had flourished in fair
Parthenope, and the sound of it had gone up to heaven, when one day
the French appeared to harass this poor city of Naples, infecting it
with books, decency and liberal notions, and, worst of all, repressing
the free and gentle art of love. But in the wide and scattered countryside
beyond the city boundaries, the older way of life is still unchanged.
Traditionally, the elder brother enters the priesthood, marries off one
of his younger brothers to continue his name and lineage, and then
settles down comfortably to live with his sister-in-law. The family
thus united lives in monotonous tranquillity, and knows only one form
of entertainment: music-making. Yet could you guess the one disrupt-
ing note which may come to trouble this sweet if uneventful existence?
—*fear!* Fear lest some spiteful neighbour should cast the *evil eye* upon
them.

The *jettatura*[2] is the *bogy-man* of the Kingdom of Naples. If a *jettatura*
should fall upon you, everything that you possess will wilt and pine
and perish. To guard against the *jettatura*, every member of the family
carries a good dozen holy relics and *agnus Dei*, and men wear *horns*
made of coral dangling from their watch-chains; some men even
wear *real* horns, eight or ten inches long, fastened round their necks and
nestling on their breasts, like a mistress' portrait, and more or less
efficiently concealed in the folds of their waistcoat. Once, when I was

[1] I sincerely hope that, by the time this part of my book has been reached, five
out of every six of the readers for whom it is *not* written will have closed it up and
set it back on the shelf. Firm in this belief, I intend to risk expounding a few ideas
which I should most hastily have obliterated from the earlier pages. May one's
trust in the perfectibility of the human spirit allow one to hope that one day someone will invent a device by which the public may be helped to select exclusively
those writers who are suited to its requirements; and by which, conversely, writers
may be enabled to reach *only* those readers whom they desire to attract? Have
you, Reader, enjoyed the works of Walter Scott and the treatises of M. Courier?
—if so, then I am writing for *you*. Did you enjoy the *Histoire de Cromwell*, or
M. Villemain's *Mélanges*, or the respective *Histoires* of M. Lacretelle or M. Raoul
Rochette?—if *that* is the case, then shut this book quickly, for you will find it
fanciful, indecent and platitudinous!

[2] Pronounced *yet-a-toura*.

coming back to Naples from Palermo, where even the biggest horns are very cheap, I was commissioned to bring back a dozen or fifteen horns of cattle, each a good three feet long, which, when I had brought them safely to their destination, were avidly seized upon and curiously mounted in gold; and soon I began to observe them, prominent among other decorations, in various drawing-rooms and bedrooms. On the sea-journey from Palermo to Naples, our *speronara* met with very dirty weather; and I, to keep my mind off being seasick, struck up a song. Whereupon the skipper and his mates swore the most uncompromising oaths, accusing me of tempting Providence, and whispering secretly among themselves that I myself might well be a *jettatore*. I took them below, and showed them the vast collection of beeves' horns which I was transporting, and in the end they grew calmer; so, to seal our pact of reconciliation, I knelt before a little statuette of Santa Rosalina, in front of which glimmered a single candle, and begged her to establish *Mutual Improvement Societies* for the enlightenment of the population of Sicily. (She replied that she would be prepared to consider it in three hundred years' time.)

Yet it was in Calabria, and blanketed in just such a fog of curious superstitions, that Paisiello, Pergolesi, Cimarosa and a hundred others first saw the light of day. No *American* sailor, I am convinced, would have taken me for a *jettatore*; America is reasonable; but what has reasonable America produced in the way of art? One of our modern writers, Vauvenargues I believe, once remarked that "the Sublime is the echo of a noble soul". But it would be even more strictly true to say that *art is the outcome of the entire culture of a race, the product of* all *its habits, including the most grotesque and the most fantastic.* In Italy, in the year 1300 or thereabouts, every head in the land was alive with speculation about the nature of *Purgatory*; thus it came about that everybody started wanting to build chapels, and, when built, to fill them with paintings of their patron saints, so that these might intercede for them, should the builders eventually turn up in that dismal region themselves; and without a single doubt, it is to nothing less than so incongruous and baroque a notion that we owe Raphael and Correggio.

Similarly, when Cosmo the Great of Florence, or the Farnese of Parma, *etc.*, by force of tyranny and a plague of spies, killed the finest joys of conversation, the first flower to blossom on the desecrated grave was *solitude*; and solitude, beneath skies as fair as those of Italy, cannot live long without love. Love in such a climate is sombre, jealous and impassioned—in short, such love is *real* love,[1] which, towards the year 1500, making its way to church and there discovering *music* (for in this land the priests have learned to seize a man by all his senses, in order to frighten the life out of poor sinners, and induce them to slip a little gift or offering into the pockets of Mother Church[2]), did see in it a way, an only way, *the* only way still free within a hostile world, to express the half-felt, fleeting shades of all its hopes and all its dull despair.

The antique *Miserere* of the Vatican, composed by Allegri in the year 1400 or thereabouts*, is, I have no doubt whatever, equally responsible for the thoroughly secular duet:

Io ti lascio perchè uniti . . .[3]

from the first act of *il Matrimonio segreto*, and for the sublime aria from *Giulietta e Romeo*:

Ombra adorata, aspetta . . .[4]

Here is a true story; it can be read at great length in certain ancient and dusty manuscripts preserved in Bologna, which, however, are by no means easy of access.[5] In the year 1273, Bonifazio Jeremei, son of a family whose sympathies were Guelph to the point of frenzy, fell violently in love with Isnelda, daughter of the famous Orlando Lambertazzi, one of the leaders of the Ghibelline faction; and unquestionably the ribald jokes bandied from mouth to mouth among the young men of the Guelph party concerning the renowned beauty

---

[1] In a land where the first condition of survival is *to be forgotten* by a dozen or more evil-minded and otherwise unoccupied Ministers of the Crown, there can be no question of enjoying the proper flattery and pleasure of being distinguished in public by the attentions of a woman of fashion. Even if this may not be the actual case in Italy to-day, it was undeniably so a hundred years ago, when the historian Giannone was murdered in prison; and though laws may change, the changes do not begin to affect traditional habits of behaviour for at least a hundred years.

[2] St Philip Neri invented the *oratorio* in fifteen-hundred-and-something. *Cf.* the monk's scene in Machiavelli's beautiful comedy, *Mandragola*. The *monk* complains that there are no more processions in the evenings.

[3] See above, p. 5.

[4] See above, p. 382.

[5] *Cf.* the *Letter* written by M. Courier (1812), concerning the ink-spot, the learned scholar Furia and the Chamberlain Puzzini*.

of Isnelda played a large part in attracting Jeremei's love towards this particular object. Despite the hatred which divided their families, they met secretly in a convent; and, forced by circumstances to avoid each other's gaze when, at this or that religious celebration, they came face to face in church, their passion, feeding on the fuel of such obstacles, blazed only the fiercer. At length Isnelda consented to receive her lover in her chamber; but one of the spies, set every evening by her brothers to watch about the precincts of the palace, came to them with the news that a stranger, young and apparently well-armed, had just been seen to force an entrance. The Lambertazzi gathered in strength, and broke down the door of their sister's room; and one of them, while she fled, struck Bonifazio in the breast with a poisoned dagger, of the kind whose use was taught in Italy by the Saracen marauders. Indeed, at the very same date as the events recorded in this narrative, the *Old Man of the Mountain*, so feared and hated by the Princes of the West, was arming his band of young fanatics, later renowned throughout the world under the title of *Assassins*, with weapons of this character. Bonifazio fell beneath the blow; the Lambertazzi bore him away into some deserted courtyard of their palace, and there concealed his body beneath a pile of broken ruins. Scarcely had they finished, and were withdrawing, when Isnelda, following the trail of blood down the countless stairways of her father's house, arrived at last within the hidden court, deserted and overgrown with weeds as tall as a man standing, in which they had hidden the body of her lover. It seemed to her that a faint spark of life still stirred within him. Now there was a popular belief that, if someone could be found whose devotion were of such a selfless quality that he or she were willing to sacrifice life itself, the victim might yet be saved by having the poison from the wound made by this lethal oriental dagger sucked out of his body. Isnelda knew the fatal properties of her brothers' weapons; yet she threw herself across the body of her lover, and drew into her own system his poisoned blood. But he remained as lifeless as ever; and not many minutes passed before she was dying also. Some hours afterwards, when her women, made anxious by her prolonged absence, at length discovered her deserted sanctuary, they found her lifeless, stretched across that other lifeless corpse of him whom she had loved.

This is the degree of love which deserves to find eternity in art.

The actual *city* of Naples, compared with Milan (and for the instant forgetting about the climate), has one peculiar glory of its own, the magnificent Casacciello,[1] and his individual artistry in performing a certain opera by Paisiello, which, I believe, together with *Nina*, is the only one which still survives in the modern repertoire. "If you have ever laughed in your life," I might say to some clumsy English *squire*,[2] whose solemn head is all one whirl of earnest arguments concerning the *Utility of Foreign Bible Societies* and the *Immorality of the French Nation*, "go to Naples and see Casaccia in *la Scuffiara ossia la Modista raggiratrice*."

Numerous different factors serve to intensify the Italian's natural leaning towards music. How is a man to *read*, for instance, when three out of every four books published are intercepted by the police, who then parade about the town with little red note-books, jotting down the name of anyone rash enough to read the one which got away? It follows that, in Italy, no one reads books; all serious discussion is suppressed; and the very unaccustomedness of reading transforms a book into a grim and Herculean labour, the merest thought of which sends a shudder down the spine of the average young man in Italy. Now a book, even though it be no more than the shoddiest of pamphlets, is a distraction from a man's own thoughts; it absorbs the residue of his emotion drop by drop, so to speak, as it is distilled from the various incidents of daily existence, before these drops accumulate and merge into torrential streams of passion. But when emotion is annihilated by immediate distraction, it has no time to make extravagant estimates of the value of anything.

Alone amid the enforced and silent solitude of booklessness, living in a land bowed low beneath the double tyranny of Church and State, in towns whose very streets are paved with spies, our poor young man knows no escape from his own depressing company save in his voice and in his crack-toned harpsichord; and further, he is driven to contemplate at length the images and impressions formed within his soul— the only *novelty* which lies within his grasp!

Our young man, then, by dint of analysing every aspect of his own emotions, comes to be aware, and more especially, to be *sensually conscious*, of subtle shades and differences which would have altogether

---

[1] The Casacciello* family closely resembles the Vestris family; the present representative, who reigns at the *teatro dei Fiorentini* (the *Théâtre Feydeau* of Naples) is the third of that name.

[2] In English in the original. (*Trans.*)

Q

slipped beneath his notice if, like his English opposite, he were to find upon his writing-desk the distracting pages of *Quentin Durward*, or an article from the *Morning Chronicle*; for nothing is less true than the fond belief that emotional self-analysis is always a delightful occupation, particularly at the first instant of taking the plunge into the depths of one's own soul. By analysis, the intensity of sorrow is a hundred-fold increased, whereas the intensity of joy is only diminished. But in Naples, as far as I was able to observe, there is precisely *one* distraction, *only* one, which the law does not forbid to those passions which the climate breeds in Neapolitan hearts, and that is *music*; and music itself, being but another expression of these same passions, thus tends only to increase their agonizing violence.

CHAPTER XLVI

Of the Peoples of Northern Europe, considered as Musicians

Music is killed by prudent reflection; the more a race is governed by its passions, the less it has acquired the habit of cautious and reasoned argument, the more intense will be its love of music.

The *Frenchman* is lively and inconstant, but he is perpetually *busy*; every career is open to his ambition; and no man thinks himself too rich to waste his energy gambling on the stock-exchange. The Frenchman may aspire to victory on the field of battle as freely as to victory in the arena of letters, for the name of Marengo rings as proudly through Europe as the name of Voltaire; and in society (that is to say, as soon as two people are joined by a third) his main concern is for his *vanity**, which he is constantly and lovingly tending, whether to pave the way for its eventual triumphs, or whether to shield its delicate constitution against potential evil. He can devote more serious cogitation to weighing the chances of a *pun* than to anything else in the world; and the prudence of cautious calculation never deserts him for an instant. Even in his wildest orgies of merriment, he never surrenders blindly, both body and soul, to the contagious impulses of the moment, utterly regardless of the consequences. In society, he has learned to make himself irreproachably charming; but only because he is *at greater conscious pains* to please society than to perform any other task.[1] The French are the wittiest, the most charming and (up to the present, at all events) the *least musical* race on earth.

By contrast, the *Italian*, with his ever-smouldering passions, or the *German*, perpetually swept upwards and onwards by the whirlwind of his vagabond imagination, and for ever weaving himself passions *from*

---

[1] "A fool sitting beside me at the *Théâtre du Gymnase*", says Guasco, "is mightily pleased with to-night's idiotic performance; and why not? He has seen nothing so amusing all the long day. Whereas I, thanks to the extravagance of my imagination, have seen many delightful things, some even of angelic beauty—but then, of course, I cut a sorry figure in a salon!"

the very threads of his own fancy—these are *par excellence* people who live and breathe in the sweet fantasies conjured up in a duet by Rossini or in some delicious aria by Paisiello. There is a difference, however, between the music of the two races; for the German, who is indebted to the icy climate of the North for a coarser physical fibre, will require his music to be *noisier*; and further, this same cold, which spreads in a frozen blast over the sighing forests of Germania, having conspired with the absence of wine to deprive him of a singing voice, while his paternally feudal government has bred him since birth in habits of limitless patience, he will automatically turn to *instrumental music* to satisfy his urge for emotional fulfilment.[1] The Italian believes in God when he is frightened, and is always tempted to turn his hand to the gentle art of swindling, because, during all the life-time he has known, he has seen himself relentlessly oppressed by the meanest and most usuriously implacable of tyrannies; whereas the German deceives no one and believes everything; and the harder he reasons, the more he believes. Herr von [Gagern], the leading jurisconsult in Germany, sees ghosts at night in his *Schloss*. The modern German has inherited from Tacitus' *Germani* an unbelievably credulous and unsuspicious nature; thus every good German, before taking him a wife, courts her *publicly* for three or four years on end. In France, if this habit were to grow common, there would never be any marriages; but in Germany, they are rarely known to be broken off. A young lady of the highest rank has been known to treat her love to a fit of the sulks, and to have up-braided him in no half-hearted fashion, for having detected in him an incautious grain of disbelief respecting the *magic bullets* of *der Freischütz*.[2] The Graf von W***, who is a young and highly distinguished diplomat, besides being a most handsome man, once mentioned in my hearing how he and his brothers, when they were about seventeen, used to fast every year without fail on the night of the 9th of November, and on the following day, set out for a certain valley in the Harz Mountains, where, their heads crowned with ivy-wreaths, and observ-

---

[1] A young man named Kreutzer, from Vienna, has recently composed an unbelievably beautiful violin-sonata; he is one of the bright hopes of music. *If* neither vanity nor avarice manages to spoil Fraülein Delphine Schauroth, and *if* she goes to Italy, she will one day become the Paganini of the piano.

[2] The Gräfin von ***, near Halberstadt. The story of *der Freischütz* is a traditional folk-tale, which Jean-Paul has turned into a charming *Novelle*, and Maria Weber into a noisy opera.

ing all the other rites laid down by tradition, they would proceed to "cast magic bullets". Later on, having gone to the Forest of Nordheim, and there, from a distance of six hundred paces, aimed at a wild boar, and (not unnaturally) missed, they would stand and gape with startled incredulity. "And yet," added the Graf von W***, "I am not more feeble-minded than another."

Thanks to his Bible, the *Englishman* dwells in a vale of perpetual gloom; and his bishops and rightful lords have forbidden him, ever since the days of Locke, to busy his head with abstract logic. If you mention some interesting discovery, or talk to him of some sublime theory, the reply is always the same: "How can I *use* that *here and now?*" His only concern lies in *practical, day-to-day utility*. Goaded inexorably onward by the pressure of incessant labour, which alone can ward off the ever-present danger of *starvation and penury**, those classes of society in whose midst the flame of pure intelligence burns brightest have not an instant of the day which may be sacrificed to art; and this is the Englishman's greatest disadvantage. A young man in Germany or Italy, for instance, knows no other call on all his endless time than the art of making love, and even those who work the hardest suffer little encroachment on their liberty, if one compares the lightness of their occupations, which never stretch beyond the early afternoon, with the harsh and barbarous labour which, thanks to the English aristocracy and Mr Pitt, burdens the wretched Briton for a good dozen hours out of every twenty-four.[1] Yet the Englishman's most striking characteristic is his shyness; and it is to this joyless aspect of his nature, bred partly by puritanism, partly by the aristocratic structure of the society in which he lives, that his love of music is largely due. It is dangerous *to expose oneself*;[2] and this fear of ridicule, which inhibits

---

[1] When I was in Liverpool, I was taken to see some fourteen-year-old children who worked sixteen or eighteen hours a day; this incident occurred on an occasion when I chanced to be walking with a party of young dandies, aged eighteen or so, not one of whom had less than £4,000 a year, nor a single idea in his thick head—not even that of throwing a shilling to these poor, downtrodden wretches. The Italian is politically crushed; but at least his time is his own; the poorest urchin in the streets of Naples is as untrammelled in pursuing the will-o'-the-wisps of his own desire as the wild boar in the forests; and to my mind, he is less wretched, and above all, less brutalized in spirit, than the Birmingham labourer. Moreover, brutalization of the spirit is contagious; the noble lord in his mansion is very far from being untouched by the boorishness of the ignorant worker.

[2] In English in the original. (*Trans.*)

every young Englishman, compels him to preserve the strictest silence concerning his emotions. But this very reticence, itself answering the exactions of a spirit of proper pride, lends itself to the encouragement of music; music is his only confidant; yet to music he will often entrust the secrets of his most intimate and personal feelings.

It is enough to see the *Beggar's Opera*, or to hear the voice of Miss Stephens, or of the renowned Thomas Moore, to be convinced that the Englishman, beneath his insensitive frame, conceals a very real vein of feeling and of love for music. This disposition, in my experience, is most noticeable in Scotland; for the Scot is infinitely more imaginative, and with this, is condemned to long, dull evenings of dreary inaction by the timeless darkness of his northern winter.

This consideration brings me back once more to the subject of poor Italy and her enforced idleness; for *a creative imagination working in the emptiness of unwanted leisure* is the first and necessary condition which produces music. On the occasion of my first visit to Scotland, I landed at Inverness; and there it chanced that my first impression was of a Highland wake, and of the old, old women keening and chanting over

This scrap of clay from which the breath of life
Has gone for ever . . .[1]

This race, I argued, must be musical. On the day following, as I rode round the crofts, I heard music welling up from all sides. Admittedly, it was not *Italian* music—no, it was something far better; for this was Scotland, and the music was native to the soil from which it had sprung. If Scotland, instead of being poor and barren, were a land of wealth and prosperity; if chance had decreed that Edinburgh should have been the seat of a powerful monarch, and, like St Petersburg, the centre of a rich and *idle* aristocracy, I do not doubt for an instant but that the subterranean springs of natural music, which well up now among the moss-grown boulders of the ancient Kingdom of Caledonia, would have been carefully caught, preserved, purified and distilled into a quintessence of *ideal beauty*, and that, in due course, the term *Scottish music* would have sounded as familiar in our ears as that of *German music* does to-day. The land which has given us Ossian, with the sombre, haunting magic of his legends, or the *Tales of my Landlord*,

[1] A literal translation of the dirge, which my guide provided for me on the spur of the moment.

the land which finds its pride in Robert Burns, might unquestionably be expected to give Europe a new Haydn or another Mozart. Yet stop a while, and think of Haydn's early years and then of Burns, brought near to death by poverty and want, and nearer by the brandy which he took to help him to forget his desperation. If Haydn had not been blessed by fate since childhood by the protection of three or four wealthy patrons, and by the interest of a powerful institution (the choir-school of the Cathedral of St Stephen), the greatest symphonist of Germany might easily have remained an incompetent wheelwright in the town of Rohrau in Hungary. But Prince Esterházy heard Haydn, and gave him a post in his orchestra; a Hungarian prince, you understand, is not at all the same sort of person as a stout and hard-headed Peer with a seat in the Home Counties. One has only to follow up the relationship between Haydn[1] and Prince Esterházy, to cease for ever to marvel at the different destinies of Haydn and of Burns; and even the ostentatious statue recently erected in Burns' memory will cease to be a wonder.

For twenty years and more, a film of the filthiest hypocrisy has been spreading like a loathsome leprosy over the life and manners of the two most civilized peoples in the world. In France, every man in power, from the lowest jack-in-office to the Minister at Court, sneers at the pious-cynical posturing of his superiors, while feeling called upon to wear a similar mask of episcopal righteousness for the benefit of his subordinates.[2] M. *** has a modest government pension, and often stands in front of the print-dealer's shop on the corner, admiring lithographs in the window; but his admiration is compulsorily graded in exact proportion to the *piety* of each artist; otherwise, should he fail to corrupt his own conscience even in this, the most frivolous of all the arts, he may be sure that, at the next ministerial purge, some faithful family friend, who spends his time submitting countless little mis-spelt reports on "morale and loyalty" to the authorities, will unfailingly see

[1] Cf. *Vies de Haydn, de Mozart et de Métastase* [by Stendhal], p. 56 [1824 edition; édition Champion, p. 51].

[2] Under the Napoleonic *régime*, a *Préfet* was known to have summoned a certain student, who was studying at Montpellier under Professor Broussonnet, into his presence, and to have brought this grave charge against him: *Sir, the thesis which you were defending yesterday is anti-catholic!* The thesis in question had dealt with a certain disease of the lower abdomen, whose first symptom was acute depression; the student should, of course, have realized that depression is a state of the *mind*, and therefore that its cause is to be sought for in the *soul*.

to it that his pension is stopped at source. Here we have one more *decency*—the *decency of hypocrisy*—come to drive yet another nail into the coffin of joy and spontaneity in France. As for England ...! Let me simply transcribe a sentence from the pen of her greatest poet:

The cant which is the crying sin of this double-dealing and false-speaking time of selfish spoilers ...[1]

Painting in France has already been done to death by hypocrisy; is music likewise to be caught and crushed in the entanglement of its tentacles?

In Italy, the hypocrite has no delight in his hypocrisy; the peril is so threatening and close that dissimulation is the merest prudence, and so ceases to be degrading.

I have been guilty of many *extravagances* in this work; and so, to excuse them, and so that it may stand as a corrective, I beg my reader to allow me to set down a *Letter* written by Mademoiselle de Lespinasse, which is not included in the *Correspondence* of the celebrated lady as it was published a few years ago.

---

[1] Preface to the concluding cantos of *Don Juan*. These final cantos contain the finest poetry which I have read for twenty years. The onslaught of Ishmael obliterates the memory of the dreariness of Cain.

AN
APOLOGY

FOR THOSE FAULTS WHICH MY FRIENDS ARE APT TO CALL
MY EXTRAVAGANCES, MY ENTHUSIASMS, MY CONTRADICTIONS,
MY *NON-SEQUITURS*, MY ... ETC., ETC.

*This Tuesday, the thirty-first day
of January, 1775.*

Indeed! I do believe that this is but another snare which you have set to bring about my downfall! Yesterday you smiled and said: To-morrow you are to see *la Fausse Magie*; I entreat therefore of your friendship, that you will write me your opinion on what you have seen. But you know too well, I replied, that I hold no opinions, and that I never judge. No matter, you insisted; I adore to hear your *impressions*, in the first place, because they are true, and in the second, because they are *extravagant*, and being so, I delight in contesting them. This observation, which you believe to be so well-founded, should have checked me in my stride; and after such a warning, I should have stopped and *argued out* a prudent, modest, closely-reasoned judgment; it would, doubtless, have been in execrable taste, and wholly unfurnished with any exact knowledge of the subject under discussion; but at least it would have left intelligent minds unshocked, if only because such minds are indulgent towards the weaknesses of others; and I should have earned thereby the admiration of fools, for a fool admires no one so earnestly as a *true dullard*. Dullness leaves a fool still king in his own realm, whereas vivifying impressions and deep, disturbing motions of the soul do but wound him and set him in a turmoil, yet never shed the least ray of enlightenment upon his spirit, nor reflect the smallest warmth within his soul.

For all that, however, caution shall be cast to the winds; I shall not respect intelligence any more than foolishness; I shall not even fear *your* judgment, for I surrender in advance. I shall seem silly, absurd, or what you will; but I shall be *myself*.

I derived pleasure, great pleasure even, from this opera, and I defy the critics one and all to prove that I was wrong. I admired the genius of Grétry; my enthusiasm made me exclaim twenty times: Never was there anything so exquisite! Never before has music been so subtle, witty and enchanting! It is as amusing, arresting and supple as the conversation of a man of brilliant gifts, who understands how to be always absorbing and never exhausting, whose style is never more eager nor more passionate than the subject demands, and whose language only seems to gain in richness for being perpetually restrained by the modest bounds of taste. Finally, I maintained, if the composer of this music were unknown to me, I should move heaven and earth to become acquainted with him from this very day. I was ceaselessly animated, ceaselessly borne aloft on wings of rapture; the orchestra seemed to speak to my heart in a language plainer than words; and again and again I cried out: *This is delightful!* Indeed, I will say it again now: it *is* delightful to spend two unbroken hours in the company of sweet and caressing sensations, truly reflecting Nature, and yet ever varied. The words, I thought, were charming; and I felt that, from beginning to end, the dramatist had had no other object than to bring out the finest qualities in the composer. The songs were distributed with much intelligence and taste; and the poet had learned the secret of making his *old men* as comic and amusing as those of Molière. Grétry has woven this particular scene into a duet which portrays its gaiety and merriment in a manner which is as lively as it is original. Anyway, what more can I say? I was enthralled, enchanted; and as I cannot criticize a thing which has afforded me so much pleasure, I have no other resource but to applaud and adore it.

Wait, though! I can see you, I can hear you already, smiling in anticipation, sure that I am about to raise Grétry above Gluck, if only because the impression of the present instant, however feeble in itself, is stronger than that of a past already distant. Is it not so? Then you shall be disappointed; and I will pray you to observe that, even when I exaggerate, my praise is never exclusive; for when I extol, the praise comes from my heart, not from my mind, and in my heart I hate disparagement; moreover, I am one of those fortunate beings whose soul can embrace two different objects, in appearance defiant opposites, and adore *both* to the point of madness: in consequence, I may say sincerely that I love and cherish the genius of M. Grétry, and that I admire and esteem that of M. Gluck. But since I am neither learned nor gifted nor foolish enough to assign rank and status to this genius and to that, I have no intention of pronouncing which is the better, nor even of comparing abilities which, in my opinion, should not be set beside one another. I am ignorant of the disparity of talent which Nature has set between them; but this I do know, that even if their degree of genius had been identical in every particular, each would have found himself compelled to make utterly dissimilar use of it, since, in opera, the comic style is not the style of tragedy.

The impression which I received from *Orfeo* held no single element in common with that which I experienced this forenoon. It was so profound, so moving, so agonizing, so absorbing, that I knew no words to express the content of what I felt; I was filled simultaneously with the yearning and with the satisfaction of passion, I was lost unless I could recollect myself in tranquillity; any stranger who had not shared the same experience as I had known, must have thought me stupid. This music claimed so close a correspondence with my soul, with the very temper of my most intimate being, that more than twenty times I was impelled to shut myself in silence and solitude in my own room, so as to renew the pleasure which I had derived from these impressions; in a word, these voices, melodies, accents made very grief a substance of delight, and I felt myself for ever haunted by those tender and lamentable strains: *I have lost thee, O Eurydice.* And what attribute of the mind may serve to conjure up comparisons between *this* and *la Fausse Magie*? How should that which merely charms and entertains be set beside an art which fills the soul, which pierces it and overturns its depths? How should wit be compared with passion? How should joyous, spirited delight be compared with that soft and melancholy mood where anguish seems a sigh of divine bliss? Ah no! I make no comparisons, lest I lose an instant of enjoyment. Yet such an attitude, to you, seems "contradiction in preference" and "disparity in judgment"! Well then, so be it! I will *not* be rational and consistent; I would rather yield to the faintest breath of sensibility, to the least tremor of every kind of feeling; and I will admonish you in the words of Diderot: "O my good friends, enough of rationality; the less we analyse, the more we shall enjoy; the charm of things which merely please and catch the fancy was never destined to submit to critical dissection; the least we owe to what we have enjoyed is our indulgence, which surely will neither corrupt our taste, nor make it less exacting."

So then, the things which I shall love shall be those which stand farthest apart, those which contradict each other most directly. I shall love Gessner, the gentle and idyllic Gessner, who shall restore my soul to calm and quietness. . . . I shall love, I shall be in love with, I shall kneel down and worship and adore *Clarissa*, who, in my eyes, stands among the most beautiful, the most powerful, the most god-like achievements of the spirit of man; I shall yield to the exaltation and the rapture distilled from every drop of beauty which dwells in the deep abundance of this masterpiece. The truth, the simplicity of this strange adventure will so enrich my imagination, that I shall finally grow to be convinced that there is not one of all the *Harlowes* with whom I have not lived and whom I have not known. The fire which burns in them will burn in me; they will awaken every passion which my soul can harbour; yet, because I admire *Clarissa*, I will not disdain *Marianne*; for here, although I shall not learn the truth of feeling, I shall discover the faithful portrait of vanity; I shall explore the depths of vanity through all conditions and degrees of men. I shall find pleasure in studying every subtle shade of vanity, described and brought to life with ingenuity and wit. When I read *Clarissa*, I shall admire the noble simplicity of Richardson; and when I read Marivaux, I shall not be ashamed to love his style, even his affectations, which are often original and amusing, and always spiced with wit.

Yes, in every branch of art I will love things apparently irreconcilable, yet which, in fact, may not be so at all, save in the minds of those who will be always *judging*, and who are afflicted with the misfortune to be insensitive to every shade of feeling. Nature, it is true, has given these poor creatures ample compensation; they are always richly satisfied with their rationality, their moderation and the logical consistency of all their tastes; their judgment is inflexible, and so they believe it to be exact; their soul is made of lead, and so they think it calm and philosophic; *they* finally, enjoy the satisfactions of self-complacency, whereas *I* am lost for ever in the trackless incoherence of extravagance and passion. It is true that these folk, so staid, so solid, so utterly *reasonable*, are scarcely aware of their own existence; whereas I am never conscious for an instant without being racked by unspeakable suffering or dazed with ineffable joy; they are bored, while I am intoxicated; but to do justice both to them and to myself, it must be confessed that, if *they* are sometimes wearisome, *I* am often exhausting.

He whose heart is chill and reasonable may sometimes exaggerate; but he whose soul is caught up in the restless tangle of passions lives in a perpetual chaos of fantastic and disproportionate extravagance; nor can it be otherwise. Both strike beyond the target; but the one has had to make an effort to do so, whereas the other is swept and driven forward by forces outside his control; the first has struggled step by step up a steep path, while the second has leapt the highest peaks without realizing that he has left the ground. Lastly, I observe this difference between exaggeration and extravagance, that those who are guilty of the former are studiously avoided, while those who indulge in the latter are rebelliously abandoned—but only to be sought after anew on the very day following; for the human soul knows no delight so rich as to be stimulated, stirred, excited . . . and such privileges are only to be found in contact with those whose passions roam at large. Such persons rouse antagonism, undoubtedly; they jar on the sensibilities and are indescribably exhausting; one may criticize them, condemn them, detest them even; but even while one does so, their attraction still persists, irresistibly, and against one's will one goes to seek their company. You may protest that my modesty seems curiously in abeyance, and that I am trumpeting my own commendation in tones so brazen that I am bound to shock the taste and fastidiousness of all who are to judge me. But I am talking to *you*, and you are my *friend* first and foremost, rather than my judge; besides, if I were to need an excuse for the Lucifer's-pride which I have just exhibited, remember that I am conducting my own defence and justification, in which special circumstances it is permissible to speak of oneself as one would normally speak only of others; there is therefore no question of appearing modest, but only of being *true*.

So let me return to my proofs; and I will add, that while I have a passionate fondness for Racine, I have discovered passages in Shakespeare which have transported me into a universe of strange delight—and yet, if ever there were *contradiction*, surely it is between these two. The reader is entranced, enthralled by the classical perfection of Racine, by the elegance, the subtlety, the charm of his language; whereas Shakespeare is disgusting and repulsive in his barbaric tastelessness, and yet, in spite of this, one is caught unawares, stunned, swept off one's feet by the power of his originality and by the nobility of his feeling and language in certain passages. Therefore, I pray you, allow me to love both one and the other. I adore the naïve simplicity of La Fontaine; but I adore also the witty, artificial ingenuity of La Motte.

Yet if I were to examine every aspect of art and letters, I should never make an end; for I should have to say that I dote upon the geniality of old Plutarch, and admire the cynical severity of La Roche-foucauld; I love the cheerful disorder of Montaigne; but I am equally fond of the ordered meticulousness and method of Helvétius.

But now I can hear you protesting; what need was there to plague me with *all* the details of your private likes and dislikes? Why did you not rather say plainly, "I take pleasure in *all* art, provided that it be *good* art"? Indeed, why not?—yet pray recall that this is precisely what I have said a hundred times, but that I have never yet persuaded you to believe me; else why should you weary me with endless repetitions, that *I praise too much*, that I am *extravagant, outrée*, that I have *no sense of proportion*? Suppose that I should set out first to prove, by *reason* and *argument*, that I am right to love the things I love—but *love* springs from the very soul itself, not from the reasoning mind. I beg you to be patient with me, while I repeat what you have often heard before: I *feel* everything and *judge* nothing; and therefore you will never hear me say that *this is good* or *that is bad*; instead, I will rather exclaim a thousand times a day: *This I love!* Yes, I love, I shall love, and I shall never cease to be in love with love while there is breath left in me; I shall love all things for the same good argument and reason as a certain great and intelligent woman once said she loved her nephews: *I love the elder because he is clever, and the younger because he is stupid.* O, how right she was! And so I shall resemble her, and say: *I love mustard because it is hot and strong, and blanc-mange because it is cool and soft.* Yet do not suspect, because I am omnivorous, because I am possessed of an insatiable appetite for affection in infinite diversity, that there is there-fore nothing in man, in art, in all the world, which I should find dis-gusting, noisome or repugnant! God in Heaven! If I were to enter into detail, there would never be an end of it . . . suffice it if I tell you just one or two of the things which I cannot tolerate. Firstly, then, verse devoid alike of thought and feeling, whose only merit lies in its vir-tuosity, like that of M. *** or M. ***; or verse which is written in a kind of precious secret code, intelligible only to the author himself and to a private circle of admirers, like that of M. *** or M. ***; or tragedies whose themes are harsh, impassioned and momentous, and whose style is puling, weak and platitudinous, if not positively un-grammatical—like those of M. *** or M. ***; or finally (since I *must* make an end of it) I might say that the precious, the *mannered*, the titillating, even the *super-subtle*, above all the *insipid*, affect me much as senna-pods or camomile-tea, or other nauseating purgatives and drugs; yet with this difference, that necessity may sometimes overcome nausea in the case of camomile and senna, but that *nothing* can make palatable the hateful insipidity of art, whose taste I do, and did, and always shall detest.

In the matter of persons, the motives governing my respective attitudes of fondness or disfavour are identical with those which determine my pleasure or repugnance relating to objects of the inanimate world; I prefer animals to fools; I prefer a man of sensibility to a man of witty phrases; I prefer a woman of deep and passionate feelings to a woman of cool and rational intellect; I prefer rustic *naïveté* to cultured preciosity; I like plain speaking better than soft flattery; and before all things, above all things, I like, I love, I *adore* simplicity and kindness and charity . . . but the greatest of these is charity. Charity is the virtue which should dwell in the breasts of all those who wield power; charity is the virtue which brings the sweetest comfort to those who suffer and are weak; charity, finally, is the virtue which redeems every failing, which consoles for every misfortune; and even if I knew that others would take advantage of it, even if I knew that *I* should suffer, were I offered the choice between the charitable kindness of Madame Geoffrin and the dazzling beauty of Madame de Brienne, I should say: give me charity, and I shall be beloved; kindness and charity are the first, perhaps the *only* gifts, in whose possession I should find delight. Unless I am mistaken, there is a greater gift still, the gift of *love*; but charity is already a kind of spiritual affection, and he who possesses it is half in love with everything that languishes in suffering and misfortune. Ah! What a wealth, an inexhaustible fountain of *such* love there is in our poor world! And he whose soul is filled to such a pitch with this great gift of kindness, pity, charity, this gift I worship, this gift I always envy—what need has *he* of pleasure or of the fleeting joys of passion? Dull lethargy will never claim *his* soul; and is not this release, this spirit-freeing prick and stimulus, the greatest charm of passion?

But, tell me, if I am to wish this virtue of charity upon anyone, should it not be first and foremost upon *you*, that you should possess it even to excess? What deep reserves of charity and indulgence must needs be hidden within your soul, if you are to read this endless, dull, exhausting *apologia*! Ah, now perhaps, you will be chary ever afterwards of loading me with silly accusations! If my *extravagances* are intolerable, they are at least less so than my justification; but remember that I was provoked; not one of my sweet, kind friends but is for ever heaping coals of fire upon my head, and so I desire to prove to them once and for all that those things which they are pleased to call my extravagances, my disparities, *etc.*, are nothing else but reason, sensibility and passion. Well, what is the outcome, the consequence of all this? Shall I whisper it in your ear? ... No, no, you would never believe me, and yet I should have betrayed the secret of my soul. Adieu; condemn me, criticize me, but do not cease to love me. The cup of my happiness shall be filled with your bounty, and I shall be sensible of nothing else.

APPENDICES

APPENDIX I

Some Notes concerning the Life and Works of Mozart[1]

THE Italians are constantly poking fun at the Germans; they think them stupid, and never tire of inventing comic anecdotes about them. I was forever finding that I had insulted the patriotic nationalism of petty politicians, and thus that I had made myself new enemies, whenever I insisted on remarking, "What has Italy produced in all the XVIIIth century that can compare with Mozart, Frederick the Great or Catherine?"

Wolfgang Mozart, he in whom the bright flame of genius shone most clearly through the enshrouding, dull preoccupations of a prosaic world, was born in Salzburg, a pretty little town lying among the picturesque, forest-clad hills which form the Northern slopes of the Italian Alps. He was a child-prodigy, and by the time he was six, he was already touring Europe with his father, who soon saw that there was profit to be got from his son's incredible virtuosity on the piano.

Mozart lived in Munich, where he married, and later in Vienna, where he was always grossly underpaid by Joseph II, who affected to prefer Italian music.

Mozart has left us *nine operas with Italian libretti*:

> *La Finta semplice*
> *Mitridate* (Milan 1770)
> *Lucio Silla* (Milan 1773)

The last two works, as far as I know, are mediocre, but full of academic niceties as such things were understood in the year 1773. How should Mozart, at the age of 17, have found the courage to break with fashionable traditions? No step could have been better calculated

---

[1] This note was inserted in the (second) 1824 edition of the *Vie de Rossini*, between the *Préface* and the *Introduction*. Readers are referred to the *Index* for the correct dates of Mozart's life and works. (*Trans.*)

to ensure failure in the opinion of those worthy critics with solid
academic trainings, who, in every city in Europe, form the bulk, and
the *noisiest* bulk, of any audience. It is precisely because of the existence
of an overwhelming majority of such people that it is so urgently to be
wished that articles in the press which deal with music should show
some traces of common-sense.

La Giardiniera
Idomeneo

Mozart wrote the latter opera in Munich in 1781, at a time when he
was madly in love. I am not sufficiently familiar with *Idomeneo* to
judge whether it betrays any particular hints of tenderness or melancholy.

Le Nozze di Figaro (1787)
Don Giovanni (1787)

In 1813, when I was in Dresden, I once met Luigi Bassi, that
wonderful old *buffo*, for whom, twenty-six years earlier, Mozart had
written the rôles of Don Giovanni, and of Almaviva in *le Nozze di
Figaro*. If I were to tell of the respectful curiosity with which I tried to
induce this kindly old man to talk, no one would take me seriously. "Mr.
Mozart", he would answer (how entrancing to hear someone who still
said *Mr* Mozart!) "Mr Mozart was an extremely eccentric and absent-
minded young man, but not without a certain spirit of pride. He was
very popular with the ladies, in spite of his small size; but he had a
most unusual face, and he could cast a spell on any woman with his
eyes ..." On this subject, Bassi told me three or four little anecdotes,
which, however, I must refrain from including at this point.

Così fan tutte (opera buffa)

The tenor aria, *la mia Doralice*, is of exquisite gracefulness, and it
strikes a new note of tenderness, infinitely superior to the finest things
in Paisiello; but the most wonderful thing is the *finale*, with its gentle
note of sighing sensuality, which is the secret of Mozart's style in all
passages where he is not overwhelmingly powerful or dramatic.
Mozart's unique position in the world of art is due precisely to his
combination of these two dissimilar qualities, dramatic power and

gentle sensuality; Michelangelo is never anything but overwhelmingly powerful; Correggio is never anything but sweetly voluptuous.[1]

La Clemenza di Tito (1792)

I do not know for certain whether it was due to the ostentatious preference displayed by Joseph II, but towards the end of his career, Mozart was moving quite perceptibly in the direction of Italian music. The distance between *Don Giovanni* and *la Clemenza di Tito* is immense.

Mozart also left *three operas with German libretti*:

Die Entführung aus dem Serail (1782)
Der Schauspieldirektor

and the masterpiece entitled:

Die Zauberflöte (1782)

The *libretto* of *die Zauberflöte* conforms exactly to that degree of charming extravagance and light, amusing fantasy which comes so easily to any French writer in search of a facile popularity; but, as we have maintained so often, this type of writing may often be ideal for the requirements of music. Music holds the secret of transforming even the cheap fancies of the vulgarest imagination into conceptions of noble grace and individual genius.

Mozart also left an almost countless number of songs, fragments of scenes, symphonies, *etc.*, and several *Masses*, of which the most famous is the *Requiem Mass*, which he composed under the shadow of the knowledge that it was for his own funeral—a foreboding which was indeed realized; he believed that the Angel of Death, disguised beneath the form and figure of an old man, had commanded him to compose this work.

Mozart surprised the secret qualities of those *wind-instruments* which are so intimately expressive of the melancholy sadness of the North. A short passage from a Mozart symphony, decked out with a couple of pages of accessory *motifs* to serve as an introduction and conclusion, would make an admirable overture to any modern opera. Born on the

[1] The *finale* in question is a perfect illustration of the contention that there is a certain type of beauty whose very essence is *tranquillity*—the beauty of Dresden, for instance, on a fine autumn day. This *finale* is one of those passages in which music comes closest to antique sculpture, seen in Rome in the lonely silence of some deserted museum.

27th of January 1756, Mozart died in Vienna on the 5th of December 1792, aged 36. If he had lived in France, he would never have earned the least degree of fame or reputation; he was *too simple*.

No *ars poetica* is of any direct value to the artist, who can only be spoiled by the reading of theories; theories are destined to influence the *public*. For instance, if the French public were well-versed in a decent theory of sculpture, it would never tolerate a statue of Louis XIV in a full-bottomed wig and with naked legs*!

APPENDIX II

List of Rossini's Compositions

STUDENT WORKS

Title	Date of Performance or Composition
Se il vuol la Molinara	
Duets for Horn	
Demetrio e Polibio	Rome, 18th May 1812 (comp. 1806?)
Mass for Male Voices	Ravenna, 1808
Il Pianto d'Armonia sulla Morte d'Orfeo	Bologna, August 1808
Two *Overtures*	
Five *String Quartets*	
Quartet for Wind Instruments	(?)
Varia	

OPERAS

La Cambiale di Matrimonio	Venice, 3rd November 1810
L'Equivoco Stravagante	Bologna, 26th October 1811
L'Inganno Felice	Venice, 8th January 1812
Ciro in Babilonia	Ferrara, 14th March 1812
La Scala di Seta	Venice, 9th May 1812
La Pietra del Paragone	Milan, 26th September 1812
L'Occasione fa il Ladro	Venice, 24th November 1812
Il Signor Bruschino	Venice, January 1813
Tancredi	Venice, 6th February 1813
L'Italiana in Algeri	Venice, 22nd May 1813
Aureliano in Palmira	Milan, 26th December 1813
Il Turco in Italia	Milan, 14th August 1814
Sigismondo	Venice, 26th December 1814
Elisabetta, regina d'Inghilterra	Naples, 4th October 1815
Torvaldo e Dorliska	Rome, 26th December 1815

Il Barbiere di Siviglia	Rome, 20th February 1816
La Gazzetta	Naples, 26th September 1816
Otello	Naples, 4th December 1816
La Cenerentola	Rome, 25th January 1817
La Gazza Ladra	Milan, 31st May 1817
Armida	Naples, 11th November 1817
Adelaide di Borgogna	Rome, 27th December 1817
Mosè in Egitto	Naples, 5th March 1818
Adina	Lisbon, 22nd June 1826 (comp. 1818)
Ricciardo e Zoraide	Naples, 3rd December 1818
Ermione	Naples, 27th March 1819
Odoardo e Cristina	Venice, 24th April 1819
La Donna del Lago	Naples, 24th September 1819
Bianca e Faliero	Milan, 26th December 1819
Maometto II	Naples, 3rd December 1820
Matilde Shabran	Rome, 24th February 1821
Zelmira	Naples, 16th February 1822
Semiramide	Venice, 3rd February 1823
Il Viaggio a Reims	Paris, 19th June 1825
Le Siège de Corinthe	Paris, 9th October 1826
Moïse	Paris, 26th March 1827
Le Comte Ory	Paris, 20th August 1828
Guillaume Tell	Paris, 3rd August 1829

PASTICCIOS

Ivanhoé	Paris, 15th September 1826
Le Testament	Paris, 22nd January 1827
Cinderella	London, 13th April 1830
Robert Bruce	Paris, 30th December 1846
Andremo a Parigi	Paris, 26th October 1848
Un Curioso Accidente	Paris, 27th November 1859
La Boutique Fantasque (ballet)	London, 5th June 1919
Rossini (operetta)	Rome, 18th May 1922

SACRED MUSIC

Messa Solenne	Naples, 19th March 1820

Stabat Mater Paris, 7th January 1842
La Foi, l'Espérance, la Charité Paris, 20th November 1844
Petite Messe Solennelle Paris, 14th March 1864
  Varia

MISCELLANEOUS

Egle ed Irene (cantata) Milan, 1814
Inno dell' Indipendenza Bologna, April 1815
Le Nozze di Teti e di Peleo Naples, 24th April 1816
  (cantata)
La Morte di Didone (cantata) Venice, 2nd May 1818 (comp. 1811)
La Riconoscenza (cantata) Naples 27th December 1821
Il Pianto delle Muse in Morte London, 9th June 1824
  di Lord Byron (cantata)
Soirées Musicales (songs and Paris, 1835
  duets)
Le Chant des Titans Paris, 22nd December 1861
Hymne à Napoléon III, etc. Paris, 1st July 1867
A National Hymn Birmingham, 1867
"Péchés de Vieillesse" (piano Paris, 1857–68
  pieces, songs, etc.)
Varia (cantatas, songs, marches, etc.)

For fuller details, see Herbert Weinstock, *Rossini*, London (O.U.P.) 1968, pp. 489–531.

BIBLIOGRAPHY

I

PREVIOUS EDITIONS OF *THE LIFE OF ROSSINI*

— *Memoirs of Rossini*. By the Author of the Lives of Haydn and Mozart. London. Printed for T. Hookham, Old Bond Street, by J. and C. Adlard, 23 Bartholomew Close. 1824. In-8vo, pp. xlii + 287.

— *Vie de Rossini*, par M. de Stendhal; ornée des Portraits de Rossini et de Mozart. *Laissez aller votre pensée comme cet insecte qu'on lâche en l'air avec un fil à la patte.* Socrate, *Nuées* d'Aristophane. Paris, chez Auguste Boulland & Cie., Libraire, rue du Battoir No. 12, 1824. In-8vo, pp. viii + 623.

— *Vie de Rosini* [*sic*]. Pseudo-second edition, deliberately put out by Stendhal in order to persuade the public that the first edition had been exhausted by the vast demand of the readers. 1824.

— *Rossini's Leben und Treiben*, vornehmlich nach den Nachrichten des Herrn v. Stendhal geschildert, und mit Urteilen der Zeitgenossen über seinen musikalischen Charakter begleitet, von Amadeus Wendt. Leipzig 1824, Verlag von Leopold Voss. In-12mo, pp. xvi + 440.

— *Vie de Rossini*, par Stendhal (Henry Beyle) . . . nouvelle édition . . . Paris, Michel Lévy Frères, Libraires Editeurs, rue Vivienne . . . 1854. In-8vo, pp. 375.

— *Vie de Rossini*, par Stendhal (Henry Beyle) . . . nouvelle édition entièrement revue . . . Paris, Michel Lévy Frères, Libraires Editeurs, rue Vivienne . . . 1864. In-8vo, pp. 375.

— *Vie de Rossini*, par Stendhal (Henry Beyle) . . . nouvelle édition . . . Paris, Calman Lévy (*Bibliothèque Contemporaine*). In-8vo, pp. 375. (1876.)

— *Vie de Rossini*, par Stendhal (Henry Beyle) . . . nouvelle édition entièrement revue . . . Paris, Calman Lévy (*Bibliothèque Contemporaine*), pp. 375. (1892.)

— Stendhal, *Vie de Rossini*, suivie des *Notes d'un Dilettante;* texte établi et annoté avec préface et avant-propos par Henry Prunières. Paris, Librairie ancienne Honoré Champion, 1922. 2 vols., in-8vo, pp. lxiv + 380; 506. (Standard critical edition in the series, *Œuvres Complètes de Stendhal*, under the direction of Paul Arbelet and Edouard Champion).

— Stendhal, *Vie de Rossini* . . . Edited by Henri Martineau. 2 vols., Paris (*Le Divan*), 1929. Pp. xxxvii + 337; 341.

— Stendhal, *Vie de Rossini*. Edited by V. Del Litto, Lausanne (Editions Rencontre) 1960.

II

ROSSINIANA

Astruc, Zacharie. "Lettre à Stendhal sur l'*Otello* de Rossini." *Le Quart-d'Heure, Gazette des Gens demi-sérieux* (Paris), 20th April 1859.

Azevedo, Alexis-Jacob. *G. Rossini, sa Vie et ses Oeuvres.* Paris, 1864.

Bacchelli, Riccardo. *Rossini e Esperienze rossiniane*. Milan, 1959.

Barini, G. "Per il Centenario del *Mosè*." *Nuova Antologia*, 1914.

— "Il Nuovo Teatro Quirino e il *Mosè* del Rossini." *Nuova Antologia*, 1915.

Bollettino del Centro Rossiniano di Studi. Thirty issues, Pesaro, 1955–1960. New series, Pesaro, January 1967–. (Articles in this journal are not listed separately in this *Bibliography*: they can be found in Weinstock, pp. 535–60.)

Bollettino del primo Centenario rossiniano. Eighteen issues, Pesaro, 29th February–15th September 1892.

Bonafé, Félix. *Rossini et son Œuvre*. Le-Puy-en-Velay, 1955.

Bonaventura, Arnaldo. *Rossini*. Florence, 1934.

Brighenti, Pietro. *Della Musica rossiniana e del suo autore*. Bologna, 1830.

Cametti, Alberto. *La Musica teatrale a Roma cento anni fa* (collected articles from the *Annuario della Regia Accademia di Santa Cecilia*, mainly published 1915–17). Rome, 1926–32.

— *Un Poeta melodrammatico romano: Appunti e notizie in gran parte inedite sopra Jacopo Ferretti e i musicisti del suo tempo*. Milan [1898].

Carpani, Giuseppe. *Lettera di Giuseppe Carpani all'anonimo autore dell'articolo sul Tancredi di Rossini, inserito nella Gazzetta di Berlino, No. 7, 1818*. Milan (G. Maspero) 1818.

— *Lettera del Professore Giuseppe Carpani sulla musica di Gioacchino Rossini. . . .* Rome (Puccinelli) 1826.

— *Le Rossiniane, ossia Lettere musico-teatrali principalmente sulla musica del Rossini*. Padua (Minerva) 1824.

Coe, Richard N. "Stendhal et les quatre Cantatrices françaises." *Stendhal Club*, III, No. 9, 15th October 1960, pp. 47–54.

— "Stendhal, Rossini and the 'Conspiracy of Musicians' ". *Modern Language Review*, LIV, No. 2, April 1959, pp. 179–93.

Cooke, James Francis. *Rossini, a short Biography*. Philadelphia, 1929.

Cowen, Sir Frederick H. *Rossini*. London and New York, 1912.

Derwent, George Harcourt Johnstone, Baron. *Rossini and some forgotten Nightingales*. London, 1934.

Desnoyers, Louis. *De l'opéra en 1847, à propos de Robert Bruce*. Paris, 1847.

Edwards, Henry Sutherland. *The Life of Rossini*. London, 1869 (largely adapte from Stendhal).

Faller, H. *Die Gesangskoloratur in Rossinis Opern. . . .* 1935.

Fara, Giulio. *Genio e ingegno musicale: Gioacchino Rossini*. Turin, 1915.

Fracaroli, Arnaldo. *Rossini*. Milan, 1941.

Gallini, Natale. "Importante inedito rossiniano: La musica di scena dell' *Edipo a Colono* di Sofocle ritrovata nella sua integrità." *La Scala: Rivista dell'Opera* No. 31, Milan, 1952.

Giorgi-Righetti, Geltrude. *Cenni di una Donna cantante sopra il Maestro Rossini, in riposta a ciò che ne scrisse nell' estate dell'anno 1822 il giornalista inglese in Parigi, e fu riportato in una Gazetta di Milano dello stesso anno*. Bologna, 1823.

Gozzano, Umberto. *Rossini: Il Romanzo dell'Opera*. Turin, 1955.

Guerrazzi, Francesco Domenico. *Manzoni, Verdi e l'albo rossiniano*. Milan, 1874.

Hirt, Giulio C. (pseud. of L. Torchi). "Di alcuni autografi di G. Rossini." *Rivista Musicale Italiana*, Vol. II, fasc. i, 1895.

Hughes, Spike. "Introduction to Rossini's *Cenerentola*." *Opera* (London), 1952.

Loewenberg, Alfred. *Paisiello's und Rossini's Barbiere di Siviglia*. 1939.

Marinelli, Carlo. "Discografia rossiniana." *Rassegna Musicale* (Rome), 9th July 1954.

Michotte, Edmond. *Souvenirs: La Visite de Richard Wagner à Rossini* (Paris 1860). Paris, 1906.

Montazio, Enrico. *Gioacchino Rossini*. Turin, 1862.

Parent de Curzon, Henri. *Rossini*. Paris, 1930.

Porter, Andrew. "A lost opera by Rossini." *Music and Letters* (London) January 1964.

Pougin, Arthur. *Rossini: Notes, impressions, souvenirs, commentaires*. Paris, 1871.

Prunières, Henri. "Stendhal et l'opéra buffa de Rossini." *L'Opéra-Comique* (Paris), April 1929.

Pugliese, Giuseppe. "Stendhal et Rossini." *La Revue Critique des Idées et des Livres* (Paris), 1920.

Radiciotti, Giuseppe. *Gioacchino Rossini: Vita documentata, opere ed influenza su l'arte*. Three vols, Tivoli, 1927–9.

—"I primi anni e studi di Gioacchino Rossini." *Rivista Musicale Italiana* (Turin), 1917, XXIV, Nos. 2, 3, 4.

Ricci, Corrado. *Rossini: Le sue case e le sue donne*. Milan, 1889.

Rognoni, Luigi. *Rossini, con un'appendice comprendente lettere, documenti, testimonianze*. Parma, 1956.

Roncaglia, Gino. *Rossini l'olimpico*. Milan, 1946, 2nd. ed. 1953.

Rossini, Gioacchino. *Lettere inedite di Gioacchino Rossini* (ed. Giuseppe Mazzatinti). Imola, 1890.

— *Lettere inedite e rare di G. Rossini* (ed. G. Mazzatinti). Imola, 1892.

— *Lettere di G. Rossini* (ed. G. Mazzatinti and F. and G. Manis). Florence, 1902.

Rossiniana (ed. by the R. Conservatorio G.B. Martini di Bologna). Bologna, 1942.

Rovani, Giuseppe. *La mente di Gioachino Rossini*. Florence, 1871.

Toye, Francis. *Rossini, a Study in Tragi-Comedy*. London, 1934.

Vatielli, Francesco. *Rossini a Bologna*. Bologna, 1918.

Viviani, Vittorio (ed.). *I Libretti di G. Rossini*. Milan, 1965.

Weinstock, Herbert. *Rossini: a Biography*. London, 1968.

III

MISCELLANEOUS

Armani, Franco. *La Scala: breve biografia (1778–1950)*. Milan, n.d.

Berton, Henri-Montan. *De la Musique mécanique et de la musique philosophique*. Paris, 1821.

Bosdari, F. *La Vita musicale a Bologna nel periodo napoleonico*. Bologna, 1914.

Burney, Dr Charles. *A general History of Music*. Four vols., London, 1776–89.

— *A musical Tour in France and Italy*. London, 1774.

Cambiasi, Pompeo. *Cimarosa*. Milan, 1901.

— *La Scala, 1778–1906: note storiche e statistiche*. 5th ed., Milan, 1906.

Castil-Blaze. *L'Opéra Italien de 1548 à 1856*. Paris, 1856.

Catalogo del Museo Teatrale alla Scala (ed. Stefano Vittadini). Milan, 1940.

Chilesotti, Oscar. *I nostri maestri del passato*. Paris, 1882.

Choron et Fayolle. *Le Dictionnaire des Musiciens*. Two vols., Paris, 1810–11.

Coe, Richard N. "Stendhal and 'Frau Mozart'". *Proceedings of the Leeds Philosophical Society*, VIII, pt. iv, 1959, pp. 254–74.

De Angelis, Alberto. *La Musica a Roma nel secolo XIX*. Rome, 1935.

De Filippis, F., and Arnese, R. *Cronache del teatro di San Carlo, 1737–1960.* Two vols., Naples, 1961.

Della Corte, Andrea. *Paisiello (con una tavola tematica)*; *L'Estetica musicale di P. Metastasio.* Turin, 1922.

Ebers, John. *Seven Years of the King's Theatre.* London, 1828.

Faustini, L. *Di Rosmunda Pisaroni: Cenni biografici e aneddotici.* Piacenza, 1884.

Fétis, François-Joseph. *Biographie universelle des musiciens.* . . . 2nd ed., 10 vols, Paris, 1873–8.

Giulini, Maria Ferranti. *Giuditta Pasta e i suoi tempi: memorie e lettere.* Milan, 1935.

Grove's Dictionary of Music and Musicians.

Heriot, Angus, *The Castrati in Opera.* London, 1956.

Hughes, Spike. *Great Opera-Houses.* London, 1956.

Mocenigo. *Il Teatro La Fenice.* Venice, 1926.

Morgan, Lady. *Italy.* 3 vols., London, 1821.

Mount Edgcumbe, Earl of. *Musical Reminiscences.* London, 1834.

Prunières, Henri. *L'Opéra Italien en France avant Lulli.* Paris, 1913.

Radiciotti, Giuseppe. "Il Barbaia nella legenda e nella storia." *L'Arte Pianistica,* Naples, 1920.

Ritorni, Carlo. *Commentarii della Vita . . . di Salvatore Viganò.* 1838.

Romani, Luigi. *Teatro alla Scala: Cronologia di tutti gli spettacoli.* . . . Milan, n.d.

Rosenthal, Harold. *Two Centuries of Opera at Covent Garden.* London, 1958.

Smith, William C. *The Italian Opera and contemporary Ballet in London, 1789–1820: A Record of Performances and Players, with Reports from the Journals of the Time.* London, 1953.

Soubies, Albert. *Le Théâtre Italien de 1801 à 1913.* Paris, 1913.

Villarosa, C. A. de. *Memorie dei compositori di Musica del Regno di Napoli.* Naples, 1840.

Weinstock, Herbert. *Donizetti and the World of Opera in Italy, Paris and Vienna in the First Half of the Nineteenth Century.* New York and London, 1963.

Fuller bibliographical indications will be found in Herbert Weinstock's *Rossini: A Biography* (1968), pp. 535–60.

NOTES

Page

Title-page *But let your thoughts* . . . Rogers' translation, lines 762–3

v   *Table of Contents.* This catalogue of singular details is Stendhal's own work.

3   . . . *you might find an opera by Rossini.* Stendhal had in fact lived in Italy with few interruptions between 1814 and 1821. During the last three years of this period he had carried on a long correspondence with his friend and literary agent in Paris, Baron Adolphe de Mareste, describing the various operas he had seen; and many of the ideas in the *Life of Rossini* were originally worked out in this form.

3   . . . *two or three others.* . . . *Vies de Haydn, de Mozart et de Métastase* (1814); *Histoire de la Peinture en Italie* (1817); *Rome, Naples et Florence* (1817); *De L'Amour* (1822); *Racine et Shakespeare I* (1823).

4   . . . *some thirty or forty inaccuracies.* . . . Perhaps a hundred would be nearer the mark. The reader is referred to Herbert Weinstock, *Rossini: A Biography* (London, 1968) for a factually accurate account of the composer's whole career.

4   . . . *to appear in English.* . . . This English edition did in fact appear: *Memoirs of Rossini, by the Author of the Lives of Haydn and Mozart*, London (Hookham), January 1824. However, it contains only about half the material which was finally included in the *Vie de Rossini*.

4   . . . . *just off the Place Beauvau.* . . . Probably a discreet allusion to the salon of the Countess Curial, Stendhal's mistress, who lived at No. 9, rue des Saussaies, at which address Mademoiselle Weltz used to give music-lessons to Clémentine Curial's daughter. Mlle. Weltz was a pupil of Federigo Massimino, who, in 1823, had opened a new music-school at 180 rue de Montmartre.

4   . . . *Montmorency.* . . . The date is probably accurate. Montmorency was a popular retreat for writers of the period, standing in relation to Paris much as Hampstead did to London.

5   . . . *barbarous treatment.* . . . Cimarosa had been an active partisan of revolutionary ideas under the "Parthenopian Republic"; when the French were expelled from Naples, he was imprisoned and condemned to death; but King Ferdinand commuted his sentence to exile. The composer died on his way abroad, in Venice, on 11th Jan. 1801. He was rumoured to have been poisoned on the orders of the King.

9   . . . *impetuous temperament.* Part at least of Stendhal's hostility towards mere "mechanical performers" on musical instruments is due to his own lamentable failure to succeed in learning to play one. On the other hand, the aesthetic ideal of "expressiveness" forms an essential part of Stendhal's sensibility, and he applies it as frequently to painting or to ballet as to music.

10   . . . *beyond the range of their technique.* The substance of this anecdote was recounted in the *Journal de Paris* in Sept. 1805, although the episode is set in Florence. The source was probably Franz Niemtscher, *Leben des k.k. Kapellmeisters Mozart*, Prague, 1798.

Page

11 ... *scurrility and baseness*. . . . Stendhal himself had been driven out of Milan in 1821 by political rumour-mongering, and his hostility to the Italian press remained unabated until the end of his life. It is to be remembered that his arch-enemy, Giuseppe Carpani, was a right-wing political pamphleteer; however, it is fair to note that Italian music-criticism at the time was inane rather than violent.

12 ... *Princess Beatrice d'Este*. Consort of the Archduke Ferdinand, son of Maria-Theresa and Governor-General of Lombardy, who kept court at Monza. Stendhal disliked and despised this royal couple, not only as symbols of the Austrian oppression of Italy, but also as the patrons of Giuseppe Carpani. Later, Beatrice's son became Francesco IV of Modena, and a model for the abominable princeling, Ranuce-Ernest IV, of the *Chartreuse de Parme*.

12 ... *Bridge of Arcola*. See *Index*, under heading *Bonaparte*.

13 ... *it is memory*. . . . Like Proust, Stendhal was deeply concerned with the part played by memory in the development of a sensibility. See the Translator's "Stendhal and the Art of Memory", in *Currents of Thought in French Literature*, Oxford, 1965, pp. 145–64.

13 ... *A friend of mine once wrote*. . . . This passage is in fact adapted from Letter XIX of Stendhal's own *Life of Haydn*.

14 ... *changes every thirty years*. Stendhal's belief that the standards of beauty change from generation to generation, as well as from country to country, formed an essential element in his "relativist" aesthetic, and constituted one of the most significant arguments which he used in his campaign against the older aesthetic of French classicism.

14 ... *Pacchiarotti*. . . . Stendhal describes a visit to the great singer in *Rome, Naples et Florence en 1817* (18th June 1817).

17 ... *galvanism*. . . . For an analysis of the philosophy of "galvanism", see A. Wolf, *A History of Science, Technology and Philosophy in the XVIIIth Century*, London, 1938, pp. 256–60. Stendhal himself was deeply interested in the relationship between physiological and emotional reactions, and was profoundly influenced by Cabanis' *Rapports du Physique et du Moral de l'Homme* (1802).

17 ... *he happens to be already preoccupied*. . . . A fundamental idea which is developed throughout the *Life of Rossini*. Music itself does no create emotion: rather it acts on the physical senses, which in their turn stimulate the imagination; and it is the power of imagination thus stimulated to embellish, transform or "embroider" emotions *already existing* in the consciousness.

18 ... *which it induces in the listener*. . . . In spite of Stendhal's quasi-materialistic belief that the essence of music lies in its physical impact on the senses, he none the less skilfully avoids any mechanistic interpretation. In fact, his analysis of the process of musical appreciation is strangely close to a modern, or phenomenological, theory of perception. Images in the mind result from the impact of material phenomena through the senses; but at the same time it is the mind alone which gives meaning or value to these phenomena. Thus perception is a constant interaction between subjective and objective.

20 ... *harmony*. . . . "Harmony", in Stendhal's use of the term, means everything that is not vocal melody.

20   ... *complex and erudite music.* Harmonic audacity had been a characteristic of Italian music at the beginning of the XVIIIth century. But in the second half of the century there had been a movement towards harmonic ingenuousness and "simplicity". The reaction to this comes after 1800, when the "new" symphonic music of Haydn and Mozart begins to influence operatic composers. Rossini studied harmony by rescoring Haydn's quartets.

24   ... *when I was garrisoned in Brescia.* .... Stendhal was stationed in Brescia in 1801, as a second-lieutenant in the 6th dragoons. He had already told the story of the "melomaniac" in the *Life of Haydn*, Letter III.

25   ... *the sextet from Elena.* Stendhal describes the sextet in *Rome, Naples et Florence* (1826), at the date of the 4th October 1816.

26   ... *Macbeth.* .... As a clamorous partisan of the Romantic, as opposed to the Classical theatre, Stendhal was an enthusiast of Shakespeare. He had seen Kean acting in London.

27   ... *the absurdity of the production.* .... It is important to remember that the *Life of Rossini* is to some extent a political pamphlet. As an opponent of the Restoration, Stendhal was hostile to all Institutions controlled by the restored monarchy—of which the *Théâtre Italien* was one. A careful examination of the evidence shows that Stendhal's accusations against Paër are grossly exaggerated, even when they are not totally unfounded. By 1822–3, the repertoire of the theatre was entirely dominated by Rossinian opera, mostly in admirable and successful productions. The only two failures had been *Torvaldo e Dorliska* (a poor opera in any case) and *La Pietra del Paragone.* See the translator's "Stendhal, Rossini and the 'Conspiracy of Musicians' ", *Modern Language Review*, April 1959, pp. 179–93.

27   ... *L'Italiana in Algeri.* .... This opera was first produced in Paris on 1st Feb. 1817, and had failed lamentably: but this had been under the previous (Catalani-Valabrègue) régime. When it was revived by Paër (27th Nov. 1821), it was immediately successful, and stayed in the repertoire more or less permanently.

27   ... *its most thunderous applause.* .... *La Pietra* was produced on 5th April 1821, and ran for three nights only. Here (but only here) Stendhal's accusations appear to be justified. The libretto was completely mutilated, and much of the music was by composers other than Rossini.

31   ... *died in Vienna in 1796.* Cf. *Index*, heading *Mozart.*

32   ... *Backstairs patriotism.* .... In the original, "le patriotisme d'antichambre" —a favourite phrase of Stendhal's.

35   ... *was an appalling flop.* .... In 1816, Stendhal published an article in *Lo Spettatore* (Milan), reviewing Mozart's *Magic Flute.* Stendhal appears to have been on good terms with Petracchi, who probably helped him to get his articles on music published in the Milanese reviews. It is a fact that Mozart has rarely achieved great popularity in Italy.

37   ... *it is a frenzy.* .... In *De l'Amour* (1822) Stendhal develops in detail this theory of the comparative effects of different national temperaments on the expression of love.

39   ... *such people.* .... This paragraph accurately describes Stendhal's own considered judgement on Rossini.

Page

40 ... *telescoping.* ... In the original, Stendhal uses the verb *syncoper*, which can have this meaning in grammar, but not in music.

44 ... *death of art in Italy.* Another of Stendhal's persistent and paradoxical theories. In a republic (*i.e.*, in a democracy) it is necessary for the stability of the state for all the citizens to devote themselves, with single-minded rationality and purpose, to the business of politics. They will therefore have no real leisure. But without leisure, art is impossible. *Ergo*, art is impossible in a democracy; it can only flourish under a tyranny.

46 ... *third-rate horn-player.* ... Giuseppe Rossini (known as *Vivazza*) in fact played both horn and trumpet; he was a member of the orchestra at the Teatro del Sole (Pesaro), and also of the military band at Ferrara. After 1789, he became official town-trumpeter of Pesaro.

47 ... *a competent seconda donna.* ... Anna Guidarini had a good but untrained natural soprano. She was a seamstress at the time of Rossini's birth. Later she made her début at the Teatro Civico, Bologna. The height of her touring career came between 1798 and 1802: she was known as "la Catalani delle seconde donne".

47 ... *from Pesaro to Bologna.* ... This is inaccurate. During his parents' tours 1798–1802, Gioacchino was left at home with his grandmother in Pesaro. In 1802, he was taken to Bologna, and introduced to Padre Stanislao Mattei, who passed him on for instruction in the rudiments of music to Maestro Angelo Tesei. But it turned out that Gioacchino was still too young and indisciplined to profit from this teaching. Between 1802 and 1804, his parents lived in Lugo; and here his father taught him the horn, Giuseppe Malerbi gave him instruction in singing, and he also learnt the cembalo. It was not until 1804, when Anna gave up the stage, that the family finally moved to Bologna.

47 ... *singing in church until 1807.* ... All this passage is a mixture of correct facts and inaccuracies. At this stage, Rossini's education was designed to train him as a singer (later he became an accomplished *tenore baritonale*); he had made his début at Ravenna in 1804, replacing Petronio Marchesi in Fioravanti's *I due Gemelli*. Between 1804 and 1805, he appears to have studied privately under Angelo Tesei, learning the violin and viola as well as singing; and from 1805 to 1806, he was taught by the famous tenor Matteo Babbini. Indeed, it was as a singer that, on 24th June 1806, he was admitted to the celebrated Accademia Filarmonica which, thirty-six years earlier, had welcomed the boy Mozart. Meanwhile, he had been earning small sums for his keep by singing soprano in various churches in Bologna. Later, he also began to be employed as recitative-accompanist in various theatres (Ferrara, Forlì, Lugo, Ravenna, Sinigaglia). It was not until April 1806 that he was admitted to the *Liceo Musicale di Bologna*, still as a soprano. His voice seems to have broken during the winter 1806–7; his last recorded concert as a treble was on 8th August 1806. At the *Liceo*, he had begun by studying the 'cello under Vincenzo Cadevagna; in May 1807, he started counterpoint under Mattei; in November 1808, he joined the pianoforte class under Gian-Callisto Zanotti, and gave up the 'cello; but by 1809, he was attending only counterpoint-classes, and that irregularly. He left in 1810.

48 ... *Il Pianto d'Armonia.* Rossini had begun composing as early as 1804 (a set of six *Sonate a quattro*), and much of the music for *Demetrio e Polibio* dates

R

from his first meeting with the Mombelli family in 1807. In 1808, however, compositions began to flow more easily from his pen. Among other things, he wrote a *Sinfonia a più strumenti obbligati*, which was later to serve as overture to *la Cambiale di Matrimonio* and later still again as overture to *Adelaide di Borgogna*. The *Pianto d'Armonia sulla Morte d'Orfeo*, for tenor and chorus, was performed by students at the *Liceo* prize-giving ceremony, 11th August 1808.

48   ... *Accademia dei Concordi*. ... A Bolognese musical society to which, in 1811 (i.e., after he had left the *Liceo*), Rossini had been appointed *maestro di cembalo* and general coach.

48   ... *Marchesi*. The Director of the *Accademia dei Concordi* was not the famous Luigi Marchesi, as Stendhal believes, but his brother, the composer Tommaso Marchesi. In 1808, the *Accademia* had, as an experiment, given Haydn's *La Creazione* (translation by Giuseppe Carpani), and the success of this venture had encouraged them to follow it with *Le quattro Stagioni*. In 1811, coached and accompanied by Rossini, the *Accademia* repeated the *Stagioni*.

48   ... *the Perticari family*. ... Costanza Perticari was the daughter of the poet Monti, and Stendhal met her in Pesaro in 1817. But it is doubtful whether Rossini knew her at all before 1818, when she invited him to conduct his own *Gazza ladra* for the opening of the new Pesaro opera-house. It was in fact the mezzo-soprano Rosa Morandi and her husband who introduced Rossini to the Marchese Cavalli, impresario of the teatro San-Mosè, and Cavalli who invited Rossini to compose a *farsa* for Venice.

48   ... *L'Equivoco stravagante*. ... This little opera was musically a success, but was removed from the stage after three days by the police, owing to the patent indecency of the libretto. As a result, Rossini, in a very bad temper, quarrelled with both cast and impresario—thus giving rise to the legend of the "quarrel" which led to *la Scala di Seta* (see below).

48   ... *L'Inganno felice*. ... Rossini's first "furore". It is worth noting that Foppa's libretto had already been set by Paisiello—thus anticipating the events of the *Barbiere*.

49   ... *many magnificent passages*. ... *Ciro in Babilonia* was, to all intents and purposes, a fiasco. The most interesting passage was an *aria del sorbetto*, written for an incompetent *terza donna* with only one passable note in her voice: middle B♭. Rossini scored all the melody in the orchestra, and allowed his singer to sing her one good note only.

49   ... *la Scala di Seta*. ... 9th May 1812. Stendhal's delightful legend is incorrect from beginning to end. To begin with, the overture described, in which the second violinists strike with the wooden parts of their bows against the lamp-stands, belongs in fact to *Il Signor Bruschino*. The story of the quarrel with the impresario is a combination (a) of Rossini's bad temper with the impresario of the teatro del Corso, Bologna (*L'Equivoco stravagante*); (b) of his annoyance with Cera, the new impresario of the San Mosè, for having given him a libretto as bad as that of *la Scala di Seta* to work on; and (c) possibly echoes of a breach of contract by Rossini, in leaving Venice for Rome before conducting the third performance of *la Scala di Seta*—although this last is unproved, and in fact improbable. *La Scala di Seta*, apart from its brilliant overture, is a disappointing opera.

49   ... *promptly set out for Milan*. ... Rossini's movements after *la Scala di Seta*

are obscure. He is alleged to have gone to Rome, to help his friends the
Mombelli family with the première of *Demetrio e Polibio* at the Teatro
Valle; but the date of this première (18th May 1812) would seem to leave
him too little time for such a journey. By July he was back in Bologna,
where he received an invitation to compose *La Pietra del Paragone* for La
Scala. He probably reached Milan by the middle of August: *La Pietra* was
given for the first time on 26th Sept. 1812.

50   ... *L'Occasione fa il Ladro*. ... The success of *La Pietra del Paragone* in Milan
accounts for Rossini having received simultaneously three commissions
for Venice: two for the San-Mosè, and one (*Tancredi*) for La Fenice.
L'Occasione (24th Nov. 1812) was a failure, and removed after five performances; *Il Signor Bruschino, ossia Il Figlio per azzardo* (late Jan. 1813),
although a much better opera, was only a qualified success. For the overture, see note above to *la Scala di Seta*.

50   ... *Ti rivedrò, mi rivedrai*. ... By a most curious slip of the pen (in view of
the argument in the next chapter: see p. 58), Stendhal reverses the order
of the two phrases as they appear in the libretto.

53   ... *his seat at the piano*. There is no foundation for this anecdote. *Tancredi*
was first performed on 6th Feb. 1813; but at both this and the subsequent
performance, Adelaide Malanotte and Elisabeta Manfredini were unwell,
and the opera was stopped half-way through Act II. The first full performance was on Feb. 12. It was not immediately a success: the "furore"
dates from subsequent performances in other cities during the weeks
following.

58   ... *the speed with which it was composed*. Rossini certainly composed the
music for *Tancredi* very fast indeed, since the première of *Il Signor
Bruschino* preceded that of *Tancredi* by not much more than ten days. The
overture, however, was simply transposed from *La Pietra del Paragone*.

58   ... *mi rivedrai, ti rivedrò*. ... Stendhal himself states that this was the first
music by Rossini he ever heard. However, there is internal evidence
from the *Lives of Haydn, Mozart and Metastasio* that he may have seen
Demetrio e Polibio as early as 1813; and probably both *L'Italiana in Algeri*
and *il Turco in Italia* by the autumn of 1814.

59   ... *scores for the flute*. ... In fact, in the passage referred to, the important
scoring is for clarinet.

65   ... *at the stirring of a finger*. Napoleon stole a vast quantity of Italian works of
art from various cities, and installed them in the Louvre. In the *Lives of
Haydn, Mozart and Metastasio*, Stendhal makes an impassioned plea that
they should be restored to Italy; but here, nine years later, he is less
engagingly idealistic.

66   ... *ma guarda e passa. Inferno* III, 51.

68   ... *German and Italian periodicals*. Stendhal had shamelessly plagiarized his
Life of Haydn from Giuseppe Carpani's *Haydine*, and it was taking him a
long while to live down the ensuing scandal. The "avowal" in this case is
less necessary; most of the *Life of Rossini* is original.

69   ... *la Testa di Bronzo*. Stendhal tells the full story of his early enthusiasm
for, and subsequent disillusion with, this opera in *Rome, Naples et Florence
en 1817*, entries 5th Nov.–5th Dec. 1816.

70   ... *a certain actress*. ... La Naldi—a *seconda-donna* who had to play the part
of Isabella at the Théâtre Louvois, 1823, since this theatre had no proper

first-class mezzo-soprano in its service. She was unhappy in the part and soon relinquished it.

71 ... *certain very clever persons.* ... See notes to p. 27.

74 ... *of reading the libretto.* Concerning the excruciating badness of the average Italian libretto of this period there is little argument, as the extracts given here will make plain. On the other hand, it must be remembered that Stendhal is using the *Life of Rossini* as a pamphlet to deliver a withering attack on the general standards of French music-criticism. Parisian music-critics at this time were normally classically-trained *literary* critics (*e.g.* Geoffroy), who regarded the music itself as frivolous and insignificant, and who in fact *did* judge an opera by its libretto. Stendhal himself, for all his vituperation, is less far removed than might at first appear from this tradition. It is notorious that he was incapable of appreciating any music unless it was associated with a verbal text: in other words, he had no notion of the dramatic powers inherent in musical form as such; he needed a *literary* source of drama (the libretto) before he could begin to appreciate the music.

85 ... *one would really like to know why?* The oath-taking scene was cut in the 1821 Louvois production because it seemed to the rather touchy French censorship of the Restoration that it offered too risky a parallel with more solemn contemporary oath-takings.

86 ... *performed in the Royal Theatres.* This is pure wishful-thinking by Stendhal. Mutilation and other forms of "arrangement" of the text and music of an opera were a standard part of contemporary practice; in fact, it was often part of a composer's contract that he should write numbers for inclusion in the operas of other composers.

86 ... *four French actresses.* ... See below, note to p. 430.

89 ... *derive some pleasure from it. L'Italiana* was first given in Venice (teatro San Benedetto) on 22nd May 1813. Stendhal probably saw it in the autumn of 1814. From 1818 until 1821, he was in close contact with liberal-carbonarist groups in Milan, who were already preaching the ideal of a united, independent, *national* Italy. There are traces of these ideas, not only in Stendhal's analysis of the opera, but perhaps also in the libretto.

90 ... *La Pietra del Paragone.* See above, thir noted to p. 49. *La Pietra* (La Scala, 24th Nov. 1812) preceded both *Tancredi* and *L'Italiana.* It is not clear why Stendhal breaks the chronological order of his narrative at this point.

90 ... *Signora Marcolini.* ... The fact is correct. Marietta Marcolini and Filippo Galli, who had already sung in Rossinian opera, both recommended the young composer to the committee of La Scala.

91 ... *Missipipì.* Strange as it may seem, the librettist (Luigi Romanelli) *does* spell it this way.

91 ... *once and for ever.* In spite of the brilliance of its score, *La Pietra* has only begun to be revived since 1960. On the other hand, Stendhal's accusations against the Paris production are here justified. Paër appears to have used *la Pietra* (5th April 1821) quite deliberately to break the irresistible vogue for Rossini opera at the expense of everything else. *La Pietra* ran for three nights, and was then removed. However, no other composer could satisfy the audience deprived of its Rossini; and by 5th June 1821, Paër was forced to admit defeat: he engaged Madame Pasta and produced *Otello.*

Page

93 ... *the case is very different*. Again we may suspect a dig at Giuseppe Carpani, particularly since this ex-journalist had attacked Stendhal about an article on *Tancredi* published in 1818, and was engaged in publishing a rival book on Rossini (*Le Rossiniane*), which appeared almost simultaneously with the *Life*.

95 ... *to play the echo*. "Echo-scenes" were one of the favourite devices in French and Italian opera of the XVIIth and early XVIIIth centuries. *Cf.* also the famous "echo-scene" in Webster's *Duchess of Malfi*.

96 ... *cut in the Paris production*. In this version, the Count tamely relates that he has lost all his fortune in a shipwreck. Stendhal's disgust is understandable.

97 ... *of her country-house*. ... *Cf.* Madame Giorgi-Righetti, *Cenni* ..., p. 19. Rossini's amorous adventures were numerous; unfortunately there are few facts by which the current gossip may be checked.

97 ... *Black Reaction*. ... Stendhal writes: "et le d ... u ... s'avançait à grands pas." Probably "le despotisme ultra".

100 ... *Giuseppe Mosca*. ... Mosca had employed the technique of the *crescendo* in a popular opera entitled *I Pretendenti delusi* (Milan 1811), and therefore Rossini was accused of having "stolen" the idea from him. In fact, the *crescendo*, used in this manner, was a symphonic device which became fairly common in opera from the end of the XVIIIth century.

101 ... *uninhibited superscription*. ... There is probably no truth in this anecdote.

101 ... *proposed to Prince Eugène*. ... Prince Eugène himself was in Russia at the time; but the General commanding in Lombardy wrote to him, asking for permission to excuse Rossini his military service as a result of the success of *La Pietra del Paragone*.

102 ... *military service*. ... Rossini later described his exemption from military service as "a clear gain to Napoleon's army".

102 ... *the laws of composition*. ... It is common at the time to find Rossini accused of "violating the laws of composition". However, Stendhal was not his only apologist: *cf.* Carpani (*Rossiniane*, p. 158); Giorgi-Righetti (*Cenni* ..., p. 26).

110 ... *a thousand francs for each work*. ... Stendhal tends to romanticize over Rossini's poverty. Admittedly, his first nine operas (up to *Tancredi*) had earned him rather less than £600 (1968 value); but after *Tancredi*, his fortunes changed radically, and he was never poor again.

119 ... *to call a genius!* This anecdote had already been retailed by Stendhal in his *Paris Monthly Review*. It is not denied by Madame Giorgi-Righetti, and would seem to accord perfectly with Rossini's character at that date.

121 ... *Demofoonte*. In the *Life of Haydn*, letter XIV, Stendhal analyses this aria in detail.

121 ... *Se cerca, se dice*. ... Similarly analysed in the *Life of Metastasio*.

124 ... *the list*. ... The reader is referred to the *Index* for the correct dates of the various composers here referred to, as also for those in the note which follows.

126 ... *on the same day*. ... The first performance of *Der Freischütz* took place in Berlin on 18th June 1821. *Zelmira* had its première in Naples on 16th Feb. 1822; it was first conducted by Rossini in Vienna on 13th April 1822.

129 ... *harmonic chiaroscuro*. ... Stendhal's concept of chiaroscuro plays an important part in his whole aesthetic, especially in painting (see Philippe

Berthier, "Stendhal et le clair-obscur", in *Omaggio a Stendhal II* (*Aurea Parma*, 1967). The transposition of a concept from painting to music is typical of Stendhal's aesthetic.

130 ... *This musical physicist*. ... *Cf.* above, note to p. 18. Stendhal was firmly convinced that the scientific classification of species and specimens could apply also to psychological phenomena.

136 ... *without further ado*. The overture to *Aureliano* had probably originated as overture to *L'Equivoco stravagante* (1811); later, Rossini used it, not only for *Elisabetta*, but also for *il Barbiere*. Three other sections of *il Barbiere*, moreover, are borrowed from *Aureliano*: the first eight measures of Almaviva's *Ecco ridente in cielo*; the introduction to Don Basilio's *La Calunnia*; and a section of Rosina's *Una Voce poco fa'*.

137 ... *Demetrio e Polibio*. ... This section contains an inextricable mixture of fact and fiction. Rossini had met the Mombelli family in Bologna in 1806–7, and had composed several separate numbers of *Demetrio e Polibio* at the request of Vicenza Viganò-Mombelli (Domenico's second wife and sister of the great choreographer), who had herself written the libretto. Since Rossini was only about fourteen at the time, it is probable that Mombelli supervised at least the scoring; the tenor Babbini also gave much advice. The opera was produced at the Teatro Valle, Rome, on 18th May 1812; and it is probable that Stendhal saw it at some time during the autumn of 1813, since he refers to it with apparently first-hand knowledge in the *Life of Metastasio* (1814). On the other hand, *Demetrio e Polibio* was not used for the opening of the new Como opera house (1813), but another opera by Mombelli, namely a resetting of Metastasio's *Adriano in Siria*: and if Stendhal did go to this opening during his stay in the town (16th–20th Sept. 1813), it would most likely have been *Adriano* that he saw. Incidentally, at the date given (June 1814), Stendhal was not in Italy at all, but in Paris.

137 ... *Contessina L.****... Probably the contessina Lechi, of Brescia. Stendhal refers frequently to the family.

141 ... *Journal des Débats*. ... The article referred to would appear to be the *Quatrième Lettre d'un Parisien sur l'Italie* (signed "D": 10th June 1823).

142 ... *There is the duet*. ... I have been unable to trace a full score of *Demetrio e Polibio*. According to Henri Prunières, the duet *precedes* the quartet in the version to which he had access; but Stendhal may well have heard a variant version.

144 ... *for some years*. ... *L'Italiana* was produced at the San Benedetto, Venice, on 22nd May 1813; *Il Turco* was given at La Scala on 14th Aug. 1814. Consequently, only some fifteen months separate the two operas.

149 ... *Di questo e quello*. ... This quartet and cantilena (in fact, the whole of Act I, sc. x of *Il Turco*, which Stendhal has just been analysing), is a borrowing from *La Cenerentola*, and consequently will not be found in modern scores.

151 ... *for the gratification of Parisian audiences*. ... The ball-room scene *was* included in the Louvois production. The only "amendment" which I have been able to trace was the transfer of the scene from *La Cenerentola*, referred to in the previous note.

151 ... *Four years later*. ... *Il Turco* was in fact not sung again in Milan until 1820–1. The original version in 1814 received twelve performances, and

was considered a disaster. The audience, struck by the similarity of the *libretto* with that of *l'Italiana*, assumed (wrongly) that the music must be similarly unoriginal.

153 ... *now found himself saddled*. ... This account is comparatively accurate. Rossini signed the contract with Barbaja (for 8,000 francs, according to himself, many years later) in the spring of 1815; during this same spring he also paid two flying visits to Naples; but he did not come into residence in that city until September. As musical director to both San-Carlo and Del Fondo, Rossini was certainly overworked. "If he had been able to, Barbaja would have put me in charge of the kitchen too," he remarked later.

153 ... *to marry his mistress*. Rossini's marriage to Isabella Colbran took place on 16th March 1822 at Castenaso, near Bologna. If it is true that Isabella had been both Barbaja's and Rossini's mistress before the marriage, no strong passions appear to have been involved, and all three remained on friendly terms.

153 ... *The Royal Personage*. ... Ferdinand IV of Naples (Ferdinand I of the Two-Sicilies). His return to Naples after the long Napoleonic exile coincided with Rossini's first arrival in the city. Stendhal's attitude towards both him and his Queen (Caroline, daughter of Maria-Theresa) is one of unadulterated, and largely justified, contempt and loathing.

154 ... *by fire*. The San-Carlo was burnt down on the night of 12th–13th Feb. 1816—some six months after Rossini's arrival in Naples. It was reopened on 13th Jan. 1817. In *Rome, Naples and Florence*, Stendhal describes in detail the gala-performance with which the theatre was reopened: it is only unfortunate that he happened to be in Rome at the time.

154 ... *who is today Signora Rossini*. ... Isabella Colbran brought a dowry of 20,000 livres a year and a villa in Sicily. The marriage was not successful, and ended in an official separation in 1837. Isabella died at Bologna in 1845, at the age of sixty.

155 ... *singing off key*. ... Isabella Colbran was a great coloratura soprano, and there is no evidence that her voice deteriorated seriously before 1822. However, being a protégée of King Ferdinand, she became a symbol of all that was politically obnoxious in the restored régime. This accounts for Stendhal's prejudice against her. It is true, none the less, that her influence turned Rossini away from *opera buffa* towards *opera seria*: after 1816, he was to write only two further comic operas in his life: *La Cenerentola* and *Le Comte Ory*.

155 ... *the principle of despotic government*. A reference to Montesquieu's *Esprit des Lois* (1748).

157 ... *a French melodrama*. ... The libretto is in fact an adaptation by the resident librettist of the San-Carlo, Giovanni Federico Schmidt (="the Tuscan-born Mr Smith"), of an Italian drama by Carlo Federici, which in its turn is based upon the English novel by Sophia Lee, *The Recess, or a Tale of Other Times* (1785).

158 ... *The opening duet*. ... The passage described is in fact Act I, sc. iv, between Matilde and Leicester, when Leicester discovers that Matilde, without his knowledge, has followed him to court.

164 ... *of its noble subject*. ... The title of the poem, *The Fifth of May*, refers to the day of Napoleon's death.

167 ... *of rational criticism.* ... Stendhal seems to have approved of the analysis given in this chapter. In a MS note on a copy of the *Vie de Rossini* belonging to Count Primoli, he commented: "Lu par hasard dopo tanti anni 209, 210, 211. I found very well, vif, clair, énergique, full of fire. 2 décembre 1839. Civ. Vec^a."

172 ... *the depths of Teutonism.* ... Despite Stendhal's exaggeration, there is some truth in this accusation. At the *Liceo Musicale di Bologna*, Rossini was already nicknamed *il Tedeschino*.

173 ... *the declamatory style.* ... According to modern critics, there is no truth in this assertion (*cf.* Weinstock, pp. 91–2).

176 ... *Il Barbiere di Siviglia.* There are perhaps more inaccuracies, myths and legends in this chapter than in any other. Here as elsewhere I am heavily indebted to Herbert Weinstock's *Rossini* (1968) for my corrections. Moreover, since the opera is so well-known, I have not thought it necessary to give the context of the quotations.

176 ... *a catastrophic flop.* Most of this anecdote is legendary. Duke Sforza-Cesarini, the impresario of the Teatro Argentina, first called on Jacopo Ferretti for a comic libretto; but the result was a text so banal that the impresario turned it down. Next, Sforza-Cesarini approached Cesare Sterbini, who had just written the libretto for the hopelessly unsuccessful *Torvaldo e Dorliska*, and persuaded him to adapt Beaumarchais' *Barbier de Séville.* Sterbini accepted with bad grace, but none the less completed the new libretto in eleven days (18th–29th Jan. 1816).

176 ... *note of explanation.* ... This can be read in Weinstock, p. 58.

176 ... *In thirteen days.* ... The contract between Sforza-Cesarini and Sterbini is dated 17th Jan. 1816. Rossini had completed Act I by 6th Feb. But on 7th Feb., Sforza-Cesarini died of a stroke, and in consequence, rehearsals were held up. In spite of this, however, Rossini completed the score and rehearsed the opera by 20th Feb. Even allowing for exaggerations, therefore, the fact is clear that Rossini must have composed and orchestrated the *Barber* in less than three weeks. Borrowings from earlier operas are not significant enough to make this feat any less astonishing, particularly since the opera originally had an overture of its own written for it, for which the *Aureliano* overture was only substituted at the last moment.

176 ... *the temptation of* shawls. ... An obscure passage, which has defeated the most expert Stendhalians: "Ce n'est pas l'amour, c'est le *shall* qui est funeste à la vertu." An alternative explanation is that Stendhal is contrasting 'natural sentiment" in love with the "English" sense of duty and strong moral obligation ("shall" = "thou shalt!").

177 ... *French music.* The *Barber* was first performed at the Louvois in Paris on 26th Oct. 1819; and on 25th Nov. 1819, Paisiello's version of the same story was also staged, so that the audiences could compare the two versions. Rossini's triumph was so indisputable that the Paisiello was withdrawn after its second performance. By 1822, this triumph had been repeated in almost every provincial city in France.

177 ... *Madame Giorgi.* ... Geltrude Giorgi-Righetti (or Righetti-Giorgi). Her comments concerning Stendhal's original article on Rossini, which include useful information concerning the *Barber*, are reproduced in the *Vie de Rossini*, ed. Prunières. Vol. II, pp. 433–74.

Page

177   ...*26th of December 1816*. ... The première of the *Barber* took place in the Teatro Argentina, Rome, on 20th Feb. 1816.

179   ...*23rd of September 1819*.... For correct dates, see above, note to p. 177. The "conversion" of the critics can be followed by taking one journal as a typical instance: Périn and Maurice's *Le Camp-Volant*. In this case, the relentless hostility of October 1819 is transformed into boundless enthusiasm by July 1820.

183   ...*platitudinous and empty*.... The guitar accompaniment to this aria is reputed to have been composed by Garcia, the original Almaviva.

185   ...*a bit of fourth-rate Gluck*.... There is some truth in the accusation, since French opera in the tradition of Gluck is based, not on the spoken language, but on the declamatory style of French classical tragedy.

190   ...*the one which Farinelli composed*.... This duet can be found as an appendix to Albert de Lasalle's edition of *il Matrimonio segreto*, Paris (Hachette) 1907, pp. 249–56:

> *Elisetta:*
> No, non credo quel che dite;
> È uno scherzo che voi fate—
> Voi mi fate delirar.
> *Il Conte:*
> Signorina, deh scusate—
> Dir vel voglio con dolcezza:
> Io non v'amo, ne pensate
> Ch'io vi posso omai sposar. ...

191   ...*in the marionette-theatres*.... In *Rome, Naples et Florence* (1826), at the date of the 10th of October 1817, Stendhal gives a long description of the marionettes at the Palazzo Fiano.

193   ...*may have some influence*.... Another example of Stendhal's theory, relating art to the material circumstances under which it is composed. The idea was destined to be worked out in detail by Taine.

193   ...*is finely done*. This aria is so difficult to perform that, in Nov. 1816, at the Teatro della Pergola in Florence, when Paolo Rosich was playing Bartolo, Pietro Romani composed an alternative: *Manca un foglio ...*, which subsequently was often sung instead of Rossini's original. This accounts for the legend that Rossini "collaborated" with Romani in writing the *Barber*.

197   ...*Nina Viganò*.... Helena Viganò, daughter of the choreographer, was a folk-singer whom Stendhal had known in Milan in 1817–18, and who had perhaps been his mistress. In 1818, she gave a series of concerts in Paris, which failed lamentably. The critics compared her voice with the dawning talent of Laure Cinti-Damoreau—which is one of the reasons for Stendhal's persistent hostility to "Mlle Cinti".

199   ...*by one Signor Majer*.... Andrea Majer (see *Index*) was an interesting Venetian musicologist and aesthetic theorist, who, however, had one unforgivable defect in Stendhal's eyes: he was a friend of the "monstrous journalist", Giuseppe Carpani.

200   ...*directors for the Opera-House*. Between 1807 and 1813, the complex of the Vienna court-theatres came under the authority of a committee drawn from the highest nobility: the *Wiener-Theaterunternehmungsgesellschaft*, or

Gesellschaft der Cavaliere, headed by Prince Joseph von Schwarzenberg. Stendhal will return to this idea of a "Noble Committee" later on: see below, p. 433.

202   ... *the old King's daughters.* Louis XV had four daughters, all musical and all ugly: Adelaïde, Victoire, Sophie and Louise. Beaumarchais taught them to play the harp.

202   ... *a gang of common malefactors.* ... A reference to a contemporary political scandal, when a liberal journalist, Jean-Denis Magalon, was condemned to thirteen months' imprisonment for an article hostile to the Jesuits and the *Congrégation*. On the 22nd April 1823 he was transferred from the prison of Ste Pélagie to that of Poissy chained in a gang of common malefactors. Chateaubriand intervened in the scandal on behalf of the unfortunate victim.

203   ... *the Prévôt des Marchands.* ... A high dignitary of the City of Paris, whose office corresponded in some respects to that of our own Lord Mayor.

205   ... *these controversies.* ... The "guerre des bouffons", or musico-political controversy, which disrupted French intellectual life in 1752.

208   ... *and there will be ballets.* ... This was the Italian fashion, and Stendhal constantly returns to the idea, even if only because Carpani thought that it was scandalous (*Rossiniane*, p. 111). On the other hand, he was bitterly opposed to the French habit of "arranging" operas (*e.g.*, Mozart's *Don Giovanni*) in such a way as to introduce the ballet-element that the public demanded. Stendhal's attitude towards the ballet is complex, and has not yet been fully studied.

209   ... *Signora de' Begnis.* ... Giuseppina Ronzi-De'Begnis retired from the part of Rosina only when she was seven months pregnant. Concerning the "struggle between the two *Barbers of Seville*", see above, note to p. 177.

210   ... *Otello.* Stendhal claims to have seen *Otello* as early as 1817. However, all his earlier judgments on the opera were distinctly unfavourable. His opinion only changed later in Paris, when he had seen Giuditta Pasta in the part of Desdemona. The whole of this chapter is full of contradictions between this early attitude and the later reconciliation.

210   ... *what one has read in books.* ... An important Stendhalian theme: namely, that the whole concept of love in the XIXth century has been corrupted by literature, and in particular by Jean-Jacques Rousseau.

210   ... *in her immortal letters.* ... Stendhal, like most of his contemporaries, firmly believed that the famous *Lettres d'une Religieuse portugaise* were the authentic heart-cry of the tormented Marianna Alcaforada. However, recent research has proved that, as scholars had long suspected, the so-called *Letters* are in fact one of the earliest novels in epistolary form, and that their "translator", the comte de Guilleragues, was in fact their author.

211   ... *literary hack.* ... The marchese Berio di Salsa was a personal friend of Stendhal; the latter, however, was not prepared to forgive a man his literary sins on any account of mere friendship.

215   ... *a barbarian like Shakespeare.* ... The "barbarity" of Shakespeare was one of the commonplaces of French literary criticism in the XVIIIth century. Voltaire himself uses the term.

217   ... *Demetrio e Polibio (1809).* ... See above, notes to pp. 48 and 137.

219 ... *The solo clarinet passage*. ... The clarinet has a melodic phrase towards the middle of the overture, which it repeats shortly afterwards. Stendhal did not include the overture in his earlier, unfavourable verdict on the opera.

221 ... *revolt against the complex*. To some extent, this prophecy may be said to have been fulfilled by Bellini.

222 ... *Viganò*. Recent historians of the ballet are coming to recognize the importance of Viganò in the development of the art of dancing. He took the highly-stylized and classical French "ballet d'action" and gave it a new direction, at once more romantic and more realistic. It was Viganò's tragedy that the later "romantic ballet" developed around the personalities of dancers such as Elssler, Grisi and Fanny Cerrito, and that a feminine style of gauze, moonlight and Sylphides supplanted his own more complex and more vigorous conceptions. In a sense, it is true to say that Viganò's ideal is restored by Diaghilev in ballets such as *Petrushka*.

222 ... *his ballet Otello*. ... It was common practice in the XIXth century, when a subject enjoyed success in one form (*e.g.* opera) to re-create it immediately in an alternative form. Stendhal's correspondence in 1818 is full of enthusiastic references to the ballet *Otello*.

222 ... *Madame Pasta*. ... Desdemona was Giuditta Pasta's first major role in Paris. *Otello* opened at the Louvois on 5th June 1821.

224 ... *of fair Parthenope*. ... The French invasion of Italy in 1799 transformed the Kingdom of Naples into the "Parthenopian Republic". The Latin phrase comes from the epitaph to Virgil's tomb.

235 ... *Alessandro Stradella*. ... Stendhal had already recounted the Stradella story in the *Life of Haydn*, Letter XX. For details of the origin of the legend, see *Groves' Dictionary*.

239 ... *A friend of mine in Bergamo*. ... Stendhal tells this story in detail in *Rome, Naples and Florence* (1826), at the date of 6th January 1817.

240 ... *in Trieste*. ... Stendhal went to Trieste for the first time in 1830. He had seen *La Cenerentola* in Milan (1817) and in Florence (1819).

243 ... *Signora Righetti*. ... Geltrude Giorgi-Righetti, a somewhat touchy soprano at the best of times, cannot have been too pleased at finding herself described as "unknown". There is every evidence (beside her own affirmation) to the contrary.

251 ... *Parleremo*. ... There appear to be several variants of the text of this famous aria. I have corrected the Italian from Ricordi's currently-published libretto (1954); Stendhal appears to have used an earlier version, or else to have quoted from memory.

257 ... *prohibited laughter*. ... Stendhal is one of the earliest writers to react against what he dimly discerned to be the threat of the Great Victorian Seriousness, which was to dominate European art from about 1830 until 1890.

261 ... *Rossini's operas in France*. ... *La Cenerentola* was given at the Louvois on 8th June 1822, with Signora Bonini in the title-part. Signora Bonini had not appeared in Paris before, and her reception was generally luke-warm. Her contract was ended "by mutual consent" in October of the same year, and Laure Cinti-Damoreau took over her parts.

266 ... *black and platitudinous*. ... Stendhal knew the play before the opera was composed, and was suspicious of the subject in advance.

Page

267   ... *for the spring season.* ... *La Gazza* was first given at La Scala on 31st
      May 1817. Stendhal was in Grenoble at the time. He probably did not
      see the opera before 1820.

268   ... *was unparalleled.* ... Milan, being under Austrian domination, was
      strongly influenced by German musical traditions. Rossini made a study
      of Winter's *Maometto II* before writing *la Gazza*, and deliberately
      scored the opera *à l'allemande*. The result (so unpredictable is the effer-
      vescent mixture of politics and art) was that the Italian critics were
      delighted, while the Austrian critics thought it worse than mediocre.

278   ... *a violent quarrel with Galli.* ... There is no evidence for this, although
      the legend was evidently widely current. *Le Miroir* (12th April 1822) gives
      a different version: "The young maestro, in a fit of distraction of the sort
      that overtakes him all too frequently, had at this point inserted a *moto di
      valza* which was agreeable indeed, but a trifle over-joyous to express the
      feelings of a father learning that his daughter is to be executed. Galli
      categorically refused to be a party to this travesty of commonsense, and
      Rossini, yielding to his entreaties, composed, some years later, one of the
      finest *arie di situazione* that have ever been heard in the theatre."

280   ... *Mi manca la voce.* ... The reference is to Elcia's aria from Act II:

> Mi manca la voce,
> Mi sento morire;
> Sì fiero martire
> Chi può tollerar. ...

299   ... *Signor Perego.* ... For examples of the work of the Milanese school of
      scene-painters, *v.* Sanquirico, *Recueil de Décorations théâtrales.*

300   ... *Mirra.* ... One of Viganò's most famous ballets. However, writing to
      Mareste on 5th Jan. 1818, Stendhal confesses that he has never seen it
      performed.

300   ... *any feeling for music.* ... Any modern listener who has heard the *Opéra
      Comique* in Paris attempting to render Italian *opera buffa* will be filled
      with sympathy for Stendhal. However, there was a further "bad habit"
      at the time, which increased the weakness of French orchestras—namely,
      that of entrusting the violas to superannuated violin-players, who simply
      restrung their ordinary violins with viola strings.

301   ... *Darmstadt.* ... The musical "Golden Age" of Darmstadt was already
      on the wane when Stendhal was writing. *Cf.* W. Saunders, *Weber*, 1940,
      p. 47.

304   ... *the secret of service.* ... The courtier concerned was Général le Comte
      Louis de Narbonne-Lara (1755–1813).

307   ... *is well-known.* ... "Vous n'êtes donc pas bon Français?" asked Louis
      XV. "Plût à Dieu, Sire, que les vers de la tragédie le fussent autant que
      moi!" replied the Duc d'Ayen.

309   ... *Tortoni's pâtisserie.* ... Tortoni's, which stood at the corner of the rue
      Taitbout and the boulevard des Italiens, remained famous until the end
      of the XIXth century.

311   ... *to their professional titles.* ... Under the Napoleonic régime, it was gener-
      ally true that all music-criticism was written by the official literary critics.
      By 1820, however, certain musicologists—notably Castil-Blaze and
      Fétis—were in revolt against this tradition.

Page

311 ...*a mere nine years.*... This is gross exaggeration. Rossini's European reputation dates from 1814–15; the *Barber* was successfully produced at the Louvois in 1819; consequently the "gap" extended over five years at the outside. Concerning the accuracy of the whole of this passage, see the Translator's "Stendhal, Rossini and the 'Conspiracy of Musicians' ".

315 ...*this vast extinguisher.*... Stendhal uses the word "éteignoir", which had a strong political significance at the period. It had been coined by the journalist Emile Babeuf (son of the notorious Gracchus, and editor of *Le Nain Jaune*) to symbolize the stifling repression of all artistic, intellectual and political enthusiasm which characterized the bourgeoisie of the Restoration.

319 ...*The Arabian Nights.*... The original French is enigmatic: "J'estime les Livres Saints comme une espèce de c*** de M*** très curieux." M. Prunières suggests *Conte des Mille et Une Nuits*, which is at least consonant with Stendhal's known feelings on the matter.

322 ...*the real composer.*... *Mosè* does in fact contain one aria (Faraone's *A rispettarmi* ...) composed by Caraffa. Rossini was given so little time to complete the score, that he had to call on Caraffa for help.

323 ...*a third revival was announced.* The anecdote has no foundation. The *Prayer* was composed by Rossini at leisure for the Lenten performances at the San Carlo in 1818.

324 ...*in the major.*... The main subject is in G minor, followed by a short episode in B flat major, sung by the chorus. Then the main theme returns in G major. See Barini, G. :"Per il Centenario di *Mosè*", *Nuova Antologia*, 1914.

327 ...*in his Aus meinem Leben.*... According to Professor Del Litto, Stendhal knew Goethe's *Aus meinem Leben* only from having read an unfavourable article about it in the *Edinburgh Review* (1816/17). However, there is evidence in the *Life of Haydn* (1814) that, even by that date, he already had some acquaintance with the book.

329 ...*awaits us one and all.*... Ironically, by 1830, it was the Italians who had adopted the French style of singing rather than vice-versa.

329 ...*le Chevalier de Micheroux.*... Son of a sometime War-Minister of the Kingdom of Naples and lover of Giuditta Pasta. Stendhal met Micheroux in la Pasta's salon in the rue de Richelieu, and very probably incorporated parts of his conversation into the *Life of Rossini*. He appears also to have borrowed freely from Majer's *Discorso sulla origine, progressi, e stato attuale della musica italiana*, Padua, 1821.

333 ...*present in the admirer.*... See above, notes to pp. 17–18.

335 ...(*18th September 1823*). This would seem to refer to an article in the *Journal des Débats* of 24th Nov. 1823, in which *Le Valet de Chambre* (libretto by Scribe, music by Caraffa) is compared unfavourably with the "simple style" of Grétry.

337 ...*the ottavino.*... The piccolo.

340 ...*Velluti.*... This anecdote appears to be substantially correct. It is interesting to note that *Aureliano* was the only part that Rossini ever scored for a *castrato*. The part of *Tancredi* is written for a female voice.

346 ...*obscure newspapers.*...*E.g.*, the *Corriere delle Dame* (31st Dec. 1819; 21st June 1823); the *Gazzetta di Milano* No. 280, 1822), etc. Stendhal himself, in his correspondence with Mareste, makes the same accusation.

In part, of course, it is justified: Rossini was constantly using borrowings from his earlier operas whenever he had to compose a new one in a hurry.

347   ... *daylight in the hall.* .... The modern practice of darkening the auditorium in order to concentrate greater attention on the stage was, in Stendhal's time, a remarkable innovation recently instituted at La Scala. It was this which enabled La Scala to achieve such effects with its décors.

348   ... *more eminently Romantic.* In 1823, Stendhal was struggling to elaborate a definition of "Romanticism" which would enable him to include Rossini, Shakespeare and Foscolo, whom he admired, and to exclude Chateaubriand, Lamartine and Madame de Staël, whom he did not.

354   ... *colouring of satisfaction.* .... It is difficult to imagine a Romeo about to commit suicide over the body of his Juliet, expressing his feelings in terms of *satisfaction*. However, Stendhal explains himself in *Notes J'un Dilettante*, No XXXV.

355   ... *(so the legend goes).* .... Unfortunately, the legend does not correspond with the facts. Paganini was already remarkable as an infant prodigy, performing on the violin at the age of eight.

356   ... *must be taken seriously.* .... See above, note to p. 257.

360   ... *arie di baule.* .... The practice goes back to the beginning of the XVIIIth century. *Cf.* Abbé Raguenet, *Parallèle de la Musique françoise et de la Musique italienne* (1702).

362   ... *the year 1822.* .... Stendhal was in Paris in October 1822. However, in October 1823 he spent a few days near Lake Maggiore, and thus was in the region of Varese.

371   ... *Madame Pasta.* Giuditta Pasta's voice did not fully mature until the season 1821–2; this explains why Stendhal is much less enthusiastic about her when writing to Mareste from Italy than when he heard her in Paris. However, as early as 2nd Nov. 1819, he notes, after hearing her sing in Stunz's *La Represaglia*: "La Pasta n'est plus reconnaissable; elle travaille sept à huit heures par jour à donner de nouvelles habitudes à son gosier." See also letter to Mareste of 22nd Dec. 1820.

374   ... *the simple manner.* See above, note to p. 221. Giuditta Pasta in fact enjoyed some of her greatest triumphs in Bellini's operas, particularly in *Norma*, which was written for her.

384   ... *nell' anima si sente.* The correct version of Petrarch's line is: "E'l cantar che nell' anima si sente."

388   ... *4th October 1819.* The première of *La Donna del Lago* took place at the San Carlo on 24th Sept. 1819. Stendhal was in Paris on this date. The anecdote which follows is probably inaccurate; it is true, however, that *La Donna* was poorly received on the first night and picked up on the second.

390   ... *O quante lagrime.* .... After 1820, when it became the habit to insert the aria *O quante lagrime* into *Otello*, an alternative aria was substituted in *La Donna*:

> Mura felici, ove il mio ben s'aggira,
> Dopo più lune io vi reveggo. ...

392   ... *(Rome 1818).* .... *Adelaide di Borgogna* was given at the Teatro Argentina on 27th Dec. 1817. It was unsuccessful. Radiciotti called it "the worst of Rossini's *opere serie* ... nothing but banality from start to finish."

Page

392 ... *It was brilliantly successful.* Given at the San Carlo on 11th Nov. 1817, *Armida* was received coldly; in particular, the critics accused Rossini of having indulged in too much heavy "Teutonic" orchestration. If *Armida* was only rarely revived in later years, however, this is due mainly to the immense difficulties of staging and casting the work.

392 ... *Amor, possente nome!* The score of this famous duet can be found in Lord Derwent's *Rossini and some forgotten Nightingales*, pp. 325–6.

393 ... *too embarrassed to praise it.* ... On 9th April 1819, Stendhal wrote to Mareste: "Rossini a fait dans *Armide* un *duo* qui vous fera bander *d'amour* pendant dix jours."

393 ... *Davide's cavatina.* ... This "cavatina" is in fact Ernesto's part in the opening quintet of the Finale of Act I.

394 ... *the absence of an overture.* ... This is not the case. Weinstock describes the beginning of the opera as follows: "*Ricciardo* [...] shows Rossini integrating the instrumental prelude into the score and the performance. The opening largo of its introduction lasts only eleven measures. Then the curtain parts and a *tempo di marcia* follows, played by a stage band. Next comes an *andante grazioso con variazioni*, after which the march is repeated and the chorus joins in. This extended four-section introduction differs greatly from the discrete overture that could be transferred from opera to opera without noticeable irrelevance." (*Rossini*, p. 90.)

394 ... *a work in the French tradition. Ermione* (San Carlo, 27th March 1819). It was indifferently received. There is no trace of the "French tradition" in the score; its only originality lies in introducing the stage-chorus (still hidden behind the curtain) into the orchestral introduction.

396 ... *a Mass.* ... The *Messa solenne*, composed by Rossini in collaboration with Pietro Raimondo (introductory overture by Mayr), and given at church of San Ferdinando, Naples, at the invitation of the Arciconfraternità di San Luigi on 19th March 1820.

396 ... *to try and identify them.* In this connection, M. Prunières recalls an incident when Lulli chanced to hear one of his own operatic arias transformed into an anthem: *Mon Dieu!* he is said to have exclaimed, *Pardonnez-moi! Je ne l'avais pas fait pour vous!*

399 ... *the Teatro San-Benedetto.* ... All this description of *Odoardo* [or *Eduardo*] *e Cristina* is pure legend. Rossini was delayed in Naples by work on *Ermione*; he was unable to reach Venice until 9th April 1819, and his new opera was due to open on 24th April. He therefore contracted with the impresario to put together an opera out of existing music which had not yet been heard in Venice. The libretto similarly was concocted by Tottola and Bevilacqua-Aldobrandini out of a text prepared by Schmidt for Pavesi in 1810. The librettists adapted Schmidt's verses to fit music from three Rossinian operas: *Adelaide di Borgogna, Ricciardo e Zoraide* and *Ermione.* However, Rossini also supplied new cembalo-accompanied recitatives and seven wholly new numbers, for which he was paid 1,600 lire. The opera was a raging success and ran for twenty-five performances. Byron described the furore in a letter to Hobhouse (17th May 1819).

405 ... *to hear too much of it.* In general, Stendhal is much less flattering about Rossini in his correspondence than in the *Life.* On 18th July 1819, for instance, he writes to Mareste from Florence: "Adieu, je vais à la *Ceneren-*

tola par la Mombelli; c'est très bien chanté; mais toujours du Rossini, c'est le pâté d'anguilles."

410 ... *against his old age.* Again, writing to Mareste, Stendhal gives a very much less romantic (but equally inaccurate) picture: "J'ai vu Rossini hier à son arrivée; il aura ving-huit ans au mois d'avril; il veut cesser de travailler à trente ans. Il est avare, et n'avait pas le sou il y a quatre ans. Il vient de placer 100 mille fr. chez Barbaglia, au sept et demi par an. Il a mille fr. par mois comme directeur *despote* du théâtre de Saint-Charles [. . .] il a 4 mille fr. pour chaque opéra qu'il fait [. . .] Barbaglia entretient ce grand homme, il lui donne gratis carosse, table, logement et *amica*." (2nd Nov. 1819.)

410 ... *stood upright on the sea.* Admiral Caracciolo, who had sided, albeit half-heartedly, with the Neapolitan insurgents, was hanged by Nelson from the yardarm in cruel and degrading circumstances on 29th June 1799; his body was cut down and dropped into the sea. Two days later, however, it reappeared on the surface, floating upright, and this was taken as a dire omen by the superstitious Neapolitans.

419 ... *CHRONOLOGICAL TABLE.* This list contains a number of errors. Some have been corrected in the text and appear between square brackets. For others, the reader is referred to *Appendix II* (list of operas) and to the *Index*.

420 ... *the peasant Tarabotto.* . . . Tarabotto appears to have been played alternately by Filippo Galli and Luigi Raffanelli, who otherwise played Batone.

421 ... *and Filippo Galli.* The original cast of *Aureliano* was as follows: Lorenza Correâ (Zenobia); Luigia Sorrentini (Publio); Giambattista Velluti (Arsace); Luigi Mari (Aureliano); Gaetano Pozzi (Oraspe); Pietro Vasoli (Licinio) and Vincenzo Botticelli (Gran Sacerdote d'Iside). Neither Galli nor Eliodoro Bianchi was concerned in this production; nor can I identify the elusive Giuseppe Fabris.

423 ... *and Matteo Porto.* . . . At the première of *Mosè*, the part of Faraone was sung by Raniero Remorini. Matteo Porto did not take over the part until a year later.

425 ... *in 1815.* Rossini's *Inno dell' Indipendenza* was sung at the Teatro Contavalli, Bologna, on 15th April 1815, in the presence of Murat. The Austrian army re-took the city the day following, and Rossini's score was lost. The "Patriotic Hymn, Naples 1820" is similarly lost: legend reputes it to have been an *Inno di guerra dei costituzionali*; but there is no real evidence that it was ever written or performed.

425 ... *Morlacchi.* . . . For a different view of Morlacchi's character, see W. Saunders, *Weber* (1940), pp. 108–19 and *passim*.

426 ... *The Utopia of the Théâtre Italien.* This chapter was written in collaboration with the Baron de Mareste.

426 ... *in his youth.* For details of the financial and administrative history of the Théâtre Italien, see A. Soubies, *Le Théâtre Italien de 1801 à 1913* (Paris 1813), and the Translator's articles "Stendhal and Frau Mozart" and "Stendhal, Rossini and the 'Conspiracy of Musicians'." During the preceding twenty-five years, the theatre had had to survive three major crises: the end of the French Revolution; the collapse of the Napoleonic

régime; and the disaster of the Catalani-Valabrègue management. It says a lot for the resilience of the institution that it survived at all.

430 ... *Le Nozze di Figaro'* ... Stendhal is totally unjust to at least two of these four singers. "Mlle Cinti", which was the stage name of Laure-Cinthie Montalant, later known as Madame Cinti-Damoreau, was destined to be one of the great glories of the XIXth century operatic stage; Mlle Demeri was a splendid, if rather un-agile soprano of the Wagnerian type, who was to hold the rank of prima-donna at La Scala for over ten years; Mlle Buffardin was a competent, if not brilliant *seconda donna*; and Mlle Blangy was probably a student from the Conservatoire on a temporary engagement. See the Translator's "Stendhal et les quatre cantatrices françaises."

432 ... *Austrian city of Vienna.* ... See above, note to p. 200.

432 ... *after three days.* In the era when stage-lighting relied mainly on candles, the sooty deposits from smoky wicks rapidly blackened the scenery. La Scala had consequently devised a type of décor which could be frequently re-painted at a minimum of cost.

436 ... *Schiassetti.* ... Adelaide Schiassetti was in fact engaged at the Louvois a few months later. She made a highly-successful début in *la Donna del Lago* on 7th Sept. 1824.

436 ... *Mombelli.* ... Ester Mombelli was likewise engaged at the Louvois shortly afterwards.

436 ... *Signor Benelli.* ... In the correspondence, Stendhal is much less flattering, describing him in his efforts at talent-scouting for the Louvois in 1818 as "tatillon et friponneau" (Letter to Mareste, 11th Dec. 1818).

436 ... *the Marchese di Santantonio.* It is interesting that all these proposed administrative reforms—reforms which, if applied, would raise the standard of the Louvois to the same exalted level as that of La Scala—had previously been suggested by Stendhal as necessary *for La Scala itself! Cf. Rome, Naples et Florence en 1817*, at the date 8th August 1818.

437 ... *two hundred and twenty boxes.* ... For further details concerning the Italian opera-houses referred to in this chapter, the reader is referred to Spike Hughes' *Great Opera Houses*, London (Weidenfeld & Nicolson) 1956.

439 ... *The teatro San-Carlo.* ... See above, note to p. 154; also Spike Hughes, *op. cit.*, pp. 180–223.

439 ... *which is even passable.* ... It is not clear to which theatre Stendhal is referring. In 1823, Rome had three lyric theatres: the Argentina (1731), the Valle (1727) and the Tordinono, renamed Apollo in 1821. The last was rebuilt in 1795, and therefore corresponds most closely to the date given by Stendhal.

441 ... *in Pavesi's Arminio.* In a letter to Mareste (23rd Feb. 1821), Stendhal refers to this performance, adding a highly unromantic comment on Giuditta Pasta: "*L'Arminio* de Pavesi est allé *alle stelle* à Venise, de compagnie avec le vieux Crivelli et la jeune Pasta qui, pour ne pas gâter sa voix par des couches, *lo piglia in c....*"

443 ... *topic of conversation.* See above, note to p. 301.

444 ... *gambling at La Scala.* ... No gambling was permitted in Milan, save at La Scala, where the profits from the tables helped to finance the produc-

tions. This scheme was instituted in 1778, forbidden in 1788, permitted again in 1802 and finally forbidden in 1815.

446   ... *passing through Paris*. ... Rossini and Isabella Colbran stayed in Paris on their way to London from 9th Nov. until 7th Dec. 1823. On 1st Dec., he had drafted a contract to compose for the Académie Royale de Musique as well as for the Théâtre Italien; and this contract had been finally signed and ratified at the French Embassy in London on 27th Feb. 1824. Rossini took up his new post in Paris on 1st Aug. 1824.

446   ... *the finest things he did*. Diderot, *Lettres à Sophie Volland*, ed. A. Babelon, 1931.

448   ... *charges of over-statement?* The *Collection Auguste Rondel* (Paris, Bibl. de l'Arsénal) has preserved numerous Sanquirico stage-designs, which remain distinctly impressive, even today.

449   ... *up into our room*. ... The change of style suggests that Stendhal is simply incorporating into his text an extract from some private letter—a typical example of his deliberately "unstudied" manner of writing.

450   ... *Dr Sangrado*. A quack doctor, who appears in Lesage's *Gil Blas de Santillane* (1715).

451   ... *Queen Caroline and Admiral Nelson*. ... Nelson's part in the suppression of the Parthenopian Republic—flirting publicly with Lady Hamilton in full view of the captured insurgents waiting for execution—is the blackest and most shameful episode in the great sailor's chequered career. See Harold Acton, *The Bourbons of Naples* (London 1956).

455   ... *in the year 1400 or thereabouts*. ... Stendhal is about two centuries out. Allegri was appointed to the Apostolic Chapel by Pope Urban VIII in 1629.

455   ... *the Chamberlain Puzzini*. Quoting from memory, Stendhal writes *Pulcini*. See the *Lettre à M. Renouard, libraire, sur une tache faite à un manuscrit de Florence* (1810), in Paul-Louis Courier, *Oeuvres Complètes*, Paris (Pléiade), 1964, pp. 248–71.

457   ... *the Casacciello family*. ... In *Rome, Naples and Florence* (1826), Stendhal gives a description of Casacciello acting the part of Domingo in the opera *Paolo e Virginia*, by Guglielmi (9th Feb. 1817).

459   ... *his vanity*. ... Stendhal constantly contrasts the extroverted vanity of the Frenchman with the introspective sensibility of the Italian.

461   ... *starvation and penury*. ... Stendhal had spent some eleven days in and around London in 1817, and a further month in Oct.–Nov. 1821. If he travelled to the Midlands or the North, it must have been during this second visit.

478   ... *and with naked legs!* The statue referred to is the one by Bosio that still stands in the Place des Victoires.

INDEX AND TABLE OF REFERENCES

(The correct or accepted spelling of proper names is given first; alternatives in brackets afterwards.)

another work, Lord Francis Jeffrey's *Essay on Beauty*; 246.

Allegri, Gregorio (*c.* 1580–1652). A relative of Correggio, he was appointed to the Apostolic Chapel by Pope Urban VIII in 1629. His works include *concertini* and *motetti* and the famous *Miserere* for nine voices in two choirs, sung in the pontifical chapel during Holy Week. See the *Musical Times*, 1885, p. 455; 455.

Alunno della Giumenta, l' (ballet). See Viganò.

Ambrogetti, Giuseppe. A *basso-buffo* of no great power, but with great gifts as an actor. He first appears in 1807, and in Paris in 1815, in *Don Giovanni*. His most famous part was that of the mad father in Paër's *Agnese*. He disappears after 1838, and is said to have become a monk; 27.

Ambrosi, Antonio. A bass singer, never in the front rank; a member of the original cast of *la Gazza* and of *Matilde Shabran*; 169, 268, 281, 423, 424, 436.

Anatole, Madame Constance-Hippolyte, *née* Gosselin (b. Paris 1793; retired 1830). French ballet-dancer at the *Opéra*. A pupil of Coulon, Madame Anatole made her *début* in 1813; subsequently she appeared (together with her husband) in Paris, Brussels, Berlin and London, in which latter city she was known as *the Goddess of the Dance*; 209.

Ancelot, Jacques-Arsène-François-Polycarpe (b. Le Havre 1794; d. Paris 1854). A popular dramatist, who began with tragedy but later turned to comedy and farce. His wife, Marguerite Chardon (1792–1875) was also a successful dramatist, under the name of Virginie Ancelot. His first tragedy, *Louis IX*, (1819) concentrated the royalist opposition to Casimir Delavigne's *Vêpres Siciliennes; Le Maire du Palais* dates from 1823; 36.

Ancillo, Giuseppe (1787–1849). Venetian apothecary and dialect poet in the manner of Buratti. Friend of Stendhal in 1820; 400.

Andromaque (tragedy). See Racine.

Anfossi, Pasquale (*c.* 1736–1797). Neapolitan composer, at first pupil, then rival of Piccinni. His works include 46 operas and 7 oratorios: his most successful achievement was *l'Incognita Perseguitata* (1773). Two other operas, *Il Curioso indiscrete* and *Le Gelosie fortunate*, both received additions from the hand of Mozart; 29, 124, 125, 318.

Annales Littéraires (periodical). *I.e., Annales de la Littérature et des Arts.* Edited by Quatremère de Quincy, Raoul-Rochette, Charles Nodier, Ancelot, *etc.* Paris 1820–28; 206.

Ansani, Giovanni (*c.* 1750–1815). Italian tenor and composer, with an international reputation in the XVIIIth century. Sang in Italy, London (1780–1), Copenhagen (1770), *etc.* Retired in 1800. See Burney, *General History of Music*; 351

Antonini, Signor. A Bolognese lawyer, friend of Stendhal; 67.

Apocalypse, The; 21, 35.

Apostoli, Francesco (1755–1816). An unsuccessful Italian official, repeatedly victim of the political troubles of his time. He was imprisoned in Corfu (1794–7); later in Sebenico and Petervaradino. Turned towards literature at the end of his career; his most successful work, the *Lettere Sirmiensi per servire alla storia della deportazione de' cittadini Cisalpini in Dalmazia ed Ungheria*, deals with his second period of imprisonment; 336.

Apoteosi d'Ercole. l' (opera). See Mercadante.

Appiani, Andrea (b. Milan 1754; d. 1817). Milanese painter, greatly favoured by Napoleon, who, in 1796, made him "commissario superiore" for procuring works of

count St. Alban (1561–1621). Philosopher and statesman, Lord Chancellor of England under James I until his disgrace. A major influence on the ideas of the French *Philosophes*, from whom Stendhal derives; 131.

Balsamina (Balzamini), Signora Camilla (b. Milan 1784; d. Milan 1810). Distinguished Italian contralto, prominent on the stages of Italy and France 1807–10; 20.

Banti, Brigitta Giorgi (b. Crema 1759; d. Bologna 1806). A street-singer, engaged by de Vismes for the Opéra (1778). A pupil of Sacchini, Piozzi and Abel, she is reputed to have learnt nothing at any time. A brilliant natural soprano, who sang in many operas by Gluck, Paisiello, Nasolini, Bianchi, *etc*. On her death, she bequeathed her larynx to the Municipality of Bologna; 329, 351.

Barbaja (Barbaïa, Barbaglia), Domenico (b. Milan 1778; d. Posilipo 1841). One of the greatest *impresari* of all time. His "discoveries" include Rossini, Bellini, Donizetti and the dancer Taglioni, besides many others. After managing the San-Carlo, he went to Vienna as manager of the *Kärnthnerthor* and *An der Wien* theatres. He himself figures in an opera, *la Sirène*, by Auber and Scribe; 152, 153, 154, 155, 163, 168, 171, 387, 439, 450.

Barbiere di Siviglia, il (opera). See Paisiello.

BARBIERE DI SIVIGLIA, IL, *ossia* ALMAVIVA, *ossia* L'INUTILE PRECAUZIONE. Opera by Rossini. Libretto by Sterbini from Beaumarchais' play *Le Barbier de Séville*. Performed at the Teatro Argentina, Rome, 20th Feb. 1816. See *Bibliography*, under entry *Giorgi-Righetti*; 40, 51, 58, 68, 103, 105, 106, 108, 153, 161, 172, 174, 176–200, 206, 207, 208, 209, 267, 271, 280, 311, 334, 401, 405, 406, 408, **422**.

Bardes, les (opera). See Lesueur, *Ossian, ou Les Bardes*.

Barilli, Luigi (b. Modena 1767; d. Paris 1824). Italian buffo-cantante, *début* in Paris in 1805. Became Administrator of the *Théâtre-Italien* in 1809, but the enterprise was financially ruinous. From 1820, he was employed as *régisseur* of the *Louvois*; 42, 268, 428.

Barilli, Marianna, *née* Bondini (b. Dresden 1780, d. Paris 1813). Wife of Luigi. A soprano who might have become one of the greatest singers of the century, had it not been for the ill-health which constantly interrupted her career. Début in Paris, 1807, as Clorinda in Guglielmi's *Due Gemelli*. From 1810, raised the standard of the Louvois to its finest peak. Died suddenly in 1813; 224, 278.

Barker, Robert (b. Kells 1739; d. Southwark 1806). English watercolour artist, the reputed inventor of the "panorama". From 1793, Barker exhibited his circular landscapes (90 feet in diameter) in Leicester Square, beginning with a "View of the Grand Fleet at Spithead". The enterprise was successful, and Barker made a fortune; 448.

Barnave, Antoine-Pierre-Joseph-Marie (1761–1793). French politician who was a distinguished member of the Left in the early days of the Revolution. A fine orator of Girondin sympathies, he entered into relations with the Court after Varennes. Guillotined under Robespierre; 208.

Baron de Dolsheim, le (opera). See Pacini, *il Barone di Dolsheim*.

Baronne de Luz (novel). See Duclos.

Barthélemy, Abbé Jean-Jacques (1716–1795). French scholar and writer, best known for his *Voyage du Jeune Anacharsis en Grèce*, an outstanding example of popularized erudition; 204.

Bassi, Luigi (b. Pesaro 1766; d. 1825). An eminent Italian *buffo* baritone, who spent the best part of his career in Prague, where he was most suc-

Benedetti, Michele. Popular Italian bass, who created the part of Elmiro Barbarigo in *Otello*. He also created parts in *Armida*, *Mosè*, *Ricciardo e Zoraide*, *La Donna del Lago* and *Zelmira*, as well as in operas by Donizetti. Sang in London in 1820; 225, 226, 320, 422, 423, 424, 425.

Benelli, Giovanni-Battista. Director of the King's Theatre, London, 1823–4. See Ebers, *Seven Years of the King's Theatre*, chapters 7–9; 429, 436.

Bentinck, Lord William Cavendish (1774–1839). English general and administrator. Served under Wellington during the Napoleonic campaigns; governor-general of Bengal (1828); later first governor-general of India. In 1814, Bentinck commanded a successful expedition against Genoa, "where he issued two proclamations which, anticipating by nearly half a century the proclamation of Italian unity, caused some embarrassment to his government"; 410.

Benzoni, Contessa Maria, *née* Querini (b. Corfu 1757; d. 1839). A famous beauty of the end of the XVIIIth century, whose *salon* Stendhal frequented in 1815 (Palazzo San-Benedetto, in Venice). She is reputed to be the heroine of the Romance *La Biondina in Gondoletta* (*q.v.*), which was set to music by Simon Mayr; 50, 67.

Béranger, Pierre-Jean de (1780–1857). French poet and song-writer. His early work is light and epicurean, his later songs biting and satirical. *Grove's Dictionary* gives a list of his libretti: 206.

Bergère, rue. See *Conservatoire*.

Berio di Salsa (Salza), Marchese Francesco Maria (b. Naples 1767; d. Naples 1820). Wealthy literary dilettante and conversationist; librettist of *Otello* and of *Ricciardo*, and a personal friend of Stendhal. See A. D'Avino and L. Solaroli, "Stendhal et le marquis Berio", in *Stendhal-Club*, III, 9, 1960; 67, 211, 213–216, 227, 232, 333, 393.

Bernacchi, Antonio (1690–1756). Bolognese male-soprano, a pupil of Pistocchi. His *début* was made about 1712; subsequently he sang in London and Italy (1716–26) and in the service of the Emperor and of the Elector of Bavaria. He was the greatest popularizer of the "embroidered" style of singing; 351, 352.

Bernard-Léon: Jean-Pierre Bernard, known as (b. Paris 1785; d. Paris, 1858). Began his career as Beaumarchais' secretary; then turned novelist, dramatist, amateur actor, and finally (1820) professional actor. One of the leading lights of the *Gymnase* between 1820–1840; 221.

Berri, Duchesse de (1798–1870). Daughter of Francis I of Naples; married Charles, Duc de Berri (second son of Charles X of France, assassinated 1820) in 1816. An energetic lady, she attempted in 1822 to stir up la Vendée in revolt against Louis-Philippe, failed, and was imprisoned for a while at Blaye; 424.

Berti, Tommaso. Tenor. Member of the original cast of *l'Occasione fa il Ladro*; 421.

Bertoletti, Milanese general; 97.

Berton, Henri Montan (1767–1844). Son of the well-known composer and conductor Pierre Montan Berton (1727–1780). As a violinist, Berton was an infant prodigy; he was a pupil of Rey and Sacchini. His first comic operas were performed in 1787, and inaugurated a series of minor masterpieces. His career was distinguished, and far more influential in French music than Stendhal would have us believe; 90, 103–108, 115, 199.

His works include:

    Aline, ou la Reine de Golconde (3 acts, Paris 1803); 103.

le Délire (1 act, Paris 1799); 103, 105.

Montano et Stéphanie (comic opera, libretto by Dejaure; 3 acts, Théâtre Feydeau 1798; his best work); 103, 105, 108.

les Rigueurs du Cloître (a "revolutionary" opera, 2 acts, Paris 1790); 105.

Virginie (opera, 3 acts, Paris 1823); 108.

De la Musique mécanique et de la musique philosophique (treatise, Paris 1821); 103.

Epître à un célèbre Compositeur français (treatise, Paris 1823). Both these treatises were inspired by jealousy of Rossini. Their hero is Boïeldieu, who, it is said, was not pleased by being thus elevated.

Besenval (Bezanval), Pierre-Victor, Baron de (1742-1794). French soldier and writer, in command of the Swiss regiment in 1789; withdrew his troops without orders when the Bastille was attacked. Author of his Mémoires de M. le Baron de Besenval (3 vols., Paris 1805); and of a number of contes, including le Spleen (see Les Conteurs du XVIIIe siècle, Paris (Flammarion) 1899); 203, 207.

Bianca, la contessa: i.e., Bianca Milesi (b. Milan 1790; d. Paris 1849). One of Stendhal's closest friends, and an aunt of his beloved Méthilde Viscontini. She was also a fervent supporter of the Milanese patriots and carbonari. See Martineau, Petit Dictionnaire Stendhalien, pp. 337–9; 33.

BIANCA E FALIERO, ossai IL CONSIGLIO DEI TRE. Opera by Rossini. Libretto by Romani, based on Manzoni, il Conte di Carmagnola. Performed at la Scala on 26th Dec. 1819; 39, 41, 397-398, 399, 402, 423-424.

Bianchi, Eliodoro (b. Cividate 1773; retired 1836). Distinguished Italian tenor, trained in Naples under Tritto.

Début at Naples in 1799, at la Scala in 1803. Rossini wrote parts for him in Ciro, Aureliano and Odoardo. Teacher of the Russian tenor, Ivanov; 420, 421, 423.

Bianchi, Luciano. Italian bass, who created the role of Orbassano in Tancredi; subsequently created parts in Sigismondo and Odoardo e Cristina; 421, 422, 423.

Bianchi, Pietro. Minor Italian architect, formerly held in great esteem by Napoleon. Architect of the San-Carlo in Naples, and of San Francesco di Paola, which is modelled on the Pantheon in Rome; 438.

Bigottini, Emilia (b. Paris 1784; d. Passy 1858). French ballet-dancer and a brilliant mime. Her career at the Opéra lasted from 1812 to 1825; but in 1828, Auber, Scribe and G. Delavigne devised for her the famous part of Fenella in La Muette de Portici; 208.

Biondina in Gondoletta, la (song). Words usually ascribed to Buratti (q.v.), but also to Antonio Lamberti. Music by Simone Mayr. See Benzoni; 196.

Blangy, Mademoiselle. French soprano, probably a music-student from the Conservatoire; 430.

Bocci, Signor. Dancer in Viganò's ballet Otello (q.v.); 230.

Boïeldieu, François Adrien (b. Rouen 1775; d. 1834). French composer, and acknowledged leader of the national school of comic opera writers in the early XIXth century. A pupil of Cherubini, he succeeded Méhul at the Conservatoire in 1817. His operas include: le Caliphe de Bagdad (1800); Jean de Paris (1812) and la Dame Blanche (1825); 90.

Boileau-Despréaux, Nicolas (1636–1711). French poet and critic, later taken as a model by Alexander Pope. His Epître à Racine is a spirited defence of Racine's Phèdre (1677) against the cabale organized by the

Duchesse de Bouillon in favour of Pradon; 25, 66, 310, 311.

Bonald, Vicomte Louis de (1754–1840). French philosopher and writer, one of the most violent reactionaries of the post-revolutionary period; he defends a mystic conception of the State based upon the divinity of the King and the political power of the Church; 93.

Bonaparte, Lucien, Prince de Canino (b. Ajaccio 1775; d. Viterbo 1840). Second brother of Napoleon; revolutionary member of the Conseil des Cinq-Cents; prepared the coup d'état of ·18 Brumaire. After a quarrel with Napoleon, he retired to Rome; 69.

Bonaparte, Napoleon (b. Ajaccio 1769; d. St. Helena 1821); 3, 12, 50, 87, 91, 97, 164–165, 176, 193, 267, 275, 285, 290, 304–305, 307, 327, 329, 330, 386, 428, 440, 441, 444, 463.

   battles: Arcola (15th–17th November 1796); Napoleon, with Augereau, Lannes and Masséna, defeats the Austrians under Alvinzy; 12, 65.

   Lodi (9th May 1796); Napoleon, with Lannes, Berthier and Masséna, defeats the Austrians under Beaulieu; 65.

   writings: Correspondance inédite, officielle et confidentielle, de Napoléon Bonaparte. Paris, 7 vols., 1819–20; 12.

   Mémoires pour servir à l'Histoire de France sous Napoléon, écrits à Sainte Hélène, par les généraux qui ont partagé sa Captivité, et publiés sur les manuscrits entièrement corrigés de la main de Napoléon. Paris, 2 vols., 1823; 307.

   see also: Las Cases; Manzoni.

Bonoldi, Claudio (b. Piacenza 1783; d. Milan 1846). Italian tenor trained under Carcani and Gherardi. Sang in Reggio and Parma, and later throughout Italy, but failed in Paris (1823). Retired 1828; 22, 420–421, 422, 423, 424, 427.

Bonoldi, Lodovico. A minor singer at the Théâtre Louvois in 1823. He sang the part of Vanoldo, Count of Seymour, in Mayr's *La Rosa bianca e la Rosa rossa*; 427.

Bordogni, Giulio Marco (1788–1856). Italian tenor, a pupil of Simon Mayr, who sang at la Scala from 1813–1815, but spent most of his career in Paris. He was one of the great teachers at the Conservatoire; 10, 427.

Borghese, la Zitella: see *Le Président de Brosses en Italie, Lettres familières écrites d'Italie en 1739 et 1740,* 3rd ed., Paris 1861, vol. II, p. 216 (*Lettre* XLIV); 187.

Bossuet, Jacques-Bénigne (1627–1704). Born at Dijon, Bishop of Condom, later of Meaux. French historian, preacher and stylist; 172, 203, 294.

Botticelli, Bartolommeo. The original Bartolo in the *Barber*. A mediocre *basso-buffo* who, in 1810, had been singing at the Louvois together with Stendhal's mistress, Angelina Bereyter; 177, 422.

Botticelli, Vincenzo. Italian *basso-buffo*, who created the parts of the High Priest in *Aureliano* and of Fabrizio Vingradito in *La Gazza*; 268, 421, 423.

Boucher, François (1703–1770). French painter of the school of Watteau and Fragonard; 448.

Branchu, Madame Alexandrine-Caroline, *née* Chevalier de Lavit (b. Cap-Français 1780; d. Paris 1850). Leading French soprano of the Opéra 1804–26); a pupil of the Conservatoire, she made her *début* at the Théâtre Feydeau in 1799; 197.

Brienne, Madame de; 471.

Britannicus (tragedy). See Racine.

Brosses, le Président Charles de (1709–1777). One of the wittiest minor writers of the XVIIIth century. Best

music by Piccinni. This work is the basis of *la Gazza ladra*; 266.

Calas, Jean (1698–1762). A merchant of Toulouse, who was condemned to death on a trumped-up charge by the *Parlement* in 1762, and executed. Voltaire shook the whole French legal system by his vitriolic denunciation of this injustice; 449.

Calas (melodrama). 3 acts in prose by Ducange and Varez. *Théâtre de l'Ambigu-Comique*, 20th Nov. 1819; 266.

Calderara, il Marchese. One of the administrators of la Scala, Milan; 433.

Calzolaja, la (ballet). See Viganò.

CAMBIALE DI MATRIMONIO, LA, opera (*farsa*) by Rossini. Libretto by Gaetano Rossi, librettist of the San-Mosè, Venice. Performed at the San-Mosè, 3rd November 1810. Rossini's first performed opera; 48, 339, **419–420**.

Camilla (opera). See Paër.

Campan, Madame Jeanne-Louise-Henriette Genest (1752–1822). Lady-in-waiting to Marie-Antoinette. Later in life, she became a well-known educationalist and principal of an Institute at Ecouen. Author of the well-known *Mémoires sur la Vie privée de Marie-Antoinette* (3 vols., Paris 1822); 203.

Campitelli, Luigi. Italian singer, one of the original performers in Rossini's cantata *il Vero Omaggio*; 425.

Camporesi (Camporese), Signora Violante (1785–1839). A well-known soprano, originally an amateur, later a professional. A pupil of Crescentini, she was a friend of Paër, and at one time gave private concerts for Napoleon. From 1816 to 1824 she sang mainly at la Scala and at the King's Theatre. Her reputation was made in operas by Mozart, Paër, and in Rossini's *Otello* and *la Gazza ladra*; 367, 397, 398, 424.

Candide, ou l'Optimisme (philosophical novel). See Voltaire.

Canonica, Luigi (b. Tesserete 1762; d. Milan 1844). Italian architect, a pupil of Piermarini. His main work was in Milan, where he built the Great Arena, the Royal Palace, the Villa Bonaparte and the Teatro Carcano. His other theatres include those at Brescia, Cremona, Modena, Sondrio and Genoa; 438.

Canonici, Giacinta. Italian soprano, leading light of the Teatro dei Fiorentini (Naples). Created the role of Berenice in *L'Occasione fa il ladro*. Later created a part in Donizetti's *La Zingara*; 421.

Canova, Antonio (1757–1822) Italian sculptor, born at Possagno. His reputation to-day is perhaps less exalted than Stendhal would have wished; his works, nevertheless, are of entrancing grace and sweetness. See Ugo Ojetti, "Canova e Stendhal", in *Dedalo, Rassegna d'Arte*, October 1922, p. 307; 11, 43, 53, 114, 189, 246, 294, 327, 331, 332, 333, 379, 418, 440.

   Venus and Adonis (sculptural group). Made for Berio di Salsa in 1794. In 1820, it passed into the hands of Col. Guillaume Fabre: 333.

Cantarelli, Maria. Italian soprano who created the role of Giulia at the première of *La Scala di Seta*. Her sister Teresa sang a *terza-donna* part in the same production. Neither made much impression; 420.

Caracciolo (Caraccioli), Francesco. Italian admiral, descendant of a very ancient Italian family which originated with Giovanni Caracciolo, favourite of Jeanne II, Queen of Naples, and assassinated in 1432. Admiral Caracciolo was hanged by Nelson on 29th June 1799 in cruel and degrading circumstances; 410.

Carafa (Caraffa), Michele Enrico C. di Colobrano (b. Naples 1787; d. 1872). Italian composer who lived mainly in Paris and studied under Cheru-

Cavaiola, la. Neapolitan folk-song, the "national anthem" of Naples; 9.

Cecconi, Anna Maria. Neapolitan contralto, who created the role of Emma in *Zelmira*. Mistress of Barbaja, she was the mother of his son Pietro; 424.

Cellini, Benvenuto (1500–1571). Italian sculptor, engraver and goldsmith, born in Florence. His *Autobiography* (which remained in MS. until 1728) is one of the most entertaining collections of reminiscences ever written; 238.

CENERENTOLA, LA, *ossia* LA BONTÀ IN TRIONFO. Opera by Rossini in two acts, libretto by Ferretti. Two *arie del sorbetto* by Agolini. First given in Rome at the Teatro Valle, on 25th January 1817; 169, 172, 187, 199, 240–261, **422**.

Cento Novelle (moral stories). See Giraldi.

C'est l'amour, l'amour (popular ballad); 32, 115.

Chabrand (Chabran), Margherita. Italian *prima-donna*, who sang in Naples 1802–1820. A pupil of Pellegrini, she created the roles of Teti (*Teti e Peleo*) and Lisetta (*La Gazzetta*); 422, 424.

Champmeslé (Marie Desmares, known as La C.) (1642–1698). Famous French actress of the XVIIth century, who created the leading rôles in several of Racine's tragedies; 310

Chant du Départ, le. One of the great songs of the Revolution. Words by Marie-Joseph Chénier, music probably by Méhul (1794); 13.

Charles II (1630–1685). King of England from 1660; 284.

Charles VI (1685–1740). Habsburg Emperor from 1711, second son of Leopold I, and father of Maria-Theresa; 258.

Chateaubriand, Vicomte François-René de (1768–1848). One of the greatest French prose-writers of the Romantic period; also a major political figure in his time. Best known to-day for his *Mémoires d'Outre-Tombe*; in their time, his *Atala* (1801) and *René* (1805) had a vast success; 93.

Chaumel, Mademoiselle. See Comelli, la.

Chauvel, Monsieur. A friend of Napoleon: 386.

Chénier, Marie-Joseph-Blaise de (1764–1811). French dramatist, journalist and politician, and brother of the celebrated poet. An ardent Jacobin during the Revolution, Chénier was elected deputy to the *Convention* by the people of Versailles; 176. His works include: *Tibère* (tragedy, 1809); 176.
See also: *Le Chant du Départ.*

Cherubini, Maria Luigi Carlo Zenobio Salvatore (b. Florence 1760; d. Paris 1842). Italian composer, later naturalized French. Director of the *Conservatoire* from 1822, and one of the greatest teachers of his time. Though not primarily a composer of opera, he has a number to his credit, including *Lodoïska* (1791); *Médée* (1797); *Faniska* (1806) and *Les Abencérages* (1813); 10, 25, 61, 131, 408.

Chigi-Albani, Prince Agostino (1771–1855); Roman aristocrat, art-patron and diarist; 101.

Choron, Alexandre Etienne (1772–1834). French scholar, mathematician, linguist, composer, *etc.*, whose writings and whose school (*l'Institution Royale de Musique Classique et Religieuse*, 1824–1830) exercised a considerable influence on French music. He wrote an *Introduction à l'étude générale et raisonnée de la musique*; 186, 434.

Cicero, Marcus Tullius (106–43 B.C.). Roman poet, philosopher and stylist; 180, 201.

Cicimarra (Ciccimarra), Giuseppe. Italian baritone, who created the part of Iago in *Otello*, and who created other rôles in *Armida, Mosè, Ricciardo, Ermione* and *Maometto II.* A regular member of the San Carlo company; 422, 423, 424.

Cimarosa, Domenico (b. Aversa 1749; d. Venice 1801). Major Italian composer of the XVIIIth century, studied under Sacchini and Piccinni and made his *début* with *Le Stravaganze del Conte* in Naples in 1772. His brilliantly successful career took him to St Petersburg and Vienna; but he was politically unwise in welcoming the republican French armies in 1799, and condemned to death. He was reprieved, but died immediately after his release from prison; 5, 6, 14, 19, 20, 22, 23, 24, 25, 29, 30, 36, 37, 38, 40, 41, 42, 50, 53, 63, 68, 77, 78, 79, 98, 103, 123, 125, 142, 144, 150, 181, 182, 186, 187, 190, 192, 193, 195, 196, 200, 241, 243, 245, 247, 249, 253, 273, 286, 301, 317, 374, 402, 408, 409, 412, 418, 425, 440, 454.

His works include:

Il Matrimonio segreto (2 acts; libretto by G. Bertati, based on comedy by G. Colman and D. Garrick; Vienna, Burg-Theater, 7th Feb. 1792); 5, 123, 128, 181, 182, 187, 188, 190, 195, 253, 351, 403, 405, 406, 455.

I Nemici generosi, ossia Il Duello per Complimento (libretto by Petrosellini; Rome, Valle Theatre, 26th Dec. 1795); 42, 98.

Gli Orazi e Curiazi (libretto by A. S. Sografi; Venice, la Fenice, 26th Dec. 1796); 41, 53, 186, 301, 364, 368, 374, 395, 418, 448.

Il Sacrifizio d'Abramo ("Oratorio"; 1786); 22.

Cinderella (opera). See Etienne. *La Cenerentola.*

Cinthio, G. B. Giraldi. See Giraldi.

Cinti, Mademoiselle (*i.e.,* Laure Cinthie Damoreau, *née* Montalant) (1801–1863). A famous French

soprano, whose reputation was still to be made in 1823. Her first engagement at the *Italiens* was in 1816; but by 1826 she was at the height of her fame, and it was for her that Rossini wrote *le Siège de Corinthe* and *Moïse.* She also contributed greatly to the success of *Le Comte Ory.* Auber wrote many rôles for her. She retired in 1843; 190, 274, 427, 430.

CIRO IN BABILONIA. "Oratorio" by Rossini. Libretto by Franceso Aventi. Performed Ferrara, 14th March 1812; 49, 339, **420.**

Clarissa Harlowe (novel). See Richardson.

Clarke, Rev. Edward Daniel. English geographer, author of the *Travels in various Countries of Europe, Asia and Africa,* London, 6 vols., 1810–23. Part I of this compendium: *Russia, Tartary and Turkey* was translated into French in 1812; 242.

Claude Lorrain (Claude Gelée, known as *Le Lorrain*) (1600–1682). French landscape painter, one of the greatest French masters of the XVIIth century; 92.

Clemenza di Tito, la (opera). See Mozart.

Clermont, Louis de Bourbon-Condé, comte de (1709–1770). French general, who received his first commission in 1733. His early campaigns were in Germany and Holland; he was at Fontenoy, and later besieged Namur and Antwerp. But he is best remembered for his disastrous defeat in 1758 at Krefeldt, by Ferdinand of Brunswick; 203.

Clotilde (ballet). See Viganò.

Clytemnestre (tragedy). See Soumet.

Coccia, Carlo (1782–1873). Neapolitan composer, pupil of Fenarola and Paisiello. *Début* in 1808 with *il Matrimonio per Cambiale*; between this date and 1819, he wrote 22 operas of which the most successful was *Clotilde* (1815). Later he was the first Professor of Composition at the

Cora (opera). See Mayr: *Alonzo e Cora*.

Coriolan (ballet). See Viganò.

Corneille, Pierre (1606–1684). The noblest French dramatist and the true father of French classical tragedy. His works include: *Médée* (1635); *Horace* (1641); *Polyeucte* (1641–3); *Nicomède* (1651). In later life, he wrote a series of critical *Examens* of his own plays: the *Examen de Nicomède* was published in 1660; 105, 188, 229, 265, 347.

Corradino (opera). See Pavesi.

Correâ (Corea), Lorenza (b. Lisbon 1771). Portuguese soprano, pupil of Pareja. *Début* in Madrid in 1790; in Venice, 1792. She sang mainly in Naples and Paris; 136, 421.

Correggio, Antonio Allegri di (1494–1534). Italian painter greatly admired by Stendhal. His finest frescoes are to be seen in Parma; 6, 175, 271, 319, 379, 404, 418, 454, 477.

Correspondance de Napoléon. See Bonaparte, N.

Corsaire, le (*Journal des Spectacles, de la Littérature, des Arts, Mœurs et Modes*). A satirical journal of somewhat spasmodic popularity which flourished between 1822 and 1852; 382.

Corso, Teatro del (Bologna). See Theatres.

Cortesi, Carolina. Italian contralto, better renowned for her beauty than for her voice. Member of the original cast of *Odoardo e Cristina*; 423.

Così fan Tutte, ossia La Scuola degli Amanti (opera). See Mozart.

Cosmo the Great (Cosimo I, Grand-Duke of Tuscany, Duke of Florence) (1519–1574). Ascended the throne of Florence after the murder of Alessandro Medici by Lorenzino. One of the most magnificent, ruthless and efficient tyrants of all times, he died peacefully in 1574; 454.

Cotugno (Cottugno), Domenico (b. Ruvo di Puglia 1736; d. Naples 1822). Italian patriot and doctor, pioneer of public hygiene and preventive medicine, especially against tuberculosis; 16–17.

Coulon, M. Ballet-dancer. He took leading rôles in London from 1821–1825; 209.

Courier de Méré, Paul-Louis (1772–1825). French classical scholar and satirist, author of brilliant and witty pamphlets against the government of the restoration. He was a pioneer of XIXth century classical scholarship: his *Prospectus d'une traduction nouvelle d'Hérodote, contenant un Fragment du Livre III et la Préface du Traducteur* (Paris 1822) created a considerable stir. Courier was murdered by his gamekeeper in 1825. See *Furia*; 203, 453, 455.

Court Theatre, Turin. See *Theatres, Teatro Regio*.

Cousin, Victor (1792–1867). French writer, philosopher, politician and scholar. His works include a major edition of Plato, which was finally completed in 13 volumes in 1840; 131

Crabbe, George (1754–1832). English poet, whose greatest works are inspired by the suffering and degradation of the poorer classes. Born at Aldeborough; 271.

Cratarol. See *Gratarol*.

Creation, The (oratorio). See Haydn.

Crébillon, Claude ("Crébillon *fils*": 1707–1777). French novelist, son of the dramatist Prosper Crébillon. Like many of his contemporaries, Crébillon is a master of prose style, and his works would enjoy a wider reputation were it not for the licentiousness of his subject-matter; 190.

Crébillon, Prosper ("Crébillon *père*": 1674–1762). French tragic dramatist, born at Dijon. His plays, together with those of Voltaire, represent the transition from classical tragedy to pre-romantic melodrama. *Rhadamisthe et Zénobie* (1711), *Atrée et Thyeste*, etc., are still very occasionally revived, 140.

S

Crescentini, Girolamo (b. Urbania 1766; d. 1846). One of the greatest of Italian male mezzo-soprani, and the last representative of the old tradition. After his *début* in Rome in 1783, he sang in Leghorn, Padua, Venice, Turin, Naples, London, Lisbon (1798–1801) and Paris (1806–1812). Cimarosa composed his *Gli Orazi* for his voice; but his greatest rôle was as Romeo in Zingarelli's *Giulietta e Romeo*; 136, 337, 354, 386.

Crivelli, Gaetano (b. Bergamo 1774; d. 1836). A well-known tenor, who had been a pupil of Aprile. His talents as an actor matched the quality of his voice. He made his *début* at Brescia in 1793; and in 1811, he succeeded Garcia at the Louvois, where he remained until 1817; 117, 135, 360, 425, 441.

Cuisinières, les (comedy in 1 act) by Brazier and Dumersan. *Théâtre des Variétés*, 14th April 1823; 261.

Curioni, Alberico (1790–1860). A distinguished tenor, reputed to have been the handsomest man on the Italian stage. He sang at the San-Carlo, and later in Barcelona and London (1821), and appeared in several of Rossini's operas, notably *Otello, la Donna del Lago* and *Pietro l'Eremita* (*Mosè*); 436.

Cymbeline (play). See Shakespeare.

Daguerre, Louis-Jacques-Mandé (1787–1851). French artist, stage-designer and inventor. He created the *diorama*, and put the finishing touches to that process of photographic reproduction (originally invented by the chemist Nicéphore Niepce) which now bears his name: the *daguerreotype*; 432.

Dalayrac, Nicolas (b. Muret 1753; d. 1809). French composer of comic operas, who made his reputation with *Le Petit Souper* in 1781. During the next 25 years, he produced 56 popular operas, none of which, however, has survived in the modern repertoire. His best works include *l'Eclipse totale* (1782); *le Corsaire* (1783); *Nina* (1786) and *Ambroise* (1793). He is rightly considered the father of the French comic opera tradition of the XIXth century; 22, 25, 80.

Dante Alighieri (1265–1321). The greatest Italian poet, born in Florence, but by no means wholly devoted to poetry, for he figured largely in the political life of his time, and was finally exiled in 1302, living the rest of his life in Verona and Ravenna; 10, 66, 198, 233.

Danton, Georges-Jacques (b. Arcis-sur-Aube, 1759; guillotined, Paris, 1794). One of the greatest, and certainly the most attractive, of the leaders of *la Montagne*. His creations include the *Club des Cordeliers*, the *Tribunal révolutionnaire* and the *Comité de Salut Public*. His quarrel with the intractable Robespierre led eventually to the death of both these notable leaders, and to the failure of the Revolution; 304.

Dardanelli, Girolama. Italian *prima donna buffa*, a member of the original cast of *Elisabetta* and of the cantata *Teti e Peleo* (Naples, 1815 and 1816); 161, 422, 424, 436.

Daru, Baron Martial-Noël-Pierre (b. Montpellier; d. Paris 1827). Another of Napoleon's great administrators, Martial Daru became *Intendant des Biens de la Couronne* in Italy in 1811, and was largely responsible for the reconstruction of Rome; 440.

Daru, Comte Pierre-Antoine-Noël-Bruno (b. Montpellier 1767; d. Paris 1829). French administrator, civil servant and writer. Pierre Daru was a cousin of Stendhal; he was also one of Napoleon's most efficient *Intendants*. His main work, the *Histoire de la République de Venise*, was published in 1819; 72.

Daubigny (d'Aubigny), Théodore Baudouin. French popular dramatist, author of farces and melodramas. Co-operated with Caigniez in writing the original version of *la Gazza ladra* (see Caigniez); 266.

David, Louis (1748–1825). French painter, politician and revolutionary. Under Robespierre, David was a sort of "Minister of Fine Arts"; later he became court painter to Napoleon; but at the Restoration, he was exiled and died in Brussels; 448.

Davide, Giacomo (1750–1830). One of the finest Italian tenors of the XVIIIth century, the elder Davide was born in Bergamo, and studied under Sala. He was the perfect master of "controlled fioriture", and sang with tremendous success throughout Europe. He was still singing well in Florence in 1802. His greatest pupils were his son Giovanni and Nozzari; 333.

Davide, Giovanni (1789–1851). A prodigious Italian tenor with a range of 3 octaves to B♭. Trained by his father, he made his *début* at Brescia in 1810. Rossini wrote parts for him in *il Turco, Otello, Ricciardo* and *la Donna*. His voice began to go in 1825, and he died as manager of the opera-house in St Petersburg; 75, 110, 118, 134, 149, 170, 173, 193, 199, 208, 225, 226, 229, 231, 263, 264, 331, 334, 343, 364, 376, 387, 389, 390, 393, 421, 422, 423, 424, 425, 436.

De' Amicis, Anna Lucia (b. Naples *c.* 1740; d. *c.* 1800). A famous XVIIIth century soprano, who began her career in *opera buffa*, but later changed to *opera seria* under the influence of J.-C. Bach. She was a member of the original cast of Mozart's *Lucio Silla* in Milan in 1773; 329, 351.

De' Angeli, Alessandro. A member of the original cast of Rossini's *Bianca*, de' Angeli came from a famous

Neapolitan family of artists and actors, one member of which, Pietro (1784–1859), was the first major historian of the Argentine; 424.

Débats (periodical). See *Journal des Débats*.

De' Begnis, Giuseppina [Claudine], *née* Ronzi (b. Paris 1800; retired 1843). A not unsuccessful *prima donna buffa*, a pupil of Garat, who made her *début* in Genoa in 1817, and in Paris two years later. She was a poor Rosina, but a good Doña Anna. On the whole she was more successful in London and Naples than in Paris. Wife of the following; 209, 311, 436.

De' Begnis, Giuseppe (b. Lugo 1793; d. New York 1849). Italian *buffo comico*. *Début* at Modena in 1813, in Pavesi's *Ser Marcantonio*. One of his greatest successes was obtained in Rossini's *Turco*. Later he became director of the opera in Bath and Dublin; 243, 422, 436.

Deceiver deceiv'd, The (comedy). See Pix, Mrs Mary.

Dedalo (ballet). See Viganò.

De' Grecis, Nicola. A minor *buffo cantante*, associated with Rossini's early works in Venice, *la Cambiale* and *la Scala di Seta*; 420, 421.

Delille, abbé Jacques (b. Aigueperse, 1738; d. 1813). French poet, one of the leading figures of the pre-romantic period. He is best known for his translations of Virgil and Milton, his horticultural epic *Les Jardins, ou l'Art d'embellir les Paysages* . . . (Paris 1782), his poem *De la Pitié* (Paris 1803), and for his astounding ingenuity in periphrasis; 21, 61, 62, 113, 124, 203.

Délire, le (opera). See Berton.

De' Marini, Giuseppe Marini, known as (b. Milan 1772; d. Santa Maria di Papua, 1829). Famous Italian actor who specialized in comedy and in character interpretations in the style of the *drame bourgeois*. His best work was done in Venice and Milan; 254, 268, 292, 296, 386, 416, 417.

Deméri (De Méri), Mademoiselle. French soprano, trained at the Conservatoire, then under Paër and Garcia. *Début* at the Louvois, 25th Feb. 1823, as Amenaide in *Tancredi*. A true Wagnerian soprano born half a century too early, she left the Louvois in Dec. 1824; from 1825–34, held rank of *prima donna* at La Scala, from which she was eventually displaced by La Malibran; 181, 427, 430.

DEMETRIO E POLIBIO. Opera by Rossini. Libretto by Signora Vincenzina Viganò-Mombelli, the sister of the choreographer. The music, which represents Rossini's earliest adventure in operatic composition, was probably written in 1806–7, and touched up by Domenico Mombelli. First produced by the Mombelli family in Rome on 18th May 1812; 137–143, 189, 217, 2224, 339, 391, 419, 421.

Demofoonte (opera). See Leo.

Dérivis, Henri-Etienne (b. Albi 1780; d. 1856). French bass, a pupil of the *Conservatoire*. *Début* at the *Grand Opéra* in *les Mystères d'Isis*, 1803. He was leading bass from 1805 to 1828, but his voice was ultimately ruined by bad training. Rossini wrote him the part of Mohammed in *le Siège de Corinthe* (1826), but his voice could not manage the new style, and he was a failure; 108, 334.

Desaix de Veygoux, Louis (b. Riom 1768; killed Marengo 1800). French general who became known in 1796. He was largely responsible for Napoleon's victories in Egypt, and instrumental in winning the battle in which he met his death; 208, 330.

Déserteur, le (drama). See Sedaine.

Destouches, Philippe Néricault, known as (b. Tours 1680; d. 1754). French comic dramatist, whose works form a link between the high comedy of Molière and the sentimental comedy of the mid-XVIIIth century. His major works include: *le Glorieux; le Philosophe marié, ou le Mari honteux de l'être* (5 acts, 1727); and *le Dissipateur, ou l'honnête friponne* (5 acts, 1736); 190.

Deux Cousines, les. French farce, author unknown. Given at the *Théâtre des Jeunes Elèves* on the 4th Nov. 1805; 92.

Deviène, François (b. Joinville 1759; d. Charenton 1803). French composer, flautist and bassoon-player, who ultimately died insane. His works include 12 operas, of which the most successful were: *les Visitandines* (1792); *les Comédiens ambulants* (1798); and *le Valet de deux Maîtres* (1799); 302.

Devin du Village, le (opera). See Rousseau, J.-J.

Dictionnaire de l'Académie Française; the standard, if conservative, reference-book of accepted French usage. 1st ed., 1694; 8th ed., 1931–5; 106.

Diderot, Denis (b. Langres 1713; d. Paris 1784). One of the greatest French thinkers of the XVIIIth century, and responsible for editing the *Encyclopédie*. His *Correspondance* with his mistress, the actress Sophie Volland, is a mine of information about the background to the intellectual life of the century: it was finally published by André Babelon in 2 vols., 1931; 446, 467.

DIDONE ABBANDONATA. See MORTE DI DIDONE.

Directeur de Troupe, le (opera). See Mozart, *Schauspieldirektor*.

Dissipateur, le (comedy). See Destouches.

Divina Commedia, la (epic poem). See Dante.

Dolci (Dolce), Carlo (b. Florence 1616; d. Florence 1686). Italian painter, a pupil of J. Vignali. His style is melodramatic, his subjects largely religious, his colouring vague and suave; 60.

Domenichino (Domenico Zampieri, known as). Italian painter (b. Bologna 1581; d. Naples 1641). A notable draughtsman and colourist of genius; 197.

Don Carlos (tragedy). See Schiller.

Don Giovanni (opera). See Mozart.

Don Juan (epic poem). See Byron.

DONNA DEL LAGO, LA. Opera in 2 acts by Rossini. Libretto by Andrea Leone Tottola, based on poem by Sir Walter Scott. Performed at the San-Carlo, Naples on 24th Sept. 1819; first given in England at the Haymarket Theatre, 18th Feb. 1823; 172, 223, 342, 352, 365, 387–391, 395, 396, 418, **423**.

Donzelli, Domenico (b. Bergamo 1790; d. Bologna 1873). Italian tenor, who made his *début* in Rome c. 1815. Rossini wrote him a part in *Torvaldo*, as did Mercadante in *Elisa e Claudio*. He sang in Vienna, Paris and London, and retired in 1841; 176, 422.

Dorat, Claude-Joseph (b. Paris 1734; d. Paris 1780). French poet of the pre-romantic period, best known for a species of short narrative poem called the *héroïde*, which he perfected; 204.

Dragonetti, Signor. A member of the Louvois orchestra, probably related to the great double-bass player, Domenico Dragonetti (1763–1846) of the King's Theatre, London; 446.

Dragonetti, Luigi (b. Aquila 1791; d. Aquila 1871). Italian patriot and orator, who emerged to fame under Murat, was deputy from 1820 until his arrest in 1827; and eventually returned to public affairs during the political ferment leading up to 1848; 452.

Drouot, comte Antoine (b. Nancy 1774; d. Nancy 1847). A baker's son who rose to be a general in Napoleon's army; later he was Napoleon's A.D.C. in Elba; and after the defeat of Waterloo, it was he who brought the French armies back to Paris; 208.

Du Belloy (Pierre Laurent Buyrette, known as Dormont du Belloy) (b. Saint-Flour 1727; d. Paris 1775). French actor, poet and dramatist. His major works include *Gabrielle de Vergy* (1777), one of the first French plays to use a mediaeval subject, and the source of many libretti; and *le Siège de Calais*, a tragedy, performed on 13th Feb. 1765; 32–33, 307

Du Bos, abbé Jean-Baptiste (b. Beauvais 1670; d. Paris 1742). French historian, aesthetician, critic and diplomat. His career in the Foreign Office ended in 1715, after which he devoted himself to letters. His major contribution lay in the revival of French aesthetic theory after the classical period, notably in his *Réflexions critiques sur la Poésie et sur la Peinture* (2 vols., Paris 1719); 246.

Duclos, Charles Pinot (b. Dinan 1704; d. Paris 1772). French novelist, wit and scholar, and one of the most entertaining minor writers of his time. His novel, *Histoire de Madame de Luz, anecdote du Règne de Henri IV* was published at the Hague, 2 vols., 1741; 288.

Ducray-Duminil, François-Guillaume (b. Paris 1761; d. Ville-d'Avray 1819). French song-writer, dramatist and exceedingly moral novelist. His novels (*e.g. Les Petits Orphelins du Hameau*, 1800) were vastly popular, and the source of countless melodramas; 19.

Du Deffand, Madame Marie de Vichy-Chamrond, Marquise du D. (b. Château de Chamrond 1697; d. Paris 1780). One of the wittiest and most intelligent Frenchwomen of the XVIIIth century. Her salon was frequented by Voltaire, Montesquieu, d'Alembert and many others.

In 1765, when she had been blind for 12 years, she developed a passion for Horace Walpole, from which resulted an amazing correspondence (Paris, 4 vols., 1812); 202.

DUE BRUSCHINI, I. See FIGLIO PER AZZARDO.

Due Giornate, le (opera). See Mayr.

Du Hausset, Madame. Lady-in-waiting to Madame de Pompadour. Her memoirs, *Les Mémoires de Madame du Hausset, femme de chambre de Madame de Pompadour* were published by Quentin Crawford (Paris 1824); 203.

Dumoustier (Demoustier), Charles-Albert (b. Villers-Cotterêts 1760; d. Paris 1801). French poet and dramatist, best known for his popular *Lettres à Emilie sur la Mythologie* (1786–98). His best play was *les Femmes* (comedy, 3 acts, Paris 1793); 40.

Durante, Francesco (b. Frattamaggiore 1684; d. Naples 1755). Italian composer, mainly of church-music. Durante was one of the greatest teachers of his time; his most celebrated pupil was Piccinni. For a list of works, see Fétis; 21, 124, 125.

Dussault, Jean-Joseph-François (b. Paris 1769; d. Paris 1824). French journalist and politician. Having made his journalistic apprenticeship with Fréron on the *Orateur du Peuple*, he became one of the early editors of the *Journal des Débats*, from which he retired in 1818; 321.

EDUARDO E CRISTINA. Opera by Rossini. Libretto compiled by Tottola, Bevilacqua-Aldobrandini and Schmidt, based on another used earlier by Pavesi. The music is largely borrowed from earlier operas —*Adelaide*, *Ricciardo* and *Ermione*. First performed Venice, 24th April 1819; 399–403, **423**.

Edwards, William Frederick (b. Jamaica 1777; d. Versailles 1842). A French doctor of English descent, and a pioneer in the study of psychological pathology. His main works include: *De l'influence des agents physiques sur la vie* (Paris 1824); and *Des caractères physiologiques des races humaines* . . . (Paris 1829); 347.

Eglantine, Philippe-François-Nazaire Fabre, known as d'E. (b. Carcassonne 1750; guillotined Paris 1794). French actor, dramatic poet and anarchistic revolutionary; his works include the famous song, *Il pleut, il pleut, Bergère*. Known as the *Chef des Pourris*, he fell with Danton and Desmoulins; 241.

EGLE ED IRENE. Cantata by Rossini. Performed in Milan, 1814, in honour of the Princess Belgioioso. Librettist unknown; 424.

Eiser. See Häser.

Elena (opera). See Mayr.

Elefanteide, l' (satirical poem). See Buratti.

Elisa e Claudio (opera). See Mercadante.

Elisabetta (opera). See Carafa, *Elisabeth in Derbishire*.

ELISABETTA, REGINA D'INGHILTERRA. Opera by Rossini. Libretto by G. Schmidt, based indirectly on *The Recess, or, A Tale of other Times*, by Sophia Lee (1785). Performed at the San-Carlo, Naples, on the 4th Oct. 1815; 16, 134, 136, 153, 157–169, 170, 172, 174, 267, 342, 359, 371, 387, 401, 407, **422**, 425, 435.

Enfant chéri des Dames. An aria, said to have been stolen from Mozart by Devièine (*q.v.*) and inserted in *les Visitandines*; 302.

Enfant de Paris (l'), ou le Débit de Consolations. Vaudeville by Lurien, d'Allarde and Armand d'Artois, given at the *Théâtre des Variétés*, 4th June 1823; 249, 261.

Ennius, Quintus (240–169 B.C.). Latin poet from whom Virgil borrowed certain lines and images, commenting cynically that "there was an occasional pearl to be found even in Ennius' dung-heap!"; 31.

she was a pupil of Metastasio. A great coloratura, renowed also for her love-affairs and her avarice. One of the wealthiest singers ever on retirement; 329, 349, 351.

Gabrielle de Vergy (play). See Du Belloy. (Opera) see Carafa; Mercadante.

Gafforini, Elisabetta. Celebrated soprano, who flourished in Italy, Spain and Portugal between 1790 and 1812. Her last recorded performance was at la Scala in 1815. Famous for comic parts; 417.

Gagern, Hans Christoph Ernst, Freiherr von (b. Wurms 1766; d. Frankfurt a/M 1852). German statesman who played a significant rôle at the Congress of Vienna. He was particularly concerned to defend the independence of the smaller European states; 460.

Gaieté, Théâtre de la (Paris). See Theatres.

Gallenberg, Graf Wenzel Robert von (b. Vienna 1783; d. Rome 1839). Austrian amateur composer, who married Giulietta Guicciardi, one of Beethoven's passions. In 1806, he took charge of the music for the court theatre of Naples, and between 1816 and 1838, he collaborated frequently with Barbaja. Grove gives a list of his ballets. See also Aumer; 314.

Galli, Filippo (b. Rome 1783; d. Paris 1853). Italian tenor, later bass. He made his début in Bologna in 1804; his first appearance as a bass was in Rossini's l'Inganno felice. Later, he acquired the reputation as the greatest basso cantante in Europe; but from 1842, he lived in Paris in great poverty; 27, 80, 91, 96, 144, 146, 149, 150, 169, 174, 175, 184, 226, 229, 244, 248, 249, 257, 268, 278, 279, 280, 293, 294, 295, 296, 297, 300, 371, 394, 406, 420, 421, 422, 423, 424, 425.

Gallianis, Teresa. Italian contralto, who sang numerous parts at La Scala in 1817–18. She created the rôle of Pippo in La Gazza ladra; 268, 290, 423.

Galuppi, Baldassare, nicknamed il Buranello (b. Burano Island 1706; d. Venice 1785). Italian composer of note, who made his début at Chioggia in 1722 with la Fede nell' Incostanza. He worked mainly in Venice, London and St Petersburg. His greatest comic operas were those written in collaboration with the dramatist Goldoni. See Grove for full list; 26, 61, 123, 124, 125, 318.

Ganganelli, Giovanni Vincenzo, Pope Clement XIV (1705–1774). His main act after his election (1769) was to suppress the Jesuits. His motives for so doing have been discussed for two centuries; and for many years it was believed that he died poisoned by his enemies; 246.

Garcia, Manuel del Popolo Vicente (b. Seville 1775; d. Paris 1832). Spanish tenor, teacher and composer, founder of a famous family. He made his début in Italian opera in Paris in 1808, in Paër's Griselda. Garcia was one of Rossini's greatest interpreters during his "Neapolitan period", and one of the most dynamic music personalities of all time; 107, 166, 170, 173, 177, 185, 208, 220, 226, 422, 427.

Gardel, Pierre-Gabriel (Gardel Jeune) (b. Nancy 1758; d. Paris 1840). Member of a famous French family of dancers and choreographers. Head of the danseurs seuls et doubles at the Opéra, 1775. His "arrangements" include the divertissements for Rossini's Siège de Corinthe. Introduced Noverre's reforms into the French ballet tradition; 452.

Garrick, David (b. Hereford 1717; d. London 1779). English actor and dramatist; pupil, later friend, of Dr Johnson. Made his début as Richard III in 1741. Director of Drury Lane 1747–76; 318, 329.

Gay, John (b. Barnstaple 1685; d.

London 1732). English poet, librettist and satirist. Best known for his *Beggar's Opera* (with Dr Pepusch), 1728; 462.

GAZZA LADRA, LA. Opera by Rossini in 2 acts. Libretto by Giovanni Gherardini of Milan, based on play by Caigniez (*q.v.*) and Daubigny. Performed at la Scala, Milan on 31st May 1817. English version by Bishop: *Ninetta, or the Maid of Palaiseau*; 41, 42, 62, 68, 122, 123, 125, 134, 135, 169, 172, 184, 229, 266–302, 311, 325, 371, 378, 398, 407, 418, **422–423**, 425, 434, 447.

GAZZETTA, LA. Opera by Rossini in one act. Libretto (bad) by Tottola. The overture was later used for *la Cenerentola*. Performed at the Teatro dei Fiorentini, Naples, 26th September 1816. Total failure; 172, **422.**

General History of Music, A. See Burney.

Generali, Pietro (b. Rome 1773; d. Novara 1873). Italian composer, who made his *début* in Rome with *Gli Amanti Ridicoli* (1802). One of the most successful composers of his generation, and one of the few whose popularity survived the advent of Rossini. He left some 60 operas, of which the best known were *Pamela Nubile* (1804) and *Adelina* (1-act *farsa*, Venice 1810); 29, 30, 36, 125, 227.

Gentili, Serafino (b. near Venice 1786; d. Milan 1835). Well-known Italian tenor, who made his *début* in 1807, and retired in 1828; 421.

Geoffrin, Madame Marie-Thérèse Rodet (b. Paris 1699; d. Paris 1777). A self-educated woman of insignificant parentage, her *salon* grew to be one of the great meeting-places of the XVIIIth century. Her admirers included Stanislas Poniatowsky, who accorded her regal honours in Warsaw in 1766; 471.

Geoffroy, Julien-Louis (b. Rennes 1743; d. Paris 1814). French scholar and literary critic, who succeeded to

the *Année Littéraire* after the death of Fréron, and later became dramatic critic of the *Journal des Débats*; 148, 311, 321.

Gerani. See Gorani.

Geremei. Historic family of Bologna, leaders of the Guelf faction, chief rivals of the Lambertazzi. The political power of the Geremei begins with Baruffaldino de' Geremei in 1217, and wanes with his death in 1252; 455–456.

Gessner, Salomon (b. Zurich 1730; d. Zurich 1788). Swiss poet, painter and engraver, whose sentimental landscape-poetry, translated by Huber (*les Idylles, poèmes champêtres*, Lyon 1762) contributed to the formation of French pre-romanticism; 468.

Gherardi, Signora Fanny, *née* Lechi. Sister of the generals Giuseppe and Teodoro Lechi, of Brescia, Fanny Lechi was a notable figure in Bolognese society. Formerly she had been the mistress of Murat, the *King of Naples*, and had followed him to Rastadt and Paris. See R. Guyot, "Murat et Fanny Lechi" in *Feuilles d'Histoire*, 1st February, 1909; 235, 236.

Gherardi, Signor Giuseppe. Husband of Fanny; 68, 102.

Gherardini, Giovanni (b. Milan 1778; d. 1861). Italian doctor, philologist and poet. His works include (apart from numerous translations from English and German), the libretto of *la Gazza ladra; la Vita di Carlo Goldoni* (1821); and *la Vita di Gasparo Gozzi* (1821); 266.

Giani, Felice (1760–1823). Italian designer, painter and illustrator, who worked in Rome and Paris. He was responsible for many of the decorations of the Tuileries; 329.

Giannone, Pietro (b. Ischitella 1676; d. Turin 1748). Italian jurist, scholar, historian and pamphleteer. His major work is a history, whose spirit foreshadows that of Voltaire: *Istoria civile del Regno di Napoli* (4 vols., 1723). His anti-clericalism led to his arrest in 1736, and to his long imprisonment, which ended in his murder through the brutality of a gaoler in Turin; 44, 299, 455.

Giardiniera, la (opera). See Mozart.

Ginevra di Scozia (opera). See Mayr.

Giorgi-Righetti, Signora Geltrude (b. Bologna 1785; d. *circa* 1849.) Italian soprano of aristocratic birth. *Début* in Rome, 1804. The original Rosina of the *Barber*. After her marriage, she sang only as an amateur, and presided over a fashionable artistic *salon* in Bologna. Her reply to Stendhal's article on Rossini (see *Bibliography*) is an important document; 177, 243, 406, 422.

Giorgone, Giorgio Barbarelli da Castelfranco, known as *il G.*) (1477–1511). Major Italian painter of the Venetian school; 236.

Giovanola (di Lodi). Italian singer who was engaged at the Louvois (1824–1825) and at the King's Theatre, London (1826–1827). At the Louvois, he played Serano in *La Donna del Lago* and Ernesto in *Ricciardo e Zoraide*, and created the part of Zefirino in *Il Viaggio a Reims*; 230.

Giraldi, Giambattista Cinzio (b. Ferrara 1504; d. Ferarra 1573). Italian writer, whose tales (*Ecatomiti*, or *Cento Novelle*, Venice 1565) provide some of the original material for Shakespeare's *Othello*, although Shakespeare probably did not use this source directly; 215.

Girard, abbé Gabriel (b. Montferrand 1677; d. Montferrand 1748). French grammarian, almoner of the Duchesse de Berri, royal interpreter in Slavonic languages. His book, *les Synonymes françois, leurs significations, et le choix qu'il en faut faire pour parler avec justesse* was published in Paris in 1736; 214.

Giraùd, Count Giovanni (1776–1834).

Roman playwright and satirical poet, a friend of Buratti and Rossi. His name recurs frequently in Stendhal's letters and diaries; 68.

Gluck, Cristoph Willibald (b. Erasbach 1714; d. Vienna 1787). German composer who came to France under the protection of Marie-Antoinette, and revolutionized French opera. His most famous work is *Orfeo ed Euridice* (libretto by Ranieri Calzabigi), first performed at the Burgtheater, Vienna, 5th Oct. 1762; French version by Moline, Théâtre de l'Opéra, 2nd Aug. 1774; 28, 104, 173, 185, 204, 206, 295, 423, 466–467.

Goethe, Johann Wolfgang von (1749–1832). German poet, *etc.*, 327. The works referred to by Stendhal are:

Die Leiden des jungen Werther (romantic novel, 1774); 210, 367, 386.

Die Kampagne in Frankreich 1792 (historical memoirs); 327.

Dichtung und Wahrheit (semi-fictionalized autobiography, 1809–1831); 327.

Goldoni, Carlo (b. Venice 1707; d. Paris 1793). Italian dramatist who began writing for the theatre in 1747. He introduced the new realist comedy into Italy, replacing the traditional *commedia dell' arte*. His influence on opera-libretti was immense (see list in *Grove*); 4, 12, 191. His works include:

Il Tasso (verse-drama). (See *Works*, 1788 edition, vol. xxvi); 12.

Les Mémoires de Goldoni pour servir à l'histoire de sa Vie et à celle de son Théâtre, Paris, 3 vols., 1787; 4.

Gorani (Gerani), Count Giuseppe (b. Milan 1740; d. Geneva 1819). Italian adventurer, writer and politician. Took part in the Seven Years' War and in the insurrection of the Corsicans against Genoa. Later, in France, he was associated with the *Encyclopédistes* and with the Girondins. His main work is the *Mémoires secrets et critiques des Cours, des Gouvernemens et des Mœurs des principaux Etats d'Italie* (3 vols., Paris 1793); 192, 287.

Goria, Mademoiselle. French singer, one of the most faithful *seconde donne* of the Théâtre Italien. Stendhal must have known her well, since she was the friend of his mistress Angelina Bereyter. She made her *début* at the Odéon on 27th Sept. 1809, in *le due Gemelli*, and was still singing at the Louvois in 1824; 427.

Gozzi, Count Carlo (b. Venice 1720; d. Venice 1806). Italian writer, younger brother of Gasparo Gozzi, whose main concern was to defend the native tradition of the Italian theatre against the innovations of Goldoni. He is best known for his *Fiabe* (1761–1765), and for his autobiographical *Memorie Inutili* (1797). The latter grew out of the need to defend himself against accusations levelled at his conduct by P. A. Gratarol, secretary to the Venetian Senate; 112, 197, 246.

Grandeur et Décadence des Romains, de la (history). See Montesquieu.

Grassini, Signora Giuseppina (b. Varese 1773; d. Milan 1850). A great Italian contralto of humble origins, trained by Marchesi and Crescentini. *Début* at Milan, 1794, in Zingarelli's *Artaserse*. The greatest triumphs of her career came in Paris. See André Gavoty, *La Grassini*, Paris 1947; 386.

Gratarol (Cratarol), Pier Antonio (b. Venice 1730; d. Madagascar 1785). Venetian lawyer and diplomat, for 34 years secretary to the Senate of Venice. In 1779, he became involved in an amorous intrigue with political consequences, and fled to Stockholm, where he published a *Narrazione apologetica*, involving Carlo Gozzi. Gozzi's reply was his now famous *Memoirs* (see *Gozzi*); 197.

Grattan, Lord Henry (b. Dublin 1746; d. London 1820). Irish statesman, whose career opened in 1775, as a member of the Irish Parliament. A superb orator, whose life-work was dedicated to the Irish cause, Grattan achieved the repeal of the English Declaratory Act (1782). After 1805, his influence was overshadowed by that of O'Connell; 452.

Graziani, Vincenzo. Italian *buffo comico*, who made his *début* at the Louvois in Paër's *I Fuorusciti di Siviglia* on 20th March 1819, and who took over the rôle of Tarabotto in the first French production of *L'Inganno Felice*. In 1825, he created the part of the Barone di Trombonok in *Il Viaggio a Reims*; 427.

Grétry, André Ernest Modeste (b. Liége 1741; d. Montmorency 1813). French composer of operas, best known for his *Richard Cœur-de-Lion*. Founder of the tradition of the *Opéra-Comique*; 22, 134, 206, 307, 345, 464–468.

 La Fausse Magie (opera in 2 acts); libretto by Marmontel; performed at the *Comédie Italienne*, 1st February 1775; 465–468.

 Lisbeth (opera in 3 acts); libretto by de Farières; performed at the *Grand Opéra*, 10th January 1797; 275.

Griselda (opera). See Paër.

Grossi, Tommaso (b. Bellano 1790; d. Milan 1853). Italian novelist and satirist, best remembered to-day for his "historical romance" *Marco Visconti* (1831). His early satire, *la Prineide*, was directed against the instigators of the Milanese mob which murdered Count Prina (*q.v.*); 115.

Guasco, Carlo. Milanese lawyer involved in politics, with whom Stendhal became friendly in 1816. See A. Maquet: *Deux Amis italiens de Stendhal: Giovanni Plana et Carlo Guasco*, Lausanne, 1964; 459.

Guercino (Guercini), Giovanni Francesco Barbieri, known as *il G.* (b. Cento 1591; d. Bologna 1666).

Mozart's patron in Vienna. Although his reign lasted only 10 years, he showed all the characteristics of the ideal "benevolent despot"; 182, 475, 477.

Joséphine, the Empress (Marie-Josèphe-Rose Tascher de la Pagerie) (b. Martinique 1762; d. Malmaison 1814). Originally married to General Beauharnais (by whom she had the son who was to become Prince Eugène), she later married Napoleon (1796), but was repudiated by him in 1809. After her retirement, she lived at Malmaison; 386.

Journal des Débats politiques et littéraires. One of the great periodicals of the XIXth century. Beginning in 1789 as the *Journal des Débats et Décrets*, it took its final title in 1814. Its early editors included the brothers Bertin, Fiévée, Geoffroy, Dussault, Hoffmann, Chateaubriand, Villemain, *etc.*; 76, 141, 206, 209, 335, 395.

Jouy, Victor-Joseph-Etienne, known as *de* Jouy (b. Jouy-en-Josas 1764; d. St Germain-en-Laye 1846). French soldier, journalist and politician. Retiring from the army in 1797, he wrote many plays and articles for the press; his libretti include Rossini's *Moïse* (1827) and *Guillaume Tell* (1829); 93.

Julius II, Pope (Giuliano della Rovere) b. Abbissola 1443; Pope 1503; d. Rome 1513). His tenure of office was notable for its military activities; he recovered most of the lost papal territories, and then, by organizing the Holy League, drove the French out of Italy; 192.

Juvenal (A.D. 60–110). Latin poet and satirist; 287.

Kant, Immanuel (b. Königsberg 1724; d. Königsberg 1804). German philosopher of Scottish origin. Author of the *Critique of Pure Reason*, etc., and founder of the school of "critical idealism"; 130, 409.

Kean, Edmund (b. London 1787; d. Richmond 1833). English actor; made his *début* as Shylock at Drury Lane in 1814. Kean was the greatest interpreter of Romantic intensity in acting; in 1818 he went as Talma's guest to Paris, and in 1828, produced *Richard III* there, to the enthusiasm of the young generation of French Romantic revolutionaries; 219, 268, 318.

Kenilworth (novel). See Scott.

King Lear (tragedy). See Shakespeare.

King's Theatre (London). See *Theatres.*

Knight, Richard Paine (b. Hereford 1750; d. London 1824). English scholar and numismatist, and a great authority on ancient art. His works include *An analytical Enquiry into the Principles of Taste* (London 1805); 246.

Kotzebue, August-Friedrich-Ferdinand von (b. Weimar 1761; assassinated Mannheim 1819). German dramatist, traitor and intriguer. By hating every man with a semblance of greatness, and by betraying his own country to the Russians, Kotzebue made himself about the best-detested man of his generation. But his dramas enjoyed some success, notably the Schicksalstragödie *Menschenhass und Reue* (1790), translated by Bursau and Mme Molé as *Misanthropie et Repentir* (5 acts, in prose, Théâtre-Français, 8 Nivôse An VII); 292.

Kreutzer, Rodolf (b. Versailles 1766; d. Geneva 1831). French violinist and composer. Became conductor-in-chief at the Académie de Musique in 1817. Besides works for the violin, Kreutzer left many operas, including *Paul et Virginie* (1791) and *Lodoïska* (1791, in competition with Cherubini); 125, 460.

Lablache, Luigi (b. Naples 1794; d. Naples 1858). Italian *basso buffo cantante* of French descent. *Début* in

Naples, 1812, as a *buffo napoletano*. His reputation reached its peak after 1830, when he was appointed singing-master to Queen Victoria; and he was one of the torch-bearers appointed to guard the coffin of Beethoven; 169, 174, 175, 193, 199, 422, 436.

La Bruyère, Jean de (b. Paris 1645; d. Versailles 1696). French writer and moralist, originally tutor, later secretary in the service of le grand Condé. His major work, *les Caractères*, appeared between 1688 and 1696; 61, 108, 186.

Lacretelle, Charles-Jean-Dominique de (b. Metz 1766; d. Mâcon 1855). French historian and journalist. Assistant editor of the *Journal des Débats* in 1790; but later exiled by Napoleon as a leader of the *jeunesse dorée*. His historical works are voluminous and tendencious: *e.g. Histoire de France pendant le XVIIIe siècle* (14 vols., Paris, 1808–26); 453.

Lady of The Lake, The (poem). See Scott; also *la Donna del Lago*.

La Fontaine, Jean de (b. Château-Thierry 1621; d. Paris 1695). French poet, universally known for his *Fables* (1668–1696). The fable entitled *l'Astrologue qui se laisse tomber dans un Puits* is in Book II, no. 13; 182, 312, 470.

Lagrange, Joseph-Louis (b. Turin 1736; d. Paris 1813). French mathematician, who began his career as artillery-instructor in Turin. His writings cover almost all branches of pure and applied mathematics, and even include an *Essai d'Arithmétique politique*; 331.

La Harpe, Jean-François de (b. Paris 1739; d. Paris 1803). French scholar and critic, a follower of the *Encyclopédistes* until the revolution turned him into a violent reactionary. His finest tragedy was *le Comte de Warwick* (1763); but he is best known to-day for his *Lycée, ou Cours de Littéra-*

ture ancienne et moderne (19 vols., 1799–1806). Another tragedy, *Philoctète* (3 acts, imitated from Sophocles, 1781) enjoyed some success in the XVIIIth century; 58, 105, 204, 266, 297, 307, 321, 335.

Lalla-Rookh (poem). See Moore.

Lambertazzi family; the leading Ghibelline family of Bologna, whose political significance, under Bonifazio Lambertazzi, lasts from 1217 until 1280; 455–456.

Lambertini, Signora Marianna. See Mombelli.

Lamennais, Félicité de (b. St. Malo 1782; d. 1854). French philosopher, whose theories passed from one extreme of total theocracy to the opposite of total, anarchistic revolution; 93.

La Motte-Houdar (la Mothe), Antoine de (1672–1731). French poet and literary polemist, deeply involved in the Querelle des Anciens et des Modernes. Best remembered to-day for his *Fables* (1719); 470.

Lampe Merveilleuse, la. Féerie-vaudeville in 2 acts, by Merle, Carmouche and Boniface, given at the *Panorama-Dramatique* in Feb. 1822; 432.

Landriani, Paolo (b. Milan 1755; d. Milan 1839). Author of *Osservazioni sui difetti prodotti nei teatri dalla cattiva costruzione del palco scenico . . .* (Milan 1815). Theatre-architect and stage-designer. His pupils included Sanquirico and Perego; 437.

Laorens = Jean-Baptiste Reinolds (*pseud.* J.-B. Guinan-Laoureins), author of the *Tableau de Rome vers la fin de* 1814 (Brussels 1816); 287.

La Rochefoucauld, François, duc de (1613–1680). French soldier, writer and moralist, chiefly remembered for his *Maximes* (1665); 470.

Las Cases, Emmanuel-Auguste-Dieudonné-Joseph, comte de (b. Revel 1766; d. Passy 1842). French historian of Spanish origins. Originally a naval officer, he became an administrator under Napoleon, and accompanied him to St. Helena, until expelled by Hudson Lowe. His *Mémoires* (originally produced in English) were published in Brussels in 1818; but his major work is the *Mémorial de Sainte-Hélène, ou Journal ou se trouve consigné, jour par jour, ce qu'a dit et fait Napoléon durant dix-huit mois* . . . (Paris, 8 vols., 1823); 91, 336, 386.

Lauzun, Armand-Louis de Gontaut, duc de Biron et de (b. Paris 1747; guillotined 1793). French general who took part in the American War of Independence (1778); his failure as commander of the republican forces in la Vendée occasioned his downfall. The *Mémoires de M. le duc de Lauzun* were published in Paris in 1822; 203.

Lavoisier, Antoine-Laurent (b. Paris 1743; guillotined 1794). French chemist and physiologist. He is best remembered for his work on the analysis and isolation of gases; but his enquiring mind took him into all branches of his chosen science; 129, 130.

Lebrun, Charles (b. Paris 1619; d. Paris 1690). Famous French painter, who was a protégé of Colbert, and one of the leading figures of the classical tradition. He was largely responsible for superintending the decoration of Versailles; 175.

Le Brunet, Jean-Joseph Mira, known as (b. Paris 1766; d. Fontainebleau 1853). French actor, whose *début* was made at Mantes in 1790. Known as *le Roi de la Bêtise*, Le Brunet's career reached its climax between 1814 and 1820; 422.

Lechi family. A vast and notable family of soldiers and scholars from Brescia, including Signora Gherardi (*q.v.*); the Contessina Lechi of Brescia, a Spanish lady, who, in her earlier career had been the mistress of Joseph II and the wife of Antonio

Lamberti; and the Generals Giuseppe and Teodoro Lechi; 137, 140, 235, 236.

Legallois, Mademoiselle. Ballet dancer; 209.

Le Kain (Henri-Louis Cain, known as) (b. Paris 1728; d. Paris 1778). French tragic actor. The son of a goldsmith, Le Kain became a protégé of Voltaire, and dominated the Parisian stage from 1750 to 1770. He was responsible for introducing some element of realism into the classical tradition; 318, 329, 330.

Lemercier, Louis-Jean-Népomucène (b. Paris 1771; d. Paris 1840). French critic and dramatist of the revolutionary and Napoleonic periods. He is best known for his historical dramas, *Charlemagne* (1816) and *Christophe Colomb* (1809), and for the first historical comedy on the French stage, *Pinto, ou la Journée d'une Conspiration* (5 acts in prose, An VIII). His other plays include: *Plaute, ou la Comédie Latine* (3 acts, verse, 1808); and *Agamemnon* (tragedy, 5 acts, 1794); 105, 285.

Leo, Leonardo Ortensio Salvatore de (b. San-Vito degli Schiavi 1694; d. Naples 1744). Italian composer who studied in Naples, and made his operatic *début* with *Pisistrato* (1714). His fame rests largely on church-music and comic opera; his best-known work is probably *Demofoonte* (San-Carlo, Naples, 1741); 21, 121, 124, 125.

Leopold II (b. Vienna 1747; d. Vienna 1792). Grand-Duke of Tuscany in 1763; Emperor in 1790. Son of Francis I and Maria-Theresa. A comparatively enlightened despot and liberal reformer; 191.

Lepeintre. A family of French actors, including Charles-Emmanuel (1785–1854), a comedian notable for his puns and impromptu wit; and his brother Emmanuel-Augustin (1788–1847), who was short and fat, and a comic dramatist as well as a first-class clown; 221.

Le Peletier, rue. See *Theatres: Opéra.*

Lesage, Alain-René (b. Sarzeau 1668; d. Boulogne-sur-mer 1747). French dramatist, novelist and translator, best known for his satirical comedy *Turcaret* (1709), and his great picaresque novel *Gil Blas de Santillane* (1715–1735); 450.

Lespinasse, Mademoiselle Julie-Jeanne-Éléonore de (b. Lyon 1732; d. Paris 1776). An illegitimate child, she lived for many years a humiliating existence, and in 1754–64 she was companion to Madame du Deffand. Visitors to the latter's *salon*, however, gradually discovered that the companion was as remarkable as the hostess, and soon her own *salon* was the glittering rival of that of her erstwhile mistress. Her *Lettres écrites depuis l'année 1773 jusqu' à l'année 1776* (2 vols., Paris 1809) were written to her lover, le comte de Guibert (*q.v.*); 202, 465–472.

Lesueur, Jean-François (b. Drucat-Plessiel 1760; d. Paris 1837). French composer, strongly influenced by Sacchini. He was a favourite of Napoleon, and professor of composition at the Académie in 1818, where he was an outstanding teacher. His most successful work, *Ossian, ou Les Bardes* (1804) earned its composer the *Légion d'honneur*; 396.

Lettere Sirmiensi (political pamphlet). See *Apostoli.*

Lettres sur l'Italie (essays). See *de Brosses.*

Levasseur, Nicolas-Prosper (b. Bresles 1791; d. Paris 1871). French bass, trained under Garat at the Paris *Conservatoire. Début* in Grétry's *la Caravanne* (1813). The mainstay of the *Italiens* and the *Opéra* from 1827 to 1853, he created rôles in both *le Comte Ory* and *Guillaume Tell*; 187, 225, 326, 427, 430.

Liparini (Lipparini), Catterina. Italian soprano with an unusually high range. Created the part of Matilde in *Matilde Shabran*. In 1819, she was engaged for a season in Paris, but had little success, save in Portogallo's *La Donna di genio volubile*; but in 1827 she created a part in Donizetti's *Otto mese in due ore*; 394, 424.

Lisbeth (opera). See *Grétry.*

Livy. Latin historian, born at Padua (59 B.C.–A.D. 19); 342.

Locke, John (b. Wrington 1632; d. Oates 1704). English philosopher, whose thought was of capital importance in the development of French liberal ideas in the XVIIIth century. Best known for his *Essay Concerning Human Understanding* (transl. by Coste, 1700); 461.

Logroscino (Lo Groscino), Bonifazio Niccola (b. Bitonto 1698; d. Palermo). Italian composer, who studied in Naples under Perugino and Gaetano Veneziano. According to *Grove*, his finales show no structural advance over those of Leo; 124, 197, 303.

Lodoïska (opera). See *Mayr.*

Lope de Vega Carpio, Feliz (b. Madrid 1562; d. Madrid 1635). Spanish dramatist of marvellous fertility, over 400 of whose plays (mainly historical and romanesque comedies or tragi-comedies) have survived; 12, 200.

Louis IX (tragedy). See *Ancelot.* There is also a play by Lemercier; *Louis IX en Egypte* (August 1821).

Louis XI. King of France 1461–1483. A sinister and cruel, but exceedingly capable monarch; 91.

Louis XIV. King of France 1643–1715; 248, 256, 304, 446, 478.

Louis XV. King of France 1715–1774; 121, 166, 299, 307, 330.

Louis XVI. King of France from 1774 until he was guillotined in 1793; 203, 304.

Louis XVIII. King of France 1814–1815 and 1815–1824. His reign was inter-

but was weak in expression. She created the parts of Amira in *Ciro in Babilonia*, Adelaide in *Tancredi*, Aldimira in *Sigismondo* and Adelaide in *Adelaide di Borgogna*; 339, 420, 421, 422, 423.

Manfrocci (Manfroce), Nicola (b. Parma 1791; d. Naples 1813). A brilliant composer in the Neapolitan tradition, who, but for his premature death, threatened to rival Rossini. A pupil of Zingarelli, he had completed two operas when he died; 29, 337.

Manners and Customs of the Indian Nations (treatise). See Heckewaelder.

Manzi, Maria (?). Member of a large family of Neapolitan singers, who created the parts of Enrico in *Elisabetta*, of Madame La Rosa in *La Gazzetta*, of Fatima in *Ricciardo e Zoraide*, of Emilia in *Otello*, of Amenofi in *Mosè*, of Cleone in *Ermione* and of Albina in *La Donna del Lago*; 422, 423.

Manzoni, Alessandro (b. Milan 1785; d. Milan 1873). Italian poet, novelist and dramatist, descended from the philosopher Beccaria. His best-known works include a novel, *I Promessi Sposi* (1827–40); two tragedies, *Il Conte di Carmagnola* (1820) and *l'Adelche* (1820–22); and his ode on the death of Napoleon, *Il Cinque Maggio* (1821); 164–165, 397.

Maometto, il (opera seria). See Winter; also Voltaire.

MAOMETTO SECONDO. Opera by Rossini, libretto by Cesare della Valle, Duke of Ventignano. Original version of *Le Siège de Corinthe*. First performed Naples, 3rd December 1820. Overture added in Venice, 1823; 134, 172, 342, 371, 394, 407, **424**.

Mara, Madame Gertrud Elisabeth, *née* Schmeling (b. Cassel 1749; d. Revel 1833). Great German soprano of the XVIIIth century, who began as an infant prodigy on the violin. In 1782, she came to Paris, where she became the rival of la Todi; and she dominated the stages of Paris and London between 1782 and 1802; 376.

Marcellus, Louis-Marie-Auguste Demartin du Tyrac, comte de (1776–1841). French politician and journalist of extreme royalist opinions, as was his son Marie-Louis (1795–1865); 93.

Marcellus, Marcus Claudius (268–208 B.C.). Roman general who became five times consul; 330.

Marchande de Goujons (la), ou Les Trois Bossus. Vaudeville in 1 act by d'Allarde and Armand d'Artois. *Théâtre des Variétés*, 31st March 1821; 261.

Marchesi, Lodovico (b. Milan 1755; d. Milan 1829). Italian male soprano. *Début* in Rome, 1774. Known as the last of the great *castrati*, Marchesi was one of the finest singers in Europe until his retirement in 1806; 48, 117, 337, 345, 351, 353, 382, 386.

Marcolini, Marietta. Italian mezzo-soprano who made her *début c*. 1805. In 1809 she was singing at la Scala. In 1811, she met Rossini, and created rôles in four of his major operas. Retired *c*. 1818; 69, 80, 87, 90, 91, 97, 100, 339, 371, 417, 420, 421, 422.

Mari, Luigi. Italian tenor, who sang mainly at La Scala (he was still singing as late as 1831), and who had an unsuccessful season in Rossinian opera at the Louvois in 1824. Created the title-part in *Aureliano* as a last-minute substitute for Giovanni Davide, who contracted measles. Act II of *Aureliano* is simplified to suit his abilities, which were less brilliant than those of Davide; 421, 436.

Mariani, Luciano. Italian bass who created the part of Oroe in *Semiramide*. In 1831, he was to create the part of Conte Rodolfo in Bellini's *La Sonnambula*; 424.

Works referred to include:

Adelasia ed Aleramo (opera seria). La Scala, December 1806; 22, 25.

Che Originali! (farsa). San-Benedetto 1798; 23–24.

Cora (Alonzo e Cora) (opera seria). La Scala 1803; 25, 35, 170, 451.

Due Giornate, le (opera semi-seria). La Scala 1801; 20.

Elena e Costantino (opera seria). La Scala 1816; 25.

Elisa (opera semi-seria). San-Benedetto 1804; 25.

Ginevra di Scozia (opera seria). Trieste 1801 (for the opening of the new opera-house); 21, 331.

Lodoïska (opera seria). La Fenice 1796; 20.

Medea in Corinto (opera seria). La Fenice 1813; 25, 170, 184, 374, 379, 451.

Misteri Eleusini, i (opera seria). La Scala 1802; 20.

Rosa bianca e la Rosa rossa, la (opera seria). Genoa 1813; 22–23, 56, 379.

Medea (opera). See Mayr.

Médée (tragedy). See Corneille.

Medici family. Ancient Guelf family of Florence which rose to power in the early XIVth century. The line died out in 1737; 87.

Mémoires de Goldoni. See Goldoni.

Mémoires de la Cour du Pape. See Burckhardt.

Mémoires de Las Cases. See Las Cases.

Mémoires [de Napoléon]. See Bonaparte.

Mémoires du Comte d'O ... See Schiller.

Mémoires d'un Colonel de Hussards, les. Comedy-vaudeville in 1 act by Scribe and Duveyrier. Théâtre du Gymnase-Dramatique, 21st February 1822; 242.

Mémorial de Sainte-Hélène. See Las Cases; Bonaparte.

Mercadante, Giuseppe Saverio Raffaele (b. Altamura 1795; d. Naples 1870). Italian composer who was a favourite pupil of Zingarelli. *Début* with

l'Apoteosi d'Ercole (San-Carlo 1819). His main reputation rests on *Elisa e Claudio* (La Scala 1821). A prolific and original composer, he was closely associated with Rossini and Meyerbeer; 125, 188, 425.

Merchant of Venice, The (drama). See Shakespeare.

Meri, Mademoiselle de. See Demeri.

Mesdames de France. The aunts of Louis XVI, who received guitar and harp tuition from Beaumarchais; 202.

Metastasio (Pietro Antonio Domenico Bonaventura Trapassi, known as) (b. Rome 1698; d. Vienna 1782). Italian poet and librettist, who lived in Vienna from 1730. His libretti were among the most popular in the XVIIIth century, some being set over seventy times by different composers. His *Artaserse* (1730) was used by Vinci; 76, 198, 200, 285.

Meyerbeer (Jakob Liebmann Beer, known as) (b. Berlin 1791; d. Paris 1864). German-Jewish composer, son of a wealthy banker. He was trained as a pianist. His main operas include *Il Crociato in Egitto* (1824); *Robert le Diable* (1831) and *Les Huguenots* (1836); 188, 191, 425.

Michelangelo Buonarroti (1475–1564). Italian painter, sculptor, architect, poet, inventor, *etc.*; 53, 134, 188, 258, 294, 319, 320, 477.

Micheroux, le Chevalier Alexandre (b. Naples 1792; d. Venice 1846). The son of Antoine Micheroux, of Liége, who had become the unofficial Foreign Minister of Naples, Alexandre was a notable amateur musician, dabbling also in liberal politics. He was probably the lover of Giuditta Pasta, at whose house he met Stendhal; 329.

Mignet, François-Auguste-Marie (b. Aix 1796; d. Paris 1884). French historian and archivist of the Ministère des Affaires Etrangères. Best known for his *Histoire de la*

quembergue 1729; d. Paris 1817). Amateur violinist and composer of aristocratic origins. *Début* with *Les Aveux Indiscrets* (1759). His greatest works come from his collaboration with Sedaine, notably *Rose et Colas* (1764) and *Le Déserteur* (1769); 206.

Montaigne, Michel de (1533–1592). French writer and moralist, author of the famous *Essais*; 470.

Montano et Stéphanie (comic opera). See Berton.

Montesquieu, Charles de Secondat, Baron de (1689–1755). French philosopher, wit and historian, best known for his political treatise, *l'Esprit des Lois* (1748) and for his history *de la Grandeur et de la Décadence des Romains*; 108, 203.

Monti, Vincenzo (b. Alfonsine 1754; d. Milan 1828). Italian poet, recognized leader of the neo-classic revival. During the troubled period in which he lived, Monti changed his allegiance repeatedly; but the quality of his verse, and his profound love for Italy remained intact; 97, 113.

Monvel (Jacques-Marie Boutet, known as) (b. Lunéville 1745; d. Paris 1812). French actor, *début* at the *Comédie Française* in 1770. Closely associated with Talma, especially during the revolution. He was also a dramatist and librettist, and father of Mlle Mars; 296.

Moore, Thomas (b. Dublin 1779; d. Sloperton 1852). Irish poet, musician and singer, who owed his early successes as much to his magnificent voice as to his poetical talent. His fame to-day rests on the *Irish Melodies* (1807–1834) rather than on the once vastly popular oriental epic *Lalla-Rookh* (1817); 15, 462.

Morandi, Rosa, *née* Morolli (1782–1824). Italian soprano/mezzo-soprano who made her *début* in 1804. Together with her husband, the composer and chorus-master Giovanni Morandi (1777–1856), she

was instrumental in getting Rossini his first commission, *La Cambiale di matrimonio*, in which she created the rôle of Fanny. She also created the part of Cristina in *Odoardo e Cristina*, and sang many other Rossinian heroines; 420, 423.

Morellet, André (b. Lyon 1727; d. Paris 1819). French philosopher and writer, a friend of Diderot and of Madame Geoffrin. His *Mémoires sur le XVIIIe siècle et la Révolution*, a valuable study of contemporary personalities, appeared in 1821; 202.

Morghen, Raffaello (b. Portici 1761; d. Florence 1833). Italian engraver, who studied in Rome under Volpato, and in 1794 founded his own school in Florence; 331.

Mori, Signorina. Member of an Italo-English family of musicians, she was born in London and could sing both contralto and soprano parts. At the Louvois, she made her *début* as Rosina in the *Barber* (6th March 1823), replacing Mlle Demeri; later she sang many Rossinian parts in Paris, including Zomira in *Ricciardo e Zoraide*, and created the parts of Marie in *Moïse*, Ragonde in *Le comte Ory* and Hedwige in *Guillaume Tell*; 427.

Morlacchi (Morlachi) di Perugia, Francesco (b. Perugia 1784; d. Innsbruck 1841). Italian composer and conductor. Studied under Zingarelli and S. Mattei, *début* with *Il Simoncino* (1803). In 1811, he was appointed to Dresden, where he tormented the life out of Weber. His best-known work is *Tebaldo ed Isolina* (Dresden 1820); 125, 188, 199, 263, 360, 425.

Morning Chronicle, The. One of the leading metropolitan morning papers of the early XIXth century. Founded 1793; 458.

MORTE DI DIDONE, LA (sometimes wrongly referred to as DIDONE ABBANDONATA). Solo cantata, written in 1811. First performed by

Ester Mombelli at Venice, 2nd May 1818. Librettist unknown; 414.

Mosca, Giuseppe (b. Naples 1772; d. Messina 1839). Italian composer. Studied at Loreto Conservatoire, *début* with *Silvia e Nardone* (Rome 1798). Prolific, facile, but without real genius. Later in life, Mosca claimed to have invented the Rossinian *crescendo*, and to have used it in *I Pretendenti Delusi* (Milan 1811); 29, 36, 100, 125, 188, 261.

Moscheles, Ignaz (b. Prague 1794; d. Leipzig 1870). German-Bohemian virtuoso pianist who studied under Salieri, and first made his reputation with his *Variationen über den Alexandermarsch* (1815). Lived largely in London and Leipzig; 345.

MOSÈ IN EGITTO ("azione tragico-sacra" by Rossini). Libretto by Tottola. 3 acts, San-Carlo, 5th March 1818. Later (1823) given in London under the title of *Pietro l'Eremita*; 16, 42, 68, 113, 125, 134, 143, 172, 280, 317–328, 342, 377, 395, **423**, 452.

Mount Edgecumbe, Richard, Earl of (b. Plymouth 1764; d. Richmond 1839). English amateur musician, and administrator of the King's Theatre, London, where his opera *Zenobia* was performed in 1800. Author of *Musical Reminiscences* (London 1825); 433.

Mozart, Wolfgang Amadeus (b. Salzburg 1756; d. Vienna 1791). Austrian composer; 10, 16, 20, 21, 29, 30–36, 37–42, 55, 56, 62, 76, 79, 103, 104, 105, 106, 107, 125, 128, 134, 142, 143, 148, 150, 153, 161–162, 177, 187, 188, 200, 214, 226, 228, 234, 242, 288, 294, 298–299, 302, 303, 316, 388, 394, 398, 403, 404, 405, 411, 418, 463, 475–478.
The works referred to include:
Clemenza di Tito, la (2 acts, libr. by Mazzola, based on Metastasio. Prague 1791); 394, 477.
Così fan Tutte, ossia La Scuola degli Amanti (2 acts, libr. by Da

Ponte. Vienna 1790); 16, 41, 476.
Don Giovanni, ossia Il Dissoluto punito (2 acts, libr. by Da Ponte. Prague 1787); 10, 20, 33–34, 35, 40, 41, 128, 229, 234, 294, 299, 300, 322, 388, 394, 403, 405, 407, 411, 418, 476, 477.
Entführung aus dem Serail, die (3 acts, libr. by G. Stephanie. Vienna 1782); 31–32, 477.
Finta Giardiniera, la (3 acts, libr. by R. Calzabigi, adapted by M. Coltellini. Munich 1775); 476.
Finta Semplice, la (3 acts, libr. by Goldoni. Salzburg 1769); 475.
Idomeneo, Re di Creta, ossia Ilia ed Idamante (3 acts, libr. by G.-B. Varesco based on Danchet. Munich 1781); 476.
Lucio Silla (3 acts, libr. by G. da Gamerra. Milan 1772); 31, 475.
Mitridate, Re di Ponto (3 acts, libr. by V. A. Cigna-Santi. Milan 1770); 31, 475.
Nozze di Figaro, le (4 acts, libr. by Da Ponte. Vienna 1786); 35, 86, 105, 106, 161–162, 214, 407, 430, 476.
Requiem (1791); 477.
Schauspieldirektor, der ("comedy with music", 1 act, libr. by G. Stephanie. Vienna 1786); 477.
Zauberflöte, die (2 acts, libr. by E. Schikaneder. Vienna 1791); 35, 477.

Müllner (Mülner), Adolf (b. Weissenfels 1774; d. Weissenfels 1829). German dramatist, one of the earliest writers of plays based on crime and detection. Leader of the *Schicksalstragödie* movement, in which form his masterpiece is *Die Schuld* (1816), translated into French by le comte de Saint-Aulaire (*l'Expiation*, 1823); 21.

Murat, Joachim (b. La Bastide-Murat 1767; executed 1815). Brother-in-law of Napoleon, and a notable soldier. From 1808 until 1815 he was King of Naples, but was obliged to abandon his realm on the fall of Napoleon; 451.

Musique mécanique (de la), et de la Musique philosophique (treatise). See Berton.

Myrrha, ou La Vengeance de Vénus (ballet). See Viganò, *Mirra*.

Naldi, Signorina. Italian soprano, daughter of the baritone Giuseppe Naldi (1770–1820), who was killed dramatically by the explosion of a pressure-cooker on 16th Dec. 1820. La Naldi came to the Louvois from the King's Theatre, London, and made her *début* in *Così fan tutte* on 19th Sept. 1820. She played Suzanne in *Le Nozze* and Isabella in *L'Italiana*, but never overcome her extreme nervousness, and retired in 1823, on her marriage to the Count di Sparra; 27, 87, 88.

Nazolini (Nasolini), Sebastiano (b. Piacenza 1768; d. *c.* 1806). Italian composer who worked chiefly in Trieste and Naples. He left some 30 operas, a few of which enjoyed a small popularity at the end of the XVIIIth century; 29.

Necker, Jacques (b. Geneva 1732; d. Coppet 1804). Swiss financier of English origins. Controller of French finances 1777–81 and 1789–90. His daughter was later to become famous as Madame de Staël (*q.v.*); 304.

Nelson, Lord Horatio (b. Burnham-Thorpe 1758; killed at Trafalgar 1805). English admiral. The inglorious incidents of Nelson's career in Italy are more familiar to Italian than to English historians; 410, 451.

Nemici Generosi (i), ossia Il duello per complimento (opera). See Cimarosa.

Neri, St Philip (b. Florence 1515; d. Rome 1595). Founder of an order of regular clergy known as the *Oratorians*, from the site of the community, which was the Oratory of San-Girolamo-della-Carità; 455.

Nero (Lucius Domitius Nero Claudius) (A.D. 37–68). Roman emperor; 411.

Nicolini (Niccolini), Giuseppe. Minor Italian operatic composer. Isabella Colbran made her *début* at *la Scala* in the première of his *Coriolano* (26th Dec. 1808), and later sang in his *Traiano in Dacia* in Bologna (teatro Communale, 1809), where she was probably heard by the 17-year-old Rossini; 29, 33, 36.

Niccolo. See Isouard.

Nicomède (tragedy). See Corneille.

Nina, ossia La Pazza per Amore (opera). See Paisiello.

Noblet, Lise Ballet-dancer. Danced leading rôles at the King's Theatre between 1821 and 1824; 209.

Noce di Benevento, il (ballet). See Viganò.

Nourrit, Louis (b. Montpellier 1780; d. Brunoy 1831). French tenor and diamond-merchant. *Début* at the *Grand Opéra* in Gluck's *Armide*. A fine singer, but cold and unambitious. His elder son Adolphe (1802–1839), a protégé of Garcia, made his *début* in 1821, and succeeded his father as leading tenor in 1826; 334.

Nouvelle Héloïse, la (novel). See Rousseau.

Nozzari, Andrea (b. Bergamo 1775; d. 1832). Italian tenor, a pupil of Davide the elder and Aprile. *Début* at Pavia 1794. His voice improved greatly towards middle-age, and he was at the height of his powers during his collaboration with Rossini (1815–20). Retired 1822; 161, 166, 170, 173, 220, 221, 226, 231, 235, 279, 322, 364, 387, 388, 392, 393, 422, 423, 424.

Nozze di Figaro, le (opera). See Mozart.

Numa Pompilius (ballet). See Viganò.

OCCASIONE FA IL LADRO (L'), *ossia* IL CAMBIO DELLA VALIGIA. *Farsa* by Rossini. Libretto by Luigi Prividali.

borated with Rossini 1824-26. An unpleasant character, but a composer of genuine talent; 20, 21, 26-29, 30, 35, 125, 221, 226.

His works include:

Agnese di Fitz-Henry (libr. based on Amelia Opie, *The Father and Daughter*). Ponte d'Altaro 1809; 27, 28, 221.

Camilla, ossia Il Sotterraneo. Vienna 1799; 28, 226, 434, 441.

Griselda, ossia La Virtù al Cimento, Parma 1798; 27.

Oro fa Tutto, l'. Milan 1793; 27.

Sargino. Dresden 1803; 27, 35.

Paër, Francesca, *née* Riccardi (b. Parma 1778; retired 1808). Italian soprano, wife of Ferdinando. *Début*, Brescia 1794. Separated from her husband and retired to Bologna in 1808; 29.

Paganini, Niccolo (b. Genoa 1782; d. Nice 1840). Italian violinist, *début* (with L. Marchesi) in Genoa 1793. A pupil of Costa, Rolla and Ghiretti, he spent his youth wildly, but soon settled down to make a fortune out of his playing; 355, 460.

Pages du Duc de Vendôme, les (ballet). See Aumer, Gyrowetz.

Paine Knight. See Knight, R. P.

Paisiello (Paesiello), Giovanni (b. Taranto 1740; d. Naples 1816). A pupil of Durante in Naples, Paisiello worked mainly in Naples and St Petersburg. "Director of National Music" under the republican government, he lost favour at the restoration, and retired from composition in 1803; 6, 14, 19, 31, 36, 51, 68, 123, 124, 125, 150, 176, 177, 178, 179, 183, 198, 243, 303, 310, 317, 402, 408, 409, 412, 440, 454, 457, 460, 476.

He left over 100 operas, including:

Barbiere di Siviglia, il (St Petersburg 1782; Paris 1789); 176-181, 198, 209, 310-311.

Molinara, (la), ossia l'Amor Contrastato (libr. G. Palomba; Naples 1788); 6.

Nina, ossia La Pazza per Amore (Caserta 1789); 457.

Piro (Naples 1787); 402.

Re Teodoro in Venezia, il (Vienna 1784); 5, 128.

Scuffiara (la), ossia la Modista raggiratrice (Naples 1787); 5, 402, 409, 457.

Pallerini, Antonia (di Pesaro). Singer and dancer at la Scala. See Ricordi, *Commentarii della vita . . . di S. Viganò,* p. 343-7; 296, 386, 447.

Pandore, la (periodical). See *Miroir, le*; 129, 148, 257.

Parlamagni, Annetta (Anna). Italian soprano/contralto, who created the part of Edoardo in *Matilde Shabran*. Still singing in Siena as late as 1835. Daughter of the following; 424.

Parlamagni, Antonio (b. *c.* 1745). Famous Neapolitan *buffo*, who was still singing with success in Rome in 1818. Created the parts of Count Macrobio in *La Pietra del Paragone* and of Isidoro in *Matilde Shabran*; 91, 421, 424.

Parmigianino (Girolamo-Francesco-Maria Mazzolo, known as *il P.*) (b. Parma 1503; d. Casalmaggiore 1540). Italian painter and engraver, strongly influenced by Correggio; 197.

PARTENOPE. Cantata by Rossini. Text by Giuseppe Genoino. Performed Naples, 9th May 1819); **425.**

Pascal, Blaise (b. Clermont 1623; d. Paris 1662). French mathematician, philosopher, theologian and writer, famous for his *Lettres Provinciales* (1656-7) and for the collection of philosophical reflexions known as *Les Pensées*; 61.

Passavant, Theophil. German traveller and moralist, author of a book on Russia; 242.

Pasta, Giuditta, *née* Negri (b. Saronno 1798; d. Blavio 1865). Italian soprano of Jewish origin. A pupil of Asiolo in Milan, she made her *début* in Brescia in 1815, but had no major success until she took Paris by storm in 1822. Her voice extended from low A to D'''. She retired *c.* 1834. See N. Ferranti Giulini, *Giuditta Pasta e i suoi tempi*, Milan 1935; 10, 16, 29, 52, 56, 58, 66, 107, 184, 208, 216, 222, 223, 226, 230, 231, 232, 234, 240, 248, 260, 277, 311, 326, 330, 336, 345, 360, 367, 371–386, 395, 397, 401, 424, 427, 429, 442.

Paul. See Richter, Jean-Paul.

Paul, Monsieur. Ballet-dancer, leading dancer at the King's Theatre, 1822; 209.

Pavesi, Stefano (b. Vaprio 1779; d. Crema 1850). Italian composer who studied in Naples. *Début* in Venice, 1803, with *Un Avvertimento ai Gelosi*; 29, 30, 36, 125, 402, 408, 425, 441.
His works include:
Arminio (Venice, 1821); 441.
Corradino (Venice 1810); 425.
Ser Marcantonio (libr. by Angelo Anelli; la Scala 1810. This is Pavesi's greatest work, and the source of Donizetti's *Don Pasquale*); 402.

Pellegrini (Pelegrini), Felice (b. Turin 1774; d. Paris 1832). Italian bass, a pupil of Ottani. *Début*, Leghorn 1795. Paër originally wrote *Agnese* for his voice. In 1826, he was succeeded by Zucchelli at the *Opéra-Italien*, and became a professor at the Paris *Conservatoire*; 27, 184, 190, 247, 253, 281, 421, 422, 427, 434.

Pellico, Silvio (b. Saluzzo 1789; d. Turin 1854). Italian patriot, poet and dramatist. One of the leading spirits of Italian romanticism, imprisoned for political reasons in the Fortress of Spielberg 1822–1830. His early tragedies include *Laudamia* (1815) and *Eufemio di Messina* (1820); 63, 435.

Perego, Giovanni (b. Milan 1776; d. Milan 1817). Italian painter and stage-designer, a pupil of Landriani. Worked mainly at la Scala. See

C. Ricci, *La Scenografia italiana*, Milan 1930; 56, 299, 448.

Pergolesi, Giovanni-Battista (b. Jesi 1710; d. Pozzuoli 1736). Italian composer. In spite of his brief existence, Pergolesi is one of the major composers of his period; 30, 43, 59, 61, 107, 121, 124, 125, 197, 303, 333, 345, 440, 454.
His operas include:
Olimpiade, l' (opera seria in 3 acts; libr. by Metastasio. Rome 1735); 121.
Serva Padrona, la (intermezzo; libr. by G. A. Federico. Naples 1733); 121.

Perlet, Adrien (b. Marseilles 1795; d. Enghien-les-Bains 1850). French vaudeville-actor and dramatist. His most successful play was a 1-act farce entitled *l'Artiste* (1821), written in conjunction with Scribe. One of his greatest rôles was in *Le Comédien d'Etampes* (*q.v.*); 221.

Perticari, Costanza (b. Rome 1792; d. Ferrara 1840). Daughter of the poet Monti, Costanza married the writer Giulio Perticari in 1812. Herself a writer of note, she lived a wild life, and in 1822 was accused of murdering her husband; 48, 111–112.

Peruchini, Signor. A friend of Stendhal in Venice; 67.

Perugino (Pietro di Cristoforo Vanucci, known as *il P.*) (b. Citta della Pieve 1445; d. Fontignano 1523). Italian painter of the Umbrian school; 48, 134.

Peter the Hermit (opera). See *Mosè in Egitto*; 318.

Petracchi, Angelo Felice. Italian impresario, originally at la Scala, later in London. See Ebers, *Seven Years of the King's Theatre*; 35, 429, 436.

Petrarch, Francesco (b. Arezzo 1304; d. Padua 1374). The first modern Italian poet; 189.

Philibert (comedy). See Picard.

Philip II, King of France 1180–1223. An energetic monarch, whose reign was stained by a violent persecution of the Jews, followed by the extermination of the Albigensians; 211.

Philoctète (tragedy). See La Harpe.

Philosophe Marié, le (comedy). See Destouches.

Philpotts (Philpott), Henry, Bishop of Exeter (1778–1869). In his youth, Philpotts wrote a number of violent pamphlets upon political matters, including a justification of the Peterloo massacre, during which he entered into collision with the more liberal-minded *Edinburgh Review* (1819–20); 11.

PIANTO D'ARMONIA (IL) SULLA MORTE D'ORFEO. Cantata by Rossini. Libretto by Girolamo Ruggia. Performed Bologna, 11th August 1808; 48, 419, **424**.

Picard, Louis-Benoît (b. Paris 1769; d. Paris 1828). French actor, dramatist and novelist, whose first comedy, *le Badinage Dangereux* (1789) was written in collaboration with Fiévée. For some time he was director of the *Louvois*. His innumerable plays include *Les Deux Philibert* (1816); he also left 25 volumes of novels, 4 of which made up the *Mémoires de Jacques Fauvel* (Paris 1823); 244.

Piccinni (Piccini), Niccolò (b. Bari 1728; d. Paris 1800). Italian composer, a pupil of Leo and Durante; *début* with *le Donne dispettose* (1754). In 1776, worsted in rivalry with Anfossi, he went to Paris, where he was elevated (against his will) to the rank of champion of the *anti-gluckistes*. Singing-master to Marie-Antoinette; 26, 31, 104, 124, 125, 204, 303, 318.

PIETRA DEL PARAGONE, LA. Opera by Rossini; 2 acts, libretto by Luigi Romanelli. Performed in Milan, 26th September 1812. Often referred to as *la Sigillara*; 27, 39, 42, 90–100, 189, 260, 339, 371, 398, 407, 417, 418, **420–421**.

Pietro da Cortona (1596–1669). Tuscan painter and architect, a brilliant and prolific artist; 39.

Pignotti, Lorenzo (b. Figline nel Valdarno 1739; d. Pisa 1812). Italian poet, fabulist and historian. His historical works, including the *Storia della Toscana sino al principato, con diversi saggi sulle scienze, lettere e arti . . .* (9 vols., Pisa, 1813–14) are more concerned with style than scientific accuracy; 238.

Pinotti, Elisabetta. Italian contralto (or *primo musico*), specializing in travesty rôles. She created the rôle of Ottone in *Adelaide di Borgogna*; 423.

Pinto (drama). See Lemercier.

Pirate, The (novel). See Scott.

Piron, Alexis (b. Dijon 1689; d. Paris 1773). French poet and dramatist. A scurrilous wit, Piron was most successful outside the rigid conventions of the *Comédie Française*. Only one of his comedies, *la Métromanie*, survives in the present repertoire; 140.

Pirro (opera). See Paisiello.

Pisaroni, Benedetta Rosamunda (b. Piacenza 1793; d. Piacenza 1872). Italian soprano, later contralto. A pupil of Pino, Moschini and Marchesi, she made her *début* at Bergamo in 1811. In spite of a disfiguring attack of small-pox, she was recognized after 1813 as the finest contralto in Italy. Retired 1831; 118, 173, 223, 364, 368, 376, 390, 393, 395, 423, 436.

Pistocchi, Francesco Antonio Mamiliano (b. Palermo 1659; d. Bologna 1726). Italian male contralto and composer. *Début* in 1675. From 1679 to 1700, Pistocchi was considered the finest singer in Europe; in 1701, he founded his school in Bologna, which spread the popularity of the *bel canto* style of singing; 351.

Pitié, de la (poem). See Delille.

Pitt, William ("the Younger") (b. Hayes 1759; d. Putney 1806). English statesman who, during the whole revolutionary period, be-

Rion de Prolhiac de Fourt, abbé de b. Saint-Flour 1759; d. Paris 1837). Archbishop of Malines. French ecclesiastical diplomat and writer, he contributed greatly to the restoration of Louis XVIII. After 1815, he retired to write a series of liberal pamphlets; 93.

Pretendenti Delusi, i (opera). See Mosca.

Préville (Pierre-Louis Dubus, known as) (b. Paris 1721; d. Beauvais 1799). French actor, originally a stonemason. *Début* at the *Comédie-Française* in 1753. He excelled in all types of parts, and was a popular favourite until his retirement in 1786; 184.

Prina, Count Giuseppe (b. Novara 1766; d. Milan 1814). Jesuit-trained Milanese lawyer and statesman. Minister of Finance from 1798, under various régimes, until 1814. His many financial reforms made him widely detested, and he was finally murdered in a riot. The *Vision of Count Prina (la Prineide)* was a vicious political satire by Tommaso Grossi (1815); 97, 115.

Principles of Taste, The (treatise). See Knight, R. P.

Profetti, Signor, Italian bass-baritone, member of the Théâtre Louvois from 1819 to 1823. His parts included Don Basilio in the *Barber*, Don Pacuvio in *La Pietra del Paragone*, Prosdocimo in *Il Turco*, and Mortimer in Mayr's *Rosa bianca e Rosa rossa*. An honest mediocrity, according to the critics; 427.

Prometeo (ballet). See Viganò.

Psammi, Rè dell' Egitto (ballet). See Viganò.

Puccitta (Pucita) Vincenzo (b. Civitavecchia 1778; d. Milan 1861). Italian composer, *début* Sinigaglia 1799. Puccitta made his reputation with *Il Puntiglio* (Milan 1802). In 1811, he became accompanist and personal composer to Madame Catalani, acquiring an unenviable reputation as a "tame musician", especially between 1815 and 1817, when she became directress of the Italian Opera in Paris. After 1817, he returned to Italy; 33, 422.

Puzzini, Monsignore. Chamberlain to the Court of Tuscany, Keeper of Manuscripts in the Library of San Lorenzo, Florence. See Courier, *Lettre à M. Renouard . . .*; 455.

Quentin Durward (novel). See Scott.

Quotidienne (la), ou la Feuille du Jour. Periodical, originally founded in 1793, which took its final title in 1815 (–1847). Its editors included La Harpe, Fontanes, Fiévée, Nodier, *etc.*; 201.

Rabelais, François (b. La Devinière 1494; d. Paris 1553). French doctor, diplomat and writer, author of *Gargantua, Pantagruel*, etc.; 255.

Racine, Jean-Baptiste (b. La Ferté-Milon 1639; d. Paris 1699). French tragic dramatist; 38, 104, 265, 297, 310, 311, 321, 416, 423, 469.

His plays include:

Andromaque (17th November 1667); 88, 265, 423.

Britannicus (13th December 1669); 265.

Iphigénie en Aulide (18th August 1674); 184, 297, 310.

Racine et Shakespeare. See Stendhal.

Radcliffe, Mrs Anne, *née* Ward (b. London 1764; d. London 1823). English novelist, whose mastery of the "Gothic" atmosphere earned her immense popularity in her time. Her best-known work is the *Mysteries of Udolpho* (1794); 28.

Raffanelli, Luigi (b. Lecce 1752). Italian *basso-buffo*, of outstanding ability as an actor. When associated with Rossini, he was already comparatively old; 420, 421.

Raison, Folie: Petit cours de morale mis à la portée des vieux enfants. Suivi des "Observateurs de la Femme". Moral-ironical essays by Pierre-Edouard Lemontey, Paris, 1816; 180.

Rambouillet, Hôtel de. Built by the Marquise de Rambouillet (rue St.-Thomas-du-Louvre) in 1615, and the site of the most famous *salon* of the XVIIth century; 113.

Raphael of Urbino (Raffaello Sanzio, b. Urbino 1483; d. Rome 1520). Italian painter; 39, 43, 45, 48, 55, 59, 80, 134, 150, 188, 217, 294, 319, 331, 440, 454.

Rapports du Physique et du Moral de l'Homme (des) (treatise). See Cabanis.

Raucourt, Mlle (Françoise-Marie-Antoinette Joséphine Saucerotte, known as) (b. Paris 1756; d. Paris 1815). French tragic actress. *Début* 1772, *Théâtre des Tuileries*. In 1808, she organized a tour of Italy with a French troupe. An extremely competent actress, but dissolute and disagreeable; 416.

Re Teodoro in Venezia, il (opera). See Paisiello.

Regnard, Jean-François (b. Paris 1655; d. Dourdan 1709). French comic dramatist, one of the successors of Molière. He left a score of minor masterpieces, of which the finest is *Le Légataire Universel* (1708); 117, 443.

Reicha, Antonin (b. Prague 1770; d. Paris 1836). French composer, teacher and musicologist. His treatises include a *Traité de Mélodie* (1814); and a *Cours de Composition musicale* (1818); 315.

Religieuse portugaise, la (novel). See Guilleragues.

Remorini, Raniero (b. Bologna 1783; d. Bologna 1827). Distinguished Italian bass. *Début*, Parma 1806. Outstanding in operas by Mayr and Fioravanti. Rossini wrote *Torvaldo* for him in 1815; 169, 174, 422.

Renégat (le). A popular novel by Charles d'Arlincourt, 2 vols., Paris 1822; 208.

Renommée, la. Periodical, founded in June 1819, upon the dissolution of *la Minerve*, by Etienne, Jay, Du Moulin and Tissot. In June, 1820 it merged with *le Courier Français*; 148, 179, 311.

Requiem. See Mozart.

Ricci, Scipione (b. Florence 1741; d. Florence 1810). Bishop of Pistoia. Ricci ardently supported the plans of Leopold II of Tuscany for subordinating the ecclesiastical to the civil authorities; the Synod of Pistoia (1786) led to rioting and to the eventual flight and disgrace of the bishop. See de Potter, *Vie de Scipion Ricci*; 246.

Ricci, Tommaso. Italian singer, member of original cast of *la Cambiale di Matrimonio*; 420.

Ricciardetto. Poem by Niccolò Forteguerri (*pseud.* Nicolò Carteromaco), 2 vols., Paris 1738. This work ran to many editions in the XVIIIth century, and is the basis of Rossini's *Ricciardo*; 393.

RICCIARDO E ZORAIDE. Opera by Rossini. Libretto by Berio di Salsa. Performed at the San-Carlo, Naples, 3rd December 1818; 172, 393–394, 400, 401, **423.**

Ricciardo Cuordileone (ballet). See Viganò.

Richard Cœur-de-Lion (1784). One of the most celebrated French operas of the XVIIIth century, libretto by Sedaine, music by Grétry. Blondel's aria, *O Richard, ô mon Roi* comes in Act I; 345.

Richardson, Samuel (b. Derbyshire 1689; d. London 1761). English writer who created the middle-class sentimental novel with *Pamela, or Virtue Rewarded* (1740) and *Clarissa Harlowe* (1747–8); 468.

Richelieu, Louis-François-Armand de Vignerot du Plessis, duc de (b. Paris 1696; d. Paris 1788). Great-nephew of the Cardinal, Richelieu was a notable soldier and Marshal of

Rosa bianca (*la*) e la Rosa rossa (opera). See Mayr.

Roscius, Quintus (*fl.* first cent. A.D.). A freed slave, who became the greatest actor in the Roman Empire; 330.

Rosich, Paolo (Pablo). Italian *basso buffo* of Spanish origins. Created the part of Buralicchio in *L'Equivoco stravagante*, and of Taddeo in *L'Italiana*. In Florence in 1816, he found Bartolo's aria *A un dottor della mia sorte* too difficult, and so Pietro Romani composed the easier alternative aria: *Manca un foglio*; 420, 421.

Rossi, Catterina. Italian *seconda donna* who created the parts of Clorinda in *La Cenerentola* and Maddalena in *Il Viaggio a Reims*. She sang at the Louvois with moderate success from 1821, her parts including Isaura in *Tancredi*, Elvira in *L'Italiana*, etc.; 243, 422, 427.

Rossi, Giovanni Gherardo de' (b. Rome 1754; d. Rome 1827). Roman scholar, poet and comic dramatist in the tradition of Goldoni. His best play was *Il Cortigiano Onesto* (1820). Trained as a banker, he was Minister of Finance from 1798–1800; 246.

Rossini, Anna. See Guidarini.

Rossini, Giuseppe (1759–1839). Father of the composer. Nicknamed *Vivazza*; 43, 46–47.

Rousseau, Jean-Jacques (b. Geneva 1712; d. Ermenonville 1778). French philosopher, novelist and musicologist. Rousseau wrote one successful operetta ("intermède"), *Le Devin du Village* (1752), translated by Burney as *The Cunning-Man* (1766). In 1753, Favart and de Guerville produced a parody of this work, *les Amours de Bastien et Bastienne*, which was later adapted by Mozart's librettist, Weiskern (1768); 15, 61, 80, 303, 305, 306, 308, 357, 358. Rousseau's other works include:

Confessions, les (posth., 1782); 15, 80.

Lévite d'Ephraïm, le; 325.

Nouvelle Héloïse, la (1761); 210.

Rubens, Peter-Paul (b. Siegen 1577; d. Antwerp 1640). Flemish painter and diplomat; 241.

Rubini, Giambattista (b. Romano 1795; d. Romano 1854). Italian tenor. A pupil of Nozzari, Rubini was engaged by Barbaja, but enjoyed no success until he appeared in Paris in *la Cenerentola* (1825). Associated with Rossini, Donizetti and Bellini. From 1830 to 1844, Rubini was recognized as one of the greatest tenors of his century. Married la Comelli (*q.v.*) in 1819; 425.

Russie, de la. See Clarke.

Sacchini, Antonio-Maria-Gasparo-Gioacchino (b. Florence 1734; d. Paris 1786). Italian composer, son of a fisherman. *Début* with *Fra Donato* (1756). Left a large number of operas, of which the most popular was the posthumous *Oedipe a Colone* (1787); 26, 31, 59, 107, 124, 125, 303, 318, 352.

Sala, Adelaide. Italian mezzo-soprano, b. *c.* 1797. She created the part of Dorliska in *Torvaldo e Dorliska*: this was one of her earliest *prima-donna* rôles. Later she had considerable success; 422.

Salieri, Antonio (b. Legnano 1750; d. Vienna 1825). Italian composer and teacher, a pupil of Tartini. Opera *début* with *Le Donne letterate* (1770). His most successful work was *La Grotta di Trofonio* (1785), but none of his operas has survived; 29.

Samandria Liberata (ballet). See Viganò.

Samson, Joseph-Isidore (b. St-Denis 1793; d. Auteuil 1871). French actor, dramatist and teacher of drama. In 1823, he was playing at the Odéon, and his reputation was still to make, since his resplendent *début* at the

member in 1780. His greatest speeches were made at the trial of Warren Hastings; 452.

Siboni, Giuseppe (b. Bologna 1782; d. Copenhagen 1859). Italian tenor, *début* Bologna 1802. Settled in Copenhagen from 1812. Father of the pianist Erik Anton Valdemar Siboni (1828–92); 170.

Sidney, Algernon (b. 1622; executed London 1682). English patriot, member of the Long Parliament (1646). An ardent parliamentarian despite his opposition to Cromwell, he was exiled in 1660, and stayed abroad until 1677. In 1682, he was implicated in the Rye House Plot, tried and executed; 284.

Siège de Calais, le (drama). See Du Belloy.

Sigillara. See *Pietra del Paragone, la.*

SIGISMONDO. Opera by Rossini. Libretto by Giuseppe Foppa. Performed in Venice, 26th December 1814; **422.**

Simond, Louis (1767–1831), French traveller and writer, author of the *Voyage d'un Français en Angleterre pendant les Années 1810–1811* (Paris 1816); *Voyage en Italie et en Sicile* (1824); 287.

Sinclair, John (b. Edinburgh 1791; d. Margate 1857). Scottish tenor, son of a cotton-spinner. Originally engaged as a regimental clarinettist, he made his operatic *début* in London in 1810. In May 1821, he sang to Rossini in Naples, and later created the part of Idreno in *Semiramide*; 424.

Sismondi, Jean-Charles-Léonard Simonde de (b. Geneva 1773; d. 1842). Swiss economist and historian. His two greatest works are the *Histoire des Républiques Italiennes du Moyen Age* (8 vols., Zurich 1807–9), and the *Histoire des Français* (31 vols., Paris 1821–44); 238.

Socrates (468–400 B.C.). Greek philosopher; 131.

Sografi, Simone Antonio (b. Padua 1759; d. Padua 1818). Italian poet, dramatist and librettist. As a writer of comedies, he was an imitator of Goldoni: *Le Convenienze teatrali* (1794) and *Le Inconvenienze teatrali* (1800) have survived. His libretti include that of Donizetti's *Olivo e Pasquale*; 117.

Solliva, Carlo (b. Casal-Monferrato 1792; d. 1843). Italian composer, a pupil of the Milan *conservatoire*. *Début* 1816 at la Scala with *La Testa di Bronzo*. Later worked in Paris, Vienna and St Petersburg; 69.

Solliciteur (le), ou l'Art d'obtenir des Places. Comedy-vaudeville, 1 act in prose, by Scribe, Dupin, Ymbert, Varnier and Delestre-Poirson, *Théâtre des Variétés*, 7th April 1817; 92.

Soubise, Charles de Rohan, Prince de (b. Paris 1715; d. Paris 1787). French soldier whose defeats (Rossbach, 1757; Wilhelmstadt, 1762) were more notorious than his victories. Happier at court than on the field of battle; 203.

Soumet, Alexandre (b. Castelnaudary 1788; d. Paris 1845). French dramatist and poet, one of the minor figures of the early romantic theatre. His two first tragedies, *Saül* (1822), and *Clytemnestre* (1822), had sufficient success to earn him his election to the Académie. Librettist of *Le Siège de Corinthe*; 36.

Spleen, le (short-story). See Besenval.

Spontini, Gasparo Luigi Pacifico (b. Maiolati 1774; d. Maiolati 1851). Italian composer, trained in Naples. *Début* with *Puntigli delle Donne* (Rome 1796). Soon after 1800, he moved to Paris, where he became director of the *Théâtre Italien*. His most successful opera was *La Vestale* (libr. by Jouy, 1807); 188, 199, 306, 307.

Staël-Holstein, Anne-Louise-Germaine Necker, baronne de (b. Paris 1766; d. Paris 1817). The daughter of the

Paris 1727; d. Paris 1781). French statesman, economist and philosopher, and one of the most notable administrative reformers of the XVIIIth century. Minister of Finance 1774–6. Leader of the school known as the *Physiocrats*; 32, 204, 304.

Uomo, l' (satirical poem). See Buratti.
Urfé, Honoré d' (b. Marseilles 1568; d. 1625). French writer, whose major work *l'Astrée* (1610–27), a vast pastoral epic in prose, is to all intents and purposes the first French novel; 54.

Vaccani, Domenico. Italian *basso cantante*, who created the part of Gamberotto in *L'Equivoco stravagante*. He was still singing in Siena in 1835; 420.
Valle, Teatro, Rome. See *Theatres*.
Vallongue, Joseph Secret Pascal-V. (b. Sauve 1763; killed Gaeta 1806). French General (engineering branch) in Napoleon's army, who was also a competent writer and poet. Fought at Aboukir Bay, Ulm and Austerlitz. Canova left a portrait of him in sculpture; 307.
Vanarella, la (ballet). See Viganò.
Variétés, Théâtre des. See *Theatres*.
Vasoli, Pietro. Italian bass, who created the parts of Don Pacuvio in *La Pietra del Paragone*, of Licinio in *Aureliano* and of Prosdocimo in *Il Turco*; 91, 241.
Vaudeville, théâtre du. See *Theatres*.
Vauvenargues, Luc de Clapiers, marquis de (b. Aix-en-Provence 1715; d. Paris 1747). French soldier and moralist; a melancholy optimist with a striking and paradoxical style; 454.
Velluti, Giovanni Battista (b. Montolmo 1780; d. Bruson 1861). Italian male soprano, trained by the abbé Calpi. *Début*, Forlì 1800. His greatest triumphs occurred between his visit

to Vienna in 1812 and his visit to London in 1825; 136, 262–265, 274, 331, 340–342, 343, 349–350, 351, 354, 355, 360, 363, 365–366, 376, 421, 425.
Venice Triumphant (Trionfo di Venezia). Painting by Veronese (*q.v.*) now in the Palazzo Ducale, Venice; 217.
Ventignano, Cesare della Valle, duca di V. Neapolitan nobleman and man of letters, renowed for his superstitions, and reputed to be a *jettatore*. He composed the libretto for *Maometto II*; Rossini is said to have made the "horn-sign" against black magic all the while he was composing the music; 394.
Venus and Adonis (sculptural group). See Canova.
Verni, Andrea. Italian bass, who created the part of Don Magnifico in *La Cenerentola*. He sang *basso buffo* parts at La Scala from 1800 to 1816. Carpani describes him as a better actor than singer; 422.
VERO OMAGGIO, IL. Cantata by Rossini, written for the Congress of Verona. Text by Rossi. Performed Verona, Autumn 1822; 425.
Veronese (Paolo Caliari, known as *il V.*) (b. Verona 1528; d. Venice 1588). Italian painter, influenced by Parmigianino. One of Stendhal's most admired artists; 217, 241, 280.
Vestale, la (ballet). See Viganò.
Vestale, la. Opera by Spontini, libretto by de Jouy. Paris (*Opéra*) 16th December 1807. A work which enjoyed great popularity between 1820 and 1830; 280.
Vestris family: famous family of singers, actors and dancers, including: Gaetano-Apollino-Baldassare (1729–1808), dancer and choreographer in Paris; his son, Marie-Jean-Augustin (1760–1842), dancer in Paris and London; Marie-Jean's son, Auguste-Armand (*fl.* 1790–1850), actor and dancer in Italy; Auguste-Armand's wife, Lucia-